NB. Les rouges font les Trouppes des Armées des Alliez, et Les bleues marquent les Trouppes Ennemies, ou francoises
Berchem
Corbeek
authever
Castel de

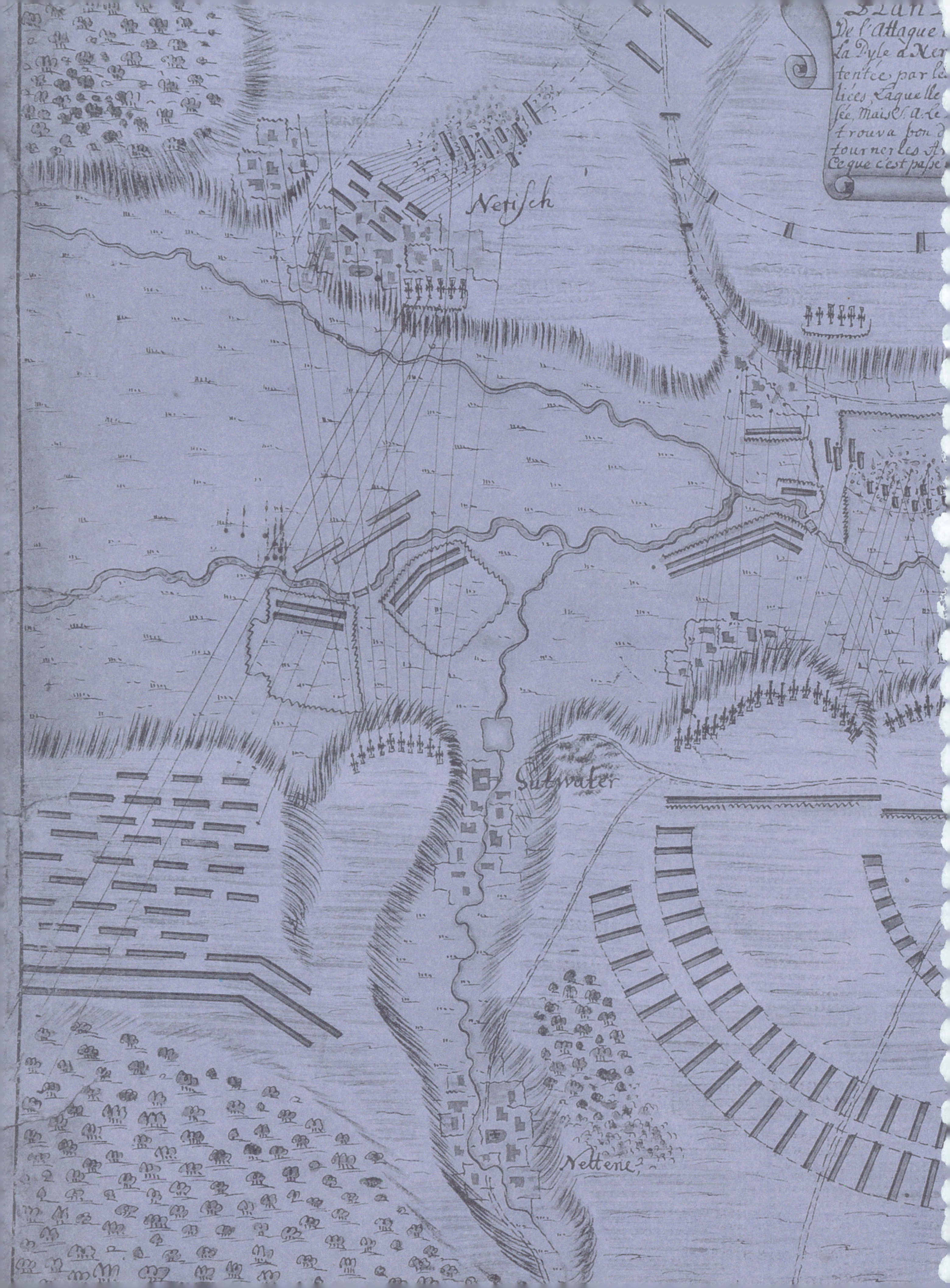
Plan
De l'Attaque
la Dyle à Ner
tentée par le
liées, Laquelle
sée, Mais S. A. Le
trouva bon d
tourner les A
Ce que c'est passé
Nerisch
Sutwater
Nettene

Marlborough

Soldier and Diplomat

The Battle of Oudenaarde, 11 july 1708.

Tapestry by Judocus de Vos after Lambert
and Philippe de Hondt, 18th century.
Blenheim Palace, Oxfordshire, UK.
The Bridgeman Art Library.

Protagonists of History in International Perspective – 2

Marlborough

SOLDIER AND DIPLOMAT

EDITED BY

John B. Hattendorf,

Augustus J. Veenendaal, Jr.,

and Rolof van Hövell tot Westerflier

KARWANSARAY PUBLISHERS

2012

Published in 2012 by
Karwansaray BV
Weena 750
3014 DA Rotterdam
The Netherlands

www.karwansaraypublishers.com

With assistance from M.A.O.C. Gravin van Bylandt Stichting and J.E. Jurriaanse Stichting.

ISBN 978-94-90258-04-7

Copy-editing by Edward Lucie-Smith
Image research and coordination by Christianne C. Beall
Design and typesetting by Jan van Waarden (RAM VORMGEVING), Asperen, the Netherlands
Maps © Karwansaray bv, designed by Rocío Espín
Lithography and printing by High Trade BV, Zwolle, the Netherlands
Printed in the EU

Contents

The Battle of Elixheim, 18 July 1705.

Tapestry by Judocus de Vos after
Lambert and Philippe de Hondt.
Blenheim Palace, Oxfordshire, UK.
Reproduced with the kind permission of
His Grace the Duke of Marlborough,
Blenheim Palace Image Library.

Introduction

By John B. Hattendorf

This volume is the second in the series *Protagonists of History in International Perspective* that focuses on major historical figures, who have been previously seen largely in their national context and not in a broad international perspective. As Europe grows more closely together, the growth of a collective historical consciousness becomes an increasingly important cultural asset. Each individual nation in Europe has historical figures that made contributions that went far beyond their own borders and deserve to be interpreted in this broader context. The War of the Spanish Succession, fought between 1701 and 1714, was one of the major conflicts in European history and John Churchill (1650-1722), the first duke of Marlborough, was a major British figure who played a wider European role during that conflict. Up to now, however, historical literature in the English language on Marlborough has almost exclusively seen him within the context of British history.[1] The research and writing that has been done in other countries and in other languages has not fully penetrated into English. The purpose of this volume and of this series is to attempt to remedy this situation by bringing together scholarly contributors from a variety of historical research perspectives. In this case, the contributors come from Austria, France, Germany, the Netherlands, the United Kingdom, and the United States of America.

The War of the Spanish Succession was a conflict between European powers over which candidate for the Spanish throne would succeed the childless Habsburg King Charles II of Spain, who had died in 1700. The basic situation was not a surprise as diplomats had been working for years beforehand to try to develop an acceptable solution to the problem. The issue centered around Spain and her wider empire stretching across the world from European possessions in Italy, the Mediterranean islands, and the southern Low Countries to colonial outposts in South America, the Pacific islands, and the Philippines. There were several candidates for the Spanish throne whose claims were similar and lay through Charles II's sisters. An alternative candidate was the Habsburg emperor Leopold I and his relations. These various choices in successors to the Spanish throne brought with them differing political consequences, all of which had implications for territorial control in Europe and around the world as well as access to the trade routes that affected the prosperity of competing national economies. Thus, the issue of who would become the new king of Spain touched on the fundamental balance of European power, while at the same time involving dynastic issues and the independence of various states and principalities as well as civil war in Spain and its territories.[2]

When the Dutch stadholder, William III, and his English wife, Mary II, succeeded jointly to the English throne in 1689, William brought with him from the Dutch Republic his clear policy of opposition to Louis XIV's expansive military and foreign policies and the basis for creating the Grand Alliance that immediately followed in the Nine Years' War, bringing together the Dutch Republic, Austria, and England to oppose France. This created a major shift in English foreign policy and united Dutch and English foreign policies together under the personal leadership and management of William III.

After the end of the Nine Years' War in 1697, William III had turned closer attention to the impending problem of the Spanish Succession. In an attempt to create a solution, William promoted the idea of partitioning the Spanish Empire between various other powers in order to maintain balance among them. This resulted in 1698 with the First Partition Treaty signed at The Hague by England, the Dutch Republic and France. In this, the two Maritime Powers of England and the Dutch Republic agreed that the Spanish crown should pass to a nephew of King Charles II of Spain, the Wittelsbach Duke Joseph Ferdinand Leopold of Bavaria, while other territories were to be divided between other Habsburg and Bourbon princes. This solution failed in February 1699, when the six-year old Bavarian duke died. A Second Partition Treaty was signed at London in 1700 in which the same powers agreed that the Archduke Charles of Austria would succeed as king of Spain. Under this agreement, the Spanish lands in Italy would go to France.

Neither of these agreements between the English, Dutch, and French had included either the Spanish or the Austrians. When Charles II of Spain died in November 1700, his will specified that there would be no partition of the Spanish Empire and that Louis XIV's grandson, Philip of Anjou, would inherit it all as King Philip V of Spain, but renounce his claim to the French throne. This situation, however, was not sufficient to create war. Initially, the French court hesitated to accept Charles II's will, thinking that the solution offered by the Second Partition treaty might avoid war and be more in France's interest. It soon became clear that Austrian objectives would not be assuaged by this solution and reports in France indicated that the Spaniards favored Philip's accession. Thus, Louis XIV announced that he had sacrificed his interests by acting on principle to accept the will in April 1703.[3] On the Dutch and English side, leaders saw this as a lack of sincerity and a deliberate breaking of their treaty agreement. Fears were heightened when Louis XIV took a series of actions that portended French blocking of Dutch and English trade as well as a possible invasion of the Dutch Republic. In 1701, William III took the initiative to reconstitute the Grand Alliance with a treaty signed at The Hague in September. Shortly after this, as relations became increasingly tense, Louis XIV's recognition of the son of the deposed King James II as the legitimate king of England, Scotland, and Ireland, added fuel to a smoldering fire. While this resulted in the recall of the English ambassador in Paris, it did not immediately create war. Historians have debated whether the outbreak of the war over the Spanish Succession was inevitable given the situation, or the result of Louis XIV's miscalculation, arrogance, or calculated intent.[4]

As tensions grew, Europe gradually divided into two opposing camps over the Spanish Succession issue. At the same time there were separate tensions in Northern Europe between Sweden, Denmark, Russia, and Saxony that might easily become entangled in the issues of Southern and Western Europe. Louis XIV initially obtained Savoy, Bavaria, and Portugal as allies for France and Spain as well as brought the Hungarian rebel leader Ferenc Rákóczi into his circle. On the opposing side, England, the Dutch Republic, and Austria worked to align the German states to their cause. Some of this was achieved through the traditional organization of the Holy Roman Empire that Austria dominated, yet also involved much diplomacy and maneuver with individual principalities. In 1700, Emperor Leopold I had tied Elector

Frederick I of Brandenburg with his promise of allowing him to take the title of King in Prussia. Other smaller principalities were tied to the allies by a complex network of subsidy treaties for the supply of troops with one or more of the principal states in the Grand Alliance.

The war began in the summer of 1701, when Louis XIV ordered his cavalry to cross the friendly territory of Savoy and to seize Milan, a territory ruled by Spain, while at the same time they were supported by French infantry who had landed in Italy and marched across the territory of Genoa to Milan. With his own Habsburg claim to Milan, Emperor Leopold ordered Prince Eugene of Savoy to counter this move. The Austrian and French armies clashed at Carpi on 9 July 1701, in the first battle of the War of the Spanish Succession.

Despite this opening clash, it took almost a year before the war became a general European conflict with the Grand Alliance formally proclaiming war against France on 15 May 1702. The interim period was a time of alignment, diplomacy, negotiation, mobilization, and preparation for a major war. This period also saw the death of William III on 19 March 1702, aged only 51. With William's death, Anne succeeded to the throne, bringing her closest personal advisers to positions of key importance. With the untimely loss of William's personal experience, knowledge, leadership, and links to the Dutch Republic, Anne turned to Marlborough to try to fill as best he could the chasm that William had left behind.

Marlborough was certainly one of the most important figures in English military and diplomatic affairs in the period 1702–10. However, the many earlier historians who describe Marlborough as if he had acquired dictatorial powers of a type that were foreign in the context of English early eighteenth-century government are mistaken. While observers sometimes characterized him in this manner, he clearly operated within the framework and machinery of English constitutional government, with its characteristic forms of court, cabinet, committee, Parliament, and governmental bureaucracy, involving both patronage and party politics.[5] He very clearly owed his position and much of his prestige as well as his own direct relationship to the Queen, to his wife Sarah's long-standing personal relationship with Anne. In this, Marlborough was not only a brilliant and successful military commander. He combined his military success and skills as a courtier and diplomat with his connections to friends and family in politics at home in a manner that enhanced his influence in London as well as on the Continent during Anne's reign. Yet, when his wife lost favour, Marlborough's position quickly collapsed.

The War of the Spanish Succession was the last of the five wars that Louis XIV had precipitated between 1667 and 1714, but it was the second of the seven Anglo-French wars that those two rival powers fought between 1689 and 1815. Thus, the war can be seen within two different broad contexts within the history of European warfare. On the one hand, it marked the end of French military domination of Europe while, on the other hand, it marked the shift to the period of an uneasy balance of power that followed with the emergence of Russia and Prussia as additional competing rivals with Great Britain, Austria, and France. In this process of shifting between two contexts, the War of the Spanish Succession shows itself as part of the continuum in the development of warfare in history. At the end of the chronological span, Napoleon had established the model of decisive battle, but in this earlier period battles were indecisive. Historian John A. Lynn has characterized these differences as 'war-as-process' for the older form of warfare and 'war-as-event' for the more modern form.[6]

In this long-term transition in the nature of warfare, the War of the Spanish Succession was a war for limited political objectives, although it involved the mobilization of huge armies on both sides for long periods of time and the large battles caused a huge number of casualties. The number of actions involving sieges and defensive fortifications far outnumbered battles in the open field. At the same time, neither the battles nor the sieges were decisive climacteric actions that ended conflict and resulted directly in peace. Due to the military limitations of the day, the War of the Spanish Succession was typical of its time and fought at a relatively slow pace on a seasonal basis, when both armies and navies could operate with optimal effectiveness. The War of the Spanish Succession was fought across Europe, from Italy to Portugal and Spain to Germany and the Low Countries, in North and South America as well as at sea in the North Sea, the Atlantic, the Channel, and the Mediterranean. The allied objective was to use their naval capabilities and their diplomacy to surround France and Spain and thereby prevent France from concentrating her overwhelming military strength for an offensive in any one theatre of the war. This strategy served to bolster France's defensive positions and to emphasise the role of the great fortresses and of positional warfare.[7] Like most conflicts of the period, the war was a long and slow war of attrition. The determining elements of conflict were relative military and naval successes combined with relative economic and financial strength and on-going diplomacy between opponents during the conduct of the war. On the allied side, in opposition to France, military success in war was also dependent upon the complex diplomatic negotiations necessary to maintain military subsidy and troop treaties.

In the context of the particular nature of the War of the Spanish Succession, Marlborough played an important international role. As a diplomat, he played a key role at The Hague, where he dealt not only with Grand Pensionary Anthonie Heinsius and Dutch military officers and officials, but also with representatives of all the allies in negotiating subsidy and troop treaties for England, directly complementing Dutch activity in this area. As a general and as the allied commander-in-chief, Marlborough based his success on his ability to co-operate effectively with the Dutch, who had the largest number of troops under his command, paid the largest share of the military effort, and controlled the army's logistics. As a field commander he was noted for promoting mobile warfare, maneuvering to engage in decisive battle, using effective operational intelligence, planning long-range logistical support, and having a remarkable ability to analyse and to react to changing tactical situations in the heat of battle. Some of these same characteristics led contemporaries to see him as impulsive, imprudent, and reckless in terms of eighteenth-century warfare. Seen at a distance of three centuries, these characteristics appear much more appropriate to warfare in the nineteenth and twentieth centuries. His ideas on this subject often could not be implemented due to the practical limitations of warfare in his time, when logistics were a major limiting factor for sieges and battles that required such massive supply support that typically allowed only one such operation to be launched efficiently in a single campaign. Nevertheless, Marlborough made an incremental improvement by being able to increase the operational tempo and in maintaining momentum from one operation to another. Typical of the era, the effects of his military success in one theatre of the war did not transfer to other theatres.[8] Success in Flanders and Germany did not bring victory in Spain.

Marlborough's ultimate achievement in becoming one of the greatest generals in British history could not have been easily foretold. He reached the greatest heights of military accomplishment without prior extensive experience in high command. Physically handsome, he rose to power through his personal service as a very successful courtier, having the talent for stylish manners and courtly conversation that easily lent itself to success in both public and private diplomacy and high-level management in government. His entire early experience and subsequent success was built upon obtaining and maintaining royal favour, and upon acting as an adviser using his deep understanding of military and international affairs. Thus, both in outlook and in temperament he was unprepared for dealing with the blow to his influence inflicted at the end of his career. He had, however, shifted with remarkable success in royal favour from James II, to William III, and to Anne, while still balancing contact with both Hanoverians and Jacobites. In all this it was his interrelated personal, political, and family connections, combined with those his wife developed, that were the key elements in reaching and sustaining his positions of power.

Aside from his natural talents as a courtier, diplomat, and soldier, Marlborough's direct personal connections with his sovereign, Queen Anne, were further supported by prevailing political interests, which gave him his substantial influence abroad with foreign princes, diplomats, and military leaders. While clearly neither the sole director of the English government nor of the Grand Alliance, he very effectively used his public image as 'the British Caesar' to develop and to maintain English interests at The Hague, where so much of the key diplomatic and military planning of the War of the Spanish Succession was done in close co-operation with Dutch leaders and representatives of other European states. In this respect, Marlborough had a unique role as a soldier and a diplomat within a European coalition, serving as a lynchpin for the Allies' complicated machinery of war.

To Her most Sacred MAJESTY
ANN
QUEEN of GREAT BRITAIN, FRANCE & IRELAND.
This MAP of
EUROPE
According to the Newest and most Exact Observations is most Humbly Dedicated by your Majesties most Obedient Servant Herman Moll Geographer.
SEMPER EADEM
NORTHERN OCEAN
Artick Circle
ICELAND
GERMAN OCEAN
NORTH SEA
ENGLISH CHANNEL
BAY OF BISCAY
WESTERN OCEAN
FRANCE
GERMANY
SPAIN
PORTUGAL
MEDITERRANE
PART OF AFRICA
The first Meridian from London
Printed for I. Bowles Printseller at ye sign of ye SCREEN over against Stocks Market and T. Bowles Print & Mapseller next to the Chapter house in St Pauls Church yard. 1708.
Sold by H. Moll over against Devereux Court, without Temple Bar. and P. Overton Map & Printseller near St Dunstans Church Fleetstreet
and by I. King Map & Printseller at ye Globe in the Poultry.

CHAPTER 1

Britain in Europe during the Age of Marlborough

David Onnekink

(PREVIOUS PAGE)
Map of Europe. An engraver, cartographer, and publisher, Herman Mol (ca. 1654-1732) came to England in 1678. Beginning as a copper plate engraver for several London publishers, he eventually began to produce his own maps, some of which were included in the works of well-known writers such as William Dampier, Daniel Defoe, and Jonathan Swift.

Print by Herman Mol, 1708.
Austrian National Library Map Department, Vienna, Austria.

In January 1712 the Duke of Marlborough attended a dinner party in London. It was organised by the 2nd Earl of Portland in honour of Prince Eugene of Savoy, who had just arrived in England. Portland had 'built last summer a noble Hall for great entertainements,' and spared no effort to impress his guests. The diner was 'a perfect garden to see, and like a Beautifull Landskipp, the variety of fruits, colours, glasses, and the gold & redd and other Colours of the China adding a new lustre to the whole, in short nothing could be more magnificent.'[1] The Earl was a lover of music, and would in 1719 be one of the founding directors of the Royal Academy of Music.[2] Hence, as an additional tribute to the great Savoyard prince, he arranged a musical performance with 'Trumpetts and kettledrum, a fit musick for such Martial genius.'[3] But behind the festive façade, the gathering had a distinctly political character. Eugene had travelled to London to obtain support from the British government for the war effort. Whereas the Tory party was resolved to end the war as soon as possible, both Marlborough and Eugene vouched to continue fighting until more favourable terms were achieved. By then, Marlborough, whether rightly so or not, was associated with Whiggism and warmongering.[4]

Strangely, Marlborough found his political allies abroad, in the Binnenhof in The Hague, rather than in Whitehall. Hence, he would have felt at ease at Portland's dinner. Next to Marlborough, Eugene and Portland, the seventeen guests, mostly noblemen, included Hendrik van Nassau-Ouwerkerk, Charles Townshend, the Earls of Dorchester, Sunderland and Devonshire, and several foreign envoys. The international character of the gathering reflected the composition of the Grand Alliance. Most, if not all of these men, were in favour of continuing the continental war against France, in opposition to the Tory government that had initiated covert negotiations with Louis XIV. The composition of the company was symbolic in more than one way. The guests embodied the second generation of advocates of Williamite foreign policy as conceived after 1689, Devonshire being the son of one of the Immortal Seven, Sunderland the son of William's prime adviser, and Portland the son of William's favourite.

During the Prince's stay in London, he was frequently seen attending the opera and dining with Marlborough, presumably also to discuss the war.[5] Of course it was those two that stood out at Portland's feast. They were the Allied heroes of the War of the Spanish Succession, internationally renowned, as follows from a Dutch pamphlet written during the time of the Peace of Utrecht and here referring to the famed Battle of Blenheim:

> *'Swabia and Francia, oppressed by the enemy's yoke*
> *Have been snatched away from him by Eugene and Marlborough*
> *And the Bavaria territory, after two battles won*
> *The name of the victors to the end of the world will come.'*[6]

Hence, by the end of the war Marlborough had transcended his status as a successful English general: he had become an international war hero. He not only symbolised Britain's commitment to European affairs, but had also been instrumental in forging international connections.[7] Britain's participation in continental warfare remained fiercely contested between Whigs and Tories, but her pivotal role in Europe could no longer be denied.[8]

The Stadholder-King William III (1650-1702).

Painting by Godfried Schalcken, 1692-1699. Rijksmuseum, Amsterdam, the Netherlands.

England after 1688

The situation had been different in 1688, when Britain's entering the European wars consisted of no less than a revolution in foreign policy.[9] Not since the late-medieval Hundred Years' War had England committed herself to grand-scale warfare on the continent. The revolution took place within several months, but it took much longer for Englishmen to come to terms with their new role – if indeed they ever really did. For the strategic shift was mainly brought about by a dynastic change. A foreign 'warrior King'[10] was instrumental in the process, rather than common consent. The purpose of William's invasion had been to draw England into a coalition against France, whereas most Englishmen, reluctantly accepting the necessity of war, viewed it as an instrument to safeguard the Glorious Revolution. Many were not even convinced, however, that such a war was necessary at all and questioned William's motives. The fact that the King primarily trusted his foreign advisers and generals hardly eased matters. Xenophobia was rife in the 1690s and naturally focused on William's Dutch and Huguenot entourage.[11] Contemporaries spoke of a 'Dutch junto,'[12] although in actual fact it was rather a mixture of Dutch, French and Germans.[13] The foreigners involved were mainly Dutch advisers, such as Everard van Weede van Dijkveld,

Willem van Nassau-Zuylesteyn and Hans Willem Bentinck, and German and French officers such as the Duke of Schomberg[14] and the Earl of Galway.

It was only to be expected that the radical change in foreign policy and the pivotal role of foreigners caused resentment. William's secretary, Constantijn Huygens junior, mentioned many quarrels between Dutch and English during the reign of William III.[15] Zuylesteyn thought that 'The English all hate us.'[16] Undoubtedly Sir John Knights spoke for many of his compatriots when complaining in the House of Commons about the 'great noise and croaking of frog-landers' in the courts of St. James and Whitehall. Opposing the 1695 Naturalization Bill, he proposed 'That the sergeant be commanded to open the doors and let us first kick this Bill out of the House, and then Foreigners out of the kingdom.'[17]

According to the dismissive notions of the imperial ambassador in London, Johann Philipp Hoffmann, these remarks were not to be taken seriously. Rather, 'The complaints are much more the result of their innate repugnancy of anything foreign.'[18] He may have been right, but probably underestimated the inflammatory potency of xenophobia in fuelling political debates in order to galvanise opposition to the government. During a controversy about the Welsh grants of the Earl of Portland in 1696,[19] Robert Price MP complained that England had become a 'Colony to the Dutch.' Why was England allying with 'our Enemies in Trade, though planted among us?'[20] There was fear that the Dutch were taking economic advantage of the war to the detriment of England. Importantly, whereas the English were trying to blockade French trade, the Dutch, always advocating free trade, wanted less rigorous restrictions, even during wartime.[21] Moreover, there was a concern that England was wasting human and financial resources in Europe only to benefit the Allies. The country Tory stalwart Sir Thomas Clarges plausibly argued during the officer's debates in 1692: 'I cannot but take notice that though we were drawn into this war by the Dutch – they being the principals – yet we must bear a greater share of the burden.'[22] Even the Earl of Marlborough tried to capitalise on the xenophobic wave in Parliament, and was in the forefront of protests against the advancement of foreign officers in the autumn of 1692.[23] William, tired of the complaints of his English generals, left the position of commander-in-chief open after 1692.[24] Until the end of William's reign, a string of controversies, such as the Irish Grants disputes, the Spanish Partition Treaties controversy and the Act of Settlement, soured relations between King and political nation. English grief culminated in the scathingly xenophobic pamphlet by John Tutchin on *The Foreigners* in 1701.[25] With the accession to the throne of Queen Anne, who pointedly referred to herself as 'entirely English,'[26] these sentiments did not disappear or lose their edge, as the new monarch continued Williamite foreign policy in broad outline. Indeed, Jonathan Swift's vitriolic *Conduct of the Allies* (1712), a derisive pamphlet attacking the Dutch, epitomised the endemic distrust of foreigners.[27]

Nevertheless, despite the rhetoric of mutual distrust and a deep-rooted antipathy to continental commitment, part of the ruling elite had started to become accustomed to the reality and necessity of Anglo-Dutch cooperation, even if the degree of that commitment remained disputed.[28] It is doubtful whether Daniel Defoe's celebrated reply to Tutchin's pamphlet, *The True-Born Englishman* (1701), stirred the hearts of many, but it is testimony to a growing awareness that English greatness was built partly on the input of foreigners.[29] As Stephen Baxter noted: 'As is the case in every great civilization, something was owed to foreigners. The Huguenots, the

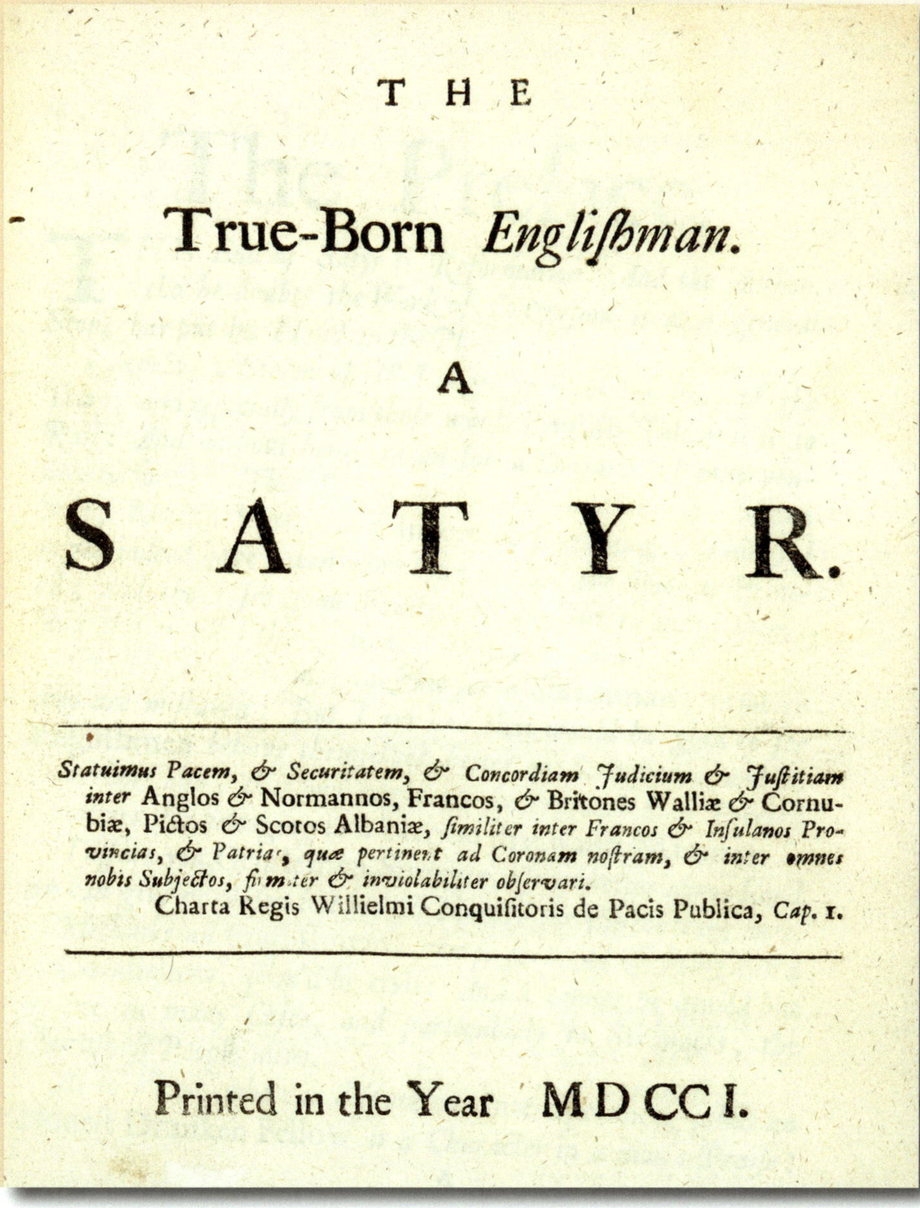
THE

True-Born *Englishman.*

A

SATYR.

Statuimus Pacem, & Securitatem, & Concordiam Judicium & Justitiam inter Anglos & Normannos, Francos, & Britones Walliæ & Cornubiæ, Pictos & Scotos Albaniæ, *similiter inter Francos & Insulanos Provincias, & Patria', quæ pertinent ad Coronam nostram, & inter omnes nobis Subjectos, fi m.ter & inviolabiliter observari.*
Charta Regis Willielmi Conquisitoris de Pacis Publica, *Cap.* 1.

Printed in the Year MDCCI.

The title page of The True Born Englishman - A Satire, by Daniel Defoe.

1701 edition, Henry E. Huntington Library, San Marino, CA, USA.

Dutch, and the German contributions to English development were all substantial. But the English made many contributions of their own.'[30] Indeed, Marlborough's own career betrayed the extent to which Britain was becoming an integral part of Europe. As an ensign, Marlborough fought against the Moors from Tangier, an English acquisition that was part of the dowry of the Portuguese Catharine of Braganza. During the Dutch War (1672–1674), Marlborough was involved in the siege of Maastricht in the United Provinces, and later was part of an English regiment in the service of the famed French Marshall Turenne. In 1690, he fought with Dutch commanders in Ireland. Hence Marlborough's training abroad and under the command of foreigners equipped him for his great task during the War of the Spanish Succession. By then, even if Marlborough's relations with the Allied commanders were frequently strained, military cooperation with foreigners had become natural for him. It had to be. Britain, in the age of Marlborough, had become a great power in Europe and could not afford to keep aloof.

England as a military power

By the turn of the 18th century it still was not obvious to many that this was actually the case. Indeed, when we look at the amount of troops, ships, finance and, last but not least, resolve, that Britain provided for the wars against Louis XIV, the Dutch still matched or even outdid the British, at least until the beginning of the War of the Spanish Succession.[31] In fact, in the years immediately after the Peace of Rijswijk, in French eyes England, torn by partisan struggle, was considered a crippled state. Louis XIV regarded the England of William III in his last years as being just as weak and vulnerable and potentially dependent on France as it had been just prior to the Glorious Revolution. As a result of the controversy about a standing army, England might easily lapse into isolationism.[32] The great standing army debates of 1697–1699, between the Nine Years' War and the War of the Spanish Succession, weakened Britain's position in the world. Britain had no distinguished military tradition, and the success of the Allies in the Nine Years' War had been to a large extent the result of Dutch engineering skills in siege warfare.[33]

Not since the days of Henry VIII had England achieved notable victories on foreign battlefields, and the great success of the Duke of Marlborough as a military genius seemed somewhat surprising. The French army, with its strategic insights and logistic capacity, offered the logical model to follow. Instead, the British preferred to rely on the local militia, viewing a standing army as a dangerous instrument in the hands of any ambitious monarch.[34] Since the 1630s every monarch who aspired to expand the standing army had been viewed with suspicion: Charles I, James II and William III had all encountered great opposition. Despite the military muscle Britain was able to develop, the army did not become an object of national pride, but was regarded as a necessary evil. The spectre of the Civil War was ever present.

However, both the British opposition and Louis XIV had underestimated British potential and resolve.[35] By the early years of the War of the Spanish Succession it had become obvious that Britain managed to sustain her military capacity, in fact she was able to do so much better than her Dutch ally. The financial and organisational foundations laid in the 1690s proved durable. Indeed, British power did not lie so much in the number of troops Britain was able to muster, but in the nation's financial capacity. From that came the possibility of being able to rely on foreign auxiliary troops.[36] At the start of the War of the Spanish Succession the British army consisted of some 40,000 British soldiers.[37] If Britain only mustered about 60,000 native troops in the peak year of 1711, it was financially responsible for an additional 114,000 foreign troops fighting all over Europe.[38] Even if this number was dwarfed by France's astounding army at the same period of 250,000 troops, it remained a significant force. Nevertheless Britain remained dependent on the Dutch and the Austrians, who delivered between about 120,000 and 135,000 troops apiece to the Alliance.[39] Britain was never able to fight a continental war successfully without the aid of a great continental power.

■ England as a maritime power

Despite her potential to influence the Balance of Power on the continent, it was at sea where Britain really developed as a Great Power. The Nine Years' War and the War of the Spanish Succession were primarily continental wars, and the navies were supportive rather than decisive. True, there were moments, such as in 1690 and 1692, when French naval power could have been instrumental in the defeat of Britain, but after 1692 the naval wars were largely over. Allied naval raids on the French coasts, for example in 1692, were failures, and with them the plans vanished for a successful descent and a quick decisive march on Paris.[40] Still, Britain would not have been able to develop a grand strategy of the magnitude it did without naval support. The alliance with Portugal and the Iberian campaign would have been unthinkable without it.[41] However it was on the Continent that the war had to be won, the fleet being merely supportive of the army. This was why Marlborough became the hero of the War of the Spanish Succession, rather than some admiral of the fleet.[42] In this sense, Marlborough embodies the whole paradox of British involvement on the continent.

It was a paradox that the political parties in Britain were unable to solve. Whereas the Whigs supported Williamite continental strategy, the Tories aspired to develop Britain as a naval, rather than a military power. This ambition was partly satisfied due to an arrangement with the Dutch. The English were contracted to deliver the largest part of the war fleet,[43] and it was during these years that England built a fleet that would surpass that of France as well as that of the Dutch Republic. Initially this naval superiority was not obvious. Until the Battle of La Hogue (1692), England remained surprisingly vulnerable to foreign invasion – as indeed the Glorious Revolution had made clear – but after the naval victory at La Hogue, the French navy was contained and therefore neutralised.

If the navy played only a supportive role in the War of the Spanish Succession, it was of primary importance in building the foundations of an overseas empire that would not fully emerge until later in the 18th century. William III and Louis XIV belonged to an older generation, they were primarily fixed on the Continent and uninterested in and largely ignorant of colonial matters. They were aware of a colonial context, but it played only a secondary role in their grand strategy.[44] During the War of the Spanish Succession, all this started to change. If Britain was emerging as a great European power, by the early 18th century it was also winning the race to become the leading world power. She would do so primarily by establishing primacy at sea and building an overseas empire.

The first step was defending the island, which was effectively achieved in 1692. By then, an Anglo-Dutch fleet had entered the Mediterranean, which facilitated a European grand strategy. Indeed, the navy was at that time still primarily active in British and European waters. Its main task was to defend Britain against foreign invasion. The Royal Navy patrolled the North Sea and the Mediterranean, the Indies and Africa being of secondary importance.[45] Britain nevertheless managed to obtain vital advantages in Spanish America, thereby outflanking the Dutch, who remained preoccupied with safeguarding their Barrier in the Spanish Netherlands.[46] The Treaty of Utrecht (1713) assigned the lucrative asiento to Britain, enabling her to carry slaves to Spanish America. Also, Britain acquired bases in the Mediterranean (Gibraltar and Minorca) to consolidate her position there. Hence Utrecht marked the emergence of Britain as a European as well as global power.

Tapestry depicting a scene during the related naval battles of Barfleur and La Hogue, 29 May and 4 June 1692.

Tapestry by Judocus de Vos, 1715-1734. Rijksmuseum, Amsterdam, the Netherlands.

The build-up and employment of such massive armies and navies would not have been possible without a powerful economy. Importantly, despite the disruptive wars around the turn of the 18th century, the growth of British commerce that had begun during the Restoration kept its momentum, fuelled by an ever expanding overseas trade.[47] The blockade of France also, it was thought, served to stimulate English domestic industries.[48] By the last quarter of the 17th century the British had overtaken the Dutch as the dominant commercial sea power. Moreover, any setbacks during or because of the war were compensated by the gains of 1713, not least by the asiento. Yet despite the importance of its burgeoning overseas and global trade, Britain's economy at this epoch remained focused on Europe rather than America. During the final stage of the War of the Spanish Succession Britain exported merchandise and products worth £942,000 to the Indies, America and Africa, against £5,520,000 to Europe – almost six times as much.[49] But the basis for a global economy was laid during these years, if only because Britain sidelined France as a colonial competitor in the New World.

■ Britain as a financial power

The concern that Eugene showed concerning Britain's commitment was a sign that Britain had now become the cornerstone of the European alliance against France. This was primarily because of the financial capital she could muster, based upon extensive borrowing, but more structurally on the fact the she was an increasingly powerful economy. The Nine Years' War witnessed the genesis of the National Debt, which in 1689 did not exist, but which by the Peace of Rijswijk (1697) had risen to £16,700,000, and by the time of the Peace of Utrecht (1713) amounted to £36,200,000.[50] Britain's capacity to continue to function with this astronomical debt compares favourably with the situation of the Dutch Republic, which by 1713 was incapacitated by a national debt of about £13,000,000.[51]

These figures are also a testimony to Britain's capacity to raise a large army. During the Civil War and after, the average spending per annum on the New Model Army had been roughly £850,000.[52] The number was actually lower during the Restoration Period, when expenditure fell to an average of £350,000 per annum.[53] This number then rose to an average of £2,500,000 per annum during the Nine Years' War.[54] Hence the expansion of the military settlement after 1688 was significant. Likewise, expenditure on the navy rose steeply after the Glorious Revolution. Between 1650 and 1680, the costs amounted to about £650,000 annually, against about £500,000 in the 1680s, rising steeply to almost £2,000,000 towards the end of the Nine Years' War.[55] In the Nine Years' War, on average £5,460,000 annually was spent on the army and the navy together.[56] On average, the British government spent about £7,000,000 per annum during the War of the Spanish Succession.[57] With a population just passing the 5 million mark around the turn of the 18th century,[58] England was a large but by no means a major country in Europe. The population of France was about 19 million around 1700. However, France, with a population four times larger, managed to squeeze out £15,000,000 in taxation, against £10,000,000 in England.[59] Although only 9% of the English national income was spent on military efforts, military spending actually consisted of about 2/3 of total government expenditure.[60]

Britain was able to finance the war mainly because of an efficient taxation system. Fiscal bureaucracy, if small by for instance French standards, grew spectacularly from 1688.[61] Direct taxation in particular proved successful, and the Nine Years' War and the War of the Spanish Succession would have been impossible without the instrument of the land tax, naturally hated by the landed classes and the Tories.[62] Between 1689 and 1713, during the wars against France, Britain was transformed into a 'fiscal military state,' a state that develops military muscle based upon its capacity to utilise fiscal instruments efficiently. This development was also made possible by the 'financial revolution.' The establishment of the Bank of England and its capacity to loan money to the government increased the monetary muscle of the government considerably.[63] It was the 'fiscal-military state' as much as the parliamentary revolution that enabled Britain to become a major power. This was a paradox, for the first required a strictly organised state but the second suggested a liberal one.[64]

Grocers' Hall, Poultry, as it appeared whilst occupied by the Bank of England, 1695 - 1734.

Print from The Bank of England from within, 1694-1900 by W. Marston Acres. Baker Library Historical Collections, Harvard Business School, Cambridge, MA, USA.

Tories and Whigs

The threat to traditional freedoms perceived as a result of these changes inevitably led to political controversy. Generally, the Tories, representing the traditional Anglican land-owning class, were averse to intervention on the Continent and preferred a naval 'blue water policy.' The Whigs, drawing power from a heterogeneous group that included territorial magnates as well as merchants in the City, and which incorporated dissenters, were more inclined to support the war as advocated by William III and later the Duke of Marlborough.[65] Such generalizations only partly do justice to the complexities of reality. For one, the Whig and Tory parties soon split in Court and Country wings. Eventually, Country Whigs and Country Tories found themselves joining in opposition to either the Court Tory or the Court Whig governments during the Nine Years' War. Yet it remains true that the continental war continued to be supported by the Court Whigs and was opposed by the bulk of the Tory Party until the Peace of Utrecht.

By 1700 parties had stabilised into powerful alliances that came to dominate British politics.[66] During the War of the Spanish Succession the 'rage of party' reached a climax, and none could escape the maelstrom of partisan struggle. Marlborough was one of the few who were averse to partisanship and he refused to make a firm alliance with either Whigs or Tories. Tragically, his policy almost inevitably bound him to the Court Whigs. This would ultimately destroy his career when the High Tories, back in power in 1710, were bent on ousting the great man. The War of the Spanish Succession was essentially a Whig war, even though men sympathetic to Toryism, such as Sidney Godolphin, played a leading role in the government. But

Queen Anne (1665-1714). Anne succeeded to the English throne on the death of William III in 1702 and became Queen of Great Britain with the Act of Union on 1 May 1707.

Painting by Edmund Lilly, 1703. Blenheim Palace, Oxfordshire, UK. The Bridgeman Art Library.

Godolphin was the exception. He was virtually the only non-partisan major office holder who maintained his position as Lord Treasurer in the cabinet throughout most regime changes (1702–1710).[67]

In 1702, after the difficult last years of William's reign during which the Whig ascendancy had evaporated, they returned to the House under a new monarch with only 190 members, against 323 Tories.[68] Queen Anne was largely sympathetic to Toryism and loathed the Whigs, not in the least because they had been so influential during William's regime. The High Tory and uncle of Queen Anne, Lord Rochester,

The Battle of Ramillies as depicted in a contemporary pamphlet.

Etching by unknown artist, 1706. Royal Library, The Hague, the Netherlands.

and the Tory stalwart Edward Seymour entered the Cabinet, as did the High Tory Earl of Nottingham, who became Secretary of State in 1702. Nottingham had played a leading role in devising a Tory strategy back in the early 1690s: one that was hardly much committed to full-scale involvement in the war in the Spanish Netherlands.[69] A blue-water strategy was advocated by the Tories: England should act as an auxiliary power, not commit herself to continental warfare but rather employ the navy effectively, and keep taxes at a low level.[70] It was hardly surprising that the alliance with the Dutch was strained by this attitude.

The tremendous victory at Blenheim in August 1704 changed all this, as it showed that the continental strategy was successful. It initiated the slow but sure comeback of Court Whigs (the 3rd Earl of Sunderland as Secretary of State in 1706, and Baron Somers as Lord President in 1708) in the government. In the 1705 elections, 291 Whigs outflanked a minority of 222 Tories.[71] The victory at Ramillies in 1706 only confirmed the validity of continental strategy. The battle at Malplaquet of 1709 was much more ambiguous. Although a victory, it was a pyrrhic one since it obtained no direct advantage, and came at a high price. By then the Whigs had become overconfident because of the military successes on the Continent, and their success planted the seeds of their fall. Shattering successes fed their ambition to conclude 'no peace without Spain.' This overconfident goal turned out to be unattainable. Although the

Whigs maintained their majority in the House of Commons in the 1708 elections, in 1710 they were massively defeated,[72] opening the way for peace negotiations upon Tory conditions.

■ The role of religion in Britain

Thus, the last decade of the 17th and first decade of the 18th century were marked by warfare against France, in order to protect British trade interests, guarantee the revolution settlement and maintain the Balance of Power in Europe. But for many Englishmen, these wars were also fought to defend Protestantism. If the wars of religion had apparently ended in 1648 with the Peace of Westphalia (or rather in 1651 with the end of the British Civil Wars), a substantial part of the British public did regard the wars against Louis XIV as essentially religious in nature. Daniel Defoe argued in 1701 that 'If we re-examine the Present State of Europe, we shall find it, as to the Interest of Religion, in worse Circumstances on several Accounts, than it ever yet was since the Treaties of Munster and Westphalia.'[73] The Catholic threat from abroad was regarded as yet another attempt to crush the English Reformation, as a phase in a 150 year old struggle. Englishmen constructed a 'confessional geography' that divided Europe into an absolutist, Catholic, therefore threatening sphere, and a free, Protestant sphere.[74] It would be futile, however, to suggest that English policymakers conducted a strictly confessional foreign policy. After all, in the 1690s an alliance was forged with the Catholic powers Savoy, Spain and the Holy Roman Empire. The 1700s saw the continuation of the alliance with the Emperor and a new alliance with Portugal. On the other hand, there was a natural inclination to join with Protestant powers, most notably the Dutch Republic.[75] And of course, English policymakers were sensitive to the idea of interventions to help coreligionists, such as the Cevennois in the south of France, who rose in revolt against Louis XIV in 1703,[76] but also the Protestant Hungarians, who rebelled against the Emperor that same year.[77]

Marlborough's role and position are a good example of the potency of religion. During the Glorious Revolution he defected and went over to William's army in order to support the Protestant cause in England. In 1708 Jurieu, Basnage and Superville, three Rotterdam ministers, appealed to Marlborough 'to incite him to secure Protestantism in France.'[78] The Duke's Protestant leanings were well known. As a staunch Protestant, it would have been difficult for Marlborough to become Governor of the Spanish Netherlands, a position that was offered to him in 1706 by the Emperor.[79]

Britain's obvious role as Protestant power having to cooperate with Catholic states put her in an awkward situation. On the one hand, she needed to maintain her position as arbiter of Europe, on the other hand she remained the leader of the Protestant part of Europe. This traditional balancing act had been part of British foreign policy ever since the time of Henry VIII and Elizabeth I, but Elizabeth in particular was also famed for her protection of Protestants, most notably those in the Low Countries during the Dutch Revolt. Likewise, Queen Anne was a beacon of hope for suppressed Protestants. In 1704 one pamphleteer tried to persuade her to intervene on behalf of the Protestant Cevennois, who had risen against Louis XIV, by appealing to this tradition. He did so by referring to 'the Piety and Justice of a Queen [Elizabeth], who maintain'd the true Religion, and reliev'd the oppressed all over Europe.'[80] He also,

The Queen Addres'd, and by new Senate told,
They'll Act with more Obedience than Her old.
Others would Swell with Pride, if thus cares'd,
But he bears humble Thoughts within his Breast
Without Concern he from his Coach alights,
To stand a Tryal which its Hearers frights.
The Dedication's excellently done,
So Mr. Cl___s-you may e'en go on!
His Entry into Oxford here is Shewn.
Attended by the Country and the Town.
The College with alacrity receiv'd
Her Son return'd, for whom acus'd She greiv'd
St. Asaphs Bishop, for his Flock's Instruction,
Allows Him Institution and Induction.
From hence the Church's Restoration rose;
And made Discovery of her Secret Foes.
The Derby Sheriff doth of him request,
That his Assize Discourse may be imprest.
The D___r and his Friends in Consultation,
How to reply to Commons. Accusation.
Into the Church the Sheriff introduces,
The D___r who laments its Foes Abuses.
The Queen bids Rochester ascend the Chair,
Fate wills that Buckingham be seated there.
Such moving Periods, and so just a Speech,
Not only Good Mens Eyes but Hearts must reach.
Her Majesty her Self of Troubles eases,
And Chuses Such Attendants as She pleases.

Playing cards depicting the impeachment of Henry Sacheverell in 1710, diamond suit.

Etching by unknown artist, around 1711.
The British Museum, London, UK.

cleverly, extended the traditional role of the English monarchs as Defender of the Faith to the Continent, thereby geographically expanding their religious jurisdiction and providing them with a justification for intervention, but at the same time pressing them to enter into continental commitments in order to defend European Protestantism.[81]

This confessional allegiance tied Britain to the Continent, although the extent to which it did so is disputed by some historians.[82] The foreign policy Britain conducted from 1689 onwards had a distinct Protestant character for many onlookers, and the Balance of Power that emerged was viewed as something mainly devised to protect Protestant interests.[83] As Protestants, the English felt themselves to be part of a transnational community. Dissenting groups may have felt this more strongly than their Anglican brethren, but Anglicans also gave substantial financial support to persecuted Huguenots, Waldensians and Palatine Protestants.[84]

Religion had also been a force within the British Isles, one that generated its own set of problems. It was a force because it provided the English with a sense of common identity and destiny.[85] By the time of Queen Elizabeth's reign, to be English meant to be Protestant and free. Yet, despite the fact that Catholicism was already by the late 16th century a waning force, in the 17th century there continued to be a paranoid fear of Catholic plots and take-overs. Notable examples are the 1605 Gunpowder Plot and the Popish Plot of 1683. The Catholic policy of James II failed miserably because it was associated with that of Louis XIV, who persecuted Huguenots after the 1685 revocation of the Edict of Nantes. However, by the turn of the 18th century these domestic fears had diminished. The Catholic threat was now mainly seen as an external one, originating in France.[86] Yet there were still intraconfessional problems to consider. The Restoration had sought to create Anglican unity by sidelining and persecuting dissenters, but William's Act of Toleration had ended this situation. By 1715 dissenters only amounted to some 340,000, of a general population of over 5 million.[87] However the Tories continued to loathe the thought of dissenters actually taking office, and launched several Occasional Conformity Bills in 1702, 1703 and 1704, in order to frustrate the dissenters and through them the Whigs. As late as 1709, Sacheverell's 'Church in Danger' campaign mobilised massive support for the Anglican settlement and led to ferocious assaults on government policy.[88] By the time of the Peace of Utrecht however relations between dissenters and Anglicans had ceased to upset the political establishment.

England, Scotland and Ireland

If partisan and religious divisions complicated the fabric of the body politic within England, relations with Scotland and Ireland added an additional dimension of complexity. The development of 'Britain' was still, in the famous words of John Pocock, 'a problematic and uncompleted experiment in the creation and interaction of several nations.'[89] The 'British problem' was a long way from being solved when the War of the Spanish Succession broke out.[90] By 1700 Wales had become almost completely integrated with England, but for Scotland and Ireland this was an entirely different matter. Three kingdoms, with different political and legal systems, confessions and cultures, could not easily be integrated. The relationship between the three kingdoms was, moreover, asymmetric, Ireland being a virtual colony of England.[91] Scotland, ever since the Union of 1603, had been equal to England but only in name. Such a complex triangular relationship was difficult at the best of times, but decidedly problematic if not potentially disastrous in hard times. This meant that every single time the British Isles – or the 'Anglo-Celtic Isles' – became embroiled in large-scale conflict, the relationship between the three kingdoms needed to be renegotiated. This became clear during the 'English' revolution of the 1640s, which many historians now interpret within a British context.[92] The problem also became acute in 1689, when part of Scotland rose in rebellion against the Glorious Revolution,[93] and Ireland became the battleground for a counter-offensive against William, a campaign that lasted for three years.[94] During the War of the Spanish Succession the British experiment reached a new stage. The Treaty of Limerick (1691) had, so it seemed, definitively subdued Ireland, and foreign invasion via Ireland had become very unlikely ever since England had established dominion at sea in 1692. Relations with Scotland remained in flux. Fundamental dissatisfaction with the rule of William III, the famine of the late 1690s and the disaster of the failed colony of Darien, for which England was blamed, strained relationships.[95] By the middle of the first decade of the 18th century Scotland had become a liability. Its refusal to guarantee the Protestant succession persuaded England to try to come to terms with Scotland. The incorporative Union of 1707 was largely the result of a package deal made by the Whigs, in which Scotland entered the Union on favourable conditions, and in turn continued to support the war and accept the succession.[96] That is not to say that Scotland necessarily recognised the Union as favourable. Indeed, profound discontent sparked the attempted 1708 Jacobite invasion, and Scotland became a breeding ground after it for Jacobitism and the most likely place for renewed invasion – as the Jacobite insurrections in 1715 and 1745 make clear.[97]

■ The threat of Jacobitism

If the Jacobite insurrections ultimately failed, Jacobite ideology provided a natural magnet for discontent with the English government and its commitment to the continental war. Originally, Jacobitism was hardly a full-fledged ideology. Its one guiding principle was the fact that it embraced the principle of divine right, and therefore substantiated James II's claim to the throne. Soon, however, Jacobitism evolved into an all-embracing counter-ideology. Whereas the Protestant and Williamite ideology of state sought a further integration with Europe, a commitment to continental warfare and an outspoken non-sectarian form of Protestantism, Jacobitism recruited successfully among those sympathetic to the old Anglican Tory regime. Remarkably, some Country Whigs were also attracted by it.[98] Whether or not Jacobitism as an ideology and as a movement was ever a real threat to Britain is disputed amongst historians.[99] If the 1690s were riddled with plots and conspiracies, possibly the only really dangerous moment was 1692, when a Jacobite revolt was planned in conjunction with a French invasion. This event proved that Jacobitism could be successful only with foreign aid.[100] Hence Jacobitism continued to provide foreign powers with leverage to intervene in British affairs, and tied Britain definitively to the events on the Continent.

As an ideology Jacobitism also penetrated the heart of the political establishment. Even Marlborough, who proved a faithful subject to William and Anne, was not insensitive to the attractions of flirting with Jacobitism, but he was certainly not alone. In the uncertain conditions of the early 1690s many did likewise, and they were motivated by pragmatism rather than ideological commitment. By the late 1700s a different situation had arisen, and England had to choose between two sharply contrasting ideological settlements. With the Protestant succession in jeopardy due to the fact that Anne had no surviving heirs, a choice had to be made between the House of Hanover, favoured by the Whigs and some Tories, like Robert Harley, and the House of Stuart, favoured by part of the Tory party including Henry St. John. The refusal of the Pretender to convert to Protestantism ultimately decided the fate of the Jacobite succession, whereas the split within the Tory party, unable to choose decisively, led to its demise after 1714.

The role of the public

All these controversies concerning religion and politics were energised by a powerful emerging public sphere.[101] Englishmen became increasingly aware of political debates and religious controversies, thanks to a massive increase in the circulation of newspapers and pamphlets. Recently, Steven Pincus has argued that Englishmen were also profoundly more interested and well-informed about foreign affairs than historians have hitherto believed.[102] The British public showed an active interest in the war. Newspapers were published several times a week with editions amounting to thousands of copies. Whereas newspapers offered more or less objective reports, pamphlets were written to persuade, and caused heated debates. Often such pamphlets were read aloud and discussed in coffee houses, and it is estimated that this manner of circulation ensured a steady reading public of tens if not hundreds of thousands of people.[103] Readers and listeners were able to form an informed opinion, which meant that British politicians increasingly felt the need to justify their foreign policy. Defeats needed to be explained, successes to be exploited to the full. It was in this context that the Duke of Marlborough was able to develop into a national hero of a kind that had not existed, one who could be publicly celebrated by pamphleteers.[104] Moreover, according to Mark Knights, under the later Stuarts England became a 'representative society,' in which numerous elections, petitions and the publication of pamphlets actively integrated a larger public with the body of the political nation. As a result, partisan contention became ever more vehement.[105] In the ideological turmoil, truth was ideologically determined, rather than a matter of fact. The public sphere significantly widened the contours of politics, but also destabilised the political system.[106]

By reading those pamphlets, the British public became involved in the political process, and it became necessary for the ruling elite to make attempts to influence an increasingly vocal voting public.[107] Such proto-democratic tendencies seemed to denote a new level of political modernisation, as did the development of administrative institutions. This institutional development gained its first major incentive in the middle of the 16th century. Although historians are reluctant now to speak of a Tudor Revolution in government in the 1530s,[108] it is clear that the middle of the 16th century saw an accelerating growth in state institutions, which continued into the 17th century and was interrupted only by the English Revolution. Whether evolution or revolution describes this development best, by 1689 this process decidedly reached a new plateau, mainly as a result of the financial revolution as described above.

Though technically not a state institution, the Bank of England (1695) played a crucial role. But the most significant change was the development of Parliament into a de facto permanent institution that was increasingly assertive. Psychologically, such a development was rooted in the experience of the Civil War, but probably stalled in the Restoration period. In the early 1690s, however, annual meetings of Parliament did much to help it develop a corporate identity. A Committee of Public Accounts was responsible for overseeing government spending and functioned as an assertive watchdog over the executive. Although accepting the prerogative of the King, Parliament was increasingly critical of the war effort, and became more active in scrutinising foreign policy.[109] By the time of Queen Anne, Parliament had considerably constrained the policy of the monarch through the Act of Settlement of 1701.[110] While it could not steal the initiative from the monarch in devising foreign policy, debates in Parliament were of vital importance, and were often regarded as being responsible for destabilising foreign policy.[111]

■ The role of the courtier

Yet despite the apparent modernity of the English state, it was also still very much an early modern state as well. We tend to see the Duke of Marlborough as a military commander, but it is easy to overlook the fact that he was also a courtier, and one who owed his position partly to the personal favour bestowed upon him by the Queen.[112] That favour in turn was partly dependent upon the relationship between Marlborough's wife, Sarah Churchill, and Queen Anne, who had developed a long-lasting friendship.[113] When that friendship ended, Marlborough's power base also crumbled. The position of the Duke and Duchess of Marlborough as royal favourites is remarkable. All the late Tudor and early Stuart monarchs relied upon favourites: Queen Elizabeth had the Earls of Leicester and Essex, and James I and Charles I had the Duke of Buckingham. This was no different for their Spanish and French counterparts: Spain and France were ruled by the great favourites of Lerma, Olivarez, Richelieu, and Mazarin throughout most of the first half of the 17th century.

The decline of this European phenomenon is generally seen to have occurred in the second half of the 17th century.[114] This also seems true for England. With the rise of Parliament and the extension of governmental institutions, the royal favourite based at court lost significance. Indeed, Restoration England was dominated by parliamentary managers, such as the Earl of Clarendon, the members of the Cabal, and the Earl of Danby, rather than by royal favourites. It was William III who reintroduced the favourite in England, first the Earl of Portland and later the Earl of Albemarle. These were only shadows of what Buckingham once was, but surprisingly they represented a return, rather than a last resurrection, of the phenomenon. Still, it was a different kind of favourite that Marlborough and Portland embodied. The essence of their role as royal favourites was their capacity to organise the war effort in conjunction with the Dutch ally. Hence England's new continental commitments were directly responsible for the re-emergence of the royal favourite.[115] The Duke of Marlborough turned out to be one of the most powerful favourites in British history, one who acquired a near-regal status. The personal favour of the monarch was crucial to Marlborough's position.

The Protestant Succession in Britain

Despite the presence of an influential courtier, around 1700 the role of the sovereign remained central to any political equation. Hence matters of succession and legality were still of the utmost importance, and it was precisely these that became problematic after 1688. The Nine Years' War, following the 'abdication' of James II and the succession of William III, has been described as a War of English Succession, but that epithet might equally apply to the War of the Spanish Succession. When Louis XIV acknowledged James III as heir to the throne in 1701, England had little choice but to defend the Williamite settlement again and declare war. With the death of the Duke of Gloucester in 1700, which left Queen Anne childless, the Protestant succession seemed uncertain. These complications show the extent to which dynasty was indeed important. Queen Anne continued to be anxious about the legitimacy of her queenship, not just for political reasons, but also as a matter of conscience. Was she entitled to the throne, or was she disobeying God by denying James III, the legitimate heir, his place on the throne?[116] Whatever her private feelings, the Queen of England needed to justify her right to the throne. Did a disputed succession weaken the standing of England in Europe? Elizabeth I, whose Protestant Succession was questioned by the Pope and the King of Spain, certainly conducted a careful foreign policy as a result. Whether this was also the case for William and Anne is more difficult to say, but there can be no doubt that there were both domestic threats and foreign complexities to deal with. The succession issue divided England internally, leading to violent partisan struggles, and also exposed the country to Jacobite invasion attempts.

England as leader of the coalition

Nevertheless to describe these conflicts as purely wars of the English succession betrays an insular approach, as they were inextricably connected to the Continent. The wars were essentially coalition wars, and it has to be emphasised that joining the Grand Alliance was a divergence of Britain's usual role. Not since the Hundred Years' War (1337–1453) had England become embroiled in large-scale conflict on the European mainland, and never before had England participated in such a broad international alliance. In retrospect it was only to be expected that the wars should instigate massive domestic opposition, and it is surprising how relatively easily Britain joined the war in 1689, and again in 1702. Before long Britain was not only a participant in the war, but had become the de facto leader of an international coalition. This was hardly the case with the Nine Years' War, where it was really William III himself who took the lead, while the Dutch army bore the brunt of the war.[117] In the War of the Spanish Succession, however, British leadership soon became clear. Ostensibly commitments were shared: the British furnished 40,000 troops and 5/8 of the fleet, against 102,000 Dutch troops and 3/8 of the fleet.[118] However, the Dutch soon were unable to meet this number of ships. An indicator of English superiority was the fact that the Duke of Marlborough was given overall command of the combined Anglo-Dutch army in the field – despite the fact that the Dutch provided far more troops. Although Marlborough's appointment was partly based upon his recognised military talent, it was primarily political in nature, aimed to please the British and commit them to the continental war.[119] Moreover, England soon developed a grand European strategy the Dutch were unable to conceive or implement, and reluctant to follow. England rapidly became the undisputed leader of Grand Alliance, although it was not until 1712, when she dropped out, that her indispensability became totally clear.

Already during the Nine Years' War Britain had evolved a grand strategy of European, even global dimensions, which matured during the War of the Spanish Succession. As argued here previously, it was never a strategy that remained uncontested among British political parties. Nor was it a grand strategy devised solely at a central level by the monarch and the secretaries of state. In practice, commanders in the field, admirals and diplomats helped to shape foreign policy.[120] The international alliance hardly simplified matters, as cooperation with the Allies was strained and difficult to coordinate. Indeed, as John Hattendorf argued: 'There was no allied strategy; there was only the separate and often conflicting views of each allied government.'[121]

Efforts were nevertheless made to streamline allied action. This was easier when William III was Stadholder-King and controlled British and Dutch foreign policy almost singlehandedly. After his death, the 'personal union' was dissolved, but Queen Anne, despite her resentment of her predecessor, decided to continue the war against France. The traditional view that Queen Anne had no interest at all in foreign policy has been recently contested. She did in fact take an active interest and kept herself informed about important matters.[122] However, she was no William III, and she did not formulate foreign policy herself. In practice, it was mainly the First Lord of the Treasury and the two Secretaries of State that were involved in the actual business of foreign policy. The Lord President of the Council, the Lord Privy Seal, the Lord Chamberlain and the Lord Chancellor were also kept informed.[123] To an important extent, the coordination of the Dutch and British war effort was streamlined through the collaboration between the Duke of Marlborough and Grand Pensionary Anthonie Heinsius, as is richly presented in A.J. Veenendaal's monumental edited correspondence of the Grand Pensionary.[124] Indeed, if Marlborough has often been praised for his strategic insight and boldness, his grandest achievement may very well have been the diplomatic coordination of Allied war efforts.

The grand coalition wars required a smooth and effective diplomatic service. According to Henry Snyder the period 1689–1714 constituted the 'formative years of the [diplomatic] service.'[125] England's diplomatic service was superior to that of their Dutch ally, due to the fact that it was much more centralised. A paradoxical result of this was, however, that diplomats in the field acquired more freedom of movement, as long as they kept in line with the desires of the Secretary of State.[126] This system has been described as the 'English plan,' and was largely initiated after 1702 by the Secretaries of State.[127] In this way, they could exclude other ministers from important information and so strengthen their position within the Cabinet. But the system was far from fixed, and in actual fact the Secretaries and the First Lord continued to compete, as would become clear in the 1712 negotiations with France.[128] Diplomats were also instructed to correspond with each other, so as to stimulate the flow of information. Whereas under William letters were read aloud in the full Cabinet Council, under Queen Anne a new practice surfaced, in which the Secretaries encouraged diplomats to write separate secret letters which contained more important information.[129] Under William III, cooperation between Dutch and English diplomats was natural, although often resented by Englishmen who felt that the King was favouring his native servants.[130] After 1702, cooperation continued, but despite the coordination at the top level between Anthonie Heinsius and the Duke of Marlborough, it went far

less smoothly. It was however informal diplomacy that was still important. William III had made use of a network of informal diplomats that conducted vital business for him.[131] His favourite the Earl of Portland had almost singlehandedly concluded the Spanish Partition Treaties.[132] Despite all complications, for two decades English and Dutch diplomacy were often cooperative and achieved notable successes.

It was during the War of the Spanish Succession that Britain was finally capable – financially, militarily and mentally – of developing a truly grand strategy, one that hitherto only Spain, France and Austria had been able to conduct.[133] In the Nine Years' War, William III had already done this to a certain extent, and his strategy was continued and extended. Before 1689, England sometimes interfered on the Continent, or waged wars with France or the United Provinces. The Spanish Succession changed all this, and necessitated a grand strategy of European proportions, as well as the construction of an international alliance. Britain was, as such, instrumental, in changing the face of European international relations.

The Duke of Marlborough discussing plans for the Siege of Bouchain with his Chief Engineer, Colonel Armstrong.

Painting by Enoch Seeman, 18th century. Blenheim Palace, Oxfordshire, UK. Photograph by Richard Cragg, reproduced with the kind permission of His Grace the Duke of Marlborough, Blenheim Palace Image Library.

■ The Spanish Succession

The problematic Spanish Succession had a long history. Already in 1668 the Emperor Leopold I and Louis XIV had made an agreement to partition the Spanish Empire in the event of the death of the childless Spanish King Carlos II. The empire included, in addition to the Spanish monarchy: Milan, Naples and Sicily, Sardinia, the Spanish Netherlands, the Italian presidii[134] and the Spanish overseas territories. Should this inheritance fall to either an Austrian or a French candidate, the balance in Europe would be disturbed. Neither the Nine Years' War nor the two Spanish Partition Treaties succeeded in solving the matter, not least because Carlos II, when on his deathbed in November 1700, made up his own mind and allotted the entire inheritance to a grandson of Louis XIV, Philip of Anjou.

The British, averse to new war, were provoked by a series of simultaneous incidents. First, Louis XIV occupied several fortresses in the Spanish Netherlands, justifying this by arguing that he was acting on behalf of his grandson. This underlined the unbreakable bond between a Bourbon France and a future Bourbon Spain. Secondly, Louis XIV acknowledged James Stuart (the 'Old Pretender') as King of England at the death of his father James II in September 1701, thereby threatening the Protestant settlement in England. Lastly, the new King of Spain assigned the lucrative asiento to a French company. On 7 September 1701 the Emperor, England and the Dutch Republic renewed the Treaty of the Grand Alliance, and in May 1702 declared war on France. A European alliance was forged relatively quickly. Initially Savoy, Portugal, Bavaria and Cologne joined or favoured the French, whereas Prussia, Hanover, Hesse-Kassel, the Palatinate, Münster and Baden joined the Allies. However, Savoy and Portugal were soon detached from France and joined the allied side thanks to a concerted effort by Austrian, Dutch and British diplomats. However, it was the British diplomats who played a leading role. In Turin it was Richard Hill, rather than his Dutch counterpart Albert van der Meer, who was able to persuade Victor Emanuel to leave France and join the Allies. In Lisbon it was the enigmatic John Methuen who outmanoeuvred his Dutch colleague, Francisco Schonenberg, and managed to conclude a commercial treaty.[135]

The war was European, but in a sense it is better described as West-European,

Verbondszaal der geallieerden, image showing the imaginary meeting of the high allies Queen Anne, the German Emperor and the States Deputy with Louis XIV.

Etching by Romeyn de Hooghe. 1702. Royal Library, The Hague, the Netherlands.

since it was not connected to the Northern War that had broken out in 1700. Denmark, Russia and Saxony had declared war on Charles XII of Sweden. The Northern War made the commitment of Prussia to the War of the Spanish Succession uncertain,[136] as the new king felt threatened by Swedish advances in Poland, but ultimately the two conflicts remained separate.[137] The theatres of war were almost exclusively in Western Europe: the Spanish Netherlands, the Rhine, Northern Italy and Spain. In the process of these grand-scale wars a new international system emerged, based on the concept of a Balance of Power. The term itself, inspired by Newtonian physics, was of English origin, and the concept was embraced primarily by British politicians. Louis XIV was disdainful, and some Dutch pamphleteers regarded it as a justification for British warmongering.[138] The Balance of Power is an ostensibly simple but in actual fact very complex term.[139] Among its many different meanings, it may simply be a literal description of a system that evolved as the result of unintended consequences. The coalitions that took shape in the later part of the 17th century to counter the threat of French universal monarchy led to a Balance of Power that crystallised eventually at the Peace of Utrecht in 1713. It can also be thought of as prescriptive.

Although William III has been described as the architect of the coalitions against Louis XIV, interestingly he never employed the term Balance of Power, instead referring to the Christian Commonwealth, a much older concept of European unity.[140] But it was Balance of Power politics, enshrined in the 1713 Treaty of Utrecht that would dominate European politics for centuries to come.

Conclusion

Between 1689 and 1713, the age of Marlborough, Britain was not only transformed internally, but also reconnected with the Continent and made an integral part of Europe. With some justification, the instigator of the process, William III, has often been described as the 'first European.' With similar justification, the Duke of Marlborough may be styled the 'first English European,' being instrumental in continuing the work of William and being the soul of international cooperation during the War of the Spanish Succession. Even his enemies in England were ready to grant him this title, though for derogatory rather than complimentary reasons.[141] The accusations in Jonathan Swift's scathing *Conduct of the Allies* turned on Marlborough's supposed self-aggrandisement and his alliance with the Dutch.

In 1688 England was still a medium and relatively isolated power, but this changed rapidly. The wars against France necessitated intervention in Savoy and an alliance with Portugal. British diplomats intervened in the Hungarian revolt to get the Emperor to show more commitment in the war against France. The British navy established permanent bases in the Mediterranean basin, such as at Gibraltar and Minorca. At the same time foreigners entered England; Huguenots were settling in Ireland, whereas Irish Jacobites in turn fled to France. Dutch and Danish troops marched in London in 1689, whilst British troops were employed in Flanders throughout the long wars. Dutch courtiers married English noble women, settled in England and acquired Irish estates. Political alliances were forged across borders. The Court Whigs found support for their policy among Dutch policy makers. Meanwhile pamphlets about the European war and the fate of European Protestantism circulated in England in unprecedented quantities. In short, Britain had transformed from an isolated and parochial island realm to the centre of Europe in only two decades.
The dinner party described at the beginning of this chapter is symbolic for this new England. Dutch, Austrian and English noblemen formed a naturally coherent group that shared a commitment to defeat France. It was also indicative of the way in which British power had developed that it was Prince Eugene who came to London to appeal to the British government to stay in the war. By the time that the War of the Spanish Succession neared its conclusion Britain had undoubtedly emerged as the centre of a European-wide coalition. It was with some justification, then, that the peace treaty of Utrecht between France and England could claim that it was for 'the advantage of their subjects, as providing (as far as mortals are able to do) for the perpetual tranquillity of the whole Christian world.'[142]

Admiral George Churchill (1654-1710), the first Duke of Marlborough's brother. He was an Admiralty Commissioner from 1699 to 1702, and a member of the Lord High Admiral's Council from 1702 to 1708.

Enamel miniature by Charles Boit, around 1700. National Maritime Museum, Greenwich, London, UK. From the Caird Collection.

Early years

John Churchill's parents, Winston Churchill and his wife, Elizabeth, had been impoverished following Winston's stalwart service of the royalist cause as a cavalry captain. They were living with Elizabeth's widowed mother, Eleanor, Lady Drake, in her ancestral home when John was born. During these early years the father, now unemployed, may have supplemented the early instruction that John received from a sequestered clergyman. At the Restoration in 1660, Winston Churchill began to recover his position and income. Appointed to the court of claims in 1662, he took his family with him to Dublin, where he enrolled John in the Dublin Free Grammar School. King Charles II knighted Winston after his return to London, appointed him to the royal household, and gave him apartments at Whitehall. About 1663, Winston enrolled John as a scholar at St Paul's School, and the boy studied there until officials closed the school in 1665 during the plague epidemic.

Arabella Churchill (1649-1730). John Churchill's elder sister, she became a lady in waiting to the Duchess of York and mistress to her husband, James, Duke of York, the future King James II. One of the illegitimate children was James or Jacques FitzJames, first Duke of Berwick, the French Field Marshal.

Painting by the studio of Peter Lilly, 18th century. Althorp House, Northampton, UK. The Collection at Althorp.

Sir Winston first found favour thanks to his eldest daughter, Arabella, who became a maid of honour in the household of the Duchess of York. Shortly afterwards the King's brother, James, Duke of York and future King, appointed John Churchill a page of honour in his household. He obtained for the 17-year old boy, on 14 September 1667, a commission as an ensign in Colonel John Russell's company of the King's Own regiment, a unit later known as the Grenadier Guards. Churchill's aunt Mrs. Godfrey, his mother's sister, was also a member of the Duke's household, and through her the young Churchill met another distant relation, a second cousin once removed, Barbara Villiers, Lady Castlemaine, King Charles II's mistress, who in 1670 became the Duchess of Cleveland.

Many biographers[2] have asserted that about 1668 Churchill had his first international experience when he went to Tangier and possibly served there for two years as a volunteer with the Earl of Peterborough's regiment in the defence of that outpost, but no contemporary evidence has yet been found to support this. However, on 10 March 1670 the Duke of York approvingly wrote to Admiral Sir Thomas Allin, who commanded the English squadron in the Mediterranean, that Churchill, one of the ensigns of the King's regiment sent to command the troops 'for recruit of your

Barbara Villiers Palmer, Duchess of Cleveland (1640-1709). The mistress of King Charles II, she was also a lover of the young John Churchill, her mother's second cousin, and he may have been the father of her daughter born in 1672.

Miniature by Jean Petitot, 1660-1680. The Royal Collection © 2011, Her Majesty Queen Elizabeth II.

squadron,' wished to continue with Allin's squadron as a supernumerary, apparently in Allin's flagship *Resolution*.[3] It is not known whether or not Churchill and his men sailed from England with Allin in July 1669,[4] but Allin records in his journal on 3 June 1670 that he 'began to victual Mr. Churchill and his men and 15 soldiers from the *William and Thomas*, a victualler.'[5] During this period Allin was involved in operations against the Algerine corsairs near Tangier as well as further away on the North African coast. On 21 June 1670 at Tunis, Admiral Allin recorded that 'I presently dispatched away... my barge with a letter and Mr. Brisbaine, Lieutenant Woodward with Mr. Churchill to the castle of Goletta...'[6] Allin returned with his flagship to England in November 1670. Shortly afterwards, on 6 February 1671, Churchill was wounded in a duel with John Fenwick in London.

In March 1671 Ensign Churchill embarked with the first company of the guards and participated in Sir Robert Holmes's unsuccessful attack on the Dutch Smyrna-bound ships anchored near the Isle of Wight. At the end of May 1672 he and his company were on board *Royal Prince*, the Duke of York's flagship. On 28 May during the battle of Sole Bay against the Dutch fleet off Southwold, Suffolk, Churchill distinguished himself by his bravery and steadiness under fire, but no details of this are known. When *Royal Prince* was heavily damaged in the battle, York transferred his flag to *St Michael*. Apparently Churchill did not follow him and stayed with most of his fellow guards who had remained on board *Royal Prince*.[7]

As a result of his exemplary conduct in battle the Duke of York wanted to promote Churchill within his household and selected him as a gentleman of his bedchamber. Overriding York's good opinion of Churchill, the King denied permission for the promotion. The basis for the King's displeasure lies in the many stories that circulated about Churchill's illicit relations with the King's mistress, Barbara Palmer, Duchess of Cleveland (bap. 1640 - d. 1709), in the period between 1671 and 1675. Few, if any, can be substantiated in detail. Churchill certainly annoyed Charles II, and this fuelled much of the common court gossip of the day. It seems that Churchill was quite probably the natural father of the Duchess's youngest daughter, born in July 1672. It is also widely believed that she gave Churchill a gift of £5,000 from money she received from the King. Despite this on 13 June 1672 Churchill obtained a military promotion, skipping the rank of Lieutenant, from Ensign to Captain in the Lord High Admiral's Regiment of Marines.[8] About this time he spent £4500 to purchase from Lord Halifax two annuities to pay £600 per year for life, thereby creating the foundation for his later fortune.

Little is known of Churchill's activities during the following year. In August 1672 he fought a duel with Henry Herbert and wounded him in the thigh, but had his own arm run through twice before Herbert disarmed him. Then in December 1672, along with a number of other English regiments, Churchill's Admiralty regiment went to France. By June 1673 he left his company and joined a dozen English officer volunteers and thirty others at Maastricht, the cornerstone of Dutch defence, and served under the command of James, Duke of Monmouth, as part of the French army under the personal command of Louis XIV. After seventeen days of siege the French King watched as Monmouth and the small English contingent, seconded by the musketeer company under Charles Ogier de Batz de Castelmore, Comte d'Artagnan (b. ca. 1611 – d. 25 June 1673), led an attack to break into the fortress. In the first three attempts the attackers were forced back, but at one point during these attacks Churchill reportedly managed to place the French flag on the parapet of a demilune. In a fourth attack, Monmouth with Churchill, d'Artagnan, and others attempted to pass an enemy barricade at one of the gates into the fortress and d'Artagnan was killed. After calling for reinforcements, Monmouth made another attempt with Churchill at his side. In this successful attack Churchill was wounded, but saved Monmouth's life. Following the surrender of Maastricht, Louis XIV publicly praised the English soldiers and, among them, personally congratulated Churchill.[9]

By the autumn of 1673 Churchill was serving with the royal English regiment in the French army in Westphalia, where he quickly came to Marshal Turenne's favourable attention. With the end of the Dutch war in February 1674 approximately 5,500 English troops remained in French service, but the numbers were soon reduced and several English regiments were combined. On Monmouth's recommendation to the French war minister Louvois, the French commissioned Churchill on 3 April 1674 as Colonel in command of the newly reorganized regiment, but he retained his rank as captain in the English army. During the campaign of 1674 under Turenne's overall command, Churchill served for a time as a volunteer on detached reconnaissance missions with Douglas's foot regiment near Heidelberg. There is no reliable evidence to credit Churchill's presence at the battle of Sinzheim on the Elsatz River some 20 miles south-east of Mannheim on 16 June, but he and his regiment were likely to have been part of the large reinforcement that joined Turenne near Philippsburg at the end of June 1674.[10]

Several months later Churchill rejoined his battalion in the French army and commanded it during the battle of Ensheim, just to the south of Strasbourg, on 4 October 1674. In that action he lost half of his twenty-two officers. Following the battle Turenne chose him, with 500 other selected officers and men, to attack the rearguard of the Austrian forces as they re-crossed the Rhine. Although no detailed reports have been found of his activities in the following months, Churchill was apparently with Turenne's army during its winter march south from Hagenau in late November and early December, around the Vosges Mountains to Belfort, and then north to Türkheim, where it fought on 25 December when British infantry distinguished themselves for their effective musketry.[11]

Marriage

Late in 1674 or early in 1675, Churchill returned to London to take up the Duke of York's long-promised appointment as a gentleman of the bedchamber, arriving with the satisfaction of having both learned much from Turenne and earned for himself a reputation for skill in combat. He took up lodgings in Jermyn Street, five doors east of St James's Street. On 5 January 1675 he was promoted to Lieutenant-Colonel in the Duke of York's regiment.[12] Shortly after returning to court he met for the first time the fifteen-year-old Sarah Jenyns (1660–1744), who in October 1673 had been appointed a member of the household of the new Duchess of York, Mary of Modena, as an attendant to her stepdaughter, Princess Anne, the future Queen. A relationship between Churchill and Sarah did not develop immediately, for in August 1675 he went on a mission to Paris, possibly to assist in obtaining a French subsidy for King Charles. From Paris he continued on to Savoy to represent the Duke of York, in company with the King's representative, Bernard Granville, on a mission of condolence, and then to Florence and Genoa.[13] Returning to London in October he was allowed to bring two trunks of silver plate duty-free.[14]

Early in 1676 the Duchess of Cleveland left the court and moved to Paris with her children. Shortly afterwards Churchill became attracted to Sarah Jenyns. Meanwhile, Churchill's debt-ridden parents were busily attempting to arrange a financially advantageous marriage for their eldest son to Katherine, the nineteen-year-old daughter and heir of the playwright Sir Charles Sedley. Nevertheless, Churchill proposed to Sarah in mid-November 1676, but Sir Winston Churchill initially opposed the marriage. When the Duke of York suggested to the French that the highly qualified John Churchill was the best choice for command of the royal English regiment in the French army, the French ambassador, Honoré de Courtin, strongly disapproved. Having full knowledge of current court gossip in London about Churchill, he reported to Minister of War Louvois that Churchill was currently more interested in seducing a maid of honour than in commanding a regiment, and later suggested that a return to Paris would allow Churchill to resume his relationship with the Duchess of Cleveland.

Churchill's relationship with Sarah Jenyns suffered from all this, but during 1677 several events occurred that changed the situation. First, in May 1677 Churchill's parents formally broke off negotiations concerning Katherine Sedley, and John agreed to join with his father in paying off the family debts. A few months later Sarah's brother died and she received a substantial proportion of her family's estates in Hertfordshire, worth up to £1,500 a year. Under these circumstances Sir Winston and Lady

Churchill approved of the match between their son and Sarah. The exact date of their marriage is unknown. Before her own marriage Sarah attended the private marriage ceremony of the Duke of York's eldest daughter, Mary, to William III of Orange, at St James's in November 1677. As part of the wedding arrangements for William and Mary, the Duke of York's master of the robes was to accompany the newly-weds to Holland to carry messages between the two courts. Even at this early stage William disliked Churchill,[15] but through the patronage of the Duchess of York Churchill purchased this position. Sarah Jenyns and John Churchill were probably secretly married shortly after this in a ceremony witnessed perhaps only by the Duchess of York.

On 18 February 1678 Churchill was promoted Colonel of one of the newly raised infantry regiments, and in order to show him further favour the Duke of York altered the date of his commission by one day, to 17 February, giving him seniority over those commissioned the same day.[16] In April 1678 York sent Churchill to the Continent on a diplomatic mission. At his departure on 5 April Sarah was still serving as a maid of honour and was being addressed by her maiden name, although she later recalled, 'I believe I was married... but it was not known to anyone but the Duchess'.[17] Leaving Sarah behind, Churchill and a west-country acquaintance, Sidney Godolphin, were directed to help settle military arrangements following England's entry into the anti-French alliance.[18] Having travelled first to Brussels, Churchill signed an agreement with the Duke of Villa Hermosa on 13 April in relation to Spanish troops. He then travelled to Breda and on to The Hague, where he began negotiations with William of Orange with instructions to offer 20,000 men and a proportionate number of guns. The negotiations encountered some difficulties with the States of Holland, with whom Churchill and William had a three-hour discussion on 19 April. Although the Dutch were unable to carry out Charles II's desires promptly, Churchill was able to return to London on 26 April with a mutual Anglo-Dutch understanding for the remainder of the war.

On 1 May 1678 Churchill was appointed brigadier of foot and given authority to enlist recruits. While he was training troops that summer he and Sarah finally made public their marriage in May or June. As a result she necessarily resigned her post as a maid of honour. In the early days of their marriage the couple lived with Churchill's parents at Minterne, Dorset, and when in London at Churchill's lodgings in Jermyn Street, where he employed seven servants. The young couple was launched on a financially sound basis. Shortly before their marriage Churchill had purchased livery, harness, and a coach to provide a fashionable lifestyle for his wife. During 1678 he sold his place as groom in the Duke of York's household, a transaction bringing him a pension of £200 in addition to his current salary as master of the robes, his two annuities, and his military pay. As a former maid of honour Sarah received an annual pension of £300. In addition, her share of the Jenyns estates at Sandridge, at St Albans, Hertfordshire, and at Agney, Kent, provided her with independent assets.

■ Duke of York's master of the wardrobe

On 3 September 1678 both Churchill and Brigadier Sir John Fenwick were ordered to proceed with their troops to Flanders. Churchill had two battalions of guards and a battalion each from the Holland regiment and the Duchess of York's and Lord Arlington's regiments. Shortly afterwards the treaty of Nijmegen was signed and

Churchill's duties turned to securing his troops in winter quarters, allowing him to return to England after only two weeks of work.

In the months that followed, English politics were dominated by events leading up to the 'Exclusion Bill' crisis. Before a new Parliament could meet, the King ordered the Duke of York into temporary exile. York and his wife left England with their household staff, and went first to The Hague, then to Brussels, where they set up residence. At the general election in 1679 Churchill, now the Duke's Master of the Robes, was elected for Newtown, Isle of Wight, on the government interest. Because of his position as a Member of Parliament he was allowed to remain in London when Parliament was in session. In May he finally went to Brussels to join York; by then Sarah was some three months pregnant and chose not to accompany him.

By June 1679 Churchill was back in London, where he fought a duel with the poet Thomas Otway 'for beating an orange wench in the Duke's playhouse.'[19] When Sir John Holmes reported this to the King, Churchill took offence at the way in which Holmes represented it, and challenged Holmes to a duel in which Holmes disarmed Churchill. In July, the King dissolved Parliament and called another, but Churchill did not stand for re-election. Instead, he chose to resume his position as master of the robes in York's household in Brussels. Churchill and his pregnant wife arrived there on 28 August. Shortly afterwards York heard that Charles II was dangerously ill. Fearing that the Duke of Monmouth might attempt to seize the throne, he decided to return to London. Travelling incognito, Churchill with other members of York's household, accompanied him. First, they went to Calais by horse, then by sea to Dover, and by land to London and Windsor Castle. On their arrival they found that the King was no longer in danger. Charles received his brother warmly, but in light of York's continuing unpopularity it was thought advisable for him to return to Brussels. After four days in London, Churchill went alone to Paris to ask for a renewal of subsidies to Charles II, and then returned directly to Brussels, where he arrived at the end of September, a few days before York and the remainder of the household returned.

By this time York was exasperated at his exile and ordered Churchill to return to London to obtain Charles's permission for him to go to Scotland. The King approved of James's new place of exile, but at the same time ordered Monmouth into exile at The Hague. After Churchill returned to Brussels, he and Sarah travelled to London. As James and his household passed through the City en route for Edinburgh, Sarah remained behind in Jermyn Street, bitterly unhappy over the separation from her husband. She gave birth at the end of October 1679 to their first child, Henrietta (or Harriot, as her parents called her).

Meanwhile Churchill had travelled on with the Duke of York to Edinburgh, where they arrived in early November. While there, he was one of York's closest advisers. At the end of January 1680 the King commanded his brother to return from exile and Churchill accompanied him to London, where they arrived on 24 February. York and his household remained in the City during the summer, hoping that the new Parliament would more readily accept his presence. Meanwhile, Churchill began to look for employment that would give him a more stable home with his family. At first York favoured Churchill being appointed as ambassador to either France or Holland, where William of Orange reportedly expressed his approval. All these plans came to nothing. When the new Parliament assembled in October, it proved strongly opposed to James's succession. By the autumn, both the King and the government had persuaded York to return to exile in Edinburgh. James sailed for Scotland on 20 October, once again accompanied by Churchill, now his principal adviser.

Sarah remained in London, but York repeatedly sent Churchill on missions to London to lobby for the end of his exile. These missions allowed Churchill to be with his family in London during late January and early February, as well as in May and part of June 1681. However, he left for Scotland on 22 June and was not with his wife when a few days later their daughter, Henrietta, died. On hearing the news, he immediately returned to Sarah's side. A few weeks later he again returned to London and was present on 29 July at the baptism of their newborn second child, also named Henrietta (1681–1733), who later married Francis, second Earl of Godolphin. Churchill left for Scotland again about 8 August, but this time made arrangements for Sarah to follow him in early September. Leaving the child behind in London with a nurse, Sarah remained with her husband for eight months with York's household at Holyrood Palace in Edinburgh. During this period she renewed her acquaintance with the Duke's sixteen-year-old daughter, Princess Anne.[20]

Early in 1682 Churchill accompanied York on a visit to Charles II at Newmarket, where York finally obtained permission to return permanently to England. The ship carrying James and his household from Edinburgh in May ran aground on shoals off the Norfolk coast and sank with a heavy loss of life. Churchill was among the few survivors, and privately told Sarah that the Duke's obstinacy and cruelty during the attempt to abandon the ship had caused unnecessary loss of life. During the summer of 1682 the court was at Windsor, but Sarah abided by the decision her husband had made after their marriage that she stay away from the King's court.

Within six months the situation at court changed. Two of Princess Anne's close confidantes were dismissed after Lord Mulgrave was accused of plotting a clandestine courtship between himself and Anne. A bedchamber woman, Katherine Cornwallis, was implicated as the Catholic who had facilitated the match. In their places Anne turned to Sarah, while the King and his brother recognized the need to avoid such situations by having Anne marry. Churchill no longer discouraged his wife from accepting a position in Anne's household, recognizing the value of Sarah's friendship with the protestant princess in offsetting his close involvement with the Catholic Duke of York.

In recognition of Churchill's service to York during his exile, Charles II created him on 21 December 1682 Lord Churchill of Eyemouth, Berwickshire, in the Scots peerage. Shortly afterwards the Churchills gave up their Jermyn Street home and took up residence in St James's Palace. Early in 1683 negotiations were under way for Anne to marry Prince George of Denmark, a younger brother of King Christian V. Since George had some military experience, Churchill was seen as an appropriate choice to escort the young prince to England, given his growing personal connections with Anne and the fact that his brother Charles had served at the Danish court. In June 1683 Lord Churchill sailed for Glückstadt, where he met Prince George and brought him back to London on 19 July for his wedding to Princess Anne. During the following weeks Sarah served as one of Anne's chaperones, and Churchill played a key role in replacing George's Danish secretary, Karl Siegfried von Plessen, with Sarah's brother-in-law Colonel Edward Griffith.

With her wedding on 28 July 1683, Princess Anne was allowed her own household, separate from that of her parents, but based on the couple's limited income. The chief position in the princess's household was that of groom of the stole, which provided £400 a year. While much political jostling was taking place among several candidates, Churchill encouraged his wife to secure the appointment as a means to promote their own advantage. Eventually, Sarah was given the post, formally inaugurating a connection that lasted for the next twenty-seven years and became the pivot upon which both their political and personal fortunes rose and fell.[21]

For the next two years the Churchills were deeply involved in court life. Churchill had given up the Lieutenant-Colonelcy of the Lord High Admiral's Regiment in February 1681, but on 21 November 1683, he was appointed Colonel of the Royal Regiment of Dragoons.[22] During that winter the Churchills left their lodgings in St James's Palace to take up new quarters with those assigned to Princess Anne and Prince George in the Palace of Whitehall, which they occupied for the next eight years. There, on 28 February 1684, Sarah gave birth to their second surviving daughter, Anne (d. 1716), named in honour of the princess, who stood as the child's godmother. Later that year Churchill acquired sufficient resources to purchase the remaining share of the Jenyns estate at Sandridge and Holywell for £11,000 and to begin repairing and extending Holywell House at St Albans as a convenient country seat to raise their family. This purchase also gave the Churchills the principal political interest for the Parliamentary seat at St Albans, and shortly thereafter the mayor announced John Churchill's candidacy. During the autumn Sarah became ill, or possibly suffered a miscarriage.

In the household of King James II

Immediately following the Duke of York's accession as King James II on 6 February 1685, Churchill was appointed Ambassador-Extraordinary to France to notify Louis XIV of James's accession and, initially, to ask for an increase in the French King's subsidy. After Churchill left London, Louis XIV gave James an unsolicited gift of 5000 livres. On receiving it, James immediately ordered Churchill to limit himself to formalities and then to return to London for the coronation.[23] Remaining in Paris from mid-February until April, Churchill reportedly told a French protestant army officer, Henri de Massue, the Marquis de Ruvigny, 'that if the King ever was prevailed upon to alter our religion, he would serve him no longer, but withdraw from him.'[24]

Shortly after returning to London Churchill was appointed a gentleman of the King's bedchamber on 22 April 1685. Then, on 14 May, he was additionally created Baron Churchill of Sandridge, Hertfordshire, taking his title from his wife's inheritance; this was one of only ten English peerages created during James's reign. The first major crisis of the reign came in June 1685, when the Duke of Monmouth returned from Holland and landed at Lyme Regis, declaring an uprising against James. When the news was received in London on 13 June, all available forces were ordered to Salisbury. Brigadier Churchill left London immediately with some 300 cavalry and reached Bridport on 17 June, Axminster on 18 June, and Chard on 19 June. Here, close to his birthplace, Churchill first came into contact with rebel forces.

After Churchill's departure from London, the Earl of Feversham was appointed commander-in-chief, with Churchill as his second in command. Offended by this appointment, Churchill wrote to Clarendon, 'I see plainly that I am to have the trouble, and that the honour will be another's,'[25] unaware that he had also just been given a commission as 'major general over all our forces as well horse as foot'[26] on 3 July

1685. As support for Monmouth waned, Feversham and Churchill brought all the King's forces together into a camp at Weston Zoyland on 5 July. On hearing of this, Monmouth moved immediately to attack them in the middle of the night while they slept in their unfortified position. The battle of Sedgemoor followed and extended into the next morning with a total victory for the royal army.[27]

Feversham reaped the main rewards of the battle. In recognition of Churchill's exemplary conduct he exchanged on 30 July the Colonelcy of the Royal Dragoons for that of the third troop of Horse Guards, and he was also appointed Governor of the Hudson's Bay Company. In the following year the Company expanded its scope of operations and moved out towards more northern regions in Canada. There, officials named the river that passes through present-day Canadian provinces of Alberta, Saskatchewan, and Manitoba with the port at its mouth on Hudson's Bay, Churchill, in honour of its Governor. Through this, he established a firm continuing interest in the development of British interests in the North American colonies, and made, in addition, a substantial profit of some £4,600 in Company shares between 1685 and 1692.[28]

After returning to his duties in the royal household Churchill quietly observed James II's increasing assertion of power. In January 1686 he was one of thirty peers whom the lord high steward, Judge Jeffreys, named to try Lord Delamere for complicity in Monmouth's rebellion. Churchill, as the most junior peer, cast his vote first; to the King's great annoyance, all the other peers followed him in voting for Delamere's acquittal. The Churchills remained passive, but quietly defensive, as the King replaced protestant office-holders. When rumours spread that Princess Anne would be declared James's successor if she become a Catholic, Anne's sister, Mary, and her husband, William of Orange, began to suspect Churchill of complicity in King James's policies. These threatening events, along with Anne's miscarriage and the death of two of her children, brought the princess into an even closer personal relationship with Sarah Churchill and at the same time with John Churchill, as Anne first began to see the need to oppose her father's policies. In the midst of all this, on 13 February 1686, Sarah gave birth to a son, John (d. 1703), initially styled Lord Churchill and from December 1702 Marquess of Blandford.

On 29 December 1686 Anne wrote to Mary to assure her that Churchill's allegiance to James II was firm, but also limited by his devotion to the Protestant cause.[29] William of Orange was increasingly worried about the situation in England and, in February 1686, dispatched a close confidant, Everard van Weede, Heer van Dijkveld, to investigate. When Dijkveld asked to meet Anne, she authorized Churchill to be her representative. Eight days after Dijkveld's departure for The Hague, Churchill wrote directly to William on 17 May 1687 to assure him of his commitment to resist conversion to Catholicism, 'I being resolved, although I cannot live the life of a saint, if there be ever occasion for it, to show the resolution of a martyr'.[30] Through this letter and his discussions with Dijkveld, Churchill established a connection upon which William built during the coming eighteen months.

Both Anne and the Churchills felt increasingly insecure. As more and more Catholics replaced Protestants in key positions, both Churchills were under threat, but John, in particular, was highly vulnerable in his position close to the King and privy to sensitive military information. Beginning in May 1687 he participated with the army's summer encampment at Hounslow, and during the autumn of 1687 he accompanied the King on his royal progress through the area that Monmouth had

IOHN DVKE OF MARLBOROVGH

raised in rebellion two years before. While visiting Winchester, the King reportedly asked Churchill how the people were reacting to his touching for the 'King's evil.' To the King's obvious displeasure Churchill bluntly replied that they saw it as paving the way for Catholicism. Immediately following this exchange, Churchill was overheard during dinner with the Dean of Winchester having a lengthy discussion on passive obedience.

In November 1687 Churchill attempted to get away from the situation by requesting command of the six English and Scots regiments in Dutch pay, then serving in the Dutch Republic. The King denied his request, wanting to transfer those forces to France under the Duke of Berwick's command, but William of Orange refused to let them leave the Dutch Republic. Then in December Churchill strongly supported Prince George in his effort to retain Lord Scarsdale as his first gentleman-in-waiting; the King dismissed Scarsdale as Lord Lieutenant of Derbyshire for his refusal to canvass electors to support the repeal of the Test and Penal Acts. Becoming increasingly worried about the safety of his family's future and fortune, Churchill placed the Sandridge estate in a trust in December 1687. In January 1688, he declined James II's personal request for his explicit support in repealing the Test Acts and Penal laws.

John Churchill, Baron Churchill of Sandridge. King Charles II first raised Churchill to the Peerage of Scotland in 1682 as Lord Churchill of Eyemouth. On James II's accession in 1685, he was given the additional title of Baron Churchill of Sandridge in the peerage of England.

Painting by John Riley, 1685-1690. Althorp House, Northampton, UK. The Collection at Althorp.

The revolution of 1688

On 15 March 1688, Sarah gave birth to her third surviving daughter, Elizabeth (d. 1714), who later married Scrope Egerton, first Duke of Bridgewater. Demonstrating the Churchills' shifting allegiances, they chose as the child's godmother Lady Lumley, the wife of one of William of Orange's strongest supporters in England. Shortly afterwards Princess Anne left London for Bath. There, accompanied by Sarah, she was recovering from illness; like many other Protestants, she was not present in London during the trial of the seven bishops and when the Queen gave birth to the Prince of Wales on 10 June. Churchill was at the army encampment; he, like many other officers, feared for his career when Catholic officers were ordered to make lists of all Catholics in their commands. By this time Churchill had long-standing connections with other protestant officers who were conspiring to defect from the King, including his former comrades from Tangier and the regiments that served with the fleet, as well as the officers who met in the Treason Club at The Rose Tavern in Russell Street.[31] In July, he made further financial arrangements to secure his family, and on 4 August 1688 he reaffirmed his intentions when he wrote to William that he was 'resolved to die in that religion that it has pleased God to give you both the will and power to protect.'[32]

The King interpreted Churchill's passivity to indicate that if his ambitions for promotion were fed, he would remain loyal as he had done during Monmouth's rebellion. In September James began to take seriously the danger of an invasion by William of Orange and ordered military and naval precautions. Even after William had landed at Torbay on 5 November, James was still preparing his forces. With Feversham as commander-in-chief of the army, the King also wanted Churchill's military skill and prestige. On 7 November 1688 he promoted Churchill to lieutenant-general with command of the larger part of the army at Salisbury. Ten days later the King left London for Salisbury, bringing with him Prince George and Churchill. En route, they learned that Lord Cornbury had defected to William with a brigade and

William for his consideration and he approved it on 14 August, appointing Marlborough to command.

As Marlborough was preparing to leave, Sarah gave birth on 19 August 1690 to their second son, Charles (d. 1692). A week later Marlborough left London, and he embarked with the fleet and troop transports at Portsmouth on 30 August. Delayed by bad weather and contrary winds, the eighty-two-ship expedition carrying about 6000 soldiers finally sailed on 17 September and reached Cork on 22 September, by which time two of William's other generals, Godard van Reede, Heer van Ginkel (later Earl of Athlone), and Ferdinand Wilhelm, Duke of Württemberg-Neustadt, had already massed 5000 troops there. The presence of a Dutch and a German general raised issues of precedence in overall command for Marlborough, who adroitly used his skills as a courtier to promote co-operation through rotating overall command on a daily basis among the three. The allied forces made an assault on Cork, taking it on 27 September. Immediately after the success, Marlborough and the allied forces turned to an assault on Kinsale. Advance forces seized the town ahead of Marlborough's arrival on 1 October, while the Old Fort, across the Bandon River, fell the following day, and the larger and better-equipped New Fort was taken under siege, surrendering on 15 October. As Marlborough had foreseen, the capture of Cork and Kinsale was a strategic stroke that denied French forces any port to support further Irish resistance. After appointing his brother Brigadier Charles Churchill as governor of Kinsale, Marlborough arranged winter quarters for the English troops and sailed for Deal, where he arrived on 28 October 1690.

In September 1690 a pamphlet entitled The Dear Bargain appeared, the first to suggest Marlborough's duplicity.[39] This recounted how since December 1688 Marlborough had made approaches to James II while serving William III and in 1690 was spurred in this by his apparent alarm that the Parliamentary election that year had seen the return of a number of crypto-Jacobites. During the months that followed Marlborough was further discredited. Suggestions were made that he misused his military position for financial extortion, and there were hints of his betrayal of Princess Anne's interests in order to gain favour with William and Mary. Marlborough was deeply disappointed not to receive any of the appointments that rumour suggested would be showered on him: knight of the Garter, master-general of the ordnance, and commander-in-chief in Ireland for the coming campaign. Instead, his military success bred envy among his rivals. Marlborough saw his promotion blocked as William gave the knighthood and the command to Dutch generals, Athlone and Waldeck, while a civilian, Henry Sidney, became Master-General of the Ordnance. When William left England for The Hague in early 1691 to preside at a Grand Alliance conference, Marlborough was left behind in London to supervise army recruitment for the coming campaign. With the King absent he became frustrated with Danby's inefficiency as Lord President and increasingly critical of the government, asking the King to return, 'after which I shall beg never to be in England when you are not.'[40]

As observers saw Marlborough apparently sliding from favour, the Jacobite agent Henry Bulkeley met Marlborough in St James's Park and, in January 1691, was received as an old friend in Marlborough's lodgings in the Cockpit. Sarah, too, renewed contact with her sister Frances, lady of the bedchamber to Queen Mary of Modena at St Germain, while Lord Ailesbury made a secret visit to her at St. Albans. Through such connections, Marlborough began a secret, personal correspondence directly with James II, and with the illegitimate son of his sister Arabella by King James, James FitzJames, first Duke of Berwick (1670 – 1734). Although Jacobite leaders distrusted Marlborough and were suspicious of his sincerity, Jacobite agents continued to maintain contact with him. They saw his connections to Anne as something of possible future use and also believed that if William continued to disregard Marlborough's ambitions, it might force him to become a sincere Jacobite supporter.[41]

In May 1691, William III returned again to Holland after a brief visit to England to open the campaign and Marlborough accompanied him to command the English corps. At the outset, Marlborough served under Waldeck, while William remained at the palace of Het Loo; then, in June, William took overall command of the allied army. Both the French and the allied armies manoeuvred, but no major action occurred. As troops on both sides began to retire to winter quarters, French troops under the Duc de Luxembourg made a cavalry attack on the allied rear in mid-September, as they marched from Leuze to Grammont. Marlborough and the English troops had already passed the scene of the attack, but quickly returned, only to have the French disengage before they could launch their attack in the only action of the campaign.[42]

At the end of October 1691 William returned to England, landing at Margate. Going by carriage, Marlborough and Bentinck, now Earl of Portland, accompanied him, as crowds welcomed their return. When the carriage reached Shooters Hill, it overturned and all its occupants were shaken by the accident. Marlborough was injured, and initially it was feared that he might have broken his neck. Soon William was involved in English politics again. Among the many issues that faced him at this time was the desire of Lord Godolphin to retire from the Treasury, perhaps to remarry. While Godolphin had grave doubts about serving William, the King found him to be one of the few Englishmen he trusted completely. In dealing with Godolphin, William turned to Marlborough to persuade him to remain in office. Although Marlborough and Godolphin had long known each other and had even worked together in the Duke of York's service as early as 1678, their close connection for the future dated from this point in 1691. This coincided with the beginning of Sarah's regular consultations with Godolphin regarding Princess Anne's affairs. As she did this, she became increasingly impressed with the soundness of Godolphin's outlook and the way in which he quietly demonstrated his deep understanding of finance, politics, and broad international relations.

■ The years of unemployment

During the remaining months of 1691, the King made it clear that he would assign Marlborough to his personal staff during the next campaign, but he would neither appoint him master-general of the ordnance nor give him the commands in Flanders that he wanted, which were given to two Dutch officers, Athlone and William's great uncle, Hendrik Trajectinus, Count zu Solms-Braunfels. Marlborough was not alone when he openly expressed his concern and privately sought to organize a mass protest among English army officers. At the same time he was involved with a similar resentment against William that appeared momentarily among members of both houses of Parliament, leading to the possibility that when Parliament returned it might force the King to dismiss his Dutch and German officials in the army and council. In this pre-session intrigue, Marlborough allied himself with dissatisfied Whigs such as Shrewsbury and Montagu and solicited support from crypto-Jacobites, but this manoeuvring failed to produce any result.

Meanwhile, in December 1691 Marlborough advised Princess Anne to reconcile herself with her father. This gesture of sentimentality earned Marlborough a pardon from James II, but remained a highly suspicious act, which, if it had become public during the invasion crisis of late April and early May 1692, might have been extremely damaging. William and Mary had certainly become suspicious of Marlborough. Giving no warning, on the morning of 20 January 1692 Secretary of State Nottingham passed to Marlborough the monarchs' message dismissing him from office and creating for him a serious financial loss of £7,000 to £11,000 in annual income. No official explanation was made, but those close to the King made it known that Marlborough's recent correspondence with James II had been discovered and that Marlborough was suspected of having disclosed to the Jacobites William's secret plan to attack Dunkirk. In addition William was said to have been offended by Marlborough's open criticism, which fuelled the jealousy between Dutch, German, and English officers, and raised the possibility of a mutiny among English officers serving under Dutch generals. Finally, mention was made of Sarah's influence in reputedly alienating Princess Anne from her sister, the Queen. William and Mary began to put pressure on Anne to dismiss Sarah, forbidding any member of their own household to have contact with Sarah. In spite of this, Anne stubbornly refused to comply. In April 1692 the Marlboroughs left their lodgings in the Cockpit and took up residence again in Jermyn Street.

On 4 May 1692 during an invasion scare Mary and the council, acting on information from Robert Young, ordered Marlborough to be arrested, with several others, on suspicion of high treason and taken to the Tower of London. Within two weeks of his imprisonment, Marlborough's one-year-old son Charles became ill and suddenly died on 21 May. After the Anglo-Dutch fleet defeated the French off Barfleur and La Hogue, Marlborough's situation eased. On 25 May he petitioned for release, as no formal indictment had been made, although the government seemed determined to prosecute him. At first the council denied his request while members examined further information, all of which proved to be based on forged letters. On 15 June Marlborough was finally released on £6000 bail, but Mary retained her suspicions and personally struck his name from the list of Privy Councillors, along with the names of those who had stood his bail.

The Marlboroughs went immediately to St Albans, but shortly afterwards Sarah left to accompany Princess Anne to Bath. When Anne returned to London in mid-October Sarah retained her nominal position in Anne's household, but in reality had retired from court to be at St Albans with her husband and children. During the winter of 1692–3 Marlborough returned to London regularly and played a leading role in making opposition attacks against the government in the Lords, convinced that the government had been deliberately plotting against him for several years. The government spy Richard Kingston reported in November 1692 that Marlborough had told him shortly after his release from the Tower: 'that King William… exercised a more arbitrary and tyrannical power than King James did; and therefore his government was not to be endured any longer, but every good man ought to lay his hand to put an end to it.'[43] As Marlborough turned more strongly toward the Jacobites at this time, he became known in their correspondence as 'the Hamburg merchant.'[44]

On 3 May 1694 a Jacobite, Major-General Edward Sackville, sent James II a translation into French of a deciphered letter that Marlborough was supposed to have written to James. It confirmed that William III's forces were preparing a landing at Camaret Bay, near Brest, and betrayed the fact that the force, under Admiral Edward Russell and General Thomas Talmash, was supposed to sail with forty ships within ten days. This document was not publicly known at the time and did not affect the outcome, though it might well have done if the French had not already known of the plan. Marlborough certainly had sufficient motives for betraying the operation, given that he was still excluded from office and jealous of Talmash as the only English officer whom William III had so far entrusted with command. However, since the original documents have not survived, it is unknown whether Marlborough actually wrote the letter.

For much of the period between 1692 and 1694 it seemed that the Marlboroughs had ended their careers at court and in public service. The death of Queen Mary from smallpox on 28 December 1694 was the first step towards change. Princess Anne, as William's immediate heir, was suddenly thrust into the limelight. In mid-January 1695 Anne took the first step toward reconciliation with the King by making a visit of condolence. A few days later she reappeared in London. Slowly, Sarah was drawn back into Anne's circle as the principal member of her household.[45] Anne persuaded William to readmit Marlborough to court, where he kissed hands on 29 March 1695, although the King remained deeply suspicious of Marlborough and offered him no employment.

As a result of Anne's reconciliation with William, the King offered her a new residence in St James's Palace. She took advantage of this offer in December 1695, and with her the Marlboroughs also acquired lodgings overlooking the park in the south-eastern corner of the palace, which remained their residence until spring 1711. In the winter of 1696–7 the discovery of a plot to assassinate the King and the subsequent arrest of Sir John Fenwick created a public scandal. In maintaining his innocence Fenwick tried to implicate Marlborough, Godolphin, Shrewsbury, and Admiral Russell as traitorous Jacobite intriguers. Enraged by the attacks on Shrewsbury and Russell, the Whigs completely discredited Fenwick. This did not interfere with Marlborough's gradual reconciliation with the King, for William had already discounted Fenwick's allegations against Marlborough.

Godolphin, who lost office over the Fenwick affair, now became even closer to the Marlboroughs and to Anne. In 1697 he spent the summer at St Albans, then followed the Marlboroughs to Anne's court at Tunbridge Wells and back to St Albans in the autumn. During this period the connections between the two families were strengthened when Godolphin's eighteen-year-old son, Francis, became engaged to Henrietta, the Marlboroughs' eldest daughter. Their marriage took place on 28 April 1698. Anne offered to provide a £10,000 dowry, but Sarah arranged for it to be divided in half, one portion for Henrietta with another, at a future date, for her younger sister, the princess's god-daughter and namesake. Soon after the marriage the newly married Godolphins moved in with the Marlboroughs at St James's Palace and Henrietta became a lady-in-waiting to Anne.

Sidney Godolphin, first Earl of Godolphin (1642-1712).

Painting by Godfrey Kneller, 1704-1710.

uation of William III's foreign policies, thus instantly creating for himself a national and international position of responsibility. He initially wanted to build a larger national government of key political leaders, including the Earls of Rochester and Nottingham as Tory party leaders, and Robert Harley as speaker, and effective leader, of the House of Commons. However, the resulting Tory government disappointed Marlborough, who had hoped to have a more widely based executive that included the Whig leader, the Duke of Shrewsbury, while being aware that Rochester and others might become major obstacles. The new government immediately committed itself to pursue William's war policy, precluding any serious consideration of the alternative policies that William might have entertained to avert a continent-wide war with France.

Campaigns and politics, 1702–1703

Shortly after the new Queen met the Privy Council on her accession day, 8 March 1702, Marlborough told the imperial envoy, Count Johann Wenzel Wratislaw, that England intended to carry forward William's commitment to the Emperor.[50] On the same day, in his role as ambassador to the States General, Marlborough made the same commitment to the Dutch in a letter to Heinsius.[51] On 9 March Anne appointed Marlborough knight of the Garter and 'Captain-General of Her Majesty's land forces and commander-in-chief of forces to be employed in Holland in conjunction with troops of the Allies', and then on 14 March master-general of the ordnance.[52] On the Queen's instructions, Marlborough travelled immediately to The Hague, leaving Godolphin as his representative and spokesman in London, although at that point Godolphin held no formal appointment.

At The Hague, with King William's untimely death, the course of domestic politics within the Dutch Republic led to the entire range of Dutch foreign relations devolving on Heinsius. No longer benefiting from William's dual positions in the two countries, the very close and direct cooperative work between Marlborough and Heinsius began. By early April, Marlborough and Heinsius obtained Dutch and Austrian acceptance to the additional article to the treaty of Grand Alliance, which bound the Allies in agreement to deny recognition of the claim of the 'pretended prince of Wales' to England's throne. At the same time the Allies secretly agreed jointly to declare war against France on 15 May.[53] At this point the English and Dutch could still not agree on who should succeed William III as the commander of their land forces when operating together. The Queen wished to have her husband, Prince George of Denmark, appointed, and she instructed Marlborough to obtain this appointment. However, the Dutch had serious reservations about George's abilities and had a variety of other, more highly experienced, senior commanders to propose, including Walrad, Prince of Nassau-Saarbrücken-Usingen, who was both a Dutch and an Imperial Field Marshal as well as the senior serving officer in the allied armies.

Marlborough returned to England to be present for William III's funeral and Anne's coronation. At the same time he and Sarah both worked to persuade Godolphin to accept appointment as lord treasurer and head of the government. War was declared as agreed earlier among the Allies on 4 May, and this was the signal for the French to concentrate their main offensive effort in Italy, while other French forces were ordered to Flanders and to the lower Rhine, creating a serious threat to the

Dutch. On 12 May Marlborough left London for Holland, but he was delayed at Margate by contrary winds until 20 May. On reaching The Hague on 26 May, Marlborough faced a difficult situation where many decisions had yet to be made. Frederick I of Prussia had offered his services for the vacant position of commanding the allied troops, but his offer was not acceptable in London. At this critical moment the Dutch saw the importance of forcing the English to commit themselves to the defence of the Republic and, for this reason, were willing to allow Marlborough a higher role. Although the Dutch had serious reservations about Marlborough's inexperience and their most senior general, the prince of Nassau Saarbrücken-Usingen, refused to serve under him,[54] the States General appointed Marlborough on 25 June Captain-General of the allied forces when they were operating together, with a salary of £10,000.[55] By a further secret resolution on 30 June 1702,[56] the States General carefully defined Marlborough's responsibilities and circumscribed his powers: the four or more Dutch field deputies who accompanied him when he was exercising this combined appointment were empowered to withhold his authorization to use Dutch troops at any time they thought prudent. The reason for this reticence was quite practical. Marlborough did not have extensive experience in such operations. The Dutch army was operating in areas well known to it and on its country's borders. In preceding years the prince of Waldeck and William III had trained and equipped the Dutch army with modern weapons, including flintlocks and bayonets fixed around the barrel. As in all allied operations in which Marlborough commanded during the War of the Spanish Succession, Dutch troops and troops in Dutch pay made up the bulk of the allied army. Its logistics, including those for English troops and foreign troops in English pay, were largely provided and transported under the management of the Dutch Raad van State, and all the heavy siege artillery came from the Dutch armouries at Delft and Dordrecht, with forward magazines at Bergen-op-Zoom and Maastricht. Any success Marlborough could have was entirely dependent upon joint co-operation with Dutch officials.[57]

During the first campaigning season of the War of the Spanish Succession, Marlborough took up his combined position with both Dutch and English troops at Nijmegen on 2 July 1702. Initially, he wanted to undertake bold offensive operations[58] by sending a detached force into Brabant and attacking the fortress at Antwerp, thereby forcing the French to withdraw from their threatening forward position. Recent experience a month earlier had shown the Dutch the danger that such detached operations posed and convinced many Dutch officials that these attempts were imprudent. Marlborough's advocacy of similar operations confirmed suspicions that many had about his lack of experience. To mollify his critics he agreed to use some of his army to support the defences at Nijmegen, but by 10 July moved with the remainder of the allied army across the Maas River to threaten the supply lines of the French army under Boufflers. Marlborough's move forced the French to retire to the west of the Maas. Then, making what was to become for Marlborough a characteristic fast march, the allied army manoeuvred the French into a position that Marlborough had designed to make it possible to bring them into a general battle on 2–3 August. The Dutch field deputies did not agree to this initiative, seeing no reason to risk the gains they had already made in forcing the French into retreat and removing the threat to Nijmegen. Now in a central position, Marlborough moved into a series of small offensive operations, taking Venlo on 25 September, Stevensweert on 2 October, Roermond on 6 October, and Liège on 29 October. These actions during his 1702 campaign removed the French threat from the Maas, placing the Allies in a strong position to begin the next year's campaign.[59]

Marlborough left the army in its winter quarters and travelled by boat down the Maas to The Hague. En route on 6 November, a French patrol from Guelder stopped Marlborough and his party to examine their documents. All but Marlborough had them. While Marlborough was being interrogated, one of his clerks, Stephen Gell, managed to slip into his hand a pass that had been intended for Marlborough's brother. After detaining them for five hours, the young officer in French service, by chance an Irishman who had deserted from the Dutch and was amenable to a deal, allowed his valuable prize to escape to cheering crowds on his arrival at The Hague on 7 November. Marlborough was grateful and generous. The young officer soon reappeared, pardoned and promoted, in Dutch service, while the clerk, Stephen Gell, had safe employment and a pension for life.

Marlborough returned to London from The Hague on 28 November. The main political issue of the moment was the first Occasional Conformity Bill; he voted for it but showed his lukewarm attitude by doing nothing else to support it. As a reward for his successful conduct in the first campaign Queen Anne created him on 14 December 1702 Marquess of Blandford, Dorset, and Duke of Marlborough. From this date Anne granted Marlborough £5,000 a year for her lifetime. He first took his seat in the Lords with his new titles on 18 December. Soon afterwards, opposition in Parliament forced the Queen to withdraw her request for payment of the grant in perpetuity to Marlborough and his heirs. Furious at this defeat, she offered from the Privy Purse an additional £2,000, which Marlborough declined.[60]

Before leaving England for the campaign of 1703, the Marlboroughs' only surviving son, John, died of smallpox at the age of seventeen. His parents were at his bedside when he died on 20 February at King's College, Cambridge. Considered to have been 'the finest young man that could be seen,'[61] he was buried in King's College chapel, where a monument to him stands. Immediately following their son's death, the Marlboroughs went, grief-stricken, to St Albans, where they seriously considered retirement. The Queen appealed to them both not to desert her and Prince George, pleading that 'we four must never part till death mows us down with his impartial hand.'[62] Meanwhile, the war situation in the Low Countries demanded Marlborough's military and diplomatic skills, and he reluctantly left for The Hague on 4 March, increasingly irritated by Tory criticism of the war effort.

In planning for the new campaign the English and Dutch generals agreed to form two armies of equal size, one on the Maas River and based at Maastricht and the other on the Rhine and based at Koblenz. First Marlborough would be with the Rhine army and capture Bonn. Then the two armies would carry out the 'great design' to seize Antwerp and Ostend, creating an independent logistical base for English forces as well as establishing allied control over the Scheldt River and the waterways that led to Brabant and Flanders. It is uncertain how far Marlborough was personally responsible for originating this plan, but he fully embraced the concept. To undertake it, the allied army divided into four separate parts in order to carry out coordinated manoeuvres and attacks that would force the French into taking risks, with potential serious losses that would benefit one or more of the allied forces. One force was to attack Ostend, a second to pass through the French lines, and a third to attack Antwerp, while Marlborough with the main allied army moved north to engage the main French army in a major battle.[63]

To carry out this plan Marlborough made a rapid tour of the fortifications on the Maas and then on 25 April began operations at Bonn, which surrendered on 15 May. By 19 May he was at Maastricht to begin the next phase. Troops and supplies were moved into place, but the plan did not come to fruition, as he had crossed the Jeker River before sufficient forage supplies were in place, and those available were quickly exhausted. Because of this the allied forces hesitated in their planned movements against Ostend, while heavy rains and bad weather hindered other plans. Taking advantage of the situation, the French under Boufflers attacked and defeated the force under the Dutch General Wassenaer-Obdam at Ekeren, just north of Antwerp, on 30 May. Dutch forces under Slangenburg were able to fight an effective action to preserve their retreating army, but the battle effectively ended Marlborough's plan. Not willing to give up entirely, Marlborough advocated an offensive attack on the main French army under Villars near Antwerp.[64] The defeat at Ekeren emphasized the risks involved, and Marlborough's advice showed his penchant for high-risk offensive operations that could be costly and uncertain.[65]

To redeem himself with his Dutch allies Marlborough agreed to a safer operation and attacked the castle at Huy, on the Maas, which surrendered on 26 August, and then moved on to Limbourg, which surrendered on 27 September. Meanwhile, the government in London ordered three of Marlborough's regiments to be detached to prepare for service in Portugal. This, along with the frustrations Marlborough felt in failing to have his 'grand design' accepted by the Dutch, began to affect his health. He returned to England on 10 November, and at Windsor he participated in the ceremonial welcome to the Austrian Archduke Karl, the Allies' candidate for the Spanish throne as King Carlos III, but known as Charles to the English..

The winter of 1703–1704 was difficult for Marlborough, with so many demands on him that he rarely had time for personal matters. During this period Sarah's strong and intransigent views on the latest version of the Occasional Conformity Bill began to irritate the Queen and to create the first beginnings of a rift between the two. At the same time Sarah began to worry about her relationship with her husband, and was disappointed not to have another child. All this led her to quarrel with Marlborough, but the demands upon him prevented him from dealing with these domestic issues directly; he tried to calm her through correspondence.[66]

Despite his varied frustrations Marlborough had shown himself during his first two campaigns with the Dutch to be a successful commander of allied forces and had effectively helped to reverse the insecure position of the Dutch Republic of two years before. The experience of the 1703 campaign, however, had underscored the need to widen the strategy of the war rather than merely deploying Marlborough in operations limited to the lower Rhine and the Maas River regions. With Portugal's entry into the Grand Alliance in May 1703, the way became clear to use the Mediterranean to support the Emperor from the south, to oppose directly French designs in Spain, and perhaps even to draw Savoy into the war as an additional ally. In all of this, England's grand strategy for the Grand Alliance was to surround France with a ring of military and naval threats that would prevent her, with Europe's most powerful army, from concentrating her strength in any one single area. If this could be implemented the combined forces of the Allies had a realistic chance of defeating a major French army, which would necessarily be reduced in strength to meet simultaneous threats from allied forces in widespread theatres. To achieve this, the Allies needed to deploy major armies in Flanders, on the Rhine, in Portugal, and in Spain, while also mounting amphibious operations in northern, western, and southern France as well as in the American colonies. Thus, the operations of Marlborough's army comprised only one of several major elements in England's grand strategy. Marlborough played an additional role in serving as the main English diplomatic negotiator at The Hague. His diplomacy focused on coordinating the wider war strategy, but he was not single-handedly directing England's war effort. Many contemporaries, particularly those abroad who did not understand the English governmental system and the complex ways in which decisions were reached within it, overestimated his personal power and attributed things to him that, in reality, were done through political coalitions and the machinery of cabinet government decision-making.[67]

■ The Blenheim campaign, 1704

At various points during the War of the Spanish Succession events within Europe threatened the viability of the English concept of grand strategy. The critical question for the allies in 1704 was whether Austria could continue as an active ally, faced on one side by a rebellion in Hungary and, on the other, by a military threat from Bavaria. This was the matter at stake in Marlborough's famous military campaign in 1704. From the outset of the war, the position of Maximilian II Emanuel, the Elector of Bavaria, was an important issue in European politics. Ambitious to raise his Wittelsbach dynasty to regal status, as his fellow Electors in Saxony, Brandenburg, and Hanover had recently done, Maximilian thought he had succeeded when his son became heir to the Spanish throne in the partition treaty of 1698. The young prince's death in 1699 destroyed this opportunity, and Bavaria, a significant military power, was willing to make an alliance with any power that could fulfill the Elector's desire. In 1702, Bavaria courted both Austria and France with this objective in mind. When the Emperor rejected Maximilian's offer of exchanging Bavaria for the Crown of Naples, Maximilian immediately aligned with France and attacked imperial positions, distracting the Emperor's forces from fighting the French. Austrian diplomats requested assistance in forcibly crushing the Bavarian threat as early as 1702, but English officials, including Marlborough, demurred. They initially preferred leaving Austria to provide a solution, hoping she could entice Bavaria into bringing her valuable forces over to the Allies.

Early in January 1704 a number of princes of the Empire met in Frankfurt to discuss the forthcoming campaign. They concluded that the war had reached a critical stage. As a number of the German princes in the upper Rhine area were threatening to shift allegiance to Bavaria and France, it was felt that the strategy of the Grand Alliance would fail unless the Emperor's forces and the German princes could co-operate and place a strong army in the upper Rhine area to oppose the French. On 26 January, Marlborough returned to The Hague to begin discussions on the forthcoming campaign. By early February English and Dutch diplomats were reporting the urgent need to solve the Bavarian problem, and both governments directed their diplomats to join in the negotiations. Marlborough returned to England on 23 February, but when the negotiations with Bavaria failed in March, the English and Dutch governments agreed to an Austrian proposal for military action on the Moselle. On 8 April Marlborough sailed from Harwich to Holland, accompanied by the Austrian envoy Count Wratislaw.[68]

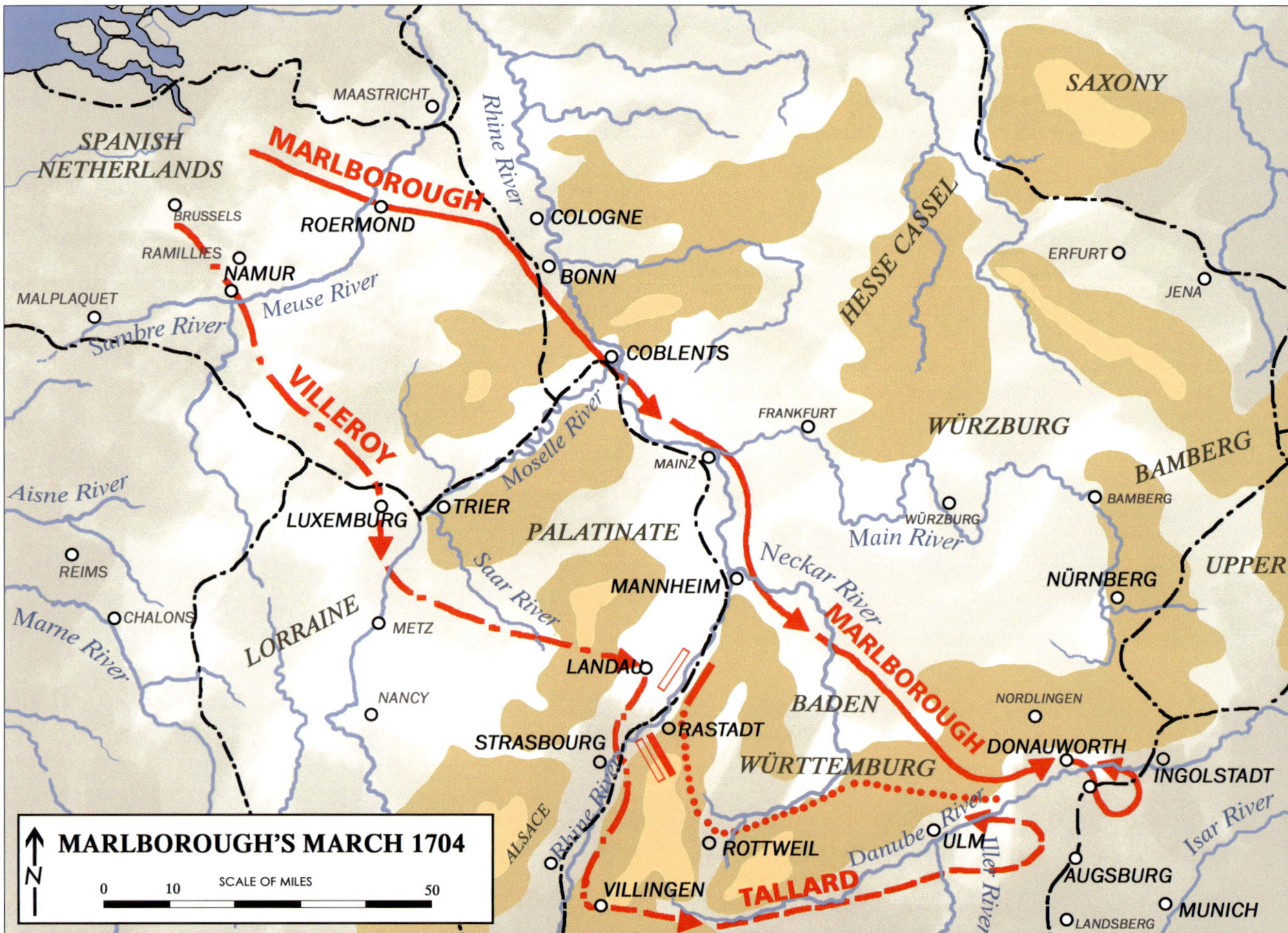
MARLBOROUGH'S MARCH 1704
N
SCALE OF MILES
0
10
50
SPANISH NETHERLANDS
MAASTRICHT
BRUSSELS
ROERMOND
RAMILLIES
NAMUR
MALPLAQUET
Meuse River
Sambre River
Rhine River
COLOGNE
BONN
COBLENTS
MARLBOROUGH
VILLEROY
Aisne River
REIMS
CHALONS
Marne River
LUXEMBURG
TRIER
Moselle River
Saar River
METZ
LORRAINE
NANCY
PALATINATE
MAINZ
FRANKFURT
MANNHEIM
LANDAU
Neckar River
STRASBOURG
RASTADT
ALSACE
BADEN
WÜRTTEMBURG
ROTTWEIL
VILLINGEN
TALLARD
Danube River
ULM
Iller River
NORDLINGEN
DONAUWORTH
INGOLSTADT
AUGSBURG
LANDSBERG
MUNICH
Isar River
HESSE CASSEL
SAXONY
ERFURT
JENA
WÜRZBURG
Main River
BAMBERG
NÜRNBERG
UPPER

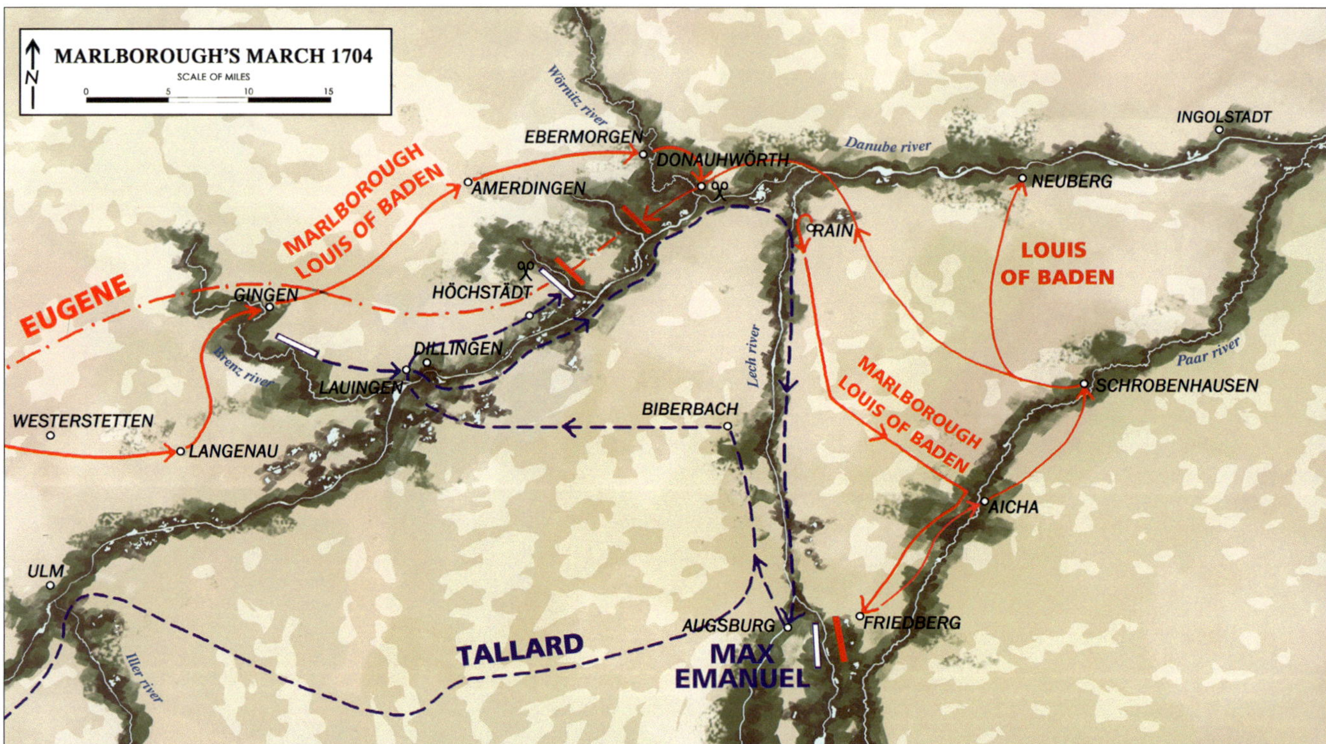
MARLBOROUGH'S MARCH 1704
N
SCALE OF MILES
0
5
10
15
Wörnitz river
EBERMORGEN
DONAUHWÖRTH
Danube river
INGOLSTADT
NEUBERG
AMERDINGEN
MARLBOROUGH LOUIS OF BADEN
EUGENE
GINGEN
HÖCHSTÄDT
RAIN
LOUIS OF BADEN
DILLINGEN
Brenz river
LAUINGEN
Lech river
Paar river
SCHROBENHAUSEN
WESTERSTETTEN
LANGENAU
BIBERBACH
MARLBOROUGH LOUIS OF BADEN
AICHA
ULM
AUGSBURG
FRIEDBERG
TALLARD
MAX EMANUEL
Iller river

With serious reservations about how far English and Dutch forces should go to support the political goals of the Austrian court within the Empire, Marlborough was instructed to press the Dutch into helping defeat Bavaria by operations on the Moselle. Meanwhile, Prince Ludwig von Baden proposed to Vienna that three armies should operate in conjunction for this purpose: one under Prince Eugène of Savoy[69] on the western border of Bavaria near Donauwörth; a second under Ludwig himself was to enter Bavaria across the Iller River south of Ulm; and the third, the Anglo-Dutch force under Marlborough, was to lay siege to Ulm. Having left The Hague for the army's field headquarters on 5 May, Marlborough agreed only to march as far as Koblenz, but conditionally to continue to the Danube and to Ulm if necessary. As the allied army moved from Roermond and crossed the Maas on 14–15 May, a French army under Villeroi began to parallel its movements 60 to 100 miles to the west to join another force under Tallard then to move from Landau through the Black Forest into Bavaria.

Although the Austrians had fully convinced the government in London of the necessity of a campaign on the Danube, and London had given Marlborough full authority to proceed with it, Marlborough decided not to reveal the full plan to the Dutch until after he had crossed the Rhine at Koblenz on 26 May. By that time French and Bavarian forces had joined in the Black Forest. Confronted with this situation, the States General agreed to the plan, reserving some forces to defend the Dutch Republic on the lower Rhine. By the time Marlborough's allied army left Wiesloch early in June, his plan was widely known. His movement to the Danube was made possible by masterly allied logistical planning and organization, especially through the work of the Dutch Raad van State and its key administrators, Adolf Hendrik van Rechteren, Heer van Almelo, and Adriaan van Borssele van der Hooghe, Heer van Geldermalsen. Camps, hospitals, bridges, food and forage, clothing, and other necessities were all supplied at short notice and in a timely manner, which facilitated their march and contrasted sharply with the greater difficulties the French faced in maintaining their own logistical support. Nevertheless, the opposing armies moved at similar speeds, averaging 6–8 miles per day when on the move.[70]

On 10 June at the army's camp at Mündelheim, south-east of Stuttgart, Marlborough met Prince Eugène of Savoy for the first time. On 13–14 June at Gross Heppach, Prince Ludwig von Baden joined them, and the three principal commanders coordinated diplomatic with military plans. As the allied armies approached the Danube, Austrian, Dutch, English, and Prussian diplomats used the military advance march to back their negotiations with the Elector of Bavaria so as to dissuade him from continuing with the French. Marlborough, himself, was also given letters of credence and full diplomatic powers for this purpose. On 20 June the Austrian envoy to England, Count Wratislaw, suggested that the Emperor bestow the greatest honour he could upon Marlborough, that of Prince of the Empire, as the Duke appeared likely to save the Empire from the Bavarian threat. By late June, although diplomats reported they had reached a tentative agreement with Bavaria, the Elector placed his army in a strategically advantageous position, giving Marlborough and English officials in London the impression that Bavaria engaged in such diplomacy only to gain time for a military advantage.

The combined allied forces under Prince Ludwig and Marlborough, amounting to some 44,000 men, moved as quickly as they could to storm the 10,000-man Franco-Bavarian garrison at the Schellenberg Heights adjoining Donauwörth on 2 July 1704.

Marlborough's march from the Netherlands to the Danube.

Maps by Rocío Espín.
TOP: Based on Wijn, Staatsche Leger, vol. 1, p. 424.
BOTTOM: based on Wijn, Staatsche Leger, vol. 1, p. 433.

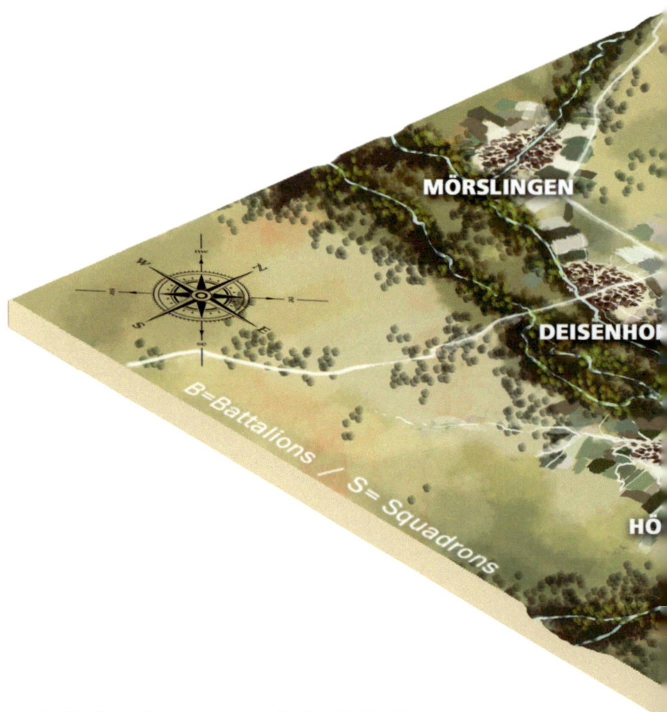

The Battle of Blenheim, 12 August 1704. Initial dispositions of Troops.

Map by Rocío Espín.

Based on Wijn, Staatsche Leger, vol. 1, p. 457.

In the action the Allies lost 1,295 men killed and 3,735 wounded, while the Bavarians and French lost 3,000–4,000 men, with 8,000–12,000 captured. This battle provided the Allies with a place to cross the Danube into Bavaria, while at the same time establishing a fortified terminal and depot for supplies coming south from Nördlingen. But it was not decisive, since French forces under Tallard had crossed the Rhine at Strasbourg and were already marching to support Bavaria before the action occurred. With this prospect of aid, the Bavarian army based at Augsburg continued to defy the Allies.

Still wanting to detach Bavaria from France and gain the advantage of the Bavarian army as part of the Grand Alliance, Marlborough sought to increase the pressure on the Elector. With allied armies in control of the Danube valley from Ulm to Passau and in a position to enter Bavaria, Marlborough began a campaign of burning and destroying the Bavarian countryside with the object of using force to back up his diplomacy. The French and Bavarian armies joined at Augsburg, creating a force of some 60,000 men, and then moved north to Biberach and west to Lauingen to try to isolate Marlborough from Prince Eugène's forces, which were approaching from the north-west. At a conference on 7 August, Marlborough and Eugène persuaded Prince Ludwig to take 15,000 troops to secure a critical alternative crossing of the Danube at Ingolstadt, while they covered the movements of the Franco-Bavarian army. When it became clear that the Allies could not succeed in detaching Bavaria from France, Marlborough and Eugène agreed to seek a battle. The two commanders made no attempt to recall Ludwig. While making a reconnaissance tour, they stopped to view the battlefield area from the Tapfheim church tower on 12 August and agreed to make a surprise assault on the Franco-Bavarian force encamped behind the River Nebel near the village of Blindheim, 5 miles north-east of Höchstädt. On 13 August NS a

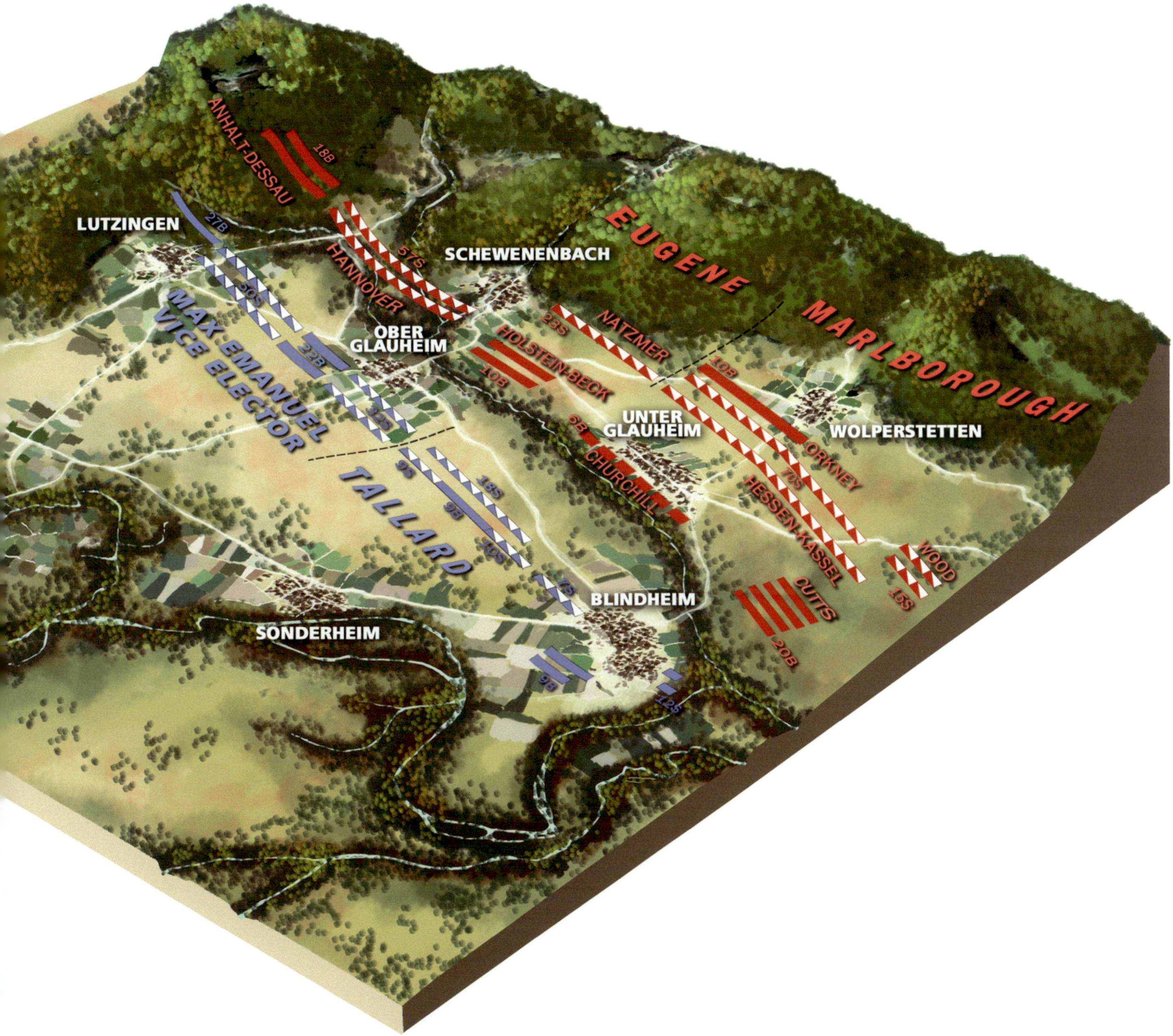

force of 52,000 men under the combined command of Marlborough and Eugène forced the 56,000-strong Bavarian and French armies under Elector Maximilian II Emanuel[71] and Marshal Tallard into a day-long battle. Typical of Marlborough's forces, 10,786, or only one-fifth, of the allied army under his overall command were British, while allied soldiers, including Dutchmen, Hanoverians, Hessians, Danes, and Prussians, made up the majority.[72]

In the battle – known ever since in English as The Battle of Blenheim and in German as The Battle of Höchstädt – Marlborough displayed his brilliance in tactical command. Although the slightly larger Franco-Bavarian army occupied a strong natural position, on higher ground behind marshy land along the Nebel River with its flanks protected on one side by the Danube and on the other by woods, Marlborough saw a flaw in its position. His army directly faced Tallard's French army, while Eugène's force was on Marlborough's right, facing troops under the Elector and

This nineteenth century silver statuette shows the Duke of Marlborough on horseback – after the Battle of Blenheim – writing his famous note to his wife on the back of a tavern bill: 'I have not time to say more, but to beg you will give my duty to the Queen, and let her know her army has had a glorious victory.'

Silver centrepiece by Robert Garrad II, 1845. Blenheim Palace, Oxfordshire, UK. The Bridgeman Art Library.

Marsin. Tallard's force did not present a single battle line, but had a weak centre with two practically independent wings, one near Blindheim and the other near the village of Oberglau. As the action unfolded Marlborough demonstrated firm and flexible control in his overall command of the action, intervening personally at critical moments when needed. In this, Eugène accepted Marlborough's overall command and willingly supported him.[73] In addition, highly capable subordinate generals took their own initiative in backing Marlborough to create an integrated, multi-national allied army that contrasted sharply with the situation in the Franco-Bavarian force under Tallard.[74]

Making his initial advance under cover of darkness, Marlborough acted to prevent the French wings from reinforcing the centre by first ordering Lord Cutts to move against the French position at Blindheim. Once the French were fully occupied, Marlborough ordered the prince of Holstein-Beck to contain the enemy wing near

Oberglau. Then he ordered his younger brother General Charles Churchill to move the allied centre across the Nebel and take up a position in an unusual formation, four lines deep with infantry battalions in close support to cavalry, on the French side of the river. In the early afternoon the French cavalry succeeded in penetrating the allied position on Charles Churchill's right flank. At this point Marlborough urgently requested Eugène to send assistance. Even though his forces were heavily engaged on the other side of Oberglau, Eugène immediately responded with a brigade of Austrian cuirassiers, who effectively drove the French back. By four in the afternoon Marlborough's forces were solidly positioned within Tallard's centre. Although Marsin's and the Elector's forces were superior in number to Eugène's, they declined to reinforce Tallard. Tallard attempted a cavalry charge, which slowed the allied advance momentarily, but Lord Orkney's battalions were able to support the allied cavalry successfully. Forced back, more than 3,000 French horsemen drowned as they tried to swim the Danube. As Tallard was trying to reach the protection of the French garrison in Blindheim, Hessian cavalry captured him. Meanwhile, Marsin and the Elector withdrew their forces toward Höchstädt and Marlborough ordered allied forces under his brother, Charles Churchill, to complete the encirclement of Blindheim, where Orkney bluffed the leaderless garrison into surrendering.[75] In the action the Franco-Bavarian army lost approximately 13,000 men, 1,150 officers, and 40 generals as prisoners, with about 20,000 killed or wounded; the Anglo-Dutch forces lost approximately 4,500 killed and 7,500 wounded; and the imperial losses were about 4,200 killed and wounded. As evening fell on 13 August Marlborough had a moment to scrawl his famous message on the back of a tavern bill that Colonel Daniel Parke, an American-born officer from Virginia, carried immediately to Sarah in London: 'I have not time to say more but to beg you will give my duty to the Queen and let her know her army has had a glorious victory.'[76]

In one of the most dramatic actions of the age, the French army suffered a major defeat for the first time in forty years and had its commander-in-chief captured.[77] Blenheim was a decisive battle in that it successfully removed the major obstacle that Bavaria presented in diverting the Allies from carrying out their broader grand strategy for the war. English leaders now turned to persuading their allies to focus on the larger task of implementing the English concept of grand strategy through several complementary theatres of war. Among the very first honours that fell to Marlborough following the victory was Emperor Leopold I's order on 28 August to create him Sacri Romani Imperii Princeps, or Prince of the Holy Roman Empire.[78] When informed of the honour Marlborough was flattered, but asked that the honour be made a substantive one with lands of a specific principality attached to the title that would give him income, status, and a vote in the Imperial Diet. The request was duly granted in the following year, when he was awarded the lordship of Mindelheim.[79]

Meeting Prince Ludwig von Baden on 25 August, Marlborough agreed to join in besieging Landau as a preliminary to the next operations in Flanders. Immediately leading the allied army back to the north, the English retraced their march from Ulm to Bruchsal. Other forces used two alternative routes to the area near Philippsburg, where they crossed the Rhine on 5–8 September and established themselves in positions favourable for a resumption of operations on the upper Rhine and the Moselle River in the following year. Marlborough's forces took Trier on 26 September, and began a six-week siege at Trarbach that ended on 20 December.

Before completing the siege at Trarbach, Marlborough began negotiations for the

English wading thro' the morass, and making the attack upon the village of Blenheim.

Engraving by Robert Wilkinson, 1710. Brown University Library, Providence, RI, USA. From the Anne S.K. Brown Military Collection.

Brigade of 10 Battallions of French foot
ye Center of ye field of Battle cut in peices be-
abandoned by their Horse, none escaping
a few Soldiers who threw themselves on ye
round as Dead to save their Lives. —
Prince EUGENE of Savoy, attacking the left Wing of ye French
Army at the Battle of Blenhiem, commanded by the Elector
of Bavaria and the Marshall Marsin whom he entirely rout-
-ed and pursued as far as the Village of Lutzingen. —

A modern view of Blenheim Palace at Woodstock, Oxfordshire.

Blenheim Palace, Oxfordshire, UK. Photograph reproduced with the kind permission of His Grace the Duke of Marlborough, Blenheim Palace Image Library.

1705 campaign. He left Weissemburg on 10 November and travelled to Berlin to negotiate a treaty with the Prussian King, Frederick I, to send 8,000 troops to Italy for the Duke of Savoy. After a week in Berlin, on 22–9 November, he travelled to Hanover, where on 2–4 December he met with Electress Sophia, allaying her doubts about him and charming her with his courtly manner. Next, in Amsterdam and then The Hague, he had extensive talks with Dutch leaders on allied plans for an offensive military campaign up the Moselle River and into Lorraine.

Marlborough finally returned to London on 25 December 1704, and on 28 January 1705 the Queen granted him the former royal manor of Woodstock, with its historical associations as the birthplace of the Black Prince and of the romantic liaisons of Henry II with his mistress, Rosamond Clifford. The grant included the Hundred of Wotton, comprising together a total of some 22,000 acres in Oxfordshire, then estimated to produce revenue of about £6,000 a year. In addition, on 5 February, Parliament approved the Queen's proposal that the grant of £5,000 made in 1702 should be made permanent for the Duke's lifetime; it also granted the funds to construct a house at Woodstock that would be not only the Duke's family seat, but a national memorial commemorating and named after the battle of Blenheim. For a symbolic quitrent Marlborough and his descendants were required to present annually to the sovereign at Windsor Castle, on the anniversary of the battle, a facsimile of the silk standard of the French royal household troops, the Corps du Roi, which Marlborough's troops had taken during the battle. In addition, Marlborough received £600 of the Blenheim bounty payment to officers serving in the battle.

About Christmas 1704 Marlborough personally chose John Vanbrugh as architect for his new house, initially to be called Blenheim Castle. A former soldier and Sir Christopher Wren's assistant at the board of works, Vanbrugh had as his assistant surveyor Nicholas Hawksmoor. In 1705 Marlborough and Vanbrugh chose the site for the building and clearing began. The Queen's gardener, Henry Wise, laid out the grounds and selected the plantings. Clearly related to Vanbrugh's design for the Earl of Carlisle's Castle Howard, Blenheim became Vanbrugh's greatest work with its 187 rooms and courtyards covering 7 acres and the cost far exceeding the initial estimate of £100,000.[80]

With his own financial position assured, Marlborough transferred the remaining portion of Sarah's inheritance from his name into her own. In March 1705 the Marlboroughs witnessed the marriage of their youngest daughter, Mary, to John Montagu (later second Duke of Montagu), an event which created a political connection through a cousin of the bridegroom to Lord Halifax, one of the Whig Junto. Sarah began to exploit this connection, creating difficulties that soon damaged her cordial relations with the Queen. Just as the public began to admire her as the person reconciling Anne to the Whigs, Sarah was actually approaching a breaking point with the Queen that eventually affected her husband's career. Although Marlborough's instincts were to stand clear of party politics, Sarah remained capable of influencing his thinking.[81]

■ The campaigns and politics of 1705–1706

Shortly after his daughter's marriage, Marlborough sailed from Harwich on 30 March. On arrival at The Hague he immediately began to initiate the military campaign that had been planned at the end of 1704. The Dutch continued to refuse him the degree of independence he wanted in commanding allied troops, while other allies were slow in producing the promised number of men.[82] Allied relations with Austria were slowed by the death of Emperor Leopold I and the succession of Joseph I, who brought new policies with him.[83] At the same time England's continuing support for the Hungarian Protestants had begun to be a major irritant in English relations with Catholic Austria, and slowed Austria's co-operation in supporting the broader aspects of allied grand strategy.[84]

While Marlborough dealt with these issues, Sarah became interested in the building works at Woodstock. In May, Godolphin employed Henry Joynes as comptroller of works and, on 9 June, authorized the first £20,000 payment towards construction of Blenheim. Vanbrugh laid the foundation stone, measuring 8 feet square, at the east end of the new building as early as 18 June. Soon nearly 1,500 men were employed on the site, constructing the building and its courtyards and creating gardens in the 7000 acre park. At this point Godolphin began to investigate the projected costs and discovered that the Queen and Parliament had made an unrealistically generous gift from a Treasury that was also funding a major war. While both Sarah and Godolphin suggested that plans be scaled back, Marlborough refused and demanded that they proceed.

By summer 1705 Marlborough realized that he could not carry out his original plans for the campaign, but decided instead to take the field with a 60,000-man force, smaller than planned. After leaving The Hague on 3 May he travelled to Maastricht, Rastatt, and then Trier. From there he and the allied army marched to Konz, where they used the nearby bridge to cross the Moselle and Saar rivers. Between 6 and 11 July, he successfully besieged Huy. That completed, he began operations to

Bronze bust of the Duke of Marlborough in the third stateroom at Blenheim Palace.

By an annoynmous artist of the British School, 19th century. Blenheim Palace, Oxfordshire, UK. Photograph by Jarrald Publishing, reproduced with the kind permission of His Grace the Duke of Marlborough, Blenheim Palace Image Library.

pass the fortified French positions and complex of earthworks, barricades, and entrenchments linking an extensive network of fortifications between Antwerp and Namur known as the lines of Brabant. In completing this under cover of darkness on 17–18 July, he captured Tienen to the west of the lines and routed a Franco-Bavarian army at Elixheim. Owing to lack of forage he was unable immediately to exploit his victory, creating indecision and further delay within the allied command. He moved into camp at Meldert and waited until mid-August to begin a new offensive, moving to cross the River Yssche and to threaten Brussels. After reaching the Yssche, he abandoned further offensives on 19 August and returned the army to Meldert, in the face of delays in bringing the artillery to bear and further indecision among the allied commanders on how to proceed.[85]

Deeply disappointed with the military campaign of 1705, Marlborough expressed his frustration to officials at home, and with greater reserve told Heinsius that he could not exercise effective command under the current restrictive arrangement.[86] Late in September 1705 the Queen revoked the Earl of Abingdon's commission as

Lord Lieutenant of Oxfordshire and replaced him with Marlborough, who eventually received his patent in 1706. At the same time Godolphin urged Marlborough to return home in order to help him deal with Parliamentary issues and help avoid political problems with the Scots Parliament, but Marlborough preferred to avoid domestic politics and turned, instead, to a diplomatic offensive in planning for the next year's campaign.

After discussions at The Hague, Marlborough travelled in October to Düsseldorf, where he met the Elector Palatine to discuss the employment of Palatinate troops in Italy, then journeyed on to Frankfurt, where on 31 October he conferred with Prince Ludwig von Baden, and met bankers and other diplomats. He then moved on to Regensburg and embarked in the Emperor's barge on 6 November for a six-day journey down the Danube to Vienna. On arrival on 13 November he assisted in arranging loans for both the imperial government and Prince Eugène's army in Italy. In preparation for his arrival, Emperor Joseph I signed on 14 November 1705 the formal diploma creating the Duke and his heirs, male or female, Princes of the Holy Roman Empire and additionally granting them the augmentation of the imperial eagle to the display of the Marlborough arms. Moreover, on 17 November Joseph raised the lordship of Mindelheim, 15 miles wide and with about 2000 inhabitants in upper Swabia from the lands confiscated from Bavaria, into the *unmittelbare Reichsherrschaft Mindelheim*, a principality and immediate fief of the Emperor. This he granted to Marlborough and his male heirs as Reichsfürst zu Mindelheim, entitling them to a seat and vote on the Diet of the Empire and the Swabian Circle.[87]

On 23 November, Marlborough and his son-in-law Charles, third Earl of Sunderland, left Vienna for Berlin, where they arrived on 31 November. There, Marlborough attempted to persuade Prussia to concentrate on the war against France as the primary threat to the peace of Europe and to maintain Prussian troops in Italy rather than fighting in the Great Northern War that involved Sweden against Saxony-Poland, Russia, and Denmark.[88] After leaving Berlin he travelled to Hanover, where he presented drafts of the bills to naturalize the dowager Electress Sophia and her son, George, the Elector, as English citizens in the event of the Queen's death and worked to convince them both of the government's intentions of maintaining the protestant succession. While in Hanover, Marlborough turned momentarily to military matters in settling a dispute among allied commanders concerning winter quarters.

After moving on to The Hague on 8 December, Marlborough joined Dutch officials in preparing for the campaign of 1706 and then returned to London on 31 January before coming back to The Hague on 25 April. Frustrated by the Dutch, he turned his initial thoughts to marching English troops over the Alps to join Prince Eugène for a campaign in Italy, but the first events of 1706 quickly shattered this idea. The French army's early offensive moves in Italy and on the Rhine made a march from Flanders to Italy impossible.[89] On 13 May Marlborough joined the allied army, which marched westwards from Maastricht on 15 May, crossing the demolished lines of Brabant at Merdorp, and was following the general course of the Méhaigne River with the thought of threatening Namur and forcing the French into battle. Meanwhile, the French had already moved out from their entrenched lines in the Southern Netherlands, expecting the Allies to be as ineffective as they had been the previous year. Advance forces from both sides reported each other's presence on 19 May, but had no exact knowledge of each other's location. Shortly after midnight on 23 May Marlborough ordered his Quartermaster-General and key staff member William Cadogan[90]

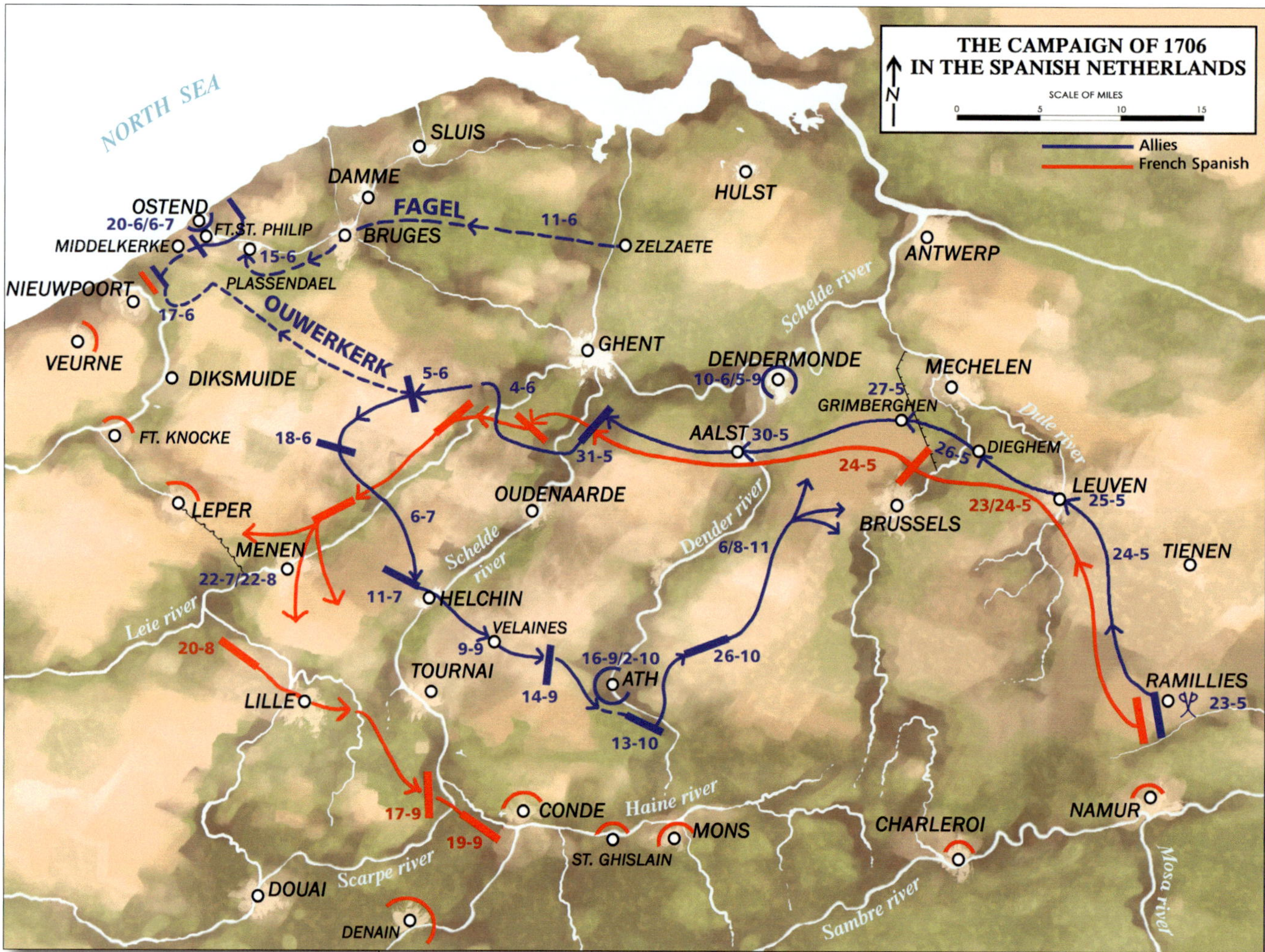

The campaign of 1706 in the southern Netherlands.

Map by Rocío Espín. Based on Wijn, Staatsche Leger, vol. 2, Atlas, map #2.

On 18 June 1706 the Emperor appointed Marlborough as Spain's Governor-General in the Southern Netherlands, using the authority Charles III had granted him and a blank patent the King had signed on 18 May. Marlborough was attracted by a post with an estimated income of £60,000 a year and much patronage, and the Queen and government in London approved. However, the Dutch made it clear that the appointment was entirely unacceptable. In their eyes the Southern Netherlands should not be returned immediately, but administered by a council under the joint direction of England and the Dutch Republic in Charles III's name. Marlborough's acceptance of the post would have divided England and the Dutch, jeopardizing Dutch plans to create an effective fortress barrier against future attack. Marlborough eventually declined the post, and instead he and George Stepney became the first two English regents of the Anglo-Dutch condominium for governing the Southern Netherlands.[94]

On Marlborough's return to London on 26 November from the victorious campaign, he was met with a torrent of rewards. Shortly thereafter the Whigs forced the Queen to assent to the appointment of Marlborough's son-in-law the Earl of Sunderland as Secretary of State. Godolphin, too, had been separated from the Tories and was now dependent on Whig support to continue in office. In reaction the Queen began to shift her reliance from Godolphin and Sarah to Robert Harley.

The Duke of Marlborough at the Siege of Lille, 1708.
This tapestry probably illustrates Marlborough receiving news of the surrender of the city of Lille on 23 October. It is unique among the Blenheim palace tapestries in showing Marlborough standing rather than on horseback. The tapestry shows in the background a view from northeast of the enceinte or outer defence works of Lille. Significantly, the view does not show the citadel, as Prince Eugene's successful siege was not completed until 9 December.

Tapestry by Judocus de Vos after Lambert and Philippe de Hondt, 18th century. Blenheim Palace, Oxfordshire, UK. *The Bridgeman Art Library.*

Despite these portents of future trouble, the victory at Ramillies helped to assuage temporarily the hostility that had steadily grown between the Queen and Sarah, but political issues soon drew them apart again.

Since Marlborough now had no surviving male heir, he requested that all honours bestowed on him in Anne's reign, including the titles of Marquess of Blandford and Duke of Marlborough, pass to his daughters, in priority of birth, and to their heirs. In addition he petitioned that the grant of £5,000 a year be made a perpetual grant on his heirs. Parliament granted these requests, which received the royal assent on 21 December 1706, 'it being intended that the said honours shall continue, remain and be invested in all the issue of the said Duke, so long as any such issue male or female shall continue,'[95] retaining the Duke's precedence as established by the letters patent of 14 December 1702. With this settled and with his political support slipping at home, Marlborough grew increasingly tired of his heavy burden as commander-in-chief and ambassador at The Hague and began to long for retirement. However, there were no ready alternative candidates to take up his posts, and he left from Margate for Holland on 2 April 1707 to open the new campaign.

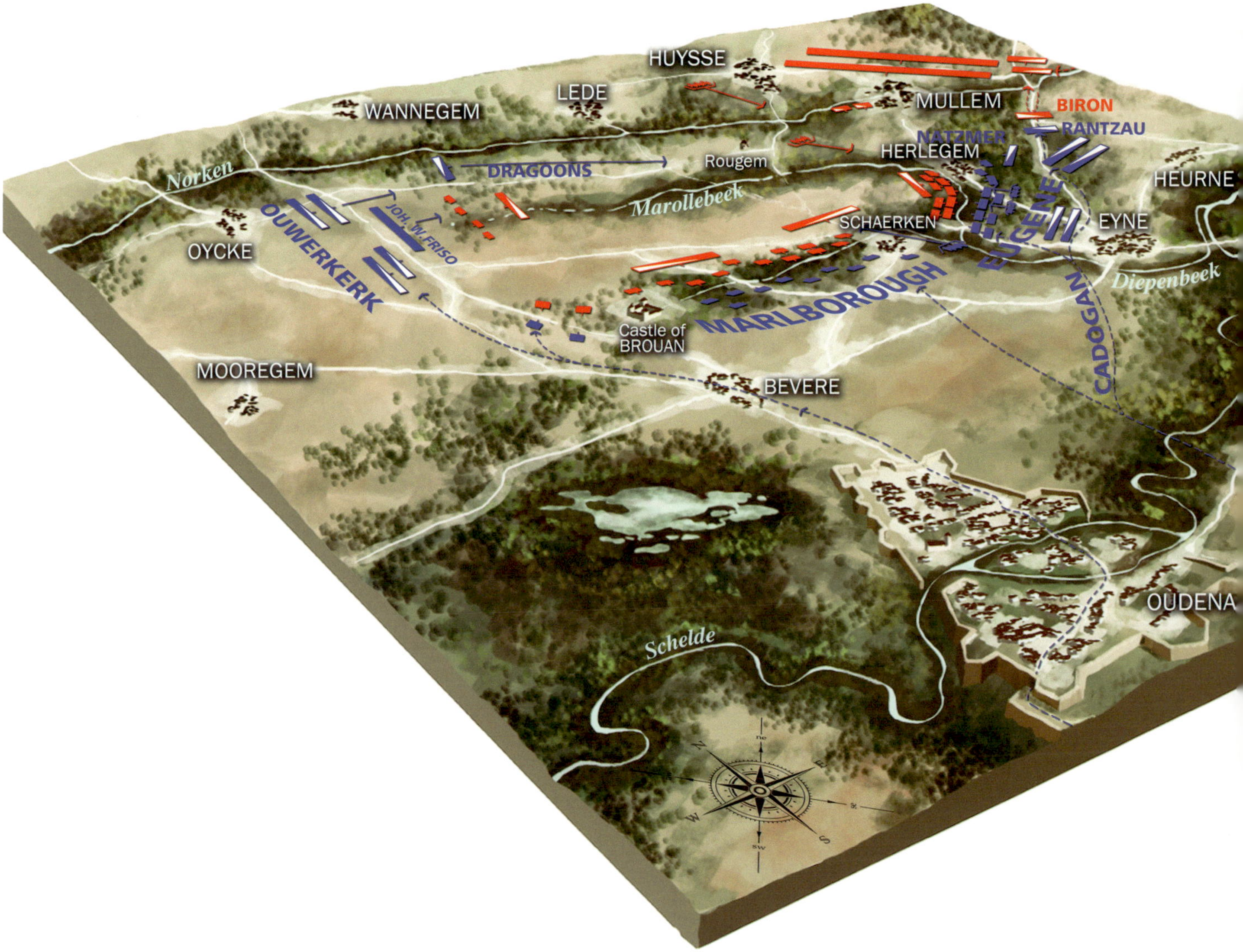

The Battle of Oudenaarde, 11 July 1708.

Map by Rocío Espín.
Based on Wijn, Staatsche Leger, vol. 2, Atlas, map #10.

The campaigns and politics of 1707

With France on the defensive along the Rhine and in Flanders, the Allies planned a strategy for 1707 in which Marlborough undertook an offensive from the Southern Netherlands into France, while Prince Eugène undertook a similar campaign from Italy, supported by the Anglo-Dutch fleets in the Mediterranean, against Toulon. Shortly after Marlborough's arrival in The Hague, allied plans for the northern theatre were delayed by events in Saxony.

King Charles XII of Sweden had marched the Swedish army into Saxony in an effort to force its Elector, Augustus, to relinquish the Polish throne to Stanislaw. The Swedish presence in Saxony raised fears that war might occur between Austria and Sweden. With this in mind the government in London ordered Marlborough to undertake a personal diplomatic mission to Charles XII in his camp at Altranstädt, near Leipzig, to prevent Austro-Swedish hostilities and to obtain Sweden's support for the Grand Alliance. Leaving the Dutch field marshal Nassau-Ouwerkerk in charge of combined allied military preparations, Marlborough went to Hanover on

24 April, then on to Altranstädt on 26 April, joining the English envoy to Sweden, the Reverend John Robinson, and his Dutch colleague, Johan van Haersolte, Heer van Cranenburg, for successful discussions with Charles XII. These laid the initial groundwork for a diplomatic agreement between Sweden and Austria that was eventually signed in the autumn. Marlborough obtained Charles XII's promise to remain neutral in the war against France, while Marlborough promised allied support for Sweden in her negotiations with Denmark and Austria, providing recognition of Stanislaw as King of Poland with guarantee for the Austro-Swedish treaty of Altranstädt. On 27 April Marlborough briefly left the Swedish camp to dine with Augustus in Leipzig. He left Altranstädt on 29 April and travelled on 1 May to Berlin, where he worked to dissuade King Frederick from making a treaty with Sweden that might distract Prussia from fighting France. After returning to The Hague on 8 May, he travelled to Brussels on 13 May, and then joined the army at Lebecq on 21 May.[96]

Meanwhile, allied military setbacks on the upper Rhine and in Spain forced Marlborough to dispatch troops under his command to support operations in those areas. The French made the first move against Marlborough's allied army, when Marshal Vendôme advanced towards Huy and forced Marlborough to guard it with his smaller force. Marlborough moved his headquarters to Meldert on 1 June, but neither the French nor the Dutch were prepared to engage in battle unless certain of the outcome. Beginning on 10 August Marlborough undertook a series of manoeuvres, based on Soignies until 31 August, then on Helchin from 7 September to 10 October, which helped maintain the Allies' position, but he was unable to undertake any siege or battle because of the need to protect the large cities of Brabant, particularly Brussels. With the campaign at an end he left the army on 14 October and went to Frankfurt on 21 October, then returned to The Hague on 3 November.[97]

Meanwhile in London on 31 August 1707 Queen Anne granted to trustees, for Sarah's benefit, a Crown lease on property in St James's Park adjacent to St James's

The Battle of Oudenaarde, 1708.

Engraving by James Hulett, 1706. Brown University Library, Providence, RI, USA. From the Anne S.K. Brown Military Collection.

Palace originally known as The Friary. Close to her lodgings in St James's Palace, Sarah initially thought of building a town house for herself. The Duke thought the site too small and her plans more costly than she anticipated, but he initially agreed to contribute £7,000 to her project on the understanding that it would eventually devolve upon the Marlborough heirs, or would become security for repaying that sum to his heirs. Disenchanted with Vanbrugh's ongoing work at Blenheim, Sarah chose Sir Christopher Wren as her architect. For one of his last works, Wren chose his son, Christopher, Jr., to assist, but made little immediate progress on the building in London.[98]

The politics of 1708 and the Oudenaarde campaign

Marlborough returned to London in November 1707 to find the ministry's work brought almost to a standstill by attacks from both parties. The failure at Toulon, the loss of Admiral Shovell at sea, the charges of maladministration at the Admiralty, and an uneventful campaign in Flanders all provided fodder for political attacks. By January 1708 it was clear that Robert Harley was attempting to replace Godolphin as first minister. When this became apparent Godolphin refused to serve in the cabinet with Harley and demanded that the Queen choose between them. During this political crisis Marlborough told the Queen that he could serve with anyone, including Harley, but Godolphin could not be persuaded to back down. As the crisis deepened Marlborough told the Queen that he would resign if Godolphin left office. Sarah, also, made the same point to the Queen, adding a request that her offices in the royal household be divided among her daughters. Still hoping that Marlborough would serve without Godolphin, the Queen waited to make her final decision. Then Marlborough pushed the point further, telling the Queen that he would resign if the Queen did not dismiss Harley.[99] Members of Parliament as well as Cabinet Ministers made it clear to the Queen that Marlborough's loss would be too much. Finally, the crisis passed on 10 February 1708 when the Queen dismissed Harley as Secretary of State, along with a number of his supporters including Henry St John. As a result of this power struggle between individual office-holders, the war policy that had been a national bipartisan one for six years now clearly became a Whig policy.[100]

From February to March 1708 the danger of a French-supported Jacobite invasion of Britain from Dunkirk delayed Marlborough's return to The Hague. He finally sailed on 29 March, clearly wanting to deal with international and military issues and to avoid if possible the party politics in which Sarah was deeply involved at home. On his return to The Hague on 10 April he and Prince Eugène participated in a series of meetings with Dutch leaders to plan the campaign of 1708. At this point it seemed that the French intended to make an attack on the Southern Netherlands their main objective, having appointed the Duke of Burgundy to command jointly with Marshal Vendôme the 110,000-strong French army in Flanders in an effort to improve the French bargaining position for a compromise peace. To meet this threat the Allies made a secret plan for Eugène to command an army on the Moselle that would appear ready to support a second army commanded by the Elector of Hanover on the Rhine, but that, in reality, would move on to Flanders to join Marlborough for a major battle with the French. This would involve all available forces, including the garrison in the allied stronghold at Brussels, relying on the waterways of Flanders instead of Brussels as the key connection to Holland. In order to complete this arrangement, Marlborough and Eugène stayed in Hanover from 26 April to 2 May for discussions with the Elector, but, in order to maintain their secret plan, deliberately deceived the Elector into thinking that the major effort would still be on the Rhine.[101]

Marlborough returned to The Hague on 6 May and then went to Brussels, where he stayed from 14 to 25 May, before returning to the army. Little happened until, suddenly, on 4 July, Vendôme's army marched from Mons in heavy rain directly towards Ghent, taking Marlborough completely by surprise. The French seized the city, with 300 English soldiers in the castle, at daybreak. By capturing Ghent, which controlled the waterways of Flanders, the French made it impossible for the Allies to abandon Brussels, as planned, since it now remained the only connection to Holland.[102]

The loss of Ghent added to Marlborough's reputation among the Dutch for imprudence. He soon recovered from this bad start to the campaign by luring the French into a major encounter at Oudenaarde on 11 July. Having pretended to be in a weak position, Marlborough employed his superior generalship and the terrain to bring new formations quickly into action, creating a continually changing tactical sit-

The Garden Front of Marlborough House, Westminster.
Built of red Dutch brick and completed in 1711, Sir Christopher Wren designed the London town house located next to St. James's Palace. The building was one of Wren's last works and the only work that he did in cooperation with his son, Christopher.

Engraving from Vitruvius Britannicus by Colen Campbell, 1715-1725. The British Museum, London, UK.
© The Trustees of the British Museum

uation in which he exploited the confusion and misunderstanding between the force commanded by Vendôme and Louis, Duke of Burgundy (elder brother of Philip V). During the action an allied army of about 80,000 under Marlborough and Eugène fought against Vendôme's and Burgundy's 85,000-man French army; the Allies lost 825 killed and 2,150 wounded, of which only 175 were British, to French losses estimated as high as 6,750 killed and 7000 captured. The battle of Oudenaarde allowed the Allies to regain the strategic initiative they had lost to the French in July and to take the offensive and put the French on the defensive.[103]

In the next operation Marlborough moved into position to take the city and fortress of Lille on 2 August; he eventually captured it, after 120 days of siege, on 10 December in one of the bloodiest actions of the time, with the total number of killed and wounded reaching 15,000 Allies and 7,000 French. In order to support this difficult operation against Vauban's masterpiece of fortification Marlborough needed extensive siege supplies and depended on supply lines, which the French methodically worked to cut off. After opening a direct and new line from the port of Ostend, a convoy sufficient to support the siege for a fortnight left there on 27 September. To protect it, Marlborough detached Major-General John Webb, and later General Cadogan, with cavalry for the convoy's further protection, having learned that a vigilant French force of 23,000 under La Motte was already attempting to waylay the supplies. In a wooded area near Wijnendael, Webb, with only 6000–8000 men – including a large Dutch contingent under General Nassau-Woudenberg – brilliantly defeated the French on 28 September. Cadogan arrived at the end of the action and the French retreated on seeing his forces. On hearing the news, a relieved Marlborough immediately sent off a

The South Portico of Blenheim Palace capped by the bust of Louis XIV that Marlborough captured at Tournai in 1709.

Blenheim Palace, Oxfordshire, UK. Photograph by Richard Cragg, reproduced with the kind permission of His Grace the Duke of Marlborough, Blenheim Palace Image Library.

note of congratulation to Webb and Cadogan. Incensed that Marlborough had given equal credit to Cadogan, Webb immediately objected, creating a political issue at home. He soon left the army and became a vocal political critic of Marlborough.
The long siege of Lille and the operations to support it took a heavy personal toll on Marlborough, putting him under continuous daily pressure for more than three months. As the operation progressed he grew increasingly irritable with both his subordinates in the English army and his Dutch colleagues. In the remainder of the campaign he was able to forestall a French attack on Brussels through manoeuvre and then retook Ghent, which fell after a fifteen-day siege on 2 January 1709. With its surrender the French at Bruges also evacuated their position. As Marlborough had intimated the previous spring at the opening of the campaign of 1708, he wanted to stay away from political struggles at home as long as possible and had advised his wife to avoid giving political advice to the Queen. Meanwhile, the Tories in the Commons passed a vote of thanks to Webb, then another to Marlborough and Eugène together, infuriating Sarah and the Whigs by giving no separate recognition to Marlborough.

The politics of 1709 and the Malplaquet campaign

From mid-December 1708 to late March 1709 Europe experienced one of the most severe winters on record. Ice choked the waterways and harbours, wildlife died, crops were ruined, and people starved. In the army, soldiers and horses died on the march and could not survive outside or in tents. In these circumstances Marlborough agreed

The Battle of Malplaquet, 11 September 1709.

Map by Rocío Espín.
Based on Wijn, Staatsche Leger, vol. 2, Atlas, map #20.

to command the army during January and most of February in order to manage the difficult logistical problems that the winter presented. Late in February Prince Eugène relieved him so that he could make a brief trip to London, where he arrived on 11 March. His stay there was short, and he returned to The Hague on 9 April.

It was probably during this visit to London that Marlborough made the first of his requests for a life appointment as Captain-General, a position he had held only at the Queen's pleasure since 1702. Increasingly exhausted by his work, seeing his prestige declining in Parliament and with Sarah's relations with the Queen increasingly strained, he realized that his military and diplomatic appointments might soon come to an end. While the success of the last campaign remained in the public mind, he thought it a good time to ask the Queen directly for the permanent appointment. The Queen demurred, replying that it would be useful to find a precedent.[104]

On Marlborough's return to The Hague he learned that Heinsius had entered peace negotiations without his knowledge, giving the impression in England that Marlborough no longer held the confidence of the Dutch.[105] Meanwhile, in Vienna the same reports led officials there to think it was Marlborough who was secretly conspiring with the Dutch against the Austrians. To end this crisis within the alliance English officials directed Marlborough to insist that an Anglo-Dutch agreement on peace was essential before any negotiations with France could be entertained. At the same time he and Eugène agreed not to discuss the Dutch barrier question[106] until the Franco-Dutch talks had been cancelled, which pressurized the Dutch into discontinuing their negotiations with the French.

When Heinsius opened barrier treaty discussions with Marlborough, the Duke was reluctant to participate, as he opposed Dutch demands. Feeling that he could not come to agreement with them, he returned to London on 1 May to ask the government to appoint a separate negotiator, who could be accountable to the Whigs. The cabinet considered several candidates and settled on Charles, second Viscount Townshend. Accompanied by Townshend, Marlborough returned to The Hague on 18 May. By that time the French had realized that they could not reach a separate peace with the Dutch and initiated general peace negotiations with the Allies. The Marquess de

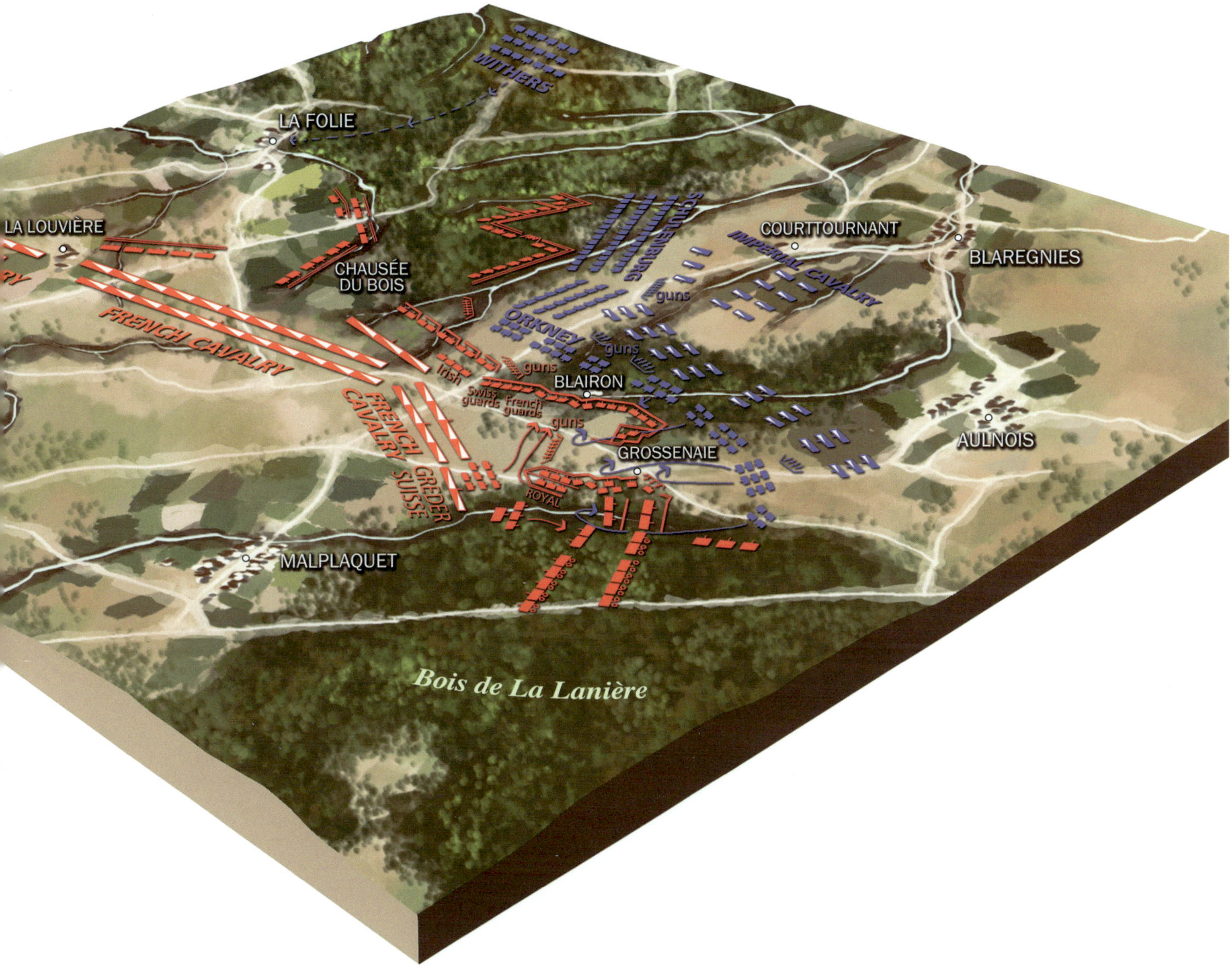

Torcy, Heinsius, Marlborough, Townshend, and Eugène were among the participants. Meanwhile, in London Sarah laid the foundation stone of Marlborough House on 24 May 1709, but the Duke was quick to remind her of the source of her funds and to ask that her project not interfere with Blenheim, 'for we are not so master of that as of the other'.[107] Initially, however, Sarah secured the money to begin the project by borrowing nearly £22,000 from the Privy Purse funds, relying on her husband's promise to her to pay the entire cost for the large house, which eventually amounted to £40,000–£50,000.

By 13 June it became clear that the peace talks had failed on one major issue. Louis XIV specifically rejected the Allies' requirement that France ensure that Philip V relinquish all parts of the Spanish monarchy to Charles III, believing this to be beyond French power. Having rejected the proposals, France began to prepare to continue military operations at a time when the Allies had been convinced that she had no choice but to accept peace. In response Marlborough, Eugène, and the Dutch began to gather their forces after the difficult winter and the shortages it produced. To open the campaign Marlborough's and Eugène's 40,000-man allied army undertook the siege of the city and fortress of Tournai,[108] which fell after sixty-nine days on

The Battle of Malplaquet.

Tapestry by Judocus de Vos after Lambert and Philippe de Hondt, 1709. Blenheim Palace, Oxfordshire, UK. Reproduced with the kind permission of His Grace the Duke of Marlborough, Blenheim Palace Image Library.

3 September with casualties mounting to 5,340 Allies and 3,800 French. On entering the citadel Marlborough saw a 30 ton marble bust of Louis XIV over the gate and ordered it to be taken down and shipped to Woodstock as a trophy. There, it dominates the top of Blenheim Palace's south portico over the taunting inscription *Europæ haec vindex genio decora alta Britanno* ('The assertor of the liberties of Europe dedicates these lofty honours to the genius of Britain').[109]

The Allies continued their military pressure on France as a means of renewing peace negotiations. By 6 September they had moved about 30 miles to the east and begun the siege of the fortress of Mons. On hearing this Louis XIV reacted violently. Declaring that the salvation of France was at stake, he immediately ordered Marshal Villars to spare no means in relieving Mons, authorizing him to engage in a major battle if necessary. Villars immediately marched from Douai to take up a strong position and established his field headquarters near the village of Malplaquet, not far from the allied armies covering the siege.

Early on 11 September 1709 the allied army of 110,000 men under Marlborough and Eugène attacked the Franco-Bavarian army under Villars and Boufflers, who were holding an extremely strong entrenched position with 80,000 men for their intended intervention in the siege at Mons. Allied forces opened the battle by storming the

The Duke of Marlborough and the siege of Bouchain, 1711.
The third of the three tapestries showing the siege, this one depicts the Duke of Marlborough receiving the news from a mounted messenger of the surrender of Bouchain on 13 September 1711. Accompanying him in the group on horseback is Colonel John Armstrong, chief engineer and surveyor of the ordnance who played a major role in the siege (second from the left), and General William Cadogan (third from the left).

Tapestry by Judocus de Vos after Lambert and Philippe de Hondt, 18th century. Blenheim Palace, Oxfordshire, UK. The Bridgeman Art Library.

French position, but were repulsed with very heavy casualties. After renewing the assault Marlborough eventually forced the French to weaken their centre to support their left wing and make a counter-attack against the Allies. Early in the afternoon he and Eugène were able to mobilize some 30,000 horsemen to advance on the French centre. The French drove the Allies back half a dozen times, until they began to give way to the huge allied cavalry force and retreat onto the plain around Malplaquet. Exhausted after a day of extremely hard fighting, the two opposing armies separated, and each remained intact without any clear victor, with each claiming a technical advantage. The cost in casualties was probably the highest for the entire eighteenth century. No exact figures are known, but it is estimated that about 24,000 Allies were killed and wounded, and approximately 15,000 killed and wounded among the French.[110] Marlborough was deeply shocked, appalled to have 'so many brave men killed with whom I have lived these eight years, when we thought ourselves sure of a peace.'[111] The experience shook the allied troops, and they ceased to be the confident force they had been before the engagement. At home both houses of Parliament voted Marlborough their thanks, and the Whigs declared this his greatest victory.

After the battle Villars and his army took up a position behind the defensive line of Rhonelle, while on 20 September the allied army resumed its siege at Mons, which surrendered on 20 October. The armies entered winter quarters in October, two months earlier than they had the previous year. In late September Marlborough resumed his thoughts about gaining a life appointment as Captain-General. In mid-September he drafted a letter to the Queen, and on 10 October he sent the final version to Godolphin to give to the Queen. On Lord Chancellor Cowper's advice, the Queen refused his request, but when Marlborough became angry, she temporized and left the matter open.[112]

Marlborough returned to London on 8 November 1709 to find that the Whigs still exaggerated Sarah's influence with the Queen. On the counterproductive advice of Arthur Maynwaring, Sarah had done things that repeatedly angered the Queen, rather than influenced her decisions. By this point, the Queen had become so irritated with Sarah that she allowed Abigail Masham to assume most of Sarah's substantive functions.[113]

Politics, campaign, and dismissal, 1710–1711

Early in January 1710 Marlborough discovered that his own relations with the Queen were no better than those of his wife. Following Lord Essex's death in January his posts as Constable of the Tower and Colonel of the Oxford dragoons fell vacant. Normally the Captain-General advised the Queen on such appointments, and Marlborough had settled upon the Duke of Northumberland and Lord Hertford as Essex's successors. On Robert Harley's advice, Earl Rivers applied to Marlborough for appointment as Constable of the Tower, but was told that another post would be more suitable. Shortly afterwards, at an audience with the Queen, Marlborough made his recommendation of Northumberland as Constable of the Tower, only to be told that it was too late as she had already assigned the post to Lord Rivers. When Marlborough asked that the appointment be cancelled, the Queen declined. Later that same day Anne wrote to Marlborough with her wish to give the dragoon regiment to Colonel John Hill, Abigail Masham's brother. Marlborough was outraged that the Queen had completely ignored his advice as Captain-General. On 14 January the Marlboroughs left London without taking leave of the Queen and went to Windsor Lodge.[114]

Godolphin and other moderate ministers were deeply disturbed by the domestic and international consequences of this quarrel. From Windsor Marlborough wrote a draft letter to the Queen declaring that he 'deserved better than to be made a sacrifice to the unreasonable passion of a bedchamber woman'.[115] Godolphin and others repeatedly urged him to acquiesce, but Marlborough was determined to vindicate himself. In order to prevent a future recurrence of the incident he wanted Parliament to vote him life appointment as Captain-General and demanded that the Queen dismiss all four members of the Masham family who were in her service. On 23 January he returned to London and began to seek political support among Parliamentary leaders for his plan. Lord Somers advised the Queen of Marlborough's intentions, and she immediately began to consult privately with party leaders, senior generals, and peers. Asking for their personal loyalty to the Crown, she pressed them to oppose Marlborough's plan. By this appeal the Queen and the Whigs won such broad and impressive support that Marlborough was forced to pretend that he had never intended to make an ultimatum. The quarrel was temporarily patched up, and Marlborough agreed to return to command the army. He departed for The Hague on 19 February and was not present in England for the outpouring of Tory sentiment that followed the Sacheverell trial and the impetus it gave to the overthrow of the Whig-dominated government.[116]

Once he had arrived at The Hague Marlborough concentrated on plans for the campaign of 1710. His initial thought was to open a siege at Douai and, when that was completed, to move on to Arras to open an avenue to the Channel coast. With this established, a joint operation with the navy could possibly follow with the objective of seizing Boulogne and Calais. As military commanders in the allied army made plans, diplomatic discussions with the French opened at Geertruidenberg on 8 March to try to resuscitate the peace proposals of 1709. At this point Marlborough was approaching his sixtieth birthday and was deeply discouraged by everything around him. News from London added to his gloom as the shift towards Tory sentiment forced more Whigs from office and the government advised foreign representatives that a change in ministers did not mean a change in England's war policy.

Sarah Jenyns Churchill, first Duchess of Marlborough (1660-1744).

Miniature by Christian Friedrich Zincke, 1711. The Royal Collection © 2011, Her Majesty Queen Elizabeth II.

On 23 April Marlborough and Prince Eugène opened siege operations at Douai with 60,000 troops that lasted sixty-three days and cost 8009 allied casualties and 2680 French casualties before the fortress fell on 25 June. Shortly afterwards Marlborough heard news that his son-in-law Sunderland had been dismissed as Secretary of State. Looking to the next phase of the campaign, he and Eugène observed that the French had destroyed all the forage near Arras, making the planned siege there difficult. In its place they first made a foray to the west of Vimy Ridge near Arras. Finding that the French did not pursue them, the allied army marched on to Béthune, opening the trenches there on 17 July for a forty-three-day siege that ended on 29 August.[117]

Just as the siege ended Marlborough learned that, nine days before, the Queen had dismissed Godolphin as lord treasurer and had opened an investigation into his ministry's financial conduct. As the Tory wave swept through the cabinet, Eugène, Heinsius, Godolphin, and the Elector of Hanover all urged Marlborough not to resign his command of the army in the middle of the campaign. Reluctantly he agreed, beginning siege operations first at St Venant from 5 to 29 September and then at Aire from 6 September to 8 November. With the campaign at an end, the allied army had gained control of a large area through its siege operations, but there was no sign that the war was any closer to an end.[118]

Portrait of the Duke of Marlborough.

Painting by Godfrey Kneller, 1712. Althorp House, Northampton, UK. The Collection at Althorp.

Marlborough left The Hague on 3 January 1711 and reached England at Southwold after a difficult three-day passage across the North Sea. The Queen received him formally and impersonally. Assuring Marlborough that she wished him to remain in command of the army for the next campaign, she strongly advised him not to seek any vote of appreciation from the new Tory Parliament. Marlborough intended to retain command, but he hesitated to agree formally in the hope that he could use his delay to maintain Sarah in her offices in the Queen's household. The Queen had made it known to her advisers that she wished to dismiss Sarah. Two of the advisers, lords Shrewsbury and Hamilton, advised Marlborough that the Queen might listen to a personal appeal from him to maintain Sarah in office. On Marlborough's advice Sarah wrote the Queen an apologetic letter, which on 17 January Marlborough personally gave to the Queen, but Anne refused to consider it.

Concerned about the effect of Sarah's dismissal on his position abroad, Marlborough asked the Queen for two weeks' grace to persuade Sarah to resign. Exasperated by the continuation of the matter, the Queen demanded that Sarah surrender her keys of office. On the evening of 18 January Marlborough delivered Sarah's keys to the Queen, formally ending her thirty year long mercurial relationship with Anne's household that had so influenced his own career.

Later that spring Sarah vacated the lodgings the Marlboroughs held in St James's Palace, and for a few weeks lived in an apartment at Montague House before moving into one of the outbuildings at Marlborough House, which was still being built. Meanwhile, Marlborough returned to The Hague on 4 March and found, as he had feared, that Sarah's dismissal and the change in ministry had seriously weakened his prestige and authority.

Marlborough returned to army field headquarters on 26 April to prepare for the campaign. Two days later preparations halted when news arrived that Emperor Joseph I had suddenly died of smallpox in Vienna on 17 April. Joseph's death meant that his younger brother, King Charles III of Spain, became Emperor Karl VI. Charles's candidacy for the Spanish throne was a fundamental basis for the Grand Alliance and had originally been the key to re-establishing a balance of power in Europe in 1701. This change in international politics created an imbalance in favour of Austria that was further complicated by the civil war within Spain and the domestic political and international treaty commitments to the idea of 'no peace without Spain.'

The campaign of 1711 was necessarily delayed while arrangements were made to elect the new Emperor. Finally, in June allied leaders held a conference to discuss the forthcoming campaign but, pointedly, Marlborough was not invited. When the campaign began, a series of complex French moves and allied countermoves took place around Arleux, a fortified position and part of what was known as the non plus ultra lines, a 160 mile series of river defences, forts, earthworks, and inundations that extended from the Channel to the foothills of the Ardennes. With only 15 miles that were not marsh, river, or flood plain, they presented an apparently impregnable defence.

Historians have debated whether Marlborough's movements at Arleux were a planned and successful ruse or merely an accident that had the effect of covering his intention to besiege Bouchain.[119] After a series of manoeuvres Marlborough with an army of 80,000 allied troops suddenly struck the lines at Arleux on 5–6 August and passed through them with few, if any, casualties. Then, instead of seeking a battle with Villars's 90,000 troops, he directed a march to nearby Bouchain and took it

A mid-nineteenth century view of Cranbourne Lodge at Windsor, which Sarah Churchill occupied in her official capacity as Ranger of Windsor Great Park, 1702-1744, and where the first Duke of Marlborough died on 16 June 1722.

Print by James Mason, around 1754. The British Library, London, UK. © The British Library Board. 014587822.

under siege on 9 August. After thirty-four days and 4080 allied and 2500 French casualties, Bouchain surrendered on 12 September. Its capture gave the Allies a launching point for the next campaign and a base from which to attack Cambrai, which blocked the allied advance into France. With this in mind, Marlborough urged the Allies, without success, to put the army in winter quarters at Bouchain.

Meanwhile, in London the ministry under Robert Harley was secretly negotiating a new basis to end the war in the light of the changed international power relationship.[120] Preparing for Marlborough's return to London, Sarah had completed Marlborough House. Marlborough left Holland on 24 November and found on his return that the Harley ministry's peace negotiations were public knowledge and that the ministry had completely abandoned the old formula of 'no peace without Spain', which he continued to support. For Marlborough, the continuation of the war was necessary in order to maintain the Protestant Succession in England.

On the heels of this political change Jonathan Swift published his Conduct of the Allies in late November, arguing that the whole war had been a Whig plot led by Marlborough and his foreign friends to enrich themselves at the expense of England's Treasury. More than 11,000 copies of Swift's work circulated, which devastated Marlborough's credibility and led to charges of corruption. In December the commissioners for the investigation of public accounts called the allied army's bread contractor, Sir Solomon de Medina, from Holland to testify that he and his predecessor, Antonio Alvarez Machado, had paid 2.5 per cent of the contract to Marlborough between 1702 and 1710 for a total of £64,410 3s. 6d. In response Marlborough asserted: 'This is no more than what has been allowed as a perquisite to the general, or commander-in-chief of the army in the Low Countries, even before the Revolution, for the service of the public in keeping secret correspondence, and getting intelligence of the enemy's motions and design.'[121]

According to Swift, Marlborough was no hero, but a friend of selfish, grasping foreigners who enriched themselves from war, the worst of whom were the Dutch, who had long been rivals to England's growth. Moreover, Marlborough had clearly profited by the war, amassing a fortune that Swift estimated at more than half a million pounds. Given the heated atmosphere of party politics during the Parliamentary recess and the charges of improper conduct that were brewing, the Queen dismissed Marlborough from all his offices on 30 December 1711.

■ Retirement and restoration, 1712–1722

In the following months Marlborough was publicly attacked from all sides in the press. When Parliament returned in January 1712 he presented a defence, but on 24 January the Commons voted by 265 to 155 that his conduct was 'unwarranted and illegal.'[122] Shortly afterwards the ministry permitted Marlborough's successor, the Duke of Ormond, the same percentage payment from army bread contracts, and the government did not pursue Marlborough's legal prosecution, although it maintained it as a threat. Treasury payments for the works at Blenheim stopped in June, and the Marlboroughs left London for Holywell House, where Godolphin joined them. There on 15 September 1712, Godolphin died from kidney failure.

With the death of his closest friend Marlborough decided to leave England, something he had been considering since October 1711. He applied to Harley, now Lord Oxford, for a pass to travel through Holland and Germany and to settle in Italy. His mention of Italy as his ultimate destination was deliberately misleading, for his main aim during his exile was to consolidate his position with the Elector of Hanover, in preparation for his succession to Anne.

Marlborough left England at the end of November 1712. On 13 December he set out for Antwerp, then travelled to Maastricht and on to Aix-la-Chapelle, where Sarah and William Cadogan, who became Marlborough's key representative in exile, joined him in February 1713. At the end of April they moved on, passing Koblenz en route for Frankfurt, where they established residence. Using Frankfurt as a base, Marlborough visited his principality of Mindelheim, for the first and only time, in the second week of June 1713. He was received with the honours due to a ruling prince and resided in the castle of Mindelburg, near Mindelheim, reporting that he 'stay'd but four days at Mindelheim, which place I liked much better then expected but not so, as to think of living there.'[123]

On 19 July 1713 Marlborough and Cadogan met Prince Eugène, who confirmed that both the Emperor and the prince of Savoy would act to prevent a Stuart restoration in Britain. On his return to Frankfurt Marlborough decided to return to Antwerp at the end of August so as to be closer at hand to England, in hope that an election would change the political landscape. The failure of this, with an increased Tory majority in Parliament and the probably unjustified speculation that Oxford would impeach Marlborough, led Mary of Modena to send a Stuart agent to contact Marlborough at Antwerp in August. For the next year Marlborough tried to develop further contacts with the Pretender's entourage as a precautionary Jacobite protection against impeachment. At the same time he continued to encourage Hanoverian opposition to the Oxford ministry.

In March 1714 the treaty of Rastatt was signed, ending the war between France and Austria. By its terms the Elector of Bavaria was restored to his lands; on 25 January 1715 the Elector's representatives took possession of Mindelheim. Marlborough

The Marlborough Column of Victory at Blenheim Palace, surmounted by a lead statue of Marlborough holding a winged victory. Erected in 1730, it stands forty metres high.

Stone column with statue attributed to either Robert Pit or Henry Cheere, 1730. Blenheim Palace, Oxfordshire, UK.
Photograph by Jarrald Publishing, reproduced with the kind permission of His Grace the Duke of Marlborough, Blenheim Palace Image Library.

petitioned the Emperor to replace his loss, but Charles VI took no immediate action. Meanwhile, although the hope of a Whig victory in the Parliamentary elections proved to be illusory, by April 1714 Sarah's homesickness and a series of illnesses among their children and grandchildren led the couple to decide to return to England in order to be near their family.[124]

With Bolingbroke and Oxford engaged in their rivalry for political supremacy in England, each began secretly corresponding with Marlborough, who offered to support whoever could safely secure the succession. In the months that followed the Marlboroughs uncovered Oxford's duplicity and arranged publication of the letters that exposed his double-dealing with Hanover. The Queen dismissed Oxford on 27 July, but Anne delayed forming a new government in hope that Marlborough could lead it on his arrival. The Marlboroughs embarked at Ostend for England on 28 July 1714 but, hampered by heavy winds and high seas, their journey across the channel took three days and four nights. While they were approaching Dover on 1 August the Queen died, and George I was proclaimed King the same day. Marlborough received a tumultuous welcome on arriving in London on 4 August, when many politicians and courtiers scrambled for his favour.

Six weeks later George I arrived at Greenwich, where the peers of the realm gathered at the riverside to greet him. On receiving Marlborough the King said warmly, 'My lord Duke, I hope your troubles are now over.'[125] The first warrant the new King signed restored Marlborough, on 4 September 1714, as Captain-General of the land forces. Then, on 26 September, he was restored as Colonel of the 1st Foot Guards, on 1 October as Master-General of the Ordnance, and subsequently as Governor of Chelsea Hospital and a Privy Councillor.

Despite this warm welcome, the Duke and Duchess were unable to re-establish the monopoly of favour they had enjoyed in the early part of Anne's rule. During the first year of the new reign, Marlborough House became the place for the Duchess to launch her granddaughter into society, while the Duke remained active in the King's inner circle of advisers and was closely involved in supervising military affairs in the inner cabinet as ministers dealt with the suppression of the Jacobite rising in 1715. Finally, late in March 1715, Emperor Charles VI reportedly gave Marlborough a new territory in place of Mindelheim, the principality of Nellenburg, with its main centre located at Stockach in Hegau, Swabia, between Lake Constance and Switzerland. Formal confirmation of this title as Fürst zu Nellenburg never materialized,[126] however, and Marlborough continued to request a replacement for Mindelheim until October 1717.

Despite Sarah's suffering her first serious illness in spring 1715, the couple frequented, in addition to Marlborough House, Holywell in St Albans and the lodge in Windsor Park – as well as visiting Blenheim regularly to oversee progress, which resumed in 1716. On 28 May 1716, shortly after the death of his 32-year-old daughter, Anne, countess of Sunderland, Marlborough suffered a paralytic stroke at Holywell. After a period of recovery at Bath, the Marlboroughs went to Blenheim, where in November, while staying in a house on the estate, the Duke suffered a second stroke, which left him speechless for a time. Although some relatively minor effects remained, Marlborough recovered. The King declined to accept his resignation and Marlborough continued to hold his offices and make occasional appearances in the House of Lords, although the effects of his illness were clear. In September 1717, the Jacobite Lewis Innes reported to the Earl of Mar that 'Lord Churchill is turned a mere child and driveller at Tonbridge, his lady, little concerned, games from morning to night.'[127] The Marlboroughs occupied Blenheim for the first time in 1719 and again in 1720–21.

The Duke of Marlborough died on 16 June 1722 at Cranbourne Lodge, Windsor. For nearly a month after her husband's death Sarah lay exhausted at Marlborough House, while arrangements were made for the Duke's lying in state. A full state funeral took place on 9 August 1722. At noon, eight horses drew a black-draped funeral car, with a suit of full armour on the coffin, through crowd-lined London streets from Marlborough House to Westminster Abbey. A procession followed that included the family mourners, seventy-two Chelsea pensioners, one for each of the Duke's years, horse and foot guards, and heralds. With an artillery salute in St James's Park and the service in the abbey, Marlborough was temporarily laid to rest in the vault at the east end of Henry VII's chapel on the same day. In his will he directed that his final resting place was to be the chapel at Blenheim, which was not yet complete. This provision was carried out twenty-two years later, on 3 November 1744.

On Marlborough's death the Barony of Churchill of Eyemouth in the Scots peerage, which had been granted for his service to James, Duke of York, became extinct, as did his unconfirmed title Fürst zu Nellenburg. By the terms of his 1705 grant from the Emperor, Marlborough's heirs retained the title Hochgeboren Reichsfürst, and by the act of Parliament of 21 December 1706 his English titles passed to his eldest daughter, Henrietta, countess of Godolphin. Her son William Godolphin, Marquess of Blandford, having died in 1731 without heirs, the titles passed at Henrietta's death, on 24 October 1733, to the surviving son of her sister Anne, Charles Spencer, who became third Duke of Marlborough. The family name remained Spencer until George, fifth Duke of Marlborough, changed it to Spencer-Churchill.

On the first Duke's death his property and investments were estimated to be worth about £1,000,000, half of which was invested in short-term loans to the Exchequer; this sum remained in a trust managed after his death by trustees, who included the Duchess, Marlborough's two former business associates, William Clayton and William Guidot, and his three sons-in-law: the Earl of Sunderland, the Duke of Bridgewater, and the Duke of Montagu.[128]

The dowager Duchess and her defence of Marlborough's memory, 1722–1744

During Marlborough's lifetime and immediately after his death a number of his friends and associates published accounts of his achievements. First among them was the Reverend Dr. Francis Hare, who was tutor to the Duke's son John, Marquess of Blandford, chaplain-general with Marlborough's army, and eventually bishop of Chichester. He was the author of pamphlets defending Marlborough's conduct in 1711 and 1712 and of *The life and glorious history of John, Duke and Earl of Marlborough... containing a relation of the most important battles* (3 vols., 1705). Also during the Duke's lifetime 'An old officer of the Army' published *A short narrative of the life of his grace, John, Duke of Marlborough, from the beginnings of the revolution to this present time, with some remarks on his conduct* (1711). Another anonymous work followed, probably by Arthur Maynwaring, and arguably completed after his death by Richard Steele: *The lives of two illustrious generals, John, Duke of Marlborough, and Francis Eugène, prince of Savoy* (1713). This work clearly reflects Marlborough's own vision of

Bust of Marlborough. This bust was commissioned by the Duchess of Marlborough for Blenheim Palace, depicting him realistically in contemporary garb and perruque. At the same time, Rysbrack did a contrasting type of bust that was more formal and stylized as a public figure, showing him as a Roman hero crowned with a laurel wreath. The Duchess presented the latter to the University of Oxford in 1730, where it is now in the Ashmolean Museum.

Marble bust by John Michael Rysbrack, 1730. Blenheim Palace, Oxfordshire, UK. Photograph by Jarrald Publishing, reproduced with the kind permission of His Grace the Duke of Marlborough, Blenheim Palace Image Library.

To
The Memory
of
QUEEN ANN
Under Whose Auspices
JOHN DUKE of MARLBOROUGH
Conquered
And to Whose Munificence
He And His Posterity
with Gratitude
Owe the Possession
of
BLENHEIM
A: D: MDCCXXXX: VI:

himself.[129] The final account by a person close to the Duke was that of Thomas Lediard, a secretary to Marlborough during his mission to Charles XII of Sweden in 1707, *The Life of John, Duke of Marlborough, with Original Letters and Papers* (3 vols., 1736; revised and enlarged, 1743). This was the first full biography, and was based on personal knowledge as well as original materials to which Lediard had access.

After the Duke's death Sarah began to concentrate on completing Blenheim as the major memorial to her husband, although it was not a place she herself enjoyed. In 1723 she had Hawksmoor design the triumphal arch at the Woodstock entrance to the grounds in order to commemorate her devotion to completing the unfinished fabric of the palace. About the same time Lord Burlington gave her the idea for the 134 foot column of victory. The first of its sort in Britain, it was built between 1728 and 1731 at the summit of the grand avenue leading from the north side of the palace, surmounted by a lead statue of Marlborough in Roman Dress, attributed alternatively to Robert Pit, an otherwise unknown artist, and to Sir Henry Cheere.[130] In 1728, after considering several authors, Sarah persuaded Lord Bolingbroke to write the inscription for the column, which incisively described the Duke's great achievements.[131] In 1733 the chapel in the palace was completed, containing the tomb designed by William Kent and executed by Michael Rysbrack. Sarah chose to have the black marble sarcophagus flanked by figures of History and Fame, crushing Envy. Below the portrait statues, each 7 feet tall and depicting the first Duke and Duchess with their two sons, John and Charles, there is a marble bas relief depicting Marshal Tallard surrendering to Marlborough in 1704. Following these commissions, Rysbrack made a portrait bust of Marlborough, and a statue of Queen Anne was installed in 1738.[132]

Having completed Blenheim, Sarah turned to defending herself and her husband in a book, written with the assistance of Nathaniel Hooke and entitled *An Account of the Conduct of the Dowager Duchess of Marlborough from her First Coming to Court to the Year 1710* (1742). In a personal justification, rather than an insider's history of Anne's reign, Sarah attempted to show that she saved the Queen £100,000 through her good management as mistress of the robes. The book's publication elicited a number of anonymous politically motivated responses that provided further details of the Duke's life and career and became sources of reference for early historians. The most important of these were James Ralph's *The Other Side of the Question* (1742), J. Robert's *A Review of the Late Treatise* (1742) and his *Continuation of the Review* (1743), and Henry Fielding's defence in his anonymously published *A Full Vindication of the Dowager Duchess of Marlborough* (1742).[133]

Sarah died on 18 October 1744, aged eighty-four, at Marlborough House. In accordance with the instructions in her will the Duke of Marlborough's remains were removed from Westminster Abbey on 30 October and sent to Woodstock. On the following day her casket followed. Two days later, on 3 November 1744, the two were buried together in the vault of the chapel at Blenheim Palace.

Statue of Queen Anne.

Marble sculpture by John Rysbrack, 1735. Blenheim Palace, Oxfordshire, UK. Photograph by Jarrald Publishing, reproduced with the kind permission of His Grace the Duke of Marlborough, Blenheim Palace Image Library.

The Battle of Malplaquet, 1709, sometimes also known as the Battle of Taniers. This name derives from Tanières or Tasnières, the name of a village southwest of Malplaquet where some of the action took place.

Engraving by Robert Wilkinson, 1710. Brown University Library, Providence, RI, USA. From the Anne S.K. Brown Military Collection.

CHAPTER 3

John Churchill, Professional Soldiering, and the British Army, c.1660-c.1760

Alan J. Guy

ROROUGH having
near La Baſſee
tier Gariſons too
ly fortified that
een the Work of a
another expedi-
THE BATTLE
OF
TANIERS
MDCCIX.
-tious march surprized the Strong Lines at Mons, in Order to Beſiege ye place
Marshall VILLARS to prevent this, having fortified his Army between two
Woods near TANIERS, his Grace attacked them, & after a very sharp dispute
(not without great Loſs) forced their Intrenchments. Whereupon he beſieged Mons
without making any Line of Circumvalation, and took it the Enemy's Army
giving him no further diſturbance that Campaign.

constant shortages of cash or credit. Military formations were fragile and hard to replace, making their leaders wary of committing them to a general action. Completing the picture was a chronic disjunction between emerging state control of the army and the entrepreneurial interest of its senior officers, an apparent lack of academic preparation for command, inchoate military staffs and the negative impact of archaic social hierarchies on the fostering of military talent. Only a military genius could free himself from such massive constraints, it was supposed and even then only for a time, after which the whole enterprise bogged down again with the coming of winter.[10]

But in reality the art of war in Marlborough's day was determinedly focused on overcoming these difficulties. By the beginning of the eighteenth century it was clear that warfare could be conducted with a defined strategic intent – 'bringing Monsieur to reason' was the concise form of words applied by Marlborough and others.[11] This was not a strategy of overthrow, inclining more to one of European collective security, but it was very ambitious both in reach and scale and involved a confederacy of allied powers. It was carried on through the flexible combination in space and time of powerful military and naval resources. No single front took priority – with the perverse exception of Spain, it might be argued. Strategy was not the product of a single mind (Marlborough's, as has sometimes been claimed),[12] but was worked out as a corporate exercise. From an English point of view, it was applied with notable consistency throughout the War. On the ground it was put into effect in ways which chime in with Claus Telp's recent analysis of eighteenth-century operational art as 'the art of war at the operational levels concerned with the conduct of campaigns with the means provided by strategy, in pursuit of the strategic objective in one theatre of war.'[13] As for the armies which made these outcomes possible, on inspection they appear much closer to an exalted classical model (the Roman army) than van Creveld would seem to allow, for by the time Marlborough arrived at high rank they too embodied 'a command system not based on any real technical superiority, that relied on standard formations, proper organization at the lowest level, a fixed repertoire of tactical movements, and the diffusion of authority throughout the army in order to greatly reduce the need for detailed control.'[14]

It is an interesting reflection on the writing of military history that for all the ink spilt in describing the Duke's personality and achievements we know more about the campaign of Xenophon and the Ten Thousand than we do about the celebrated march to the Danube in 1704.[15] This may be accounted for by the fact that much of eighteenth-century military custom and practice was conveyed by word of mouth or example, as opposed to a discernible induction programme or analysis, and as a consequence some essential components of the scene – the instrumental features of early-modern warfare – have receded from view. The existence of contemporary treatises dedicated to tactics and military engineering has at least made it possible for modern authorities to produce combat studies which convincingly demonstrate fighting techniques.[16] In particular, a series of drill-books issued by royal authority have allowed us to construct a definitive account of the eighteenth-century British army's regimental training and small-unit tactics.[17] Administrative arrangements in the part-privatized regimental economy of the day are harder to pick out, but even these can be extracted from a mixture of official documentation and private correspondence.[18] Much less understood are the multiple activities through which the armies of Marlborough and the generals of his time overcame the besetting frictions of war. Much of that achievement was founded on grinding physical effort – not at all exciting for the readers of military history books – and it is the voices from the lower ranks, few and far between as they are, which speak of it most clearly. For each year of his Compendious Journal, Sergeant James Millner of the 18th Foot entered data of significance to him as a soldier in a marching regiment, this being his concluding analysis of the Blenheim campaign: 'The *tedious* [my italics], but ever glorious, memorable and victorious Campaign of 1704, was in Length Thirty Weeks and One Day, commenced the 24th Day of April, and ended on the 20th of November; of which our Corps, with the Grand Army, and apart, to, in and back from Germany, march'd and sail'd Ninety-one Days, and therein Three Hundred Ninety-two Leagues, or One Thousand One Hundred and Seventy-six Miles English.' That is to say, in one campaigning season Marlborough's army marched over half the distance Xenophon and his comrades traversed in two years.[19] In his book Millner faithfully recorded the army's peristaltic pulsations across the landscape: the long marching, the man-handling of cannon, pontoons, bread wagons, warlike equipage and 'all other necessary Utensils of War'; the digging of trenches and the 'making and bringing of Fascines, Gabions, Pick-axes, Mauls, Hurdles and such like Necessaries, for the expeditious carrying-on of a Siege'; the heat of the sun, or the thunder, lightning and driving rain that knocked tents flat in seconds, sending thousands of gallons of water through what until then had seemed a well-chosen camp site. These were the authentic rhythms of early-modern military life, experienced from the ground up. Whatever the season the armies Marlborough led spent all their waking hours, and doubtless many night-time ones too, engaged with them.[20]

Taking the Habsburg army of c.1680-1740 as a research model, Erik Lund has made an imaginative attempt to recover this military world in rich detail, reinfusing, as he would put it, the arcane vocabulary of Sergeant Millner with meaning. Lund demonstrates that the armies were intimately connected to their parent societies – not isolated from them in a bubble of combat-related specialism. They possessed an in-built knowledge-base which enabled them to mobilize a wealth of practical skills from among their own ranks. The officers whose 'labour histories' he reconstructs are revealed as proven managers of a skilled and disciplined workforce. Their shared expertise, as much civilian as military in origin, comprehended what would now be called human resource management, estate management, animal husbandry, topography and soil analysis, forestry, practical botany and hydraulics.[21]

If they had not been able to apply these competencies in methodical, scientific and predictable ways, early-modern armies would scarcely have been able to advance a league or cross the first wet ditch they came to, let alone successfully conduct marches and countermarches of hundreds of miles, or span the great waterways of Flanders and the Balkans. Neither could they have completed an operational deployment, nor fought a battle with clear tactical purpose, nor kept up the industrial-scale resourcing of a siege. Mastering these contingencies was, we suggest, the quotidian task of the working general. Among dozens of examples we can find of Marlborough in a conventional soldierly mode, the veteran Sergeant Wilson recorded an incident of a different kind which points up the Duke's understanding of how the outwardly mundane aspects of military activity required close personal management by the commander, and his sure touch when dealing with them. In Germany or Flanders local peasants could be made to labour in their thousands for the army for free, but

not so the soldiers, who were clearly in a position to strike a bargain. In 1706 they were levelling the French lines near Courtrai when,

> 'His Grace, coming along the line to see the workmen, said in a very jocose manner: Work my lads. Work and levell the lines to perfection, for I'll give you my promise, whilst the Wars hold and I am yo'r Gen'll, they shall not be raised again." Upon w'ch the workmen reply'd, "My Lord. May it please Y'or Grace. That is very well but that is not all. For if Your Grace thinks fitt we shall be glad of our money for levelling the same." To which His Grace replied, "What? Is nothing to be done without money?" "No", replied the men, "and that Your Grace well knows." "Very well", replied he, "Lett yo'r work be levell'd t'night and you shall be paid tomorrow." The w'ch the men performed and His Grace was as good as his word.'[22]

■ Learning the Business

In public, Marlborough always tried to appear confident, focused and aggressive in action. Right from the start he declared that he was not prepared to stay with an army that did nothing but devour forage.[23] He would not give the enemy time to breathe if he could help it,[24] or lose a moment in pressing his advantage.[25] 'I knew he never slipp'd an opportunity of fighting whenever he could come at them', reminisced Captain Robert Parker of the 18th Foot.[26] Marlborough could shed copious tears at the sight of the dead and wounded, but this is no reason to think that his four great battles – five if we count the attack on the Schellenberg – went any way other than he had intended, and with that came a basic willingness to accept the butcher's bill.[27] For all his purported coolness and self-command, he exposed his person recklessly in action in a manner which seemed more appropriate to the warfare of the preceding age[28] – behaviour not at all resembling what we see in the decorative Blenheim tapestries that are so often called upon to illustrate his heroic deeds.[29] That he understood the high stakes he was playing for is clearly seen when he paused to consider the misfortunes of others. Hearing news of the disaster at Almanza ('as bad as may be') he urged his old comrade Lieutenant-General Thomas Erle to keep his spirits up in the hope that things would turn out all right in the end and, 'comfort yourself the best you can under a misfortune to which the best men of our profession are always liable.'[30] Similarly, when rumours reached camp of the overthrow of Charles XII of Sweden by 'the Mosecovit' at Poltava in June 1709 Marlborough confided in Godolphin, 'what a malincolly reflection is it that after a constant success for ten years, he should in two hours mismanagement and ill success, ruin himself and country.'[31] But even in the case of a fighting general like Marlborough, the hours actually spent in battle, or even the approach to it, were few in number, and on most campaigning days the problems confronting him were literally more down to earth.

How did John Churchill learn the soldier's trade? That was a question raised very early on by someone who could actually have asked him, yet who does not seem to have done so, and which has never been answered fully.[32] Other than a handsome presence and a willingness to put himself in harm's way by actions that would bring him to the notice of the great (a pre-requisite for advancement in a patronage-based society) we know almost nothing about Marlborough's early military life. It seems he was taught the manual of arms by a Cromwellian veteran and he seems to have

Field Marshal Sir John Ligonier, later first Earl of Ligonier (1680-1770). Born in France to a Huguenot family, Ligonier became a naturalized Englishman and volunteered for service in the British Army. He served in many battles and sieges during the War of the Spanish Succession, including the Schellenberg, Blenheim, Ramillies, Oudenaarde, and Malplaquet. In 1712, he became governor of Fort St. Philip, Minorca. From 1759 to 1763, he was one of Marlborough's successors as Master General of Ordnance.

Painting by Sir Joshua Reynolds, 1755-1757. National Army Museum, London, UK. Reproduced by permission of the Council of the National Army Museum, London.

owned a schoolboy copy of Vegetius' De Re Militari, though Sir Winston Churchill wondered whether John's Latin had really been up to mastering it.[33] If the regiment is to be regarded as the school of the soldier and active service the best place to study, then a subaltern's tour of duty in the frontier garrison of Tangier should have supplied him with the required instruction in looking after hard-bitten veterans, keeping up their discipline, maintaining garrison routines and conducting the petite guerre characteristic of that dangerous outpost – some 'real soldiering' in the parlance of a later age. We are also told that he competently administered a battalion as its lieutenant-colonel commanding, an important milestone in any professional officer's road to high rank.[34] However, as Sir Winston wisely pointed out, even Marlborough's celebrated command apprenticeship under the great Turenne could be reduced to a series of opportunities to observe a military genius in action and learn 'in a responsible but subordinate position, every detail of active service.' This is an example of what Don Higginbotham, speaking of the military education of George Washington, has labelled the 'tutorial method', characteristic of the emergence of great professions such as medicine and the law, and which in the military sphere consisted of discussions with battle-tested veterans, some independent book-learning, observation and practice under arms.[35] Getting beyond that simple formula is problematic, though Lund has shown from his detailed work on the Habsburg armies that a standard seventeenth-century military curriculum could include organizing the marches of the army and its train of cannon and baggage; reconnaissance and mapping; amassing munitions, purchasing provisions and seeing to the supply of forage; siting camping grounds and headquarters; intelligence and security duties and, in preparation for higher grades of responsibility, a mixture of diplomatic and political work. This knowledge had to be communicated without the benefit of a formally constituted staff corps, in place of which senior commanders selected and trained their military family on a highly personal basis. As the well studied career of John Ligonier (a British commander-in-chief in the next generation) confirms, a combination of staff, administrative and quasi-political assignments – in Ligonier's case major-of-brigade, assistant adjutant-general and adjutant-general in Spain (1711-12) and the lieutenant-governorship of Minorca (1713) – constituted successive rites of passage to high command.

Marlborough's principal staff officer, who acted alongside him in battle, was his Quartermaster-General, William Cadogan. Cadogan was recognizably a chief-of-staff, provided that term is understood as meaning a personal relationship to the commander and not a bureaucratized command system. He was often entrusted with independent command, intelligence duties, diplomatic missions to the allied powers and sensitive political transactions at home. Marlborough and Cadogan were themselves supported by generals of horse and foot, each with their own cadre of majors-of-brigade, junior staff officers, aides-de-camp and messengers. In the heat of the action at Ramillies, General Richard Ingoldsby recalled being visited by ten of these people (a pardonable exaggeration, perhaps) followed by the great Cadogan himself.[36] As the Prince de Ligne later pointed out, by now armies had reached such a level of sophistication that career opportunities must be provided for organizers and managers just as much as for warriors of the traditional kind.[37] Marlborough, and Cadogan also it would be fair to say, were striking combinations of both.[38]

John Churchill as he appeared in 1668 when he was an ensign in the regiment of French Guards.

Engraving after Adam Frans van der Meulen. Published by Godefroy, Paris around 1788. Brown University Library, Providence, RI, USA. From the Anne S. K. Brown Military Collection.

An Undiscovered Country? Marlborough's British Army

The characteristics of the English troops (strictly speaking the designation 'British' would be anachronistic for the period) were well appreciated in Marlborough's day. The quality of manpower, horseflesh and equipment were considered excellent by European standards: 'I never saw better horses, better clothes, finer belts and accoutrements', famously declared Prince Eugene, 'but money, which you don't want in England will buy clothes and horses, but it can't buy that lively air I see in every one of those troopers' faces.'[39] Marlborough's own opinion was 'that English horses, as well as English men, are better than what can be had anywhere else.'[40] He praised his soldiers when he got the chance, 'the troupes I carry with mee are very good and will doe whatever I will have them.'[41] Clearly he was proud of them.[42] He was solicitous of their needs, and alongside that he understood their distinctive shortcomings and the logistical arrangements these entailed, for the English (and we might infer the Dutch, for there were always more of them in the field) were unable to march without a ready supply of bread, while the Germans, who were used to starving, couldn't march without the English.[43] Interested in hard cash as he was, Marlborough was anxious that his English troops were paid on time and in full.[44] He had an insider's appreciation of their 'moral economy,' as we have seen. He did his best to see that old soldiers got a snug billet at home when they were no longer fit to serve.[45] A proud and sensitive man in his own right, he was aware of the Englishman's notoriously high opinion of himself, degenerating at times into insolence and a contempt for all foreigners, but which, under good officers, was capable of being expressed in formidable fighting power. As Daniel Defoe put it, hailing victory at the Schellenberg:

'An Englishman has something in his Blood,
Makes him love Fighting better than his food
He wil be sullen, lay him down and die
If he cannot Come at his Enemy
But, let him loose, you fill his Soul with Joy,
He's ravish'd with the Thoughts of Victory'[46]

Most likely the Duke would have concurred with those sentiments.

By now we are speaking of an army acclimated to war in the campaigns of William III, at ease with the practicalities of life in the field and made up of reliable officers and seasoned personnel – contemporary opinion being that it took one year to fashion a recruit and five to make a veteran of him. With the exception of hotspots like Tangier, or the disciplined ranks of the Anglo-Dutch Brigade, the regular army of John Churchill's youth had been a very far cry from that ideal. Not that the British Isles had failed in the past to bring forth legions of fighting men, for they had long been a good recruiting ground for European armies of varying professionalism, effectiveness and confessional allegiance. Officers from England, Scotland, Wales and Ireland had over two centuries become part of an international fraternity of arms – though of the rank-and-file despatched overseas, few who went returned again other than as cripples or beggars, which alone must cast doubt on any attempt to claim that there was deep-rooted continuity in the British military experience.[47]

Yet, with the arguable exception of the New Model Army, England's domestic armed forces in the seventeenth century were laggardly in developing styles of command, leadership and organization suitable for a new age of European conflict.[48] The quasi-gendarmerie of Charles II and James II hardly seems up to the scheme of empire-wide military domination sometimes attributed to it.[49] Yet for all its scruffiness and ill discipline, this was not the 'toy army' of repute – like many armies established for the purpose of repressing its own people, it had no organized rival in the land and was greatly feared as a result.[50] To the relief of many it folded in upon itself in 1688 when an influential group of career officers of the type earlier favoured by King James opted to desert him. Their motives varied from zeal for the Protestant cause and a wish to uphold the liberties of England through to raw selfishness, for having bought their commissions they feared a remodelling of the English military establishment in the Roman Catholic interest along the lines of that currently being played out in Ireland by the Earl of Tyrconnel, King James' lieutenant-general there. Whatever the case, James' field army of some 30,000 dwindled to a remnant of 4,000 which, unhelpfully for the peace of the realm, he disbanded on the spot. Of his officers, only around one-third remained loyal; another third left the army by retirement or compulsion, and the remainder joined William of Orange. For his part William had neither time nor inclination to remake an English army from scratch, so the latter group, John Churchill prominent among them, carried on in post – useful officers perhaps, but touched by dishonour.[51] The new monarch had an understandably low opinion of their commitment and professionalism, and the condition of the English regiments sent to Ireland and the Low Countries proved him correct. Their numbers were inadequate. Pay and equipment were lacking. The men proved to be very bad at looking after themselves on operations, which was scarcely to be wondered at for, as onlookers noted, many of them were little more than boys. Even at this distance, the condition reports made by one of King William's reviewing generals at Dundalk camp in October 1689 make for depressing reading: 'hardly any good officers, and an entire absence of good order...'; 'too much bad company, and debauchery and drinking...'; a colonel 'too easy on the officers, who are the most negligent that can be imagined...'; 'the officers know nothing and entirely neglect the service, the soldiers are worse...'.[52] This sorry state of affairs would take time to sort out as well as lengthy and positive exposure to Dutch methods, the hard knocks of continental warfare, and an infusion of trusted officers from the Anglo-Dutch Brigade, of which there were never enough.

There exists a revealing snapshot of 'M. de Marlbrouck' in July - September 1689, trying to bring a sense of order to the units assigned to his command as a lieutenant-general in Flanders under the not unsympathetic gaze of William's veteran general Prince Waldeck. All things considered he is doing his best, thinks Waldeck, though Marlborough was never to be so exact a disciplinarian as William of Orange.[53] It was fortunate therefore that in one key area of expertise – infantry drill and tactics – a framework of instruction was in place equal to that of any army in Europe and the English infantry were arguably the best armed. The regulations William found in operation, together with successor publications in 1690 and 1702 which remained in force during Queen Anne's reign formed part of a series issued from the middle years of Charles II. Varying over time in the emphasis given to changing combinations of weapons – pike, matchlock, flintlock, bayonet and grenade – they had nonetheless succeeded in establishing a core of common practice that made it possible to assimilate the most important new weapons-system of the day – the flintlock musket and socket bayonet – and then to facilitate the devastating platoon fire techniques favoured by Marlborough. Platoon fire, learned from the Dutch, seems to have been the one major departure from arrangements that had long existed. Everything else – the army's evolutions, manoeuvres and marches – remained the same. '[We] come closest to the mark', says John Houlding, who has looked deeply into the matter, 'when we conceive of Marlborough's battalions as essentially those passed on and trained up in the campaigns of William, differing only in that they were newly and uniformly armed and able to lay down a most formidable and destructive fire; in so far as speed of movement, variety of manoeuvre or suppleness are concerned, they were only marginally better than those of William, or no better at all.'[54]

William III was not an army 'reformer' in the widely understood sense of that term. He had trusted subordinates from his own army to do that gritty sort of work for him in respect of his own as well as his English troops. But he understood and vigorously enforced the cardinal virtue of discipline – officer discipline especially – and in his use of trusted reviewing generals, sent on circuit to inspect and report on the state of individual regiments, he anticipated a key feature of royal control over the land forces exercised by the Hanoverian kings after 1714.[55] In the meantime it was characteristic of Marlborough that his main concern seems to have been to keep the existing system going and maximise results, not to tinker with it.[56] He tried to ensure that officers attended their duty, and that wherever possible those who did so should be preferred over those who did not, which was common sense but not always easy to bring about.[57] He worked hard to keep hold of the reins of military patronage, and having had free run in that department for a long time he was most resentful when his near-monopoly was challenged.[58] Conversely, he recognized that he had to defer on occasion to the claims of political or social pre-eminence, and he did so with all his customary politeness.[59] One time this resulted in the absurdity that Lord Wharton, who had never been a soldier at all, was appointed colonel of a newly-raised regiment of dragoons on the Irish Establishment where, as Lord Lieutenant, he had independent authority and many people to satisfy in the line of military appointments, evidently starting with himself.[60]

Overall, Marlborough's approach to the prevailing culture of proprietary command seems to have been that it was helpful in saving public money. The proliferation of single-battalion regiments in the British army (contrasted with the multi-battalion European model), each with its full quota of field officers and a proprietary colonel who set the tone of the whole unit, for good or ill, multiplied the patronage opportunities available to government. Some resultant loss of central control, and the negative impact of jobbery and nepotism were more than off-set by the private funding which was on offer to raise, equip and maintain the formations created under this system.[61] As for the time-honoured traffic in officers' commissions which formed a major part of proprietary culture, though Marlborough did his best to prevent them being sold to minors,[62] his approach was also conservative, and much more relaxed than William III's had been, since he felt that it kept the business within the regimental family to the part-exclusion of Parliamentary interest,[63] and it was also a way of providing for the upkeep of sick and maimed officers or their widows and orphans in an age when pensions were small and hard to come by.[64] Yet wherever possible Marlborough insisted on the claims of valour and seniority, whether in army or regimental command. In this connection he tried, not altogether successfully, to limit the pernicious custom of satisfying officers' clamour for promotion by awarding them brevets, which, without carrying with them any increase in salary, afforded their holders a higher rank in the army than in their own regiments, and which led to disputes over the exercise of command and the subverting of established claims for preferment.[65]

As a career professional, who had himself spent time in the exercise of regimental command, Marlborough must also have become aware over time of what to us still remains the dark side of army life, where soldier and civilian interacted socially and economically in ways which seem very alien from the perspective of professional armed forces in today's developed world. There is no indication that he either paid much attention to these issues or wished to 'reform' them, other than a characteristic wish to reward the deserving and help soldiers and their dependants in the limited financial way he could: arrangements of this kind were best left to the regimental family, as before.[66] But as John Childs has inferred, unfortunately without being able to find a great deal of contemporary evidence in support,[67] the many skills and trades we know to have been contained in the army and which were of such practical use in wartime continued to be exercised in the parallel civilian world by off-duty soldiers who 'moonlighted' to boost their meagre pay, provide economic support to the parent unit and, in worst cases, contribute to the mercenary benefit of their officers and non-commissioned officers.

Glenn Steppler's study of the army's domestic arrangements in the 1760s-90s, based on the records of the Foot Guards serving in London, confirms the existence of this self-sustaining military economy and the many compromises with what we would nowadays perceive as military efficiency which kept it functioning. Given our current lack of knowledge it is perhaps not unreasonable to read his findings backwards to a time when public funding for the armed forces was even more precarious than in the reign of King George III and personal ethics more flexible.[68] The sinister moral environment of Marlborough's time is balefully illuminated by the military career of Colonel Francis Charteris of the 3rd Foot Guards. Charteris sold what was nicknamed 'the protection of the Guards' to London's insolvent debtors by enlisting them as soldiers. This gave them legal protection from their creditors, yet they rarely went on duty for more than a few minutes at a time, and were instead permitted to continue in their civilian avocations. For the privilege, Charteris extracted payment from them many times over, operating through the sergeants and corporals who managed the dirty end of the business and who, as a matter of course, expected to be plied with drink and gratuities by the recruits on parade days. He pocketed the men's government enlistment bounty; he extracted bribes to protect them from being drafted overseas on active service; he colluded with bailiffs and duns so that his clients had to keep applying to him for paid assistance or, if an individual proved too troublesome, he sold him to the man's creditors in the style of Jonathan Wild the thief-taker. Even if a soldier was able to compound for his debts, Charteris gouged him one last time by making him buy his way out of the regiment.[69] Such goings-on among Her Majesty's own Household Troops in the capital city of the realm make an extraordinary contrast to, say, the heroism of Rowe's brigade at the Blenheim palisades. The rogue colonel's protection racket eventually became so gross that it attracted the attention of Parliament, and it would surely be wrong to infer that it represented a typical slice of army life under Anna Augusta. Nevertheless it is still to be wondered whether, in some milder form, off-colour arrangements of this kind might have permeated much of the domestic existence of the military. And if more research into the daily routine of the tragically anonymous common soldiers is needed, that is even more the case for the army's women, who performed the essential gendered tasks of washing, scavenging, cooking, nursing and mending for their menfolk, yet about whom we know next to nothing.[70]

Legacies

What was Marlborough's legacy to the British army, its public image, and its next generation of commanders? The close of the war of the Spanish Succession was marked by large-scale disbandments and a breaking-up of the military community. At the war's height (1709) up to 70,000 men, a mixture of volunteers and conscripts, were entered on the English Establishment, plus another 12,000 in Ireland. By contrast, in 1715 the English Establishment was fixed at under 16,000 officers and men, with an additional 12,000 in Ireland. The latter remained the official quota until 1769, but for most of the post-Succession War period the English Establishment hovered only between some 18,000 to 26,000 men, by no means all of them actual 'boots on the ground.' Regimental precedence in the order of battle was fixed on the principle that newly-raised formations would be the first to be disbanded; the survivors were nicknamed the 'Old Corps', a designation satirically applied to the Whig magnificoes and their men of business who ran the country through to the 1760s. In this settled environment, political stability and proprietary right – expressed in military terms by the money officers paid for their commissions, the private funds they invested in their regiments and the secure financial return they felt they were entitled to make from them – remained intimately connected. They were also jealously guarded, even against the growing authority of the Crown, though so much political heat had been released from the system by the close of hostilities, by the defeat of the 'Fifteen' and the passing of the Septennial Act (1716) that factionalism in the military, whilst by no means absent, and occasionally noisy and petulant, was much less threatening than it had been in Marlborough's time.[71] In terms of basic organizational effectiveness, the unit drills and tactical arrangements perfected during the war were maintained for years, though they could only be practised on a diminished scale, seeing that the soldiers were scattered in country quarters, or lodged here and there in crowded towns, in troop or company strength – often less. Houlding has tellingly characterized this relentless degradation of Marlborough's veteran formations as 'the friction of peace.'

As for the human factor, the fate of thousands of demobilised rank-and-file remains obscure. There had been immense wastage even during the war; military administrators, logisticians and curious Members of Parliament had all struggled to come to terms with it.[72] In the field armies, plaintive calls for daily returns of men under arms speak to the difficulties of manpower audit in the early-modern age. Arrangements for the pensioning-off of old or worn-out soldiers, their transfer to garrison invalid companies or to The Royal Hospital Chelsea, though benevolent from a seventeenth-century perspective, hardly seem to qualify for the term 'resettlement' bestowed on them by the leading scholar of Queen Anne's army.[73] The eccentric Colonel Henry Hawley thought that it was so important to retain old soldiers' skills in peacetime that it was worth hauling them round the country in wagons, but this was hardly a system that could have been kept going for long.[74] As for the officers; the provision of regular half pay (from 1699) meant that in theory there was now in existence a pool of military talent to call upon in any future emergency, but proprietary colonels were keener to fill regimental vacancies with their friends, clients and dependants than to accommodate a superannuated hero. Even for those fortunate enough to be able to soldier on into the long peace of the 1720s and 1730s in the safe haven of the Old Corps it was plain that when the crisis finally arrived numbers of them had been rendered useless by the passage of time. In Henry Hawley's own dragoon regiment (he was a major-general by now) there were in 1741 two lieutenants unfit to serve, the one 'laid up with palsie', and the other unable to mount his horse – a notable handicap for a cavalryman. In a sample of other regiments ordered on active service were to be found a lieutenant-colonel aged near 80, 'through infirmitys unable to attend the service,' subalterns of 30 or 40 years' standing laid low by amnesia, deafness and the gravel, and captains from their fifties to their eighties crippled by gout and rheumatism. Lieutenant-Colonel Humphrey Bland, who had served in Flanders and Spain, was so worried about this loss of accumulated knowledge and the (pardonable) ignorance of a new generation of officers that he published a compendium of sound practice and advice, *A Treatise of Military Discipline* (1727) which became the eighteenth century's standard military textbook. In that sense at least, the technical professionalism of Marlborough's army attained some measure of permanence.[75]

But with the departure of the human relics of the age of Marlborough came the ending of the directly communicated legacy of his great actions. Historical studies of the Duke's campaigns were a mainstay of the professional soldier's bookshelf, vying with Julius Caesar and Vauban, certainly until the mid-1750s, by which time disappointments in the War of the Austrian Succession had somewhat dented the self-confidence of the British military, but continuing strongly thereafter. They might have encouraged an aggressive turn of mind. Nevertheless, what would be done from now on would for the most part have to be done by younger men, who would benefit from the accelerated promotion offered by active service in an expanding wartime army and exposure to novel military techniques and literature.[76] That said, something of the old ethos endured in stereotypical forms which even today can be identified in stock military 'types.' Take for example Joseph Addison's 'Captain Sentry', '... a Gentleman of great Courage, good Understanding [and] invincible Modesty' who had left the service in 1711. Having acquitted himself gallantly in several engagements he had felt obliged to give up a way of life 'in which no Man can rise suitably to his Merit, who is not something of a Courtier as well as a Soldier.' One of the founding members of the fictional Spectator Club, the Captain was 'never overbearing, though accustomed to command Men in the utmost Degree below him; nor ever too obsequious, from a Habit of obeying Men highly above him.'[77] The implied opposites – and these from a Whig author it should be noted, not a Tory – are instructive. By the 1730s, these contrasts were becoming more sharply etched, though the stereotype himself remained constant, even down to his physical appearance. Thus, the Universal Spectator's 'Captain Platoon' was a

> '... *gentleman distinguished by the name of Old Flandercan ... he served under the Duke of Marlborough in all his Campaigns, and ever since the Peace he had been on Half Pay. The Captain had good Sense, but a rough Carriage and Manner of Expression; he is so unfashionably blunt as to speak as he thinks, but speaks as scarce any but himself does. He pays no deference to Titles, but will tell a Peer he wants Sense, and a Lady she wants Modesty, yet his Satire, though Severe, is not*

obliged to put up with such excesses for fear of being left undefended against something much worse.[83] In the Duke's day, senior officers in particular seem to have revelled in a rattling, immoral lifestyle. Everyone knows the story of the swashbuckling Colonel Daniel Parke who carried Marlborough's famous pencilled note from the field of Blenheim home to London, and how he gallantly declined the customary reward of 500 guineas in favour of a miniature of Queen Anne, if only to receive both the miniature and 1,000 guineas as his recompense. Unfortunately, on close examination it would appear that Parke may have had no right to claim the army rank of colonel at all, and his life, which ended violently, was scandalous by any standard. In 1712 one of Marlborough's most trusted lieutenants, General George Maccartney, was under suspicion of rape and political murder,[84] as well as having taken part with General Thomas Merydith and Brigadier Philip Honywood in drinking damnation to the ministry and taking pot-shots at an effigy of Robert Harley (December 1710), an exploit which got them all cashiered. From 1706 onward even the faithful William Cadogan had been part of a gambling ring which placed bets on the outcome of military operations in which he had a major role as quartermaster-general. He had also connived with others to skim money sent abroad to pay the forces.[85]

The fact that these brave officers repeatedly put themselves in great danger on behalf of Queen and country might have entitled them to some charitable consideration, but instead it came to be believed by many that such gentlemen lay too heavy on the land.[86] Not for the last time, moral opprobrium lent weight to what was otherwise a tendentious and politically motivated campaign of abuse. The main target was Marlborough himself, and it is doubtful whether his reputation has ever fully recovered from its merciless deconstruction by Jonathan Swift in two issues of The Examiner in 1710-1711.[87] In Marlborough's case the enduring stereotype was arguably not so much that of the too-powerful soldier, rather that of the over-mighty subject with a fancy foreign title and a palace funded by the taxpayer.[88] But however underhand or misdirected these criticisms were in the Duke's case, there was to be a significant long-term impact on the command superstructure of the army.

In point of fact, Marlborough at no time enjoyed untrammelled military power. That, in theory, belonged to the Sovereign, whether that person was Queen Anne, who could not have been expected to lead her troops in battle, or King George I who certainly could, seeing that he had held high military rank. Furthermore, until his death in October 1708, Queen Anne's consort, Prince George of Denmark, had been invested with the resounding title of Lord High Admiral and Generalissimo of the Land Forces. Marlborough's title of Captain-General was honorific, signifying a particular distinction in public life. By virtue of military genius he had raised it to a level equivalent to a secretaryship of state. The appointment became very important to him. In a distracted state of mind he several times requested the Queen to confer it on him for life – a colossal political blunder – but without success.[89] Reinstated as Captain-General by George I, Marlborough ably directed operations from London during the 'Fifteen', but soon after fell victim to the first of a series of crippling strokes, so that for all practical purposes the role fell into disuse, effective command passing to Cadogan. But hounded as he was by charges of financial impropriety, personal unpopularity in the officer corps and political opposition, Cadogan was forever prevented from becoming anything greater in name than eldest lieutenant-general on the staff. In 1723, during one of the King's periodic absences in Hanover, ambition got the better of him and he took to styling himself commander-in-chief, itself an inferior distinction to Captain-General. This, it was thought, was going too far. The designation was not confirmed,[90] and during many years of their respective reigns, King George I and his son King George II – who as a young man had served under the Duke and who at Dettingen in 1743 led his own army in battle (to the chagrin of his field commander, Marlborough's old comrade the Earl of Stair) – did without a Captain-General or commander-in-chief at all. In peacetime, the army could safely be managed by a junior minister, a few civilian clerks and a committee of general officers. When, as a wartime exigency, a new Captain-General, William Augustus Duke of Cumberland, was finally appointed, the experience proved not to be a happy one – quite the contrary in fact, for what had at one time seemed dangerous in the hands of a commoner was believed to be even more so when in the hands of a King's younger son at a time when the heir to the throne was a minor. Cumberland had been designated Captain-General in 1745, aged twenty-three and ranking only as a junior major-general at the time. He relinquished the appointment, along with all his other military commands, at the time of his disgrace in 1757. What was for him a personal disaster proved to be a lucky stroke from a political point of view. His de facto successor in command of the army, Field Marshal Lord Ligonier, though a distinguished veteran of twenty-three battles and nineteen sieges, a capable field commander and gifted administrator, was not the larger-than-life character that Marlborough or Cumberland had been. He was altogether more rococo than baroque; sociable, worldly-wise, popular in the service, urbane to the point of cunning and a keen spotter of military talent. (Among his protégés were Forbes, Howe, Amherst and Wolfe, which could in turn signalize them as heirs of Marlborough's genius, transmitted through their clever old chief, though this is hardly a conjecture that should be insisted on). While Ligonier gathered to himself quite as many of the strings of military organization as Marlborough had done, his role remained strictly to advise, not to command. In cabinet he was a team player, collegiate, definitely subordinate to that most civilian of warlords, William Pitt the Elder. He was effectively government's chief-of-staff (though not at the time labelled as such), hardly a role that Marlborough could have been said to have performed. But this was how the interface between government and the military needed to be managed in future – if possible, that is. As for the glamorous appellation of Captain-General, the notion of conferring it on Ligonier (to guard against the sudden return of Cumberland to his father's favour, one wonders?) was quickly dropped. Both it, and its holders, had had a troubled history; now was a good opportunity to let it fade away. It has not been revived.[91]

Plan of the Siege of Kinsale in October 1690.

Drawing by unknown artist. The British Library, London, UK.
© The British Library Board. Blenheim Papers, 61343B.

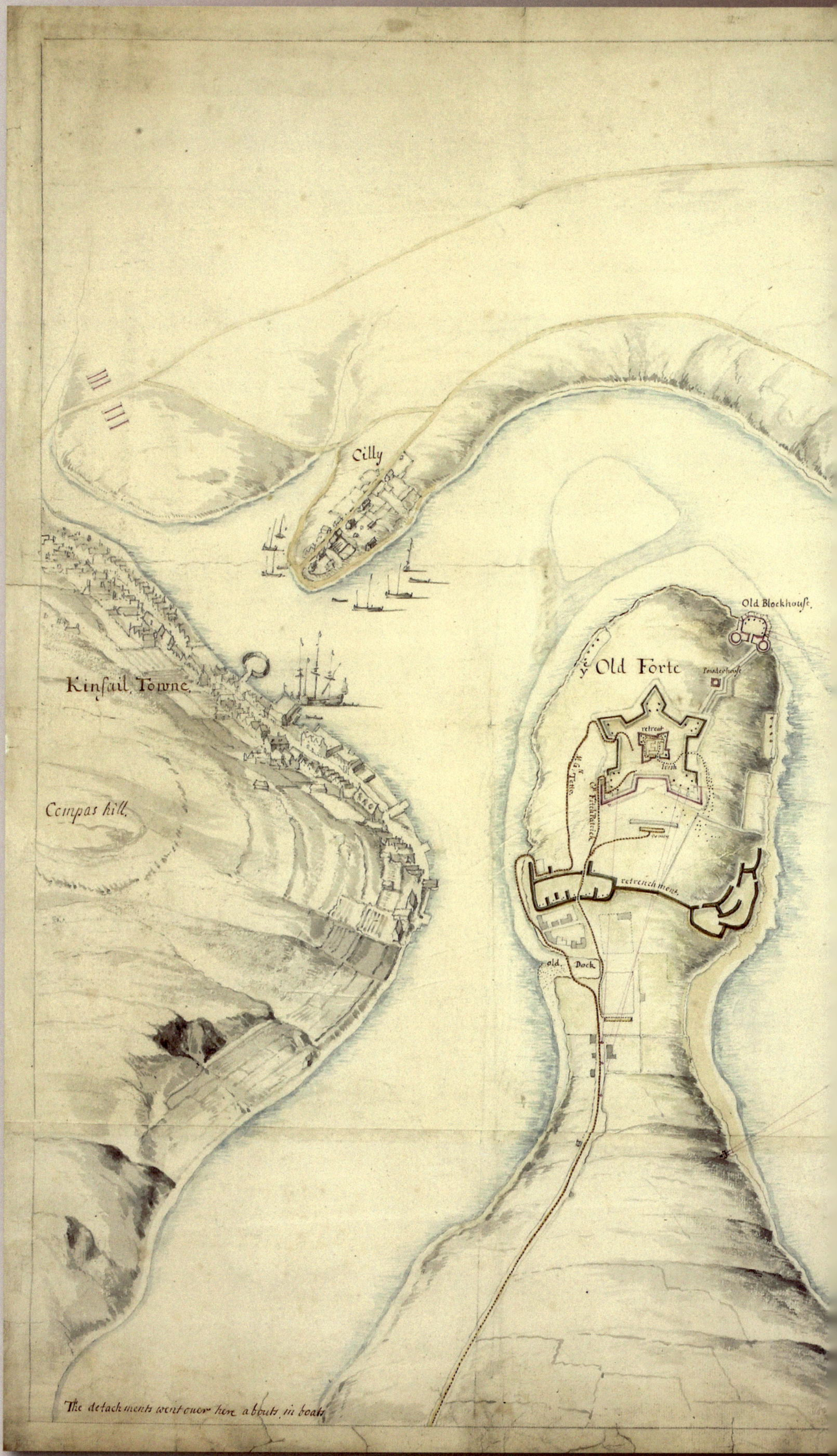

CHAPTER 4

Marlborough and Siege Warfare

Jamel Ostwald

For Marlborough's biographers, siege warfare is a problem. On the one hand, the Duke of Marlborough is admired by many modern military men because of his constant quest to seek out and fight the decisive field battle.[1] His victories at Blenheim and Ramillies in particular attest to his ability to master the battlefield. His constant focus on seeking battle, as illustrated in his correspondence and as highlighted by his various biographers, further reinforces the point. On the other hand, it is also well known that Allied forces under his overall command conducted five times as many sieges as field battles. Herein lies the problem, for the laudatory literature on Marlborough revolves around his recognition of how a decisive battle could theoretically end the war in a single day, yet in the minds of his admirers nothing could be further from this quest for decision than the plodding pace of trench attacks on fortified positions. How then to explain why Marlborough undertook so many sieges, and how should one treat these sieges? His biographers resolve such questions with a threefold approach – first, they castigate those who willingly pursued a positional strategy of siege warfare, second, they blame difficult allies for forcing the Duke to besiege these many fortresses, and finally, they argue nonetheless that Marlborough was a master not only of field warfare, but of siege craft as well. All three of these claims are based on a shaky understanding of the nature of siege warfare in the 'age of Marlborough.'

Siege Warfare in the Marlborough Literature

Despite the recognition that 'few periods of military history can have been more dominated by siege warfare,' Marlborough's biographers show little interest in the subject.[2] The Marlborough literature, focused as it is on the Duke's perpetual quest for battle, gives sparse coverage of his many sieges. Dozens of pages are spent analyzing his battle tactics and manoeuvres, while the fortresses and sieges that stymied his advances on a dozen occasions are relegated to brief, stereotyped treatment. In the campaign narratives, one day of battle is given more treatment than a year's worth of sieges. Even the pursuit after a victorious field combat receives barely a nod in comparison to the minutiae of tactical manoeuvres on the battlefield. The 1706 campaign is typical in this regard, where the tactical details of Ramillies receive more coverage than the entire rest of the campaign, post-battle pursuit and the subsequent four sieges combined.[3] The standard biography by David Chandler even gives the inconsequential battle of Oudenaarde nearly as much discussion as the epic four-month siege of Lille. Of the dozens of publications dedicated to the Duke over the past century, only two focus squarely on siege craft, and it was not until 2007 that one expressed sustained interest in siege warfare on its own terms.[4]

The explanation for the literature's lack of attention to siege craft is obvious when one considers how siege warfare itself is portrayed: battle's offensive potential is constantly contrasted with the attritional stalemate of siege warfare.[5] Winston Churchill gave one of the more straightforward examples of this disdain when he apologetically informed his readers of the need to 'accustom [you] at this point to the routine and ritual of siege operations in this period; for unhappily these pages must speak of many.'[6] David Chandler is foremost among recent historians to refer to positional warfare as an 'abortive' form of warfare.[7] Sieges are further marginalized by narratives and generalizations that consistently revolve around the success or failure of Marlborough's quest for battle.[8] Scholars contend that a strategy relying on sieges was doomed to indecision and those who willingly engaged in it are declared ignorant of the true art of war.

Little surprise, then, that an explanation is needed to justify Marlborough's frequent reliance on siege craft. His supporters justify his record by arguing that these sieges were forced on the unwilling commander by his Dutch allies. Chandler wrote that Marlborough 'was often forced by his allies or overall circumstances into undertaking numerous sieges in the Flanders theatre.'[9] This line of argument goes back to Marlborough's days, when his earliest supporters insisted that the Duke was an unwilling besieger, in part because of Tory accusations that he was profiting from these sieges by drawing out the length of the war. And although the Duke's political opponents lambasted his involvement with siege craft, his biographers have noted a silver lining. While they bemoan the many sieges he was 'forced' to undertake, they make a virtue out of this vice, praising the breadth of Marlborough's genius for his success in both battles and sieges and repeating the contemporary saying that Marlborough won every battle he fought and captured every town he besieged. In this view, Marlborough was 'no less a master of siege and maneuver' than battle.[10]

■ Siege Warfare in the Age of Vauban

While the Marlborough literature has only begun to change over the past few years, a generation of scholars has vastly improved our understanding of siege warfare in early modern operations. Most attention has been devoted to the development of trace italienne style fortifications which replaced towering, thin medieval stone walls with stouter, earth-backed ramparts set low within an often labyrinthine network of ditches and outworks. As *Figure 1* illustrates, the basic principles of this style of military architecture were to hide the curtain walls from direct fire, to place multiple vertical obstacles between the attacker and defender, and to maximize the amount of defensive firepower by creating intersecting fields of cannon and musket fire from curtain walls, outworks, and covered ways.

With the possibility of hundreds of garrison troops pouring down fire from the multi-level parapets, besieging troops would be required to spend weeks and perhaps months capturing the covered way, breaching outworks and curtain walls, crossing one ditch after another, wresting outworks away from tenacious defenders, and finally storming a breach in the curtain wall. All these efforts forced besiegers to expend limited resources and precious campaign time. The widespread diffusion of such defensive innovations initiated a subsequent effort to improve the success of sieges and shorten the delays such defences imposed. By the late seventeenth century the French military engineer Vauban represented the epitome of this art. According to the voluminous literature, Vauban introduced trench parallels, trench cavaliers and ricochet fire to return the advantage to the offensive.[11] With these tactics and others, Vauban systematized earlier techniques by improving every detail of the siege, coordinating the precise fire of a few dozen cannon with the shovelling of dirt. *Figure 2* provides an illustration of these principles as they were applied at Ath in 1697, an attack judged by many to be Vauban's finest.

The result, in theory at least, was an ultra-efficient attack that promised a rapid capture with only minimal loss of life. How well Marlborough mastered the Vaubanian siege will be the focus of the rest of this chapter.

Figure 1 Gunpowder Fortifications

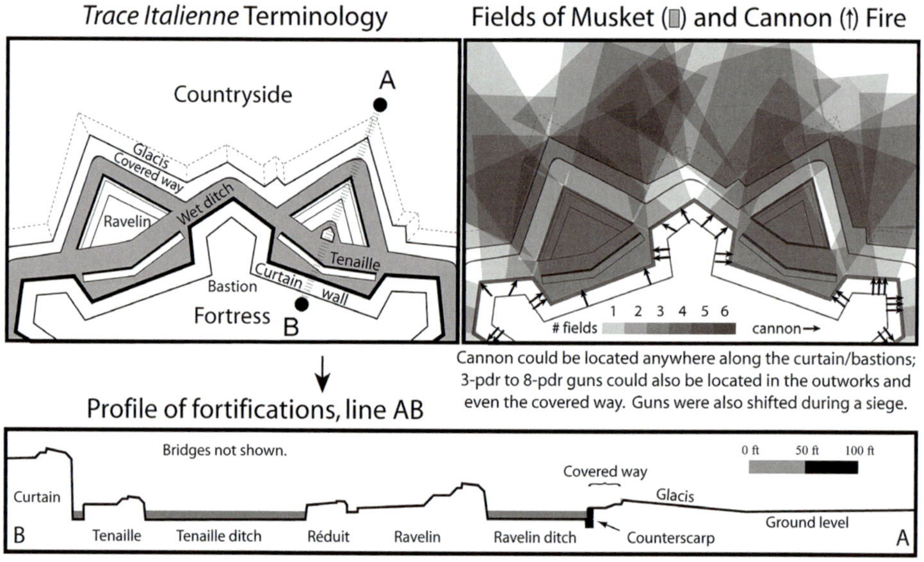

Figure 2 Vauban's Siege of Ath, 1697

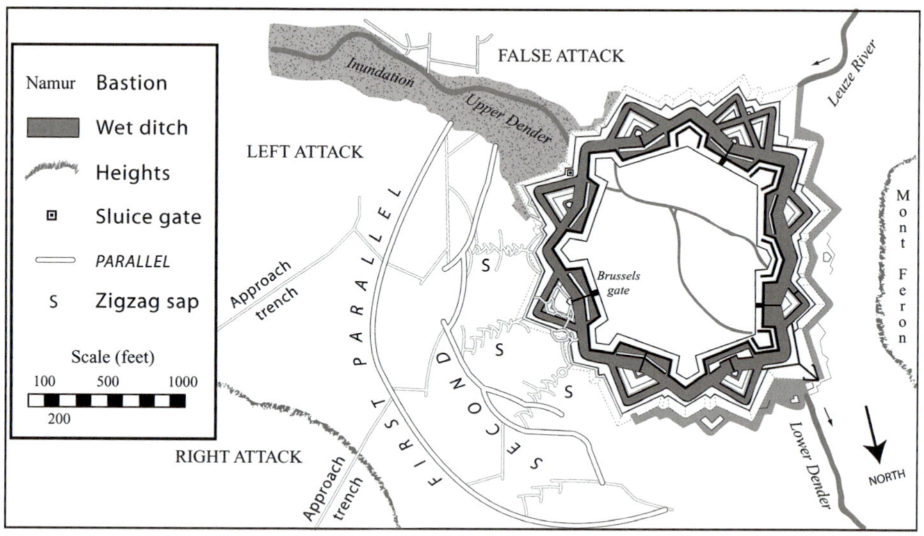

Marlborough's Early Experience of Siegecraft

Any understanding of Marlborough's role in the sieges of the War of the Spanish Succession requires an appreciation of how little John Churchill's early career prepared him for the kind of state-of-the-art siege craft he would face at the peak of his career. Although Churchill's formative years parallel the decades when Vauban brought the siege attack to a new level of efficiency, he, like most English soldiers, had little direct experience of the details of a siege à la Vauban. An overview of his career to 1700, a look at the English experience with siege warfare, and an appreciation of how Vauban's efficient siege technique evolved over time all serve to illustrate that Marlborough would find his early experiences of little use when dealing with the sophisticated sieges late in the War of the Spanish Succession.

Although it was impossible to completely avoid siege warfare in the 17th century, John Churchill had little direct exposure to state-of-the-art siege techniques over the course of his early career. His baptism of fire began in the English outpost of Tangier in 1668, where his garrison skirmished with Berber raiders for several years until he returned to England in 1671; formal siege craft was out of the question in this frontier on the margins of 'civilized' Europe. A few years later Captain Churchill would find himself serving under the Duke of Monmouth in French service, a post which placed him at the Sun King's siege of Maastricht in 1673.[12] There are extremely few sources regarding Churchill's activities in this period, but we do know that at the siege of Maastricht in particular he received public commendations for bravery from his commander and even from Louis XIV himself. More important here than his bravery is the question of what lessons he learned of siege craft. The siege of Maastricht may be best known as the scene of the death of the real-life musketeer d'Artagnan, but for military historians the 1673 siege is notable for the introduction of Vauban's system of trench parallels. Thus Churchill was one among many to witness a small slice of siege history, and this siege would even be the subject of a mock re-enactment at Windsor Castle a year later.[13] We should not, however, overestimate the impact of this experience. The Vaubanian siege as it is known today was a sophisticated system that developed over the course of several decades, with different elements tested out at various sieges, Maastricht 1673 being only the first stage of many. Trench parallels were hardly the totality of Vaubanian siege craft. His second tactic, the use of trench cavaliers, would be first implemented at Luxembourg eleven years later, his ricochet fire would first be utilized at Ath in 1697, and it was only in his 1704 manual dedicated to the Duke of Burgundy that he presented a full accounting of his systematized system of attack. Most of these events took place well after the future Duke's formative period and Vauban's system was in fact only codified while Marlborough was leading allied armies in the War of the Spanish Succession. Nor did the use of these three tactics necessarily indicate an acceptance of Vauban's emphasis on efficiency. Even more important to Vauban's system was his decades-long inculcation of the need for preparation, application and evaluation into the minds of his engineers. Vauban's siege was a mindset and a process, not a simple formula that could be blindly applied by just anyone.[14] As an English officer cutting his teeth in the 1670s, Churchill's French service was too early and too fleeting for him to experience fully Vauban's systematization of the siege attack.

Just as significant is the French environment that Churchill was exposed to during the Dutch War. Fighting under the famous marshal Turenne, he experienced several campaigns conducted by an offensive-minded commander seeking to manoeuvre and fight the enemy in the open field, most notably in the winter campaign of 1674 which led to the battle of Türckheim.[15] The great French marshal gained a reputation for his offensive-minded operations, prompting Marlborough's biographers to remark that Turenne's vigorous attitude must have surely rubbed off on the young Churchill.[16] While this is likely to be true, what goes unnoted is that the Turenne model was, critically, quite the opposite of the Vaubanian mindset as far as the proper conduct of a siege was concerned. Turenne and many other French generals had a long history of disdaining engineers, as Vauban complained again and again, and it is likely that Marlborough's frequently expressed dislike of sieges and engineers had been stoked by Turenne's own dismissal of their expertise.[17] In the 1650s Churchill's royal patron James Stuart, Duke of York noted how Turenne and other French officers took personal control of the attack:

> *'wee had not so much as one single Ingeneer, nor did I ever observe them to be made use of at any other place, but only as overseers of the work... And not only from my own observations, but by what I have learn'd from others who haue had more experience and seen more seruice then myself, I find and am settled in my opinion, That no Generall ought wholly to confide in any Ingeneer for the carrying on of a Trench.'* [18]

This dismissive attitude towards engineers would continue throughout the seventeenth century and well into the eighteenth. In this environment it is hardly surprising that Vauban constantly strove to improve siege tactics in order to overcome such resistance.[19] Vauban would have some success in this regard, with the siege of Maastricht seeing the beginning of his ascendancy which lasted till the turn of the century. However, what was just as predictive of future siege craft was the difficulty chief engineers had reigning in the more vigorous impulses of the general officers, particularly their desire to sacrifice additional lives in general storms of the covered way rather than await the results of the more certain technique of sapping. At Maastricht, in fact, Louis forced Vauban to storm the covered way before he felt prepared to do so, prompting the engineer to complain of such conduct years later: 'This siege was extremely bloody due to the faults of several [important] people which must not be named.'[20] Many contemporaries praised the brave demeanour of troops storming the covered way, but Vauban himself had quite a contrary opinion of its necessity. In short, the siege of Maastricht taught contradictory lessons, depending on one's outlook: either how engineering techniques could preclude the need for brute force techniques, or, from the generals' perspective, how a vigorous storming of the covered way could accelerate the capture of fortifications. As Marlborough's later conduct would prove, he learned the latter of these two lessons.

Back in England, Churchill would continue to rise through the ranks under his new sovereign William of Orange, gaining his first direct command over a siege fifteen years after the end of his Flanders campaigns. Williamite forces would spend several years subjugating Jacobite supporters in Ireland, and in 1690 this offered the newly-minted Earl of Marlborough his first opportunity for independent command. While his monarch's forces were bleeding heavily at Limerick and while much of England was in a panic due to the likelihood of a French invasion thanks to the naval defeat at Beachy Head, Marlborough devised a risky plan to take 5,000 troops from England to descend on the south-eastern coast of Ireland, in order to prevent any future French reinforcements to the theatre. The two targets were the ports of Cork and Kinsale, and William's approval set the project into motion. The first objective was a weakly defended place, whose garrison commander had refused an order to burn it and retreat in order to cover the withdrawal of Louis's forces back to France.[21] Cork's defenders relied upon a few insignificant forts beyond the limits of the town city defences, but the main defence was the river surrounding the town on all sides. The garrison's task was made even more difficult by the high ground which allowed an attacker to view the interior of the town, while the garrison of 4,500 was considered too small to guard its perimeter. Marlborough's forces, reinforced to a strength of 12,700 men, with the Duke of Württemberg as alternate commander, disembarked their ships' cannon nearby and within three days had breached the town's medieval walls. Facing a storm on two fronts, the Irish commander quickly capitulated with his garrison at the end of September.

Next Marlborough and Württemberg moved their forces southward to Kinsale.[22] Although its port was not as useful as Cork's, Kinsale could boast slightly better defences, though the town itself was protected only by its medieval stone wall with several towers and bastions. Like Cork, it too was commanded by neighbouring heights. It immediately surrendered as the Williamite forces approached. The location's real strength lay with two forts that guarded the harbour, the Old (James) Fort and the newer Charles Fort. Both of these were pentagonal trace italienne-style works, though their small size limited the firepower the garrison would be able to muster against any besiegers.[23] The Old Fort, garrisoned by some 400 men, was successfully stormed by an Anglo-Danish contingent on 3 October. The stronger New Fort had a 1500 man garrison. Its recalcitrance forced Marlborough and Württemberg to open trenches and wait for their thirty cannon and thirteen mortars to be transported overland to the site. After ten days of open trenches and three of bombardment from eight breaching guns and two mortars, Charles Fort surrendered with the honours of war.

Marlborough acquitted himself well in these two endeavours. Ireland, however, was a poor training ground to learn Continental-style siege craft. Few of its fortifications were up to continental standards: most consisted of small forts and towns with medieval stone walls, only occasionally flanked by angled bastions, while neither Cork nor Kinsale's fortifications boasted even a single ravelin or other outwork.[24] Outworks shielded curtain walls from besieger cannon fire, provided defenders in the covered way with an additional layer of supporting fire from behind and from the flanks (possibly including a few small cannon), and created one more obstacle to overcome before reaching the main wall. Attacking small forts, particularly those without revetted covered ways and outworks, with only a handful of cannon was simply not comparable to the scale of siege craft being conducted on the Continent.[25] Those few Gaelic strongholds that were up to continental standards, namely Limerick (in 1691 at least) and Athlone, were attacked while Marlborough was out of theatre. Nor was Ireland very conducive to Continental-scale siege operations, since the rivers were of little use for heavy transport, while the roads and horses were abysmal by more civilized standards. Tactically, operationally and logistically, these sieges demanded far less skill than the sieges Marlborough had witnessed in the 1670s, and less still than those conducted by the Allies in the 1690s.

There were other opportunities for the Earl to gain more significant siege experience, but he would miss them all. In 1691 William's Dutchman Godard van Reede-van Ginkel would achieve what his master was unable to, capturing the fortified towns of Athlone and Limerick. These were among the most competently conducted attacks in William's Irish war, but Marlborough missed them both, as he was instead marching and encamping to little effect in the Low Countries. William would shift Britain's full effort to the Low Countries theatre in 1692, and following the advice of the 'Dutch Vauban' Menno van Coehoorn, would conduct only four sieges, most remarkably the 1695 siege of Namur which required the amassing of 300 guns and more than 50,000 men. Notably absent from all of these was Marlborough, for his discontent with William's Dutch ways earned him temporary exile from Court in 1692. He would spend the rest of the Nine Years' War as a mere spectator while his Continental peers gained further experience in siege craft across the Channel. Direct personal experience is not a guarantee for competency, much less mastery, but it was a real benefit given the ever-increasing specialization of siege craft that occurred in the late seventeenth century.[26] Winston Churchill bristled at William's suggestion that rable to what Marlborough faced in Ireland: poorly-fortified towns, often still with their medieval walls, which were totally reliant upon a few small forts and the occasional château for their protection. Only the strongholds of Maastricht and Antwerp could boast strong works, and neither was besieged.[38] No surprise then that when faced with more than 100 cannon and 20,000 men or more, the defences of these bicoques (as Vauban disparagingly termed them) were quickly obliterated and their garrisons forced to surrender. Seeking a silver lining in their rapid capture, a French newspaper noted that these works were:

> *'besieged by an army four times as large as would have been necessary for a similar siege... the enemy also used an extraordinarily large siege train for such a small place. This shows how formidable the French troops are, and how much the enemy feared engaging them in close combat; when cannon and bombs capture places, there is little glory for the besiegers, and the method is so costly that a State cannot take many fortresses in this fashion without ruining itself in very little time.'* [39]

Starting in 1706, however, the Allies no longer faced dilapidated Spanish fortifications but Vauban's *pré carré* blocking their advance to Paris. A comparison of the attacks on Kinsale and Tournai illustrate the degree of the challenge now facing Marlborough and the Allies. Of these fortresses, only Tournai and Bouchain saw Marlborough exerting a sustained, direct influence, and even here much of his attention was focused beyond the siege lines. For most of these later, more challenging, sieges, Marlborough relied on others to conduct their works.

Of equal importance to the question of who had overall command at each siege was that of who conducted the actual attacks – those who supervised the trenches day after day. Marlborough was not the only busy commander, which is why every siege commander relied on a chief engineer, and further devolved authority to lower-ranking general officers who served as commanders at each attack.[40] In turn each commander of the approach would be served by his own engineer (called a 'director of the approaches'), as well as by lower-ranking generals who supervised each day's labours.

Unlike a field battle where the commander could keep the entire unfolding battle under his direct observation and rush in when necessary, there was a whole constellation of subordinates that minded the innumerable details of a siege. Historiography's obsessive focus on Marlborough has seen to it that their names and particularly their deeds have gone unnoted. Most important were the chief engineers, and as we have already seen, the English had very few to offer. Coehoorn, the Frisian infantry officer William elevated during the Nine Years' War to master-general of Dutch artillery and director-general of the engineers, would continue to serve after the Stadholder-King's death, and would conduct all of the Allies' Low Countries sieges until his own death in early 1704. His attacks were dramatic not only for his reliance on massive firepower, but also for the fireworks his prickly personality sparked off. The Frisian firebrand quibbled with the Duke (and with other Dutchmen) at almost every one of these sieges.[41] After a brief interlude under the Liégeois infantry brigadier Jean Gérard Baron de Trognée, two other Huguenot technicians, Guillaume le Vasseur Des Rocques and Lucas Du Mée, would direct the remaining sieges in Flanders.[42] These Dutch directors would be assisted by Dutch and German subordinates, and at least 275 engineers of all ranks saw service in Dutch pay at some point of the War of the Spanish Succession, with the number available in any single year of

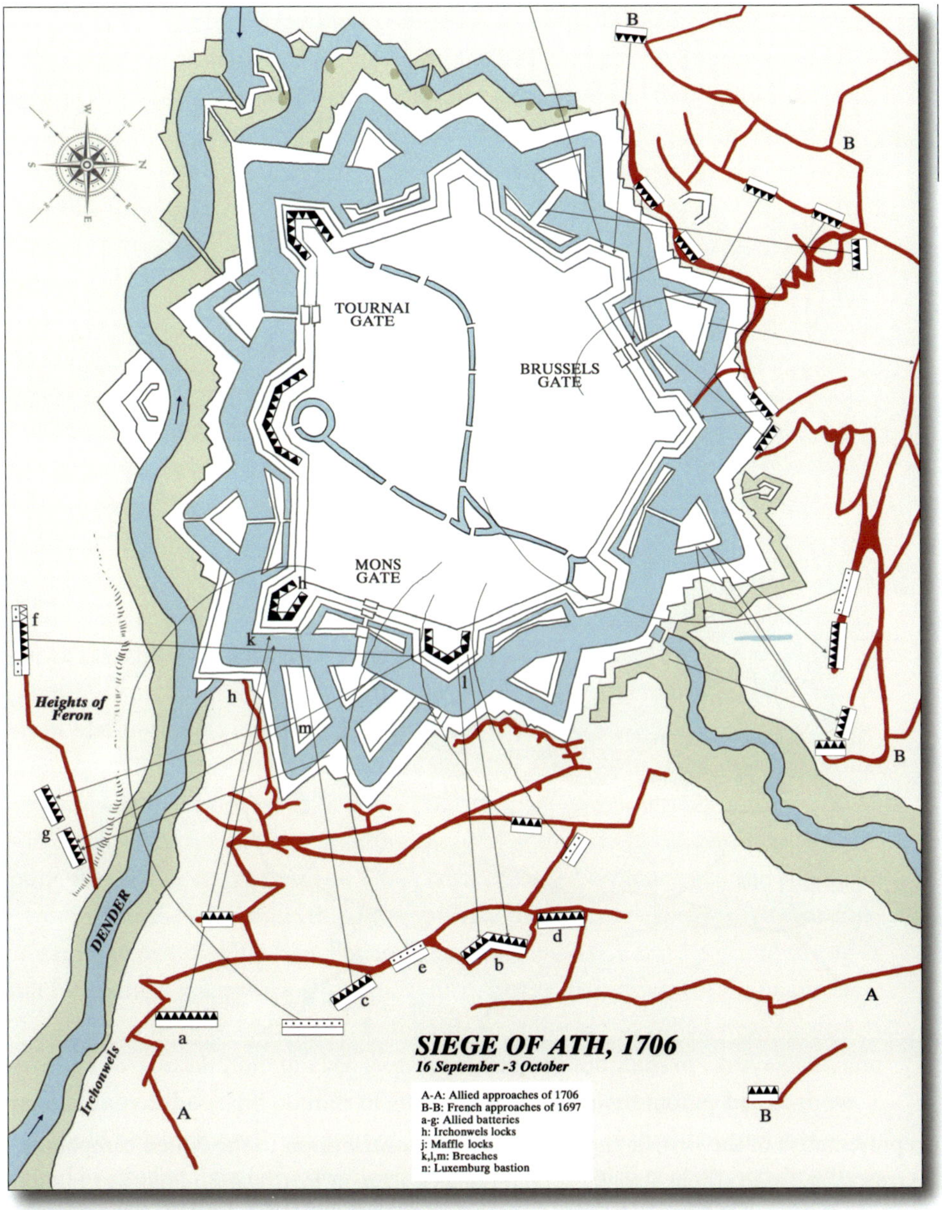

The Siege of Ath.

Map by Rocío Espín.
Based on Wijn, Staatsche Leger, vol. 2, Atlas, map #5.

the Spanish Succession conflict ranging between forty and eighty.[43] Marlborough's own correspondence highlights England's inability to provide enough engineers for its own domestic needs, much less contribute significant numbers to the coalition cause.[44] Contemporary accounts of the Flanders theatre, particularly those that discuss the details of siege craft, make practically no mention of the four English engineers most frequently identified as running the sieges: Holcroft Blood, John Armstrong, Richard King, and Michael Richards.[45] John Armstrong in particular is singled out by Chandler and others for his contributions during the war, and particularly in the 1711 attack on Bouchain, a task which earned him three depictions in the Blenheim tapestries. According to Chandler, Marlborough gave Armstrong the 'major share of the responsibility for continuing the siege operations.'[46] Delving deeper we soon discover that this was limited to completing the lines of circumvallation around the town in order to cut off French communication with those within, an admittedly challenging task.[47] In fact fieldwork of this sort appears to be relatively

The
SIEGE of TOURNAY
July ye 8th 1709.
A. Benoist Inv.
Published according to Act of Parliament.
C. Du Bosc fe.

When we add in the outlays made by the Dutch to repair the many barrier fortifications they had just obliterated (and those they captured more easily), as well as the fact that the Dutch also had to pay contributions to preclude French raiding parties, it is hardly surprising that the Dutch faced an immense burden. Adding up all the extraordinary costs of these many sieges, the role of British arms in the sieges diminishes to only part of a much larger coalition whole. Declaring Marlborough a master of siege craft ignores the reality that his Dutch subordinates were the real practitioners.

The 1709 bombardment of Tournai.

Engraving by Claude Du Bosc, from The Military History of Prince Eugene and of John Duke of Marlborough *by John Campbell, 1736-1737.*
The British Library, London, UK.

■ Marlborough's Real Role

If the Dutch provided the majority of the siege commanders and troops, supplied practically all of the siege technicians, and covered the many extraordinary expenses, what of Marlborough? An examination of one of the only major sieges under his direct command, the attack on Tournai's town and citadel in 1709, provides a concrete example of not only Marlborough's limited role in its capture, but of the less-than-masterly conduct of its approaches. The Duke's own preferred target, the West-Flanders fortress of Ieper, was vetoed by his allies, and Tournai was duly invested on 27 June. The town was one of the strongest in the Low Countries with layers of outworks, including several large horn works, as well as a pentagonal citadel defended by a complex system of subterranean countermines. Its garrison of 7,000 men, however, was thousands fewer than these imposing defences required, courtesy of a feint performed by the Allied army in the run-up to the investment which led the French commander Villars to withdraw reinforcements from the town. Marlborough commanded the sixty-battalion siege army, although only seven of these regiments were British, while Prince Eugene commanded the observation force. Ground was broken at three attacks on 27 June, none of which were commanded by English generals, and as usual the Dutch (and Spanish) provided the vast majority of the technicians.[56] Unlike most other sieges Marlborough apparently oversaw the trenches in person: all of his correspondence during the attack on the town is dated from the 'camp before Tournai,' but for the citadel's siege he moved his camp twelve miles away to the town of Orchies for forage and to keep a closer eye on Villars' manoeuvres. The reliance on the Dutch engineers continued. Des Rocques broke his leg before the trenches were opened, yet his plan of attack was followed despite this perfect opportunity for Marlborough to discard it and conduct his own.[57] Marlborough did not, however, insist on the engineering recommendation to have the three attacks coordinate their efforts, as one observer complained that each attack knew almost nothing about what the other two were doing.[58]

Structural weaknesses inherent to the period's siege craft also hindered Marlborough's command. His early estimates of the duration of the siege were no better than the engineers: early expectations of a quick capture were premature, though the town itself would fall after only three weeks of siege.[59] Engineering disputes festered. As soon as the injured Des Rocques returned to service, his subordinate Du Mée vociferously sniped at the pace of his superior's attacks, a dispute that only the siege commander could have resolved, and which was only conclusively resolved when Du Mée was fatally wounded attacking the citadel.[60] The engineers continued to suffer significant casualties, as they did at every siege, but more telling is the fact that at this siege the engineers complained of physical violence directed against them by the infantry

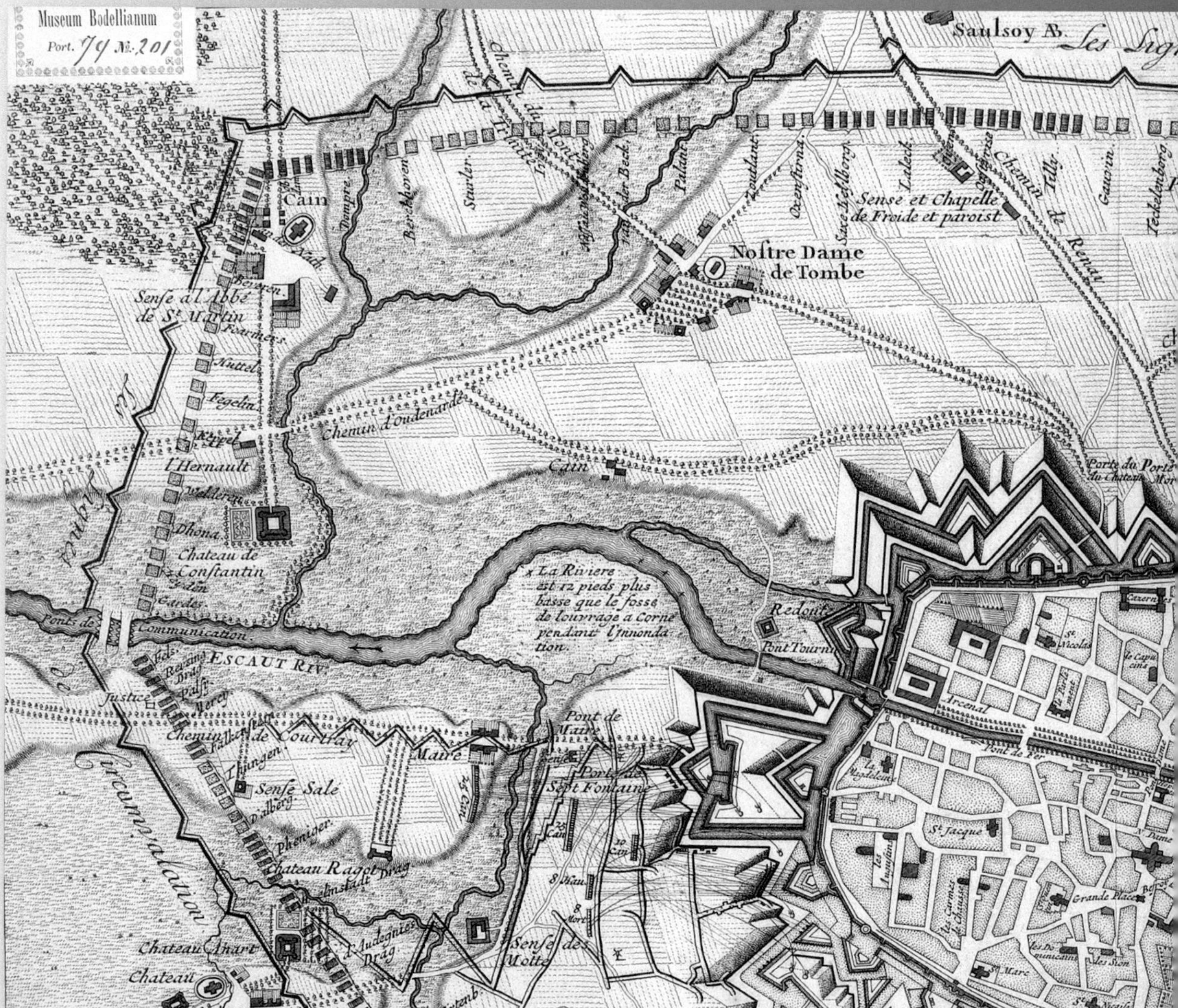

Museum Bodellianum
Port. 79 No. 201
Saulsoy
Les Lignes
Cain
Senſe et Chapelle de Froide et paroiſt
Noſtre Dame de Tombe
Senſe d'l'Abbé de St Martin
Chemin d'oudenarde
Cain
l'Hernault
Chateau de Constantin
La Riviere est 12 pieds plus basse que le fosse de louvrage a Corne pendant l'inondation.
Redout
Pont Tournant
Pont de communication
ESCAUT RIV.
Justice
Chemin de Courtray
Pont de Marre
Marre
Port de Sept Fontain
Senſe Sale
Chateau Ragot
Chateau Ghart
Chateau
Senſe de Molte
Froienne
Fontaine St Eloy
Attaque du General Schulenbourg
Porte de Lille
St Jacque
Arcenal
Grande Place
Faubourg d'Orcq
le Val Comanderie
Chat. de Marliere ou Marquain
Orcq
Fontaine de Desnouville
Chemin de Lille
Les Lignes de Circumvalation.
Croix Notre Dame
A. Speel Batterien.
B. Keetels daar de Mortiren in ſtaan.
C. De Batterie daar de bres mede zal gemaakt worden.
D. Galderien. of. Conter Mynen.
E. Het werckje dat geheel plat zal geschoote worden, om dat het ons in de weege legt.
F. Waar door men in den graft zal komen om de Citadelle te beſtormen.
G. De France haar Linie.
H. Een werckjen dat de Francen gemaakt hadden om ons het naderen ſo veel als het mogelyk was te beletten.
Troupes Campées entre le haut et bas Escaut, du côté de Lille.
Total
29 Batt.
28 Esq.
59 Bat.
Troupes campées entre le haute et bas Escaut, du côté de Mons et d'Ath.
30 Batt.
31 Esq.
59 Esq.
I. Daar de Bres zal zyn.
K. Daarſe den 25 Aug: op ſoude gestormt hebben.
L. De Ketel die ondermynt is geweeſt.
M. De Muur die de Francen hebben late ſpringen
N. De batterien die de bres ſullen maaken.
O. De groote keetel van mortiren en hobitſers.
P. Daar de hant mortiren ſtaan.
Q. Een kaſemat daar de francen nog uit ſchieten
ACAD. LUGD. BAT. BIBL.

Map showing the Siege of Tournai in 1709.

Engraving, 18th century, published by Nicolas Visscher. Leiden University Library, Leiden, the Netherlands. From the Bodel Nijenhuis Collection.

officers in the trenches.[61] Marlborough's hand was also missing during the confusion caused by his shift from the siege camp to Orchies, which led to a night of trench work without a single general directing their approaches.[62] Nor did Marlborough's control over the siege extend to forcing the infantry generals in the trenches to follow the advice of the artillery officers; the result was inefficient cannon fire and much wasted powder.[63] As for the countermines, the Saxon approach commander Schulenburg complained of how little the engineers were prepared to capture them, but here too Marlborough seems just as impotent sitting in his camp at Orchies and despairing of success.[64] The Dutch general Albemarle, who served as Marlborough's go-between while he was at Orchies, summarized its management thus: 'order and good conduct are lacking.'[65] About most of these missteps and mistakes the siege commander's correspondence is silent, and it is in fact only in Dutch sources, which were directly responsible for the siege, that the most significant blemishes appear. Given all these errors, it is perhaps as well for Marlborough's reputation that he played such a limited role in the attack, although one should certainly question whether his position as siege commander demanded that he spend more time focusing on its details.

Yet the siege was successful, and in relatively short order, as was almost every other siege of the war. Its success was due less to the technical expertise of its commander, than to their brute force tactics and luck. Following Coehoorn's method, Marlborough had 'all the artillery that anyone could ask for in a siege,' and opened fire on the town and its works with more than 130 cannon and 40 mortars; garrison sources described being 'attacked by the most frightful artillery ever seen before a place.'[66] The final surrender of the citadel on 3 September was particularly fortunate for the Allies, most participants estimating that its countermines could have allowed it to hold out for a month longer had its supplies lasted. In short, the Allies attacked an imposing but under-garrisoned, under-supplied fortress with overwhelming firepower and undistinguished trench works. It was a successful siege, but hardly a masterful one.

Surveying all of the Allied sieges, we must be more precise in identifying exactly what each ally contributed to the many coalition successes. Generally speaking, we can locate Marlborough's main involvement at the operational level. First, as commander of Allied forces he played a determining role in the selection of targets, though he had to balance his own projects with those of his allies. He then manoeuvred the Allied field army into a position whereby an investment force could surround and cut off a French garrison from outside support, and coordinated the transport of supplies and labour to the site as needed.[67] In the larger sieges particularly he remained with the observation force and covered their trenches from French relief. But we should also recall that almost every Spanish Succession siege was successful, regardless of who commanded the covering army. Only four of the thirty-five sieges in Flanders were unsuccessful – a success rate of 90% – and in only one of these cases did a relief force play a critical role in ending the siege.[68] When Marlborough was in the observing force he undoubtedly maintained close correspondence with those on-site, mostly through word-of-mouth if the lack of communication preserved in the Blenheim papers is any indication. From time to time he visited the trenches in order to make a personal reconnaissance of their progress, and was obviously involved in councils of war where important decisions were made. His most active contribution was his frequent direct intervention in councils of war to press for a rapid capture of whatever place was under siege at the time, often cajoling, browbeating and overruling his engineers in the process. To this end he might oversee its pivotal junctures, such as a general storm of the covered way (as he did at Menen). At the end of sieges, he usually approved the terms of the capitulation as well. In general, however, he kept his eye on the larger operational picture, uneasily leaving the details to his more siege-savvy coalition partners.

■ Conclusion

By the dawn of the eighteenth century the real challenge of siege craft was not simply to capture a place, but to minimize the costs of its capture. Judging a contemporary's expertise in siege craft thus depends on first choosing sides – is it enough to capture a town, or to do so without making numerous mistakes? More controversially for the period, contemporaries disputed which mistakes were most costly – the cost of recklessly-sacrificed lives or of needlessly-lost time? Marlborough avoided delays wherever possible, intervening forcefully at certain critical points of the siege in order to accelerate its pace. Opening the trenches as soon as possible, opening fire on the garrison as soon as possible with the maximum number of artillery pieces available, bombarding the town indiscriminately as well as the works, and storming the covered way were the stages most amenable to non-engineer pressure. Through his many tactical choices Marlborough clearly sided with the vigorous camp rather than with the efficiency-minded engineers. These tactical choices violated the cult of efficiency promoted by Vauban, but they led to success. Success, however, is a far cry from mastery.

To pierce almost completely through Vauban's vaunted *pré carré* in five years was an impressive military feat, even if it does not electrify those thirsting for decisive victories in the open field. Judged by his individual actions, however, Marlborough was not a 'master' of siege warfare. Marlborough's limited exposure to siege warfare early in his career encouraged a vigorous, anti-engineering mindset, and while his explicit rejection of many of Vauban's efficient tactics worked well against Spanish bicoques in the war's early years, they were less-well suited to the fortifications of Vauban's iron frontier. Though the Dutch engineers were never given the full authority to conduct their attacks as they saw fit and were frequently forced into using brute force tactics, the Duke could not ignore them altogether. The resulting uneasy hybrid of trench parallels, overwhelming firepower and vigorous storms did the job, and the Dutch picked up most of the tab. After the Allies entered the confined, fortress-dotted theatre of northern France in 1708, casualties steadily mounted as Marlborough's operational brilliance became secondary to the brute force clearing of Vauban's *pré carré*. This was an allied effort to be sure, but one headed up by the United Provinces' generals, engineers, artillery and troops. The Duke's greatest personal contribution to this effort was to manoeuvre the Allied army into a position whereby the more technically-skilled and better-equipped Dutch could then capture the French fortresses that blocked their advance – by 1706 there was no other option. In this context, Marlborough's command of the covering force was an intelligent division of labour that allowed each ally to contribute its own particular strengths in order to bring Louis XIV to heel.

CHAPTER 5

Marlborough, the Allies, and the Campaigns in the Low Countries, 1702-1706

'By thes difficultys you may see the great disadvantage a confederat army has'

John M. Stapleton

Marlborough's relationship with his coalition partners during the War of the Spanish Succession is one of the more complex and arguably least understood aspects of the Marlborough story.[1] Few historians would deny that Sir John Churchill, First Duke of Marlborough was one of the period's great battlefield commanders.[2] His battlefield victories alone suggest a commander of great tactical skill, and when considered together with the capture of more than twenty-five towns by siege, Marlborough's record as an army commander is truly remarkable; that he accomplished so much at the head of a coalition army is extraordinary.[3] The Confederate Army – the contemporary name for the allied military organization in the Low Countries – comprised formations drawn from the military establishments of the Dutch Republic, England and a host of Scandinavian and German principalities. According to his greatest biographer, Winston Churchill, Marlborough 'held the Grand Alliance together no less by his diplomacy than by his victories' using his oft cited charm, good-manners, and persuasiveness to assuage the most troublesome of his allied colleagues.[4] The same qualities that made Marlborough an excellent diplomat are listed amongst his most important assets as a coalition commander; assets which allowed him to command the Confederate Army to victory on the battlefield.[5]

Nevertheless, Marlborough's battlefield victories – and historians' obsession with them – have obscured the lack of unity within the Confederate Army's headquarters during Marlborough's early campaigns and his consequent disappointments during those same campaigns. From the time he took command of the Confederate Army in late June 1702 through the conclusion of the stormy 1705 campaign, Marlborough found it virtually impossible to build operational consensus with his Dutch coalition partners. Almost from the start, senior Dutch generals found fault both with Marlborough's operational concepts and with his leadership style, which in turn led to escalating friction between the commander-in-chief and his Dutch allies.

The literature surrounding his first campaigns and his character as a commander is itself contradictory. Although some of Marlborough's biographers laud him for his diplomatic skill and his ability to 'handle' difficult allied generals, they also acknowl-

Baron Menno van Coehoorn (1634-1704). An innovator in weaponry for siege warfare and in fortification design, Coehoorn was the counterpart in the Dutch Army of the French Army's Vauban. Coehoorn became a Lieutenant-General of Infantry in the Dutch army in 1694, Inspector-General of Fortifications in 1695, and Master-General of the artillery in 1697.

Painting by Theodoor Netscher, late 17th century. Rijksmuseum Twente, the Netherlands.

edge that his Dutch coalition partners frequently vetoed his operational schemes, which in turn fostered discontent within the allied high command.[6] One vein of this Anglophone literature attributes this 'Dutch obstructionism' to Marlborough's penchant for battle as contrasted with their apparent preference for siege operations.[7] Emphasizing his martial genius, these authors posit that Marlborough's battle-centric operational schemes represented a break from traditional, siege-driven logistically constrained ones. For them, Dutch obstruction reflected military backwardness and conservatism as contrasted with Marlborough's imagination and genius.[8] Other biographers take this thesis further, maintaining that obstruction was fostered by jealousy of Marlborough's position as commander-in-chief – being an Englishman in command of a confederate army –and of his military genius. Sir John Fortescue, for example, when describing the reason for Marlborough's early operational failures opines: '[a]s to his actual work in the field, we have often only the wreck of his finest conceptions, ruined as they were by the jealousy, selfishness, timidity and conceit of smaller men.'[9]

The Anglophone literature has expended much ink damning Dutch generals for obstructing Marlborough's plans, but little exploring why they might have done so. For such a confident literature, it is noteworthy that not a single biography of Marlborough written in the past twenty-five years contain Dutch primary sources beyond B. van 't Hoff's edited correspondence between Marlborough and Holland's Raadpensionaris Anthonie Heinsius, let alone Dutch secondary literature.[10] The absence of Dutch sources in the Anglophone literature – particularly as it relates to Marlborough's relations with Dutch generals and officials – calls into question the veracity of its conclusions on that subject. Only an examination of Marlborough's generalship from both the Dutch and English perspectives can shed light on the sources of friction between Marlborough and his Dutch colleagues.

Marlborough's experience was at the centre of that tension. Marlborough's approach to war with his emphasis on bringing the enemy to battle – a change heavily emphasized in the Marlborough literature – caused far less discord between him and his Dutch coalition partners than has been portrayed. Instead, Marlborough's inexperience at the operational level of war – exacerbated by the idiosyncrasies of his generalship – was the greatest source of friction between Marlborough and his Dutch allies. Although his lack of command experience beyond the regiment is widely acknowledged in the historiography, few of his biographers are willing to concede that it might have had an adverse effect on his military judgment in certain situations. Instead, they chose to explain his inexperience away, couching it more positively by looking ahead to his victories at Blenheim and Ramillies rather than at his less auspicious early campaigns. J.R. Jones' 1993 biography of Marlborough exemplifies this reasoning when he explains how Marlborough's inexperience actually gave him an advantage over his more seasoned Dutch colleagues:

> *'His Dutch contemporaries – Overkerk, Ginkel, Slangenburg – had vastly more military experience, but it was experience of a somewhat disheartening and mentally deadening kind, acquired as subordinates of William in a series of bloody campaigns of attrition that had achieved no more than a precarious containment of the French army. They did not believe, as Marlborough did, in the practical possibility of total victory; they had not developed the tactical and strategic ingenuity to work out the methods by which it could be achieved. Like their French counterparts they were tied to conventions and rules of war that Marlborough and Eugène... were to shatter.'* [11]

Like the mass of the Anglophone Marlborough literature, Jones discounts the Dutch general officers' wealth of experience – many of them having served as general officers in two major Low Countries' *wars* against the same foe to Marlborough's two *campaigns* – while downplaying Marlborough's comparatively limited campaign experience. What is more, while Marlborough may have believed in 'total victory,' it was arguably not the practical possibility Jones suggests.[12]

Marlborough's inexperience had a very tangible effect on his relations with his Dutch allies, particularly during his early campaigns. While his command style – characterized by his reluctance to heed the advice of his more seasoned Dutch subordinates – exacerbated the friction, his inexperience played a far more fundamental role in fostering conflict – particularly as it pertained to the conduct of operations – than any other factor. The States General's imposition of restrictions on Marlborough's command authority, the Dutch generals' vetoes of Marlborough's operational schemes, and even the personality clashes between Marlborough and certain Dutch generals were all affected in some way by decisions Marlborough made which reflect his inexperience as an army commander. Only when the friction between Marlborough and the Dutch generals threatened to rupture the Anglo-Dutch alliance, did the States General finally take action. Its decision to meet with Marlborough and the Dutch generals in the fall of 1705 after the conclusion of that unsuccessful campaign did more to foster greater allied cooperation than anything Marlborough himself did as its Commander-in-Chief

■ Generalship, experience, and the art of war in the Low Countries

When Marlborough arrived in Nijmegen on 2 July 1702 to take command, senior Dutch generals were sceptical of his ability to lead the Confederate Army, and with good reason. While he was an experienced officer in the general sense, Marlborough had never commanded an army of the size, composition, or the political complexity of the Confederate Army. For his part, he adapted to his new role well, though he soon found the challenges of coalition command frustrating. Within weeks of his arrival at the Confederate Army's camp at Dukenburg, an exasperated Marlborough – aggravated by the delays caused by the late arrival of allied contingents, the slow preparation of magazines to sustain the army, and his general lack of control over events – wrote to his friend and confidant, Sidney, first Earl of Godolphin: 'By thes difficulties you may see the great disadvantage a confederat army has.'[13]

As the Confederate Army's commander, Marlborough was following in the footsteps of Stadholder-King William III, though Marlborough's apprenticeship at his hand was limited both in depth and duration. Diplomatically, Marlborough already possessed considerable experience when William III named him Extraordinary Ambassador to the United Provinces and commander of the English expedition sent to the Low Countries.[14] During this visit, he was introduced to the organs of the Dutch state and its most important officials, first of all Holland's Raadpensionaris Anthonie Heinsius. As Augustus J. Veenendaal's chapter in this volume describes, Marlborough and Heinsius quickly developed a strong working relationship, and ultimately a friendship of sorts.[15] During these negotiations, Marlborough made a favourable impression on Dutch government officials, which in part explains their enthusiasm for nominating him Commander-in-Chief of the Confederate Army after

William III's death. Politically and diplomatically, Marlborough seemed an ideal choice to succeed the Stadholder-King as the coalition army's military commander.[16]

Militarily, however, Marlborough was an unknown. True, he was an experienced soldier having campaigned during both the Dutch and the Nine Years' Wars, but his experience did little to prepare him to command the army assembling in the Low Countries. Military experience was a vital part of a general's education in the latter 17th century and Marlborough possessed little as a general officer at the time he assumed command of the army.[17] Most of his command background was at the company and regimental levels; his time commanding larger formations – brigades, army wings, or even independent corps – was limited when measured against his Dutch counterparts.[18] His most important experience as a general officer came during his tenure with the Confederate Army itself in 1689 and again in 1691. Although he showed he was a conscientious administrator, he commanded the English force for only two campaigns.[19] Worse, Marlborough participated in only one campaign with William III as the Confederate Army's Commander-in-Chief. Thus, he had little opportunity to see first-hand what it was to be the Confederate Army's Commander-in-Chief.[20] William III, by comparison, had been mentored by more experienced soldiers like Count Georg Friedrich von Waldeck and Prince Johann Moritz von Nassau-Siegen when he first took command of the Dutch Army in 1672. He learned the art of warfare both through experience and his mentors' tutelage.[21] Marlborough enjoyed no such mentorship, nor such experience.

Although a number of the Confederate Army's senior officers, including William himself, commented on Marlborough's skill and potential as a field commander, his limited experience left him far less prepared to command the Confederate Army than many of his rival Dutch officers (and even some of his English colleagues).[22] Churchill argues that Marlborough's experience was impressive, nonetheless. In his biography of Marlborough, he wonders:

> *'Was [Marlborough's] service then so scanty? Tangier, Sole Bay, Maestricht, at least two campaigns under Turenne, Sedgemoor, and... Walcourt and Cork, certainly constituted a record of varied experience, of hard fighting and invariable good conduct by land and sea, in almost every rank from an ensign to a Lieutenant-General in independent command.'* [23]

But historians overlook that while Marlborough's experience was varied, it was also limited to the *tactical* level of war. He had very little experience organizing marches, coordinating operations, or planning campaigns, all skills practiced by general officers, and almost no experience serving within the Confederate Army in the Low Countries. Indeed, compared to his Dutch counterparts, Marlborough was 'only half qualified' given his experience.[24]

Most Dutch general officers, on the other hand, had far more experience than Marlborough, both on the battlefield and serving within the Confederate Army's organizational hierarchy. That fact alone explains William III's preference for Dutchmen and other continental officers for the Confederate Army's most important posts. For example, Godard van Reede van Ginkel – after 1692 First Earl of Athlone – had far more experience than Marlborough, under whom he would serve in 1702. Athlone was a Lieutenant-General at the time Marlborough was sacked in February 1692. Six years older than Marlborough, Athlone began his military career in the late

1650's with the cavalry and, like the Englishman, gained his formative military experience during the Dutch War.[25] But whereas Marlborough's experience mostly was limited to regimental and brigade command, Athlone commanded at every level in the Dutch and Allied armies, advancing from Colonel to Major-General during the course of the Dutch War, and ultimately rising to General of Cavalry by the Nine Years' War's conclusion. Athlone had extensive combat experience having participated in every campaign of the Dutch War; during the Nine Years' War he commanded troops both in Ireland and the Low Countries.[26]

Athlone's extensive combat experience is matched by his gradual rise through the ranks of the Dutch Army and the larger coalition military organization. Unlike Marlborough, Athlone grew into his various jobs and was entrusted with greater and greater responsibility as he gained experience. His military career mirrored the careers of many Dutch general officers of his generation: all earned their spurs under William III's command, most during the Dutch War. Like Athlone's, their experience was long and tough, rising through the company-grade ranks in five or more years and through the field-grade ranks after a decade of mostly wartime experience before being entrusted with greater responsibilities. Many of his contemporaries such as Prince Walrad von Nassau-Saarbrücken, Hendrik van Nassau-Ouwerkerk, Jacob van Wassenaer-Obdam, and Frederik Johan van Baer-Slangenburg, had served under William III during the Dutch War as field-grade and junior general officers. By the end of 1691, the Nine Years' War's third year and the end of Marlborough's apprenticeship-in-arms, these soldiers averaged between eight and ten campaigns in the Low Countries, five or more of them as general officers, more than three times Marlborough's command experience. But while Marlborough's removal from his posts in 1692 ended his wartime experience until 1702, these same officers continued to campaign – and to learn. By 1697, they had another six years of campaigning under their belts and were firmly grounded not only in the tactics of the battlefield, but in the operational complexities of warfare in the fortress-dotted Low Countries, as well. They had participated in sieges, had commanded foraging operations, had led contribution raids, had invested towns and had commanded wings of the army in battle. All of this while part of a very unique, idiosyncratic, confederate military organization.

In comparing Marlborough's experience to the experience of his Dutch contemporaries, one is struck by his lack of sustained practical military experience. In his memoirs published in the 19th century, Sicco van Goslinga – a Dutch field deputy who accompanied Marlborough during several campaigns[27] – recognized this void when he described Marlborough's weaknesses as a commander, thus:

> '*The Duke is a profound dissembler, all the more dangerous that his manner and his words give the impression of frankness itself. His ambition knows no bounds, and an avarice that I can only call sordid, guides his entire conduct... Sometimes on the eve of an action, he is irresolute or worse; he will not face difficulties, and occasionally lets reverses cast him down: of this I could give several eye-witness accounts... He is not a strict disciplinarian, and allows his men too much rein, who have occasionally indulged in frightful excesses. Moreover, he lacks the precise knowledge of military detail which a Commander-in-Chief should possess* [emphasis mine JS]. *But these defects are light when balanced against the rare gifts of this truly great man.*' [28]

GENERAL GINCKEL,
CREATED EARL OF ATHLONE,

Goslinga's recognition that Marlborough lacked certain military knowledge is supported by Marlborough's own career path and the notable absence of campaign experience as a general officer. In fact, most English officers lacked the campaign experience of their Dutch counterparts, an important reason why William III relied so heavily on Dutch, German, Huguenot and other foreign officers for the Confederate Army's most important posts. But by the conclusion of the Nine Years' War, many Englishmen had proven their ability within the Confederate Army's ranks: Lieutenant-Generals Sir Henry Belasis, James Butler, 2nd Duke of Ormonde, Charles Churchill, and the Huguenot Henri de Ruvigny, Earl of Galway all emerged from the Nine Years' War with more campaign experience than Marlborough.[29] In many ways, Marlborough's absence from the army after the 1691 campaign made him less qualified than other candidates militarily, but his political connections – both in England and the Dutch Republic – coupled with his diplomatic ability ensured his selection as William III's successor.

Marlborough, the Dutch Republic, and Command of the Confederate Army

When the States General announced its decision to appoint Marlborough Commander-in-Chief of the Confederate Army, Athlone expressed his discontent and concern, proposing instead that he should hold a rank equal to Marlborough's, rather than a lower one. Other generals were angry. The Prince of Nassau-Saarbrücken – the Dutch Republic's senior army commander – refused to serve with Marlborough, and sent one of his aides – Major-General Daniel Wolf von Dopff – to consult with Marlborough in his stead.[30] Consequently, the States General put safeguards in place to ensure the safety and proper employment of its troops while under Marlborough's command. Initially, it assigned *gedeputeerden te velde* – 'field deputies' – to the army as had been done when William III commanded the army. However, even greater strictures were placed on Marlborough. The States General added the caveat that all proposed operations must first be approved by the ranking Dutch general before any action was to be taken. According to one Dutch historian, this part of their resolution reflected the States General's concession to Dutch generals like Athlone who were hesitant to give Marlborough untrammeled control of the, predominantly Dutch, Confederate Army.[31]

The extent of Marlborough's authority as the Confederate Army's Commander-in-Chief is a topic of considerable importance and controversy in the Marlborough literature. Many Anglophone historians are critical of the arrangements under which Marlborough exercised his command, focusing on his lack of control over the formulation of operational strategy and the cumbersome processes he had to follow to assuage his coalition partners. Especially puzzling and troubling for modern day historians is the role the Republic's field deputies played in that process.[32] Understanding their role, both in relation to Marlborough's command of the Confederate Army, as well as to the Dutch Republic's military and political institutions, will clarify the character of the system under which he operated while identifying the origin of the opposition to Marlborough's plans.

The constraints imposed on Marlborough were directly tied to the Dutch state's executive and administrative bodies, especially the States General and the *Raad van*

Godard van Reede, Heer van Ginkel, Amerongen, and Middachten, Earl of Athlone (1644-1703). A Dutch General of Cavalry in 1692, he was appointed a Field Marshal in the Dutch Army in October 1702. Earlier, he had accompanied William III to England in 1688. In 1692, William III granted him the titles of Earl of Athlone and Baron of Aughrim in the Irish peerage to recognize his success in commanding William's army in Ireland during 1690-1691.

Painting by Godfrey Kneller, around 1692. Castle Amerongen, Amerongen, the Netherlands. Reproduced with the permission of Stichting Kasteel Amerongen.

ough's plans at various times, was driven by their military assessment of the situation, not the field deputy's. How Marlborough and the Dutch generals understood the conduct of operations and the potential for achieving their aims as balanced against their risk to the army lay at the crux of their disagreements. For both Marlborough and the Dutch generals, this was based on their collective experience as officers.

A clash of personalities, outlook, or of experience? Marlborough, the Dutch generals, and the Confederate Army at war

The 1702 campaign highlights Marlborough's shortcomings as a coalition commander at that point in his career. When he took command of the Confederate Army in late June 1702, the war's first campaign in the Low Countries had already been underway for several months. Late in March, prior to Marlborough's appointment, the States General determined that securing the fortresses on the Rhine and Meuse rivers, the traditional invasion route into the Dutch Republic, would best serve its security needs and had divided the Confederate Army into smaller corps aimed at that end.[53] By late June, Prince von Nassau-Saarbrücken's small coalition force had captured Kaiserswerth, the first step toward opening the Rhine. But Boufflers' French army, operating between the Meuse and Rhine Rivers, had chased the main army under Athlone back to Nijmegen and continued to pose a threat not only to that city but to allied communications along the Rhine, as well.[54]

Marlborough's arrival brought a notable change to the allied headquarters and its personnel to the Confederate Army. Marlborough appointed William Cadogan and Adam de Cardonnel his Quartermaster-General and Personal Secretary respectively. Cardonnel had served on William Blathwayt's staff during the Nine Years' War and had been Marlborough's personal secretary since 1692.[55] Cadogan was a more problematic selection, however. In common with Marlborough, Cadogan's military experience hardly prepared him to be Quartermaster-General. Although he had extensive experience as a company-grade officer during the Nine Years' War, he had none as a staff officer. The Quartermaster-General's judgment was of vital importance to the army's operations, being responsible not only for collecting intelligence but preparing the army's order-of-battle, and its route-of-march. Marlborough's over-reliance on Cadogan's advice became a serious concern for many Dutch generals, particularly their own veteran Quartermaster-General Dopff.[56]

Almost from the time of Marlborough's arrival at the army, he and Athlone clashed over the Confederate Army's prospective operations. Their first disagreement came in early August 1702 when Athlone refused to acquiesce to Marlborough's proposed attack on Boufflers' and Tallard's forces as they retreated through a defile near Peer in Brabant.[57] Although the Allies appeared to possess the tactical advantage, Athlone reminded Marlborough of the operation's ultimate objective – the capture of the Meuse fortresses – and battle's inherent unpredictability. A lost battle would place Dutch security in jeopardy. Marlborough reluctantly agreed and the French army was allowed to retreat unmolested.[58] On the surface, Marlborough seemed pleased at the result as his letter to Godolphin shows:

Adriaan van Borssele van der Hooghe, Heer van Geldermalsen (1658-1728). A member of the Raad van State *– Council of State – since 1692 and a Field Deputy, 1702-1711, he was largely responsible for the logistics of the Allied Army.*

Etching by Jacobus Houbraken, from Vaderlandsche Historie vol. 18, by Jan Wagenaar, 1758. Utrecht University Library, Utrecht, the Netherlands.

> *'When I write my last, I was very near an opinion that wee might have engaged the French before I could write againe. Wee were near enough to have done it, if the right and left had been of a mind. But wee are contented with what we have done, which is the obliging them to retier upon the Demer, soe that wee have it in our power to attacq what place wee please upon the Meuse.'* [59]

But his letter to his wife Sarah suggests otherwise. Marlborough writes: 'These last three or four days have been very uneasy, I having been obliged to take more *pains than I am able to endure*.'[60] Clearly hurt by Athlone's decision, Marlborough chafed at being forced to follow his advice and at his apparent reluctance to risk the Confederate Army in battle.[61]

His animosity toward Athlone was not new. During the Nine Years' War, William III chose Athlone to command the Allied forces in Ireland, a command coveted by Marlborough himself.[62] As the 1702 campaign wore on, the relationship between the Confederate Army's two senior commanders deteriorated as Marlborough demanded greater operational control. Geldermalsen, the Council of State's field deputy, grew concerned. He wrote to Heinsius:

Earl Cadogan

'From [Mr. Hop], you will learn I must add two particular things, the first that I have begun to realize that the moods of our two generals, the Counts Marlborough and Athlone, are not entirely in agreement [original underlined]*; the former being hotter than the latter, and day by day acts as though he is the general here, whereas at Nijmegen matters would have been decided by the generals of the State* [i.e. the Dutch generals]*; if he does not push this matter too far, then what has occurred hitherto is not too serious, but I have the honor of communicating this to you in advance, as something that I have begun to fear.'*[63]

Instead of openly discussing his proposed operations with Athlone and the army's senior generals – thus benefiting from their experience – Marlborough more and more tried to coax them into battle, which usually did little more than antagonize the generals creating even more frustration within the high command.

The 'missed opportunities' of Marlborough's first campaign highlight the growing rift between Marlborough and the Dutch generals but not for the reasons often cited. According to the literature, the difference of opinion between Marlborough and the Dutch generals grew from his desire to bring the French army to battle and the Dutch generals' desire to avoid it. But such a simplistic assessment overlooks the root of their opposition to Marlborough's operations. Instead, many of the Dutch generals – including Athlone – did not oppose battle under the right circumstances. They also understood, in a way Marlborough likely did not, that battles could seldom be forced on an unwilling foe. Twice during the 1702 campaign the Allies offered battle to the French and on both occasions its commander declined to engage. On 20 August, Marlborough very nearly intercepted elements of Boufflers' army as it attempted to attack a supply train from Eindhoven, but he withdrew before the Allies could attack. Then on 22 August near Helchteren, Marlborough tried to surprise his army again when it pursued the Allied army too close through constricting terrain. Hoping to take advantage of the French army's disorder as it tried to deploy, Marlborough ordered General Obdam with the cavalry of the Allied right wing to attack the French army's left, but delays coupled with the softness of the terrain forced the plan's postponement. Daybreak on 23 August found both armies in order-of-battle prepared for combat, but neither side attacked the other. Instead, taking advantage of the reprieve, Boufflers cautiously retired during the night of 23/24 August.[64]

The incident at Helchteren led to numerous recriminations both by Marlborough and his contemporaries, and later by historians. The traditional narrative, based solely on Marlborough's correspondence, blames the Dutch – especially Obdam – for this second missed opportunity to fight the French in the field.[65] Marlborough's letters, and his criticism of Obdam, are damning. Writing to Godolphin, he explains:

'I have but to[o] much reason to complain that the ten thousand men upon our right did not march as soon as I sent the orders, which if they had I believe wee should have had a very easy victory, for their whole left was in disorder. However, I have thought it very much for her Majesty's Service to take noe notice of it as you see by my letter to the States. But my Lord Rivers and almost all the generall officers of the right were with mee when I sent the orders, soe that notwithstanding the care I take to hinder it, thay doe talke.'[66]

General William Cadogan, first Earl of Cadogan (1675-1726). Cadogan served as Marlborough's chief of staff, quartermaster general, and chief of intelligence. He additionally served as a British envoy to the Dutch Republic and Flanders, 1707-1711. He became Earl of Cadogan in 1718 and succeeded Marlborough as Commander-in-Chief of the British Army after Marlborough's death in 1722.

Painting attributed to Louis Laguerre, around 1716.

© National Portrait Gallery, London, UK.

Hendrik van Nassau, Heer van Ouwerkerk and Woudenberg (1640-1708). Nassau-Ouwerkerk had accompanied William III to England in 1688 and served as the king's Master of Horse. In 1696, he became a Major-General of Cavalry in the Dutch Army and was promoted to General in 1701, and then to Field Marshal in 1704.

Painting after Godfrey Kneller, 1700-1724. Palace Het Loo, Apeldoorn, the Netherlands. On loan from the Geschiedkundige Vereniging Oranje-Nassau.

> *'I must teach you a general maxim; that is if you find yourself in a delicate situation, or need to decide on a battle or some great or hazardous enterprise, if you are resolved to do it, neither consult your generals, nor call a great council.'* [74]

Marlborough's distaste for councils-of-war seems an odd perspective for the commander of a coalition army. Though William III also was loathe to adhere to their decisions, he nevertheless saw utility in them not only as a source for ideas, but as a formal way to allow his generals to present their views.[75] Marlborough's contempt for them, as evidenced by his comment to Goslinga, may suggest his own insecurity as commander-in-chief. Whether he feared stirring up opposition to his operational schemes, did not care to hear others' contrary opinions, or feared he somehow would demonstrate his ignorance of military matters, Marlborough's dislike for councils-of-war, let alone consulting his senior generals, appears more of a weakness than strength, particularly in the leader of a coalition army. By keeping his own council, Marlborough failed to utilize an important asset – the Dutch generals' wealth of campaign experience – while at the same time stirring up resentment and opposition from those same officers.

Marlborough's inexperience and his reluctance to work closely with his Dutch counterparts were not the only problems facing Marlborough and the Allies in 1703. Athlone's death in February of that year deprived the Confederate Army of one of its ablest commanders and Marlborough of the council he needed, however reluctantly. Even worse, Athlone's death, together with Nassau-Saarbrücken's in late 1702, exposed hitherto hidden rivalries amongst the Dutch Republic's senior generals that would exacerbate Marlborough's command difficulties. The deaths of these two Dutch Field Marshals in quick succession left that post vacant. Jacob van Wassenaer-Obdam, and Hendrik van Nassau-Ouwerkerk – both Generals of Cavalry – were the obvious candidates for the post but both were equal in seniority. Complicating matters was the fact that neither would serve as the other's subordinate, thus placing the States General in an awkward position politically. Rather than choosing one candidate over the other however, the States General instead promoted neither, assigning each to separate field armies. Ouwerkerk would serve with Marlborough's army in Brabant, while Obdam commanded the Scheldt Army with other Dutch generals. The General of Infantry position, also vacant, posed similar challenges for the States General. Four generals were eligible for the one vacant slot: Lieutenant-Generals Slangenburg and Noyelles were the most likely candidates, but Lieutenant-Generals Salisch and Coehoorn also coveted the position. Ultimately, the States General promoted both Slangenburg and Noyelles, creating a first and second General of Infantry, the former to serve with Obdam and the latter with Marlborough and Ouwerkerk.[76]

By creating in essence two armies built around two separate groups of senior generals, the States General unintentionally exacerbated the rift between Marlborough and Confederate Army's Dutch officers. Even more problematic than the physical division of forces were animosities within the Dutch officer corps the States General's decisions exposed. Known to be strong willed, undiplomatic, and difficult to work with, Slangenburg was widely disliked amongst the senior Dutch officers. Noyelles, Salisch, and Coehoorn all refused to serve under him; the even-tempered Heinsius even called him a 'difficult man.'[77] The States General's inability to make difficult decisions inadvertently divided the Confederate Army into factions. Marlborough's

onsieur Naßau.
D'. Auverquerque

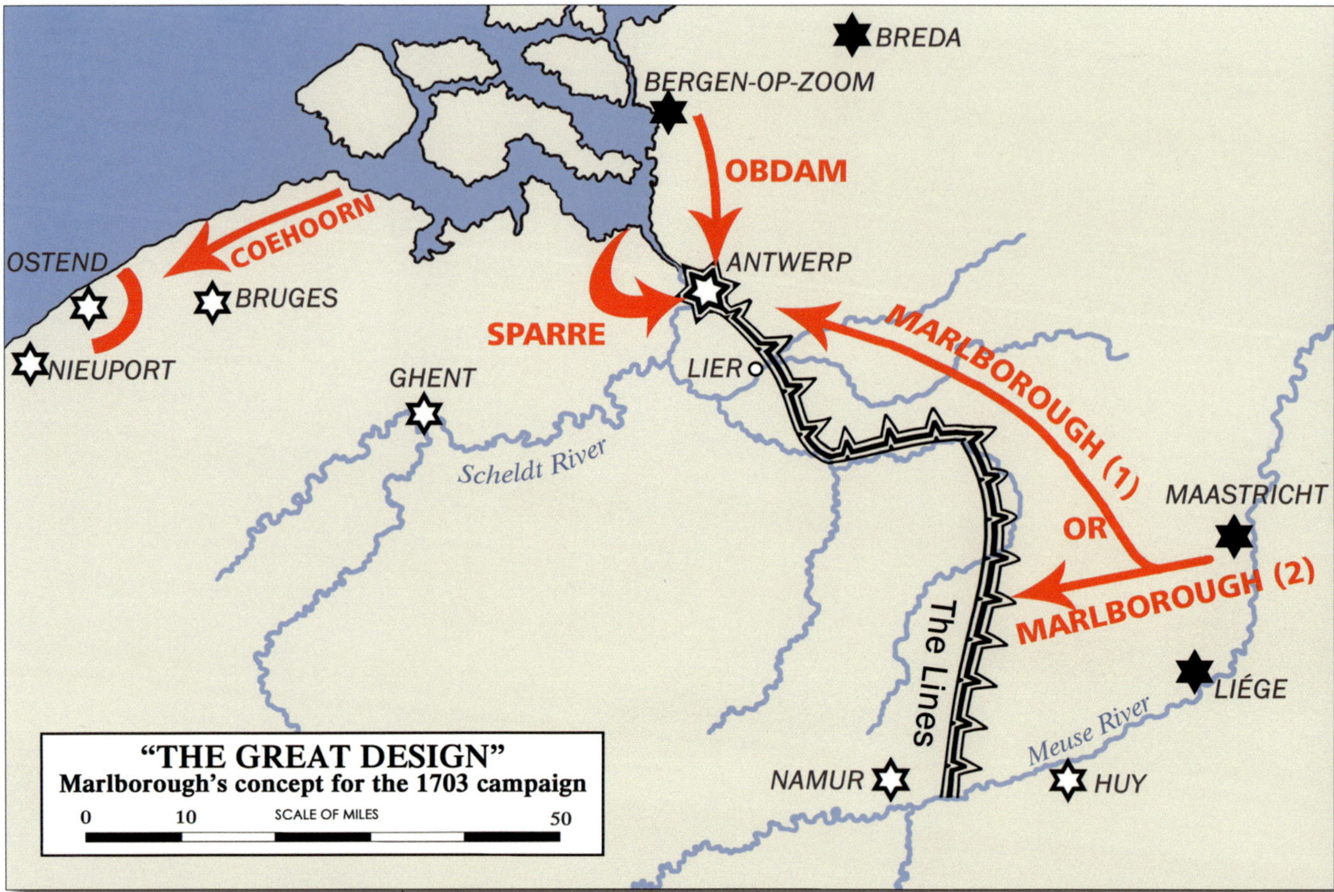

The Great Design.
For the 1703 campaign, Marlborough attempted to shift the centre of gravity of the Allied armies from the Rhine to Flanders. His overly ambitious plan involved first capturing Bonn, then shifting his focus westward to Flanders with the aim of capturing Antwerp and Ostend, but too few troops were allocated for operations planned in Flanders, revealing his inexperience in operational warfare.

Map by Rocío Espín.
Based on Winston Churchill's Marlborough, his life and times, book 1, page 662.

inexperience further exacerbated this divide. Even during the 1702 campaign, Marlborough had begun referring to the mostly Dutch generals who opposed his plans as the 'Left Wing' and those who supported him as the 'Right Wing,' connotations based loosely on the positions of the Dutch and British contingents in the Confederate Army's order-of-battle, respectively. The States General's division of the army high command formalized this schism further as Obdam's largely Dutch Scheldt Army – later commanded by Slangenburg – became the hotbed of Dutch opposition to Marlborough's operations. By the campaign's end, Slangenburg's opposition directly threatened the unity of the Confederate Army if not the Anglo-Dutch alliance itself and ultimately set the stage for the stormy events of the 1705 campaign.[78]

The plan and conduct of the 1703 campaign demonstrate Marlborough's inexperience in operational warfare. First, its goals were overambitious, centring on two separate objectives, each on opposite flanks of the Low Countries Theatre of Operations. Marlborough's plan, dubbed the 'Great Design,' would open with a siege of Bonn on the theatre's extreme eastern flank, an operation designed both to placate the Allies and to better open communications with the Holy Roman Empire.[79] Once he captured Bonn, Marlborough would shift his focus westward to Flanders, with the aim of capturing Antwerp and Ostend. Almost immediately Marlborough's ambitious plan ran into difficulties, however. Although Bonn fell to the Allies early in the campaign (15 May), implementing the second part of the plan – the attack on Antwerp – proved problematic. The attack on Antwerp called for Marlborough and Coehoorn to launch diversions in Brabant and western Flanders respectively, while Obdam breached the Lines of Brabant – a line of field fortifications covering the Belgian frontier – and invested Antwerp. Once Obdam was through the Lines, Marlborough's main army would follow to cover Obdam's siege operations.[80]

But shifting the allied centre of gravity from the Rhine to Flanders proved far more difficult than Marlborough had anticipated, while his distribution of forces to complete the operation turned out to be overly optimistic. Too few troops were allocated for operations in Flanders: roughly 40,000 of the Allies' 95,000 troops in the field were earmarked for Coehoorn's diversion and Obdam's siege of Antwerp leaving the remaining 55,000 men in Marlborough's diversionary force.[81] The bulk of the troops earmarked to attack Antwerp, furthermore, were to be transported by ship from Bonn to Bergen-op-Zoom.[82] When it became evident that Obdam's Scheldt Army would not be ready for operations on schedule, Marlborough grew impatient. Rather than wait for Obdam's troops to arrive, he suggested that Coehoorn besiege Ostend with his Flanders army – approximately 10,000 men – while his own army on the Maas created a diversion in the direction of Huy to allow time for Obdam's army to concentrate.[83] He then proposed besieging Huy while Coehoorn was conducting his own siege of Ostend. These suggestions reveal an alarming ignorance of siege operations; not only did Marlborough fail to recognize that the two armies were too small to besiege both places simultaneously, but he made no account for the time it would take to assemble the artillery, equipment, and labourers necessary to conduct a siege, let alone two. Not surprisingly, the veteran engineer Coehoorn refused, much to Marlborough's chagrin.[84]

There were other problems. Marlborough refused to remain idle waiting for Obdam's army to complete its concentration despite the Dutch generals' warnings and Coehoorn's refusal to besiege Ostend. The original plan required Marlborough's army on the Meuse to hold Villeroi's main Franco-Spanish army in Brabant through demonstration. But holding his army through demonstration was problematic because Villeroi enjoyed the benefit of interior lines and field fortifications, which would allow him to send detachments to Antwerp while trailing Marlborough's main army from the shadow of the Lines. From its camp at Maastricht, Marlborough could do just as much to pin Villeroi as any move toward Huy would do and he would be closer to Obdam if he needed support. But Marlborough was unconvinced. He determined that only by directly threatening Huy could he pin down Villeroi's troops effectively. Thus, despite objections from Ouwerkerk, Albemarle, and the other Dutch generals, Marlborough marched on Huy. To many Dutch generals, his march south was nothing more than show; in Wijn's words, 'to lend force to [Marlborough's] arrival in the army.'[85] Albemarle for one worried that his refusal to listen to the advice of his allies was a harbinger of things to come, and undermined the operation's chances for success. Ultimately, Albemarle's observations proved accurate.[86]

Although it would be an exaggeration to blame Marlborough for Obdam's defeat at Ekeren, his reluctance to heed the Dutch generals' warnings contributed to that defeat. As the Dutch generals had foreseen, Marlborough's march to Huy did not pin French forces in Brabant as he had predicted. Instead, while Villeroi matched Marlborough's motions – close enough to the Lines to gain succour there if necessary – he sent detachments from his army to reinforce Bedmar's Franco-Spanish army defending Antwerp. Coehoorn's demonstrations in Flanders were not sufficiently strong to weaken Bedmar's army; he still had plenty of troops to face the Allies when, prematurely, Obdam advanced on the Lines in late June. When Marlborough realized what was afoot, he was too far away to intervene. Marshal Boufflers and General Bedmar launched their spoiling attack on Obdam's forces at Ekeren on 30 June. The Scheldt Army – commanded well by Slangenburg after Obdam fled the field – managed to fight its way out of encirclement and stave off disaster. But the loss of almost 1,800 troops brought the Great Design to an inauspicious close. Worse, it placed General Slangenburg, one of the army's most seasoned – and most difficult – generals in command of the Scheldt Army.[87]

Despite the collapse of his Great Design, Marlborough remained intent on salvaging something from the campaign. Initially, he hoped to force the Lines before Antwerp but this proved both unpopular and impractical.[88] In the council-of-war that followed, Marlborough pushed for renewing the attempt on Ostend, but his plan was opposed by all of the senior Dutch officers including Coehoorn.[89] Consequently, Marlborough and the allies shifted their operational focus to the Maas valley with the aim of taking advantage of the Confederate Army's strength in numbers. On 15 August, Marlborough and the army invested Huy, and after eleven days, the modest but important fortress fell to coalition forces.[90]

The vehement divergence of opinion over Marlborough's plan to force the Lines of Brabant in the wake of Huy's capture caused a crisis within the Confederate Army's high command. The army's 'Right Wing,' led by Marlborough, favoured an attack on the Lines of Brabant while the 'Left Wing,' represented by Slangenburg – now commander of the former Scheldt Army – and the Dutch generals, preferred to besiege Limbourg. On 24 August 1703, Marlborough held a council-of-war at his headquarters in Val Notre Dame to discuss the plan. His scheme, as described by Churchill, called for a general attack on the Lines between the Méhaigne River and the fortified town of Zoutleeuw. Deploying the whole Allied army over a six-mile front where the French defences were weakest, Marlborough argued, would give the Allies an advantage since the enemy did not have the troops to meet such a wide assault. If the French remained in the lines, a battle would ensue that, Marlborough argued, would be to the Allies' advantage. If the French retired, the allies would have their bridgehead into the heart of Brabant.[91] In the words of historian Ivor Burton, Marlborough's plan 'illustrated all of Marlborough's genius in perceiving the strategic possibility that escaped others.'[92] Marlborough and his supporters maintained that if they did not make this attempt now, given the Allies' numerical advantage and the weakness of the lines at this place and at this moment, then the war in the Low Countries might grind to an unbreakable stalemate. To give their sentiment weight, the ranking British and allied generals who supported the plan signed Marlborough's memorandum.[93]

The Dutch generals, led by Slangenburg, were unconvinced, however. They argued that the Lines were only as weak as the army that occupied them, and that even if they were comparably weaker than other sections of the Lines, they would give the French army occupying them a significant advantage.[94] Furthermore, Slangenburg argued, with the entire allied army concentrated together, Villeroi would be able to concentrate all of his forces against the allied attack. Finally, he argued, what should be done once the Lines were breached if they were successful? What was the larger operational objective? Namur would be too difficult to attack this late in the season and the French army had plenty of good defensive positions from where they could defend against a breakthrough. A siege of Limbourg, on the other hand – though less bold – would enable the Allies to control more territory and provide a stepping stone for future operations.[95]

Adolf Hendrik van Rechteren, Heer van Almelo (1656-1731). An aristocrat from Overijssel, he served as a field deputy of the State's General with the army in 1702-1703. Thereafter, he served as a Dutch diplomatic envoy to a number of German principalities from 1703. In 1705 Van Rechteren was elevated to Count of the Holy Roman Empire. Later, he was a delegate at the Utrecht peace negotiations and then the negotiations over the Barrier Treaty in 1714-1715.

Painting by unknown artist, in or around 1705. Photograph by Hans Westerink, reproduced with the kind permission of the Count van Rechteren Limpurg.

With both sides deadlocked, the States General intervened. It agreed with Marlborough that there was more to be gained by forcing the Lines than by a siege of Limbourg or some other secondary operation. However, it left the final decision to proceed with Marlborough and the States General's field deputies who were on the spot and better placed to make that decision. To learn more, Marlborough and the deputies agreed to reconnoitre the lines. What they found undermined Marlborough's plans. Most of those who took part in the reconnaissance believed an assault would produce casualties but little operational advantage. Even those who still supported an attack admitted that the allies would suffer at least 6,000 casualties in an assault on the Lines. The field deputies' assessment only widened the divide between the Left and Right Wings as Marlborough and many of the British generals accused the Dutch of cowardice.[96] Further reconnaissance of the Lines did little to change the opinions of the two parties. Frustrated, Marlborough conceded to Dutch demands for a siege of Limbourg, but complained to Heinsius that he 'would much sooner dye' than serve another year trying to gain the unanimous consent of the Dutch generals.[97]

Few Dutch officers blamed Marlborough directly for this quarrelsome state of affairs. Many believed the problem of unity stemmed from the combination of the divisive undercurrents within the senior Dutch officer corps and the command constraints imposed by the States General, coupled with Marlborough's inexperience as an army commander. Adolf Hendrik van Rechteren-Almelo, a field deputy from Overijssel, recognized the Confederate Army's structural problems.[98] Virtually everyone in the army praised the quality of the troops, leadership, and administration but no one could see a way to make the army work smoothly, and so take advantage of these strengths. He likened the army to a house 'nicely furnished,' but one 'where nothing is in its proper place, and if one moves about it, all will fall into disorder.'[99]

Albemarle believed Marlborough's inexperience was at least partially to blame for the army's difficulties. Part of the so-called 'Left Wing,' Albemarle saw no operational utility in forcing the lines in 1703. Writing to Heinsius, he recognized that 'Marlborough is both capable and full of good will, but because of his ignorance of the local topography he cannot always form his own opinion.' Seeking the opinions of others, Albemarle added that Marlborough was often supported by people who also know nothing of the theatre's topography, but in whom he confides, nevertheless. As a result, Marlborough frequently makes the wrong decision or changes a sound decision agreed to the day before. Frustrated by the events of the campaign, Albemarle concluded his missive with the comment a book should be written about this someday.[100]

Daniel Wolf von Dopff, the Dutch Army's Quartermaster-General concurred with Albemarle's assessment.[101] One of the most knowledgeable officers in the army with regards to the theatre of operations and the local terrain, Dopff had served as one of the Dutch Army's quartermaster-generals since the Dutch War and was William III's quartermaster-general throughout the Nine Years' War. In his letter to Heinsius dated 26 August 1703, Dopff noted that not only was Marlborough following the advice of men with little knowledge of the theatre of operations, but that in doing so, he had reversed sound plans that had been made in consultation with more experienced officers. Consequently, fruitful opportunities had been lost.[102] Although neither Dopff nor Albemarle directly stated it, Cadogan was the target of their criticism. The Duke's over-reliance on his Quartermaster-General, and other British officers with little knowledge of the theatre of operation's intricacies, compromised both Marlborough's judgment and his ability to formulate sound operational plans.[103]

The crisis of command within the Confederate Army reached its zenith during the 1705 campaign. Marlborough's victorious Blenheim campaign in 1704 gained him both greater prestige and confidence as an army commander. But it also indirectly fostered even greater friction in the allied headquarters as Marlborough demonstrated both his best and his worst characteristics as an army commander. From the assault on the Lines of Brabant on 18 July 1705 to the abortive attack on Villeroi's army at Overijssche a month later, Marlborough paid little heed to the concerns of his Dutch allies, nor did he follow any of their well-reasoned advice. Following the Confederate Army's assault on the Lines of Brabant and the defeat of Villeroi's cavalry at Elixhem on 18 July 1705, consensus broke down again between Marlborough and the Dutch generals over how best to cross the swollen Dijle River to engage the French army beyond. After a reconnaissance of the riverbank where Marlborough intended for them to cross, Slangenburg, Albemarle, and Dopff reported that the area selected for the crossing was poor, and after consultation with other Dutch generals, proposed an alternative crossing point which promised a better chance for success. When Slangenburg and the Dutch generals briefed the Commander-in-Chief as to their findings, he would not be moved. Instead, Marlborough followed Cadogan's advice who, unlike the Dutch generals, foresaw 'no difficulties' with the original spot.[104]

The action on the Dijle on 29-30 July 1705 further soured relations between Marlborough and the Dutch generals and set the stage for his public row with Slangenburg three weeks later. Again, as Slangenburg and Dopff had predicted, the crossing proved far more difficult than Marlborough and Cadogan had foretold. The assault's leading elements – comprised largely of the Dutch troops – managed to cross pontoon bridges across the Dijle without incident, but Villeroi was not surprised and launched vigorous counterattacks against the bridgehead. Although the Dutch forces in the bridgehead held off these French attacks, the English bridgehead soon was in trouble. Marlborough, who was supposed to bring the main body of the army across the Dijle to support the assault, arrived more than two hours late at the point of departure. When he heard the news of the British difficulties, he called off the assault, forcing Ouwerkerk, Slangenburg and the Dutch troops still across the river to withdraw on their own.[105] When they learned of Marlborough's decision, they were furious. For the Dutch generals, particularly Slangenburg, Marlborough's failure to consult with any of them before calling off the operation exemplified the manner in which Marlborough treated his Dutch allies. Albemarle wrote angrily to Heinsius of Marlborough's conduct, accusing him of treating the Dutch generals 'like children,' providing them with little or no information of his operational intentions. Worse, his correspondence suggests that he tried to pin the blame for the operation's failure on the Dutch when clearly this was not the case.[106] In his letters to Heinsius, Marlborough continued to rail against councils-of-war claiming that 'they destroy the secrecy and dispatch upon which all great undertakings depend' the implication being that openness with his allies was a threat to security, a statement dangerously close to an accusation of treason.[107]

The friction between Marlborough and the Dutch officers finally came to a head in mid-August. Marlborough had planned an audacious operation to turn the French army's position behind the IJssche Brook which called for the bulk of the army's centre and right wings to engage the enemy's front, while an allied detachment from the left flank attacked the French right flank. The mass of the allied army – including Ouwerkerk and the Dutch troops on the left – arrived at their assigned positions between 7:00 AM and 10:00 AM and waited. The flanking detachment commanded by Marlborough's brother got bogged down in the Forest of Soignies during its march and only reached the battle area between 5:00 and 6:00 PM and then, not on the flank as planned but against the French right front of its order-of-battle.[108]

At 5:00 PM, Dutch field deputies called a council-of-war to discuss the army's course of action given the day's late hour. With the army still unprepared to attack and a brook intersecting the Confederate Army's line of retreat if the battle were lost, the generals and deputies discussed their views for the coming battle with Marlborough. Marlborough and Ouwerkerk still wanted to press the attack, though Ouwerkerk admitted the enemy position would be a tough nut to crack.[109] Slangenburg and the Dutch generals – to include Ouwerkerk's subordinates – opposed an assault, however. Slangenburg was especially critical of the plan and Marlborough's conduct of the oper-

ation thus far. The details of Marlborough's plan, which called for the Allies to assault the French position opposite the IJssche Brook via four crossing points, had not yet been revealed to the army's subordinate commanders. Ouwerkerk and the rest of the army's centre and right sat in its order-of-battle opposite Villeroi for seven hours without any orders; time – Slangenburg argued – that should have been taken preparing for the assault. Furthermore, the French positions were more formidable than they had been led to believe. When asked about Marlborough's 'design,' Slangenburg replied that up to that point he knew nothing of a design. He stated that he would do his best to carry out the attack as ordered but he would not give it his endorsement.

Action of the Dijle River, 29-30 July 1705. The crossing of this river proved far more difficult than Marlborough and Cadogan had predicted. The debate over this undertaking further soured relations between Marlborough and the Dutch generals and set the stage for Marlborough's public row with General Slangenburg three weeks later.

Drawing by unknown artist, 1705. Atlas van Stolk, Museum Het Schielandshuis, Rotterdam, the Netherlands.

Then the field deputies asked the opinions of Ouwerkerk's subordinate commanders, Lieutenant-Generals Tilly and Salisch, and both agreed with Slangenburg's assessment. Ultimately, all the Dutch generals save Ouwerkerk agreed to make the attack if ordered, but none would take responsibility for the consequences.[110] Not surprisingly, the field deputies relented and withdrew their support for Marlborough's assault.

The field deputies' decision to withdraw its support had wide ranging consequences for Marlborough, the Confederate Army, and for Slangenburg. Marlborough was outraged and blamed Slangenburg for the operation's failure, angrily writing to Godolphin:

> *'When I had write thus far I toke the resolution of not letting the post go, believing I should have engaged the enemy as yesterday, which I certainly had done if it had been in my power. But all the Dutch generals except Monsieur Auverkerk were against it, so that the deputys would not consent to our engaging, not withstanding we were in battaile* [order] *within canon shot of the enemy; and I assure you that our army were at least one third stronger than theirs. We are now returning, for we can't stay longer then the bread we have braught with us will give us leave. It is impossible to make the warr with advantage at this rate.'* [111]

Although one can understand Marlborough's frustration, this letter – like so many of Marlborough's letters – says little about why his plan met such vocal opposition. He seems utterly oblivious to the fact that bad luck – the failure of the flank march to arrive in the right place – rather than the Dutch generals, led to the failure of an otherwise sound operation. Marlborough's demeaning command style, which not only left many of the army's most seasoned Dutch generals out of the operational planning process but blamed them when things went wrong, resulted in their resenting him, particularly the blame he heaped upon them for the failure of *his* operations. It is no wonder that they were unwilling to stick their necks out given their past history with him.[112] By the campaign's conclusion, the command situation within the Confederate Army had reached a crisis, a crisis Marlborough could not solve alone. Only the States General could take the necessary steps to restore unity within the Confederate Army.

The most significant casualty of the 1705 campaign was Slangenburg himself. Never popular within the Dutch senior officer corps, Slangenburg was an easy sacrifice for the States General to make. Marlborough had the firm backing of Parliament and the Queen. For the States General to support Slangenburg would be to undermine the Anglo-Dutch alliance, something their 'High and Mightinesses' were not prepared to do.[113] Although Slangenburg tried to convince others of the righteousness of his position, ultimately he was sacrificed in the interests of allied unity. In September, at the States General's request, Slangenburg took leave from the Confederate Army never to return.[114] In an effort to build unity within the army in the wake the campaign's frustrations, the States General organized a meeting between Marlborough and the Dutch generals to discuss both groups' grievances. On 21 September in Turnhout, Marlborough met with Willem Buys – *Pensionaris* of Amsterdam – and other representatives of the States General in order to resolve the issues of command and the field deputies' authority.[115] Removing the deputies or limiting their power was impossible; but the States General were prepared to allow Marlborough to approve which deputies would accompany him on campaign, just as William III had done.[116] This compromise pleased Marlborough and led to – in the words of Richard Holmes – 'a remarkable period of Anglo-Dutch military cooperation.'[117]

Conclusion

It would be easy to reach the conclusion that Slangenburg and the field deputies were the only obstacles preventing the decisive victory that Marlborough had sought for so long. After all, the following year he won a remarkable victory at Ramillies, followed by an equally remarkable pursuit that led to the collapse of the French position in the Spanish Netherlands. But Ramillies led neither to the end of the Spanish Succession

War nor to even greater field victories, as Marlborough had believed would be the case. Instead, the Englishman still found it supremely difficult to bring the enemy to battle. After 1706, Marlborough fought only two major battles – Oudenaarde in 1708 and Malplaquet in 1709. Neither brought Louis XIV to the negotiating table. Instead, siege operations dominated the war in the Low Countries and Marlborough's attention; operations whose success relied heavily upon the expertise of his Dutch coalition partners.

When Marlborough took command of the Confederate Army in July 1702, he faced a steep learning curve. Having never commanded an army of the political complexity of the Confederate Army, Marlborough found it difficult to build support for his operations during his early campaigns. From the start, his Dutch subordinates were as sceptical of his ability as he was of theirs. Marlborough's infatuation with the promise of battle coupled with his ignorance of the operational level of war caused many of his Dutch colleagues to doubt his wisdom as a commander, particularly when his operations needlessly put the mostly Dutch Confederate Army at risk. Why Marlborough disregarded the operational perspective of his more experienced coalition partners is difficult to understand and the sources provide few clues. His poor opinion of Athlone, for example, may have been the product of their shared history. But his unwillingness to bring any Dutch general into his confidence during his first campaigns is puzzling, and seems at odds with good generalship. Marlborough's refusal to acknowledge Coehoorn's advice regarding a siege of Ostend in 1703, for example – advice from a soldier recognized as one of the period's great siege warfare experts – is astonishing, particularly given Marlborough's scant experience in siege operations up to that point. Whatever the cause, his command style and operational outlook frustrated the Dutch general officers who served with him.

The States General's sacrifice of Slangenburg, coupled with its relaxation of the strictures it imposed on Marlborough's command authority allowed him to conduct operations more to his liking, while sending a powerful message to the senior Dutch officer corps. The great victory at Ramillies marked a turning point in the Allies' fortunes in the Low Countries. It also marked a turning point as the war devolved into costly, positional warfare. From 1707 to 1711, Marlborough waged the very war his Dutch colleagues had tried to convince him was necessary. Their expertise in siege warfare – as contrasted with Marlborough's ignorance of the same – highlights their importance to the allied war effort and to the Confederate Army, while demonstrating the complexity of military operations in the age of Louis XIV. As Marlborough gained experience campaigning in the cockpit of Europe, he came to appreciate more and more the perspective of his Dutch allies. Although historians often disparage the Dutch for their caution and conservatism, their expertise in warfare as it was fought in the Low Countries made Marlborough's victories possible.

him. His modest office next door to the meeting hall of the States of Holland on the *Binnenhof* in The Hague, became the nerve centre of the coalition against the universal monarchy of King Louis XIV of France.[3]

Heinsius was not a party man, hence his popularity with both opposing sides, Orange men and republicans. His position as Grand Pensionary was never in doubt after the death of William. He may have had little charisma, and may have been more of a very able civil servant than a real leader, who would push through his own opinions, but he was certainly well-respected everywhere, highly intelligent and very well versed in national and international politics. He was no fierce enemy of France, but very cautious about the real intentions of the French. His own experiences with

Meeting room of the States of Holland, now the 'Eerste Kamer' of the Dutch Parliament. The portrait of Heinsius is high on the wall at the left.

The Dutch Eerste Kamer, The Hague, the Netherlands. Photograph by Ton Sipman.

French politics since 1672 made him suspicious of French promises, but he was not in favour of a complete destruction of France. He was absolutely uninterested in personal glory; if possible he remained in the background and let others bask in the sunshine of glory and success.[4] He may have been slow at times, prone to hesitate even, but his method of persuasion with well founded arguments generally worked. Sometimes this slowness exasperated his contemporaries. Marlborough came to recognize this trait of the Pensionary: 'but he is in his nature so timorous that he will never contradict whatever the inclinations of 116 [the States] may be.'[5] Even if this is a bit exaggerated, there is some truth in the Duke's remark about Heinsius's slowness and timidity, although in many cases the Pensionary managed to bring differing opinions in line with his own ideas. That this took time was only to be expected, and delays could hardly be avoided in a governmental system such as that of the Republic.

But when it was really needed Heinsius could act quickly, for example by sending Dutch troops to Scotland to help suppress the Jacobite insurrection of 1715. The Dutch Republic was at that moment desperately in need of support from the British government in their endless negotiations with the Emperor about the Dutch Barrier in the now Austrian Netherlands.[6] By rigorously executing the obligations of the States General as expressed in the Anglo-Dutch treaties, that guaranteed both the Protestant Succession in England and the Dutch Barrier in the Austrian Netherlands, Heinsius more or less forced King George I to honour his part of the deal. It worked and the English representative at the negotiations began to support the Dutch side without reservations.

Marlborough and Heinsius

Marlborough and Heinsius must have known each other already personally before the beginning of the first campaign of the War of the Spanish Succession, as Marlborough had commanded the English forces in the Southern Netherlands for some time during the earlier War of the League of Augsburg, also known as the Nine Years' War, from 1689. It is not hard to believe that both men met somewhere at The Hague or *Het Loo* – William's favourite country retreat – during the early years of that conflict, although there is no written record. However this may be, Marlborough fell out of favour with King William in 1692 and although reconciled in 1698, got his new command only after the death of William in the Spring of 1702, when Queen Anne named him commander of all English forces and ambassador-extraordinary to the States General in The Hague.[7] The States followed soon with Marlborough's appointment as Lieutenant-Captain-General, or commander in chief of all the Dutch land forces, an exceptional honour for a man, a foreigner moreover, who at that time still had to prove his abilities as a commander. These duties brought him in close contact with Anthonie Heinsius, after William's death the unchallenged leader of the Dutch Republic.

Marlborough and Heinsius at work

The Grand Alliance was signed in The Hague on 7 September 1701; Heinsius, Marlborough and Count Goes, the Imperial Ambassador, were the signatories. The first few letters from Marlborough, written from England and from Dieren, one of the King's country houses and hunting lodges in Gelderland, date from 1701.[8] There are only a few answers from Heinsius preserved from this year, but both men must have met frequently in The Hague, as that town – officially only a village – was the nerve centre of the Dutch Republic and the heart of the Grand Alliance between England, the States General, and – somewhat more distant – the Emperor. It was in 1702, the year the real War of the Spanish Succession began in Western Europe, that the close collaboration between the two men started to blossom in earnest. Marlborough was then 52 years of age, Heinsius nine years his senior, already an old man judged by the standards of the time. Yet, despite frequent illnesses, the Pensionary was to live on for 18 more years!

Office of the grand pensionaries of Holland from the outside. It is situated on the ground floor in the left corner with the curtains drawn.

The Dutch Eerste Kamer, The Hague, the Netherlands.
Photograph by Ton Sipman.

Frequent correspondence between the two men started in earnest in 1702, with 65 letters in total, of which only nine were from Heinsius. There are also quite a few that appear to have been lost. Marlborough generally wrote in English, unless he dictated to his secretary Adam de Cardonnel, as he knew that the Pensionary had no trouble in reading English. English was not yet the universal world language of today, of course, and Heinsius was one of the few Dutch statesmen who were able to read and even write English. However that may be, Heinsius always writes to Marlborough in French, never in English. The correspondence really took off in the next year, with a total of 93 letters, of which 20 are from Heinsius, and the number of letters continued to grow over the years, to a maximum of 125 in 1705, with 49 from Heinsius.[9] From that year on, the total ran generally between 115 and 120, in most years evenly divided between the two protagonists. Only the year 1711 shows a sharp downturn, reflecting Marlborough's loss of political clout in England, with 75 letters altogether, of which 34 were from the old Pensionary. Altogether 1000 odd letters between the two statesmen have survived, not counting the many, especially from the earlier years, that have been lost.

Not all the negotiations between the two friends had to be conducted by letter. The two men met in The Hague at least twice every year, before and after the annual campaign, and when things were really pressing, Marlborough came from the battlefield or crossed the North Sea to meet the Pensionary in The Hague in person. Sometimes he stayed for a week or two, sometimes less, and now and then for just a few days before sailing for England after the campaign had ended, or when starting for

The 'Mauritshuis', next door to the government buildings of the 'Binnenhof', where Marlborough was lodged until 1704 when it burned down.

The Mauritshuis, The Hague, the Netherlands. Photograph by Ton Sipman.

'However, those are his weaknesses that do not measure up to the great talents of this truly great man.'[44] It is a great pity that Heinsius never wrote anything that comes near to Goslinga's sketch of Marlborough's character. He must have heard similar rumours about his duplicity and avarice, not only from Goslinga himself, who was a trusted colleague of the Pensionary, but also from others. Jacob Hop and especially Johan van den Bergh, one of the Dutch caretakers in the Condominium in Brussels, often wrote about the exactions of Marlborough and especially his lieutenant William Cadogan, who, although married to a rich burgomaster's daughter of Amsterdam, was considered far more greedy – corruptible even – than his master.

Later historians think they have noticed a certain cooling of the correspondence between the two men after this delicate affair, but close reading of their letters does not give much food for this idea. Indeed, when Marlborough's position in England seemed to be threatened by the new Harley-Oxford ministry in 1710, he came even closer to Heinsius. After the death of Emperor Leopold on 17 April 1711, Marlborough wonders what should be done now, with the political situation so completely changed with King Charles III now being Emperor Charles VI. He gives his own ideas and thoughts to Heinsius and desperately asks for his advice, ending in a cry from the heart: 'For God sake lett me hear from you.'[45]

■ A personal or a political friendship

There is very little personal to be found in their correspondence, nothing unusual as far as Heinsius is concerned. His letters, no matter to whom, are always short and businesslike, impersonal even, and with little or no mention of his own personal feelings. There is hardly any emotion noticeable in his correspondence. Marlborough is more open, shows his feelings more often, as he did after the frustrating Moselle campaign of 1705:

> *'I am so uneasy at all the follys and villonys I have met with whilst I was on the Moselle, that I should be extreamly obliged to you if you could find some proper person to be in my post when this campagne is ended, so that I might be quiet in England, where I would use my utmost endeavours to serve the publick cause and the States in particular, to whome I wish as much as success as any subject they have.'*

Heinsius apparently took this complaint seriously enough, as he answered immediately:

> *'You have good reasons to be angry about all that has happened to you at the Moselle, but not so much as to want to retire from the command for the next year. I do hope that you will not think about it anymore and that the good God will bless you so much during this campaign that you will continue with pleasure for the next year.'*[46]

As has already been noted before, this was not the only occasion when Marlborough, utterly frustrated by the disunion among the generals and the lack of support from the Allies threatened to step back, but every time he let himself be persuaded to remain in charge.

Only in cases of sickness even Heinsius loses his usual distance somewhat: 'I learned from a note from Cardonel that you have been ill. I hope that it will be over by now and that you are recovered.' That is about as far as Heinsius ever went, but compared to what Marlborough writes when he hears that the Pensionary is ill, it is almost next to nothing: 'I was sorry to see by the last post that you were not well. I wish with all my heart this may find you in perfect health. The good of the common cause cannot at this time bare your being sick.'[47]

■ The end of a nine years' friendship

Marlborough was divested of all his offices on the last day of 1711. The correspondence between the two men, who had worked together so closely for nine years, then stopped abruptly. After that fateful day the Duke wrote only one more letter to Heinsius, on 8 February 1712 (N.S.). He added as a kind of apology:

> *'For my own part I am taking measures to retier, and since I cannot be otherwise usefull, you shall be sure of my prayers, and I beg the justice of you to beleive that next to my own country, the States will have my earnest wishes and prayers for their prosperity, as also that yourself may be for ever happy.'*[48]

Heinsius never answered this one. The Pensionary lived for nine more years, happy or not, but he did never write Marlborough again. After this kind of farewell, only two later letters from Marlborough to Heinsius are known, both to recommend officers in the favour of the Grand Pensionary, one from 1713 and one from a year later. Both are rather impersonal, especially the last one written in French from Antwerp; both are very businesslike, but one little opening line in the 1713 one – from Frankfurt – gives a faint indication of Marlborough's feelings: 'I am persuaded it is unnecessary I should make any excuse for my silence since my coming out of England, you knowing it is occasioned neither by want of respect or inclination.'[49] Again, no answer from Heinsius is known. But Heinsius never wrote letters without a purpose, and with the Duke living in retirement there was no reason for him to answer the few letters that Marlborough sent him. He was not the man to put his pen to paper when there was no necessity. He never wrote just for the fun, and all his letters are about politics or military matters, never anything personal.

Conclusion

The question remains: were they true friends, colleagues or just working together for the common good? I would opt for the latter. Heinsius had very few personal friends, if any at all. From the vast number of his correspondents, only a few names – those of regents who were probably a little bit closer to him than the rest – stand out: Arnold Joost van Keppel, Earl of Albemarle, Adolf Hendrik van Rechteren-Almelo, Sicco van Goslinga, Arent van Wassenaer-Duvenvoorde and maybe Bruno van der Dussen, the Pensionary of Gouda and a distant relative, but these are about all. Heinsius lived for his work, for the welfare of Holland and the United Provinces, for the common good, and for the peace of Europe, and he had no personal distractions. He had no women, no country houses, no yacht, and no other pleasures to keep him from his duties. Work came first and last no matter what. He could collaborate with Marlborough possibly better than with most others, but they never became close personal friends in the modern sense of the word. With a statesman like Heinsius, that was just impossible. They valued each other's qualities and they needed each other to reach their common goal: the security of the Dutch Republic and that of England, and an end to the French threat to the stability of Europe. As soon as one of them lost his position and his influence in political or military matters, there was no reason to continue a correspondence that had lost its usefulness. In their time this was nothing unusual. Friendship for life, the romantic notion that would only begins to be seen towards the end of the eighteenth century, was something Heinsius and Marlborough did not know about. Friendship was based on reciprocal usefulness, and as soon as that usefulness was over, the friendship ended quietly, without either party being offended or disappointed. Even without their being friends in the more modern sense, theirs was a rare example of a close relationship between two men working together. On one side the cold, businesslike burgher regent, and on the other the flamboyant nobleman, two extremes maybe, but collaborating to create an extremely well-oiled machine that functioned as long as both remained in office. After Marlborough's downfall, apparently neither felt inclined to continue a relation that had lost its importance.

Where the relationship between Great Britain and the Dutch Republic since the days of William III as Stadholder-King was concerned, Heinsius' motto had always been *si collidimur frangimur*, or *when we collide we will break.* The wily old politician was right about this. Indeed, for a long time the two nations could not do without the other. But when the new Harley-Oxford ministry in London decided to go its own way in the negotiations with France without recourse to The Hague, the old alliance was broken, to the great disappointment of the grey Pensionary, who must have felt left out in the cold by these upstarts in the British government. The Peace of Utrecht as finally concluded – without much cooperation from Heinsius – was a great disappointment for him. Fortunately the estrangement between the two nations did not last long. The death of Queen Anne and the access to the British throne of the Elector of Hanover as King George I changed things for the better when the new King decided to renew the old alliances with England's long time ally across the North Sea, very much assisted in this by Heinsius.

CHAPTER 7

Marlborough as an Enemy

Clément Oury

In April 1674, the defence of Alsace, which had been conquered by France thirty years earlier, had been entrusted to Henri de la Tour d'Auvergne, Marshal Turenne, then considered the best of Louis XIV's generals. At that point, Turenne had a reduced number of troops at his disposal, the King having decided to focus the offensive in other regions. Turenne's campaign was marked by three victories: Sinsheim, in the Palatinate, in June; Entzheim; and especially Türkheim, in Alsace, on 4 October and 5 January. First he crossed the Rhine, to prevent an invasion. Next, he was forced to return to Alsace, where he watched as his enemies took possession. Finally, he completed a bold winter march across the Vosges Mountains, ruining imperial plans for an invasion and driving off the opposing army. This campaign showed his mastery of the terrain, his mastery of the art of manoeuvring and of the indirect style, and especially his audacity – all at a time when campaigns ended in the fall. It is today considered Turenne's masterpiece.[1]

In the ranks of Louis XIV's army were some British troops, whom Charles II had not repatriated after the signing of the peace treaty between England and the United Provinces.[2] In 1674 some of those regiments, now financed by France, participated in the defense of Alsace. Such was the case of the regiment under young John Churchill. Turenne quickly took note of him for his courage, and Churchill earned himself the nickname of '*bel anglais*.' The example set by the French Marshal, his taste for quick actions and for manoeuvres that sometimes ran against established principles, undoubtedly had a decisive influence on John Churchill's military education. Almost thirty years later, Churchill would return to the Continent to 'teach the French their own lessons.'[3]

For Louis XIV and his kingdom, the Duke of Marlborough played the role of fearsome enemy during the War of Spanish Succession, triumphing over French generals and armies, invading French territory, seeking to impose a humiliating peace. How, then, was he perceived by the French of his time? To find out, we need to study both the image that political and military leaders had of him and the judgments of courtiers and residents of Paris. The lack of sources keeps us from penetrating much further into the deeper strata of French society. An analysis of Marlborough's image will in turn help us understand how the French viewed their own army, or even their own regime. To carry it out, we can examine correspondence between the various personalities at Versailles and the army (princes, ministers, and generals),[4] the memoirs of generals and courtiers, and the pamphlets then circulating in the capital.

Henri de la Tour d'Auvergne, Vicomte de Turenne.

Painting by Charles Le Brun, 17th century. Versailles, France.

Marlborough's Image in France during the War of Spanish Succession

The French seem not to have reacted in any particular way on learning the name of the captain-general, who would command Allied troops in Flanders. Until that point, the Duke of Marlborough had never taken full command, except ten years earlier when he led a corps of a few thousand men against the Jacobites in Ireland.[5] His nomination seemed the result of diplomatic manoeuvres. For the Marquis de Sourches – whose memoirs record the day-to-day consensus at court – Marlborough was imposed by default. The Dutch had rejected the Elector of Brandenburg, whom they had already tangled with over territorial matters and who, if given this command, could have pretended to the title of Stadholder. By comparison, Marlborough was but an 'anxious man, and who certainly is no more valuable in war than those over whom he is preferred.'[6]

Operations in 1702 and 1703 quickly earned the English general the reputation of a war commander 'who liked to fight'[7] and who 'lives for occasions to acquire glory,'[8] as opposed to the prudence and reserve of the States General. Still, the French saw nothing to suggest that Marlborough could decisively turn army fortunes in the Allies' favour. Louis XIV's subjects believed their troops unshakeable. We mustn't forget that nobody at the beginning of the eighteenth century, even among the Sun King's oldest officers, could remember seeing a French army routed. The last true defeats dated back to the war against Spain, which had ended in 1659. Despite a few notable setbacks (like the loss of Namur to William III, in 1695), the French seventeenth century, or Grand Siècle, was dominated by French victories, from the battle of Rocroi, which began the reign of Louis XIV, to the sometimes ineffective but always grand battles of the Nine Years' War (or War of the League of Augsburg).

This presumption among French soldiers is apparent in the memoirs of Marquis de Chamlay – a French officer who at court acted as a sort of chief of military staff to Louis XIV, preparing maps and proposing campaign plans.[9] On 17 August 1704, with a battle in Bavaria looking more and more likely, Chamlay was reassuring. The united forces of Marshals Tallard and Marsin would be 'more or less invincible.'[10]

> *'Let us hope that lord Marleboroughͭ [sic] [shall confirm] that the Germans have retained their custom of letting themselves be beaten by the French... It would be a novelty to see an enemy army get the better of ours.'* [11]

That 'novelty' had in fact been witnessed four days earlier, on the battlefield of Blenheim, but news of it spread only a few days later. The first reports arrived in Versailles on 20 August, but they were still unclear and contradictory, for two reasons. First, the battlefield lay at a considerable distance. Mail from the French army had to travel nearly seven hundred kilometres, over the rugged terrain of the Black Forest. Next, the French could hardly accept the news of so resounding a defeat. At first, some even believed that it was the Imperial army, led by the Prince of Baden, that had been beaten.[12] As new, more detailed information arrived, fear and disbelief seized the court:

'Rumors unclear and unreliable abounded, as, for example, that eleven battalions had been cut to pieces on the battlefield, in addition to the twenty-six that had been taken prisoner whole; that the cavalry and gendarmerie, the King's elite troops, had yielded, putting up no resistance... It all seemed incredible.' [13]

But Louis XIV remained stoic. He did not want news of the defeat to stop court ceremonials. The celebration scheduled for the birth of his great-grandson, for the triumph of the Seine and the Tagus over the Thames and the Danube, was to go on as planned.[14]

Despite the gravity of the defeat, the King seems to have considered Blenheim an incomprehensible anomaly, one that cast no doubt on the French army's superiority. Two weeks before the battle of Ramillies, then, Louis XIV could still write to the Duke of Villeroi: 'My troops, when more or less equal in numbers [with the enemy], have lost no [battles] during my reign.'[15] Events in Bavaria – a theatre of operations where the French lacked experience – were neglected, while the good results of the campaign of 1705 seemed to show that they were a mere digression.

That is why some in France could still at this date deny the military ability of the Duke of Marlborough. 'He is an adventurer mortified by the scant success of his campaign, and who now seeks only to risk everything,'[16] wrote Villeroi after the English general's lacklustre performance in Flanders in 1705. His thirst for combat was attributed to vanity and a desire to please. Michel Chamillart, Secretary of State for War, supported the marshal's opinion:

'You shall have no trouble getting me to say that I have but a mediocre opinion of the Duke of Marlborough's abilities. In my view, what he did during this campaign has destroyed the great opinion generally held of him after the battle of Höchstädt, where the victory should be attributed to pure chance, rather than to the ability of the enemy generals. It is true that they were able to take advantage of our faulty deployment of troops.' [17]

During the same period the King of Spain, Philip V, could write to his grandfather, Louis XIV: 'My lord Marlborough is but a braggart, and we can only hope that his bragging will soon come to an end.'[18]

Not until the victory at Ramillies did the Duke of Marlborough acquire the status of a great general in the hearts and minds of the French. News of the battle of 23 May 1706 plunged the court into a state of stupefaction, much as the defeat two years earlier had. 'I was at Versailles. Never had there been such anxiety, such consternation,'[19] wrote Saint-Simon. Marquis de Sourches, meanwhile, wrote of a 'dreadful bit of news.'[20] The Princess Palatine too evoked the atmosphere at Versailles after the announcement: 'We have a pressing need for consolation, for I have never seen such misfortune in the thirty-five years that I have been in France. Not a day goes by that we do not hear some new piece of bad news.'[21]

From 1706 onwards the captain-general managed to undermine the morale of the French soldiers and officers, and thus their offensive capacity. In the wake of Ramillies the French army found itself in a state of psychological dejection, which in large part explains their inability to defend Brabant and Flanders. The Duke of Vendôme painted an edifying picture on his arrival in the Low Countries:

'I shall do my best to raise morale [among the troops], but it will be no small undertaking. If, that is, I can carry it out, for everybody here is ready to doff his hat on hearing the name of Malboroug [sic] *[…]. Still, I have not lost all hope that I can bring them around by delivering some good speeches and setting some good examples, and I can assure you that I shall leave no stone unturned. To be frank, however, the task is even more difficult than I had imagined.'* [22]

Louis-Claude-Hector, Duc de Villars, Marshal of France (1653-1734).

Painting by Hyacinthe Rigaud, 1714.
Palais de l'Institut, Paris, France.

Consternation in the military and at court was matched by a true fascination with the victorious general. Several captured officers endeavoured to meet the Duke of Marlborough. Certain Frenchmen even sought pretexts to visit the allied army. Paparel, a banker meeting Vendôme's army in Flanders on business in September 1706, requested Vendôme's permission to cross over to the enemy camp, 'to see the famous general.'[23] Marlborough's victories dominated every discussion. Everyone had a point of view and an explanation to offer. The Princess Palatine went as far as to say that 'those who believe in witchcraft will think that [Marlborough] made a pact with the devil to enjoy such unprecedented good fortune.'[24]

The Duke of Vendôme was very popular in the French army. His arrival brought some comfort to the troops in Flanders, and their disappointment and consternation were all the greater after their defeat at Oudenaarde. The army's physical trials might have been less this time than after Blenheim and Ramillies, but morale nevertheless reached new lows. The correspondents of the Secretary of State for War described 'dejected' soldiers,[25] now appearing to lack all discipline and composure.[26] Come September even Vendôme had to admit that distress among his soldiers was such that he could no longer vouch for them.[27] The court, now accustomed to disasters, could no longer muster surprise at the news. The first reports that it received of the battle of Oudenaarde suggested that the French army had been utterly vanquished.[28] This was in fact an exaggeration, for the troops had certainly retreated to safety behind the canal to Bruges in Ghent.

The period from the battle of Ramillies to the fall of Lille was marked by a serious crisis of confidence in France's military leaders. Songs and other satirical works flourished, evoking the humiliating defeats with ferocious humour. If the Duke of Marlborough or Prince Eugene made an appearance, the reason was not so much to acknowledge their talents, as to mock the failings and failures of the French generals. Satire, it's true, denigrates better than it glorifies. The figure of Marlborough serves essentially to ridicule the false bravura of Villeroi[29] or the inappropriate piety of the Duke of Burgundy.[30] It thus masks a criticism of the regime, by denouncing the roles of military men and courtiers. The songs showed no respect even for the royal family. The sacred person of the Duke of Burgundy, grandson to the King and heir to the crown, was dragged through the mud.[31] Finally, certain texts continued to question the English general's talent, insisting instead on the shortcomings of his adversaries:

'Marlborough, you owe not to yourself
Your double victory
It is to Tallard, to Villeroy
That all your glory belongs.
You owe a general compliment
To the one and the other general.' [32]

C.L.H. M[l]. DUC DE VILLARS. 1714.

Almansa, in 1707. Finally, after Vendôme's fall into disgrace, Marlborough faced Marshal Villars, whose victories in Bavaria, on the Rhine, in the Cévennes, and in the Dauphiné had more than demonstrated his talents. His second-in-command at the battle of Malplaquet, Marshal Boufflers, was throughout his career a valorous warrior. He was named Marshal of France in 1693, emerged victorious at Ekeren, and heroically defended Namur in 1695 and Lille in 1708.

The extent of the captain general's success cannot be explained by the mere ineptitude of his enemies. Should we thus attribute it to some new style of combat, based squarely on attack? Marlborough's taste for offence shows up first in his tactics. In three of his principal victories it was the Allied troops who marched out to confront the entrenched French, whereas the battle of Oudenaarde represents an encounter between moving troops, Allied and French. This choice allowed him to decide where the brunt of the battle would take place. At Ramillies, for example, he was thus able to dispatch a maximum of troops to his own left, practically withdrawing his right wing. Villeroi seems not to have noticed the deployment – despite warnings from several subordinates – and let his troops deploy evenly throughout the battlefield. The criticisms that rained down on Villeroi after the battle harped on that mistake and ridiculed French generals whose 'savoir-faire is exhausted once [the army] is ranged for battle in two lines.'[46] The generals of Louis XIV nevertheless quickly noted the danger of letting Marlborough decide how a battle would unfold tactically. At Oudenaarde Vendôme tried to make amends by taking the offensive (but the Duke of Burgundy prevented part of his forces from engaging in combat), and at Malplaquet Villars built up a strong reserve, so as to be able to send in forces wherever the captain-general applied his pressure.

Marlborough's taste for attack also showed in his strategy. Though active at a time dominated by wars of position and punctuated by sieges and lumbering army manoeuvres, the captain-general loved battles.[47] At first, his audacity unquestionably surprised the French generals. On the eve of the battle of Blenheim most French officers were convinced that the Allies would never dare cross the Nebel right in front of them.[48] Also, in 1706 Louis XIV did not believe that the Allies would wish to attack his army on open ground.[49] Here again we see that the warnings of Blenheim had gone unheeded.

Still, can we consider that Marlborough had a totally new vision of combat – of combat as an instrument for the destruction of the opposing army – and that the generals of Louis XIV saw it as a mere symbolic advantage, useful at best for conducting sieges? In truth, the French too believed in following up battle with pursuit of the enemy. Of course, that meant actually being able to pursue him! Marshal Luxembourg was severely criticized after his victory at Neerwinden, precisely for his inability to capitalize on the victory.[50] The Duke of Vendôme, meanwhile, vaunted himself for having chased down the enemy for three days after the battle of Calcinato in 1706.[51]

Incidentally, we mustn't carry too far this opposition between a Marlborough hungry for battle and overly prudent Frenchmen eager to avoid it. In 1706, it was Villeroi who engaged the English general, who then hastened to accept the challenge. That same year the Duke of Orléans wanted to withdraw lines protecting the siege of Turin to meet Prince Eugene's army in open country.[52] His proposal, though rejected by a council of war held on the spot, was later approved by Versailles. Sometimes Louis XIV himself was the one calling for battle. It was on one such occasion, in 1701, that he replaced the overly prudent Marshal Catinat with Villeroi, who had promised to engage Prince Eugene rapidly – with well-known results.

Having at last learned that it was best not to offer him battle too early, the French generals tried to turn Marlborough's taste for combat against him. In 1708 Prince Eugene found himself in command of an army on the Moselle, with orders to act in concert with Marlborough's troops, and draw the French troops into a great battle.[53] On learning of Eugene's arrival in the Spanish Low Countries, the Duke of Vendôme set up a plan to counter that possibility, proudly proclaiming to Louis XIV: 'I am convinced that they will join together; and if their plan is to have another Hocstet, they just might have miscalculated. I say to you that we shall beat them.'[54] During the first part of the campaign (up to the taking of Bruges and Ghent) Vendôme deliberately adopted a slow strategy, in which he restricted all of the Allied army's movements, knowing that Marlborough didn't much like those 'kinds of wars.'[55] The campaigns of Villars in the Spanish Low Countries, imposed, it's true, by France's defensive attitude, had no other purpose. They were to reduce to a minimum the activities of a general who loved battle – and had a political need to win.

Indeed, it was perhaps his political status, and his independence in commanding his troops, that best distinguished Marlborough from the French commanders. It is often said in keeping with Saint-Simon, that the generals of Louis XIV paid the price for a 'stratégie de cabinet,' in which the operations of the French armies were controlled directly from the court by the King and the Secretary of State for War.[56] The generals at the head of the armies, it is claimed, had but little room to manoeuvre. Their autonomy was limited to logistical matters, with all big decisions requiring royal approval. Finding themselves, in the words of Saint-Simon, 'swaddled,' they were thus incapable of reacting quickly to enemy manoeuvres.[57] This view has recently been called into question by numerous works, which have endeavoured either to describe the activity of a French political or military leader (Marshal Luxembourg, Chamillart, Chamlay[58]) or to study a particular war (the Nine Years' War, the War of Spanish Succession[59]). They show that the Sun King, though demanding to be informed of every operation, no matter how small, was aware that his generals needed great autonomy, especially in emergencies. He did not hesitate to send very detailed instructions to his army chiefs, but he often specified that they were to be taken as advice and adapted to the circumstances.

The strategic blockage of the French generals – and a blockage it was indeed, with the French often showing themselves incapable of countering Marlborough's determined movements effectively – manifested itself at another level: at the head of armies in mid-campaign, between various generals of equal rank. It was a frequent problem at the end of Louis XIV's reign. The armies were too big for a single man to command. To harness their military superiority, the French had to combine armies.[60] And so Marshal Tallard had to cooperate with Marsin in 1704, and Vendôme with Berwick in 1708. Adding yet another layer of complexity to the military needs were political considerations. In 1704 and 1706 the French generals had to cooperate with Maximilian II Emanuel, Elector of Bavaria in 1704 and governor of the Spanish Low Countries in 1706. In 1708 Vendôme had to cooperate with Burgundy, so as not to injure the military prestige of the French king's grandson. The problem was that most of the time Louis XIV refused to grant supreme authority to a single man, believing instead that the various commanders should arrange matters between themselves. When the first conflict arose, then, everybody wanted the King to play referee –

Kettledrums of the Gardes du corps du Roy.

Print / watercolour by Jacques-Antoine Delaistre, from Infanterie et Gardes françaises, vol. III, 1721.
The Army Museum, Paris, France.
© Paris - Musée de l'Armée,
Dist. RMN/Image musée de l'Armée

hence the appearance of the *stratégie de cabinet*, to the great dismay of Louis XIV. At the heart of almost every French defeat we find a problem of coordination between war chiefs: debate between Villeroi, Tallard, and Marsin before the departure of French troops for Bavaria, in June 1704; disagreement between Tallard and Marsin in the days before the battle of Blenheim, leading to the fateful decision not to join the armies; discord before the battle of Turin between, on the one hand, the Duke of Orléans and, on the other, Marsin and the Duke de La Feuillade; conflict between Vendôme and Burgundy at Oudenaarde and between Vendôme, Burgundy, and Berwick during the siege of Lille. At Ramillies, however, Villeroi was sufficiently incompetent to be beaten without that problem. After the disastrous campaign of 1708 Louis XIV decided at last to grant full command of his principal army to one man, Villars.

Marlborough undoubtedly suffered far more than his French adversaries from the difficulties of multiple commands. He led an army born of an unquestionably more mismatched alliance than that of France, Spain, and Bavaria. He was thus constantly forced to settle disputes between the commanders of troops from the Dutch Republic, Prussia, and even the Palatinate – this in addition to handling the often strained relations with the delegates of the States General and the effects of political dissent in

Officers and flags of the French Guards.

Print / watercolour by Jacques-Antoine Delaistre, from Infanterie et Gardes françaises, vol. I, 1721.
The Army Museum, Paris, France.

England. Despite all such handicaps, however, Marlborough's authority over his army often outstripped that of the French commanders over French armies. Whether repelling them with his military aura or dissuading them as a skilful negotiator, Marlborough often managed to neutralize those who sought to undermine his authority. Hence, Marlborough was successful in 1704 when he rid himself of the Prince of Baden by offering him the siege of Ingolstadt. Marlborough achieved his greatest successes while commanding his army alone, or while accompanied only by Prince Eugene, with whom he maintained perfectly cordial relations.

In comparison with his adversaries, then, Marlborough appears neither as a second-rate general facing blunderers nor a general whose radically new military ideas upended all the tactics and strategies of the French. Aside from his unquestionable talents as a warrior, what made Marlborough a fearsome enemy, with far greater freedom of action than his French counterparts, was his ability to inhabit several roles that reinforced one another: namely, those of war chief, politician, and diplomat. But the very interdependence that served him so well during the war would also be his downfall. The collapse of his political allies in England brought about the withdrawal of his military command, despite his exceptional record. As for the generals of Louis XIV, all they needed to hold on to their posts was to keep the sovereign's confidence.[61]

Marlborough: Man of War, Man of Peace?

The multiplicity of the Duke of Marlborough's duties made him a key figure in eventual diplomatic negotiations, as the French were quick to grasp. Aware that the captain general could favour or block any attempt to cease hostilities, they often tried to approach him and win him over to the cause of peace.

It should be noted that in its first years Louis XIV had wanted to put an end to the war. He had never wanted it in the first place. He was behind the first diplomatic approaches to the Allies, in 1705. The first to be approached for negotiation were the Dutch, deemed the least interested party in pursuing what for them was a costly war. France nevertheless remained prudent. The time for official negotiations had not yet come, and discussions were kept discreet, so as to plumb opinion and determine the demands of each combatant. It was thus not possible to use official ambassadors, and French diplomacy resorted to parallel agents, whose professions gave them occasion to meet various heads of the Alliance. In 1705 the role belonged to Marquis d'Alègre, a French officer taken prisoner during the battle of Elixheim on 18 July 1705.[62] He was empowered by Marquis de Torcy, Secretary of State for Foreign Affairs, to discuss with the Dutch various diplomatic solutions, all based on a partition of the Spanish empire, and including in particular the neutralization of the Low Countries, compensations for the Archduke, and commercial advantages for maritime powers.[63]

The first task assigned him was to meet with Marlborough, so as to bring the English in on the informal negotiations. To win him over, the French officer, after some customary talk of the benefits of peace, was to deplore the mistrustful, even hostile, attitude of the States General towards the English general. Insisting on the natural solidarity between military commanders faced with civilian power, d'Alègre was to go as far as criticizing the Dutch for their refusal to take any risks and their desire to force Marlborough to 'make war by their method' – that is, without recourse to battle![64] Finally, d'Alègre was authorized to offer the Englishman, in the name of the King, the sum of two million livres. His instruction insisted that it was 'the only way to win [Marlborough] over' but nevertheless prudently recommended that d'Alègre not make the offer unless the captain-general seemed disposed to accept.[65] The venality with which the French credited the Duke of Marlborough had formerly seemed an obstacle, since the Duke stood to gain financially from the war, but now it could serve as an argument for peace.

The Marquis did indeed meet with Marlborough, in the Allied camp, in November 1705. He also managed to reach Holland, where he met with various politicians, notably Heinsius and the Pensionary of Amsterdam, Buys. Negotiations soon reached an impasse, though they dragged on into April 1706. In fact, the Allies were dissatisfied with Louis XIV's concessions and preferred to await the outcome of their military operations. Though all professed their desire for peace, the Marquis d'Alègre's successive interlocutors refused every advance. Each maintained that he was unable to decide without the consent of the other parties. Thus the Dutch declared themselves unwilling to agree to anything without Marlborough, whose demands were supposed to be greater than theirs. Marlborough himself, meeting again with d'Alègre in December 1705, declared that he could decide nothing without the consent of Queen Anne and of the States-General.[66]

Though the work of the Marquis d'Alègre bore no fruit, other talks were undertaken in the course of 1706. There were no less than four negotiations carried on in

Standard of the company of household troops belonging to the Duke of Harcourt.

Print / watercolour by Jacques-Antoine Delaistre, from Infanterie et Gardes françaises, vol. III, 1721.
The Army Museum, Paris, France.
© Paris - Musée de l'Armée, Dist. RMN / image musée de l'Armée

parallel, often without previous consultation. If for the first three Versailles and a few Dutch politicians had taken the initiative, the last was launched by Elector Maximilian II Emanuel of Bavaria – and once again Marlborough played a starring role. The Elector's position in the summer of 1706 was especially precarious. The battle of Blenheim had lost him his hereditary states. The battle of Ramillies, meanwhile, had just cost him his authority over most of the Spanish Low Countries, where he had been governor in the name of Philip V.[67] His political clout seemed as likely to evaporate as the Spanish regiments theoretically under his command. He thus took the initiative to compensate for his military setbacks through an intense campaign of diplomacy. From June to August he sent emissaries to the kings of Prussia, Sweden, and

Spain.[68] At the same time he opened channels to Ouwerkerk, and especially to the Duke of Marlborough. The Elector's first proposals for the captain-general were relatively limited. He would agree to deliver Luxembourg, Namur, Charleroi, and Nieuwpoort in exchange for guarantees of his titles and territories. Discussions quickly took on greater importance. The agent handling transmissions between Marlborough and Max-Emanuel, President Antoine Sersanders, a Flemish magistrate, soon assured the French that the Duke of Marlborough himself was offering to work for peace, through this new line of negotiations. Thus informed, Louis XIV encouraged the Elector to pursue that line.[69] Once again, so as to smooth the negotiations, Louis XIV permitted the Elector to offer the Duke of Marlborough the two million livres brought up by Marquis d'Alègre.

But this line of negotiations fared no better than the previous three. The Duke of Marlborough had no intention of carrying on secret diplomacy – always keeping the Allies informed of the dealings – and his chief objective was probably to pry the Elector away from the French alliance, gleaning a few fortified positions in the process.[70] But Chamillart, Secretary of State for War, accused Marlborough of encouraging the negotiations, which were under his complete control, so as to focus French attention on them and more effectively obstruct the other peace talks underway.[71]

The failure of this episode did not stop Marlborough from opening similar negotiations, in 1708, with Marshal Berwick. Relations between uncle and nephew had remained friendly and solid throughout the war. We might attribute this to family ties or, as Arsène Legrelle believes, to Marlborough's desire to maintain relations with representatives of the court of Saint-Germain – i.e., with the court of the Pretender in exile.[72] Still, it was because of his special relationship with Berwick that the Duke of Marlborough tried to open a new line of negotiations, in August. The two were geographically close at the time, each observing from his own camp the events of the siege of Lille. The exchange between opposing commanders of missives necessary for the armies' daily operations could hide correspondence on a more important subject. The first proposals that the English general sent to his nephew contained no truly novel idea. Indeed, Marlborough suggested only that the French make offers to the Dutch, which he could then support once he had received them. These proposals, which Berwick forwarded immediately to the court, were received with great caution. September saw a sporadic exchange of letters, to no real effect.[73] Already burned by negotiations with the Elector, Chamillart feared above all that the English general was only playing for time.

Matters took a different turn after 30 October. A new letter from Marlborough introduced the idea of a truce in the Spanish Low Countries – though the citadel of Lille had not yet fallen. The Duke of Burgundy would thus be able to transmit peace proposals to the Dutch delegates accompanying the army, to Prince Eugene, and to Marlborough himself. These would necessarily be passed on to their respective governments – i.e., to the three major members of the Alliance.[74] This dazzling manoeuvre would thus prove to all of Europe that peace was possible. To end his letter, Marlborough expressed the hope of enjoying 'the friendship... promised two years ago by the Marquis d'Alègre'[75]: i.e., the two million livres.

Torcy and his agents were fairly enthusiastic. Chamillart was much less so, yet it was he who was charged with drafting a reply for Berwick to transmit to Marlborough. In Chamillart's view, no truce was conceivable unless the French first accepted the Allies' publicly stated 'preliminaries,' which included French renunciation of the

Standard of the French Queen's Dragoons.

Print / watercolour by Jacques-Antoine Delaistre, from Infanterie et Gardes françaises, vol. V, 1721.
The Army Museum, Paris, France.

Spanish crown. By renouncing it right away, however, the French would no longer be able to renounce it as a concession, and thus could bargain for nothing in exchange. Chamillart therefore demanded that new secret discussions be held, on a basis more favourable to France, before any truce.

The Duke of Marlborough found the reply quite irritating, and negotiations got bogged down once again, continuing all winter but producing nothing new. In March 1709 Torcy decided to break them off in favour of another, more promising channel for discussions, once again going right through Holland. Exchanges between Berwick and Marlborough came to a definitive end with the latter's departure for London, in April.[76]

In his memoirs[77] the Duke of Berwick expresses his certainty that these negotiations could truly have borne fruit. It is difficult today to form a definite opinion on the matter. Was Marlborough sincerely in favour of peace, did he fear the English public's lassitude over the war, or was he simply sounding out French opinion? What is certain is that Marquis Torcy truly believed in the possibilities offered up by the captain-general's proposals, and that Chamillart's distrust largely explained the failure of the discussions. In this way, the episode represents yet another skirmish in the long struggle between the two ministers, both of whom sought control over decisive negotiations.

In Torcy's view, the negotiations could continue through other channels. He had sent Grand Conseil President Rouillé, an experienced negotiator, to Holland, to hammer out terms similar to those proposed with Marlborough. In the minister's optimistic reports, Marlborough still seemed an ally for peace:

> *'The Duke of Marlborough will not hamper the negotiations, whatever particular interest he seemed to have in continuing the war. There can be almost no doubt that he now wants peace, perhaps because his enemies in England are increasing in number and he fears that some turn in his fortunes will give them the means to overwhelm him, or perhaps because he is jealous of the reputation that Prince Eugene of Savoy has earned for himself at his expense, or perhaps because he is disgusted by the defiance of the Dutch towards him and their persistent opposition to his becoming governor of the Low Countries, a post that the Archduke has tried several times to give him. In any case, whatever new reason he might have, we should believe that he wants peace. Over the past several months he has taken several eager steps to make it known.'* [78]

Unfortunately, Dutch demands went well beyond what Rouillé had been authorized to offer in the name of the King. It was Torcy himself who would have to leave for Holland, and there he went in May 1709. Marlborough joined him on 18 May. Torcy sincerely hoped that the Duke's arrival at the negotiating table would help moderate Allied demands. This time Louis XIV had planned to offer him three to four million.[79] The Minister was grievously disappointed. Marlborough could not – or, if Torcy's memoirs are to be believed, would not – play the role of intermediary. Instead, he allowed, or encouraged, Prince Eugene to present new demands, such as the cession of all of Alsace, and the talks ran aground.[80]

It was a decisive episode, cementing Marlborough's image for the French as a warmonger. In his memoirs Marshal Villars considers him, along with Eugene, as wholly responsible for the end of negotiations, because it was his exaggerated assurances, his promises to 'seek battle at any price' and to 'penetrate the kingdom,' that had persuaded the Dutch not to shilly-shally.[81] Hostility towards Marlborough is evident also in the instructions sent by Torcy in 1710 to the two new French negotiators.[82] They describe Marlborough in particularly harsh terms. He is portrayed as a liar and a manipulator, talking peace, pretending that he is only obeying his own government, while inciting the States General to war, 'because it is in his interests.'[83] The French envoys are warned to believe him no further:

> *'He will assure the plenipotentiaries of his zeal to serve the King. They should respond honestly to his claims to be frank and show good faith. But... His Majesty is absolutely convinced that Marshal Uxelles and Abbot Polignac will not also be fooled.'*[84]

The French could indulge in such severe criticism because in March 1710 Marlborough no longer appeared as the key to all negotiations. First of all, he had lost his credibility, 'his speeches fool no one in England, no more so than in Holland'[85]. That the Allies had gotten bogged down militarily, as shown by the mitigated success of Malplaquet, helps explain the disillusionment. Moreover, despite his still considerable political weight, Marlborough was no longer truly able to influence the hawks or doves in his country, or even to modify the clauses of an eventual peace treaty.[86] The Tories' victory in Parliament a few months later would only confirm his decline. For the first time, as a result, Louis XIV and his Secretary of State for Foreign Affairs planned to offer the Duke no reward.

The Duke of Marlborough's image would not improve later. French diplomatic and military leaders delighted in his political decline. In 1711 Villars attributed progress in peace to the death of Joseph I – who left as his sole heir Archduke Charles, pretender to the Spanish crown – and to 'a few clouds forming in England over the fortunes of lord Marlborough.'[87] Marshal Noailles, meanwhile, delighted in seeing Queen Anne turn away from a general whose 'murderous ambition... sacrificed the people to his own interests.'[88]

At the time there was no strict separation between matters of war and matters of peace. The generals leading the armies were also the diplomats discussing the treaties, whether before the war (as with Tallard in London during talks for the partition treaties), after the war (as with Villars and Eugene in 1714, setting terms for the Treaty of Rastatt), or during the war (as with Boufflers and the future Lord Portland during the Nine Years' War[89] or the Elector, Berwick, and Marlborough during the War of Spanish Succession). For this reason the French, in taking the first steps towards peace, could hope that the captain-general would prove a valuable ally. His courtesy towards his French prisoners,[90] as well as the concern he might have had for the Pretender,[91] showed that he had no preconceived aversion to France. He had a reputation for enriching himself off the war, certainly, but the French hoped to persuade him to accept the idea of peace in exchange for millions. The disillusionment was only bigger in 1709, when it was revealed that he held a hard line against the kingdom of Louis XIV. He was thenceforth saddled with the black reputation of a greedy warmonger, which helped paint the unflattering picture of him that would endure in French posterity.

■ Marlborough and Posterity in France

France lost interest in the Duke of Marlborough rather quickly after his disgrace. On his death, in 1722, the reign of Louis XIV already seemed far in the past, so deep were the ruptures brought about by the regency of the Duke of Orléans. Saint-Simon himself, who in his *Memoirs* dwells at length on the campaigns of the War of Spanish Succession, saw fit to write Marlborough an epitaph of just two paragraphs, underscoring the extraordinary career of a man 'of the minor nobility and quite poor' who rose to become 'an English peer, captain-general of the armies, ...prince of the Empire and Mindelheim.' For the rest, thought Saint-Simon, 'his life and acts are so well known that one may pass on in silence.'[92]

He nevertheless permits himself a judgment on Marlborough's military qualities, calling him the 'most fortunate captain of his century.'[93] But it is a half-hearted tribute. The luckiest he might have been, but not necessarily the most talented. In fact, if we exclude Voltaire, who frankly admired him,[94] most eighteenth-century French historians interested in the period of the War of Spanish Succession preferred to see Marlborough as a general more deft than brilliant.

Even French military thinkers of the eighteenth century – a century rich in strategic thought – hardly paid him any attention. They preferred examples from antiquity, of course, but when they did mention generals contemporary with Louis XIV they cited names like Condé, Turenne, Luxembourg, Prince Eugene, and even Vendôme and Villars – but not Marlborough.[95] Napoleon too neglects him. In speaking of the need to delve into the campaigns of great generals, so as to learn the art of war, he cites only Gustavus-Adolphus, Turenne, Prince Eugene, and Frederick of Prussia as examples for modern times.[96]

Still, even if he did not put him in the same rank as those four, Bonaparte seems to have held Marlborough in high esteem. *Mémorial de Saint-Hélène*, the diary kept by Count de Las Cases during his stay with the deposed Emperor, contains several of Napoleon's thoughts on the English general. Napoleon calls him a 'great general,'[97] but what he finds truly remarkable about Marlborough is his sagacity and his ability to be both 'captain and diplomat.'[98] For Bonaparte, talk of the English soldier was above all a chance to criticize Wellington, whom he considered a man 'of no foresight, no generosity, no faith,' in every way unworthy of comparison with his illustrious predecessor.[99]

Moreover, it was under the Empire that was published the sole biography of Marlborough ever to appear in France – except, of course, for translations of works from English. It is very favourable to the man it describes and is the work of an abbot, Du Tems. Writing at a time when England was widely detested, the author went to some trouble to justify his work. His very first sentence assures the reader that there is no question of admiring the United Kingdom, for 'every great man belongs to all peoples and to all centuries,'[100] and Marlborough 'boasted of belonging by his origins to the French nation[101] – or so pretends the Abbot. His purpose, he continues, is essentially pedagogical:

> *'Though they have no need to look beyond their borders to find great masters in the art of victory, the French would not object to learning the art of war from Marlborough…, those who seek a career in negotiation shall also find in him a great master, for he was as great a statesman as he was a captain.'* [102]

The bold parallel with Napoleon can be rather surprising, yet it was Bonaparte himself who ordered the *Imprimerie Impériale* (the imperial print shop) to publish the work.

Despite this exceptional backing, exaltation of Marlborough seems not to have been well received in France. The *Moniteur*, a periodical that essentially functioned as the 'official journal' of the Empire, was extremely harsh in its criticism of Du Tems's biography.[103] It took up the traditional accusations of cupidity and criminal ambition and refused to consider Marlborough a great general, because he had faced only blunderers.[104]

Most nineteenth-century authors were hardly kind to Marlborough. A very complete study of the War of Spanish Succession, published in 1830, purports that he 'had no genius for war'![105] The century's great dictionaries insist on the villainy of a man who owed his career entirely to his relations with women (whether his sister or his wife) and to his many acts of treachery. The French refused to forgive his abandonment of James II, in 1688. And thus in 1873 the *Grand dictionnaire universel* of Larousse painted an exceedingly cruel portrait:

'Born into an obscure family, and setting out under humble circumstances, he attained the highest positions through shrewdness. His rise was due to more than military talent, with low intrigues and treachery playing an equal, if not greater, role. Marlborough is the exemplar of the ambitious man, of the courtier who shrinks not even from infamy, and for whom no dishonour can come of profit.' [106]

Likewise, Michelet, in his famous *Histoire de France* (1877), finds in him 'the sickly pallor and duplicitous air that betrays the base soul.'[107] It goes without saying that Sarah Churchill is treated no better than her husband.

The following century would prove less hostile to the Captain-General. In the 1930s Hilaire Belloc's biography[108] was translated from English. (Should we read into this a renewed interest among the public in the English army, which fought on French soil during the First World War?) The biography written by Winston Churchill, however, went untranslated until 1949 – and by then it was the descendant rather than the forebear that interested the French.

Despite this, and though lacking the nineteenth century's acerbic bite, French historiography in the second half of the twentieth century was hardly free with its praise for Marlborough. The English general was rarely crowned with laurels in the manner of Condé or Turenne. His entry in the *Dictionnaire du Grand Siècle* states that he was not a 'war chief of genius.'[109] Jean-Christian Petitfils's biography of Louis XIV considers that, while he was 'an excellent soldier as well as a fearsome tactician,' Marlborough had neither 'the audacity nor the military genius of Prince Eugene.'[110] And, of course, it does not refrain from insisting on his venality, his taste for intrigue and for war.

Surprisingly, Prince Eugene often gets a wholly different treatment during the same period. From the nineteenth to the twentieth century the 'great Eugene'[111] was considered 'one of the greatest captains of modern times,'[112] a 'prince full of audacity and vigour... a philosopher... a patron.'[113] Prince Eugene was nevertheless no more in favour of peace than Marlborough! The explanation for this state of affairs is perhaps given by Michelet, who considers that this general, 'the youngest son of the house of Savoy, but son of the Count of Soissons and of one of Mazarin's nieces, may be called French.'[114] Should we infer that French historians prefer to have been beaten by an expatriated countryman than by a foreigner?

Perhaps the tarnish on captain-general's military reputation results merely from the unflattering song that caught on throughout France and immortalized him. For a time after the battle of Malplaquet rumour spread through the French army that Marlborough was dead.[115] As a result the song *Malbrough s'en va-t-en guerre* ('Marlborough's off to War') spread within certain regiments. It mockingly describes the general's departure for the front and his wife's wait for the eventual news of his death. The song did not become truly popular until the end of the eighteenth century, when Marie-Antoinette learned it from her children's nurse. During the Revolution the people of Paris seized on the song for its celebration of an aristocrat's death. In 1792 it was sung under Marie-Antoinette's windows, so as to remind her of the death of her brother Leopold II.[116] Napoleon himself hummed it often.[117] Today it is a 'classic' children's song.

Over time, with the fading of the Duke of Marlborough's memory, the song's meaning has in fact changed. Originally intended to ridicule the imprudence of a general seeking to conquer France in a matter of months, the nursery rhyme now

Marlborough s'en va-t-en guerre - 'Marlborough's posterity'.

Print by Pellerin and Co. MuCEM (Museum of European and Mediterranean Civilizations), Paris, France. © RMN. Photograph by Franck Raux.

MALBOROUGH S'E

Malborough s'en va-t-en guerre,
Mironton, mironton, mirontaine
Malborough s'en va-t-en guerre,
Ne sait quand reviendra, ter.

Il reviendra à Pâques,
Mironton, mironton, mirontaine,
Il reviendra à Pâques.
Ou à la Trinité. ter.

La Trinité se passe,
Mironton, mironton, mirontaine,
La Trinité se passe,
Malborough ne revient pas.

Madame à sa tour monte,
Mironton, mironton, mirontaine,
Madame à sa tour monte,
Si haut qu'elle peut monter.

Elle voit venir son page,
Mironton, mironton, mirontaine,
Elle voit venir son page,
De noir tout habillé.

Beau page, ah ! mon beau page,
Mironton, mironton, mirontaine
Beau page, ah ! mon page,
Quelle nouvelle apportez?

Aux nouvelles que j'apporte,
Mironton, mironton, mirontaine,
Aux nouvelles que j'apporte,
Vos beaux yeux vont pleurer.

Quittez vos habits roses,
Mironton, mironton, mirontaine,
Quittez vos habits roses.
Et vos satins brochés.

Monsieur Malborough est mort,
Mironton, mironton, mirontaine,
Monsieur Malborough est mort,
Est mort et enterré.

J'l'ai vu porter en terre,
Mironton, mironton, mirontaine,
J'l'ai vu porter en terre,
Par quatre officiers.

L'un portait sa cuirasse,
Mironton, mironton, mirontaine,

Propriété des Éditeurs. (Déposé.)

A-T-EN GUERRE.
92
L'un portait sa cuirasse,
L'autre son bouclier.
L'un portait son grand sabre,
Mironton, mironton, mirontaine,
L'un portait son grand sabre,
Et l'autre rien ne porta.
A l'entour de sa tombe,
Mironton, mironton, mirontaine,
A l'entour de sa tombe,
Romarins l'on planta.
Sur la plus haute branche,
Mironton, mironton, mirontaine,
Sur la plus haute branche,
Le Rossignol chanta.
On vit voler son âme,
Mironton, mironton, mirontaine,
On vit voler son âme,
Au travers des lauriers.
Chacun mit ventre à terre,
Mironton, mironton, mirontaine,
Chacun mit ventre à terre,
Et puis se releva.
Pour chanter les victoires,
Mironton, mironton, mirontaine,
Pour chanter les victoires,
Que Malborough remporta.
La cérémonie faite,
Mironton, mironton, mirontaine,
La cérémonie faite,
Chacun s'en fut coucher.
Les uns avec leurs femmes,
Mironton, mironton, mirontaine,
Les uns avec leurs femmes,
Et les autres tous seuls.
Ce n'est pas qu'il en manque,
Mironton, mironton, mirontaine,
Ce n'est pas qu'il en manque,
Car j'en connais beaucoup.
Des blondes et puis des brunes,
Mironton, mironton, mirontaine,
Des blondes et puis des brunes,
Et des châtaines aussi.
Imp. Lith. Pellerin et Cie à Epinal, Fournisseurs Brevetés de S. M. L'Impératrice.

somewhat ironically deplores the misfortunes of war. While the 'Malbrough' of the song is extremely well known in France, nothing of the sort can be said about the historical personage. And while biography and military history have recently come back into style, no monograph on Marlborough has yet appeared. His black legend, and historiography's refusal to acknowledge his exceptional talents, helps explain the fact. The time seems to have come to pay attention to an enemy whom Voltaire called the 'deadliest man for France to arise in centuries.'[118]

CHAPTER 8

'The only thing that could save the Empire'

Marlborough, the States General, and the Imperial States: Diplomacy and Military Strategy in the War of the Spanish Succession and the Great Northern War, 1700-1711

Bernhard R. Kroener

John Churchill, Duke of Marlborough.

Painting by unknown artist – possibly Jan Frans van Douven or Adrian van der Werff, around 1715. Wittelsbacher Ausgleichsfonds, Munich, Germany.

In February 1700, a division of Saxon troops launched an assault on the Swedish positions in Riga; in November 1700, Charles II, the last Habsburg on the Spanish throne, died. These two events happened at a great distance from each other, in southwest and northeast Europe, and, at first sight, do not seem to be connected.[1] Nevertheless, they would cause two military conflicts to develop simultaneously that were to change fundamentally the European tectonics of power. Historical research, nevertheless, normally argues for an explicit separation of the Great Northern War (1700-1721) and the War of the Spanish Succession (1701-1714).[2]

Indeed, considering their origin and the history of how they developed, there is no doubt these are two clearly separate historical events. However, as regards the concomitant different visualisations of threat and the resulting strategic and operational decision-making processes, this diagnosis is not warranted, at least not for the European powers that were situated at the interface of the two conflicts. On the contrary, every change in the political and military power balance in the Baltic Sea area and in the southeast of Europe had an immediate effect on the military strategy of the powers united in the Grand Alliance.

Visualisations of Threat

The skirmishes in the Baltic Sea area directly affected the strategic interests of the Maritime Powers, Great Britain and the Dutch Republic. While in London interest lay in the delivery of urgently needed armaments to help maintain the fleet – especially timber, pig iron, tar and hemp – what was traditionally also of vital importance for the Dutch Republic was the Baltic Sea trade as it supplied the population with basic food, grain and fish.[3] For the North German courts, especially Hanover and Brandenburg, which still vividly remembered the horrors of the Thirty Years' War waged only fifty years earlier, the prominent issues lay not only in their mutual rivalry but also in the different political ways they viewed matters of security and national defence. Denmark and Saxony-Poland, by contrast, were only occasionally involved in both conflicts. The Hofburg Imperial Palace feared that, in view of the

Max Emanuel II (1662-1726), Elector of Bavaria.

Joseph Vivien, Bavarian National Painting Collection, Munich, Germany.

initially decided to join the Maritime Powers because of financial considerations.[12] The Elector of Saxony and King of Poland was engaged in the Northern War. The clerical Electors of Trier[13] and Mainz[14] opted to join the powers making up the Grand Alliance, in view of the promises of assistance that had been made and the prospect of financial support. Electoral Palatinate, ruled by the Emperor's brother-in-law, held a firm position in the anti-French alliance.[15]

As members of the Imperial Federation, the armed Imperial States were at the same time subjects of their respective Imperial Circles. A union of Imperial States of greater or less importance, the Circles had since the 16th century formed the regional organization for the Imperial defence. Whereas in the 18th century the North German Circles each could no longer muster effectiveness because of the dominance of armed or foreign powers as Imperial States (Denmark, Sweden, Brandenburg-Prussia, England-Hanover, Saxony-Poland), the western and south-western Imperial Circles occasionally gained supra-regional importance as they combined forces in their Circle associations.[16]

Like the smaller and less powerful electors, the armed Imperial States could only successfully throw their foreign political weight about during the conflicts that involved the large powers, if they succeeded in becoming indispensable partners by supplying troops. But even the armed Imperial States were not able to independently recruit and maintain the large number of soldiers necessary to comply with their political requirements.[17] The great powers, like the Dutch Republic, therefore tried to bind the larger Imperial States to themselves, or at least to persuade them into well-disposed neutrality, by contractual warranties of regular payments in return for support.[18]

Recruiting and hiring out contingents meant an increase in revenue for the Imperial Electors and to some extent gave them scope for developing their own foreign policies. However, given the coalition partners' different war goals, the operational mobilization of the separate contingents required the permission of the powers in whose payment the troops were. The subsidy contracts that were concluded under these conditions were based on a tradition that goes back to the late Middle Ages. They improved the security of those territories whose military means did not allow them to pursue their own independent politics of interest, in addition to helping them to develop their own foreign goals. For them, the subsidies formed a natural tool in international relations.[19]

Even contemporaries acknowledged that the subsidy policies did not do much to reinforce the defensibility of the Empire. Instead, they first and foremost served the interests of the large powers and the Armed Imperial States. At the same time, these states sought to enlarge their territorial power base and to increase the size of their permanent armies. The Empire, as a result, tended to develop into a federal union of the more powerful states. Ultimately, this would inevitably lead to the collapse of the Imperial Federation.[20]

As an alternative to this, the less powerful states in the west and the southwest of the Empire developed a military organization based on the articles of association of the Circles, under the leadership of the Elector of Mainz. In defensive terms, it served to protect their territories.[21] Since the 1670s, its members had been united by a commonly felt threat of French annexation. They hoped to recover Alsace and Lorraine from France by going to war and creating a security zone that would permanently protect their territories against French attack.[22]

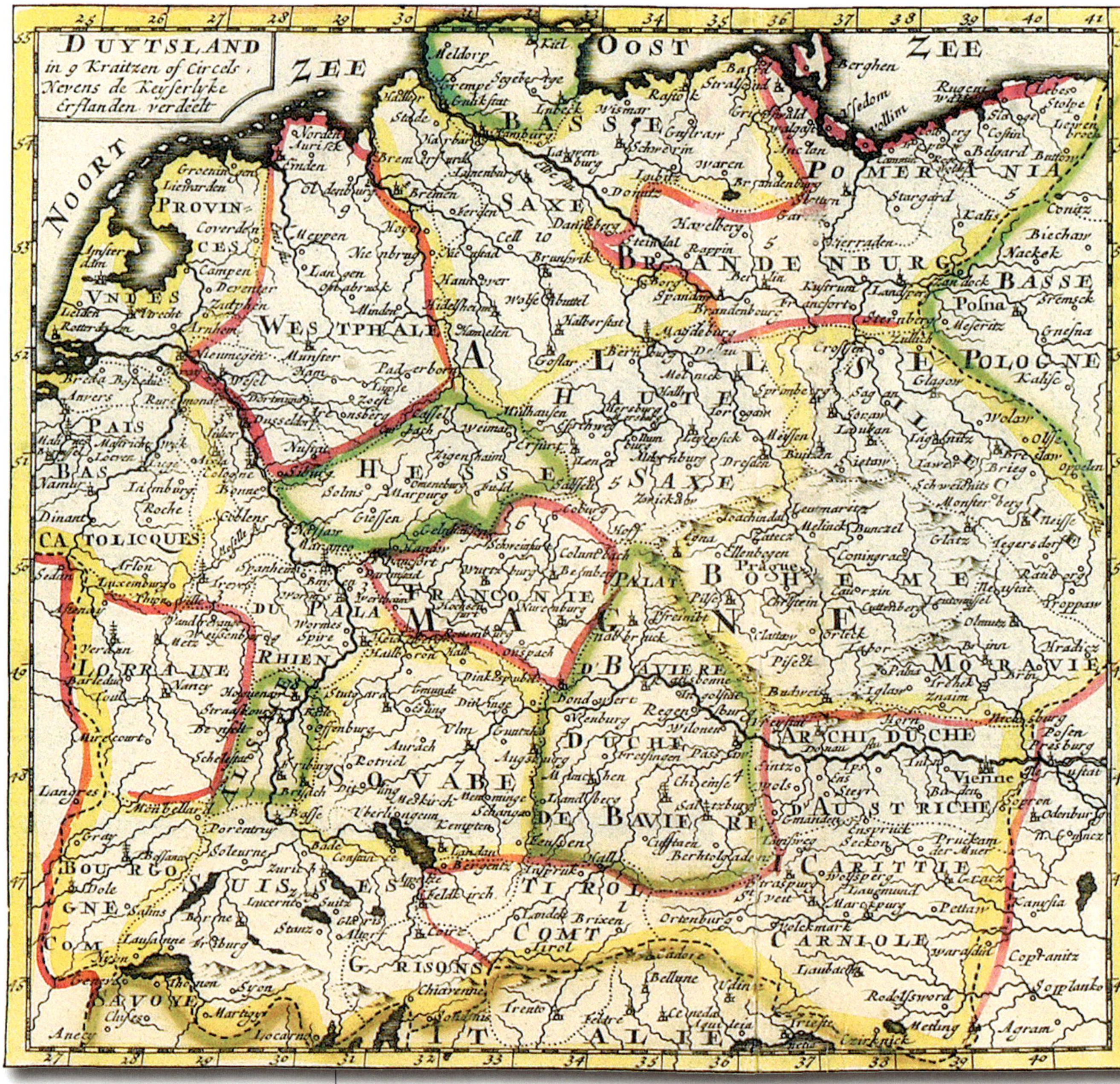

Das Alte Reich und seine Kreiseinteilung. 'A map showing the old German Empire and its territories'.

Hand-coloured engraving by Pieter Schenk, 1706. The Wehrgeschichtliches Museum, Rastatt, Germany.

When one observes their war goals in more detail, it is seen that even the large powers that were united against France and the States General aimed at differing goals, which directly affected the troops they brought into the field. For instance, the Habsburg heir wanted to receive the undivided Spanish inheritance, while the Maritime Powers were only prepared to grant him the outer areas that Spain possessed in Europe, Italy and the southern Netherlands. From the perspective of London, the fate of the Spanish mother country and its overseas properties had to remain uncertain until the peace treaty.[23] In the tradition of William III, the military defeat of France was seen as the prerequisite for a territorial re-organisation on the continent and in the New World.[24]

Besides unrestricted trade with the West Indies, the States General for their part aimed at the limited goal of protecting their territory against France. The restoration

'An imperiled Europe begs for help from Brittannia, who is accompanied by Freedom and Religion'.

Grisaille by Adriaen van der Werff, 1697. The Royal Archive, The Hague, the Netherlands. Reproduced with the permission of Stichting Archief van het Huis Oranje-Nassau.

of the Spanish Netherlands and an adequate, militarily defended barrier were in this respect considered strategic apron protection.[25] A large-scale deployment of Dutch troops to defeat France was therefore not in their interest.

Planning of operations and structures of leadership

In planning the operations of allied armies every partner jealously sought to achieve maximum success with the least possible effort. The States General, for example, were quite willing to demonstrate their military power, but they were not prepared to

A Paris Chez I. Mariette rue St. Iacques aux Colonnes d'Hercules.
Monsieur le Prince Louis de Bade
General des Armées de l'Empire.

expose their army to a pitched battle against the French armies. The demand of the government in The Hague, that the joint commander-in-chief could only deploy the armed forces for the security of the States General, seems plausible from this perspective, but it interfered with achieving a true combination of forces and, thus, with establishing the Alliance's united operational command. The coalition armies operating far away from each other were thus at a disadvantage against the uniform leadership structure of the French army fighting on the inner lines.[26]

If the war goals of the states united in the Grand Alliance of The Hague were heterogeneous, and if, too, the conditions under which they agreed to deploy their troops were extremely varied, the personalities involved in the military command were also very different. On the side of the Emperor, but by no means undisputed in the circle of consultants around the ageing Leopold I, were Prince Eugene of Savoy, who covered the south flank in Italy, while Ludwig Wilhelm Margrave of Baden, the conqueror of the Ottomans, led the contingents of the Imperial army on the Upper Rhine. On the Lower Rhine the supreme command was in the hands of Dutch generals while Brandenburg commanders were occasionally also entrusted with this task.[27]

The unexpected death of William III, who for decades had been the soul of the anti-French opposition, and the accession to the throne of his sister-in-law Anne, aroused fear among the Allied cabinets that Great Britain might back out of its obligations to the continental alliance. The appointment of the Earl of Marlborough, one of the 'best and wisest leaders in this country,' as the Emperor's ambassador in London described him, guaranteed that the Court of St James would remain the engine of the anti-French Alliance.[28]

On his first visit to The Hague in March and April 1702, the States General decided to transfer command over the field troops to Marlborough. Given the imminent threat to the Netherlands and the numerical superiority of their troops, which were twice the number of the English expedition corps during the whole war, it is not surprising that clear restrictions were imposed on the Earl as to his freedom in exercising the supreme command.[29] In the 18th century, supreme command was also subject to other criteria, originating in the structure of the European peerage. Members of governing dynasties claimed the supreme field command by virtue of their birth. In the social perception of their time, corresponding military skills were ascribed to them. At the same time, a different seniority and the political power of the sovereign served could – if both parties held the same rank – lead officers who did not have the necessary leadership qualities to lay claim to the supreme command. Under these circumstances it could sometimes be wise to change the supreme command on a regular basis.[30]

Thus, Marlborough found himself confronted with a great number of challenges. For instance, as the commanders of the strongest contingent at the theatre of war, some Dutch generals initially treated his claim to the leadership with considerable reserve.[31] The increasing number of troops that Great Britain financed over the next years through subsidy contracts with the Allied powers reinforced his political-strategic importance on the Continent. It is against this background that Marlborough gradually gained larger operational freedom and finally succeeded in reinforcing his political claim to the leadership in the war council of the Allied army.[32]

In July 1702, he took over supreme command over the joint Dutch, British and Imperial States' troops that had come together in the Netherlands as the 'Deputy Captain-General of the Republic.'[33] The title he received clearly shows from which

Margrave Ludwig Wilhelm of Baden-Baden (1655-1707), Imperial Field Marshal.

Engraving by the firm of Antoine Trouvaine, around 1700.
The Wehrgeschichtliches Museum, Rastatt, Germany.

Louis-Claude-Hector, Duc de Villars, Marshal of France.

Engraving by Georg Friedrich Schmidt after Hyacinthe Rigaud, 18th century. The Wehrgeschichtliches Museum, Rastatt, Germany.

position and by whose orders he had to act. More than any other contemporary general Marlborough personified the unity of politics and warfare. Although he agreed with Anthony Heinsius, the Grand Pensionary, on fundamental ideas about political aims, he had to accept a war strategy from the cabinet in The Hague that initially imposed severe restrictions on his operational actions.[34] Nevertheless, through clever manoeuvres he succeeded in driving away the French troops from the Lower Rhine and, therefore, from the areas of the Elector of Cologne, who was an ally of France. After the capture of Liège, Louis XIV finally also had to dismantle the Meuse line towards the end of 1702. The not inconsiderable successes of the first campaign year furnished him with the title of Duke of Marlborough. He undoubtedly welcomed this title, as it put him on a social level on a par with his rank of supreme commander-in-chief.

Diplomacy and conduct of war

After the first months of campaigning, London was already feeling annoyed at the restrictive conduct of war embraced by the States General. They were only prepared to place their expensive auxiliary troops at the disposal of the British for defensive strategies. The Imperial ambassador used the general feeling to turn the attention of English statesmen to theatres of war within the Empire, especially those in upper Italy.[35] For his part, Marlborough regretted the restrictions that the field deputies of the States General had imposed on his conduct of war, yet he nevertheless wanted to adhere to a close pact with the Netherlands as a basis for the Alliance. Moving the main actions to the south of Germany would have made Marlborough more dependent on the Court in Vienna, which could not be in the interest of London.[36]

By 1702, The Hague had also recognized the strategic connection between the different theatres of war and had shown their willingness to support the Imperial troops under Ludwig Wilhelm, Margrave of Baden, with 15 battalions under the command of General Goor. France fought within inner lines and could therefore only be defeated, if the Allied succeeded in carrying out simultaneous attacks from different sides. Thus it made sense to start another theatre of war in the Iberian Peninsula. Portugal joined the Grand Alliance in 1703. King Pedro II pledged – through providing military means – to help put Archduke Charles, the son of Emperor Leopold I, onto the Spanish throne. In the Flemish theatre of war, however, the States General's regionally oriented concepts of security did not allow for a further fanning out of forces – for example, a campaign along the Moselle.[37]

In September 1702, Bavarian troops took the free Imperial city of Ulm in a surprise attack and thus brought out into the open the Wittelsbach Elector Maximilian Emanuel's support of France.[38] A few months later, Victor Amadeus, Duke of Savoy was persuaded to join the Alliance. This brought about a sudden change in strategic tectonics. The Imperial and Circle troops, which had recently taken the fortress of Landau (10 September 1702)[39] and gained a gateway into Alsace and Lorraine, found themselves threatened in the rear by Bavarian troops. Savoy's disloyalty to France, on the other hand, not only endangered the French Mediterranean coast, but also formed a considerable threat to France's core provinces with the threat of allied support for the rebellious Camisards in the Cévennes Mountains of south-central France.[40]

This situation marks the starting point for the war year of 1703 that would lead to a severe crisis for the Allies. In view of the immense costs of their 100,000-strong army, the largest contingent of the Alliance, the Dutch Republic persisted in maintaining a defensive strategy in order to achieve their limited war goals. As the general commander-in-chief who represented the joint strategic viewpoints of the Alliance,

Marlborough tried to diminish the pressure on the fronts in Italy and at the Upper Rhine through a diversionary action.[41]

His campaign plan therefore provided for a full-scale attack on the last French positions along the Rhine – the conquest of the fortress of Bonn on 15 May 1703 – and a comprehensive offensive to take Antwerp and Ostend. With this, the Netherlands would have been protected against the threat posed by the French troops by means of a sufficiently broad cordon sanitaire. The realization of this 'great design' would also, finally, have brought everlasting fame to Marlborough as a general strategist and would have brought the Empire some necessary relief.[42]

The defensive, cautious and cost-conscious conduct of war demanded by the States General caused rising tension among the Maritime Powers. The States General finally vetoed the powerful offensive attack planned by Marlborough. The field campaign in the Netherlands in 1703 was authorized only to maintain the status quo.

In the meantime, the Alliance's situation in the Empire and Italy had seriously deteriorated. The Imperial army in Italy was blocked by superior French troops. In the summer, not only was Landau lost again but so too were the fortresses of Kehl and Breisach that protected the Rhine crossings. As a result, a French army under the command of Marshal Villars had been able to cross the Rhine. The army had moved through the Black Forest in Germany and joined the troops of the Bavarian Elector. Together, they had inflicted a crushing defeat on the Imperial troops at Höchstädt (21 September 1703).[43] An uprising in Hungary and the loss of Passau to the French and the Bavarians resulted in the blockade of the Danube, the central supply line to Austria, cornering the Emperor.

It could now not be ruled out that French and Bavarian troops might launch a pincer attack on Vienna from South Germany and Upper Italy. It was nevertheless doubtful if the Franco-Bavarian forces would have been capable of such a concerted action over great distances. It was however conceivable that an attack could be launched from Bavaria on the South German Imperial Circles and thus in the rear of the forces that were deployed at the Upper Rhine. There was a risk that this threatening scenario might induce individual allies such as, for instance, the Swabian and Franconian Imperial Circle, to flee into neutrality. This, in turn, would have been sufficient to cause the front on the Upper Rhine to collapse.[44] In view of this threat, the fortress war in the Netherlands became of secondary importance. It was decided in Vienna to consolidate the front in Italy on the basis of what had been achieved so far. In 1704, for France, Bavaria, and Austria the heart of the war was located in the south of Germany while on the Iberian Peninsula, a Spanish-French army succeeded in taking the initiative.[45]

The campaign of 1704

With Margrave Ludwig Wilhelm von Baden's suggestion for a relief attack by troops of the Maritime Powers along the Moselle, he returned, in the beginning of January 1704, to a plan of action from the previous campaign year.[46] This plan aimed at stabilizing the position of the Electors of Trier, Mainz, and the Palatinate, whose territories were of strategic importance and who experienced the French threat very intensively.[47] At the same time, Ludwig Wilhelm, in his capacity of Chief Commander of the Imperial Army, also claimed the exclusive supreme command over the units that were to be sent from the Netherlands.[48]

These plans fitted in with an essentially defensive orientation of the conduct of war on the part of the front of the Imperial Circles united in the Nördlingen Association. Worried about the territorial integrity of their lordships, they could only mobilize their united war efforts towards a limited operational goal.[49] Against this background, the defence of the Stollhofener and Ettlinger lines – dilatory and financed with limited means – as a part of the Upper Rhine barrier against France represents a military performance that is not to be underestimated.[50] Marlborough was under no illusions either that in the light of the deteriorating financial position and the different views of each of the regents in The Hague about the war, the States General would continue their strategy of defensive border protection.

The plan to shift the focus of the warfare to the south of Germany, whereby in particular the area between the Moselle and the Danube was looked upon as a place from which to start offensive action, was discussed again. In the light of the dangerous situation and imminent threats of 1704, Marlborough supported the plan although he made it clear that he would certainly not subordinate himself to the supreme command of Ludwig Wilhelm.[51]

The double threat of the Franconian and Swabian Circles in both the east and the west and the increasing costs of the war had led to a war-weariness in the Imperial Circles. Under these conditions Ludwig Wilhelm just advocated a quieting down of affairs at the Upper Rhine front. For his part, Marlborough did not want to see his freedom of action restricted again by a plan of war that was orientated toward defence. Given the situation in the year 1704, he could only achieve military success if he were given freedom of operational action and could adopt an offensive approach.

The following example illustrates the strategic operational dilemma of the Alliance. While the States General and the Nördlingen Association had a preference for the primacy of a defensive border protection, London and Vienna were convinced that victory over France could only be achieved through offensive conduct of war.[52] In order not to meet with fundamental resistance from the States General, planning for the 1704 operation was done in three steps. First, it was explored if relief troops could be sent along the Moselle, then it was calculated if recapturing Landau was feasible, and finally, a campaign along the Danube was secretly agreed on.

Due to the attitude of the States General, Marlborough could at first only command the troops of the German Imperial States that stood either in a subsidy relation with Great Britain or were politically dependent on the country. Apart from the contingents of Brunswick-Lüneburg , under the Elector of Hanover, these were the troops of the Landgrave of Hesse-Kassel and of other less powerful Imperial States. In every single case, the content of the respective subsidy treaties determined the conditions under which troops were to be sent into the field. The Brandenburg corps, for example, which Berlin had placed at the disposal of the Emperor and the Maritime Powers, was not to be deployed as auxiliary troops, but rather as a contingent on the same standing with the Allies.[53]

The States General, who were responsible for the maintenance of the army, were at first left to believe that in 1704 Marlborough would operate along the Moselle and the Meuse in order to cover the borders of the Southern Netherlands. It was not until London had applied pressure that the Republic agreed to an autonomous deployment of the troops commanded by the Duke. The Hague assumed that the troops would

Prince Eugene of Savoy-Carignan (1663-1736).

Mezzotint by Stephan Maystetter, 1700. Württemberg State Library, Stuttgart, Germany.

secure the middle Rhine line, the area between Coblenz and Landau.

Stephan Maystetter excud. Aug. Vind.
EUGENIUS FRANCISCUS
Herzog von Savoyen, etc. etc. General Feld-Marschall.
Principis Eugenÿ faciem, gladiumq; minantem,
Turca prius vidit, sensit, et obriguit.
Nunc aquilam fugiens gallus, cantare nec audet,
Nec potis est Tanti Signa videre viri.

With Marlborough's decision to enter into combat – 'to march where Britons had never marched before' – he took a tremendous risk.[54] If the project failed – and this was quite possible given the distances to be marched, the uncertainties as to provisions, and the lack of information about the opponent's possible actions – Marlborough's military, political, and personal future would likewise fall to pieces. He took the risk, as this could free him from the shackles of the States General's policy, with its restrictions on his conduct of war that he had experienced during the previous campaign in the Netherlands. Only a victory bearing his name would reinforce his position in national politics, promote the fortunes of his House, and satisfy his military ambition. No doubt, Marlborough also recognized the strategic importance of a campaign into Bavaria, which – in contrast to a spreading out of troops along the Meuse and Moselle or a defence on the Upper Rhine front – could give a decisive turn to the war. 'I hope this expedition I am Making into Germany may be of great advantage to the Queen's affairs; I am sure it is the only thing which could save the Empire and if I succeed, I hope it may secure 16 [= Godolphin] and 86 [= Marlborough] from the malice of their ennemies,' the Duke told his wife Sarah on 7 May 1704.[55]

That the diplomatic preparations for the 1704 campaign went so successfully is undoubtedly due to the harmonious cooperation based on mutual trust between Marlborough, the Imperial ambassador in London Count Wratislav, and Prince Eugene of Savoy as President of the Court War Council (Hofkriegsrat).[56] Wratislav and Marlborough very skilfully managed to convince the States General to agree to split the jointly financed Dutch-English Army. This decision meant a profound break with the traditions of William III. Marlborough made it quite clear to the responsible parties in The Hague that London, in close cooperation with the Court in Vienna, had already prepared plans for a campaign. With this, the traditionally close relationship between Great Britain and the States General showed its first cracks. In the coming years, the dividing line between contending viewpoints ran between those who advocated offensive operations to decide the war and those who favoured a defensive policy that maintained the status quo.

In the early summer of 1704, Allied troops, with their backbone formed by British units, marched towards the south. A little later, they were followed by a Danish corps. At the same time, the Elector of Saxony announced that he had to withdraw his troops from the Imperial army in order to protect his own territory against Swedish attacks. Different visualisations of the nature of the threat as well as hopes that the opponent's weakness might be used to develop their own power directly affected the balance of power in the various theatres of war. When the middle-ranking powers were simultaneously hit by the War of the Spanish Succession and the Great Northern War, the two large-scale European conflicts visibly intersected.

At the beginning of the 18th century, these powers were not yet in a position to maintain sufficiently large armies in peacetime to defend their country borders. It was only when the threat of war increased that they armed and mobilized, recruitment for which was done in the European mercenary market. Following the Peace of Travendal in August 1700, Denmark had found herself obliged to maintain an army that was numerically too large for her financial resources. Yet, in view of the continued Swedish threat, Danish statesmen thought it unwise to disarm the troops. In such a situation it seemed logical to hire the troops out to other warring powers in return for subsidies. The right to call the troops back at any moment for the defence of their own country had also been negotiated by Poland and Brandenburg in their subsidy contracts with the Maritime Powers.[57]

For that era, not only did the diplomatic preparations constitute a masterly operational and logistic achievement, but also the conduct of the 1704 campaign was likewise an amazing performance. It was crowned by the military success at Höchstädt/Blenheim.[58] The higher-ranking Imperial General, Field Marshal Ludwig Wilhelm Margrave of Baden, had initially advocated negotiating with Bavaria and France to reach a political solution. By doing this, he had meant to serve the interests of the

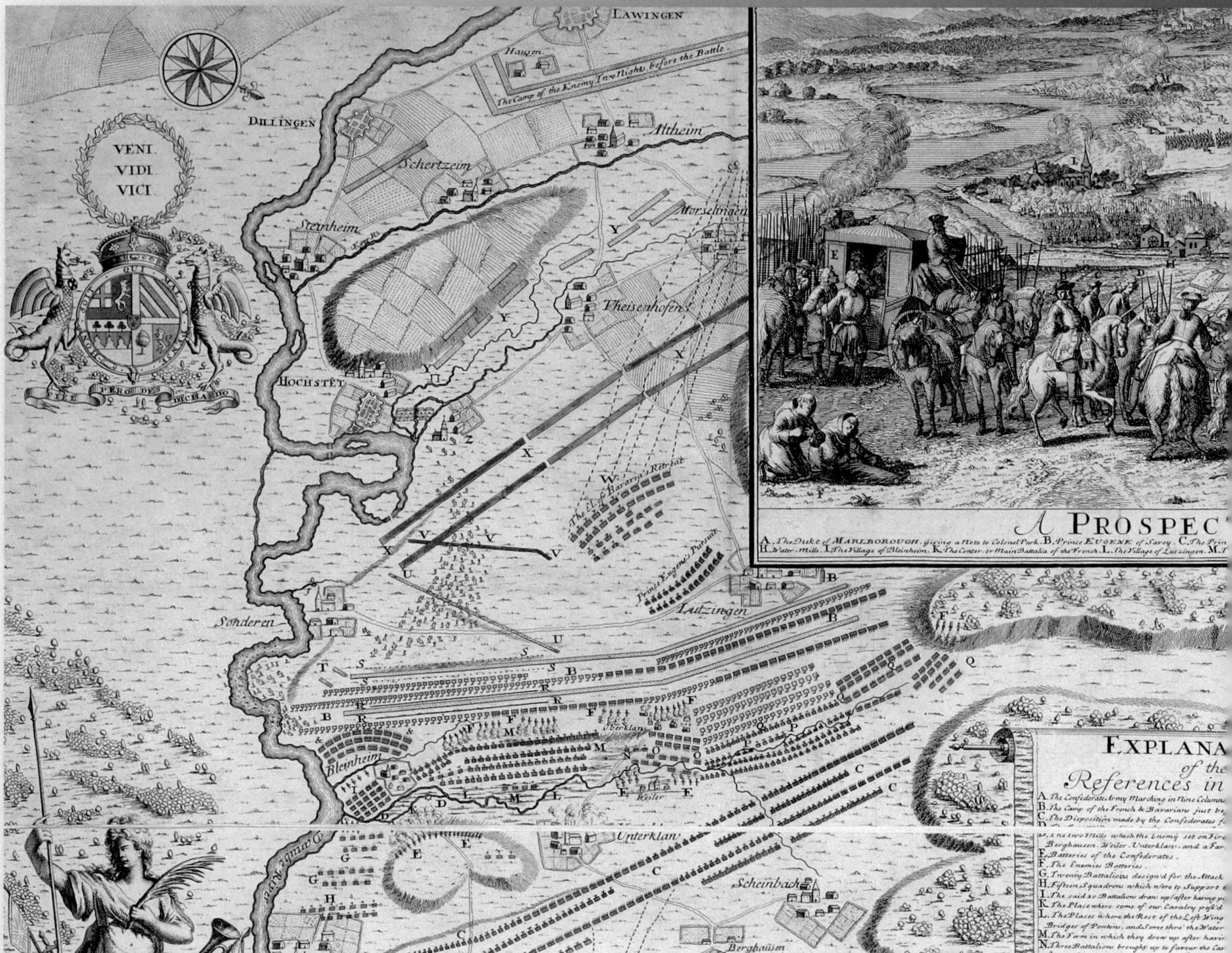
LAWINGEN
The Camp of the Enemy Two Nights before the Battle
VENI
VIDI
VICI
DILLINGEN
Altheim
Schertzeim
Steinheim
Theisenhofen
HOCHSTET
Sonderen
Lutzingen
Bleinheim
Unterklau
Scheinbach
Berghausen
Wolperstette
Gremen
Schwenningen
Dapfheim
Munster
Appershoven
Pragstal
The Camp of the Confederates the Night before the Battle
A PROSPECT
EXPLANA
References in
A most Exact and Accurate
PLAN
of the Several Attacks at the Famous
BATTLE of BLEINHEIM
And of the Incampments of both Armies
Before & after the Battle
The whole Survey'd upon the Spot by the
Quarter-Master General Assisted
by the Best English Ingeneers
and Corrected & Approved
by all the Generals.
LONDON
Sold by DAVID MORTIER
Book Man and Print Seller
in the Strand at ye Sign of
Erasmus's Head near the Savoy
ORDER of BATTLE of the CONFEDERATE ARMY as they March'd up to the ENEMY, the 13th Aug. 1704. N.S.
The Duke of MARLBOROUGH, Capt Genl of the Queen of Great Brittain's Forces.
Prince EUGENE of Savoy, Field Marshall of the
Corp of Reserve

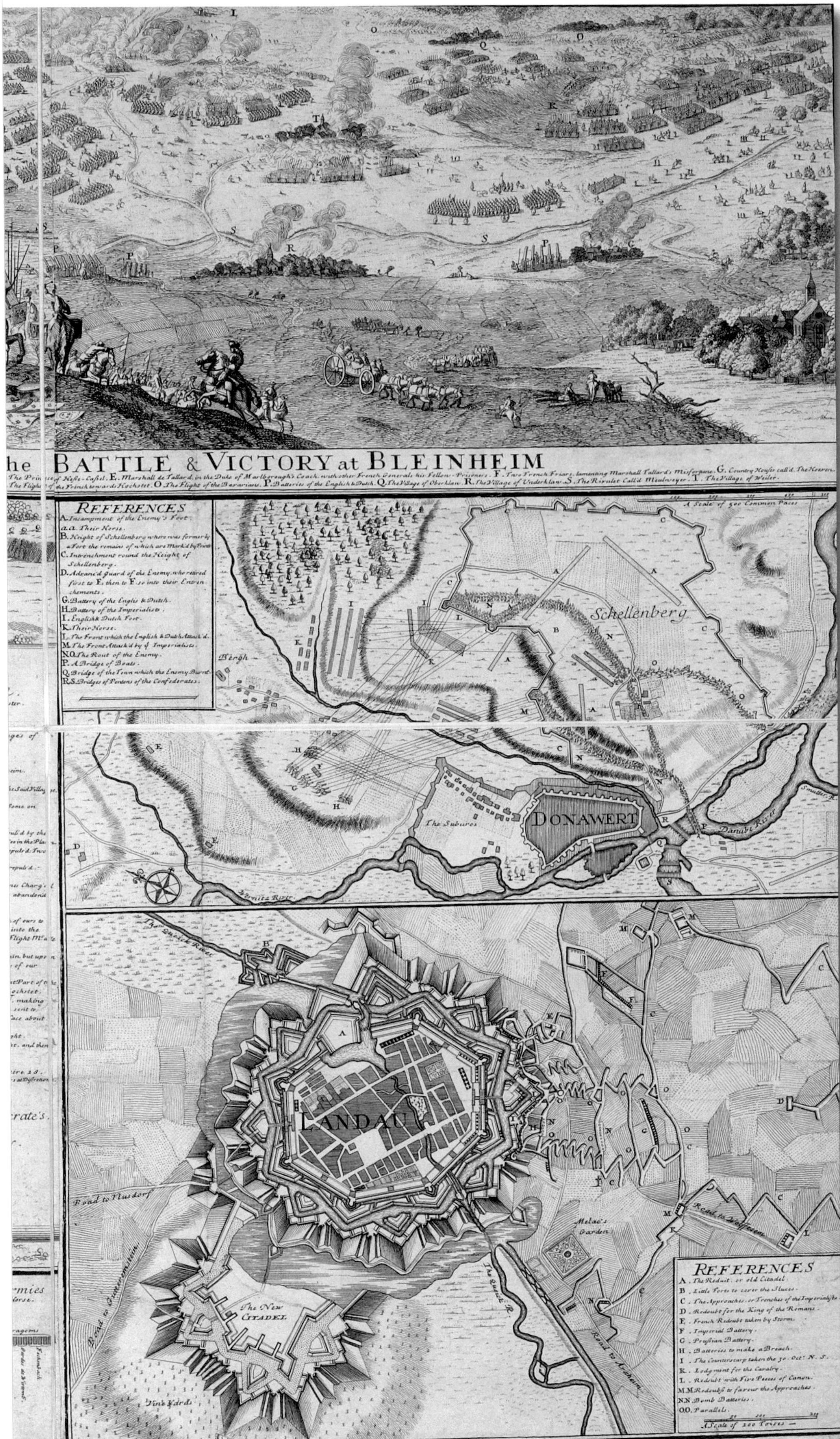

A most Exact and Accurate Plan of the several attacks of the famous Battle of Blenheim.

Engraving by David Mortier, 1705.
The British Library, London, UK.
© The British Library Board. 28620.(3.).

Johann Wilhelm II (1658-1718), Elector Palatine.

Painting by Adriaen van der Werff, 18th century.
Bavarian National Painting Collection, Munich, Germany. © bpk | Bayerische Staatsgemäldesammlungen.

reduced from a partner to a petitioner.[64] Because of the various agreements that Frederick I had entered into to supply troops to the Emperor, the States General, and Great Britain, Prussia was not at any time able to deploy its some 25,000-strong army of subsidy troops as a cohesive, Prussian-led contingent in any particular theatre of war.

The Allied subsidies for Prussia, of which two-thirds had to be supplied by London and one-third by the States General, enabled the additional deployment of 8,000 Prussian troops. Through the deployment of these troops, Berlin hoped to get a guarantee from Great Britain for the security of the Brandenburg territories that were threatened by the Northern War. In addition, Berlin hoped for diplomatic support in its attempt to acquire the inheritance of the Princes of Orange. As far as the Maritime Powers and the Emperor were concerned, Brandenburg served as an 'isolator between the flare-ups on this and on the other side [that] had to be kept on board at any price.'[65] It was only on the surface that subsidies served to pay for the deployment of troops. They were always part of a political concept of security that promised mutual benefit.[66]

Both the political journalism of the Late Enlightenment and a nationally-oriented historiography have until the middle of the 20th century labelled the hiring out of troops as a 'trade in soldiers,' seeing this as a private affair through which royalty financed its boundless representation costs. However, in the 18th century, the army was just as much a tool for the violent attainment of international goals as it was an instrument in diplomacy.[67]

This principle is clearly illustrated through the example of Brandenburg-Prussia. At the beginning of the War of the Spanish Succession, King Frederick I had tried to establish Prussia as an independent partner within the Alliance by requisitioning contingents of troops that, after being deployed, operated independently. In this sense Berlin had exerted military pressure on the Duchy of Saxe-Gotha-Altenburg to break off all relations with France and to join the Alliance. A less powerful Imperial state, Gotha bowed to the supremacy of the neighbouring states and declared its willingness to hire out troops to Brandenburg-Prussia. A number of regiments from other Imperial States, such as Hesse-Kassel and the Electoral Palatinate, were similarly placed in the service of Prussia. As part of contractual agreements with the Court at Berlin, the expenses for maintaining these army units were paid by the Maritime Powers.[68] Since Berlin was continuously able to increase the strength of its troops, it also continuously expanded its supremacy in Northwest Germany.

For the campaign of 1705, Brandenburg-Prussia supplied – besides the 8,000 men that were to be deployed in Italy in accordance with the November 1704 treaty – an additional 12,000 men from the 'old corps' were deployed at the Upper Rhine. They consisted of 8,000 men of contractual troops that were directly subordinate to the Emperor and 4,000 men from the Prussian contribution to the Imperial army. Lastly, 5,000 men of the so-called 'treaty of accession' troops fought in Flanders. Since the beginning of the war these had been financed by the Maritime Powers and were not to be transferred to other theatres of war without permission from London and The Hague.[69]

On the one hand, the wide distribution of these contingents made it possible to lend military support to the territorial interests of Brandenburg in the west and south. On the other hand, it also meant that almost its entire army was financed by the partners of the Alliance. Yet, if the Northern War were to spread and pose a potential threat to the central provinces, it had to be possible to quickly transfer the troops to

King Charles XII of Sweden.

Painting by David Krafft, 1706-1707.

the north. That is why the November treaty of 1704 was initially agreed on for just one year.[70] In London, Marlborough's diplomatic skills antagonized those who envied him while in the Empire his reputation grew. Sophia, the Princess Electress of Hanover, wrote to her confidant Leibnitz: 'In England they are mistaken to say that the Duke of Marlborough has travelled from court to court merely to receive gifts.'[71]

In 1705, Prussia's territorial and financial claims and the distinctly less flexible Imperial politics of the young Emperor Joseph I – since his succession in Vienna – caused tensions to increase. In order to mediate in this situation, the English general, meanwhile proclaimed an Imperial Prince and made Prince of Mindelheim in Swabia, was called in. Prussia had withdrawn the 12,000-strong 'old corps' from the Upper Rhine in view of the critical stage that its worsening relationship with the Imperial Court had reached and because of the opaque situation in the northeast.[72] Having completed the campaign in the Netherlands in the late autumn of 1705, Marlborough started out again on an extensive diplomatic mission that would take him to the Palatinate Court, Stuttgart, Saxe-Gotha, and eventually Berlin. Towards the end of December 1705, the November treaty was renewed with one year and the Prussian contingents stayed at the endangered Italian theatre of war for another year. Immediately before the start of the 1706 campaign the Elector Palatine could be induced to enlarge his contingent, an extra 3,000 man could be obtained from Saxe-Gotha and finally, the Landgrave of Hesse-Kassel was persuaded to provide 10,000 men for the Upper Italian front. All in all, the Maritime Powers financed a total of 28,000 men of the army in Italy.[73] It is undoubtedly thanks to Marlborough's diplomatic skills and his reputation that the prerequisites as to personnel and logistics for the Allied victory in the battle of Turin (7 September 1706) were met.[74] Thanks to the victory won by Marlborough at Ramillies (23 May 1706), Lombardy, Flanders, and Brabant had by the start of 1707 been freed of their enemies while the 'old corps' had been returned to the side of the Maritime Powers.[75] After his victory at Fraustadt (1706) over the King of Poland and Elector of Saxony, the Swedish King Charles XII had pitched camp at Altranstädt, a few miles from Leipzig. The Northern War had again moved dangerously close to the War of the Spanish Succession. News about the Swedish troops being encamped in the Empire and about the young and charismatic Swedish king appearing before Leipzig evoked, with uncanny topicality, distant memories of Breitenfeld and Lützen in the European courts.[76]

Given the breakthrough achieved a few months later by a French army led by Villars into South Germany and the fact that this brought the Swedish and French troops dangerously close, the Allies had grown increasingly fearful that at the last moment France could be saved by Swedish arms. The Maritime Powers therefore sent the Duke of Marlborough in April 1707 to explore the intentions and plans of Charles XII. As the Duke had not been given specific instructions, the outcome of their several hours tête-à-tête concerned primarily the atmosphere between the two. As a result, Charles XII confirmed in his view not to seek an alliance with France, but rather to fight Russia.[77]

Marlborough had stopped off in Hanover on his outward journey in 1707; his return trip took him once again to Berlin. Hanover and Prussia were at the seam between the Great Northern War and the War of the Spanish Succession. Since Georg Ludwig's electoral right had not yet been acknowledged by the Electoral College and, further, as his claim to the British throne was also as yet insecure, he was firmly in the camp of the Alliance. But it was not at all certain whether the chronically precarious financial situation of King Frederick I would dissuade him from becoming a military partner on the side of Sweden.[78] The Prussian-Swedish 'eternal' alliance of 16 August 1707 did not dispel these fears. With the Swedes marching off eastwards and the eventual destruction of their army at Poltava (8 July 1709) came, evidently, a bloody end to the nightmare of the European cabinets.[79] As the Northern War moved eastwards, Brandenburg lost the partner she needed for her policy of vacillating between West and East, a development that Marlborough knew how to use in masterly fashion to benefit the goals of the Grand Alliance. Prussia needed the support of the Maritime Powers to enforce its territorial claims and henceforth, as it was unable to maintain them, had to hire out its troops.[80]

Conduct of war under the primacy of the coalition tactics: defensive or offensive

While the Swedish threat had diminished by 1707, the Allies suffered a reversal of fortune in the south and the east after the successes of the past year. The campaign of 1708 was meant to steer the war into the direction of peace. After the death of Ludwig Wilhelm von Baden and the hapless interlude in command of Margrave Christian Ernst von Bayreuth, the Elector of Hanover now held rank as a Protestant Imperial general field marshal with a status comparable to Eugene's as a Catholic Imperial field marshal, and to Marlborough's, as the general commander-in-chief of the troops of the Maritime Powers. At the beginning of 1708, these two commanders visited the Elector of Hanover in Hanover in order to discuss the plans for the next campaign.[81] Just as Ludwig Wilhelm von Baden had been in 1704, so too in 1708, Georg Ludwig of Hanover was left in the dark concerning his partners' real plans.

Setting offensive goals, as they had done when they had been plotting against the Elector of Bavaria, Eugene and Marlborough aimed to break through the French front of fortresses in Flanders. This would help to open up the way to Paris and predispose Louis XIV towards peace. As a result of the concomitant weakening of the Allied troops at the Upper Rhine, Georg Ludwig feared that the South German Imperial Circles would be overrun by French armies. On the basis of these assumptions he could at most agree to a diversion along the Moselle. Conversely, he rejected the idea of deploying Austrian troops reinforced with contingents from the Upper Rhine front in Flanders.[82]

The behaviour of Eugene and Marlborough in 1704 and 1708 showed some amazing correspondences. Their biographers have first of all pointed to resemblances of a personal nature to account for their joint military and political successes.[83] Meanwhile, it has gone unnoticed that with their principle of taking the offensive, both generals followed a belief about strategic power politics that was in line with their assignment. On this account, the States General had been left in the dark in 1704 by Marlborough about his operational plans, while Margrave Ludwig Wilhelm could not forbid a functional division of the assignment into a defensive and an offensive component.

By contrast, the Elector of Hanover did not just have the intention, in 1708, to distinguish himself militarily. By defending the Empire he also sought to gain the political approval of the Electoral College for his rank of Elector.[84] As ordered by the Reichstag, Georg Ludwig led the Imperial army whose task it was to protect the frontal Imperial Circles. Given the practical possibilities, they were successful in accomplishing this, even though they were hindered by the malfunctioning of the states and the unwieldy leadership and command system. On account of the orders they had been given by the Circles, the Imperial army did not anticipate being deployed to take the offensive. The troops would just be used to provide cover and to besiege.

It was, however, not so much the generals' own personal characters that determined their conduct but the orders that each, in his respective position, received from his political superiors and the military means they had at their disposal to execute them. As had happened in 1704, in 1708, too the different offensive and defensive concepts of the Allied partners clashed. While Vienna and London wanted to fulfil the military preconditions for a favourable peace, both the Imperial States and, incidentally, the States General, aimed at a military safeguard for their territorial integrity. Given the expansionist French politics of the previous thirty years, this type of armed border protection only promised to be a success for the central states and the Imperial territories if a strategic glacis was placed before their own dominions so they would have time to take diplomatic and military countermeasures in case of a hostile attack. On the Upper Rhine, these considerations shaped the plans for the recovery of Alsace, the Free County of Burgundy, and parts of Lorraine. Even the Duke of Savoy and the Protestant cantons of the Swiss Confederation did not want to give up the idea of an effective barrier. In a similar way, the regents in The Hague tried to use the Spanish Netherlands in part or wholly as a barrier against France.[85] Thus, Dutch, British and Austrian interests only corresponded with regard to the liberation of the Spanish Netherlands. As long as these were not completely in the possession of the Allies, the States General rejected a further attack on French territory.[86]

■ Power politics, obligations to the Alliance and hope for peace

Due to the exhaustion of France, which the defeat of Oudenaarde (11 July 1708) and the loss of Lille had made manifest, Louis XIV saw himself forced to explore the possibilities for peace.[87] Encouraged by the Allied superiority in the Flemish theatre of war, the States General asserted maximum claims. Apart from the right to occupy French border fortresses, these referred to the fortresses of the Spanish Netherlands, even those on the Rhine (Bonn) and the Moselle (Trarbach). The Hague was presumably trying to develop a joint defence strategy together with the frontal Imperial Circles.[88] The idea found in older research that the Netherlands sought rapprochement with the Imperial Alliance because of the difference of opinion between the Maritime Powers that had become obvious during the recent years of war is not tenable.[89] London needed the support of the States General to enforce a Protestant succession to the throne, and Marlborough was therefore appointed to meet the demands of the government in The Hague, which was also being courted by France with similar concessions. His task was to conclude a renewed border contract on the basis of the States General's demands.[90]

Vienna laid claim to the totality of the Spanish inheritance and, in the interest of the Empire, demanded, though less emphatically, a barrier that was in no way inferior in scope to that of the Netherlands.[91] In The Hague, Prince Eugene and Marlborough, in close communication with Pensionary Heinsius, put forward the demands

GEORG. I.

burg-Prussia were increasingly desirous to divide, with the Tsar's permission, the German possessions of Sweden among themselves and to thus bring about a territorial re-organization of northeast Europe.[97] Marlborough, who was seen in Berlin as an honest broker of the Brandenburg interests and as someone for whom even 'the king and his House showed special devotion,' advised the Prussian ambassador Grumbkow to let the Northern matters alone until peace had been made in the west.[98]

In the summer of 1709, the Prussian crown prince (later King Frederick William I) made an appearance in the western theatre of war. His father, King Frederick I, had asked the Duke of Marlborough, as the preceptor of his son, not to tutor him in military matters only. But only a short while later the relaxed relations between Marlborough and Frederick I were troubled by news about the peace talks, which had been held without the participation of the Prussian representative. At the wish of the Dutch Republic, Prussian claims on the Orange inheritance had, barring the Principality of Neuchâtel, been left out of account.[99]

Feeling aggrieved and given the distant prospect of finding compensation in the Baltic Sea area, Prussia entered into secret negotiations with France at the beginning of 1710, while threatening to withdraw its troops from the western theatres of war. The diplomatic game was not meant to lead to Prussia's secession from the Grand Alliance, but to sensitize the great powers to the claims of Frederick I.[100] Complaints about the lack of attention for their interests were also brought by the diplomatic representatives of the other partners of the Grand Alliance – Savoy, Portugal, Hanover, and the Nördlingen Association of the Imperial Circles – that had not been involved in the negotiations of the larger powers. The prospect that France could reject the peace treaty led to a war-weariness in England and the States General – which had borne the main burden of the war – that became more and more politically explosive.[101] The armed Imperial States and the frontal Imperial Circles were not mistaken in fearing that their claims would become so many items of compensation in the eyes of the larger powers and might be sacrificed to dynastic and political interests related to both military security and trade. The Dutch Republic sought to press their own demand for an extended barrier against France, hinting that in return they would show themselves more accommodating about the situation on the Upper Rhine.

George I at the time he became King of Great Britain in 1714.

Painting by the studio of Godfrey Kneller, around 1714. © National Portrait Gallery, London, UK.

■ The collapse of the Alliance

Even before the final breakdown of the peace negotiations, there were forebodings, in London, of domestic political upheaval, which were bound to damage the reputation of Marlborough as the resolute political representative of Great Britain in the Grand Alliance. Given the war-weariness that was spreading in both the Dutch Republic and, increasingly, in England, France saw an opportunity – even after the breakdown of the negotiations at Geertruidenberg in the summer of 1710 – to strengthen its position through a war of attrition against the Allies. The fact that the situation in northeast Europe was becoming acute necessitated consultations to avoid the two conflicts intertwining, which could be achieved by deploying a neutral corps in which both the Maritime Powers and the armed Imperial States would participate.[102] Hence, Hanover, Prussia and Saxony tried hard to leave their troops at the western

CHAPTER 9

Friendship and Realpolitik: Marlborough and the Habsburg Monarchy

Michael Hochedlinger

Military historians, especially those working on the early modern period, are accustomed to the most incredible cases of rivalry and obstructionism between generals and officers of the same camp. Altercations over rank and precedence were even more likely to erupt and paralyse the war effort when combined armies of two or more coalition partners took the field. The War of the Spanish Succession, however, affords one shining example of the very opposite. The oft extolled and indeed remarkable friendship between John Churchill, Duke of Marlborough, and his Austrian counterpart, Prince Eugene of Savoy (1663-1736), not only put its stamp on Anglo-Austrian military cooperation. It also served as a strong binding agent for a political partnership which, despite the diverging interests of London and Vienna, was to last for more than a decade. Marlborough's fall from power signalled the imminent break-up of the alliance which, literally, left the Austrian Habsburgs and the Dutch alone on the field of battle. Almost inevitably, therefore, a chapter on 'Marlborough and the Habsburg Monarchy' amounts to portraying the unusual partnership between the English Duke and the Savoyard Prince in Austrian service.

Prince Eugene of Savoy.

Painting by Jacob van Schuppen, 1718. Rijksmuseum, Amsterdam, the Netherlands.

Up to a point the excellent working relationship between Marlborough and his 'famous comrade' (W.S. Churchill) served as a substitute for the centralized allied high command that was lacking. Indeed, both Eugene and Marlborough were not merely soldiers. They also dominated the foreign policies of their home countries and defined the strategies they then had to execute militarily. However, the institutional, political and social framework within which they had to operate, the 'political cultures', as it were, in London and Vienna differed considerably, something that is often forgotten by historians. The situation in London was much more complex with Court, Parliament and public opinion bringing their influence to bear on the decision-making process. In Vienna, by contrast, there was no representative body and no *vox populi* to affect foreign policy as defined by the Emperor and his advisors behind closed doors.

Contemporary pamphlets and commercial art were quick to popularize the Anglo-Austrian tandem. The imagery is telling. Medals representing Eugene and Marlborough in antique Roman armour were coined during the war to celebrate the military triumphs of 'Castor and Polux redivivus'. But like the mythological demigods of Graeco-Roman legend, Marlborough and Eugene were quite different characters. What they shared was a passion for ostentatious building projects which secured them a place in art history – and the eternal gratitude of tourist industries in both England and Austria.

eign subsidies (to be provided by the Maritime Powers) and foreign troops supplied by the more potent German princes in return for money but, even more importantly, for political support. Hanover and Brandenburg, for example, owed their elevation to electoral and royal status to the Emperor's never-ending demand for 'cannon-fodder.'

After the end of the Nine Years' War (1697) and the Great Turkish War (1699), the Emperor enjoyed but a short period of peace. The Spanish question was looming, as the Madrid branch of the Habsburg family was nearing extinction. By force of arms France had already secured important Spanish outposts along its eastern frontier but it was obvious that the Sun King's appetite had not yet been appeased, and of course the Habsburgs in Vienna could not be ignored. Beginning in 1668 partition treaties had parcelled out the Spanish inheritance on paper – well before His Catholic Majesty effectively departed this life.

In 1698/99 the Maritime Powers and France took care of the 'Spanish Question.' First by declaring chief heir the Bavarian elector's minor son, with Versailles and Vienna getting their minimum portion, then, after the electoral prince's untimely death, by awarding Spain and the Spanish Netherlands to the Emperor's second son Charles (1685-1740), Naples-Sicily and Lombardy to the French Bourbons (June 1699). This was not at all to Leopold I's liking, since the Spanish possessions in Italy, especially Lombardy, were, and remained, the heirlooms for which Vienna showed the greatest interest – above all for geopolitical reasons.

It was the dying Spanish king himself who frustrated all these schemes in his last testament (October 1700). In order to spare his monarchy partition he declared Louis XIV's grandson, Philippe d'Anjou, his universal heir, and the French king, much to the irritation of the Maritime Powers, hurried to cancel his treaty obligations and entered upon the rich inheritance. French troops occupied Lombardy and invaded the Spanish Netherlands, where the stadholder, the elector of Bavaria Max Emanuel, put up no resistance. A pro-Habsburg conspiracy in Naples was crushed.

The Renewal of the Grand Alliance

As early as November 1700 it was clear that the Emperor would send troops to northern Italy to get his foot in the door. Only in summer 1701 did the fighting begin. Expectedly, the Italian army under Prince Eugene, the hero of the last Turkish War, proved much too weak to drive the superior French back, but his first minor victories no doubt supported a simultaneous diplomatic offensive in London and The Hague. Initially both England and the United Provinces, fearing a French offensive into the Netherlands, had recognized Philippe d'Anjou as new king of Spain, but on 7 September 1701 the Grand Alliance was signed in The Hague to renew the anti-French coalition between the Emperor and the Maritime Powers soon to be joined by German princes and several Imperial Circles. While Spain and its colonies should be left to Philip V of Spain on condition that the crowns of Spain and France would never be united, the Austrian Habsburgs were to receive the Spanish Netherlands and the former Spanish possessions in Italy to build up a territorial barrier against further French expansion.

At this point Marlborough and Eugene of Savoy had barely heard of each other. While the latter was struggling to hold out in Italy, the former was just beginning to relaunch his career. The Imperialists were fully aware of Marlborough's upcoming predominance under the reign of Queen Anne, and the Emperor's representative in London, the Bohemian Johann Wenzel Count Wratislaw (1669-1712), was ordered to cajole the new Captain-General as best he could. From June 1702, Marlborough at the head of an expeditionary force operated successfully against the French in the Meuse-Lower Rhine region. It was from Belgian Limburg that the English general, on 4 September 1702, congratulated Eugene upon his recent 'victory' (in fact a draw) at Luzzara; it was their first direct contact recorded.[4] More spectacular was the capture of Landau in the Palatinate, one of Vauban's masterpieces, in September 1702. The presence of Joseph, king of the Romans, Emperor Leopold's elder son, had given the siege additional weight.

Yet this was the last major success for the allied cause before disaster struck rather massively. After many months of tergiversation, Max Emanuel of Bavaria, ambitious beyond his means, finally opted for the French cause in September 1702. As early as 1701 his brother Joseph Clemens, the Elector of Cologne and Prince-Bishop of Liège, had set a bad example by calling French troops into his territories. Bavaria's defection opened up a new and very dangerous front in the back of the Upper Rhine defence line, but also threatened the neighbouring Austrian provinces to the south and east of the electorate.

The entire Rhine barrier was on the verge of collapsing when, in 1703, the French not only took Breisach, Kehl, and Landau but also managed to break through the Black Forest and join forces with Max Emanuel. The Franco-Bavarians successfully defeated allied punitive expeditions and even launched a major counter-offensive by invading Austrian Tyrol in summer 1703.

In northern Italy the Imperialists, ill equipped and inferior in number, had got trapped in a dangerous stalemate. In early 1703, therefore, Eugene rushed to Vienna to request more support for a theatre which, after all, was vital to Habsburg's grand strategy. Promoted president of the *Hofkriegsrat*, the Emperor's central military authority, he was to return to Italy only in 1705. In the meantime, Eugene's army corps proved unable to prevent the French from rapidly advancing north towards the Tyrol where Max Emanuel was beginning to spread himself out. While a Tyrolese uprising soon kicked the Bavarians out of the alpine province, the French attack from the south was stopped by a 'diplomatic revolution': Eugene's cousin, the Duke of Savoy, at last changed sides and joined the Grand Alliance (October/November 1703). Then, few may have suspected that Savoy was to become Austria's most dangerous – and ultimately successful – rival over the control of northern Italy.[5]

For the time being, Savoy's defection clearly weakened France's position, while a decisive diplomatic success scored by the Maritime powers involved new obligations for the Austrian Habsburgs. In May 1703 Portugal joined the Allies whose war aims were now extended to include the complete expulsion of the Bourbon king of Spain and the enthronement of the Emperor's second son Charles, as Lisbon would not tolerate a predominant Bourbon neighbour. In September 1703 the 18-year-old Archduke left Vienna for Portugal – significantly via London. Charles was little more than king by the grace of the Maritime Powers, sponsored by English and Dutch money, transported by the Anglo-Dutch fleet and supported by an expeditionary force for which the English and Dutch paid. But the gain of Gibraltar in 1704 and of Barcelona (and Catalonia) in 1705, providing the English fleet with two important naval bases, also had a positive effect on the Austrian war effort in Italy.

Prospects in Spain were more than spoilt by a large-scale revolt in Hungary led by

Joannes Wenceslaus S.R.I. Comes
Wratislaw de Mitrovicz S.C.
Rq. Maj. Act. Cons. Int. Camer. Reg. Bohem.
Cancellar. et Magnus Prior Melitensis.

Ferenc Rákóczy (1676-1735), whose family had a longstanding tradition of anti-Habsburg activities. Large parts of the kingdom soon escaped the Emperor's control. Tax receipts dried up and incursions by Hungarian insurgents terrorized Austria's eastern provinces for years to come. Even Vienna was in serious danger and had to be surrounded by a new outer wall protecting the suburbs.

But the Rákóczy-rebellion, soon sponsored by Louis XIV, also cast a dangerous shadow over the Emperor's relationship with the Maritime Powers, especially with England, and this not only because Austrian regiments were recalled from the Rhine to bolster the front in Hungary. Godolphin furiously complained at one point that the Emperor was thinking of nothing but the Hungarian problem.

The insurrection was multifaceted and had economic, social, political but also religious overtones. The fate of Hungarian Protestantism in particular did mean something to the Maritime Powers. As early as 1705, Marlborough warned the Emperor's representative in London that his fellow countrymen regarded the rebellious Hungarians as their persecuted brothers. The English envoy to Vienna, the poet-diplomat George Stepney (1663-1707), was the Hungarians' passionate advocate against the Emperor's supposed popish and Jesuitical penchant. In order to demonstrate willingness to compromise, Vienna had to accept several English and Dutch attempts at 'mediation.' It was only after 1707, when the Hungarian rebels decided to formally dethrone the Habsburgs as kings of Hungary that sympathy for the Magyars waned. As late as 1709 Rákóczy and his followers tried to establish contact with Marlborough who, while keeping the Austrian ally informed, assured them that both the Queen and the States General 'ont fort à coeur les souffrances des pauvres peuples de Hongrie.'[6]

Winston Churchill, while calling Leopold I a Catholic despot and Austria's policy in Hungary unjust and illegal, strongly disapproved of the Dutch and English interference in the Emperor's domestic affairs.[7] The Hungarian revolt finally broke down in 1711 but the formal peace treaty concluded between the sovereign and his rebellious subjects set dangerous bounds to Habsburg absolutism and state-building capacities.

Johann Wenzel Count Wratislaw.
In 1701, Emperor Leopold I sent Count Wratislaw (1669-1712) to London to persuade William III to recognize Austrian claims to the Spanish Crown, then represented the Emperor in the negotiations at The Hague that concluded the Grand Alliance. In 1703, he was recalled from London to Vienna to accompany the Archduke Charles to England en route to Spain. He remained in London as both Charles's and the Emperor's envoy. In 1704, he accompanied Marlborough and Prince Eugene on campaign, returning to Vienna after the victory at Blenheim.

Engraving by unkown artist, around 1705. Austrian National Library Portrait Collection, Vienna, Austria.

■ The Blenheim Campaign of 1704

Such was the bleak political and strategic background against which the famous campaign of 1704 needs to be seen. Allied grand strategy had actively created a multitude of theatres in order to force the French king to divide and overstrain his forces, but the Austrian ally had reached its limits much earlier. The Hungarian danger seemed all the more problematic, as to the west of the Austrian heartlands, Bavaria remained undefeated and prepared to join forces with Rákóczy in the east. In fact, Max Emanuel invaded Upper Austria early in 1704. No doubt: the elimination of the Bavarian threat was of paramount importance – to the safety of the Habsburg lands but also to the allied war effort at large. For almost two years the small electorate had successfully prevented the Allies from concentrating on their principal enemy – France.[8]

A first concentric attack on Bavaria had failed in September 1703. Eugene and the Emperor's chief diplomat and former envoy to London, Count Wratislaw, were convinced that for a decisive blow substantial support from the Maritime Powers was

needed. While the Dutch remained anxious not to weaken the allied performance in the Belgian theatre of war and consequently were hesitant to supply troops for an offensive against Max Emanuel, Vienna hoped that Marlborough could be talked into leaving his quarters around Maastricht and marching south. Even a meeting between Duke and Prince in The Hague was envisaged, but in the end it was Wratislaw alone who persuaded the English commander-in-chief. Joint allied operations, it was rumoured in order not to scare the Dutch, were to be directed against Landau or the Moselle valley, while in reality it had become clear by April 1704 that Marlborough would advance to the Danube. In preparation for this advance, the logistics for it were organized from The Hague by the Council of State of the Dutch Republic. On 20 May 1704 the Duke's army corps finally broke camp and marched south via Bonn, Andernach, Koblenz, Mainz, Darmstadt and Heidelberg, reaching the Danube near Ulm on 29 June.[9]

A serious problem remained: Who would act as co-commander on the Imperialists' side? The Duke and Wratislaw had clearly hoped for Eugene who in fact left Vienna in late May. The supreme commander in southern Germany, however, was Margrave Ludwig Wilhelm von Baden (1655-1707), Eugene's cousin but also – as the Emperor's *Generallieutenant* and *Reichsgeneralfeldmarschall* – his senior. Once a most active and daring commander-in-chief against the Turks (1689-1692), hence his eloquent nickname 'Türkenlouis,' he had become overly cautious and defensive-minded. Furthermore, he had not given up hopes of winning Max Emanuel over without risking a bloody battle and thus did not really qualify for carrying out the allied grand design against Bavaria.

Eugene and Marlborough met for the first time on 10 June 1704 at Mundelsheim near Marbach am Neckar. It was 'love at first sight.' 'The two generals', Winston Churchill enthused, 'spent several hours in each other's company. Then at once began that glorious brotherhood in arms which neither victory nor misfortune could disturb, before which jealousy and misunderstanding were powerless, and of which the history of war furnishes no equal example.'[10]

On 13-14 June 1704 Eugene, Marlborough, Ludwig Wilhelm von Baden and Wratislaw met at Groß Heppach to finalize the strategic plan. Ludwig Wilhelm reserved for himself and Marlborough the more prestigious attack on the Bavarian electorate, while Eugene was to mount the guard along the Rhine. Max Emanuel had just received French reinforcements and another French army was preparing to cross the Black Forest. Wratislaw who, as a sort of liaison officer, had accompanied the Anglo-allied army corps on its way south stayed with Marlborough as Eugene's confident and participated in the campaign despite his legendary obesity.

On the Schellenberg near Donauwörth (2 July 1704) Ludwig Wilhelm and Marlborough managed to inflict a crushing defeat upon the Franco-Bavarians. However, they paid a heavy prize and failed to exploit their success, apart from ravaging Bavaria, while at the same time last-minute negotiations with Max Emanuel were under way. Eugene complained that even Marlborough now showed little energy, and the Duke found himself on increasingly problematic terms with Baden.

Eugene meanwhile proved unable to prevent the French beyond the Rhine from breaking through to the Bavarian elector. At the head of a substantial part of his army he at least dogged their footsteps and marched towards the Danube. On 11 August 1704 Eugene and Marlborough joined forces and got rid of Ludwig Wilhelm von Baden who marched off to besiege Ingolstadt. On 13 August 1704, at Höchstädt-

George Stepney (1663-1707), English Diplomat and Poet.
A member of the literary Kit-Cat Club in London, Stepney served as England's diplomatic envoy to the Holy Roman Empire from 1701 to 1706 and to the Dutch Republic in 1706-07.

Painting by Godfrey Kneller, 1705-1708.

Letter from the Duke of Marlborough to Charles III of Spain, informing the king of the victory at Blenheim.

Letter by John Churchill, 1704. Austrian National Archives, Vienna, Austria.

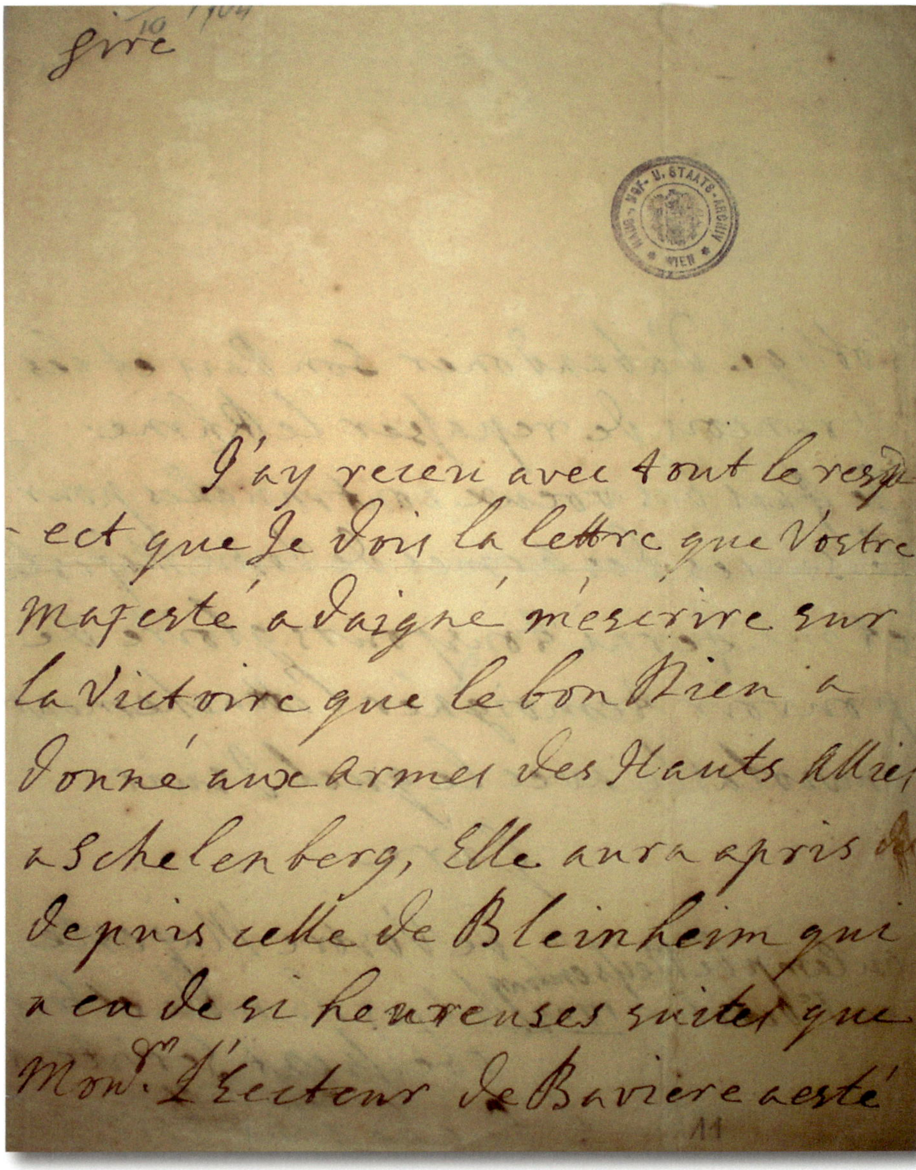
Sire

J'ay receu avec tout le respect que je dois la lettre que Vostre
Majesté a daigné m'escrire sur
la Victoire que le bon Dieu a
donné aux armes des Hauts Alliés
a Schelenberg, Elle aura apris
depuis celle de Bleinheim qui
a eu de si heureuses suites que
Mons.r l'Electeur de Baviere a esté

Blindheim, soon transmogrified into 'Blenheim', the allied forces routed the Franco-Bavarian army. Together with the remnants of his forces Max Emanuel fled to France, leaving his country to ten years of Austrian occupation. Over the following decade Bavaria was squeezed dry to help keep the Emperor's spluttering war machinery going.

Marlborough's march to the Danube had no doubt been instrumental in solving the Bavarian problem, and it was he who had carried the day by crushing the French centre during the battle. Eugene had been unable to make any progress against the enemy's left wing, which saved the Franco-Bavarians from complete annihilation. '*Had the success of prince Eugene been equal to his merit*', Marlborough wrote to his wife on 14 August, 'we should in that day's action have made an end of the war.'[11] Or as Addison put it: '*Fam'd Eugenio bore away, only the second honors of the day.*'

After the elimination of Bavaria, Marlborough's army marched north, but the English captain did not return home until after, travelling to Berlin and Hanover in person, he had tightened the bond with the two most important suppliers of subsidy

Joseph I, Holy Roman Emperor in imperial regalia. The eldest son of Emperor Leopold I, Joseph (1678-1711) ruled as emperor from 1705 to 1711.

Painting by unknown artist, 18th century. Kunsthistorisches Museum, Vienna, Austria.

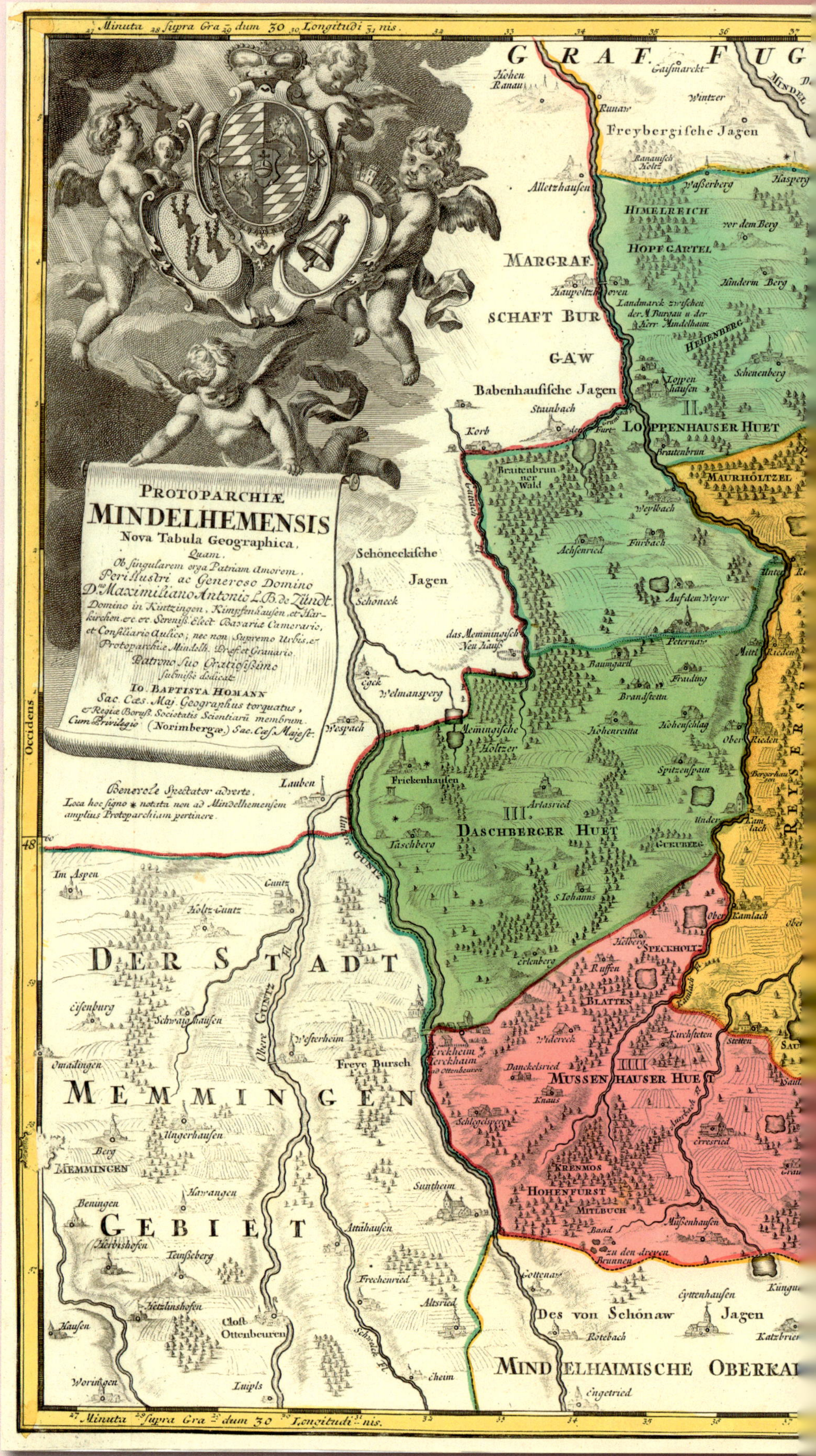
PROTOPARCHIÆ
MINDELHEMENSIS
Nova Tabula Geographica,
Quam
Ob singularem erga Patriam amorem
Perillustri ac Generoso Domino
Dno Maximiliano Antonio L.B. de Zündt
Domino in Kintzingen, Kimpfenhausen, et Harkirchen, etc. etc. Sereniss. Elect. Bavariæ Camerario, et Consiliario Aulico; nec non Supremo Urbis et Protoparchiæ Mindelh. Præf. et Granario
Patrono Suo Gratiosissimo
submissè dedicat
IO. BAPTISTA HOMANN
Sac. Cæs. Maj. Geographus torquatus, et Regiæ Boruss. Societatis Scientiarū membrum.
Cum Privilegio (Norimbergæ) Sac. Cæs. Majest.
Benevole Spectator adverte.
Loca hoc signo ✱ notata non ad Mindelhemensem amplius Protoparchiam pertinere.
Minuta Supra Gradum 30 Longitudinis
Occidens
GRAF. FUG
MARGRAF. SCHAFT BURGAW
Babenhausische Jagen
Freybergische Jagen
HIMELREICH
HOPFGARTEL
II. LOPPENHAUSER HUET
MAURHÖLTZEL
Schöneckische Jagen
III. DASCHBERGER HUET
IIII MUSSENHAUSER HUET
DER STADT MEMMINGEN GEBIET
MEMMINGEN
Freye Bursch
Des von Schönaw Jagen
MINDELHAIMISCHE OBERKA
Obere Guntz Fl.
Schwaab Fl.
Clost. Ottenbeuren
KRENMOS
HOHENFURST
Lauben
Frickenhausen
Memingische Höltzer
SPECKHOLTZ
BLATTEN

A map of Mindelheim.

Map by J.B. Homann, 1715. Austrian National Archives, Vienna, Austria.

Reichsfürst (Prince of the Reich) by diploma predated 14 November 1705 and, thirdly, the Emperor turned Mindelheim into an immediate principality with seat and vote at the Imperial Diet (predated 17 November 1705). The formal investiture took place in Innsbruck in late April 1706. Mindelheim was supposed to yield £ 2,000 per year, while the Emperor, by way of exception, reduced the enormous chancellery fees to an absolute minimum. As Marlborough's proxy, George Stepney took possession of the principality in May 1706. Its double status as a direct Reich principality and an Austrian sub-fief was anomalous, yet so was the entire cause.[15]

Curiously, Marlborough was not the first famous soldier to reign over Mindelheim. Between 1467 and 1586 the lordship had been in the hands of the Frundsberg family. Georg von Frundsberg (1473-1528), Charles V's famous lansquenet leader, was born and died in Mindelheim.

Up and down

Militarily, 1706 was a much better year than 1705. Marlborough beat the French at Ramillies (23 May 1706), and the Austrians were not idle either. For the Monarchy – which had faced bankruptcy in 1703 – the upward trend started with a (private) English loan of £250,000 redeemable within six years, secured by Silesia's tax yield and bearing interest at 8 per cent. Subscription began in March 1706; the Prince-Consort and Marlborough signed for £20,000 respectively with other prominent figures following in their wake.[16]

The 1706 loan was modest but sufficient to finance the provisions for Eugene's Italian army thus enabling him at last to break the deadlock, relieve Turin besieged by the French (7 September 1706) and expel them from Lombardy – a truly decisive success. Further north Ramillies put the Allies in control of most of the former Spanish Netherlands which the Dutch were quick to integrate into their barrier strategy and commercial policy. In a counter-move Vienna offered Marlborough the vacant stadholdership – 'one of the rightest thoughts', Godolphin wrote, 'that ever came from the emperor's counsels' and very much to Marlborough's taste.[17] But the scheme foundered due to strong Dutch resistance. A provisional administration in Brussels dominated by the Dutch ran Belgian affairs, officially in the name of Charles III of Spain who in 1708-9 renewed the offer made to Marlborough two years earlier. Again nothing came of the project but such a strong mark of confidence at least served to bind Marlborough even more closely to the House of Austria. In the end, Eugene was made stadholder of the Austrian Netherlands in 1709, while the English and Dutch signed an agreement giving the States General control over a series of Belgian fortresses.

For Vienna, Spain had always been a secondary theatre, but after the expulsion of the French from northern Italy London expected its ally to change course rapidly. An invasion of Provence should divert French attention from Spain where the allied cause was on the defensive. But while Eugene agreed to strike against southern France, the Austrians could not be dissuaded from at the same time conquering Naples which was still in Bourbon hands. In May 1707, 10.000 Imperialists marched off to southern Italy. By early July 1707, they had taken the city of Naples and most of the kingdom and in early 1709 Austrian troops bullied the Pro-French Pope Clement XII into accepting Habsburg supremacy over Italy.

Eugene's march into Provence in summer 1707 went much less smoothly despite support from the Anglo-Dutch fleet. At the end of August 1707 Eugene was forced to raise the siege of Toulon. As a consequence London insisted on more substantial and direct Austrian help for the wavering allied position in Spain. A convention signed in April 1708 obligated the Emperor to send 4.000 troops to the Peninsula for which the Queen paid. English public opinion and, under its pressure even Marlborough and Queen Anne, had been clamouring for Eugene as commander-in-chief in Spain. The Emperor refused but at least sent his second best general, Guidobald Starhemberg (1657-1737).[18] Eugene was designated for the Belgian theatre to which Vienna's attention naturally turned after the triumph in Italy.

In 1707 the Habsburg Monarchy had also lived through very dark moments in the east, not only because of the ongoing Hungarian revolt. The Great Northern War threatened to spill over into the Habsburg orbit, when in 1706 the Swedish king Charles XII invaded neighbouring Saxony and made himself at home there. Charles soon intervened on behalf of the protestants in Silesia and France did its very best to drag him into the war. Marlborough's short visit to the Swedish army camp at Altranstädt in April 1707 helped to ease the tension and made clear that no Franco-Swedish alliance was in the making. An accord of 1 September 1707, negotiated by the Emperor's indefatigable chief diplomat Wratislaw, removed the Swedish threat to the Habsburg Monarchy in return for minor concessions to the protestant cause in Silesia.[19]

The ideal opportunity to reciprocate came in the 1708 campaign. In April 1708, Eugene and Marlborough met in The Hague with Grand Pensionary Heinsius to arrange for close military cooperation in Belgium. The prince would concentrate a substantial army composed of Austrian and German subsidy troops which, officially, were to operate along the Moselle but in the event joined the Anglo-Dutch forces around Brussels.

These forces came too late to help Marlborough against a French offensive which took Ghent and Bruges, thus plunging the Duke into deep depression. But the arrival of Eugene well ahead of his troops was a sufficient moral boost to redress the situation. On 11 July 1708 the victory of Oudenaarde opened a string of allied successes. With Eugene's reinforcements the Grand Alliance now disposed of more than 100,000 troops in the Belgian theatre and could set about demolishing one by one Vauban's ring of fortresses along the Franco-Belgian border. Lille fell in October 1708. The French responded by peace initiatives which in the long run effectively sowed the seeds of discord among the Allies; the war-weary Dutch seemed the first to succumb to French temptations. High level peace talks in The Hague during the first half of 1709 in which Marlborough and Eugene participated delayed the start of the campaign. The French conceded what the Allies had demanded; Vienna, having reached its war aims by early 1709, was particularly pitiless, claiming not only the entire Spanish inheritance but also a substantial shift of the Franco-German boundary line in Alsace, Lorraine and along the Rhine. In June 1709 negotiations were broken off, as Louis XIV, though prepared to sacrifice his grandson the king of Spain, refused to take an active part in his ousting.

Marlborough and Eugene took much blame for not having put an end to the bloodshed – and the bloodiest encounter of the war was yet to come. The battle of Malplaquet (11 September 1709) was too costly – the Allies lost 7,800 dead – to pass for a real success. Peace negotiations were resumed in 1710 but despite a more mod-

Johann Wenzel, Count Gallas and Duke of Lucera. Count Gallas (1669-1719) served as the emperor's diplomatic representative in London, 1705-1711. In addition, he negotiated troop subsidies with Mainz in 1708 and the Dutch Republic in 1707-1708.

Mezzotint by John Smith after Godfrey Kneller, 1707. Austrian National Library Portrait Collection, Vienna, Austria.

erate attitude on the Austrian side again broke down. Successful, if bloody sieges in northern France orchestrated by Eugene and Marlborough in what was their last joint campaign did not deliver the hoped-for death-blow to the French; unusual military success in Spain proved a one-off. Very soon Charles III, the allied puppet king, saw himself confined to a small strip of land in Catalonia.

Marlborough's fall and the end of the Anglo-Austrian alliance

From the summer of 1710, Habsburg foreign policy had to confront problems of an even more fundamental kind. The dismissal of Marlborough's son-in-law Lord Sunderland as Secretary of State signalled the downfall of the Whig government (August 1710) and the rise of the Tories, who had always opposed the war. Eugene persuaded his brother-in-arms not to resign, the Emperor's envoy to the English court, Gallas, was put on the alert, and, finally, Joseph I intervened personally to emphasize the Captain-General's centrality to the common war effort. But though of necessity 'Whiggish' as far as English domestic politics were concerned, Vienna could not be sulking and had to establish a tolerable working relationship with the new government. Queen Anne made it clear that the war in Spain had to be continued vigorously, and the removal of the Duchess of Marlborough from court did not at once entail her husband's dismissal. In March 1711 Marlborough again assumed command in the Belgian theatre, while, this time, Eugene remained on the Rhine.

Marlborough took Bouchain in September 1711 but was then ordered to move into winter quarters before the really 'hard nuts' such as Cambrai and Arras could be tackled. In summer 1711 France and England agreed on peace preliminaries; first hints at exploratory talks had reached Vienna via Marlborough earlier that year. But soon the English Captain-General was no longer in a position to do his Austrian friends a good turn. Shortly after his arrival in London in November 1711 Marlborough found himself stripped of all his offices – and accused of peculation. Austria's most important agent in England was thus neutralized.

It remains doubtful whether Marlborough, had his career not come to a sudden and bitter end, would have been able to stop Britain's course towards peace. In April 1711 a dynastic disaster had entirely changed the international situation: Joseph I had died of small pox without leaving a male heir. His brother Charles was to succeed him in the Hereditary Lands as well as on the Imperial throne. Luckless as king of Spain, the last male Habsburg returned home on an English ship (ironically H.M.S. *Blenheim*) leaving his wife and troops for a last stand against the Bourbon rival (September 1711).

Among the Allies there was, understandably, no enthusiasm for a repeat performance of Charles V's 16th century *monarchia universalis*, as, during a short visit to Vienna, Lord Peterborough, the former English commander-in-chief in the Peninsula, made clear with characteristic bluntness (April 1711). He suggested that Spain and its colonies should be entrusted to the Duke of Savoy, while the Austrian Habsburgs were to be indemnified with Spain's former possessions in Italy. Wratislaw was quite prepared to take such a scheme into consideration, but Charles still ruled out any partition of his Spanish inheritance.[20]

The Emperor had not only lost Marlborough as intermediary and informant at the English court but also his official representative, Count Gallas. As instructed, the

Joannes Wenceslaus Comes a Gallas, &c.
G. Kneller S.R.Imp & Angl. Eques Aur. pinx. 1707.
I. Smith fec.

latter had intervened massively on behalf of the Whigs but had obviously gone too far in his propaganda activities. Neither the new men in power nor the Queen had been spared in his reports intercepted by the English, and Gallas – now *persona non grata* – had to leave the country (December 1711).

The rift in Anglo-Austrian relations came in a particularly critical phase of the war. In January 1712 peace talks were to begin in Utrecht, and the Emperor, unwilling to end the conflict without having achieved his aims, seemed increasingly isolated. Charles VI now played his trump card and sent Eugene to London, as Marlborough had demanded (January 1712). Bad weather rather than massive Tory intrigues almost thwarted the journey. The crossing was extremely stormy, and talks with the Queen and her ministers remained fruitless. Of course, the war hero, always with Marlborough at his side, was received with great enthusiasm by the public, not, of course, by Tory partisans such as Jonathan Swift who criticized both Eugene's physical defects and his excessive thirst for glory which allegedly torpedoed any peace settlement. 'A natural tincture of Italian cruelty in his disposition' and the occupation of arms, Swift remarked caustically, had extinguished 'all pity and remorse' in the prince.[21]

As the Tory government would not listen to Austrian arguments, a decisive military strike seemed the very last chance to block the road to peace. An embittered Eugene left London at the end of March to continue military operations where Marlborough had been forced to break off. The Savoyard succeeded his friend as commander-in-chief of the Dutch forces, while the English army corps, mostly German subsidy troops, came under the orders of the Duke of Ormond who was instructed not to venture his troops while negotiations with France were going on. A huge scandal ensued, when this leaked out. After an Anglo-French armistice had been signed (August 1712), Ormond left the allied army to occupy Dunkirk which the French sacrificed as a pawn. His Prussian, Hanoverian, Danish and Saxon contingents, however, refused to join him and were taken over into Dutch pay.

Despite such chaotic conditions Eugene had managed to take Le Quesnoy (July 1712), sending raiding parties even down to Paris. The turning point came when the French defeated a Dutch army corps at Denain (24 July 1712). On 11 April 1713, France, England, the United Provinces, Portugal, Savoy and Prussia concluded peace at Utrecht. The Emperor's delegates refused to agree to conditions which Vienna could not but regard as outrageous, fabricated, Eugene of Savoy was foaming, by Oxford and Bolingbroke, their cronies and whores.[22]

Britain, too, had a score to settle with the Austrian partner. Viscount Bolingbroke summed up a long-standing critique of the ally, when he declared that the Habsburg Monarchy 'expects everything and does nothing.' He could never think of Austria, he continued in a most drastic parable, 'without recollecting the image of a man braiding a rope of hay while his ass bites off the other end.'[23] Yet, at closer scrutiny, Britain's self-image as the generous paymaster of the anti-French coalition calls for substantial qualifications, at least from a narrowly Austrian perspective. Vienna calculated that between 1706 and 1712 the English ally had, under varying titles but not as direct subsidies to the Emperor, granted £ 2,000,000, but only a fraction had actually been paid. In fact, £ 900,000, mostly for the maintenance of the Imperial army in the Belgian theatre (1709-11), still remained unsettled. In 1717, the Emperor renounced his claims in return for a part payment of only £ 130.000.[24]

If one looks at national troop strengths, England's very own war effort (which

A view of the city of Mindelheim.

Detail from a map by J.B. Homann, 1715. Austrian National Archives, Vienna, Austria.

traditionally focussed on the fleet) seems even less impressive. In 1710 26.000 English soldiers were earmarked for Flanders and 19.000 for Spain. The Dutch Army numbered 137,000 men, nationals and auxiliaries, and most of them were serving in the Southern Netherlands, while the Emperor's army establishment stood at 133.000 men of whom, however, less than a third could be deployed in theatres prioritized by the English: Spain, the Netherlands and the Rhine. 50.000 were still tied down in Hungary, 31.000 in Italy.[25]

■ The loss of Mindelheim

With Spain lost for good – the Empress-Queen had left Barcelona on H.M.S. *Blenheim* in March 1713 with the Imperial troops following in July – Italy and Belgium neutralized, the Rhine front was the only theatre of war where the Austrian hawks could demonstrate their determination to carry on. Militarily, the 1713 campaign in Germany was a disaster, but politically the Emperor's steadfastness did pay off. The peace treaties of Rastatt (6 March 1714) and Baden (7 September 1714) contained much more favourable conditions and secured Charles VI not only the former Spanish Netherlands but also Milan, Naples, Sardinia, and Mantua.

Marlborough had left England in December 1712, travelling first to Belgium, then to Aachen and finally to Frankfurt where he and the Duchess were to stay for a couple of months. He remained in contact with his Austrian friends. In June and July 1713 he met up with Eugene at Heidelberg and Mainz. Their meetings were not merely about the good old days, as Marlborough was obviously trying to pose as minister-in-exile. In summer 1713 the Emperor decided to go along with a most secret plan the Duke had brought up to overthrow the Tories with the help of the Elector of Hanover, Queen Anne's heir presumptive. Of course, nothing came of it.[26]

To a large extent such dubious initiatives were simply moves to support more personal projects, especially in relation to Mindelheim. So far, Marlborough – who from 1705 proudly signed his letters 'Prince et Duc de Marlborough' – had shown no particular attachment to his principality. It was only in June 1713 that the exiled general paid a (very short) first and last visit to his fief which a Baron Joseph von Imhof (1667-1738), an Augsburg patrician in Habsburg civil service recommended by Prince Eugene, had administered for him since 1706. A recent portrait by Godfrey Kneller (who also subscribed to the loan of 1706) had to make up for the absent prince.

In 1709 Marlborough had managed to secure the right of succession through the female line not granted under the 1705 diploma and which the Imperial Diet had flatly refused in 1706. This was an important point, the Duke's only son having died in 1703. But no formal document had yet been issued to implement this concession technically. In February 1713 Charles VI instructed his representative at the Utrecht peace talks, Count Philipp Ludwig Sinzendorf (1671-1742) to confirm that Mylord-Duc should be allowed to transmit his principality to his daughters and their male descendants as promised by Joseph I.[2]

One year later, however, Marlborough's princely career came to an end. Under massive French pressure the peace treaties of 1714 stipulated the full restoration of the exiled Elector of Bavaria. Implicitly, this included the town and lordship of Mindelheim. There is an undated petition in German which Marlborough must have addressed to the Emperor in the summer of 1714, when the peace of Baden had not yet been finalized. In it he implored Charles VI to ensure that the treaty contain a saving clause for Mindelheim.[28] In vain, in December 1714 the Emperor informed the Duke that he was no longer prince of Mindelheim.

Marlborough, now rehabilitated and back in England, had to face the facts. In a letter to Charles VI dated 14 January 1715, he was at pains to present himself as a good loser. 'Je ferois volontiers,' he declared, 'un plus grand sacrifice pour le bien et le repos de l'Empire.'[29] Ten days later, the Bavarians again took possession of Mindelheim.

In reality, Marlborough would not throw in the towel; the British envoys to Vienna were instructed to put pressure upon the Austrian ministry. As late as 1717 he bombarded his Austrian friends with letters to procure him at least some compensation for the loss of Mindelheim, preferably in cash. Charles VI is said to have considered investing the Duke with the south German county of Nellenburg, old Habsburg territory near Lake Constance, or, at a pinch, with some Tyrolean lordship. Nothing came of these projects (despite allegations to the contrary[30]), and the published correspondence between Marlborough and Prince Eugene ends in 1715. Much the same must be true of their friendship. While by 1716 Anglo-Austrian relations had been normalized, Marlborough had lost his political influence. Several strokes forced him into retirement, while Eugene's career reached its apex.

Rumours that the English general had really been invested with Nellenburg would not die down. In July 1940, newspapers from the Lake Constance region reported that the ancestor of Britain's unwavering premier, Winston Churchill, had become prince of Nellenburg after 1715. It was with great relief that, following consultations with the Haus-, Hof- und Staatsarchiv in Vienna, this hoax could be cleared up: 'Seien wir froh,' journalists appeased their audience, '*daß W[inston] C[hurchill] keinen deutschen Namen trägt. Es wäre für uns wahrlich keine Ehre!*'[31]

Little did they know that the Marlborough family had continued to hold the title of 'Prince of Mindelheim' (and it does so today!). Not content with formal tinsel the Marlboroughs had in 1825 even approached Chancellor Metternich through the channel of the British embassy in Vienna to remind the House of Austria of promises made to the first Duke after his expulsion from Mindelheim. The Holy Roman Empire, however, had ended its days in 1806, and the family could only produce letters by Emperor Charles VI and Eugene of Savoy printed in Archdeacon William Coxe's edition of the Blenheim Papers then hot off the press.[32] The Austrian side distrusted the evidence produced and seemed furious at the way in which the family was acting – an obvious example, Vienna diagnosed, for the well-known 'coarseness' of the English nation![33] George Canning's sabotage of the 'Metternich system' was taking its toll.

■ Bibliographical Note

The relationship between Marlborough and Prince Eugene has repeatedly attracted the attention of both British and Austrian historians, yet they rarely go beneath the surface. After older works such as John Campbell's *The military history of the late prince Eugen of Savoy and of the late John Duke of Marlborough 1701-1706* 2 vols., 1736-7, came the Austrian officer-archivist (later general) Alexander Kirchhammer (1847-1909) with his very superficial 'Prinz Eugen von Savoyen und John Churchill Herzog von Marlborough', in: *Organ der militärwissenschaftlichen Vereine* 24 (1882), 443-64. The British lieutenant-general Sir George MacMunn followed in 1934 with *Prince Eugene*, twin Marshal with *Marlborough*. Gustav Otruba, *Prinz Eugen und Marlborough. Weltgeschichte im Spiegel eines Briefwechsels*, aims at a broader audience, but is useful as a handy catalogue of the published correspondence between Eugene and Marlborough from 1702 to 1715. Hans Schmidt, 'Prinz Eugen und Marlborough', in Johannes Kunisch, ed., *Prinz Eugen und seine Zeit. Eine Ploetz-Biographie*, does not afford any new insights. An art historical detail in Marlborough's relationship with Austria is examined by Peter Barber, 'Marlborough, Art and Diplomacy: The Background to Peter Strudel's Drawing of Time revealing Truth and Confounding Fraudulence', in: *Journal of the Warburg and Courtauld Institutes* 47 (1984), 119-35.

Eugene's private papers were unfortunately dispersed at his death in 1736, but his military correspondence is printed in Friedrich Heller-Hellwaldt, *Militärische Correspondenz des Prinzen Eugen von Savoyen*, and in the monumental *Feldzüge des Prinzen Eugen 1697-1736*, 20 vols., Vienna, 1876-1891, an incredibly detailed narrative of Eugene's military campaigns published by the *Kriegsarchiv* (Austrian War Archives). It is unlikely that all letters to and from Marlborough preserved at the *Haus-, Hof- und Staatsarchiv* in Vienna, among them a considerable number of autographs, have already been published or even consulted. The (formal) correspondence with Leopold I and Joseph I (mostly in Latin) is in *Staatenabteilungen England Varia* 6. This collection includes some letters to Wratislaw, but the main bulk of the latter is in *Große Korrespondenz* 69/b. Letters to Sinzendorf are filed in *Große Korrespondenz* 63/1 (M). *Kriegsakten* 196 includes correspondence with Leopold I and Wratislaw as well as the latter's reports from the Blenheim campaign of 1704. More important still is the correspondence – also in Kriegsakten 196 – between Marlborough and Charles III (Charles VI as Emperor after 1711). Isolated pieces of correspondence between

Marlborough and Eugene, but also between Wratislaw and his court are to be found in *Österreichisches Staatsarchiv*, Vienna, *Kriegsarchiv Alte Feldakten*, and the War Archives' collection *Curiosa*.

The definitive biography of Prince Eugene is by the German Max Braubach, *Prinz Eugen. Eine Biographie*, 5 vols., Vienna, 1963-1965, is based on broad archival studies in many European collections. It replaces the two volumes by Alfred von Arneth, *Prinz Eugen von Savoyen*, 3 vols., Vienna, 1858. There are two shorter, but solid, biographies in English by Nicolas Henderson, *Prince Eugene of Savoy. A Biography*, London, 1964, and Derek McKay, *Prince Eugene of Savoy*, London, 1977. The massive older literature on Eugene is surveyed in Bruno Böhm, *Bibliographie zur Geschichte des Prinzen Eugen von Savoyen und seiner Zeit*, Vienna, 1943.

Churchill's monumental biography of his ancestor, largely based on the Blenheim Papers remains the best starting point from an English perspective: Winston S. Churchill, *Marlborough. His Life and Times*, new ed., 2 vols. Chicago, 2002. Eugene plays only a very marginal role in David Chandler, *Marlborough as Military Commander*, 3rd ed., Staplehurst, 1989. The bulk of the correspondence between Marlborough and Prince Eugene is to be found in English publications: William Coxe (1748-1828), *Memoirs of John Duke of Marlborough with his original correspondence collected from the family records at Blenheim*, 3 vols., London, 1818-1819 (German translation in 6 vols. Vienna, 1820-2); General Sir George Murray (1772-1846), ed., *The letters and dispatches of John Churchill first Duke of Marlborough from 1702 to 1712*, 5 vols., London, 1845. It contains 157 letters which Marlborough addressed to Eugene and four letters by Eugene to Marlborough. B. van 't Hoff, ed., *The Correspondence 1701-1711 of John Churchill First Duke of Marlborough and Anthonie Heinsius, Grand Pensionary of Holland*, The Hague, 1951, does not provide the confidential view of the Austrian ally one might expect. Horst Kospach, 'Englische Stimmen über Österreich und Prinz Eugen während des Spanischen Erbfolgekrieges,' in: *Mitteilungen des Instituts für Österreichische Geschichtsforschung* 73 (1965), 39-62, is disappointing.

There is no adequate 'diplomatic history' of Vienna's policy during the War of the Spanish Succession, drawing together both the enormous body of (older) literature and the rich archival depots in Austria and beyond. An Austrian equivalent to John B. Hattendorf's *England in the War of the Spanish Succession. A Study of the English View and Conduct of Grand Strategy 1702-1712*, New York and London, 1987, remains to be written. Oswald Redlich, *Österreichs Großmachtbildung in der Zeit Kaiser Leopolds I*, Gotha, 1921, and his *Das Werden einer Großmacht.* Österreich 1700-1740, Baden, 1938, are by far the best introduction. See also Leopold Auer, 'Österreichische und europäische Politik um das spanische Erbe', in Elisabeth Springer and Leopold Kammerhofer, eds., *Archiv und Forschung. Das Haus-, Hof- und Staatsarchiv in seiner Bedeutung für die Geschichte Österreichs und Europas*, Vienna and Munich, 1993, 96-109. Onno Klopp, *Der Fall des Hauses Stuart und die Succession des Hauses Hannover*, 14 vols., Vienna, 1875-1888, was allowed to make extensive use of Austrian archival sources. Linda & Marsha Frey, *A Question of Empire. Leopold I and the War of Spanish Succession*, New York, 1983, have consulted material from a series of European archives. Leopold Auer, 'Zur Rolle Italiens in der österreichischen Politik um das Spanische Erbe,' in *Mitteilungen des Österreichischen Staatsarchivs* 31 (1978), 52-72, highlights the centrality of Italy within Habsburg grand strategy.

There are several unpublished post-war doctoral theses on Austro-English relations during the War of the Spanish Succession which do not always meet modern standards: Margarethe Geyer, *Die Gesandtschaft des Grafen Wratislaw in London bis zum Abschluß der Großen Allianz vom 7. September 1701*, Vienna, 1948; Erika Skall, *Die Entstehung der Großen Allianz 1701*, Vienna, 1950; Elisabeth Mach, *Johann Wenzel Graf Gallas, kaiserlicher und königlich-spanischer Botschafter am Hof der Königin Anna von England 1705-1711*, Vienna, 1966; Elfriede Mezgolich, *Graf Johann Wenzel Wratislaw von Mitrowitz. Sein Wirken während des Spanischen Erbfolgekrieges*, Vienna, 1967. Elke Jarnut-Derbolav, *Die österreichische Gesandtschaft in London 1701-1711. Ein Beitrag zur Geschichte der Haager Allianz*, Bonn, 1972, is the best treatment available. Strangely, even the two standard biographies of Emperors Leopold I und Joseph I are by American historians: John P. Spielman, *Leopold I of Austria*, Rutgers NJ, 1977 and Charles Ingrao, *In Quest and Crisis: Emperor Joseph I and the Habsburg Monarchy*, West Lafayette, Ind., 1979.

Military history has been equally neglected by post-1945 Austrian historiography. Michael Hochedlinger, *Austria's Wars of Emergence 1683-1797. War, State and Society in the Habsburg Monarchy*, London, 2003, has short diplomatic and military narratives. The 300th anniversary of the battle of Höchstädt-Blindheim (Blenheim) stimulated important research. There is a splendid exhibition catalogue Johannes Erichsen and Katharina Heinemann., eds., *Brennpunkt Europas 1704. Die Schlacht von Höchstädt*, Ostfildern, 2004, and an in-depth study by Marcus Junkelmann, *'Das greulichste spectaculum'. Die Schlacht von Höchstädt 1704*, Munich, 2004.

The opening of a new front in the Mediterranean in 1694 was an event with great consequences for Great Britain and its navy. It was a Dutch idea. Sending naval squadrons to the Iberian Peninsula and into the Mediterranean for the protection of trade and shipping to the Levant and to fight the Barbary States was almost a tradition in the Dutch Republic. At the opening of the Nine Years' War in 1689, William III, the Stadholder-King, would have liked to send a squadron to the Mediterranean right away, but the French fleet in Brest prevented this by an unexpected operation in Irish waters. Immediately after the French defeat in the battles of Barfleur and La Hogue (May 29 and June 1-3, 1692), William III suggested operations in the Mediterranean to his ministers in London, but in vain. The Stadholder-King felt that allied sea power in this area would enhance the overall allied strategy. He considered that the diplomatic and strategic benefits of such a move would be equal to any comparable support of trade and shipping.[1]

In 1694 William III and the Dutch Republic finally had their way. In early April political and naval authorities in Amsterdam as well as Grand Pensionary Heinsius stressed the desirability of fleet operations in the Mediterranean.[2] Meanwhile the Brest fleet had joined the fleet from Toulon in that area. William III therefore ordered the allied fleet to enter the Mediterranean. What followed was as novel as the theatre of action itself. Despite highly vocal objections from naval administrators and admirals on board the ships, the allied fleet was not to return home for winter quarters but must remain at Cadiz. The Spanish authorities had made this suggestion and offered to pay the extra costs for the fleet remaining away from home all winter. For the first time the English fleet wintered at a foreign naval base. It was the first step in Britain's subsequent search for its own fleet accommodation abroad, a crucial element on its road to later world-wide naval supremacy.

An uneasy naval alliance

The two former enemies, England and the Dutch Republic, had fought three consecutive wars at sea. Their naval conflicts ended in 1674. Thereafter, Louis XIV's pursuit of supremacy in Europe, starting in the late 1660's, drove the two countries into each other's arms, resulting in the two treaties of 1674 and 1678, the first of a commercial, the second of a defensive nature. In 1678 both countries promised to support each other in case of attack upon the other's territory. The terms of the defensive treaty described in detail the aid each power had to render to the other, should either be invaded by a third. The attacks or the preparations for attack were restricted to Dutch and English territories in Europe. The support could consist of troops and/or ships. Princely bonds were established by Stadholder William III's marriage to Mary, the English king's niece. During the 1680's France continued its policy of territorial expansion, and a Europe-wide conflict was unavoidable when the Stadholder became king of England as well. Louis XIV did not accept the deposition of James II nor did he accept the Protestant succession.

This so-called Nine Years' War was fought on land and at sea. The pattern of Anglo-Dutch cooperation was laid down in an official agreement signed in May, 1689.[3] At sea the partners were to contribute warships at a ratio of five to three, five from England for each three from the Republic. On land, the ratio was reversed, three soldiers from England for each five from the Republic. These ratios had already

Naval actions during Marlborough's campaigns.

Map by Rocío Espín.

been mentioned in the treaty of 1678. The command structure, voting in councils of war and other details were stipulated as well. Both countries, from now on called the two Maritime Powers, started a cooperation to which each had to get accustomed. The North Sea had been their familiar common battle ground, but this would now for both fleets become a backwater. France was the enemy; it had its main fleet concentrated at Brest, a strong naval base on the Atlantic Ocean near the entrance to the Channel. The mercantilist policies of Colbert had provided France with a strong battle fleet along with a merchant marine and that made him a true protagonist of sea power according to the late nineteenth-century naval philosopher A.T. Mahan.[4] Much to the surprise and annoyance of the Maritime Powers, France for the moment dictated naval strategy. The French navy successfully landed troops in southern Ire-

The Battle of La Hogue, 3-4 June 1692.

Painting by Adriaen van Diest, late 17th century. National Maritime Museum, Greenwich, London, UK.

of fighting ships. In England, the invasion scare now faded away. The Maritime Powers had gained superiority in the Channel and the Atlantic. In a Dutch doggerel after the battle, a Frenchman is saying:

> *'Alas, our admirals where are they,*
> *5,000 pieces of guns,*
> *the entire transport fleet,*
> *the entire battle fleet?*
> *Damned, all has been set on fire and in flame.*
> *Ha, Holy Louis, ah Our Lady.*
> *Mercy. My Lord, we are your prisoners.'* [8]

After the two battles it proved difficult for the victors to exploit the situation. Blockading Brest meant dealing with many limiting factors such as wind, tide and complexities of navigation. It would only become standard practice much later, from 1758-1759. In 1693, the preferred English scheme to thwart the French naval threat was to capture Brest by landing troops there and thus eliminate the Atlantic fleet.

This never occurred. On the contrary, bad strategic and tactical manoeuvring by allied naval forces gave the French the opportunity to combine their two fleets off Cadiz. On June 20, 1693, they surprised a huge convoy of 150 Dutch and English Levant ships near Cape St. Vincent.[9] The allied losses were heavy. Yet the French did not follow up this victory. The entire French fleet simply disappeared into the Mediterranean, thus illustrating the French government's lack of a consistent strategy in which the navy was to play a major role. Downplaying the navy as a major fighting force – though not officially embraced – was France's sole consistent policy in warfare at sea from 1693 onwards. French warships were increasingly deployed in squadrons raiding hostile targets such as merchantmen, fishing vessels, whole convoys, and overseas trading posts. Economic warfare had become France's preference.

This strategy disgusted the English naval establishment, which longed to fight the set-piece battle that now consistently eluded them, but William III showed the way to respond to the new situation. He envisaged the western Mediterranean as a new front in the Europe-wide war against Louis XIV. He saw strategic possibilities which lay 'beyond the mental horizon of most English ministers', as N.A.M. Rodger states in his *Command of the Ocean*.[10] In some ways, William III envisaged a new role for his two navies. This conflict was different from previous ones, in which the Dutch and English had been involved. These wars were fought and decided at sea. The decision in the present war would be made on land. This was already obvious to most politicians and military experts. Yet naval forces could play an essential role in arriving at the final decision. Command of the Mediterranean was crucial to any war in which France was the enemy of Spain or any of the Italian states. Controlling the sea, the allied fleet could be useful in besieging fortresses and in supplying the armies of France's enemies. However, one thing had become clear during the first four years of the war: in this conflict navies now had only a complementary function. The southern Netherlands, Germany and northern Spain were the main battlegrounds of the Nine Years' War and not the sea. England only slowly became aware of the extra potential of naval operations against France and later against Spain.

Another interesting aspect of this war was the gradual erosion of the position of the Dutch Republic as one of the leading sea powers. It was the consequence of the two Anglo-Dutch treaties of 1678 and 1689, and of William III's prominent role in maintaining and establishing a balance of power on the continent. The Dutch contribution to the war on land was greater than that made by the English, and William III was in command of allied troops. Dutch naval officers, however, had to accept as a fait accompli English dominance in naval affairs. This was difficult for the old hands, who had fought victorious battles in the Third Anglo-Dutch War of 1672-1674. The treaty of 1689 stipulated that the senior commander of an Anglo-Dutch squadron would always be an Englishmen. This stipulation had its logic, but the text of the treaty created a situation in which no Dutch flag officer would ever command joint squadrons or detachments. That was an insult in Dutch eyes and a guarantee of friction.

Hence cooperation was touchy, in particular in the aftermath of the Beachy Head defeat. Hardly any of the allied officers could speak or understand the language of their opposite numbers. In 1692, Admiral Russell had both an English and a Dutch secretary, the Dutchman also acting as an interpreter. From 1691 Admiral Van Almonde proved to be the correct choice to command the Dutch naval forces. He had the right talents to function productively with his English colleagues. His tactical suggestions at sea regularly found willing ears.[11]

Grave Monument of Lieutenant-Admiral Philips van Almonde (1644-1711). The Admiralty of Amsterdam appointed van Almonde Lieutenant-Admiral of Holland in 1692, and in 1708, the Admiralty at Rotterdam additionally appointed him Lieutenant-Admiral, the highest position by tradition. He commanded the Dutch naval force in the combined Anglo-Dutch fleet in both the Nine Years' War and in the first portion of the War of the Spanish Succession.

Sint-Catharijnekerk, Den Briel, the Netherlands. Photograph by Ton Sipman.

The Dutch, in general, slowly adjusted to playing second fiddle. For the people of the Netherlands, the army was now much closer to them than the navy, which operated further and further away from their home ports. Jean Bart's raids in the North Sea and the dire need of more convoys to protect both mercantile shipping and fishing vessels were more frequently discussed in the Netherlands than battle fleet operations in distant waters. Meanwhile, in 1694, the Dutch and English naval authorities switched their main attention to new activities in the Mediterranean and the problem of a fleet wintering abroad.

■ A successful adventure: the allied fleet in the Mediterranean (1694-1695)

The southern front in Louis XIV's warfare was north-eastern Spain. French troops had occupied great parts of Catalonia. Barcelona was their wished for prize and they besieged the city from land and sea. The arrival, however, of the allied fleet in the Mediterranean during the summer of 1694 immediately turned the tables, changing the military situation. The joint Anglo-Dutch-Spanish fleet counted 75 ships-of-the-line and was superior to the combined Brest-Toulon fleet, which speedily retreated into Toulon. The Allies were then able to liberate Catalonia. The presence of the Allies also had its impact upon the activities of the Barbary corsairs. The security of mercantile shipping to and from the Levant was greatly enhanced.[12]

The Anglo-Dutch fleet remained in the Mediterranean for two years. A successful attack on Toulon was deemed impossible. Meanwhile the other French fleet was locked up in Brest, thus opening the door for allied operations elsewhere. The French fleet was not only impotent in the Mediterranean, but was virtually absent from the Channel as well.

For the winter of 1694-1695, the Spanish government offered hospitality at Cadiz to the English and Dutch warships and their crews. Earlier, Port Mahon on Minorca had been mentioned as a possible base. Cadiz became England's first experience of a situation where her main fleet wintered over and refitted in a foreign port. John Ehrman called this 'the most interesting administrative event of the war'.[13] Ships of all rates, including the largest, were involved. Cadiz Bay was certainly not an ideal location, lying partly open and undefended. Shore leave for the allied men was very restricted. Admiral Russell was housed ashore, disgruntled about the hardships of his exile. He would rather have been at home and was often full of spleen. British relations with the Spanish authorities were far from cordial, in contrast to the experience of their Dutch colleagues. Spain and the Republic had made an agreement about the presence of the Dutch vessels, with Spain promising to pay the costs. Two instalments were paid, but not the four others that were due, out of a total of £190,000. The yield from a Scheldt toll in the Spanish Netherlands was the security for payment. England on the other hand financed the stationing of her fleet in Cadiz completely from her own funds.

On November 18, 1694, the English issued the first order to begin the refit of vessels at Cadiz. The English did the work all on their own. Local circumstances were adverse, but as Ehrman neatly formulated it, 'the officers and men set to work methodically and with some vigour, with that consciousness of their superiority to their surroundings which distinguishes the Royal Navy in the ports of Southern Europe.' This was possible thanks to adequate preparations made at home by the naval administrators in British dockyards. They supplied everything: victuals, slop cloths, and materials for refitting the ships, skilled workmen included. The first stores ship sailed for Cadiz on September 22, 1694, carrying fifty loads of oak timber, three sets of careening gear with six pumps, 48 masts, and so on. Five more stores

Admiral Sir George Rooke (1650-1709) commanded combined Anglo-Dutch naval forces in both the Nine Years' War and the War of the Spanish Succession.

Painting by Michael Dahl, around 1705. National Maritime Museum, Greenwich, London, UK.

vessels sailed in early December. The rest followed in February 1695. These five vessels had on board 47 shipwrights, caulkers, smiths, and bricklayers as well. The four oakum boys sent to Cadiz should not be forgotten. In this way, a repair yard on English lines was established in a foreign harbour. Provisioning the crews sufficiently turned out to be more difficult and time consuming. The financial side was covered by the Bank of England, which had just been incorporated in May 1694 for the purpose of lending money to the government. Hence the Navy was able to pay for its materials promptly.[14]

The refitting and resupplying of the Dutch contingent was a different story. Victualling the Dutch ships was part of the Dutch-Spanish agreement, a temporary relief for the Dutch captains. The first four supply ships from the Netherlands did not arrive until February 1695, and others got there even later. The Dutch contingent counted 24 ships-of-the-line and almost 9,000 men. Severe frost and adverse winds caused delays at home, but the principal reason for the delay was a lack of coordination among the five Admiralties. None made any preparations before October. Significant arrears both in receiving state subsidies and in paying bills to suppliers of victuals or materials had created problems in the navy's finances. Victuals and naval stores could hardly be ordered on credit. At Cadiz, according to Admiral Russell, the unready state of Dutch ships was simply caused by 'their constant want of provisions and their thriftiness in not allowing their ships to be cleaned.'[15]

William III's new strategy of opening a new naval front was successful only in 1694 and 1695. The second winter at Cadiz was not a success. Many things went wrong. At the top of the list came an early and unexpected departure of the Toulon fleet for Brest. In late March 1696, the allied ships left Cadiz to return home. The pre-1694 situation was soon restored. Catalonia fell and Barcelona was taken by the French in 1697, after a siege and a bombardment by a small naval squadron and the galley fleet.[16]

When the next war broke out in 1702 and the Mediterranean became straightaway the most important naval front, English politicians and naval leaders immediately considered a base for the navy in that region an absolute necessity. In retrospect, one can look upon the fleet's wintering at Cadiz in 1694-1695 as the commencement of Great Britain's future desire to occupy naval bases in those regions of the world that were or would be vital for its trade and shipping interests. Amsterdam had triggered this development.

No consistent strategy

In the course of the Nine Years' War, naval warfare increasingly became a thing on the fringe of the major events, all of which took place on shore. For two years (1694 and 1695), the allied fleet had frustrated French attempts to capture Catalonia, but only temporarily. Neither side had a consistent policy of using its naval forces to their utmost. Meanwhile something curious took place. Intense building programs, started in 1689, had resulted in navies that were bigger than ever before. The number of English ships-of-the-line had increased from 83 to 112 in 1695; the Dutch from 52 to 72, and the French numbers grew from 89 to 119.[17] The French navy was still substantially larger than the English and only one-third smaller than the combined forces of the Maritime Powers. The Dutch, the smallest of the three, in 1696 deployed their greatest naval force ever. The fleet, the North Sea squadron and the convoy ships

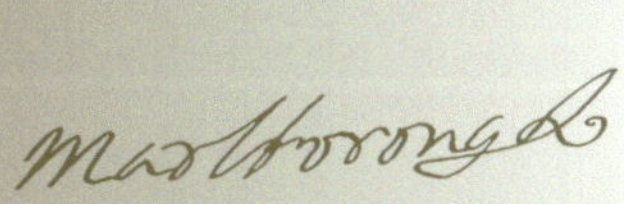

amounted to 115 vessels manned by 24,369 men and boys.[18]

A large scale naval battle did not take place after Barfleur and La Hogue in 1692. The allied naval forces were mostly split up in smaller contingents and deployed in a great variety of operations. From 1695, France more or less dissolved its main fleet. Paris gave priority to state coordinated privateering in order to hurt the enemy's seaborne trade as severely as possible. Strong squadrons of men-of-war and privateers audaciously attacked English and Dutch shipping, even well-protected convoys of merchantmen.[19] This policy scored great successes, in particular the operations of Jean Bart. The French followed the same policy in the western Atlantic and in North American waters. The Maritime Powers found it difficult to respond to these French activities. One striking example is De Pointis' raid of 1697 which created havoc amongst allied shipping. His force, made up of seven ships-of-the-line and fourteen privateers attacked Cartagena and captured merchant ships, while eluding English squadrons near Cuba, Newfoundland, and at long last in the Channel. De Pointis brought enormous booty into Brest in late August 1697, though with debilitated ships and crews.[20]

In the Channel, the allied fleet was superior to the French as of 1695. The lack of a serious opponent, however, and the unlikelihood of a major battle made large men-of-war somewhat redundant. In the absence of set-piece battles, naval barrages blasting coastal fortresses and the harbour fortifications at Brest, St. Malo, Dunkirk, and some other places were among their few alternative uses. Bombardments and occasional landings of troops became a regular allied business. France was kept on the alert and was forced to maintain troops along her seacoasts. In a parallel sense, destruction of or damage to English and Dutch harbour facilities were the most serious things France could now threaten. Rumours of a French invasion plan in 1696 briefly caused confusion in allied naval circles.[21]

In this situation it was unavoidable that the Maritime Powers gave the greatest priority to the protection of mercantile shipping. Mutual protection of shipping in the western hemisphere, for instance, had not been stipulated in the Anglo-Dutch treaty of 1689. The Dutch, much alarmed by the successes of Dunkirk privateers, kept increasing the numbers of smaller warships in the North Sea. In 1694 the English Parliament, spurred by their merchants and ship-owners, passed a Convoys and Cruisers Act, which created a sort of second navy to protect the commercial and shipping interests of England.[22] This Act was clear testimony to England's growing awareness of how important trade and shipping had become to the country.

A demonstration of sea power in 1700

The peace of Rijswijk in 1697 did not last long. Expectations for a lasting peace were low. The problem of the Spanish Succession was in the offing. France's opponents would certainly not voluntarily accept a member of Louis XIV's Bourbon family on the throne at Madrid, ruling a vast overseas empire as well. War was to break out again in 1702. The growing tensions around the issue of the succession added to the conflict in northern Europe. The official interlude of five years between the two wars was not in fact very peaceful.

Even more than events during the last phase of the Nine Years' War, the Great Northern War (1700-1721) demonstrated from its start the influence that sea power could exert in areas bordering on the sea. The Maritime Powers grasped this sudden opportunity. The safety of their shipping interests in the Baltic was at stake, a threat that by tradition put the Dutch in particular on the alert. In 1700, free passage through the Sound was in danger. Denmark and Sweden were at loggerheads once again. Problems with the borders between southern Denmark and the county of Holstein were the cause of the conflict. The young Swedish king Charles XII was all too eager to intervene, of course, on Holstein's side. Both England and the Republic had guaranteed the observance of a 1689 treaty concerning Holstein. When the Danish army started operations along its southern border Sweden threatened to land troops near Copenhagen. The English and Dutch governments decided, under the circumstances, to send a joint naval force to the Sound under the overall command of Admiral Sir George Rooke. The Dutch contingent of thirteen ships-of-the-line under Admiral Philips van Almonde was slightly stronger than the ten English ships under Admiral Rooke, illustrating that Dutch interests in the region were preeminent. The two men were on good terms with each other.

In June 1700, the allied forces arrived at Gothenburg and slowly advanced to the northern part of the Sound. Both the Danish and the Swedish navies were stronger than the combined allied squadron. The Danes forbade the Allies passage through the Sound. A process of negotiation and careful manoeuvring finally resulted in a Swedish-allied joint effort, while the Danes retreated behind the defences of Copenhagen. The stubbornness of the Danish king and his refusal to observe the 1689 treaty were finally broken by a Swedish invasion and two light bombardments of Copenhagen by Rooke's and Van Almonde's ships. On August 18, 1700, a new treaty was concluded. The Swedish evacuation was supervised by the allied naval forces, which having done that, sailed home. Peace and free passage of the Sound were restored by clever diplomacy and a restricted use of violence.[23]

Convoying, another aspect of sea power

Dramatic shows of force were important instruments of sea power in time of peace, but convoying also had potential for achieving the goals of nations. While most of the larger warships were kept in reserve, smaller units did convoy services on regular trading routes. In earlier days the Dutch navy had started a system of accompanying merchant ships to a number of commercial destinations. Merchants and ship-owners were entitled to a certain amount of protection in the frame of fiscal arrangements between the state and traders. The Dutch Admiralties provided regular convoys on routes to and from, for instance, the White Sea, the Iberian Peninsula and the last leg of sailing home from the East Indies. Every year this service was available at mutually agreed times, resulting in regular shipping patterns. Safe transport of silver and gold from Lisbon or Seville to Amsterdam was a traditional matter of concern and so drew convoy protection. Naval captains liked the service since they earned a certain percentage of the value of the bullion.

With its growing overseas trade, the English need of regular protection for shipping became a factor in naval policy there as well. The Levant trade was one of the most flourishing sectors of English foreign trade, as were the Iberian connections, fed by the exchange of Newfoundland dried cod for dried fruits and wines. An undisturbed import of naval stores from the Baltic was increasingly important. Thus in

The Action at Vigo Bay, 22 - 24 October 1702.

Engraving by Peter Schenk, 18th century. Maritiem Museum Rotterdam, Rotterdam, the Netherlands. From the Collectie De Jonge.

England too the provision of naval convoys evolved after 1660 into a reliable system of support for merchantmen, not only by convoying but also by patrolling at fixed stations. The majority of fighting ships were dispatched to southern Europe and the Mediterranean. As was the case with the Dutch, no warships were employed to convoy merchantmen to the Baltic. In London, ship-owners and merchants were in touch with naval authorities about how convoys were to be organized. The result was a partnership between these groups and the state in which the navy functioned as an instrument to further the interests of both.[24]

In this context the abandonment of Tangier in 1684, seems odd. It, as well as Bombay, had been part of the dowry of Catherine of Braganza, the Portuguese princess who had married the English King Charles II in 1662, and it provided England with a permanent naval presence in the Mediterranean. Tangier, however, turned out to be ill-suited as a base because most warships were too large to be accommodated and it was not well equipped to provide stores and provisions.[25] In peacetime and in the relations with the Barbary States, Tangier was not needed, but the experience of the Nine Years' War had taught a different lesson.

In wartime, the normal convoy system could not be continued in its entirety. Naval squadrons only took care of earmarked merchant fleets such as the Levant convoy or special groups of vessels sailing home from the Baltic through the Sound. Increasing numbers of losses to French privateers stimulated the trading interest to ask for better and more protection. The Cruisers and Convoys Act of 1694 had been a tangible result. Five cruising squadrons operated around Ireland and England, covering passing convoys. During the War of the Spanish Succession (1702-1713), which followed after a short and uneasy peace, the overall situation was no different. French privateering successes were even greater and the complaints from ship-owners and merchants in London were even louder. The result was a second Cruisers and Convoys Act in 1708. This act removed 43 warships, their armament precisely formulated, from fleet use and assigned them as convoy escorts and cruisers at specified home stations.[26] The action put an end to protests from the trading interest for the rest of the war. Whatever tangible effects the 1708 Act may have had, the total value of English imports and (re)exports remained rather stable. In 1700, the value of imports was £5,849,000 with the value of exports and re-exports £6,419,000 and in 1713 the figures were £5,352,000 and £6,433,000 respectively.[27] It is perhaps noteworthy that the Navy's failure to provide adequate protection had been used in 1708 by opponents of the government to attack the Admiralty. The most powerful man on this board was Admiral George Churchill, Marlborough's brother.[28]

The start of another war in 1702 and its naval strategy

In October of the first year of the War of the Spanish Succession, the Maritime Powers dealt a severe blow to their French and Spanish opponents. The two were staunch allies opposed to the appropriation of the entire Spanish empire by the grandson of Louis XIV, who now reigned in the Iberian kingdom as Philip V. The Spanish silver fleet with the accumulated wealth from several previous years, protected by a strong French squadron, arrived safely on the coast of northwest Spain at Vigo Bay in late September, 1702. At least it seemed the ships arrived safely. However, the principal English and Dutch battle fleets, which happened to be on their way home after a failed campaign against Cadiz, were on the spot. They hesitated only briefly before forcing the entrance of the bay on October 22. The enemy was taken by surprise and unprepared. The complete French squadron of fifteen ships was annihilated by fire or by capture. Several Spanish galleons were burned and six were captured. It was a great financial loss for the enemy.

The allied success was just in time. In the Netherlands several verse mongers did their work. The relief was great. Two stanzas serve as an example:

'Eleven galleons, loaded with silver.
Those have we carried quickly away from here,
And those that were stranded there.
All fell into our hands.
And this trembles the whole of Spain, by its noise.

The French vessels do not get away either,
But they do not escape their fate, dead sure,
Five taken, And sunken four,
And eight consumed by flame and fire.
What we all watched with delight'.[29]

come to power in 1710. The relations between the military leaders of England and the Republic deteriorated. Old-hand Job de Wildt, secretary of the Amsterdam Admiralty and the leading Dutch naval administrator, died in 1704, and was not replaced by anyone of his quality. The Dutch were falling back in their provision of annual naval contingents, failing to meet the quotas agreed to in the naval treaty of 1689. English lists of vessels deployed, however, mentioned only those ships that sailed entirely under English command. Those under Dutch command were not included and these were an increasing number.[33] The English became less careful in appointing commanders who were at least equal in rank to their Dutch colleagues, a very sensitive point of honour. In June 1706, Admiral van Almonde relinquished his command, when it became clear that his opposite number would be of lower rank. The Dutchman sailed home as a passenger on board an English warship. There had been other incidents of this nature in previous years, without provoking quite such an ostentatious Dutch reaction. English authorities and officers on the spot treated the Dutch contingents more and more as a support fleet and not as equal partners.[34]

The Mediterranean scene

The key issue of the war was the question who would rule Spain. France and Spain, Portugal, several Italian states and of course the Emperor were all involved. Armies were to play the main role in this. The party that could move troops and munitions freely over the sea and organize amphibious assaults might have a trump card. A French fleet blockaded in Toulon or able to sail at will then was a crucial factor in this contest. The Maritime Powers greatest fear was the Mediterranean fleet joining the one at Brest. The attempt to conquer Cadiz, designed to prevent any union of the two, had, however, been an utter failure. Other attempts to acquire a stronghold on the Spanish coast for the same purpose were to follow. The Nine Years' War had taught the Allies the value of a naval base in this region, so close to the centre of fighting. The main naval activities would be in and around the Mediterranean, all others being subordinated to this. Smaller vessels were to be used for the protection of the route to Flanders and for a sort of blockade of Dunkirk, as well as for convoy services and operations in the West Indies and North America.

An important consequence of the victory at Vigo was Portugal's adherence to the alliance in 1703. This new ally provided facilities to overwinter on the Tagus in Lisbon. Some Dutch warships took up that option as early as the winter of 1703-1704. Not much had been done by the allied fleet that year. The allied warships had arrived late in the Mediterranean, had visited some Italian ports and provided convoys for Levant traders. The French and Spanish coast was left undisturbed, while the French fleet withdrew to port when the allied fleet appeared.

More was to happen in 1704. Both the Brest and allied fleets arrived early in the Mediterranean. At first, the French evaded action while Admiral Rooke failed to take Barcelona. Then the Allies grasped the lucky opportunity of Gibraltar being almost undefended. In early August, English and Dutch marines were landed. The small and ruined fortress was captured in the name of Charles III, the Austrian claimant to the Spanish throne. Only much later would Gibraltar's great potential be recognized.

Plan showing the combined English and Dutch fleet lifting the French siege of Gibraltar.

Engraving by Pierre Husson, 1704. Maritiem Museum Rotterdam, Rotterdam, the Netherlands. From the Collectie De Jonge.

The naval battle of Malága

The capture of Gibraltar provoked an almost immediate effort by the combined Brest-Toulon fleet to try to retake it. On August 24 the battle of Malága took place. It was a fierce and bloody fight between almost equal adversaries. The allied fleet had 53 ships-of-the-line and a number of bomb vessels. The French probably had at least 50 capital ships plus more than 20 galleys. The latter could give a tow or other help to a ship in trouble, but could not be used on this occasion because of their limited firepower. The French had some very large ships carrying 104 guns. The largest English ships had 96 guns and the Dutch ones even less. The Allies had the advantage of the wind, though the weather was rather calm. The fleets fought in parallel lines, the three squadrons more or less opposite each other, all according to line tactics. At the end of the day-long battle several allied ships had run out of shot and powder. Bomb vessels had not been used before in a sea fight. They turned out to be valuable; one of the largest French ships was set on fire by their bombs and they scored some very damaging hits. No ship was sunk or captured on either side, though a Dutch vessel sank a few days later. The battle was therefore indecisive. The next day the French forfeited the chance for victory when the wind changed in their favour. They remained in line, but were only prepared to fight if the Allies gave battle, which they

The Battle of Vélez-Málaga, 24 August 1704. The battle was the largest naval battle during the War of the Spanish Succession. It took place off the coast of southern Spain. Indecisive in tactical terms, it became a strategic victory for the Anglo-Dutch forces, as the French fleet at Toulon did not emerge again in full strength during the remainder of the war.

Painting by Isaac Sailmaker, 1704. National Maritime Museum, Greenwich, London, UK.

did not. The English and Dutch ships retired to Gibraltar but the French did not give up. They decided to try to reduce the fortress at Gibraltar by a siege on the land side and a blockade by a naval force. This effort lasted several months, until a gale blew the blockading ships out to sea. The siege ended abruptly in March 1705.[35] It was only then that the English and Dutch could finally consider Gibraltar to be theirs.

Gibraltar was not equipped to accommodate a fleet wintering over because its anchorage was too unprotected. Lisbon continued to serve that purpose. Each winter a number of allied warships used the harbour on the Tagus. Yet the capture of Gibraltar, plus the strategic victory at the battle of Malága, combined, as they were, with major successes on land – Marlborough's and Eugene's victory at Blenheim-Höchstädt, both events that also took place in August 1704 – were nevertheless cause for much rejoicing in London and The Hague.

The annual preparations for yet another campaign in the Mediterranean had become a routine. The navy's role was now fully complementary. From 1705, more expeditionary troops were on board and their commanders often began to overrule the admirals. Lengthy discussions in councils-of-war became normal. The capture of Barcelona in 1705 was largely at the instigation of the generals. An attack on Toulon, which would have eliminated the French fleet, was constantly postponed. Instead of

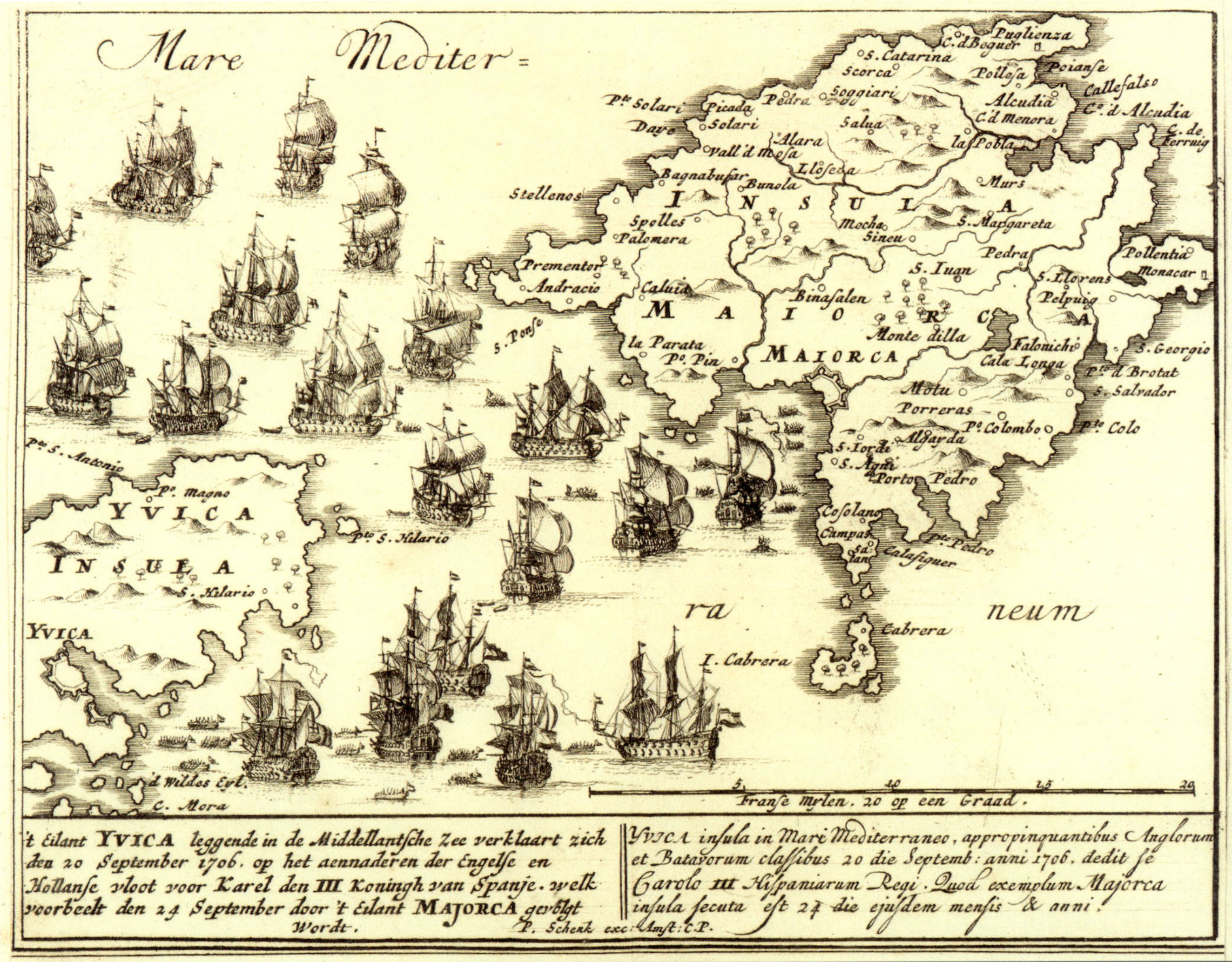

The Islands of Majorca and Ibiza declare for King Charles III, 20 September 1706.

Engraving by Peter Schenk, 18th century. Maritiem Museum Rotterdam, Rotterdam, the Netherlands. From the Collectie De Jonge.

this, more cities along the Spanish coast were occupied, though mostly only for a short while. In July 1707, the long awaited attack on Toulon finally took place. It was a land and sea assault, in which the navy was much more successful. English and Dutch bomb vessels shelled the harbour intensively, whereupon the French scuttled their warships in shallow water with the intention of raising them later. The land attack was ineffective. The troops could not continue the siege. The result that counted, however, was the de facto elimination of the Toulon fleet. Through this, allied naval forces gained full control of the western Mediterranean. They now had the ability to provide transportation and naval support for allied armies wherever and whenever these were needed. The French were unable to raise any major opposition.

In 1708, a usable naval base for the English and Dutch fleets in the Mediterranean was still a major priority for the Maritime Powers. After having supplied the army in Catalonia and capturing Sardinia, the allied command was urged by Charles III, the Habsburg pretender to the Spanish throne, to attack Minorca, the most westerly island of the Balearics. The other two large islands, Ibiza and Majorca, had already been taken in October 1706. Port Mahon on Minorca probably offered the best harbour in the western Mediterranean. According to a Dutch seaman's saying the Mediterranean had only four good harbours: June, July, August, and Port Mahon.[36]

Gerhard Callenburgh (1642-1722).
The Admiralty of Rotterdam appointed Callenburgh a Vice-Admiral in 1689 and Lieutenant-Admiral in 1697. He served at sea until 1704.

Painting by Johannes Vollevens, 1718. The Mauritshuis, Willemstad, the Netherlands. From the collection of the Rijksmuseum, Amsterdam, the Netherlands. Photograph by Ton Sipman.

A combined operation of naval and army contingents succeeded in conquering the island. It was soon obvious that Britain intended to keep Port Mahon. It was an attractive naval base, no more than 300 miles from Toulon.[37]

From a wider perspective and in light of hindsight one can easily say that the capture of Gibraltar and Port Mahon were the most important naval events in the War of the Spanish Succession, in particular in the Mediterranean. The capture of Port Mahon occurred in a phase of the war when the allied fleet was drastically decreasing in size. From 1707 onwards both the British and Dutch contingents became smaller and smaller, and their employment less and less spectacular and useful. Naval operations followed the war on land and consisted, as mentioned earlier, of the transportation and supply of troops.[38] An occasional assault was made in southern France in 1709. Plans were formulated for another attack in Sicily. Convoys of grain vessels for a hungry France were intercepted. The situation in Spain was no longer favourable, and changed dramatically when in 1711 the Emperor died leaving Charles III his most likely successor. In September 1712 an armistice put an end to naval operations.

■ Irritation amongst allied naval leaders

The growth of English self confidence and the rise of a new generation of political and naval leaders resulted in decreasing consideration for Dutch war efforts and a neglect of the implementation of the 1689-treaty stipulations which were still in force during this war. This created tension between the Maritime Powers, aggravated by the circumstance that the Dutch were not fulfilling their agreed quotas of ships. The Dutch on their side complained about English haughtiness and disdain, while the English complained about Dutch touchiness. Dutch flag officers felt humiliated by the stipulation of 1689 that each naval detachment had to be commanded by an English officer. This officer had to have a rank higher or at least equal to that of his Dutch counterpart. Admiral Van Almonde's withdrawal in 1706 when the stipulation was violated proved to be a critical event. The same disdain for Dutch feelings was displayed again a year later. The only Dutch flag officer in the Mediterranean suddenly died on July 9, and a captain became the highest ranking Dutch officer in the combined fleet. Another flag officer had to come from the Republic. It was Jan Gerrit Baron van Wassenaer, Vice-Admiral and a man with a great fighting reputation. He arrived in Gibraltar on October 10, just when the English Admiral Sir Cloudesly Shovell was about to leave for England. The English admiral announced his own immediate departure to his new colleague, the wind being too favourable to be missed. At this point, Rear-Admiral Sir Thomas Dilkes took command of the winter forces. Shovell assumed that Van Wassenaer would become Dilkes' opposite number. But that was not what the Dutchman thought proper: as a vice-admiral he would not serve under a rear-admiral. Doing so would be a sign of disrespect for his masters, the States General. Most English officers were surprised by this refusal, and tried in vain to change Van Wassenaer's mind. Shovell said it was now too late for another English command arrangement.

After the meeting Van Wassenaer assembled his ships, gave instructions for the winter period, wrote to the States General, and sailed to Lisbon on board a Dutch first rate. He arrived there on November 19. He was in a desperate mood. His hurried voyage from the Republic was fruitless. The need to maintain respect for his masters had given him no other option. The Hague fully approved his actions. On April 7, the English vice-admiral Leake arrived, but it was not before May 5 that the two vice-admirals sailed to the theatre of war in the Mediterranean.[39]

For an officer of a higher rank to serve under a lower allied colleague is still a touchy proposition in modern times, but was even more so in an era when the assumed honour of the state, and in its wake, the personal pride of an officer were at stake. The behaviour of Van Wassenaer also has to be placed in the perspective of rapidly declining Dutch naval power, growing English irritation with the Dutch and English disrespect for their ally. The Republic was no longer considered an equal partner.

■ There was more than the Mediterranean

In the Nine Years' War, Amsterdam and William III had been the great instigators of making the Mediterranean one of the centres of warfare against Louis XIV. Marlborough followed in their footsteps. He was a true advocate of such a strategy. In 1702 a direct attack on Toulon was very much his preference. Such an attack in the soft underbelly of Europe would divert French troops from other fronts. The strategy paid off in many ways, but the military situation in Spain and Italy hindered a full concentration on Toulon.

After the battle of Malága and the scuttling of the Toulon fleet, the Maritime Powers no longer had any serious naval opponent. No further naval battle of significance could be expected. In 1707, the French effectively abandoned their main fleet in favour of royal squadrons with a privateering mission; such squadrons had already been operating since 1702.[40] Dunkirk was their most important base, with St Malo second. Forces of five, six or more warships in combination with a number of 'private' privateers cruised in the North Sea, the Channel, the Soundings, and also in the Atlantic Ocean near Brazil, in the West Indies and the seas off North America. They were hard to combat. The Maritime Powers concentrated their forces upon Dunkirk, but their blockades were seldom water tight. After an escape a long, often fruitless chase followed. For example in 1711 a French squadron under Duguay-Trouin from St Malo captured Rio de Janeiro with a force of seven ships-of-the-line and six frigates. Also part of his record was the earlier capture of three English East Indiamen off Ireland in 1695. On October 2 1706, Forbin, from Dunkirk with his force of seven small men-of-war, attacked a Dutch convoy of seventy merchantmen sailing home from the Baltic and Norway. The six Dutch escort vessels successfully kept Forbin away from the convoy itself, but lost three ships in doing so. Before this fight, Forbin had been cruising and capturing ships in the North Sea throughout the entire summer.[41]

Because of the geographically widespread nature of French activities, both the English and Dutch naval authorities faced heavy demands for the protection of shipping and of the fisheries. The Mediterranean remained the primary concern, though the fleet stationed there gradually became smaller and smaller. The Dutch deployed most of their other warships in the North Sea, the Channel and, during the summer season, also used them for the protection of their homeward-bound East Indiamen. The English admiralty sent their ships to a greater variety of destinations: the West Indies and North America, the Soundings, Dunkirk and the North Sea, Ireland, coastal patrol and convoy in home waters and convoy of trading ships going abroad. The numbers deployed increased in the course of the war, in particular those in the western Atlantic and in convoy service abroad.[42]

One example of the yearly routine in naval activities clearly shows the general pattern. In June 1710 six Dutch warships, 4th- and 5th-rates and frigates, escorted 270 herring vessels to the fishing grounds off England and Scotland and to the Shetland Islands. They also brought 25 Scottish merchantmen safely into Edinburgh. The commander's ship log refers frequently to the presence of numerous, mostly small French privateers, trying to pick one or more herring vessels out of the group. Despite all his best efforts, Commander Cornelis van Brakel, the grandson of the man who towed the 'Royal Charles' from the Medway to Holland in 1667, had lost at least six herring vessels by the time he returned home in mid-September.[43]

■ Conclusion

The fruits of a number of successful campaigns in North America by British naval squadrons and by colonial and expeditionary troops, some in amphibious operations, were harvested in the peace treaty of Utrecht in 1713. Negotiations had been started in 1710. Britain's goals in the grand strategy were reached. Nova Scotia, the whole of Newfoundland, Hudson Bay, and the island of St Kitts in the Caribbean were added to the other British North American possessions.

The outcome of the war in Europe was an independent Spain, though with a Bourbon king, a severely weakened France and a Dutch Republic with a more stable southern border secured by the so-called barrier towns. Britain and the Republic kept their traditional commercial privileges in Spain. But Britain got more than the territories overseas. It did not return Gibraltar and Port Mahon to Spain. These places were to become British naval bases in the Mediterranean. The lesson of Tangier had been learnt and Amsterdam's advice from 1694 had been taken to heart. This was the start of the establishment of a network of British naval bases and, correspondingly, the first step to British naval dominance. Now trade and shipping could and would expand widely in whatever direction British merchants and shippers chose.

Great Britain had been the ascending power in the two long wars, the Dutch Republic the declining one. The Dutch state had lived beyond its means. To maintain a great army of more than 100,000 men for 24 years, interrupted for only five years by a shaky peace, and to equip fleets manned by 11,000 to 24,000 men and armed with 2100 to 5000 guns were too much for a country of hardly 2 million people, despite all its commercial and financial strength.

The Nine Years' War and the War of the Spanish Succession were Europe-wide conflicts. Overseas establishments were still only marginally involved. The struggle on land was decisive, but not entirely. The fact that England – after 1707 Great Britain – was protected from the danger of invasion by its navy was crucial for this country's role in the two wars. Additionally, the fact that French troops were diverted from other tasks and kept occupied by the constant threat of an allied landing on one or other of France's coasts was a naval contribution highly appreciated by Marlborough and his generals. The situation in the Mediterranean would have been completely different without the almost continuous presence of the Maritime Powers' fleet. The allied blockade of hostile ports and interception of enemy convoys hampered hostile imports and exports, weakening French economic and financial strength in particular. Navies played a complementary, but essential role in the two wars.

Malága in 1704 turned out to be the last great battle in a long series of naval battles that had begun with those of the Anglo-Dutch Wars. After that the development of naval battle tactics, which until then had progressed at a rapid rate, came to a standstill. During the next three to four decades all navies became smaller and less significant in the conflicts among states that were the norm of eighteenth century Europe.[44]

JOHANES DUX MARLBURII S.R.I. PRINCEPS &C.
Unbounded Courage and Compassion Joind.
Tempring each other in the Victors Mind.
Alternatly proclaim him Good and Great,
And made the Hero and the Man Compleat.

CHAPTER 11

A European general in the English press: The print image of Marlborough in the Stuart realms

Tony Claydon

John Churchill, 1st Duke of Marlborough.

Etching by unknown artist, 18th century.
© National Portrait Gallery, London, UK.

For almost any major figure of the late Stuart era, an analysis of the person's presentation in the press would be essential for a comprehensive consideration of their life. This was an age of print, so we need to understand how people were depicted in published works. For Marlborough, press image was even more important than usual. He was a leading statesman in the first years after the 1695 lapse of pre-publication censorship in England, and in the first decades when the nation was divided into stable but antagonistic parties. He consequently faced frequent and partisan comment in print, and his public image became the essential stuff of political belief, identity and debate. In the closing years of Queen Anne's reign, it is only a slight exaggeration to claim the Duke's virtue or vice was *the* point of contention between Whigs and Tories. Marlborough thus helped to usher in a modern style of politics in which media-constructed personality plays at least as much role as issues or ideology in public dispute. Certainly, figures had been lauded and vilified in the press before. Yet up to this point, government control of publication had prevented the image of individuals becoming polarised in the sustained way that Marlborough's became, or – alternatively – censorship had broken down in conditions of such overwhelming crisis that images could not function as the Duke's did.[1] Marlborough was therefore one of the first figures whose disputed print *persona* structured a stable partisan politics.[2] Within this process, the international context – the problem of presenting a figure of pan-European significance to an English audience – was key.

Marlborough's press image to 1710

Marlborough burst into the press during his first German and Flemish campaigns. He had had a print presence before this (William's propagandists had published his 1688 letter to James II explaining his shift of allegiance at the revolution, and he had been lionised as the capturer of Cork in 1690), but it was not until the opening years of the war of Spanish Succession that he became a central figure in published iconography.[3] Of course, the Duke's dramatic success on the battlefield explained this sud-

den prominence. Yet it is important to probe deeper and to examine exactly how his image was constructed, because this helps explain why he became so controversial later on. Despite its originally non-partisan nature, the initial print celebration of Marlborough had to cope with particular rhetorical problems that ultimately fractured his public presentation.

Press response to the Duke's victories came in four principal forms. The first were immediate reports of his triumphs. Some of these were battlefield dispatches printed by order of the royal court to convince the public of the successful prosecution of the war. Others appeared in newspapers. These made the general's conquests some of the earliest events to be covered by a daily press: it was only after the *Daily Courant's* launch in 1702 that any long-standing periodical appeared more than three times a week. The second class of publication encompassed narratives of whole campaigns. Often written by those serving in Marlborough's forces (and in particular by the Duke's chaplain, Frances Hare) these combined day-by-day coverage of military manoeuvres with panegyrics of the commander in chief.[4] A third genre of pro-Marlborough material was the praise in the large number of thanksgiving sermons for his victories. The English state traditionally marked armed success with a national day of celebration that required every congregation to hear a suitable sermon, and the early part of Anne's reign was no exception. Much of this pulpit rhetoric was published, either as part of the regime's war propaganda or by individual preachers wishing to memorialise God's blessings – and most included passages praising Marlborough's service.[5] Finally, the Duke was lauded in quite astonishing quantities of poetry. It was the self-appointed duty of poets to celebrate national victory, but England's poor military showing in the seventeenth century had left them little opportunity to display their art. After Blenheim, however, they compensated rapidly. Addison's hugely popular *The campaign*, which expounded Marlborough's triumph on the Danube in over twenty pages of rhymed pentameters, was imitated by numerous other authors of diverse talent.[6] One might mention a fifth species of celebration – pictorial prints – but in truth these were disappointingly conventional. Although produced in reasonable numbers and no doubt purchased and displayed by an adoring public, they tended to comprise a simple portrait of the general – framed, bewigged, and armoured – but with little text beyond his name and list of titles.[7]

Despite the variety of this material, the basic image of Marlborough was consistent across the genres. For poets, preachers and pamphleteers, the Duke had 'retreiv'd the ancient glory of the English nation' after decades of shameful failure, and comparisons were made with heroes of much earlier eras.[8] Writers also agreed about the means of this success. They said Marlborough was inspirational in his personal bravery, he kept the coolest head in terrifying situations, and he demonstrated an astonishing capacity for lightning marches. So authors used 'courage' as a key head when describing the general's character, they spoke effortlessly of 'brave Marlborough', or lauded the 'Bravery of that *Matchless General*.'[9] The Duke's battlefield calm was most memorably praised in a passage of Addison's *Campaign*. This poem described how he had surveyed 'the field of death' at Blenheim 'in peaceful thought', and compared him to an angel directing a violent storm by divine command.[10] This was widely seen as the literary highlight of the piece, and was echoed in many other descriptions of the general's demeanour.[11] Marlborough's marching was noted in all genres. The speed of his armies was praised as far back as the Cork campaign in 1690, but under Queen Anne this became his chief motif. Dispatches stressed that victories had been achieved by quick manoeuvres seizing strategic ground, campaign narratives were catalogues of brilliant relocations, and sermons praised marches greater than any others in history.[12]

Thus far, Marlborough's image was straightforward, if occasionally hyperbolic. One could argue it was rooted in the realities of the Duke's achievements. Hard-nosed military historians have praised the general's bravery, his coolness under fire and the brilliance of his strategic marching.[13] Other features of the coverage, however, posed more difficulties. Two particular contexts for the Duke's military adventures had to be handled with care, and polemicists never found an absolutely satisfactory way to parry their disruptive potential.

The first was Marlborough's relationship with Queen Anne. Despite care to identify the reigning monarch closely with England's military effort, it proved difficult for the press to present this effort without diminishing the ruler in comparison to her general. Most obviously, this was because of Marlborough's personal role in the success. His string of victories between 1704 and 1711 was too consistent to be the result of luck; the astonishing scale of some of them against the odds told the same story; and there was evidence – gleefully reported in the press – that England's allies saw him as vital to the continued progress of the confederate cause.[14] As a result, it was virtually impossible to praise victory without lionising Marlborough, and this always risked overshadowing Anne in the press coverage. Similarly, Marlborough was physically present at the battles and in the rapid manoeuvres between them that so often explained their outcome. This meant there was an active, detailed and exciting narrative to tell about his exploits, which magnified his print presence at the expense of the passive, sit-at-home Queen.

The problem was exacerbated by newspaper coverage. Frequent publication, coupled with the fact that Marlborough's triumphs occurred on the far side of an only sometimes navigable Channel, meant campaign stories unfolded in stages. This focussed public attention on the Duke as readers got regular updates on his progress and as initially sketchy reports of victories were followed by fuller accounts of the triumphs. For example, coverage of Blenheim in the thrice-weekly *Post Man* started with outline reports of the battle in the issue for August 10-12. This whetted the public appetite for more information, which the paper satisfied over the next week. It expanded coverage in its August 12-17 editions with a more detailed account of what had happened, with praise of Marlborough's personal genius, and with reports of the rejoicing in the Netherlands. It then developed the story further in its next issue by printing the Duke's message to the King of Prussia that assessed the strategic situation in Germany after the victory. *The Daily Courant* did not persist with the story every morning after its first coverage on August 11, but within ten days it recorded the relief of England's allies, tidying up operations in Bavaria, and the commander's thinking on the next objectives of the campaign.[15] With information about the fighting emerging in this way, readers' anticipation kept Marlborough and his triumphs centre-stage. As one observer of the coverage after Blenheim put it: 'fresher Reports have still brought the better news, and the Success proves every day greater and greater.'[16] By contrast, Anne's press persona had little to do. Papers reported the queen receiving dispatches from her hero, and ordering public thanksgivings for his latest conquests, but of course this was all reactive.[17]

A related problem was Marlborough's prominence on the title pages of pamphlets. Understanding that journal-fed interest in the Duke would be the 'hook' for purchases, publishers printed his name prominently on the front of their productions, and this was important because they produced title pages in extra quantities for promotional public posting. Unfortunately, such advertisements for Marlborough occurred even on publications emerging from the heart of the monarch's regime. Thus although the word 'QUEEN' was the largest word on the front of William Sherlock's official thanksgiving sermon for Blenheim, which had been preached before Anne in St Paul's cathedral in London, the phrase 'under the Command of the Duke of MARLBOROUGH' was also prominent; whilst the work's Irish equivalent – William King's sermon before the Lords Justices in Dublin – had the word '*MARLBOROUGH*' written larger than the lower case 'Her Majesty's forces' (this last phrase being the only title-page reference to Anne).[18] In a similar vein, the front pages of a string of thanksgiving prayers for military victories – works whose lengthy titles summarised the official reason for the celebration – all stressed in attention grabbing italics that it had been 'the Duke of *Marlborough*', or '*John, Duke of Marlborough*', who had commanded the triumphant armies.[19]

There were attempts to prevent Anne being overshadowed, but they were not entirely successful. A common tactic was to present her general's actions as service to his queen. The Duke himself did this in his public statements, and the press both reproduced these expressions of fealty, and expanded them.[20] So virtually every poem, and virtually every thanksgiving sermon, had a passage explaining that Marlborough's success magnified Anne's glory. Some writers also praised her wisdom in choosing such a servant, or reassured the reader that there could be no jealousy between two people so utterly united in the same cause.[21] Another tactic was to stress the role of providence in Marlborough's victories, and to praise Anne's piety as the chief cause of divine favour.[22] Again, some writers used tropes of glorious female military leadership from the past, and applied them to the current situation to bolster the Queen's image. Anne was therefore equated with Elizabeth I, who had displaced her generals and admirals in popular memory of her battle with Spain.[23] The Queen was also presented as a new Deborah, the divinely-favoured leader of Israel who had triumphed during the nation's military struggle to survive in the Holy Land in the period of the biblical judges. This scriptural parallel was particularly encouraged in the 1704 thanksgiving sermons for Blenheim since the specially-composed liturgy for divine service had Deborah's story as the Old Testament lesson.[24]

Yet despite these efforts, Marlborough's press presence troubled royal image-making. The notion of service reminded the reader of the Duke's triumphs and emphasised his magnificent magnanimity as much as it promoted his patron; and the image was difficult to sustain with anything like the interest or length of glorious military narratives. As a result, references to Anne – even as the original cause of Marlborough's success – could get squashed at one end of duke-centred analysis.[25] Discussion of providence allowed praise of Anne's Christian virtue, but it sometimes tripped over into near-millenarian hymns to godly victories which apotheosised her general as heaven's great instrument. One of the ripest examples here came from Edward Fowler, the bishop of Gloucester, preaching at the Blenheim thanksgiving in 1704. He ended his address with the hope that the battle might mark the final defeat of 'Powers of Darkness'; and he praised Anne's commitment to the war, the church, and public piety as part of this hope. Yet he also presented the Queen's greatest success as the appointment of a general of unequalled skill, whose history of personal battlefield escapes suggested he was being specially protected by God for his apocalyptic task.[26] Meanwhile Andrew Archer, preaching on the same day in Tunbridge Wells, said the

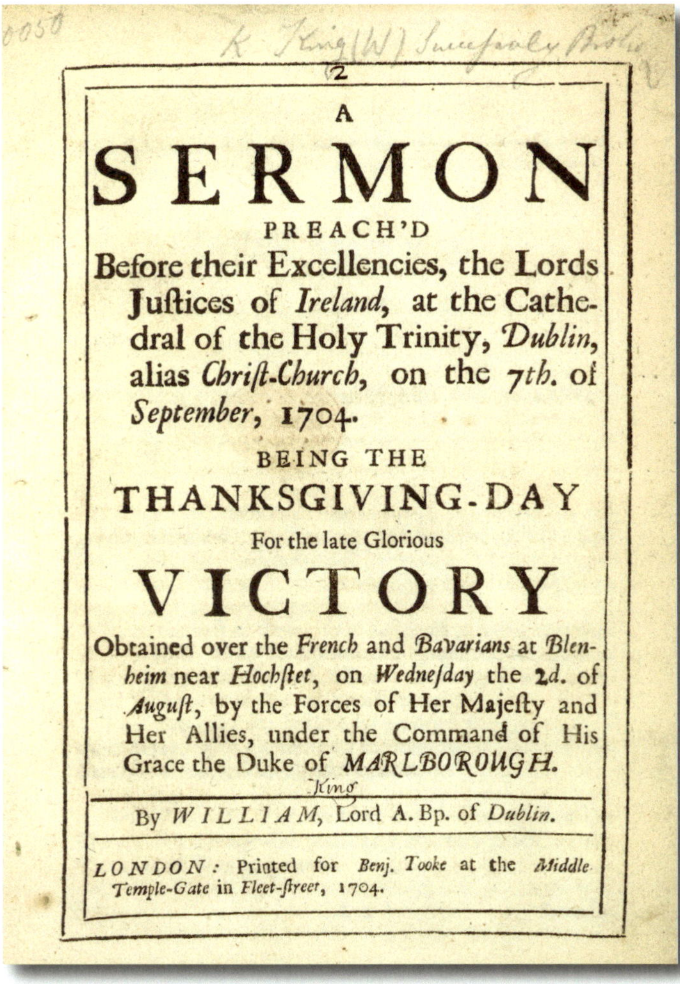
A

SERMON

PREACH'D

Before their Excellencies, the Lords Juſtices of *Ireland*, at the Cathedral of the Holy Trinity, *Dublin*, alias *Chriſt-Church*, on the *7th.* of *September*, 1704.

BEING THE

THANKSGIVING-DAY

For the late Glorious

VICTORY

Obtained over the *French* and *Bavarians* at *Blenheim* near *Hochſtet*, on *Wedneſday* the *2d.* of *Auguſt*, by the Forces of Her Majeſty and Her Allies, under the Command of His Grace the Duke of MARLBOROUGH.

By *WILLIAM*, Lord A. Bp. of *Dublin*.

LONDON: Printed for *Benj. Tooke* at the *Middle Temple-Gate* in *Fleet-ſtreet*, 1704.

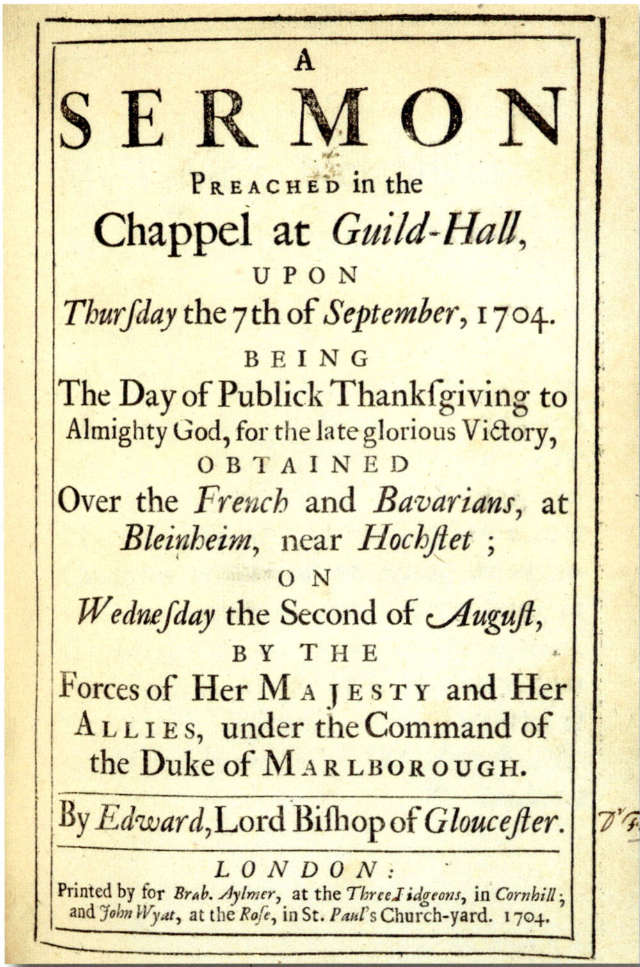
A

SERMON

PREACHED in the

Chappel at *Guild-Hall*,

UPON

Thurſday the 7th of *September*, 1704.

BEING

The Day of Publick Thankſgiving to Almighty God, for the late glorious Victory,

OBTAINED

Over the *French* and *Bavarians*, at *Bleinheim*, near *Hochſtet*;

ON

Wedneſday the Second of *Auguſt*,

BY THE

Forces of Her MAJESTY and Her ALLIES, under the Command of the Duke of MARLBOROUGH.

By *Edward*, Lord Biſhop of *Glouceſter*.

LONDON:

Printed by for *Brab. Aylmer*, at the *Three Pidgeons*, in *Cornhill*; and *John Wyat*, at the *Roſe*, in St. *Paul's* Church-yard. 1704.

(left) Title page of A sermon preached before their excellencies the lords justices of Ireland at the cathedral of the Holy Trinity, Dublin... 7th September, Dublin 1704.

Print from a pamphlet by William King, 1704. The British Library, London, UK. © The British Library Board. 4475.cc.70.

(right) Title page of A sermon preached at Guild-Hall, upon Thursday, the 7th September, London 1704.

Print from a pamphlet by Edward Fowler, 1704. The British Library, London, UK. © The British Library Board. 696.f.10.(14.).

extraordinary success of 'Her Majesty's Arms' demonstrated the divine hand at work, but re-enforced the point by speaking of God's gifts to Marlborough of 'Counsel, and Wisdom, and Understanding … Courage and Magnanimity', and of heaven's special protection of him 'in the Day of Battel.'[27]

Reference to earlier female leaders also helped less than might have been hoped. Elizabeth had not had to deal with a dominant, unequivocally successful commander (her forces had been led by a number of generals and admirals, all flawed); and she had been physically active enough to construct some sense of personal command (at least rallying her troops against the Armada at Tilbury). She had, therefore, built a myth of active individual leadership that it was hard for the Marlborough-facing and semi-invalid Anne to imitate. Comparison between the two rulers therefore relied on stressing the scale of the early eighteenth century victories, rather than the Queen's personal role in them: and this, of course, put the spotlight back on her general.[28] Deborah was similarly problematic. Although this female judge had been the ultimate authority in Israel in her time, close reading of the scripture revealed that it had been her general Barak who had actually scored the nation's victory. The two figures were presented as near-equal agents in a providential deliverance, so equating Anne with Deborah could lead to a flattering identification of Marlborough as our '*Brave and Valiant Barak*'.[29]

The Duke therefore threatened to overshadow his ruler whatever was done to avoid this. A second problem was finding a comfortable relationship between Marlborough and the English nation. Although the Duke's victories could be celebrated as restoring England's military pride, the actual circumstances of his command meant writers could not convey unalloyed patriotism. Most clearly, Marlborough's forces were always an alliance from many states and nations opposing Louis. At Blenheim the general was in direct command of an Anglo-Dutch army, and had the support of another German force; and his other campaigns drew on soldiers supplied by the Netherlands, Denmark, Austria, Prussia, and other princes of the Holy Roman Empire. The multi-national nature of the armies also meant the Duke had to work closely with foreign commanders. He forged a close relationship with Prince Eugene of Savoy-Carignan, whom the press fully recognised as a co-commander of the allied armies; but also worked with many minor German princes and Dutch generals, whose names featured prominently in print reports for their valour, for their tragic deaths, or both. Beyond this, Marlborough's strategies and war aims were only questionably English. As other chapters of this work make clear, he was not gaining new territories for Anne, nor repulsing an enemy from English shores. Rather he was engaged deep in Flanders or Bavaria, and his objectives were to save Germany from French invasion, to construct a barrier to defend the Dutch, and to return the Spanish Netherlands to their Habsburg claimant. All this might be defended as serving England's interests, but only if audiences thought France was such a pressing threat that Anne's realm had to join with anyone who would combat Versailles.[30] Ironically, Marlborough's success in containing Louis began to undermine that conviction as the war continued. If France had been sufficiently cowed, some (particularly the Tories) asked, might the Duke now be fighting more for foreign than English causes?[31]

As with the relationship with the Queen, press writers tried to contain these difficulties, but again with only limited success. The obvious tactic to reconcile a national celebration of the Duke with the international context was to boast of English leadership of a pan-European cause. In a variety of ways, writers suggested that England's glory was magnified by Marlborough's service to a great consort of peoples, and that this made his country the effective arbiter of the continent's fate.[32] To drive this point home, writers insisted that the other nations recognised the cause of their deliverance. The great Englishman was universally thanked as the saviour of nations. As so often, Addison's *Campaign* set the tone with its description of the mighty Austrian Emperor laying aside his grandeur to travel to Marlborough's camp after Blenheim and to embrace the victor in profound gratitude.[33] Yet whilst such writing allowed patriotic pride in the Duke's achievements, difficulties remained. This kind of rhetoric provided only an ambiguous celebration of Marlborough's Englishness, and it further complicated his relationship with Anne.

To start with, stressing the Duke's Europe-wide significance associated him ever more closely with people overseas. As he marched across a continent for its salvation, he was depicted in what might (for some readers) be suspiciously close collaboration with foreigners. The Duke's own printed words stressed his reliance on European allies, especially his co-commander Eugene of Savoy: his very first and otherwise brief report from Blenheim said of Eugene that he could not 'lay too much praise of the Prince's good conduct, and the Bravery of his troops.'[34] This close personal association with Savoy was emphasised and celebrated by others, from newspaper reports of the generals' co-ordinated manoeuvres, to the poet Thomas Gibson, who paired his Marlborough epic with a Latin effort praising the Habsburg prince as a '*Christian*

Hanibal.[35] Of course, this writing used Marlborough's relationship with foreign commanders as a microcosm of the Grand Alliance, and so emphasised England's leadership of a united confederacy. Yet there was a potential danger here, illustrated by the 1709 poem *Alcander*. This talked of Eugene and Marlborough's swords 'united in one Fight' but also suggested it was the cause the Englishman shared with Savoy, and the honour and excitement of fighting with his friend, which dragged him away from a life of domestic happiness in his home country. At one level this passage was a harmless poetic conceit to underline selfless duty, but it might inadvertently hint that Marlborough put foreign priorities above his own nation. This was particularly the case as the poet pleaded rhetorically with the Duke to keep himself out of danger, so that England did not lose its great protector.[36]

Similarly, repeated stress on Europe's gratitude to Marlborough might raise questions about who was actually gaining from his actions. Lists of the nations that had been saved by the Duke tended to leave England out. Naturally this was because writers wished to present their country as the generous benefactor of others, but it could leave the impression that Anne's subjects were taking on the burdens of war whilst the advantages went to those overseas. When foreign gratitude tipped over into a language of reliance on Marlborough, the danger was even greater. Take, for example, Leonard Welstead's poem celebrating the Duke's return to England in 1709. This had a personified Holland praising Marlborough as her 'Worthiest Friend', but also claiming her security depended on his presence – since when he was absent from the Low Countries, French generals grew bold. Building on these assumptions, Welstead had Holland hoping Marlborough would return soon, but in a note of hostility to foreigners that we will see becoming typical of Tory writers (Welstead was a Tory at this point) the poet suggested that the Dutch would stoop to dishonesty to ensure this happened. 'Holland, the VICTOR to detain, prepares / Imagin'd Dangers and dissembled Fears.'[37] As so often in the pre 1710 writing on Marlborough, the sour note was fleeting, and the rhetorical risk to the Duke's image may have been unintentional. Nevertheless, highlighting his importance to foreigners was double-edged. Serving nations overseas, he might be seen as their captive.

Another problem with presenting Marlborough as the leader of an international cause was its ever-darker eclipse of Anne. As he was shown rescuing foreign rulers from France, and receiving their praises, he became at least the equal of – perhaps even dominant over – people who technically outranked him within the hierarchies of European nobility. This potentially raised him to the same level as his queen: and it might even put him above her if it left the impression that Anne ruled England, but the Duke led Europe. This danger could surface in the most casual line. Richard Chapman's Blenheim sermon to his Hertfordshire parish talked of Marlborough relieving Savoy, a 'Prince no less brave': but whilst this was meant to praise the courage of all who had fought, it ended up presenting the English duke as the saviour of a prince, and moreover a man who embodied the entire Habsburg cause.[38]
The problem emerged in a more structured way when Marlborough was shown as an equal of rulers in narratives of his campaigns. Reports had him meeting with sovereigns and being handsomely entertained by them: as for example in the negotiations, dinners, and troop reviews in Holland and Northern Germany as Marlborough began his progress towards Blenheim.[39] Writers also had the Duke constructing armies from battalions led by ranks of European nobles or taking surrenders from city magistrates who were technically the representatives of great monarchs.[40] Per-

John Churchill, 1st Duke of Marlborough.

Engraving after Godfrey Kneller, 1703.
© National Portrait Gallery, London, UK.

haps the most striking instance was Francis Hare's account of Marlborough's early meeting with the Archduke Charles Habsburg. This was the confederacy's candidate for king of Spain, and he might have insisted on the respect due to that office (for all that his claim was pretty theoretical, given that his rival was actually ruling in Madrid). Instead however, Hare had him give Marlborough a sword, and acknowledge he was a poor prince who had little else to offer.[41] Still more disturbing questions about Marlborough's rank were raised when writers referred to his own principality of Mindelheim in Swabia. This had been created for him by the Habsburgs as a reward for his services, but it technically raised him to the status of sovereign ruler. If this further muddied his relationship with Anne in the public mind (and deepened his association with foreign lands), the prominent title page references to Marlborough as 'Prince of the Holy Empire', or even as a prince of the 'Sacred Roman Empire' may not have been entirely helpful.[42]

Uniting all these difficulties was one particular rhetorical comparison. Making the obvious parallel with the last man to lead a European confederacy against France, the Duke was presented as the successor to William III. The press stressed that William had promoted Marlborough, and now depicted him replacing the prince of Orange as the last great hope of European liberty. The image had extremely wide currency. It surfaced in a variety of written genres (including plodding verse to celebrate the battle of Oudenaarde, and the parliamentary act granting Marlborough the manor of Woodstock, where Blenheim Palace would be built), and it could unite authors divided on almost everything else.[43] In 1706 William Atwood and Mathew Prior had an intense poetic spat. This was driven by their respective attachments to Whig and Tory factions, and was played out in nit-picking criticism of grammar in their rival odes to Anne's victories – but for all this, there was little to choose between their presentations of Marlborough. Atwood talked of the general appearing just as William's death had made many despair for liberty, and of his matching Orange's 'Pattern of Glory.'[44] Prior talked of him inheriting William's sword, and using it to the same effect in terrifying Louis XIV.[45]

At first glance, the comparison between William and Marlborough was logical. Both men were active military leaders of virtually the same alliance, on virtually the same battlefields. Yet for all the ease of the parallel it was disturbing. First, it again aggrandised the Duke by presenting him as successor to a king. This may have been even more unsettling to those who remembered literary treatments of William and Mary and noticed similarities with the writing on Marlborough and Anne. For both 'couples' writers constructed gendered teams, with the male element fighting evil on the battlefield, whilst the female's piety called down divine blessings.[46] This presented the general as at least the equal of his ruler, and unceremoniously bundled Anne's actual partner, George of Denmark, off the field. More concretely, to associate Marlborough with William was to tie him to someone whose own loyalty to England had been questioned. The Dutch ruler had been attacked for favouring the interest of his homeland over those of his new realm, and his commitment to land battles with France in Flanders had been used as evidence.[47] Anne herself may have tried to capitalise on the disquiet at the start of her reign with her coronation statement that she knew her heart to be 'entirely English.'[48] If Marlborough was the new William in print culture, therefore, similar doubts might arise about his patriotism. Why did he imitate his predecessor in fighting for the security of the Netherlands, spending so much time abroad, and working more closely with foreigners than the English?

JOHN DUKE of MARLBOROUGH. HER MAJts GENERALISSIMO in FLANDERS &c.
QUEEN
t'Amsterdam by I. Temmen y 15 Dec: 170

Marlborough's press image after 1710

So far we have charted potential dangers in Marlborough's early press image. Yet these remained largely latent before 1710. To that point, support for the war was largely bi-partisan: the Duke was praised across the political spectrum as the successful champion of a national cause, and off-notes were fleeting. Tory writers may have been concerned at the Duke's ever-closer alliance with the Whigs in the first decade of Anne's reign, but their early strategy was to construct alternative heroes rather than attack Marlborough. The Tory-leaning Admiral, George Rooke, who had captured Gibraltar in 1704, was pressed into service, especially by the High Church poet and polemicist William Pittis; whilst John Philips (fellow of the Tory hothouse, Christ Church, Oxford) answered Addison's *Campaign* with a poem stressing Robert Harley's role in securing the Blenheim victory.[49] After the failed peace negotiations of 1709 and 1710, however, war re-entered party politics with catastrophic consequences for Marlborough. Tories began to condemn Whigs for prolonging a conflict which they thought had become unnecessary for England (Louis was now too weak to attack her); which they feared might result in an over-mighty Austria replacing an over-mighty France; and which they supposed brought political and financial advantage to their political rivals. As this happened, the Duke – as the leading military figure of the day, and as a Whig ally – found himself the target of sustained attack.[50] As we have noted, this came to structure the whole substance of party debate: as this occurred, the European dimension of Marlborough's career was crucial.

To an extent, the Duke suffered from a simple re-surfacing of an earlier pattern of dispute. In the last years of William's reign, Tories had resisted the Whigs' desire to remobilise against Louis XIV, fearing a new war would increase a public debt which had already led to heavy taxes, and had expanded mechanisms of credit which they feared their political enemies controlled. As part of this campaign, Tory writers had accused Whigs of stoking international tensions, in order to support the bloated military state on which they had fed through the 1690s.[51] Charles Davenant's 'Tom Double' pamphlets enlivened this attack by creating a fictional character – Double – who had creamed off profits of war (state contracts, confiscated Irish land, gains trading gilts, pilfered military payments and so on) and so had risen far above the honest country gentry whom he had taxed mercilessly.[52] Once Tories recommenced their criticisms of conflict after 1710, these old images re-emerged. Crucially, however, the established elements of Marlborough's press *persona* ensured the old tropes attached to a real, rather than a cartoon, character. As we have seen, the Duke's print presentation could feed suspicion that he had climbed illegitimately far through social ranks, and that he was happier helping foreigners to attack France than serving the interests of his homeland. The first element was directly paralleled in Davenant's portrait of Tom Double. The second had very close affinities, since it allowed Marlborough to be portrayed as the advocate of a damaging and unnecessary war. As a result, the Duke acted as a magnet for pre-existing discourse, so one party re-cast his print image to match that of Double. As this occurred, Marlborough became an iconic totem of party dispute, debated in terms of personal ambition and of war-mongering betrayal of his country.

One 1710 pamphlet, *Reasons why the duke of Marlborough cannot lay down his commands*, catches the transition. At the time it was written, Harley's new Tory administration had just replaced the Whigs with whom Marlborough had built close ties (indeed the tract was dated two days after the fall of Godolphin, the Duke's chief political ally). One line of Whig attack on the new government was to exploit the Duke's glittering reputation, and suggest England's great general would resign in disgust at the new ministry. Our tract countered this; but in a way which perverted the Marlborough's greatness to undermine him. There was, its author assured the audience, no chance that the Duke would leave his post. England was safe because he was a man of exemplary loyalty, honour and gratitude, and a man who fully understood his interest. The general would therefore continue to serve because of his duty to the Queen, but also in thanks for what he had received for his earlier service – and it was under this head that the knife turned. The author listed what Marlborough had, in fact received. This included the ducal title, the principality in Mindelheim, numerous gifts from foreign princes, appointments as ambassador extraordinary and generalissimo, court posts at St James', the manors of Woodstock and Wooton, five hundred pounds annual income from the post office, large shares in monies earmarked to raise troops and pay soldiers, and a string of offices and pensions for his wife.[53] This list, of course, brought Marlborough close to Double. Here were exactly the sort of hierarchy-busting, and foreign-tainted, perquisites of government that had built the corrupt career of Davenant's creation – and the parallel was re-enforced as Davenant himself reprised his popular character. In a pamphlet published around the same time as the *Reasons why*, Double explained how his vicious career had continued to advance under Anne. Whilst the fictitious Whig did not directly claim Marlborough as an accomplice, Double did suggest 'Great Men' had become his captive around 1708 (when Marlborough had successfully urged Anne to work with Whigs alone). He also charged that the general's campaigning in Flanders had been a pro-Dutch ploy to drain resources from the honest Tory strategy of attacking Spain's overseas empire, and he admitted he had blocked investigations into military payments – an area where we will soon see the Duke in deep trouble.[54]

These threatening winds of 1710 became a tempest the following year with the appearance of Jonathan Swift's *Conduct of the allies*. This hugely influential pamphlet ranged wider than an attack on Marlborough, becoming an effective Tory manifesto. It accused the Whigs of prolonging the war to feed their avarice and ambition, and charged that England's foreign allies had drained her resources to defend themselves. The English, the author asserted, should not have been involved as principle combatants, and should have attacked France and Spain's maritime interests rather than raising massed armies to protect foreigners in Flanders. In a crucial passage Swift put Marlborough in the dock. Asking why the English had become 'the *Dupes* and *Bubbles* of Europe', he explained the Queen had temporarily become the captive of her commander.[55] The Duke was a man of boundless 'Appetite for Wealth and Ambition,' who had insisted on a mass continental land war because it gave him opportunities for military glory and gifts from foreign princes.[56] War had also raised a vast army whose supplies its general could embezzle, and created an expensive and indebted government to benefit his Whig and monied friends. In all this, Swift picked up the themes of the Double tracts, but also played on the troubling elements of Marlborough's own press image. Swift's Duke was a man who had overshadowed the Queen till she could not longer bear the 'Tyranny and Insolence' of this servant.'[57] He was also a man who winked at the 'several gross Impositions from the other *Powers*' because he was in league with Dutch and Germans to profit from Britain's gold and blood.[58] Making the key link back to William III, Swift also stressed the parallels between Marlborough's war and the battles of the 1690s. These too had been fought by mass English forces in Flanders; and they had been led by a general who 'although a King of *England*, was a Native of Holland' and so did not have Britain's interests truly to heart.[59]

Swift's pamphlet was a huge popular success. It sold at least five editions by the end of 1711, and forced Whig writers to answer its charges. For some time the party's press output was heavily influenced by the need to respond point by point.[60] Yet for all its extraordinary impact, the coverage of Marlborough in Swift's piece merely parroted an attack which had been mounted in the Tory press since the fall of the Whig ministry, and certainly contributed to the Duke's sacking by the Queen at the end of 1711. Swift echoed, and would be echoed in, numerous productions which made the same basic points, and which continued to exploit the difficulties in the general's earlier portrayal. So, the rewards of war had allowed Marlborough to overshadow his monarch. He was a subject of huge ambition who had forgotten what was due to his sovereign, a man who had invaded 'exhorbitant power.'[61] He was a man who was driven by insatiable avarice. He had hoarded the perquisites of office and had defrauded the English taxpayer of their money.[62] In this last charge, accusations of corruption in the management of military budgets were central. Late in 1711, the commissioners for public accounts in the Tory-dominated parliament accused Marlborough of improperly receiving two and a half per cent of the monies for the bread supply contract to the army: publication of the reports fed a campaign for closer investigation and arraignment.[63] The Duke was also accused of using diplomatic influence to prolong the war that enriched him. The case here was built on retrospective accounts of peace negotiations at The Hague in 1709 and Geertruidenberg 1710. According to Tory writers, there had been a potential settlement in both these years, since confederate success had pushed Louis towards reasonable terms, but the Duke and his Whig allies had scuppered this, acquiescing in exorbitant Dutch demands that had alienated French diplomats.[64]

The Tory press campaign also took up Swift's suggestion that Marlborough was aligned with foreign interests. The Duke had not only prolonged the war for his personal gain, but also so that his Dutch and Austrian friends could go on pursuing their own national interests using English resources. Even more perniciously, he became an agent of those foreign powers at the centre of Anne's government. One colourful 1710 pamphlet illustrates the tone well. *The secret history of Arlus and Odolphus* was a thinly disguised allegory of Harley's fall in 1708, relating the court politics of the kingdom of 'Grandinsula' and renaming the chief characters (often only marginally with the substitution of a few letters) in the authentic British events. Within the drama, the vital scene came as Fortunas (Marlborough) hit upon the key argument to persuade a reluctant Empress (Anne) that she must part with her trusted servant Arlus (Harley). Fortunas said he could no longer work with Arlus, but crucially stressed that if he had to resign, this would do far more damage than the simple loss of his services. Fortunas claimed that any successor to him as general of the Empress' forces would find it hard to gain 'such Absolute Necessary Confidence, and Power from her Allies, as they had been pleas'd to Honour him with', and these allies' dismay at his loss of office might lead them to seek a separate peace with the common enemy.[65] Here Marlborough's illegitimate influence over Anne was bound to his complicity with overseas rulers. He ganged up with them to bully his sovereign into dismissing a loyal minister and perverted the court from its true patriotic course. This

LIKE COACHMAN, LIKE CAUSE: or, AN EMBLEM, *Of what we must expect, if* Low-Church *gets uppermost.*

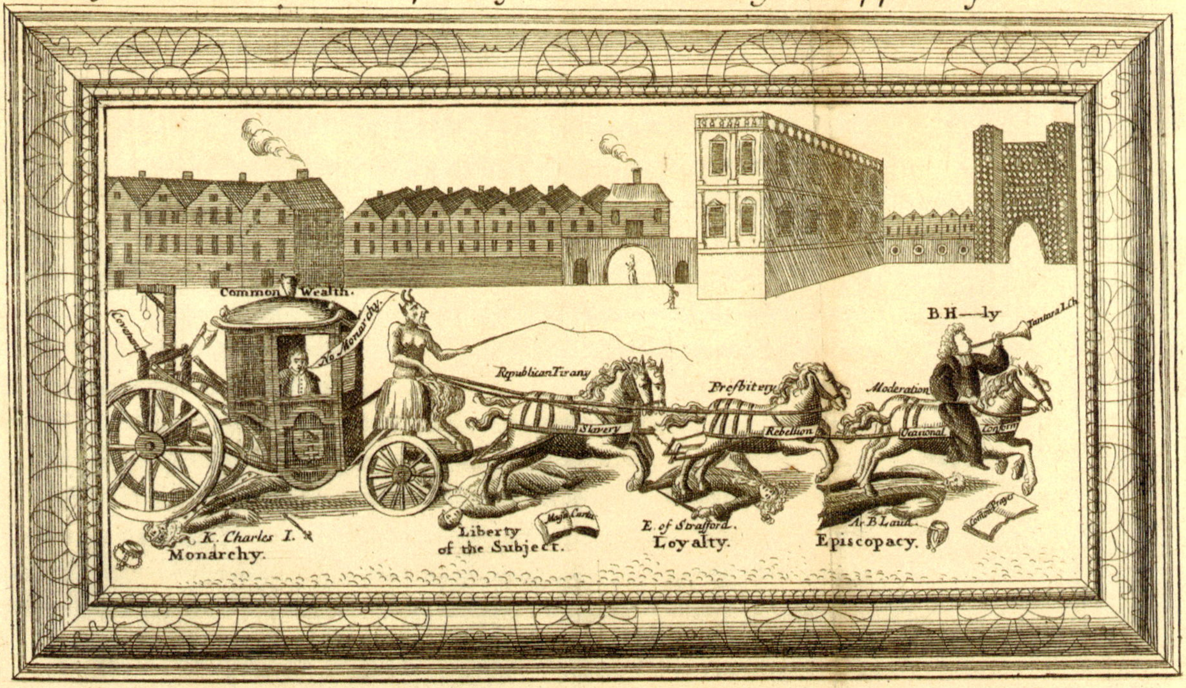

EXPLANATION.

In days of old when men had any awe
Of God, and paid Obedience to his Law,
Were more ambitious to be Good than Great,
They then Obey'd their King for CONSCIENCESAKE,
As God's Annointed and as One whom He
Had by a Wise, a Just, and Good Decree
Seated with Power on the Regal Throne;
And therefore SUBJECT unto Him alone:
He did they knew by Jure Divino sway
The Royal Scepter, therefore did obey,
And their sincere Allegiance to him pay.
Nothing could then provoke them to rebell,
Because a Rebell's Doom they knew too well.
Thus it continu'd 'till the World at last
Did after many years and ages past
Grow more Licentious, Wicked, and Profane,
And Men more Base and Turbulent became;
Scorning the poor Restraint of Government,
In spite of Heaven they grew fully bent
To throw aside the Sneaking Servile Yoke,
Oppose their King and God himself provoke.
And thus RESISTANCE came at first in Vogue,
Rebells were Honest, Loyal Subjects Rogues.
The Devil highly did commend the Motion,
The which he back'd with this accursed Notion;
That Kings by Nature were no more than they,
Like them a Vessel made of Common Clay:
And thus at length in Arms whole Nations rose,
And did their King, and God himself oppose.
And so alass a Bloody Crew of Old
Of Great Brittania's Offspring, we are told,
Under the Saint-like Mask of Reformation
Did sadly ruin both the Church and Nation,
It's Grievances pretending to redress
When I durst say they thought of nothing less.
Religion Liberty was all the Cry,
And to secure the Laws, their King must die.
These Sons of Belial this infernal Crew
Both King and Subject did at length undo;
And Liberty it self a Victim fell
By those Accursed Instruments of Hell.
And then the silly Sotts when 'twas too late,
Bemoan'd their wretched and unhappy State,
And Gods assistance did again implore,
Whom they so basely had despis'd before;
Who did their Church and Monarchy restore.
But some there are alass, who not content
With any sort or kind of Government,
To Egypt back do cast a longing Eye,
Hope to be fool'd once more before they die.
Let such impartially but view this print,
And I am sure they'll say there's something in't
The Devil drives, the Patron of Rebellion
Is in the Coach, and H—ly rides Postillion.
The Steeds are fierce, and such become the Cause:
See under feet th' Crown, our Liberty, & Laws.
Behind the Covenant and Ropes you see,
To shew the Nation what their Doom must be,
Should Whigism once get the upper hand;
The good the wholesom Laws of this our Land,
Nay and the Church we seem so much to prize,
Must to those Rebels fall a Sacrafice:
And that same Liberty which now we boast
We may be sure will be for ever lost.
Let who will say there's nothing in this print,
I'll swear the Devil and OLD NOLL is in't.

John Churchill, 1st Duke of Marlborough.

Miniature (Enamel on copper, 93 x 63 mm) by Christian Friedrich Zincke, 1710.

CHAPTER 12

'The British Caesar'

John Churchill, 1st Duke of Marlborough, and the Visual Arts

Richard Johns

John Churchill was once one of the most recognisable men in Europe. His ambition at the Restoration court and early distinction in battle made him the subject of public and artistic scrutiny from a young age; and as his fame and rank grew towards middle age – then as it soared in the months and years after the Battle of Blenheim – so did the pictorial record of his life. From the simple likeness used to illustrate a penny broadside celebrating the history and achievements of 'The British Caesar', to the more intimate, and intricate, portrait miniatures prized by the Duke's closest family and friends, such as that produced by Christian Friedrich Zincke around 1710, to the high-minded history paintings and tapestries that adorned the state rooms of Blenheim Palace, images of the Duke of Marlborough and his military exploits permeated every level of European culture during the first quarter of the eighteenth century.

Diplomatic and military historians, whether examining the cause and effect of early modern warfare or enquiring into the successes and failures of Marlborough's leadership, frequently cite the rich visual culture of the period as a more-or-less faithful record of the Duke's appearance, character and military career. Within the history of art, meanwhile, the collected iconography of the Duke of Marlborough has a less-prominent but nonetheless considerable significance. Art historians are likely to be less concerned with Marlborough's innovative deployment of foot and cavalry at the Battle of Blenheim, for example, than with how the subsequent representation of Blenheim and other campaigns provided a vehicle for novel ideas about history painting and portraiture; or with how such images contributed to the establishment of the modern military hero as a distinctive cultural model.[1]

This chapter seeks a common ground between these two very different perspectives. Focusing on John Churchill's legendary status as the most powerful soldier of his age – a 'British Caesar', no less – the pages that follow consider how the visual arts, and the industry that supported them, engaged with one of the most enduring narratives of British military history. It wasn't only Marlborough's reputation as a great strategist, or his success in battle, that encouraged his contemporaries to evoke comparisons with Rome's most famous dictator. The Duke's controversial pursuit of power, the international reach of his reputation, his ambiguous relationship with the monarchy, and even his political (if not actual) downfall, all encouraged supporters and detractors alike to draw parallels between the two formidable statesmen.

The BRITISH CÆSAR:

O R,

The History, and Glorious Achievements of JOHN *Duke of* MARLBOROUH, *Prince of the* Empire, *and Captain-General of the* Confederate-Forces.

FORTUNE, that design'd to raise this great *Heroe*, caus'd him to ascend by gradual Steps, while Nature agreed to make that his Delight, which She design'd to make his Glory.

His Youth was always addicted to Martial Studies, and his Prudence was conspicuous to his Honour, in perfecting the Soldier: With these Accomplishments he set forward and distinguish'd himself through every Post, from a *Colours* to a *Truncheon*; which has not for many Years been so successful in the Hand of an *English* General; that we may now very well bestow on him, the Titles of the *Empire*'s Saviour, *Europe*'s Deliverer, and the Darling of his Country: And as he first signaliz'd himself in the *French* Service, so they may have now the Honour, if they please, to applaud his Conduct.

Tho' King *Charles* had, for Merit he saw in him, created him Colonel of Dragoons, and added to't the Title of Lord *Churchill*, yet was there no Opportunity of War to shew how well he deserved those Honours: Nor yet that of Lieutenant-General conferr'd by King *James*, but in a Cause where Honour, Conscience, and Religion oblig'd him to quit that Prince's Service, as he himself did the Nation soon after.

King *William* being seated on the Throne, and having declar'd War against *France*, after creating him Gentleman of the Bed-Chamber and Earl of *Marlborough*, sent him to command the *English* Forces in *Flanders*, where he signaliz'd himself at the Battel of *Walcourt*, and Heading a Detachment of *English*, gave a Check to the Progress of the Marshal *d'Humiers*, who had advantagiously attack'd the Confederate Army; and in the end, forc'd him to retreat, with the loss of many Men slain, and some Cannon and Ammunition: And this Year, in *October* 1689, having ended the Campaign, he returned to *London*.

In 1690, he was sent with some Forces under his Command, to reduce the two Harbours of *Cork* and *Kingsale* in *Ireland*, then in the Hands of the *Irish* Rebels; at the first of which Places he arriv'd on the 21st of *September*, and the next Day entring the Harbour, was opposed by the Enemy, who had a Battery of 8 Guns there; but his Lordship sending 3 Arm'd Boats ashore, they soon made the *Irish* quit their Guns. On the 23d, He order'd the greatest part of the Land Forces up the Passages, six Miles from *Cork*, headed by the Duke of *Grafton*; and the same Day order'd Major-General *Tettau* with a Party of 1000 Men, to attack one or both of the New Forts, and New *Shannon* Castle, which the *Irish* perceiving, set Fire to the Suburbs, and retired hastily into the Town; whereupon the *English* possess'd themselves of New *Shannon* Castle, and planted some Guns there. On the 26th, the Duke of *Wirtemberg* join'd the Army before the Town, and on the 27th, they took Possession of the *Cat Fort*, the Enemy having abandon'd it without a blow struck, and from thence raised a Battery which ply'd both the City and Fort; besides another Battery above the Fort, and one at *Red-Abby*. These soon made a Breach in the City Wall, so that his Lordship order'd all things for an Assault, which was prevented, by the Enemies beating a Parley; yet not accepting the Terms offer'd them, the firing was renew'd, and having enlarg'd the Breach, the general Assault was just going to be given, when the Besieged to prevent it, beat a second Parley; and at length the Earl of *Tyrone* and Colonel *Riccaut*, being sent from the Governour, were glad to accept his Lordships Conditions; and the Garrison consisting of 4000 Men, were made Prisoners of War, both Officers and Soldiers; and the next Day the *English* enter'd *Cork*. From thence on the 28th of *Sept.* his Lordship sent a Detachment of Horse and Dragoons immediately to summon the Town and Forts of *Kingsale*, upon whose Approach, the *Irish* retreated into the Old and New Forts; and on the first of *October*, his Lordship set out with the Army, and arrived the next Day before *Kingsale*; and having taken up his Camp, gave Directions to make the necessary Approaches: General *Tettau* was order'd to attack the old Fort which he took, and made the Garrison Prisoners: From thence his Grace sent to summon the New Fort, but was answer'd by the Governour, *'Twould be time enough to talk of that a Month hence:* Therefore on the 5th, his Grace order'd the Trenches to be open'd, and Batteries to be raised. When a Breach being made, and a Storm threaten'd, the Enemy beat a Parley; and the Garrison consisting of 3500 Men, were to march out with their Arms and Baggage, and be conducted to *Limerick*. So that his Lordship having perform'd this Signal piece of Service with great Gallantry and Success, thereby as it were finishing the War in *Ireland*, he returned again to *England*; arriving at *Kensington* the 28th of *Oct.* following, where he received that favourable Welcome from their Majesties, which his great Services deserved. How he came a Year after to lay down his Employments, is still a Secret; but 'tis certain, King *William* was at a great loss to supply his Vacancy, and that he ever retained an Esteem for his Lordships Political and Military Abilities, which his Majesty sufficiently express'd, as soon as time and better Information had dissipated the Prejudices which had been whisper'd against him; which appears by his Majesty's prudent fore-sight in creating him before his Death, Plenipotentiary and Commander in chief of the *English* Auxillaries.

Our most Gracious Sovereign Queen *Anne*, under whose auspicious Reign his Grace has done such Signal Services for his Country and the Common Cause, as are hardly to be parallel'd; being unanimously seated on the Throne of her Ancestors, sent him with the Title of Ambassadour Extraordinary, and Plenipotentiary to the States of *Holland*: where, after several Conferences, he made a Speech condoling them on the Death of the King, and also tending to confirm the Alliances which his Majesty had so prudently begun, highly pleasing to the States; so that having finish'd his Negotiations, he returned to *England* again the 5th of *April* following; where giving her Majesty a satisfactory Relation of his Embassy, and settling his Affairs, on the 12th of *May* he set out for *Holland*; and soon after from thence to the Army, where he arrived the 2d of *July* before *Nimeguen*: The States having sent Orders to all their Generals and other Officers to obey him, constituting him *Generalissimo* of all their Forces. Having drawn the Troops together, he march'd the Army over the *Maese*, which River he repass'd again the 28th, taking in the strong Castle of *Grevenbroek*, following the *French* so close, that they were oblig'd to quit the *Spanish Guelderland*; but not being able to bring them to an Engagement, he order'd next the Town of *Venlo* to be besieged, where the Lord *Cutts* heading the *English*, took the Fort of St. *Michael* Sword in Hand, which occasion'd the Town soon after to surrender, being conducted to *Antwerp* with their Arms and Baggage, but without Cannon or Mortars: Upon which his Lordship order'd the Troops employ'd in that Siege to march immediately and invest *Ruremond*; where having open'd their Trenches, and firing furiously upon the Place, the Garrison thought fit to capitulate, and surrender'd the 6th of *October*, on the same Terms with *Venlo*, and were conducted to *Lorrain*. Also at the same time he caus'd *Stevenswaert* to be attack'd, which surrender'd by Capitulation.

Nor did these Successes satisfie his Ambition; but when People concluded he had done sufficient for one Campaign, and that 'twould end here, his Lordship, by a surprizing March arriv'd before *Liege*, where the Chapter and Magistracy sent Commissioners to him to treat of a surrender of the Town, which being readily granted, the Articles were signed on both sides, and the next Day the Confederates took Possession of the whole Town; six Days after the Trenches were open'd before the great Citadel, and by the 23d having made a sufficient Breach, the Counterscarp was attack'd with such Fury, that the *French* could not defend it; when instead of lodging themselves thereon, as was only designed the Confederates got into the *Cover'd way*, passed the Ditch, mounted the Breach, and took the Place by dint of Sword, Monsieur *de Violaine*, who five Days before sent word to his Lordship, It would be time enough to think of a Surrender six weeks hence; was so surprized at this vigorous Attack, that he immediately beat a Parley; but the Allies being already entered, would not hearken to it, and had killed all they met, had not the *French* thrown down their Arms and begg'd Quarter: This Cittadel being thus taken, the Conquest was soon compleated by the Surrender of the *Chartreuse*, upon honourable Terms, the Garrison being conducted to *Antwerp*.

On the 3d of *November* (N. S.) The Confederate Army separated near *Liege*, and his Lordship came the same Day to *Maestricht*, where he embark'd immediately on the *Maese* for *Holland*; where he had a narrow Escape from a Party of the Garrison of *Gueldre*, who seiz'd the Boat, and having examin'd the several Passports, without knowing his Lordship, having first riffled the Trunks, and made his Guard of Foot Prisoners, they retired with their Booty, leaving him to pursue his Voyage: This reached the *Hague*, where the People were in the greatest Consternation; but upon his Arrival there the sixth following, the People expressed the greatest Demonstrations of Joy imaginable for his Escape and safe Arrival: And having received the Compliments of all the Foreign Ministers and Persons of Quality upon his Glorious Campaign, he embark'd for *England*, and arriv'd at *Whitehall* the 28th following: and on the 23d of *December*, the Queen was pleased to declare before a Committee in Council, That she was so well satisfied with the Eminent Services of my Lord of *Marlborough*, that she intended to make him a Duke.

The next Year 1703, His Grace passed over early for *Holland*, his Presence being highly wanted there, to settle the necessary Measures for opening the Campaign on the *Lower Rhine*; and having resolved to begin it with the Siege of *Bon*, he set out on the 11th of *April* for the Army, where giving Directions for the Siege, caused the Place to be invested on the 24th (N. S.) and by the 13th of *May* being ready to storm the Town, having made one furious Assault, the *French* unwilling to stand a second, beat a Parley the 14th, and surrender'd the Place on honourable Conditions.

Soon after the Surrender of *Bon*, his Grace returned to the Main Army, and marched towards *Liege* to follow the *French*; who, upon the Confederates advancing to *Niendorp*, retired with great Precipitation to *Bockworm*, not daring to stand the Hazard of a Battel; whereupon his Grace formed a Resolution of attacking them in their Lines, and had certainly executed it, with the same Success he has done lately, had he not been over-ruled by the State-Deputies.

Therefore on the 16th of the following Month, he caused *Huy* to be invested Fort *Pickard* and St. *Joseph* surrendred, and were made Prisoners: and on the 25th, the Castle having stood one Assault, beat a Parley, and surrender'd next Day Prisoners of War.

On the 10th of *August*, his Grace gave Orders for investing *Limburg*, and on the 20th, followed himself to forward the Siege, where he found the Confederates already Masters of the Lower Town, and their Batteries being finish'd by the 27th, the Breach was so wide, that all things were preparing for a general Storm, which the *French* perceiving, beat a Parley; but all the Conditions they obtained, were to be made Prisoners of War, the Garrison consisting of 1400 Men.

And now his Grace being informed of the King of *Spain*'s Arrival at *Dusseldorp*, he left the Army to wait on his Majesty.

With whom he proceeded to the *Hague*, and from thence returned to *England* the latter end of *October*.

In *January* following, the States representing by their Envoys, that the coming of his Grace to the *Hague* might be of great Advantage to the Common Cause: Her Majesty was pleased to direct his Grace to go thither; and having had several Conferences with the Deputies of the States in Relation to some private Affairs; he left that Place on the 11th of *February*, and arrived again the 24th at *London*.

In the Year 1704, His Grace form'd that Great Project of Delivering the *Empire*; *viz.* his unexpected March to *Germany*, the which he had imparted but to Three Persons in *England*, the Queen, Prince, and Lord Treasurer; and not to above as many in *Holland*; nor to One of the *Imperial Court*, till he was ready to put it in Execution: In order to which, he embark'd on the 19 of *April*, for the *Hague*; where on the 23 of *May* he had a Preliminary Conference with the Deputies, about the Measures to be taken that Campaign: On the 2 of *May* his Grace had another long Conference with them, wherein he open'd his Project; and the next Day with the *States General* themselves, to whom he made a lively Representation of the imminent Danger that threaten'd the *Empire*, and indeed all *Europe*, if an immediate Check were not put to the Progress of the *French* and *Bavarians* in *Germany*; adding, that being now entire Masters of the *Maes*, and all *Spanish Guelderland*, a small number of Forces were able to secure their Territories: These Reasons, supported by the Reputation of him that deliver'd 'em, made so great an Impression upon the whole Assembly, that all Affairs relating to the ensuing Campaign were at this one Conference determin'd: So that without more delay his Grace took leave, and on the 5th set out towards *Ruremond*; giving Order, for the *English* and other Troops posted thereabout, to join, and march towards *Coblentz*. Having review'd the *Dutch* Army at *Maestricht*, and order'd the Troops on all sides to March, he advanc'd on the 18th to *Bedbourg*, and by the 25th to *Nieuderff*, near *Coblentz*; on the 26th, with the Horse and Dragoons, he advanc'd to *Brauback*, the next Night to *Nasletten*, and the 28th to *Smalbach*; where the Foot had Orders to follow, as close as was consistent with the Artillery and Baggage: On the 29th his Grace march'd to *Cassel*; on the 30th he gave the Troops some Rest, and on the 31st pass'd the *Maine*, and encamp'd that Night at *Grosterbont*.

On the 1st of *June* he advanc'd to *Quingenbergh*, the next Day to *Weinheim*, and the 3d to *Ladenburgh*; where the Troops pass'd the *Neckar*, and encamp'd on the River side: Here his Grace thought necessary to halt for 2 Days, as well to give his wearied Troops Rest, as not to leave too far behind the rest of the Auxiliary Forces. On the 6th he march'd from *Ladenburgh* to *Wiselock*, the 7th to *Eppingen*, and the next Day to Great *Gardach*, where several of the Artillery-Troops join'd his Grace. On the 9th he march'd with the Horse to *Monblesheim*, where Prince *Eugene* came to Dine with his Grace the next Day; at which time met two of the Greatest Men of the Age, equal in Merit and in Fame; part of the Day pass'd in Conferences between 'em, wherein the mutual Esteem they had for each other before, grew into a strict Friendship and Confidence, which appear'd in all the Operations of the Campaign; the next Day his Highness march'd with the Duke to *Great Heppach*; where Prince *Eugene* view'd the Army, and was highly pleased: On the 13th Prince *Lewis* of *Baden* had an Interview with his Grace; where they settled the Operations of the Campaign: On the 14th his Grace march'd to *Ebberspach*, and the 18th to *Grosseisen*; on the 21st his Grace decamp'd from *Grosselsen* to *Launsheim*, and the next Day made a motion to join P. *Lewis* at *Westersletten*. The 24th the Army march'd from thence to *Elschingen* near the *Danube*, where they halted 3 Days; and on the 28th march'd to *Gingen*, within 2 Leagues of the Elector of *Bavaria*'s Army; and the next Day the *English* Foot and Artillery join'd them: On the 30th they march'd, and encamp'd at *Belmershofen*, and that Day continu'd their March in sight of the Elector of *Bavaria*'s Army; who rightly judging his Grace intended to attack *Donawert*, sent a great Detachment of his best Troops to reinforce that Post: The next Day his Grace advanc'd at 3 in the Morning with 6000 Foot, and 30 Squadrons of *English* and *Dutch* Horse, besides 3 Battalions of *Imperial* Grenadiers, the rest of the Army following under P. *Lewis* with all possible diligence; but the Way being bad, his Grace cou'd not come to the River *Werntz* till Noon, having pass'd the same by 3, at the Head of the Cavalry, and view'd the Intrenchments, gave Orders for the Attack, which was begun by the *English* and *Dutch*, with unparallell'd Bravery, before the *Imperialists* came up; and met with such vigorous Resistance, that they were twice repuls'd: But after an Engagement of an Hour and half, the *Imperialists* by that time being come up, the Intrenchments were forc'd, with a terrible Slaughter of the Enemy; pursuing them to the *Danube*, where a great part follow'd the Example of their General Count *D'Arco* and the other General Officers, who saved themselves by swimming that River; leaving behind them 15 Pieces of Cannon, all their Ammunition, Tents, and Baggage, and 13 Colours. During the Fight, his Grace gave his Orders with the greatest Presence of Mind, and exposing his Person to the greatest Danger. The Loss of the Enemy was computed to be 300 Men, nor was the Confederate's much less; which was abundantly made up by gaining so compleat a Victory, which gave an Entrance into the Duke of *Bavaria*'s Country, and forced him to retire under the Cannon of *Augsburgh*; sending Orders to his Garrison at *Donawert* to set Fire to the Town, burn the Bridges, and so retire. But his Grace advancing, they durst not stay to execute his Orders: So that the Confederates entred the Town, and found there good Magazines. The next Day his Grace passed the *Danube* near that Place, and encamped at *Mertingen* in the Elector of *Bavaria*'s Country; the 6th his Grace observed for a Day of Thanksgiving: His Grace resolving to improve this Advantage, order'd the Count *Frize*, with 4000 Men, and 12 Pieces of Cannon to pass the *Lech*, and take Post in the Country of *Bavaria*; being reinforced next Day with 6000 Men more; And the whole Army came and encamped with their Right at *Hamiter*, and their Left at *Ginderkingen*, near the River; and upon the first notice of their beginning to pass it, the Garison of *Nicuburgh* abandoned that Place, and his Grace ordered a Detachment to take Possession of it: After which, his Highness decamping from *Ginderkingen*, ordered *Rain* to be invested; the same Night the Trenches were opened, and the Approaches carried on with so good Success, that by the 16th in the Morning the Garrison desired to capitulate, and the Articles being agreed to, they marched out next Day, and were conducted to *Augsburg*: The same Day his Grace decamped, and came to *Ousterhausen*, and on the 18th continued his March to *Aicha*; and having rested there 2 Days, advanced to *Roerbach*, and from thence to *Fridberg*, within a League of *Augsburg*; where his Grace received Advice from Prince *Eugene*, that Marshal *Tallard* was arrived the 28th at *Villengen*, and that his Highness was upon the March to observe him.

In the mean time, his Grace and Prince *Lewis* finding the Duke of *Bavaria* inflexible, and that all he said on the account of Accommodation, was to gain Time, resolved up the Siege of *Ingoldstadt*; likewise ordering a strong Detachment to Burn and Plunder his Country as far as *Munich*. Thereupon they marched back from *Fridbergh* toward *Aicha*, Burning all the Villages between those two Towns which they had spared before; and from thence advanced to *Hogenwaert*. On the other hand, the Marshal *Tallard* with 12000 Horse and Foot joined the Elector at *Biberach* on the 21st of *August*, with design to pass the *Danube* at *Lawingen*, and fall on Prince *Eugene*, who was by this time encamped at *Hochstet*: This Project of their's, brought forth the Battel of that Name: For upon notice of their Motions, his Grace resolved to return toward *Donawert*; and at Pr. *Eugene*'s request, sent him a strong Detachment to reinforce him, under the Duke of *Wirtembergh* and General *Churchil*, directing them to use all imaginable Diligence; with promise, that he would soon be with them, with the rest of the Army, and accordingly on the 10th continued his March toward *Rain*. Prince *Eugene* now being assured of the Enemy's Design, and that they advanced that Day as far as *Steinheim*, with intent to attack him the next, sent to acquaint his Grace thereof, and hasten his March. On the 11th, his Grace decamped by Two in the Morning, with design to rejoin Pr. *Eugene* that Evening, which was happily effected.

The 12th at break of Day, his Grace with Pr. *Eugene* went to view the Enemy's Army; who advanced, and encamped on a very advantagious Post on a Hill; their Right extending to *Bleinheim*, and their Left to *Lutzinghen*; having before them a Rivulet whose Banks were high, and the bottom marshy: Notwithstanding which, it was resolved by his Grace and Pr. *Eugene* to give them Battel before they had fortified themselves in that strong Camp; whereupon that very Night all the necessary Dispositions were made, and the heavy Baggage sent to *Donawert*.

The next Morning early, being the 13th of *August*, a memorable Day, in which the Fate of the *Empire*, or rather all *Europe*, was decided; the Confederate Army began to march, filing off in 9 Columns, and by Six presented themselves before the Enemy's Camp; when his Grace and Pr. *Eugene* being posted on an Eminence, called to them all the Generals, and gave them the necessary Orders for the Day: And then the Army advanced on the Plain, and were drawn up in Order of Battel: By Nine the Cannon began to play on both Sides; and every thing being disposed, his Grace gave Orders for the General Attack, which was begun on the Left, by three quarters after Twelve. Major General *Wilks* made the first Onset with Five *English* Battalions, supported by my Lord *Cuts* and General *Saint-Paul*, with 11 other Battalions, and 15 Squadrons, under Major General *Wood*: The first 5 Battalions charged at the Village of *Bleinheim*, to the very Muzzles of the Enemy's Muskets, but were forced to retreat: While this Brigade rallied, that of *Ferguson* commanded by himself, attacked the Village of *Bleinheim* on the Left, but with no better Success. The *English* Foot having thus begun the Engagement, the Horse of that Wing passed the Rivulet, and fell pell-mell over-against the Center of the main Battalia of the Enemy: In a word, all passed, and drew up in Order of Battel, as well the Ground would permit; the Enemy keeping themselves quiet on the Hill they were possessed of: But our Cavalry advancing, they moved, and charged our Men with a great deal of Fury; who being besides flanked by the Fire from behind the Village of *Bleinheim*, the first Line of Horse was put into disorder; but Lieutenant General *Bulow* brought up the Second Line, and charged the Enemy with such Vigour, that he drove them to the very Hedges of *Bleinheim*; this gave time to the Cavalry of the Left Wing to rally, and forming themselves entirely in order of Battel, charged the Enemy's Horse, and routed them. While these things passed, Marshal *Tallard* caused Ten of his Battalions to advance, to supply the Defects of his Cavalry, and try a last Effort; which the Prince of *Hesse* and other Generals perceiving, caused also three Battalions of our Infantry to advance, to sustain the Horse; and then began a terrible Fire, in which at first our first Line was a little disordered. But renewing the Charge, entirely broke, and routed the Enemy's Horse; who abandoning their Foot, those Ten Battalions were entirely cut to pieces. Marshal *Tallard* rallied once more his routed Cavalry, and finding Things in this desperate Condition, resolved to draw off the Foot and Dragoons from *Bleinheim*; and and thereupon sent to Marshal *Marsin*, to keep the Enemy in Play, to favour their Retreat: But *Marsin* answered, That he had already too much upon his Hands, (having to do with the Duke of *Marlborough* in Person) to spare any Troops: In the mean time, the Confederate Cavalry finding an Expedient to attack the *French* Horse on their Right Flanke they totally dispersed them: Part of them endeavoured to gain the Bridge they had on the *Danube*; the other, among whom were the *Gens d'Arms*, were so closely pursued, that, those who escaped being killed, threw themselves into the *Danube*, where most of them perished. The Marshal *Tallard* was himself enveloped with Runaways, and taken by the Prince of *Hesse*'s *Aid de Camp*.

While these things passed on the left, his Grace caused the Village of *Overklaw* to be attacked, where the Prince of *Holstein-Beck*, who commanded the Onset, was repulsed, and himself taken Prisoner: being sustain'd by some *Danish* and *Hannoverian* Horse, they charged a second time, but with the same success; till his Grace having himself brought up some Squadrons, supported by the Body of Reserve in a third Attack, caused the Enemy to retire; when returning to the Centre, he found the Day there decided in his Favour. By this time the Elector of *Bavaria* was perceived, making his Retreat from the Village of *Lutzingen*, and the *French* Cavalry wholly dispersed, that our Troops were Masters of all the Ground between the Enemy's Left, and the Village of *Bleinheim*, those 28 Battalions and 12 Squadrons of Dragoons, finding themselves cut off from the rest of their Army; and despairing of making their Escape, they laid down their Arms, and surrender'd at Discretion: Prince *Eugene* in the Right, had more to do with the Elector of *Bavaria*, were things were at one time in an ill Condition; but his Highness, by his great Prudence and Conduct, retrieved all again, and gave it the Name of a Compleat Victory on his part; nor must we do less than give him his share of the Glory, as we must a little extol the Conduct of his Grace, by whom the whole Action was in a manner managed and directed: They both exposed their Persons to the eminent'st Dangers; and his Grace narrowly escap'd being killed by a Cannon-Ball which grazed under his Horse's Belly.

The Enemy's Loss, according to their own Confession, amounted to near 40000 killed, wounded, or taken Prisoners; with 113 Pieces of Cannon, 24 Mortars, 129 Colours, 171 Standards, 17 pair of Kettle-Drums, 3600 Tents, 34 Coaches, 300 Laden Mules, and other rich Booties; with the loss of our side, 4485 Men killed, 7525 wounded.

And now we come to the Consequences of this great Victory: On the 6th of *August*, the City of *Augsburgh* sent forthwith to desire his Grace's Protection, as did also the City of *Memmingen* on the 20th; and also the Enemy returning to the *Rhine*, his Grace resolv'd to follow them, leaving General *Thungen* to carry on the Siege of *Ulm*; where he first drove them over the River *Queich*, and then over the *Lauter*, by which the Confederates had it in their Power to form the Siege of *Landau*, which was invested on the 12th of *September* by Prince *Lewis*, whilst his Grace and Prince *Eugene* covered the Siege, the Day before which *Ulm* surrendered to General *Thungen*.

On the 22d of *October* the present Emperour, then at the Siege of *Landau*, came to *Croon-Weissenburg* to visit his Grace, and see his victorious Troops: of which his Grace having notice, he drew the Army up in two Lines, and receiving his Majesty at the Left Wing of his Army, waited on him along the Line, and saluted him with a tripple Discharge of the Artillery and small Arms; after which his Grace, by a tedious March through a mountainous barren Country, leaving most of his Troops at *Croon-Weissenburg*, arrived the 28th of *October* at *Tryers*, which City the *French* abandoned upon his Approach: Having possessed that important Post, he summoned a great Number of Pioneers to work on the Fortifications, and the 31st went and viewed the Ground above *Saar*, in order to mark out a Camp for the Horse to cover those Work-men, and the next Day went towards *Traerbach* to take a narrow view of that Place, and having given the necessary Directions for carrying on the Siege, the Care of which was committed to the Prince of *Hesse*; he returned the next day towards *Landau*, where he found the Besiegers Masters of the Counterscarp; and on the 8th of *Nov.* arrived at *Croon-Weissenburgh*, from whence he sent the *English* into Winter Quarters, and began his Journey to *Berlin* on the 15th, where he arrived on the 22d; having been received in all the Towns through which he passed with extraordinary Marks of Respect, and was met without the Town by the King's Great Chamberlain, the Field Marshal and other Nobility; and that same Evening, had Audience of his *Prussian* Majesty and the Queen, and the 24th was entertained at Dinner by the Prince Royal, who, on the 26th set out with his Grace for *Hannover*; his Grace being infinitely well satisfied with his Entertainment, and the Success of his Negotiation at that Court: On the 1st of *Decemb.* his Grace, with the Prince Royal, arrived at *Hannover*, where he was received with all imaginable Demonstration of Respect from that Elector, the Princess *Sophia*, and the whole Court: On the 5th, his Grace began his Journey to *Holland*, and arrived at *Naerden* the 9th, and on the 11th set out for the *Hague*, being saluted with a triple Discharge of all the Cannon, and the loud Acclamations of the People: And on the 15th of *December*, having finished some Dispatches, he returned to *England*, bringing over with him the Marshal *Tallard*, and other *French* Generals, and the Colours and Standards taken at *Hochstet*.

His Grace, on his Arrival at St. *James*'s, was received with the highest Welcome, both from the Queen, Prince, and Nobility; and the next day coming to the House of Peers, he was complimented with an Address from the Lord Keeper, as also by a Committee from the House of Commons, he ascribing his Victory to the Bravery and Merit of his Troops.

His Grace was also invited by the Lord Mayor and Court of Aldermen to Dine with them in the City, where he received the like Congratulations on his great Successes: On the 11th of the same Month, the House of Commons came to this unanimous Resolution; That an humble Address should be presented to her Majesty, that she would be pleased to consider of some proper Method to perpetuate the Memory of the great Services performed by his Grace; which was done by settling the Mannor of *Woodstock*, and Hundred of *Wooten* to him and his Heirs.

And on the 26th of *March* following, his Grace set out for *Holland*, and arrived at the at the *Hague* the 2d of *April* following; and having regulated the Operations for the ensuing Campaign: He set out for *Maestricht*, where he held a Council of War with Monsieur *Auverquerque* and the other Generals; and having viewed the *English* Troops encamped along the *Maese*, on the 15th of *May* he passed that River, in order to march for the *Moselle*; and on the 17th arrived at *Coblentz*, from whence he went to confer with Prince *Lewis* at *Rastadt*, giving Orders in the mean time for the Troops to continue their March: His Grace having settled Matters with the Prince of *Baden*, arrived the 27th at *Triers*, and having assembled all the Forces in that Neighbourhood; the *English* passed the *Moselle* at *Igel* the 3d of *June* following, and the *Dutch*, and others in *English* and *Dutch* Pay passed the *Saar* at the same time, and so all the Forces joined. His Grace advanced by the Defile of *Tavern*, and came within a Mile of *Syrk*, and the next day took the Camp at *Elest*, Marshal *Villars* retreating before him: But the *Germans*, by their Slowness (to say no worse) having baulk'd the Campaign on that side; mean time the *French* having taken *Huy*, and invested *Liege*, the State Deputies were not a little Importunate with his Grace to march back for the *Netherlands*, where their Troops might be better employed, as it has appeared since; for upon his Grace's return, the *French* quitted the City of *Liege*, and his Grace also re-took *Huy*: After which, having informed himself of the Condition of the Enemies Lines, he resolved to attack them e're they were made stronger by further Detachments from the *Moselle*; and therefore it was resolved, that Monsieur *Auverquerque* should pass the *Mehaigne*, and face the Lines, to give the Enemy a Jealousie they were to be attacked on that side, while his Grace should attack them at *Heylesheim*: This Stratagem succeeded, according to his Grace's Opinion (though contrary to the Opinion of some other Generals, who were against those Measures) for the Enemy drew their Main Force that way: In the close of the Evening, his Grace sent a Detachment under Count *Noyelles* of 20 Battalions and 30 Squadrons, to advance silently toward *Heleshein*, and at *Tattoo* followed with the rest of the Army, at which time Monsieur *Auverquerque* was also to march back again, and second the Attempt in Conjunction with his Grace.

By break of Day, the Detachment under Count *Noyelles*, being come to the Lines, forced their Passage with little Opposition, and got over with so much Diligence, that 3 Regiments of *French* Dragoons were obliged to retire in great Disorder: Immediately after Monsieur *Allegre* appeared with a strong Body of Horse and Foot, and advanced with great Resolution to attack Count *Noyelles*, but his Grace being already got over, with good part of the Horse of the Right Wing, and having formed them, attacked the Enemy with such Bravery, that after a sharp Dispute of 2 Hours, he obliged them to retire with considerable Loss; thereupon he immediately ordered a Detachment to *Tirlemont*, where they made the Regiment of *Montluc* Prisoners: another Detachment advanced and seized *Deist*, which the Enemy abandoned, and the Magistrates sent to beg his Graces Protection.

There were taken Prisoners in this Action, 2 Lt. Gen. 1 Maj. Gen. and above 100 Officers, and 2500 Private Men, 15 Pieces of Cannon, 20 Standards or Colours, and a great part of the Enemy's Baggage: besides they lost 1000 Men on the Spot. After the Action, his Grace marched to the Camp at *Park-Abby* near *Louvain*, where we now leave him to pursue his Conquests.

IOHN DUKE of MARLBOROUGH

L O N D O N: Printed and Sold by *John Nutte*, near *Stationers*-Hall, M DCC V.

■ After Kneller

The British Caesar, from a Broadside published by John Nutt in London, incorporating a portrait of John Churchill, 1st Duke of Marlborough.

Etching by Michael van der Gucht, 1705. The British Museum, London, UK.

One of the earliest surviving and least public images of Marlborough is a family portrait painted by John Closterman in the early 1690s. Now hanging on the stairs at Blenheim Palace, the painting was conceived for the more modest surroundings of Holywell House, the Jenyns's Hertfordshire seat and, from 1677, John and Sarah Churchill's marital home. Closterman, having learned his trade first in his native Osnabrück, then in Paris with the French court painter François de Troy, travelled to England in 1681 following the death of the pre-eminent court painter Peter Lely. As one of only a handful of artists capable of succeeding Lely, Closterman enjoyed a long and successful career in England, producing erudite, classicizing portraits for a select group of literary and aristocratic patrons.[2] He painted Marlborough on more than one occasion, including in around 1705 the large equestrian portrait that now hangs in the great hall of the Royal Hospital at Chelsea, but it is this earlier family group that represents the artist's most original contribution to Marlborough's pictorial legacy.

Given the preponderance of military iconography on view elsewhere in this chapter, it is striking how little reference is made in Closterman's painting to Marlborough's already distinguished military career. Marlborough's public life may be hinted at by his unconventional position, towards the edge of the composition, and by the distant landscape that separates him visually from the intimate circle formed by Sarah and the couple's five children, but he remains firmly within the orbit of the family. Meanwhile, Sarah, resplendent in blue, silver and gold, takes centre stage as the matriarch of a blossoming family, as issues of dynasty, good breeding and conjugal harmony are privileged over other, more worldly claims of individual distinction. Notwithstanding the apparent intimacy of the scene, Closterman's painting also aspires to the highest forms of group portraiture, as established in England during the 1630s by the Flemish artist Anthony Van Dyck. More specifically, the heavily draped classical architecture and the rich attire and co-ordinated body language of the sitters in Closterman's painting recall one of the most ambitious and most celebrated of all family portraits: Van Dyck's extraordinary depiction of the 4th Earl of Pembroke and his family, at Wilton House. Closterman even gives the Marquess of Blandford, the couple's eldest son, the same swaggering pose as his older counterpart in the Pembroke group; but his response is in every other way more restrained than Van Dyck's monumental wall-sized painting. The result is a model of aristocratic domesticity that would inspire the portraits of later dukes and their families at Blenheim, by the likes of Thomas Hudson and Joshua Reynolds.[3]

The painting was commissioned around 1693, while the Churchills were biding their time at Holywell in the wake of the Earl's recent dismissal and imprisonment for his alleged involvement in secret negotiations to restore James II. Closterman's carefully staged family portrait thus coincided with a period of temporary retirement for the pair; but also with a moment of great expectation as the focus of political attention shifted towards Anne following the death of Mary II. The artist conveys this critical episode with a timely display of familial affection, portraying the Marlboroughs as leading members of what was increasingly recognised as a court-in-waiting. Even the playful symbolism of the orange blossom beside the couple's second daughter, Anne, dressed in orange, would have been understood in an age noted for its love of allegory and allusion as a playful visual (and botanical) declaration of the family's

John Churchill, 1st Duke of Marlborough and his family.

Oil on canvas (282 x 142 cm) by John Closterman, 1695. Blenheim Palace, Oxfordshire, UK. The Bridgeman Art Library.

His Grace John, Duke of Marlborough, Marquis of Blanford, Earl of Marlborough, Baron Churchill, of Sandridge and Baron Churchill of Aumouth; Captain-General of all Her Majesty's Forces; Master General of the Ordnance; One of ye Lords of Her Majestys most Honourable Privy-Council, and Knight of the most Noble Order of the Garter. Her Majestys Ambaſsador Extraordinary and Plenipotentiary to the States General of the United Provinces and General of the Confederate Armies.

G. Kneller S. R. Imp. & Angl. Eques Aur. pinx. 1705 — I. Smith fec. — 157 — Sold by I. Smith at ye Lyon & Crown in Russel-street Covent-Garden.

commitment to the Protestant succession, and to the Revolution principles inaugurated by William of Orange in 1688. It is a delicate gesture, childish even, but one that deliberately unites the Marlborough name and the nation's recent royal past within a single history, while suggesting for both a healthy and fruitful future. By fusing the overarching dynastic concerns of the early modern elite with a relatively novel ideal of intimate family life, Closterman's portrait represents a recently ennobled family on the cusp of its prime: youthful, loyal and ready to assume an even more prominent role in the life of the nation.

Among the dozens of portraits of Marlborough produced during his lifetime, the most numerous by far was the 'head-and-shoulder' format – a type of portrait associated most closely at the time with the studio of the celebrated German artist Godfrey Kneller, and with the burgeoning print culture that developed in tandem with Kneller's phenomenal success as a painter. A frequent collaborator with Kneller was John Smith, one of the most influential printmakers and publishers of the day.[4] Smith's individual success lay in his ability to translate Kneller's refined society portraits into high-quality, affordable images for a growing print-buying public. Few such images proved as successful as the mezzotint portrait of Marlborough, taken from a painted likeness by Kneller, which Smith produced and sold at his Covent Garden shop a few months after the Battle of Blenheim.

Marlborough's likeness is framed by a courtly full-bottomed wig, lace cravat and out-of-date plate armour (an emblem of soldierly prowess that remained fashionable in portraiture long after it ceased to be worn into battle), over which he wears the collar and Great George of the Order of the Garter. Kneller's portrait thus combines a general air of aristocratic gravitas and fashionable refinement with the more exclusive trappings of military and political authority that locate the sitter at the heart of the nation's affairs. In Smith's translation of the image, these attributes are accentuated by the publisher's preference for (and obvious mastery of) the relatively novel technique of mezzotint, a form of printmaking that was particularly well-suited to reproducing the softened lines and polished appearance of Kneller's celebrity faces. Finally, the authority assumed by Kneller's portrait is affirmed, in its engraved state, by a lengthy inscription which across five lines of close text relates the many titles and offices that Marlborough had accumulated to date.

To a later generation of artists and writers on art, the physical characteristics exemplified in Smith's mezzotint became known as the 'Kneller mask' – a social disguise available to anyone with the means to order a head-and-shoulder from the artist or one of his many imitators. At the time, however, the restorative touch of Kneller's brush (delicately translated here by the printmaker) was valued as proof of the artist's unparalleled ability to capture a 'good likeness.'[5] The elusive question of what exactly constituted a 'good likeness' around the turn of the eighteenth century is foregrounded by a chalk drawing, made around the same time, now in the collection of the British Museum. The drawing, a close study of a man's face turned slightly to one side, appears to have been sketched from life and for many years was thought to be a preparatory study by Kneller for an earlier portrait of Marlborough. Kneller certainly made the image, but the identity of the sitter has since been questioned (primarily, it seems, on the basis of the likely age of the man portrayed).[6] As well as pointing to the paradoxical nature of any likeness (as an essential, but all-too-fragile component of any portrait), the uncertainty that results from the 'loss' of the sitter highlights the distinctive social and pictorial conventions that underpinned even the

John Churchill, 1st Duke of Marlborough.

Mezzotint by John Smith after Godfrey Kneller, 1705.
The British Museum, London, UK.
© The Trustees of the British Museum.

Study for a portrait of an unknown gentleman (formerly identified as John Churchill, 1st Duke of Marlborough).

Black, red and white chalk on paper (368 x 238 mm) by Godfrey Kneller, 1715-1720. The British Museum, London, UK.

most scrupulously observed likeness in Kneller's England. For the artist and his contemporaries, the flawless oval face, double chin and large, heavy eyes exemplified in this drawing and in Smith's mezzotint embodied a particular ideal of aristocratic masculinity (well-fed, well-bred and eminently self-assured), onto which the peculiarities of an individual's face could be mapped by the skilled artist. Far from being an anonymous, all-pervading mask, these conventional physical signs were understood implicitly as essential attributes of a 'good likeness.'

Smith's high-end reproduction of Kneller's portrait was among the first to appear

John Churchill, 1st Duke of Marlborough.

Engraving by unknown printmaker after Godfrey Kneller, 1705.
© National Portrait Gallery, London, UK.

after the Battle of Blenheim, and it soon became the standard image of Marlborough as Britain's warrior Duke. The publisher also produced a smaller version of the print, such was its popularity, and when the original copper plates used in the printmaking process began to wear, causing the image to fade, they were reworked by the publisher to keep up with the unceasing demand for Marlborough's likeness. Each new edition was subtly different to the last, revealing a slight shift in the pose or dress of the sitter, a new inscription, or a less-voluminous wig in line with the latest fashion. The cumulative impression is of a semi-official image that was being reviewed and refined as Marlborough's fame increased. Meanwhile, the Kneller-Smith head-and-shoulder prompted countless unofficial copies, by which means Marlborough's like-

ness became familiar to an ever-growing public. The result, far more than a mere physical resemblance, is a compelling and far-reaching image of John Churchill as the archetypal soldier-politician of Queen Anne's Britain. In this respect, at least, a 'good likeness' is precisely how we ought to understand Kneller's original portrait.

The fruitful collaboration between Kneller and Smith resulted in another print of Marlborough, which, representing the Duke on horseback, drew upon a well-established tradition of equestrian portraiture that had been favoured by princes and generals throughout Europe during the previous century. In Smith's print, horse and rider occupy an area of raised ground beside a classical ruin, while to the left a cavalry squadron rides from the middle distance towards a battlefield in the valley below. If the inclusion of a rearing charger signalled the consummate horsemanship and martial prowess of its rider, the presence of a second figure, a young black servant carrying the Duke's helmet, sharpened the effect by bringing to mind one of the most emphatic expressions of stately authority in the history of British art: Van Dyck's renowned equestrian portrait of Charles I with his equerry Seigneur de St Antoine, painted for the King in 1633 (restored to the Royal Collection after 1660).[7] But all is not as it first appears with Smith's mezzotint, which recalls Van Dyck's iconic image of Stuart kingship in another, less expected way.

Smith's mezzotint survives in several different states, having undergone a similar transformation as Pierre Lombart's 'Headless Horseman' of the mid-seventeenth century. Lombart's celebrated engraving is perhaps the best-known example of the common practice of reworking a printing plate to maximise its relevance and commercial value. It was first issued during the 1650s for the Council of State as a portrait of Oliver Cromwell on horseback, composed more or less directly from Van Dyck's equestrian portrait of Charles I. In the decades that followed, Lombart's copper printing plate underwent repeated transformations at the hands of successive publishers and was reissued with the identity of the rider alternating between Cromwell, Charles I and Louis XIV – and once (inspiring its popular name) with no head at all.[8] Following a similar pattern, Smith's mezzotint of Marlborough on horseback was initially published around 1689 after a once-celebrated life-size portrait by Kneller of the renowned mercenary and commander of William III's army in Ireland, Frederick Schomberg, Duke of Schomberg.[9] Following the German Duke's death at the Battle of the Boyne, Smith reworked the original copper plate, substituting Schomberg's head with a portrait of King William. Several years later, after Blenheim and after Marlborough had been made a Prince of the Holy Roman Empire, the same plate was altered for a second time and republished for a Continental audience as a portrait of the triumphant Duke, with a new inscription given only in French and complete with the Caesarian legend: *Je suis venu, j'ay veu, j'ay vaincu.*

As well as indicating the sizeable investment required to produce a prestigious print of this kind (and thus the commercial advantage to the publisher of reworking an existing image), the changing identity of the rider also lays bare the conventional nature of military portraiture at the turn of the eighteenth century: the likeness at the centre of the image may change, but the visual apparatus of power remains intact. The final version of the plate confirmed Marlborough's military credentials, associating him with a succession of princes and generals which, the accompanying inscription implies, reached back to the dawn of the Roman Empire. Moreover, Smith's decision to obliterate the features of William III suggests that by 1704 not only had Marlborough's reputation eclipsed Schomberg's formidable military legacy, but also, just

Frederick Schomberg, Duke of Schomberg, on horseback.

Mezzotint by John Smith after Godfrey Kneller, 1689.
The British Museum, London, UK.
© The Trustees of the British Museum.

two years after William's death, a high-end image of the triumphant English Duke was judged by the publisher to be of greater commercial value even than a portrait of the late King-Stadholder himself. As Marlborough's international fame increased, so did the reach and relative value of his likeness.

But there were limits. One of the very first images of any kind to elevate Marlborough to the status of national hero appeared on a medal struck in 1703 by the Royal Mint to commemorate the capture of Bonn, Huy, and Limbourg during the opening stages of the War of the Spanish Succession.[10] Marlborough appears on the reverse, on horseback and attended by a female figure who, kneeling, offers the keys to the

John Churchill, 1st Duke of Marlborough on horseback, design for an allegorical portrait.

Oil on canvas (93 x 74 cm) by Godfrey Kneller, 1706.

Hampton Court, to turn his attention towards a grand decorative scheme for the interior of Marlborough's new Oxfordshire palace. Such a scheme, Buckeridge imagined (presumably with Andrea Mantegna's *Triumphs of Caesar* from Hampton Court in mind), ought to depict a momentous triumphal procession, with the Duke riding god-like in a gilded carriage, surrounded by the spoils of war and with '*Albion Rejoycing and the World in Awe*.'[13] A few years later, the court physician and poet Richard Blackmore issued a similar proposal, this time addressed to the leading Soho weaver John Vanderbank, in which he described in excruciating detail a succession of increasingly implausible scenes of victory that could be turned into tapestries for 'Blenheim's lofty Walls'.[14] The fantastical painted and woven scenes described by Buckeridge and Blackmore may have been exaggerated for poetic effect, but such was the scale and ambition of John Vanbrugh's vision for Blenheim, that the palace that emerged from the medieval parkland over the next two decades would eventually become every bit as sensational as the two poets had imagined, and more, combining architecture with portraiture, history painting and allegory in the grandest of ways.[15]

The Marlboroughs' taste for luxurious wall hangings became apparent as soon as their thoughts first turned to the decoration of their new palace. Among the Duke's earliest tapestry commissions, ordered within weeks of the start of building at Woodstock, in 1705, was a set of eight set-piece military scenes depicting the life of a contemporary (though non-specific) army.[16] From the drinking, smoking and whoring of an army at rest in *The Camp*, to the disciplined labour of *The Siege*, to the point-blank violence of *The Skirmish* and *Pillage*, the *Art of War* tapestries reflected the seasonal exercises and operations of modern European soldiery, setting the tone of martial iconography that would eventually define every aspect of the palace.[17]

The series was not new to Marlborough. It had been designed by Lambert de Hondt for the Elector of Bavaria in the 1690s, and subsequently adapted for other royal and aristocratic patrons across Europe, including William III who ordered a set in 1700. The tapestry industry during the seventeenth and early eighteenth centuries operated within a highly evolved market, typically involving artists, agents, workshop owners and weavers, and it was not unusual for successful tapestry designs, or cartoons, to change hands several times or be adapted to meet the different requirements of consecutive patrons. Marlborough had the *Art of War* series personalised for Blenheim by inserting the Churchill arms into the decorated borders of each panel and, more decisively, by having his own portrait incorporated into the design for the fifth scene in the series, *The March*, which consequently portrayed the Duke as a Commander-in-Chief surrounded by half a dozen of his generals, all on horseback. Six further sets of the modified tapestries were woven around the same time, one for each of Marlborough's own generals. For their part, it was a substantial cultural and financial investment – one that signalled not only a shared taste for the work of some of Europe's most highly skilled craftsmen, but also a collective commitment to Britain's recent military affairs and, at that moment, an unquestioned loyalty to Marlborough as their leader.[18]

In November 1708, as the fighting season extended into winter, Marlborough commissioned the weaver and textile merchant Judocus de Vos to produce a new set of tapestries depicting the three most significant allied victories of the war so far: Blenheim, Ramillies and, most recently, Oudenaarde. The three tapestries were woven in De Vos's Brussels workshop, just a short distance from the towns and battlefields that provided their subject. Based on original designs by Lambert de Hondt, who for the purpose drew freely on his own *Art of War* designs, the Victories tapestries were among the earliest and most exclusive decorations designed specifically for Blenheim Palace. Over the next three years, while hopes for the timely completion of building work at Woodstock remained high, the series was extended to twelve panels, ten of which survive more or less intact in the state rooms at Blenheim (see view of the Third State Room, p. 340).

Historians of the War of the Spanish Succession tend to accept the Blenheim *Victories* as a contemporary and therefore broadly accurate account of Marlborough's campaigns – encouraged, it seems, by the designer's evident understanding of military matters and the extraordinary degree of detail that is woven into each of the wall-sized panels. In devising the series, De Hondt and his workshop were able to draw upon a wealth of visual and literary sources, including up-to-date maps, published battle plans, eyewitness accounts of the fighting, and even portraits of the principal figures, to give each panel a sense of historical legitimacy that sets the *Victories* apart from the artist's earlier *Art of War* series and other comparable tapestries.

The Battle of Blenheim in progress, with Marshall Tallard captive in Marlborough's coach in the foreground.

Etching by Jan van Huchtenburg, 1704. The British Museum, London, UK. *© The Trustees of the British Museum.*

As Jeri Bapasola has shown in her excellent account of the tapestries at Blenheim, De Hondt paid particular attention to the tactical execution of the war under Marlborough's leadership.[19] Whether it is the laying of fascines in the middle-distance of the Donauwörth panel (a theme carried over from the *Art of War* series), the use of pontoon bridges across the Scheldt at Oudenaarde, or the extraordinary logistical achievements of Marlborough's army at Bouchain and Lille, the Blenheim *Victories* present a carefully observed and richly detailed account of the Duke's successful management of the war. Exceptionally, in the first of two panels relating to the siege and surrender of Lille, Marlborough's innovative approach to provisioning his army even provides the principal foreground subject, which centres on a convoy of 'Marlbrouks' – narrow, large-wheeled carts said to have been conceived by Marlborough to navigate terrain that had been flooded by the enemy.

For all this attention to detail, the tapestries owe as much to the conventions of western military art, and to the related practices of landscape and history painting, as they do to the documented history of any of the events depicted. The extent to which such pictorial concerns as composition, perspective, gesture, and even a 'good likeness,' determine the range of meanings conveyed by De Hondt's designs is nowhere more apparent than in the panel depicting Marlborough's triumph at Blenheim, arguably the single most iconic moment of the entire war. The left side of the tapestry comprises a distant view of the battle, mapped across an extensive Bavarian landscape. The Danube and the town of Höchstädt are clearly visible, as are the artillery, infantry and cavalry – their respective roles at different stages in the battle condensed within a single, unified prospect. The whole scene, complete with burnt-out buildings and the bodies of dead and injured soldiers, is rendered with astonishing detail using the best available wool and silk threads. In front of this battle-scarred landscape, the moment of victory is represented in the foreground as a gathering of social equals, far removed from the smoke and noise of the battle. As France's Marshal Tallard and his deputies approach Marlborough and his entourage on horseback, the opposing generals acknowledge one another with the same good manners as two old acquaintances at a New Year hunt. In this way, the bitter power struggle between Europe's most powerful armies, played out so violently in the background, culminates in a single polite exchange between statesmen. In the lower left corner of the same panel, an ensign of the King's Own regiment (recalling Marlborough's own professional beginnings as a young grenadier) arranges a trophy of regimental drums and colours captured from Tallard's defeated army. This time-honoured ritual of victory extends to the elaborate decorative border, where the paraphernalia of war, ancient and modern, is assembled in the same conventional manner, interspersed with the arms of those towns captured during the battle.

As a group, the ten surviving *Victories* present a succession of expertly crafted panoramas, against which the particulars of one battle after another may be plotted and scrutinised at a forensic level. At the same time, the viewer, already immersed in the martial iconography of Blenheim Palace, is invited to take a longer view of the war – to survey each campaign from the same elevated perspective as the Duke and his generals as they receive intelligence, despatch orders and accept the surrender of the enemy. The dual register of the Blenheim *Victories* – between the detail and the general – finds a parallel in a double portrait by the Flemish-born artist Enoch Seeman, showing Marlborough with his chief engineer, Colonel John Armstrong (see also the portrait on page pp. 34 and 340). The hierarchical, conversational dynamic of Seeman's painting suggests a corresponding balance between tactical scrutiny and strategic vision, here focused on the interaction between Armstrong, Marlborough and the viewer around a plan of the siege of Bouchain.

As well as offering a compelling vision of Britain's recent military past, the Blenheim *Victories* also confirmed John and Sarah Churchill's membership of an international cultural elite which, like the polite encounter between Marlborough and Tallard in the *Blenheim* panel, transcended the more immediate contest that provided the tapestries' principal subject matter. Textiles from the best workshops in Brussels and Antwerp were counted among the most prestigious forms of contemporary art, more exclusive (and considerably more expensive) than the work of even the most sought-after living painters. Both the *Art of War* series and the Blenheim *Victories* continued a long and distinguished tradition of military textiles that reached back to antiquity and which since medieval times had been valued among the very highest forms of pictorial decoration, reserved for the grandest interiors.[20]

The significance of Homer's description of Helen at her loom recreating the various struggles between the Trojans and the Achaeans, or of the numerous *Trojan War* tapestries that it inspired among the courts of Renaissance Europe, was not lost on Marlborough's generation, many of whom were more than willing to recognise Marlborough as heir to the military heroes of a mythical classical past. As well as appealing to the authority of the ancients, however, Marlborough and his Flemish designers would also have been keenly aware of another, more immediate precedent for the *Victories*, in the seven battle scenes that Adam Frans van der Meulen had contributed to the celebrated *Histoire du Roi* tapestries produced for Louis XIV at the Gobelins manufactory.[21] That a form of display so closely associated with the military ambitions of the Sun King during the 1660s and 1670s could now be harnessed to commemorate the thwarting of Bourbon designs in Europe can only have added to their appeal for Marlborough and his supporters.

The Battle of Blenheim.

Brussels tapestry from the workshop of Judocus de Vos after Lambert and Philippe de Hondt, 1708-1709. Blenheim Palace, Oxfordshire, UK.
Reproduced with the kind permission of His Grace the Duke of Marlborough, Blenheim Palace Image Library.

The diligently researched battlefield detail, the artfully choreographed encounters between generals, and the serial format of the *Victories* have all played a significant role in determining how the seasonal campaigns in Flanders, from Blenheim to Bouchain, have been (and continue to be) understood. Whether showing the Duke issuing orders mid-battle, the novel transport of army provisions, or the formal acceptance of victory, De Hondt's designs repeatedly placed in the foreground the strategic vision that underpinned the success of the allied campaigns. The result is a compelling pictorial narrative describing the war on land as a succession of innovative allied victories, led at every turn by a dynamic English Duke.

The Third State room at Blenheim Palace with the Battle of Oudenaarde tapestry in situ, with one of two panels representing pillage from the Art of War *series to the left. Enoch Seeman's portrait of Marlborough with Colonel John Armstrong hangs above the fireplace.*

Blenheim Palace, Oxfordshire, UK. Photograph by Jarrald Publishing, reproduced with the kind permission of His Grace the Duke of Marlborough, Blenheim Palace Image Library.

After Malplaquet

The intimate correlation between the progress of the war and the weaver's loom was demonstrated by Count Zinzendorf, imperial ambassador at The Hague, in a letter to Marlborough congratulating the Duke on his most recent victory, at Malplaquet, in September 1709. Writing just a few days after the battle, Zinzendorf remarked that the Duke's latest victory, by far the bloodiest encounter of the entire war (and not the most obvious subject for a decorative wall-hanging) would make '*une bonne adjonc-*

tion pour la tapisserie.'[22] In the event, De Hondt and De Vos represented Malplaquet in a relatively conventional fashion, with Marlborough on horseback (although, unusually, with his back to the viewer) surveying the battlefield from a distance as he issues orders to a mounted officer. Significantly, however, and in contrast to the Blenheim panel, the middle distance focuses on the serried ranks of the allied forces as they move into position, and on the opening salvoes of the battle, rather than on the violent conclusion of the day's events. Only the massed infantry and heavy fortifications of the French army give an indication of the ferocity of the fighting that would ensue. Given the exceptionally heavy losses that day, we might even detect a sense of political expediency in Zinzendorf's hurried recommendation that the experience of Malplaquet be incorporated as soon as possible into the triumphal sequence of events established by the earlier tapestries in the series – as if it were only through the act of representation that the battle could finally be assimilated into the master narrative and designated a victory.

The costly and controversial campaign of 1709 was also one of three battles chosen for an ambitious decorative scheme devised and executed by the French painter Louis Laguerre for the Duke and Duchess's Westminster residence, Marlborough House, shortly after the completion of the building in 1711. Laguerre may have

The dining room at Blenheim Palace with the silver centrepiece in commemoration of Marlborough's famous victory at Blenheim in the foreground.

Blenheim Palace, Oxfordshire, UK. Photograph by Jarrald Publishing, reproduced with the kind permission of His Grace the Duke of Marlborough, Blenheim Palace Image Library.

The Malplaquet staircase at Marlborough House (overpainted heavily in the twentieth century).

Paintings by Louis Laguerre, 1712. The Marlborough House, London, UK. Photograph by Richard Johns.

seemed an unlikely proponent of the allied cause. Born at Versailles in the 1660s, where his father was keeper of the royal menagerie, he attended the *Académie royale de peinture et de sculpture* in Paris, where he acquired a thorough understanding of the Academic battle painting of Charles Le Brun and Van der Meulen, before travelling to England around 1684 – working at first alongside Verrio at Windsor then, as his reputation grew, at the country houses of some of England's most prominent aristocratic patrons.[23] Laguerre would go on to decorate the saloon ceiling at Blenheim with an allegorical celebration of Marlborough's triumphant military career, but his first assignment for the Duke and Duchess was to adorn the hall and formal staircases of Marlborough House with a series of wall paintings commemorating the allied victories at Blenheim, Ramillies and Malplaquet.

The Marlborough House murals draw on many of the same pictorial conventions as the earlier *Victories* tapestries at Blenheim Palace, revealing a similar concern for the kind of topographical and documentary detail that had helped to distinguish De Hondt's textile designs from earlier Renaissance models. In other respects, however, Laguerre's scheme offers a very different impression of the allied campaigns, with an unsettling emphasis on the physicality and violence of eighteenth-century warfare. Climbing either of the two staircases at Marlborough House, the visitor is greeted at every turn by the grimacing faces and unsheathed daggers of soldiers engaged in hand-to-hand combat, and by the contorted bodies of the naked and the dead that litter the foreground. Such details, when they appear at all in the Blenheim *Victories*, are invariably seen from a distance: one of a hundred far-off particulars that make up De Hondt's scrupulously observed prospects. In Laguerre's painted decoration, by contrast, war is an altogether more tumultuous affair, experienced at close quarters.

East wall of the Ramillies staircase at Marlborough House (overpainted heavily in the twentieth century).

Paintings by Louis Laguerre, 1712. The Marlborough House, London, UK. Photograph by Richard Johns.

The marked change of register between the Blenheim *Victories* and Laguerre's Marlborough House murals may be explained, in part, by the shifting fortunes and public perceptions of the Duke himself during the later stages of the war. In the months after the allied victories at Blenheim and Ramillies, the captured colours of the Bavarian and French armies were paraded through the streets of London and displayed as trophies in the Guildhall; medals were struck and garden statues cast in Marlborough's honour; and the virtues and military achievements of the 'British Caesar' were heralded from pulpits and printing presses countrywide. In this context of patriotic optimism, it can only have seemed fitting that the most conspicuous expression of the nation's gratitude, the newly endowed Blenheim Palace, should feature a suitably grand narrative foregrounding Marlborough's commanding role. It was under similar circumstances that Christopher Wren was commissioned to design a fashionable new dwelling in Pall Mall (a stone's throw from the Queen's apartment at St James's Palace) befitting the Marlboroughs' status as one of the most powerful couples in the land. By the time their new townhouse had been completed, however, Fortune's Wheel had turned against them both, as the heavy toll of Malplaquet was followed by the public ignominy of Sarah's dismissal from the royal household and the Duke's removal from office amid accusations of corruption, mismanagement and cowardice. Although officially celebrated as another great triumph, the huge losses sustained by the allies in the campaign of 1709 emboldened Marlborough's critics, as Whiggish enthusiasm for the war and the security it once promised increasingly gave way to Tory-led calls for a negotiated peace and doubts over Marlborough's competence. Even more damaging for the Duke personally was the growing belief that he had profited on a grand scale from the war while avoiding any personal danger and,

The Battle of Malplaquet.

Engraving by Claude Dubosc after Louis Laguerre, published by Thomas Bowles and Henry Overton, 1717.
The British Museum, London, UK.
© The Trustees of the British Museum.

The Battle of Blenheim.

Engraving by Louis Duguernier after Louis Laguerre, published by Thomas Bowles and Henry Overton, 1717.
The British Museum, London, UK.
© The Trustees of the British Museum.

worse still, that he had deliberately prolonged hostilities for his further enrichment. Such a sustained attack on Marlborough's conduct and moral character called for something more than a repeat of the well-rehearsed triumphalism of the *Victories* tapestries.

Laguerre's extraordinary response finds a sharp focus in his depiction of the Battle of Ramillies, which plays out across the walls of the west stairs at Marlborough House, beginning with the opening encounter of the battle on the ground floor, and culminating alongside the upper flight of stairs on the west wall with the defeat and pursuit of the enemy. Marlborough appears at the centre of the largest painting, on the east wall. Conspicuous on a white horse, the Duke remains fully composed as he gestures downward, towards the lifeless body of a British officer killed in action. More specifically, Laguerre represents a well-documented and critical episode of the battle during which Marlborough's aide-de-camp, Colonel James Bringfield, was killed by a cannonball while helping the Duke to remount after his previous horse had fallen – the missile, by all accounts, passing through Marlborough's legs and killing the Colonel outright. Some reports even suggest that his head was taken clean off. Bringfield's sacrifice earned him a brief posthumous fame and a modest monument in Westminster Abbey, but his widely reported demise – and Laguerre's vivid dramatisation of the event on the stairs at Marlborough House – also served to reaffirm Marlborough's own commitment to the fight and selfless disregard for his own safety in the face of extreme danger.

Laguerre's pictorial declaration of Marlborough's physical valour found a close journalistic parallel in the earliest detailed account of the Duke's military career. *A short narrative of the life and action of his Grace* was published anonymously in 1717 as a vindication of Marlborough's good character following a succession of attacks by, according to the author, scurrilous hacks in various 'base pamphlets' (foremost of which was the popular Tory journal *The Examiner*).[24] The author of the biography, traditionally identified as Daniel Defoe, claimed to be 'an Old Officer in the Army' who had served under Marlborough. With the assured voice of the eye witness, Marlborough's old comrade compared the Duke's actions to those of other great figures of history – Caesar, Hannibal, even Moses – who had inspired the discipline and respect of their followers by leading by example, from the front. The pamphlet's stated aim was to counteract the prevailing image of the allies' former Commander-in-Chief as a dangerously ineffective soldier and self-serving politician. It is suggestive of a shared project that the author's evocative description of Marlborough and his soldiers surrounded by 'the Stinks of Mortality,' and of the ugly spectacle of 'Men and Horses dying and dead together' on the battlefield, resonates so powerfully with Laguerre's recently completed murals. If the public had been witness to such brutal sights, the author insists, or shared 'the daily danger and expectation of Death' experienced at first hand by Marlborough and his men, then the Duke's patriotism and personal virtue would be seen to be beyond question and the malice of his critics would be exposed. At Marlborough House, the visitor could see what he meant.

In the same year that the unnamed officer's vindicatory biography was issued, Laguerre's designs found a wider audience as a series of high-quality engravings published by Thomas Bowles and Henry Overton, complete with 'a short account of what was most remarkable' provided in English, Latin and French.[25]

But it was when experienced within the context of Marlborough House, alongside the exceptionally refined stairs and surrounding architecture of one of eighteenth-

BLENHEIM
Sonderen
Klaw
Lutzingen

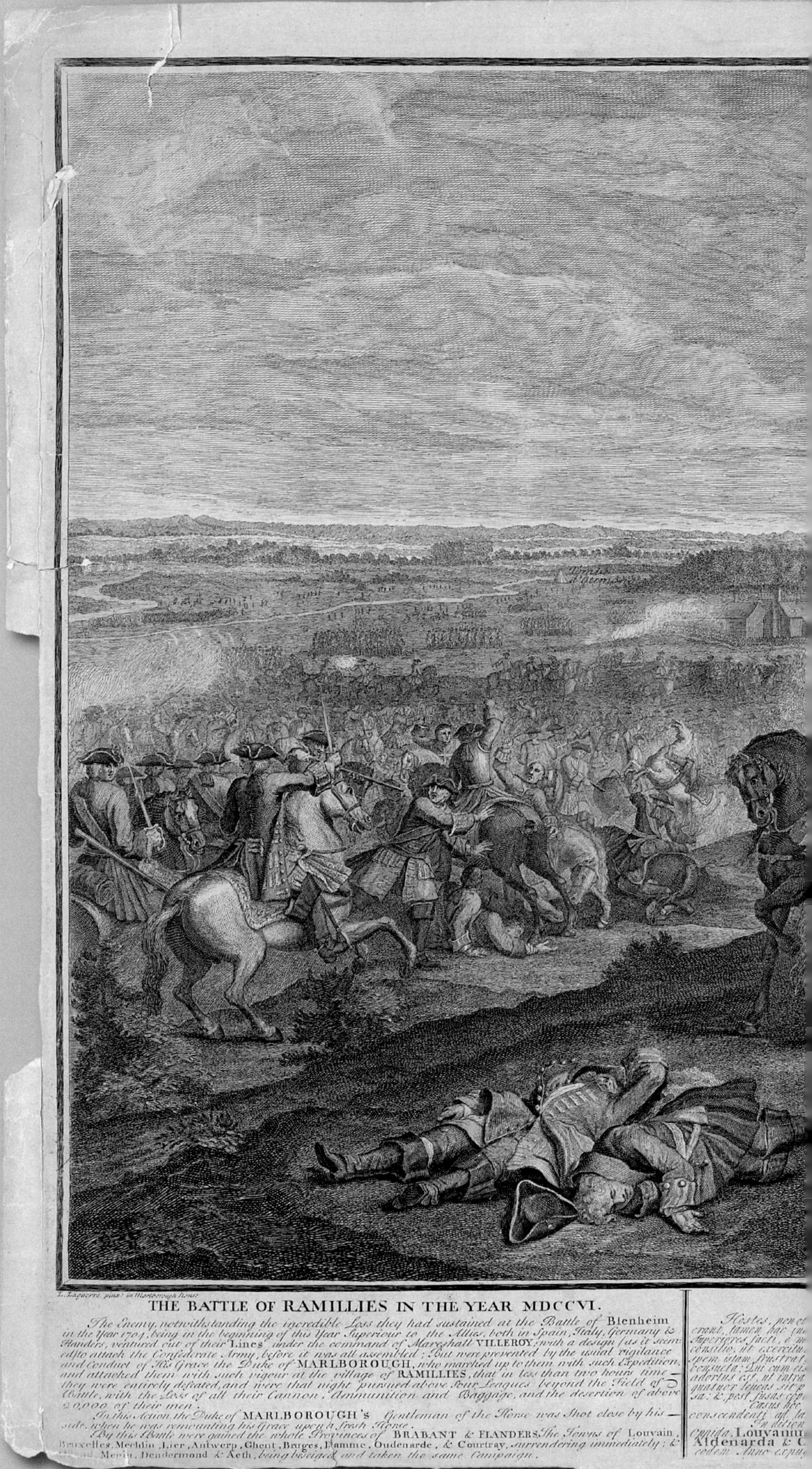

The Battle of Ramillies.

Engraving by Claude Dubosc after Louis Laguerre, published by Thomas Bowles and Henry Overton, 1717.
The British Museum, London, UK.

Ramillies
Offuz
Autre Eglise
RAMILLIENSE ANNO MDCCVI.
LA BATAILLE DE RAMILLIES L'ANNÉE MDCCVI.
Printed for & Sold by CARINGTON BOWLES, No 69 in St Pauls Church Yard, LONDON.

1705, had been dead for almost a decade and the responsibility for painting the hall fell to a native painter of growing reputation, James Thornhill. The English artist's credentials for such an important undertaking were amply demonstrated by other notable commissions: at Chatsworth for the Duke of Devonshire and, more recently, in the painted hall of the new Royal Naval Hospital at Greenwich, the first phase of which had been completed two years earlier, in 1714. For the lower hall ceiling at Greenwich, the artist's most high-profile undertaking thus far, Thornhill had devised a scheme that centred on the posthumous figure of William III introducing the personification of Peace to a grateful Europe while stamping on French Tyranny. At Blenheim, Thornhill called upon a similar repertoire of mythological and allegorical characters.

The best account of the hall ceiling was written by the artist himself for his patron, the Duchess of Marlborough. Thornhill's design centres on a simple encounter between a military hero and a grateful nation, set within a large oval and against an enormous painted triumphal arch – in keeping with the classical splendour of the surrounding architecture:

> *'Brittannia sitting on a Globe, giving ye Laurel to a Hero that is introduc'd by a beautifull Genius who presides over him; He is attended by Constancy holding a Dagger in his hand over a fire. Brittannia is guarded by ye 4 Great Cardinal Vertues, viz, Prudence, Temperance, Fortitude & Justice, At ye feet of Brittannia is Peace, wth her Olive branch, and Plenty, wth her Cornucopia of Fruits.'*[28]

Overhead, the winged figure of Fame heralds the hero's arrival, directing her clarion towards 'the 4 Quarters of the Earth' as Clio, the muse of history, looks on from the top of the oval and records the year upon which (above all others) Marlborough's fame rested: '*Anno Memorabile 1704*.' The artist's own matter-of-fact explanation of the ceiling serves as a useful reminder that unlike some of the more obscure Ovidian scenes that adorned the ceilings of other country houses, the allegorical rhetoric in the hall and elsewhere at Blenheim was never intended to be ambiguous or difficult to understand. Even the great battle plan that the eponymous 'Hero' presents to the Minerva-like figure of Britannia, attracting the amazement of both Hercules and Mars, the God of War, is large enough and sufficiently detailed to be read with ease from the ground below.

Thornhill's remarkable contribution to the decoration at Blenheim has been overshadowed by the artist's subsequent quarrel over money with the Duchess (whose distaste for the opulence of Blenheim, and impatience towards the artists and craftsmen whose work she oversaw, are well documented), and by his replacement as the painter of choice at Blenheim by the French artist Louis Laguerre.[29] Nevertheless, the hall ceiling survives as one of the most sophisticated attempts to elevate Marlborough to the exalted realm of panegyric hitherto reserved for gods and kings. It also marked the centre of a martial iconographic programme that would define every aspect of the decoration at Blenheim, and which would eventually reach beyond the main building, deep into the surrounding parkland.

The visual language of military triumph is everywhere apparent at Blenheim, from battlefield spolia (in the form of a giant marble bust of Louis XIV, removed from the gates of Tournai and displayed triumphantly above the south front at Woodstock) to the stylised exploding grenades and trophies that give the palace its

The Duke of Marlborough presenting a plan of the Battle of Blenheim to Britannia, painted on the hall ceiling at Blenheim Palace.

Painting by James Thornhill, 1716-1717. Blenheim Palace, Oxfordshire, UK. Photograph by Jarrald Publishing, reproduced with the kind permission of His Grace the Duke of Marlborough, Blenheim Palace Image Library.

The Duke of Marlborough flanked by personifications of Time and Truth.

Engraving by Pieter Tanjé after Adriaen van der Werff, 1722. The British Museum, London, UK.

unmistakable silhouette. In the decade following Marlborough's death, Sarah Churchill made two significant additions to the Blenheim estate. To mark the entrance to the park from the adjacent village, she built a triumphal arch (known today as Woodstock Gate), designed by Nicholas Hawksmoor and loosely modelled on the Arch of Titus in Rome. Further to the north and west, she also erected a giant Doric column, 134 feet high and topped with a larger-than-life lead figure of a Roman general – not, strictly speaking, a portrait, but the same abstracted 'Hero' found in the painted allegories of Kneller and Thornhill.[30] Inspired by Trajan's Column in Rome and, closer to home, Robert Hooke's Monument to the Great Fire of London (and anticipating Nelson's Column in London's Trafalgar Square by more than a century), the 'Pillar of Truth' also incorporates a lengthy inscription on all four sides of its massive pedestal. A transcription of the successive Acts of Parliament in which the estate and palace had been granted to Marlborough fill three sides of the pedestal (in a fastidious, even obsessive affirmation of the legal foundations of the place); the fourth offers an official account of the Duke's military and political career from his

(PREVIOUS PAGE)
Monument to John Churchill, 1st Duke of Marlborough.

Sculpture by John Michael Rysbrack and William Kent, 1733. Blenheim Palace, Oxfordshire, UK.
Photograph by Jarrald Publishing, reproduced with the kind permission of His Grace the Duke of Marlborough, Blenheim Palace Image Library.

appointment as William's representative in Holland at the outbreak of the War of the Spanish Succession to the endgame of Bouchain a decade later (written, somewhat surprisingly, by the Duke's old antagonist Henry St John, Viscount Bolingbroke). The combined inscriptions amount to a grandiose *apologia* for the Duke's military life – a textual affirmation, should one be required, of the patriotic and personal narratives that underpinned and gave contemporary meaning to the classical figure atop the pillar, and which informed every aspect of the architecture and decoration at Woodstock. The sculptural decoration and the further architectural projects commissioned by Sarah for Blenheim after the Duke's death extended the victorious rhetoric of the palace to an unprecedented, monumental level, creating, in effect, a *via triumphalis* – a triumphal way for the British Caesar in the heart of the English countryside.

The same commemorative impulse that inspired the 'Pillar of Truth' at Blenheim found a wider expression through a number of elegiac prints that were issued following the Duke's death. Representative of the more sophisticated among them is a small engraving designed by the Dutch artist Adriaen van der Werff. The combination of a female figure illuminated by the sun, personifying Truth, and an older figure with a scythe, embodying Time, rehearses a stock-in-trade theme of early modern allegorical art, only in this instance, the Truth unveiled by Time is nothing less than a good likeness of Marlborough – one more variation of the head-and-shoulder portrait that twenty years earlier had become synonymous with its subject's unblemished public virtue.

The combined decorations at Blenheim Palace and Marlborough House constitute some of the most ambitious and prestigious works of art ever produced for an English patron. Together, they can be understood as integral components of the great town and country houses they adorn – reciprocal spaces within the political and physical geography of early eighteenth-century Britain. Individually, and as a group, they attempt to balance a documentary concern for the detail of Britain's recent military past with a desire to convey a perceived broader truth about the execution of the war under the virtuous leadership of an unflinching English Duke. Tapestry, modern history painting, allegorical ceiling painting and monumental sculpture (all forms of art more closely associated at the time with the French court and, for the most part, executed by foreign artists and craftsmen) combine in a forceful visual testimony to Marlborough's conduct and constancy during the War of the Spanish Succession. These works, by some of the most celebrated artists of the day, also endowed grand-scale narrative art with a new importance, inaugurating a national sense of cultural, as well as military superiority that continued to gather momentum as the eighteenth century progressed. On closer examination, however, the imagery associated with Marlborough's military career reveals itself to be far more provisional and, at times, more fragile than is often supposed. Reading this diverse body of imagery as part of a changing, contested history of Britain's recent military past – rather than as an uninterrupted celebration of aristocratic heroism – invites us to speculate on the limits of the Duke's personal iconography of power, and raises deeper questions about the role of the visual arts in the construction of individual and national mythologies as Britain took on the cultural and military might of Louis XIV's France.

The great monument to Marlborough in the chapel at Blenheim constitutes a final chapter in the official iconography of John Churchill. It is the creation of two of the leading artists of their generation: the architect and garden designer William

Kent, who conceived the allegory and designed its pyramidal architectural support, and the brilliant Flemish sculptor Michael Rysbrack, who was responsible for realising Kent's grand design in a combination of four different types of marble.[31] The result of their collaboration is an imposing, if somewhat melodramatic structure that towers over the visitor and dominates the private chapel at Blenheim. It was commissioned by the dowager Duchess in 1733, when issues of dynasty were once more to the fore as her grandson, Charles Spencer, succeeded as third Duke. Crowning the monument, in front of a large obelisk, is a carved figure of the Duke, represented life-size and all'antica. In skilled hands, the enduring materials and distinctive colour tones of stone sculpture could convey a timeless ideal of patriotic virtue, exemplified here by the fixed, imperial gaze and Roman military uniform of Rysbrack's carving. Marlborough is flanked by the Duchess and their two sons, neither of whom had survived into adulthood. Beneath the mourning family group, the twin personifications of History and Fame herald the Duke's immortality, while beneath, a dragon – representing the personal and political attacks ranged at Marlborough – is crushed once and for all under the weight of a black marble sarcophagus. Finally, for the carved relief on the pedestal, Kent returned to the moment that more than any other encapsulated the patriotic myth of Marlborough, when the victorious English general accepted the French surrender from Marshal Tallard after the Battle of Blenheim. The composite nature of Marlborough's monument draws together the various elements that had defined the image of the Duke of Marlborough at various moments throughout is his adult life: devoted father and husband, unrivalled strategist, fearless leader of men, and loyal subject. All are brought together, in death, within a single unified monument.

Churchill, W.S., *Marlborough: His Life and Times*, 2 vols. (London, 1947).

Churchill, W.S., *Marlborough: His Life and Times*, 2 vols. (Chicago, 2002).

Churchill, W.S., *Marlborough*, Gekürzte Ausgabe, 2 vols. (München, 1968).

Clark, G.N., *The Dutch Alliance and the War against French Trade 1688–1697* (New York, 1923).

Cobbet, *Parliamentary History of England 1688–1702*, 12 vols. (London, 1806–1812).

Claydon, T., *William III and the godly revolution* (Cambridge, 1996).

Claydon, T., *The English Print 1688-1802* (New Haven & London, 1997).

Claydon, T., *William III: profiles in power* (Harlow, 2002)

Claydon, T., *Europe and the Making of England, 1660–1760* (Cambridge, 2007).

Colley, L., *Britons. Forging the Nation 1707–1837* (New Haven & London, 1992).

Coombs, D., *The Conduct of the Dutch. British Opinion and the Dutch Alliance during the War of the Spanish Succession* (The Hague, 1958).

The Correspondence of Henry Hyde, earl of Clarendon, and of his brother Laurence Hyde, earl of Rochester, Singer, S.W., ed. (London, 1828).

Corns, T., ed., *The royal image: representations of Charles I* (Cambridge, 1999).

Corvisier, A, *La France de Louis XIV 1643-1715. Ordre intérieur et place en Europe* (Paris, 1979).

Corvisier, A., *Louvois*, (Paris, 1983).

Corvisier, A., ed., *Histoire Militaire de la France*, I, des Origines à 1715 (Paris, 1992).

Corvisier, A., *La bataille de Malplaquet 1709. L'effondrement de la France évité* (Paris, 1997).

Coutau-Bégarie, H., *Traité de stratégie*, 4th ed. (Paris, 2003).

Coward, B., ed., *A Companion to Stuart Britain* (Malden, 2003).

Cox, B., *King William's Joint Venture.* (Assen, 1995).

Coxe, W.J., *Memoirs of John Duke of Marlborough with his original correspondence collected from the family records at Blenheim,* 3 vols. (London, 1818-1819).

Coxe, W.J., *Memoirs of John Duke of Marlborough with his original correspondence collected from the family records at Blenheim and other authentic sources,* 6 vols. 2nd edition, (London, 1820).

Coxe, W.J., *Memoirs of the Duke of Marlborough, with his original correspondence, collected from the family records at Blenheim and other authentic sources,* 3 vols. New ed., revised by John Wade (London, 1847-1848, 1873-1876, 1897, 1905-1908).

Craig, R., *England in the 1690's: Revolution, Religion and War* (Oxford, 1999).

Craske, M., *The Silent Rhetoric of the Body: A History of Monumental Sculpture and Commemorative Art in England, 1720-1770* (New Haven & London, 2007).

Croft-Murray, E., *Decorative painting in England 1537-1837*, vol. 1: Early Tudor to Sir James Thornhill (London, 1962).

Crowhurst, P., *The Defence of British Trade 1689-1815* (Folkestone, 1977).

Dalton, C. *English Army Lists and Commission Registers 1661-1714*, 6 vols. (London, 1898-1901).

Dangeau, P. de Courcillon, marquis de, *Journal du marquis de Dangeau, avec les additions inédites du duc de Saint-Simon.* Soulié, Dussieux, Chennevières, and Feuillet de Conches, eds., 19 vols. (Paris, 1854-1860).

Delmarcel, G., *Flemish tapestry from the 15th to the 18th century* (Tielt, 1999).

Dickson, P.G.M., *The Financial Revolution in England: A Study in the Development of Public Credit, 1688–1756* (Aldershot, 1993).

Dotzauer, *Die deutschen Reichskreise in der Verfassung des Alten Reiches und ihr Eigenleben (1500-1806)* (Darmstadt, 1989).

Downie, J., *Robert Harley and the press: propaganda and public opinion in the age of Swift and Defoe* (London, 1979).

Duchhardt, H., *Balance of Power und Pentarchie 1700-1785* (Paderborn, 1997).

Duclos, J.L.N., *Mémoires secrets de Duclos.* Petitot and Monmerqué, eds., 2 vols. (Paris, 1829).

Duffy, C., *Siege Warfare: The Fortress in the Early Modern World 1494-1660* (London, 1979).

Duffy, C., *The Fortress in the Age of Vauban and Frederick the Great 1660-1789* (London, 1985).

Duffy, C., *The Military Experience in the Age of Reason* (London, 1987).

Duke, A.C., and Tamse, C.A., eds., *Britain and the Netherlands VI: War and Society* (The Hague, 1977).

Dutems, J.-F.-H., *Histoire de Jean Churchill, duc de Marlborough*, 3 vols. (Paris, 1806).

Duvivier, F.F., *Observations sur la Guerre de la Succession d'Espagne,* 2 vols. (Paris, 1830).

Earle, E.M., ed., *Makers of Modern Strategy* (Princeton, 1943).

Ehrman, J., *The Navy in the War of William III 1689–1697: Its State and Direction* (Cambridge, 1953).

Elton, G.R., *The Tudor Revolution in Government: Administrative Changes in the Reign of Henry VIII* (Cambridge, 1953).

Elze, W., *Der Prinz Eugen. Sein Weg, sein Werk und Englands Verrat* (Berlin, 1940).

Erichsen, J., and Heinemann, K., eds., *Brennpunkt Europas 1704. Die Schlacht von Höchstädt* (Ostfildern, 2004).

Evertsz, U.A., and Delprat, G.H.M., eds., *Mémoires relatifs à la guerre de succession de 1706-1709 et 1711 de Sicco van Goslinga, député des Estats-Généraux* (Leeuwarden, 1857).

Falkner, J., *Marlborough's Sieges, 1702-1711* (Stroud, 2007).

Feckl, K.-L., *Preußen im Spanischen Erbfolgekrieg* (Frankfurt am Main, 1979).

Feldzüge des Prinzen Eugen von Savoyen, Nach den Feld-Acten und anderen authentischen Quellen, 23 vols. (Wien, 1876-1892).

Fluchère, H., *Laurence Sterne, from Tristram to Yorick: An Interpretation of Tristram Shandy* (Oxford, 1965).

Fockema-Andreae, S.J., *De Nederlandse Staat onder de Republiek* (Amsterdam, 1961).

Foot, M., *The Pen and the Sword: A Year in the Life of Jonathan Swift* (London, 1966).

Fortescue, J., *Marlborough* (London, 1932).

Foxcroft, H.C., *The Life and Letters of Sir George Savile, marquess of Halifax* (London, 1898).

Fouw, A. de, *Onbekende raadpensionarissen*, ('s-Gravenhage, 1946).

Francis, A.D., *The Peninsular War, 1702–1713* (London, 1975).

Francis, A.D., *The Methuens and Portugal 1691-1708* (Cambridge, 1966).

Frey, L., and Frey, M., *A Question of Empire. Leopold I and the War of Spanish Succession* (New York, 1983).

Frey, L., and Frey, M., *Frederick I: The Man and his Times* (New York, 1984).

Frey, L., and Frey, M., eds., *The Treaties of the War of the Spanish Succession: An Historical and Critical Dictionary* (London & Westport, Conn., 1995).

Fruin, R., *Geschiedenis der Staatsinstellingen in Nederland tot den val der Republiek.* Colenbrander, H.T., ed., with an introduction by I. Schöffer ('s-Gravenhage, 1980).

Geerds, R., ed., *Die Mutter der Könige von Preußen und England. Memoiren und Briefe der Kurfürstin Sophie von Hannover* (Ebenhausen & München, 1913).

Geikie, R., and Montgomery, I.A., *The Dutch Barrier, 1705-1719* (Cambridge, 1930).

Geyer, M., *Die Gesandtschaft des Grafen Wratislaw in London bis zum Abschluß der Großen Allianz vom 7. September 1701* (Wien, 1948).

Gibbs, V., ed., *The English peerage* (London, 1932).

Gibson, E., *The Royal Academy of Music 1719–1728* (New York & London, 1989).

Glete, J., *Navies and Nations: Warships, Navies and State Building in Europe and America, 1500-1860* (Stockholm, 1993).

Glozier, M.R., *The Huguenot Soldiers of William of Orange and the Glorious Revolution of 1688: The Lions of Judah* (Brighton & Portland, 2002).

Glozier, M.R., *Marshal Schomberg, 1615–1690: 'The Ablest Soldier of His Age': International Soldiering and the Formation of State Armies in Seventeenth-Century Europe* (Brighton & Portland, 2005).

Goncourt, E. and J. de, *Histoire de Marie-Antoinette* (Paris, 1858).
Gorman, F., *The Long Eighteenth Century. British Political & Social History 1688–1832* (New York, 1997).
Gothaisches Genealogisches Taschenbuch der Gräflichen Häuser (Gotha, 1763-1942).
Great Britain. Parliament. House of Lords, *Journals of the House of Lords, beginning anno primo Henrici octavi* (London, 1771-).
Great Britain. Parliament. *The Parliamentary history of England, from the earliest period to the year 1803: from which last-mentioned epoch it is continued downwards in the work entitled, "The Parliamentary debates",* edited by William Cobbett and T.C. Hansard, 36 vols. (London, 1776-1833).
Great Britain, Public Record Office, *Calendar of state papers, domestic series, of the reign of Charles II,* 28 vols. (London, 1860-1930, 1968).
Great Britain, Public Record Office, *Calendar of state papers, domestic series, of the reign of James II,* 3 vols. (London, 1960-1972, 1979).
Great Britain, Public Record Office, *Calendar of Treasury books,* 1660-1718, *preserved in the Public Record Office,* edited by William A. Shaw, 32 vols. in 64 (London, 1904-1943).
Great Britain. Royal Commission on Historical Manuscripts. *Report on the manuscripts of Allan George Finch, Esq., of Burley-on-the-Hill, Rutland.* 5 vols. 71 (London, 1913-2004).
Great Britain. Royal Commission on Historical Manuscripts. *Calendar of the Stuart papers belonging to his majesty the king, preserved at Windsor Castle,* 7 vols., 56 (London, 1902–23).
Great Britain. Royal Commission on Historical Manuscripts. *Seventh report of the Royal Commission on Historical Manuscripts.* (London, 1879).
Green, D., *Blenheim Palace* (London, 1951).
Gregg, E., *Queen Anne* (London & Boston, 1980).
Griffiths, A., *The Print in Stuart Britain 1603-1689.* Exhibition catalogue, British Museum (London, 1998).
Grimblot, P., ed., *Letters of William III, and Louis XIV and of their ministers etc. 1697–1700* (London, 1848).
Gruber, I., *Books and the British Army in the Age of the American Revolution.* (Chapel Hill, 2010).
Guibert, J.-A.-H. de, *Écrits militaires, 1772–1790* (Paris, 1977).
Guy, A.J., *Oeconomy and Discipline: Officership and Administration in the British Army, 1714-1763* (Manchester, 1985).
Haintz, O., *Karl XII. von Schweden,* 3 vols. (Berlin, 1958).
Hantsch, *Reichsvizekanzler Friedrich Karl von Schönborn 1674-1746. Einige Kapitel zur politischen Geschichte Kaiser Josefs 1. und Karls VI.* (Augsburg, 1929).
Harris, F.A., *Passion for Government. The Life of Sarah, Duchess of Marlborough* (Oxford, 1991).
Harris, T., *Politics under the late Stuarts. Party Conflict in a divided Society 1660–1715* (New York, 1993).
Harris, T., *Restoration: Charles II and his kingdoms, 1660-1685* (London, 2005).
Hartley, J. M., *Charles Whitworth: Diplomat in the Age of Peter the Great* (Aldershot, 2002).
Hartmann, P.C., *Die Finanz- und Subsidienpolitik des Kurfürsten Max Emmanuel von Bayern und der kurbayerische Gesandte in Paris, Comte d'Albert – Fürst Grimberghen* (München, 1967).
Hassinger, E., *Brandenburg-Preußen, Russland und Schweden 1700-1713.* Veröffentlichungen des Osteuropa-Institutes München, vol. II (München, 1953).
Hattendorf, J.B., *England in the War of the Spanish Succession: A Study of the English View and Conduct of Grand Strategy, 1702-1712* (New York & London, 1987).
Hatton, R.M., *Charles XII of Sweden* (London, 1968).
Hatton, R.M., *Georg I. Ein deutscher Kurfürst auf Englands Thron* (Frankfurt, 1982).
Hatton, R.M., ed., *Louis XIV and Europe* (London, 1976).
Hatton, R.M., and Anderson, M.S., eds., *Studies in Diplomatic History: Essays in Memory of David Bayne Horn* (London, 1970).
Hatton, R.M., and Bromley, J.S., eds., *William III and Louis XIV: Essays 1680-1720 by and for Mark A. Thomson,* (Liverpool, 1968).
Haute, G. van den, *Les Relations Anglo-Hollandaises au Début du XVIII Siècle d'après la Correspondence d'Alexandre Stanhope 1700–1706* (Louvain, 1932).
Hawkins, E., *Medallic Illustrations of the History of Great Britain and Ireland to the Death of George II* (London, 1885).
Heller-Hellwaldt, F., *Militärische Correspondenz des Prinzen Eugen von Savoyen* 2 vols. (Wien, 1848).
Henderson, N., *Prince Eugene of Savoy. A Biography* (London, 1964).
Heuser, E., *Die Belagerungen von Landau in den Jahren 1702 und 1703* (Landau, 1894).
Hibbert, C., *The Marlboroughs* (London, 2001).
Higginbotham, D., *George Washington and the American Military Tradition* (Athens GA & London, 1985).
Hilsenbeck, *Johann Wilhelm Kurfürst von der Pfalz, vom Ryswicker Frieden bis zum Spanischen Erbfolgekrieg 1689-1701* (München, 1905).
Hinrichs, C., *Friedrich Wilhelm I. König in Preußen, Jugend und Aufstieg* (Hamburg, 1941).
Hochedlinger, M., *Oberösterreich im Spanischen Erbfolgekrieg 1702-1706* (Wien, 1993).
Hochedlinger, M., *Austria's Wars of Emergence 1683-1797. War, State and Society in the Habsburg Monarchy* (London, 2003).
Hoefer, F., ed., *Nouvelle biographie générale depuis les temps les plus réculés jusqu'à nos jours,* 46 vols. (Paris, 1857–1866).
Hoff, B. van 't, ed., *The Correspondence 1701-1711 of John Churchill First Duke of Marlborough and Anthonie Heinsius Grand Pensionary of Holland* (Utrecht, 1951).
Hohrath, D., and Rehm, C., eds., *Zwischen Sonne und Halbmond. Der Türkenlouis als Barockfürst und Feldherr* (Rastatt, 2005).
Holmes, G., *British Politics in the Age of Anne* (London, 1967).
Holmes, G., *The Trial of Doctor Sacheverell* (London, 1973).
Holmes, G., *Augustan England: Professions, State and Society, 1680-1730* (London, 1982).
Holmes, G., *The Making of a Great Power. Late Stuart and early Georgian Britain (1660–1722)* (London & New York, 1993).
Holmes, G., ed., *Britain after the Glorious Revolution 1689–1714* (London, 1969).
Holmes, R., *Marlborough: England's Fragile Genius* (London, 2008); also published under the title *Marlborough: Britain's Greatest General* (London, 2009).
Hopkins, P., *Glencoe and the End of the Highland War* (Edinburgh, 1998).
Hoppit, J., *A Land of Liberty? England 1689–1727* (Oxford, 2000).
Hora Siccama, J., *Aantekeningen en Verbeteringen op het register op de Journalen van Constantijn Huygens den Zoon* (Amsterdam, 1915).
Horn, R., *Marlborough: A survey of panegyrics, satire and biographical writings, 1688-1788* (Folkestone & New York, 1975).
Hornstein, S., *The Restoration Navy and English Foreign Trade 1674-1688* (Aldershot, 1991).
Horwitz, H., ed., *The Parliamentary Diary of Narcissus Luttrell 1691–1693* (Oxford, 1972).
Houlding, J.A., *Fit for Service: The Training of the British Army, 1715-1795* (Oxford, 1981).
Hüttl, L., *Max Emanuel: Der Blaue Kurfürst, 1679-1726. Eine politische Biographie* (München, 1976).
Huygens, C., *Journaal van Constantijn Huygens den Zoon, van 21 Oct. 1688 tot 2 Sept. 1696,* 5 vols. Werken van het Historisch Genootschap (Utrecht, 1876-1883).
Ingrao, Charles W., *In Quest and Crisis: Emperor Joseph I and the Habsburg Monarchy* (West Lafayette, Ind., 1979).
Israel, J., *The Dutch Republic: Its Rise, Greatness and Fall, 1477-1806* (Oxford, 1995).
Jany, C., *Geschichte der Preußischen Armee vom 14. Jahrhundert bis 1914,* 4 vols. (Osnabrück, 1967).
Japikse, N., ed., *Correspondentie van Willem III en van Hans Willem Bentinck,* 5 vols. ('s-

Hattendorf, J.B., 'The Rákóczi Insurrection in English War Policy, 1703-1711', in: *Canadian American Review of Hungarian Studies*, VII (1980), 91-102.
Hattendorf, J.B., 'Churchill, John, first duke of Marlborough (1650–1722)', in: Matthew, H.C.G., and Harrison, B., eds., *Oxford Dictionary of National Biography* (Oxford, 2004). Oxford Biography Index Number 101005401.
Hattendorf, J.B., 'Churchill, George (*bap.* 1654, *d.* 1710)', in: Matthew, H.C.G., and Harrison, B., eds., *Oxford Dictionary of National Biography* (Oxford, 2004). Oxford Biography Index Number 101005399.
Hebbert, F.J., 'Major-General John Richards (1667-1709)', in: *The Journal of the Society for Army Historical Research*, 81 (2003), 8-25.
Hefford, W., 'Some problems concerning the Art of War tapestries', in: *CIETA Bulletin*, 41-42 (1975), 105-16.
Hendrix, S., 'In the Army: Women, Camp Followers and Gender Roles in the British Army in the French and Indian Wars, 1755-1765', in: Groot, G. de, and Bird, C.P., eds., *Sexual Integration in the Military* (New York, 2000).
Höbelt, L., 'The Impact of the Rákóczi Rebellion on Habsburg Strategy: Incentives and Opportunity Costs', in: *War in History* 13 (2006), 2-15.
Horn, R.D., 'Marlborough's First Biographer, Dr Francis Hare', in: *Huntington Library Quarterly*, 20, (1957), 145-62.
Houlding, J.A., 'Bland, Humphrey', in: Matthew, H.C.G., and Harrison, B., eds., *Oxford Dictionary of National Biography* (Oxford, 2004). Oxford Biography Index Number 101002607
Hussey, J., 'Marlborough and the loss of Arleux, 1711: accident or design', in: *Journal of the Society for Army Historical Research*, 70 (1992), 5-14.
Hutton, R., and Reeves, W., 'Sieges and Fortifications', in: Kenyon, J., and Ohlmeyer, J., eds., *The Civil Wars: A Military History of England, Scotland and Ireland, 1638-1660* (Oxford, 1998), 195-233.
Johnston, S.H.F., 'Letters of Samuel Noyes, Chaplain of the Royal Scots, 1703-4', in: *The Journal of the Society for Army Historical Research*, 37 (1959).
Jordan, J., 'The Siege of Kinsale, 1690: The Danish Report', in: *An Consantóir*, 15 (1954-1955), 58-65.
Junkelmann, M., 'Feldzug und Schlacht bei Höchstädt', in: Erichsen, J., and Heinemann, K., eds., *Brennpunkt Europas 1704. Die Schlacht bei Höchstädt-the Battle of Blenheim* (Ostfildern, 2004), 54-67.
Kirchhammer, A., 'Prinz Eugen von Savoyen und John Churchill Herzog von Marlborough', in: *Organ der militärwissenschaftlichen Vereine* 24 (1882), 443-64.
Klein, T., 'Die Erhebungen in den weltlichen Reichsfürstenstand 1550-1806', in: *Blätter für deutsche Landesgeschichte* 122 (1986), 137-92.
Kopperman, P.E., 'The British High Command and Soldiers' Wives in America, 1755-1783', in: *Journal of the Society for Army Historical Research*, 60 (1982), 14-34.
Kospach, H., 'Englische Stimmen über Österreich und Prinz Eugen während des Spanischen Erbfolgekrieges', in: *Mitteilungen des Instituts für Österreichische Geschichtsforschung* 73 (1965), 39-62.
Kroener, B.R., 'La planification des operations militaires et le commandement supérieur. La crise de l'alliance franco-bavaroise à la veille de la bataille de Höchstädt', in: *Forces Armées et Systèmes d'Alliance. Histoire Militaire Comparée*, no.1 (Montpellier, 1983), 165-89.
Kroener, B.R., 'Militärischer Professionalismus und soziale Karriere. Der französische Adel in den Europäischen Kriegen 1740-1763', in: Kroener, B.R., ed., *Europa im Zeitalter Friedrichs des Großen, Wirtschaft, Gesellschaft, Kriege.* Beiträge zur Militärgeschichte, 26 (München, 1989), 99-132.
Kroener, B.R., '"Das Schwungrad an der Staatsmachine"', in: Kroener und Pröve, eds., *Krieg und Frieden. Militär und Gesellschaft in der Frühen Neuzeit* (Paderborn, 1996), 1-23.
La Barre Nanteuil, H. de, 'La guerre de siège sous Turenne', in: Gambiez, F., ed., *Turenne et l'Art Militaire* (Paris, 1978), 143-48.
Lane, M., 'The Diplomatic Service under William III', in: *Transactions of the Royal Historical Society*, 4th series, X (1927), 87-109.
LeFevre, P., 'John Churchill and Piercy Kirke. Fresh Light on the Early Careers of two Restoration Officers', in: *N & Q*, 31-3 (1984), 338-39.
Liddell-Hart, B.H., 'Letter to the editor and C.T. Atkinson's response,' *Journal of the Society for Army Historical Research*, 14 (1936), 118-19.
Loeber, R., and Parker, G., 'The military revolution in seventeenth century Ireland', in: Ohlmeyer, J., ed., *Ireland from Independence to Occupation 1641-1660* (Cambridge, 1994).
Lossky, A., 'International Relations in Europe', in: Bromley, J.S., ed., *The Cambridge Modern History: The Rise of Great Britain and Russia* (Cambridge, 1970).
Macinnes, A., 'William of Orange – 'Disaster for Scotland'?', in: Mijers, E., and Onnekink, D., eds., *Redefining William III: The Impact of the King-Stadholder in its International Context* (Aldershot, 2007).
MacLachlan, A.D., 'The Road to Peace 1710–1713', in: Holmes, G., ed., *Britain after the Glorious Revolution 1689–1714* (London, 1969), 197-215.
Maltby, W.S., 'Origins of a global strategy', in: Murray, W., Knox, M., and Bernstein, A., eds., *The Making of Strategy: Rulers, States and War* (Cambridge, 1994).
Manning, R.B., 'Styles of Command in Seventeenth-Century English Armies', in: *The Journal of Military History*, 71 (2007), 671-99.
Mason, A.S., and Barber, P., '"Captain Thomas, the French engineer", and the teaching of Vauban to the English', in: *Proceedings of the Huguenot Society of Great Britain & Ireland*, 25 (1991), 279-87.
Mathis, F., 'Neue Aspekte zur Planung des süddeutschen Feldzuges von 1704', in: *Mitteilungen des Österreichischen Staatsarchivs*, 27 (1974), 141-69.
Mathis, F., 'Marlborough und Wratislaw. Eine politische Freundschaft als Grundlage des Sieges von Höchstädt 1704', in: *Mitteilungen des Instituts für Österreichische Geschichtsforschung* 83 (1975), 114-43.
McJoynt, A., 'Marlborough', in: Margiotta, F., ed., *Brassey's Encyclopedia*, 657.
Mikoletzky, H.L., 'Die große Anleihe von 1706. Ein Beitrag zur österreichischen Finanzgeschichte', in: *Mitteilungen des Österreichischen Staatsarchivs* 7 (1954), 268-93.
Milne, J., 'The Diplomacy of Dr. John Robinson at the court of Charles XII of Sweden, 1697-1709', in: *Transactions of the Royal Historical Society,* Fourth series, XXX (1948), 75-93.
Morrill, J., 'The British Problem', in: Bradshaw, B., and Morrill, J., eds., *The British Problem c. 1534–1707. State Formation in the Atlantic Archipelago* (London & Houndmills, 1996).
Mulloy, S., 'French engineers with the Jacobite Army in Ireland, 1688-1691', in: *The Irish Sword*, 15 (1983).
Neubauer, M., 'Österreich und seine Geschichte im Werke Winston S. Churchills', in: *Österreich in Geschichte und Literatur* 12 (1968), 189-96.
Nishikawa, S., 'The SPCK in Defence of Protestant Minorities in Early Eighteenth-Century Europe', in: *The Journal of Ecclesiastical History* 56-4 (2005), 730–48.
Noorden, C. von, 'Die preußische Politik im spanischen Erbfolgekrieg', in: *Historische Zeitschrift* 18 (1867), 297-358.
Nordman, C., 'Louis XIV and the Jacobites', in: Hatton, R.M., ed., *Louis XIV and Europe* (London, 1976), 82-111.
Onnekink, D., 'Anglo-Dutch diplomatic cooperation during the opening years of the War of the Spanish Succession (1702–1704)', in: Jongste, J.A.F. de, and Veenendaal, A.J., Jr., eds., *Anthonie Heinsius and the Dutch Republic 1688-1720* (The Hague, 2002), 45-63.
Onnekink, D., '"Dutch counsels": The Foreign Entourage of William III', in: *Dutch Crossing*, 29 (2005), 5–20.
O'Reilly, A., 'A Fall from Grace: Vendôme, Bourgogne, and the Aftermath of Oudenaarde', in: Money, D., ed., *1708, Oudenaarde and Lille*

(Cambridge, 2008), 73-84.
Ostwald, J., 'The 'Decisive' Battle of Ramillies, 1706: Prerequisites for Decisiveness in Early Modern Warfare', in: *Journal of Military History*, 64 (2000), 649-77.
Otruba, G., 'Die Bedeutung englischer Subsidien und Antizipationen für die Finanzen Österreichs 1701-1748', in: *Vierteljahrschrift für Sozial- und Wirtschaftsgeschichte* 51 (1964), 192-234.
Oury, C., 'La bataille d'Audenarde du côté français', in: Money, D., ed., *1708, Oudenaarde and Lille* (Cambridge, 2008), 44–57.
Oury, C., 'La prise de décision militaire à la fin du règne de Louis XIV: l'exemple du siège de Turin, 1706', in: *Histoire, Économie et Société.* (2010) no. 2, 23-43.
Perjés, G., 'Army Provisioning, Logistics and Strategy in the Second Half of the 17th Century', in: *Acta Historica Academiae Scientiarum Hungaricae*, 16 (1970), 1-51.
Pincus, S.C.A., 'Republicanism, Absolutism and Universal Monarchy: English popular Sentiment during the Third Dutch War', in: MacLean, G., ed., *Culture and Society in the Stuart Restoration. Literature, Drama, History* (Cambridge, 1995).
Pocock, J. G. A., 'British History: A Plea for a New Subject', in: *The Journal of Modern History* 47 (December 1975), 601–21.
Poldervaart, A., 'Het konvooi tot bescherming van de haringvloot onder leiding van kapitein Cornelis van Brakel in 1710', in: *Netwerk, Jaarboek Visserijmuseum 2003.*
Price, J.L., '"A State Dedicated to War": The Dutch Republic in the Seventeenth Century', in: Ayton, A., and Price, J.L., eds., *The Medieval Military Revolution: State, Society and Military Change in Medieval and Early Modern Europe* (London, 1995).
Riedenauer,E., 'Kaiserliche Standeserhebungen für Angehörige des Militärstandes von Karl V. bis Karl VI.', in Lindgren, U., *et al.*, eds., *Sine ira et studio. Militärhistorische Studien zur Erinnerung an Hans Schmidt* (Kallmünz, 2001), 65-83.
Rogers, M., 'John and John Baptist Closterman: a catalogue of their works', in: *Walpole Society*, 49 (1983), 224–79.
Roorda, D.J., 'Le secret du Prince. Monarchale Tendenties in de Republiek 1672–1702', in: Roorda, *Rond Prins en Patriciaat* (Weesp, 1984).
Roosen, 'The origins of the war of the Spanish Succession', in: Black, J., ed., *The Origins of War in Early Modern Europe* (Edinburgh, 1987), 151-75.
Schlip, H., 'Die neuen Fürsten. Zur Erhebung in den Reichsfürstenstand und zur Aufnahme in den Reichsfürstenrat im 17. und 18. Jahrhundert', in: Press, V. and Willoweit, D., eds., *Liechtenstein – Fürstliches Haus und staatliche Ordnung. Geschichtliche Grundlagen und moderne Perspektiven* (Vaduz, München & Wien, 1988), 249-92.
Schmidt, H., 'Prinz Eugen und Marlborough', in: Kunisch, J., ed., *Prinz Eugen von Savoyen und seine Zeit* (Freiburg im Breisgau & Würzburg, 1986), 144-62.
Scott, H.M., 'Marlborough', in: Parker, G., and Cowley, R., eds., *Reader's Companion to Military History* (Boston, 1996), 287.
Scouller, R.E., 'Marlborough's administration in the field', in: *Army Quarterly*, 95-96 (1967-1968), 197-208, 102-13.
Showalter, D., 'Churchill', in: Frey, L., and Frey, M., *The Treaties of the War of the Spanish Succession.*
Sicken, 'Heeresaufbringung und Koalitionskriegsführung im Pfälzischen und im Spanischen Erbfolgekrieg', in: Duchhardt, H., ed., *Rahmenbedingungen und Handlungsspielräume europäischer Außenpolitik im Zeitalter Ludwigs XIV.* Zeitschrift für Historische Forschung, Beiheft 11 (Berlin 1991), 89-134.
Simms, J.G., 'Marlborough's Siege of Cork', in: Hayton, D.W., ed., *War and Politics in Ireland 1649-1730* (London, 1986).
Snapper, F., 'Koning-stadhouder Willem III en de commerciëel-financiële structuur van de Republiek', in: *Tijdschrift voor Zeegeschiedenis*, 8 (1989).
Snyder, H.L., 'The duke of Marlborough's request of his Captain-Generalcy for life: a re-examination', in: *Journal of the Society for Army Historical Research*, 45 (1967), 35-52.
Snyder, H.L., 'The British Diplomatic Service during the Godolphin Ministry', in: Hatton, R.M., and Anderson, M.S., eds., *Studies in Diplomatic History* (London, 1970), 47-68.
Snyder, H.L., 'Arthur Maynwaring, Richard Steele, and *The lives of two illustrious generals*', in: *Studies in Bibliography: Papers of the Bibliographical Society of the University of Virginia*, 24 (1971), 152-62.
Spiers, E.M., 'George, Prince, second duke of Cambridge (1819–1904)', in: Matthew, H.C.G., and Harrison, B., eds., *Oxford Dictionary of National Biography* (Oxford, 2004). Oxford Biography Index Number 101033372.
Stapleton, J.M., 'Grand Pensionary at War: Anthonie Heinsius and the Nine Years' War, 1689-1697', in: Jongste, J.A.F. de, and Veenendaal, A.J., Jr., *Anthonie Heinsius and the Dutch Republic*, 199-227.
Stapleton, J.M., 'The Blue-Water Dimension of King William's War: Amphibious Operations and Allied Strategy during the Nine Years' War, 1688-1697', in: Trim, D.J.B., and Fissel, M.C., eds., *Amphibious Warfare 1000-1700: Commerce, State Formation and European Expansion* (Boston, 2006), 330-34.
Stein, 'Festungen und befestigte Linien des 17. und 18. Jahrhunderts am Oberrhein', in: Press, Reinhard und Schwarzmaier, eds., *Barock am Oberrhein*, Oberrheinische Studien 6 (Karlsruhe, 1984), 55-106.
Stephens, H.M., 'Frederick, Prince, duke of York and Albany', in: Matthew, H.C.G., and Harrison, B., eds., *Oxford Dictionary of National Biography* (Oxford, 2004). Oxford Biography Index Number 101033372.
Symcox, G., 'Britain and Victor Amadeus II – or: the Use and Abuse of Allies', in: Baxter, S., ed., *England's Rise to Greatness* (London, 1983), 151–84.
Thomson, M.A., 'Self-Determination and Collective Security as Factors in English and French Foreign Policy, 1689-1718', in: Hatton, R.M. and Bromley, J.S., eds. *William III and Louis XIV: Essays 1680-1720 by and for Mark A. Thomson* (London, 1968), 271-86.
Thomson, M.A., 'Parliament and Foreign Policy, 1689-1714', in: *idem*, 130-39.
Thomson, M.A., 'Origins of the War of the Spanish Succession' in: Hatton and Bromley, eds., in: *idem*, 140-61.
Troost, W., "To Preserve the Liberty of Europe'. William III's Ideas on Foreign Policy', in: Onnekink, D., and Rommelse, G., eds., *Ideology and Foreign Policy in Early Modern Europe (1650–1750)* (Aldershot, 2011).
Veenendaal, A.J., [Sr.], 'The opening phase of Marlborough's campaign of 1708 in the Netherlands: a version from Dutch sources', in: *History*, 35 (1950), 34-48.
Veenendaal, A.J., [Sr], ' Kan men spreken van een revolutie in de Zuidelijke Nederlanden na Ramillies?', in: *Bijdragen en Mededelingen voor de Geschiedenis der Nederlanden*, 7 (1953), 198-214.
Veenendaal, A.J., Jr., 'Des Rocques', in: Frey, L., and Frey, M., eds., *The Treaties of the War of the Spanish Succession: An Historical and Critical Dictionary* (London & Westport, Conn., 1995), 132-33.
Vertue, G., 'Notebooks II', in: *The Volume of the Walpole Society*, 20 (1932).
Watson, P., 'Churchill, John II' in: Henning, B.D., and History of Parliament Trust (Great Britain), *The House of Commons, 1660-1690.* 3 vols. (London, 1983), II, 69.
Wilson, P.H., 'New Approaches under the Old Régime', in: Mortimer, G., ed., *Early Modern Military History, 1450-1815* (London, 2004), 135-54.
Wood, S., 'Ligonier, John', in: Matthew, H.C.G., and Harrison, B., eds., *Oxford Dictionary of National Biography* (Oxford, 2004). Oxford Biography Index Number 101016653.
Zernack, K., 'Der grosse Nordische Krieg', in: Zernack, K., ed., *Nordosteuropa* (Lüneburg, 1993).
Zwitzer, H.L., 'The British and Netherlands

Armies in relation to the Anglo-Dutch Alliance, 1688-1795', in Raven, G.J.A. and Rodger, N.A.M., eds., *Navies and Armies: The Anglo-Dutch relationship in War and Peace, 1688-1988* (Edinburgh, 1990), 33-48.

Reference Notes

Introduction

[1] See the major English language biographies of Marlborough by Lediard, T. (1736); Coxe , W. (1819); Alison, A. (1852); Wolseley, G. (1894); Atkinson, C.T., (1921); Fortescue, J. (1932); Churchill, W.S. (1933); Ashley, M. (1939); Rowse, A.L. (1956); Burton, I.F. (1968); Barnett, C. (1971); Chandler, D.G. (1973); Bevin, B. (1975); Thomson, C. (1979); Jones, J.R. (1993); Hibbert, C. (2001); and Holmes, R. (2009).

[2] Hattendorf, J.B., 'Die Ursprünge des spanischen Erbfolgekrieges'

[3] Thomson, 'Origins of the War of the Spanish Succession' in: Hatton and Bromley, eds., *William III and Louis XIV*, 145.

[4] See, for example, Baxter, *William III*, 379-401; Thomson, 'Louis XIV and the Origins' in: Hatton and Bromley, eds., *William III and Louis XIV*; Roosen, 'The Origins,' in: Black, ed., *The Origins of War*; Troost, W., *William III*, 253-262.

[5] Hattendorf, *England in the War of the Spanish Succession*, 21-51.

[6] Lynn, *Wars of Louis XIV*, 361-71.

[7] Hattendorf, *England in the War of the Spanish Succession*, 53-75; Lynn, *Wars of Louis XIV*, 368-69.

[8] Lynn, *Wars of Louis XIV*, 370-71.

1 Britain in Europe during the Age of Marlborough

[1] Nottingham University Library [NUL], Portland Papers, PwB 79.

[2] Price, Milhous and Hume, *Italian Opera*, 2–4; Gibson, *The Royal Academy of Music*, 24.

[3] NUL PwB, 79.

[4] John Drummond to Heinsius 20 October 1711, Willem Buys to Heinsius 22 December 1711, in Veenendaal, Jr., *Briefwisseling Heinsius*, XII, 604-05.

[5] NUL PwB 79; Luttrell, *A Brief Historical Relation of State Affairs*, VI, 712-13.

[6] *Op de Vrede tot Uytrecht …* .

[7] Cf. Simms, *Three Victories and a Defeat*, 44.

[8] On criticism of this international reputation of Marlborough, see Jones, *Marlborough*, 220–21.

[9] Gibbs, 'The Revolution in Foreign Policy', 59–79.

[10] Rubini, *Court and Country*, 14, 24.

[11] Alphen, G. van, *De Stemming van de Engelschen*; Craig, *England in the 1690's.*

[12] The image of William as a foreigner intervening for his own purposes has also stuck in English historiography. For a good overview, see Vallance, *The Glorious Revolution*, 293–94.

[13] Onnekink, D., "Dutch counsels".

[14] However, technically Schomberg was a Huguenot. On Huguenot soldiers see Glozier, *The Huguenot Soldiers*; Glozier, *Marshal Schomberg, 1615–1690.*

[15] E.g. Huygens, Constantijn, *Journaal*, I, 79.

[16] Huygens, *Journaal*, II, 341.

[17] Quoted in *The Parliamentary History of England*, V, 857; Alphen, G. van, *De Stemming van de Engelschen*, 184.

[18] Quoted in Alphen, G. van, *De Stemming van de Engelschen*, 126.

[19] See Onnekink, *The Anglo-Dutch Favourite*, ch. 7.

[20] *A Speach for repealing Grants in Wales for Bentinck 1696*.

[21] Clark, *The Dutch Alliance and the War against French Trade.*

[22] Horwitz, *The Parliamentary Diary of Narcissus Luttrell*, 304.

[23] Alphen, G. van, *De Stemming der Engelschen*, ch. 4. Cf. Childs, *The British Army of William III*, 75ff.

[24] Childs, *The Nine Years' War and the British Army*, 69.

[25] Tutchin, *The Foreigners.*

[26] *Cobbet's Parliamentary History of England etc. 1688–1702*, VI, 5.

[27] Swift, *The Conduct of the Allies*. On English opinion of the Dutch, see Coombs, *The Conduct of the Dutch..*

[28] Cf. Hoppit, *A Land of Liberty?*, 136.

[29] Defoe, *The True-born Englishman.*

[30] Baxter, *England's Rise to Greatness 1660–1763*, viii.

[31] Onnekink, 'Anglo-Dutch diplomatic Cooperation'.

[32] Tallard to Louis 31 March 1698, 3 April 1698, in Grimblot,, *Letters of William III, and Louis XIV*, I, 323, 343.

[33] On engineering, see Chandler, *The Art of Warfare*, part IV.

[34] Schwoerer, *No Standing Armies!*

[35] After the Nine Years' War, the French Count Tallard wrote to Louis XIV about England that 'this kingdom must be considered as a country destitute of resources for many years to come', Tallard to Louis 3 April 1698, in Grimblot, *Letters of William III, and Louis XIV*, I, 343.

[36] Brewer, *The Sinews of Power*, 42.

[37] Childs, *The British Army*, 103.

[38] Jones, *War and Economy*, 11.

[39] Jones, *War and Economy*, 29. On the strength of the army of the States General, see Wijn, *Staatsche Leger*, I, 25 and appendix 1-3.

[40] Cf. Jones, *Britain and the World*, 19, 21. On the English fleet, see Ehrman, *The Navy in the War of William III.*

[41] On the war in Iberia, see Francis, *The Peninsular War.*

[42] Cf. Jones, *Marlborough*, 234.

[43] For every three warships the Dutch provided, the English delivered five. Stork-Penning, *Het Grote Werk.*

[44] Typically, when discussing the Spanish Partition Treaty, discussions focused on continental

affairs, the Indies being only discussed at the very end of the negotiations. See for instance Louis XIV's letter to Count Tallard of 25 April 1698, in Grimblot, ed., *Letters of William III, and Louis XIV*, I, 419-29.

[45] Simms, *Three Victories and a Defeat*, 75.

[46] Nimwegen, O. van, *De Republiek der Verenigde Nederlanden.*

[47] Hoppit, *A Land of Liberty?*, 318.

[48] Gorman, *The Long Eighteenth Century*, 52.

[49] Simms, *Three Victories and a Defeat*, 74.

[50] Brewer, *The Sinews of Power*, 30.

[51] Aalbers, *De Republiek en de Vrede van Europa*; Aalbers, 'Holland's Financial Problems'.

[52] Wheeler, *The Making of a World Power*, 82.

[53] *Ibidem*, 88–89.

[54] Childs, *The British Army of William III*, 269, appendix C.

[55] Wheeler, *The Making of a World Power*, 59, 65.

[56] Holmes, G., *The Making of a Great Power*, 439.

[57] Brewer, *The Sinews of Power*, 30.

[58] Wrigley and Scofield, *The Population History of England*, 196.

[59] Jones, *War and Economy*, 29.

[60] Brewer, *The Sinews of Power*, 40-41.

[61] *Ibidem*, 66-67.

[62] *Ibidem*, 95.

[63] Dickson, *The Financial Revolution in England; Roseveare, The Financial Revolution.*

[64] Brewer, *The Sinews of Power*, xvii.

[65] Gregg, *Queen Anne*, 133; Harris, *Politics under the late Stuarts.*

[66] Kishlansky, *A Monarchy Transformed*, 317–19.

[67] For an analysis of Godolphin's career, see Sundstrom, *Sidney Godolphin.*

[68] Holmes, *The Making of a Great Power*, 423.

[69] Wood, A Study of Anglo-Dutch Relations in the Grand Alliance; Haute, G. van den, *Les Relations Anglo-Hollandaises*; Onnekink, 'Anglo-Dutch diplomatic Cooperation'.

[70] Kishlansky, *A Monarchy Transformed*, 320.

[71] Holmes, *The Making of a Great power*, 423.

[72] *Ibidem.*

[73] [Defoe], *The Danger of the Protestant Religion*, 7.

[74] Claydon, *Europe and the Making of England.*

[75] Thompson, *Britain, Hanover and the Protestant Interest.*

[76] See for instance Marlborough to Heinsius 25 June 1704, and Heinsius to Marlborough 3 October 1704, in: Hoff, B. van 't, *The Correspondence*, 112-13, 139-40; see also the correspondence of the English ambassador in Turin, Richard Hill, in Blackley, *The Diplomatic Correspondence*; Symcox, *Victor Amadeus II;* Symcox, 'Britain and Victor Amadeus II'.

[77] Ingrao, *In Quest and Crisis*, 123–60.

[78] Cerny, *Theology, Politics, and Letters*, 130.

[79] Jones, *Marlborough*, 132 ff. Staunch opposition from the Dutch also played a role in Marlborough's decline. Veenendaal, [Sr.], *Het Engels-Nederlands Condominium*, 29 ff.

[80] Boyer, *The Lawfulness*, 7.

[81] *Ibidem*, 10.

[82] Thompson, *Britain, Hanover and the Protestant Interest*; Claydon, *Europe and the Making of England*; Claydon, 'Protestantism, Universal Monarchy and Christendom', 129–47; Pincus, *Protestantism and Patriotism*; Pincus, *1688. The First Modern Revolution.*

[83] Thompson, *Britain, Hanover and the Protestant Interest.*

[84] Nishikawa, 'The SPCK in Defence of Protestant Minorities'; Hoppit, *A Land of Liberty?*, 215; Claydon, *Europe and the Making of England.*

[85] Hoppit, *A Land of Liberty?*, 214.

[86] Colley, *Britons*, 5.

[87] Hoppit, *A Land of Liberty?*, 220.

[88] *Ibidem*, 223.

[89] Pocock, 'British History'.

[90] On the complications of new British historiography in this period, see Claydon, '«British» History in the Post-Revolutionary World'.

[91] Morrill, 'The British Problem', introduction.

[92] I.e. Royle, *The Civil War.*

[93] On this, see Hopkins, *Glencoe.*

[94] Childs, *The Williamite Wars.*

[95] Macinnes, 'William of Orange – Disaster for Scotland?'; Riley, *King William.*

[96] On the Union, see Macinnes, *Union and Empire*; Brown, *The Union of 1707.*

[97] Szechi, *1715*, New Haven, 2006.

[98] Goldie and Jackson, 'Williamite Tyranny'.

[99] Szechi, *The Jacobites.*

[100] Cf. Szechi, *The Jacobites.*

[101] For a good overview of this, see Atherton, 'The Press and Popular Political Opinion'.

[102] Pincus, *1688*; Pincus, 'Republicanism, Absolutism and Universal Monarchy'.

[103] Simms, *Three Victories and a Defeat*, 53. On pamphleteering, see Joad, *Pamphlets and Pamphleteering.*

[104] Simms, *Three Victories and a Defeat*, 44, 54.

[105] Knights, *Representation and Misrepresentation*, 3.

[106] On this subject, see Knights, *Representation and Misrepresentation.*

[107] Cf. Zaret, *Origins of Democratic Culture.*

[108] Famously argued by Elton, *The Tudor Revolution in Government.*

[109] Black, *A System of Ambition?*, 46.

[110] Thomson, 'Parliament and Foreign Policy. See also Black, *A System of Ambition?*, 51.

[111] Black, *Parliament and Foreign Policy*, 39.

[112] Kishlansky, *A Monarchy Transformed*, 318–19.

[113] Harris, *Passion for Governmen*; Bucholz, *The Augustan Court*, ch. 6.

[114] Brockliss and Elliott, *The World of the Favourite.*

[115] Onnekink, *The Anglo-Dutch Favourite.*

[116] Gregg, *Queen Anne.*

[117] Onnekink, 'Anglo-Dutch diplomatic Cooperation'.

[118] Wood, 'A Study of Anglo-Dutch Relations', 75; Wijn, *Het Staatsche Leger*, I, 25 and appendix 1-3.

[119] On the question of military leadership, see Wood, 'A Study of Anglo-Dutch Relations', 77–87.

[120] Hattendorf, *England in the War of the Spanish Succession*, 46.

[121] Hattendorf, *England in the War of the Spanish Succession*, 47.

[122] Gregg, *Queen Anne*, 136ff.

[123] Black, *A System of Ambition?*, 70.

[124] Veenendaal, Jr., ed., *Briefwisseling Heinsius.*

[125] Snyder, *'The British Diplomatic Service'*, 47.

[126] There were actually two secretaries of state, one for the northern and one for the southern regions of Europe; Ellis, 'British Communications and Diplomacy', 159–67.

[127] MacLachlan, 'The Road to Peace 1710–1713'.

[128] Earl of Nottingham to Richard Hill, 3 March 1704 in Blackley, *The Diplomatic Correspondence of the right honourable Richard Hill.*

[129] Lane, 'The Diplomatic Service under William III'.

[130] Roorda, 'Le secret du Prince'.

[131] Onnekink, *The Anglo-Dutch Favourite.*

[132] On British grand strategy in the War of the Spanish Succession, see Hattendorf, *England in the War of the Spanish Succession.*

[133] Italian port cities in Spanish possession: Porto Ercole, Orbitello, Telamone, Monte Argentaro, Porto Santo Stefano, Porto Longone and Piombino.

[134] On these negotiations, see Francis, *The Methuens and Portugal.*

[135] On Prussia in this period: see Frey and Frey, *Frederick I: The Man and his Times.*

[136] See Andrew Lossky's ideas about a tripartite division of Europe, which assured the separation of the Habsburg-Ottoman War, the Northern War and the War of the Spanish Succession in his 'International Relations in Europe'.

[137] For Louis's dislike, see his declaration at the renunciation of the French crown by Philip V in 1713. For Dutch discontent, see the pamphlet *Korte Schets van 's Lants Welwezen,* 1714.

[138] Luard, *The Balance of Power*; Sheehan, *Balance of Power.*

[139] Troost, "To Preserve the Liberty of Europe".

[140] Jones, *Marlborough*, 226–27.

[141] Quoted in *A Collection of Treaties between Great Britain and other Powers*, I, 341.

2 Courtier, Army Officer, Politician, and Diplomat

[1] This chapter is a revised and reformatted version, with additional source annotation, of the biographical sketch that was first published in Mathews, C., and Harrison, B., eds., *The Oxford Dictionary of National Biography* Oxford, 2004, XI, 607-33.

[2] Lediard, *Marlborough*, I, 21;Coxe, *Memoirs*, I, 3-4; Alison, *Life*, I, 4; Wolseley, *Marlborough,* I, 63-66; Churchill, *Marlborough*, I, 55-56; Atkinson, *Marlborough and the British Army*, 37-38; Fortescue, *Marlborough,* 6-7; Ashley, *Marlborough*, 16; Rowse, *Early Churchills,* 154; Chandler, *Marlborough as a Military Commander*, 5-6; Barnett, *Marlborough,* 39; Bevin, *Marlborough*, 23; Jones, *Marlborough,* 14; Hibbert, *The Marlboroughs*, 8

[3] TNA: ADM 2/1746, fol. 61.

[4] LeFevre, 'John Churchill and Piercy Kirke,' 338. No paybook has yet been found for *Resolution* for the period July 1669 to November 1670 to ascertain exactly Churchill's capacity on board the ship.

[5] Anderson, *Journals of Sir Thomas Allin,* II, 171.

[6] *Ibidem*, II, 174.

[7] Atkinson, *Marlborough and the British Army,* 42-44; *Calendar of State Papers, Domestic, 1671-72,* 609.

[8] Dalton, *English Army Lists,* I, 127-28; *Calendar of State Papers, Domestic, 1671-72,* 218, 222.

[9] Atkinson, *Rise of the British Army,* 46-49.

[10] *Ibidem*, 50-53.

[11] *Ibidem*, 54-66.

[12] Dalton, *English Army Lists,* I, 180.

[13] Bell, *Handlist of British Diplomatic Representatives*, IT44, SAV 28.

[14] *Calendar of Treasury Books, 1673-1675.*

[15] Baxter, *William III*, 150.

[16] *Calendar of State Papers, Domestic, 1677-78,* 17, 18 February 1678.

[17] Wolseley, *Marlborough,* 1, 195.

[18] *Calendar of State Papers, Domestic, 1678,* 2, 7, 26 April 1678

[19] *Seventh Report*, HMC, 473a.

[20] Harris, *A Passion for Government*, 29-30.

[21] Harris, *A Passion for government*, 34-36; Gregg, *Queen Anne*, 29-30.

[22] Dalton, *English Army Lists,* I, 301.

[23] Lachs, *Diplomatic Corps*, 61, 115.

[24] *Burnet's History*, I, 486.

[25] *Correspondence of Henry Hyde*, I, 141.

[26] Dalton, *English Army Lists,* II, 49; *Calendar of State Papers Domestic: James II, 1685*, doc. 1128, 3 July 1685.

[27] Chandler, *Sedgemoor*; for Churchill's role see 6, 22-24, 30, 33, 48, 52, 61, 64-66, 116, 126, 154.

[28] Thomson, *First Churchill*, 48; See also, Webb, *Lord Churchill's Coup.*

[29] Brown, *Letters of Queen Anne*, 20.

[30] Coxe, *Marlborough*, I, 10.

[31] Childs, *The Army of James II*, 148-50.

[32] Churchill, *Marlborough,* I, 240 with facsimile of original document.

[33] *Correspondence of Henry Hyde*, II, 211, 214.

[34] Churchill, *Marlborough*, I, 299.

[35] Foxcroft, *Life of Halifax*, II, 203.

[36] See Onnekink, *Anglo-Dutch Favourite.*

[37] *Burke's Peerage:* 'Marlborough'.

[38] Churchill, *Marlborough,* I, 281; BL, Addit. MSS 61,101: William III to Marlborough, 3/13 September 1689.

[39] Hopkins, 'Aspects of Jacobite Conspiracy', 266.

[40] Churchill, *Marlborough,* I ,349.

[41] Hopkins, 'Aspects of Jacobite Conspiracy', 268-69.

[42] Childs, *Nine Years' War*, 164-72.

[43] HMC *Finch MSS*, IV, 501.

[44] Hopkins, 'Aspects of Jacobitism,' 313, f. 42.

[45] Harris, *A Passion for Government*, 74-76.

[46] Gregg, *Queen Anne,* 120-21.

[47] Hattendorf, 'Die Ursprünge des spanischen Erbfolgekrieges', 109-22.

[48] Raa, F. ten, *Het Staatsche Leger,* VII, 450.

[49] Hattendorf, 'Die Ursprünge des spanischen Erbfolgekrieges'.

[50] Jarnut-Derbolav, *Die Österreichische Gesandtschaft*, 68.

[51] Hoff., B. van 't, ed., *The Correspondence*, 10: Marlborough to Heinsius, 8/19 March 1702.

[52] Dalton, *English Army Lists,* V, 15.

[53] Raa, F. ten, *Het Staatsche Leger,* VII, 177-78.

[54] Lamberty, *Mémoires,* II, 147.

[55] Wijn, *Het Staatsche Leger,* I, 111-12.

[56] This secret resolution of 30 June 1702 is printed in full in Wijn, *Het Staatsche Leger,* I, Appendix 9: 696-98; A draft of the instructions to the field deputies dated 7 July 1702 is printed in the same volume, Appendix 10: 699-702. See also Veenendaal, Jr., *Briefwisseling Heinsius,* I,

316: Heinsius to Athlone, 1 July 1792; I, 325-26: Heinsius to Athlone, 7 July 1702.

57 Nimwegen, O. van, *De subsistentie*, 331-44.

58 For Marlborough's predilection for swift movement and surprise, see Scouller, 'Marlborough's Administration' and his *The Armies of Queen Anne.*

59 Wijn, *Het Staatsche Leger,* I, 117-22, 180-89.

60 Gregg, *Queen Anne,* 164-66.

61 *Memoirs of ... Ailesbury*, II, 558.

62 Brown, ed., *Letters... of Queen Anne*, 125.

63 Wijn, *Het Staatsche Leger,* I, 260-71

64 On Villars as Marlborough's opponent, see Vogüé, *Villars;* Sturgill, *Villars*; Ziegler, *Villars.*

65 Wijn, *Het Staatsche Leger,* I, 271-85, 292-309, 344-58.

66 Snyder, *Marlborough-Godolphin*, I, passim.

67 Hattendorf, *England in the War of the Spanish Succession,* 54-75.

68 *Ibidem.*

69 On Eugène, see among others, Braubach, *Prinz Eugen*; McKay, *Prince Eugene*; Ortruba, *Prinz Eugen und Marlborough.*

70 *Ibidem.*

71 For the Bavarian perspective, see Hüttl, *Max Emanuel,* 363-74.

72 Hattendorf, 'English grand strategy in the Blenheim campaign'; Mathis, 'Marlborough und Wratislaw'.

73 Braubach, *Prinz Eugen,* 2, 69-71.

74 There have been many important studies of this campaign and battle, among them are Wijn, *Het Staatsche Leger,* I, 455-70; Verney, *Blenheim;* Green, *Blenheim*; Chandler, *Marlborough;* Chandler, *Blenheim Preparation*; Tincey, *Blenheim*; Spencer, *Blenheim*, and the richly illustrated museum exhibition catalogue: Erichsen and Heinemann, *Brennpunkt Europas, Höchstädt.*

75 Cra'ster, ed. 'Letters of the First Lord Orkney,' 307-11.

76 Snyder, *Marlborough-Godolphin*, 1, 349. On Parke, see Miller, *Colonel Parke of Virginia.*

77 For a French view of Blenheim and its effects, see Lynn, *Giant of the Grand Siècle*, 9, 234, 529, 595; Lynn, *Wars of Louis XIV*, 290-94.

78 BL, Add. MS 61143, fol. 153*v.*

79 Barber, P., 'Marlborough as imperial prince, 1704–1717'.

80 Green, *Blenheim Palace*; Bond and Tiller, *Blenheim: Landscape.*

81 Harris, *A Passion for Government,* 113-19.

82 Wijn, *Het Staatsche Leger,* I., 537-650.

83 Ingrao, *In Quest and Crisis*, 31-77.

84 Hattendorf, 'The Rakoczi Insurrection in English War Policy, 1703-1711'.

85 Wijn, *Het Staatsche Leger,* I, 635-50.

86 See for examples, Marlborough's letters in Hoff, B. van 't, *Correspondence,* 205-09; Snyder, *Marlborough-Godolphin,* I, 482.

87 Barber, 'Marlborough as imperial prince, 1704–1717'.

88 Frey and Frey, 'Foreign Policy of Frederick I'.

89 Wijn, *Het Staatsche Leger,* II, 16-23.

90 On Cadogan, see Watson, *Marlborough's Shadow.*

91 Ostwald, 'The 'decisive' battle of Ramillies, 1706'.

92 Spens, *George Stepney*, 274-80.

93 Wijn, *Het Staatsche Leger,* II, 55-136.

94 Spens, *George Stepney,* 302-15; Veenendaal [sr.], *Het Engels–Nederlands condominium,* and idem, 'Kan men spreken van een revolutie in de Zuidelijke Nederlanden na Ramillies?'

95 6 Anne cap. 7.

96 Milne, 'The Diplomacy of Dr. John Robinson'; Koningsbrugge, *Tussen Rijswijk en Utrecht*, 144-46; Hatton, *Charles XII,* 224-26.

97 Wijn, *Het Staatsche Leger,* II, 199-213.

98 Harris, *A Passion for Government,* 149-50; Tinniswood, *His Invention So Fertile*, 335-36, 364.

99 Gregg, *Queen Anne*, 258-59.

100 Holmes, *British Politics,* 71-75.

101 Veenendaal [Sr.], 'The opening phase of Marlborough's campaign of 1708'; Wijn, *Het Staatsche Leger,* II, 265-82.

102 Wijn, *Het Staatsche Leger,* II, 282-93.

103 *Ibidem*, II, 294-316.

104 Snyder, 'The duke of Marlborough's request'.

105 Stork-Penning, *Het Grote Werk*, 217-19, 265-69, 286-88.

106 On this subject, see Geikie and Montgomery, *The Dutch Barrier*, 90-147.

107 Snyder, *Marlborough–Godolphin*, III, 1269.

108 The place is called Doornik in Dutch; see Wijn, *Het Staatsche Leger,* II, 482-510.

109 Green, *Blenheim Palace,* 249.

110 Wijn, *Het Staatsche Leger,* II, 523-55; Corvisier, *Malplaquet*, 121-24.

111 Snyder, *Marlborough–Godolphin*, III, 1381.

112 Snyder, 'Marlborough's request'.

113 Harris, *A Passion for Government,* 157-62.

114 Gregg, *Queen Anne,* 300-03.

115 Snyder, 'Marlborough's request', 77.

116 Holmes, *Trial of Doctor Sacheverell.*

117 Wijn, *Het Staatsche Leger,* II, 575-668.

118 *Ibidem,* II, 669-60.

119 Hussey, 'Marlborough and the loss of Arleux'; see also Holmes, *Marlborough,* 456-58; Chandler, *Marlborough as Military Commander,* 287-91.

120 Hattendorf, *England in the War of the Spanish Succession,* 238-48.

121 Cobbett, *Parliamentary History*, VI, 1051–2.

122 *Ibidem*, 1077.

123 Barber, 'Marlborough as imperial prince', 70.

124 Gregg, 'Marlborough in Exile'.

125 Churchill, *Marlborough,* II, 627.

126 *Gothaisches Genealogisches Taschenbuch,* 530-35.

127 HMC *Stuart Papers*, V, 35

128 Harris, *A passion for government;* TNA: PRO, PROB 11/583, fols. 305–50: Marlborough's will and last testament.

129 Snyder, 'Arthur Maynwaring, Richard Steele, and *The lives of two illustrious generals*'.

130 Green, *Blenheim Palace,* 177, 278. No contemporary documents have been found to identify the artist with certainty; while no other sculpture by Robert Pit is known, Cheere was a well-known figure.

131 Green, *Blenheim Palace,* 168-77; Horn, *Marlborough: a Survey,* 524-25. The inscription was first published in a pamphlet in 1731 and reprinted in Lediard, *Marlborough,* III, 438-45.

132 Webb, *Rysbrack*, 93-96, 163-64.

133 For a printed bibliography, see Horn, *Marlborough: A Survey,* 544-51. This can now be supplemented with additional titles from *Eighteenth Century Collections Online* http://mlr.com/DigitalCollections/products/ecco/

3 John Churchill, Professional Soldiering, and the British Army, c1660-c1760

[1] Smyth, *A History of the Lancashire Fusiliers*, 281-83, 376-78. As a result of a maladroit intervention by Sir Hudson Lowe, the gifting process proved to be far from straightforward, but the volumes finally ended up in the Regiment's possession.

[2] Aguilar, *The Military Maxims of Napoleon*, 44-45. See also Luvaas, *Napoleon on the Art of War*, 29-41. According to Hilaire Belloc, *The Strategy and Tactics of the Great Duke of Marlborough*, 4: 'Napoleon seems to have looked upon Marlborough as an equal, and therefore to have set him even above that other great captain, Frederick of Prussia, whose military genius he so greatly admired. Napoleon read and re-read (commentating continuously in his own hand) Marlborough's campaigns; he proposed them as a model.'

[3] See, for example, Paret, *Makers of Modern Strategy*, where the Duke does not even appear in the index. The predecessor volume, Earle, *Makers of Modern Strategy*, mentions Marlborough only in the context of how unlikely it would be for a modern general to combine political with military command in the way the Duke was believed to have done; 204.

[4] Horn, 'Marlborough's First Biographer'; Harris, 'The Authorship of the Manuscript Blenheim Journal'; see also Holmes, *Marlborough*, 218-19.

[5] Holmes gives due weight to these symptoms and their ominous significance; *Ibidem*, 308-09.

[6] Wolseley, *The Life of John Churchill, Duke of Marlborough*, II, 426, 444. Interestingly, the Duke of Wellington is not included among the representative 'makers of modern strategy' either—see note 3 above.

[7] Burton, *The Captain-General*, 199.

[8] The Marquis de Brezé in his *Reflexions sur les Prejugés Militaires*, quoted by Duffy, *The Military Experience in the Age of Reason*, 140.

[9] For an imaginative attempt to make use of them, see Carpenter, *Military Leadership in the British Civil Wars*, 22-27 and *passim*.

[10] See, *inter alia*, Van Creveld, *Command in War*, 17-57, especially 54; Perjés, 'Army Provisioning, Logistics and Strategy'; Wilson, 'New Approaches under the Old Régime', and Duffy, *op. cit., passim.*

[11] See Pincus, *1688: The First Modern Revolution*, 296, and a breathless cluster of Marlborough letters to various correspondents, dated 3 June 1706 in the immediate aftermath of Ramillies in: Murray, *Letters*, II, 54.

[12] 'In the campaigns themselves, the Duke of Marlborough normally made England's strategy, and his views came to dominate the alliance as a whole'; Maltby, 'Origins of a global strategy', 166. For the formulation of strategy in general, see Hattendorf, *England in the War of the Spanish Succession,* especially 21-112; Thomson, 'Self-Determination and Collective Security', 271-86.

[13] Telp, *The Evolution of Operational Art*, 2. For a case study, see Hattendorf, 'English Grand Strategy and the Blenheim Campaign of 1704'; also Burton, *op. cit.*, 97-98.

[14] Van Creveld, *op. cit.*, 56; see also Luttwak, *The Grand Strategy of the Roman Empire,* 2-3.

[15] Anyone who doubts this should consult Lee, *A Greek Army on the March, passim.*

[16] See, for example, Chandler, *The Art of Warfare.*

[17] Houlding, *Fit for Service.*

[18] See, for example, Scouller, *The Armies of Queen Anne*, *passim*, and Guy, *Oeconomy and Discipline.*

[19] Millner, John, 'Serjeant in the Honourable Regiment of Foot of Ireland', 141; Lee, *op. cit.*, 3.

[20] *Ibidem*, vii and *passim*. For other voices from the ranks, see Chandler, ed., *A Journal of Marlborough's Campaigns during the War of the Spanish Succession,* and Chandler and Scott, *Journal of Sergeant John Wilson*. Examples of these movements reconstructed from marching orders and other data, are provided by Stansfield, 'Early modern systems of command', *passim.*

[21] Lund, *War for the Every Day*, *passim*. For the practical application of specialist knowledge by a representative military 'virtuoso', see Stoye, *Marsigli's Europe*, especially 119-44, where the conduct of war along the Middle Danube against the Turks is studied. The ambitious scale of these operations is more than comparable to Marlborough's march to the Danube in 1704.

[22] Chandler, *Journal of John Wilson*, 61.

[23] Marlborough to Godolphin, 23 Aug/3 Sept 1703, Snyder, *Marlborough-Godolphin*, I, 237.

[24] Marlborough to Robert Harley, 3 June 1706, Murray, *Letters*, II, 554.

[25] Marlborough to Harley, 4 July 1704, *ibidem*, I, 342.

[26] Chandler, *Military Memoirs: Robert Parker and the Comte de Mérode Westerloo*, 115.

[27] For a forthright commentary, see Burton, *op. cit.*, 60-61.

[28] Barker, *The Military Intellectual and Battle*, 157-59.

[29] Wace, *The Marlborough Tapestries*, 69-70.

[30] Marlborough to Duchess Sarah, 4/15 May 1707, Snyder, *Marlborough-Godolphin*, II, 770; same to Erle, 20 June 1707, Murray, *Letters,* III, 428.

[31] Marlborough to Godolphin, 4/15 Aug 1709, Snyder, *Marlborough-Godolphin,* III, 1331.

[32] ''T was worthy a particular Enquiry, How *England* came to Breed so Great a Soldier as his Grace. . . in the unactive, lazy reign of a Prince [Charles II] under whom he pass'd his Youth', Hare, *The Life and History of John, Duke and Earl of Marlborough*, cited in Horn, *Marlborough: A Survey*, 139-40. Hare was Marlborough's personal chaplain and historiographer and travelled with him on campaign, but that is as far as the enquiry seems to go.

[33] Webb, *Lord Churchill's Coup*, 15; Churchill, *Marlborough*, I, 46.

[34] Webb, *op. cit.*, 21-25, 40; Holmes, *op. cit.*, 58-61.

[35] Churchill, *op. cit.*, I, 106; Higginbotham, *George Washington*, 14.

[36] Lund, *op. cit.*, 144-46, 200-02. For the development of the army staff under William III, including the emerging importance of the post of Quartermaster-General, see Waddell, 'The Administration of the English Army in Flanders and Brabant', 179-95. For Sir John Ligonier see Whitworth, *Field Marshal Lord Ligonier,* 29-32. For up-to-date assessments of Cadogan's role, based on recent archive discoveries, see Holmes, *op. cit.*, 211-19, and Stansfield, *op. cit.*, *passim*,

together with his prosopographical survey of the command hierarchy. For Cadogan's political work on the Duke's behalf, see Gregg, 'Marlborough in Exile'. Cadogan's diplomatic missions for Marlborough are a constant feature in Hoff, B. van 't., *The Correspondence.* Lord Orkney's recollections of Ramillies are in Cra'ster, 'Letters of the First Lord Orkney': Orkney to one of his brothers, 24 May 1706, 315.

[37] Charles-Joseph, Prince de Ligne, cited by Duffy, *op.cit.*, 65.

[38] As Hilaire Belloc long ago pointed out in the case of Marlborough; *op. cit.*, 8.

[39] Churchill, *op. cit.*, I, 775.

[40] Marlborough to Robert Harley, 24 Nov 1704, Murray, *Letters and Despatches*, I, 544.

[41] Marlborough to Duchess Sarah, 4/15 May 1704, Snyder, *Marlborough-Godolphin*, I, 296-97.

[42] '. . . the Governor [of Liège] was taken in the breach by an English lieutenant, by which you may see the Queen's subjects were first upon the breach. This has been an action of great vigor, soe that it is impossible to say to[o] much of the bravery that was shown by all the officers and soldiers.' Marlborough to Godolphin, 12/22 Oct 1702, *ibidem*, I, 126.

[43] Same to same, 25 June/6 July 1704, *ibidem*, I, 331. For the comparative strength of Dutch and English forces on the Continent, see Zwitzer, 'The British and Netherlands Armies', 37.

[44] Marlborough to Godolphin, 1/12 Sept 1704, Snyder, *Marlborough-Godolphin*, I, 368; 1/12 July 1706; *ibid.*, II, 608-09.

[45] Adam Cardonnel (Marlborough's private secretary) to Colonel Hales, 27 July 1703, Murray, *Letters and Despatches*, I, 152; Marlborough to the Commissioners of the Royal Hospital, Chelsea, 24 Jan 1707, *ibidem*, III, 300.

[46] Duffy, *op. cit.*, 30-32; Defoe, 'A Hymn to Victory', cited Horn, *op. cit.*, 48.

[47] For a detailed survey of these developments see Manning, *An Apprenticeship in Arms*; also Childs, *Nobles, Gentlemen and the Profession of Arms*, especially v-xv.

[48] Manning, 'Styles of Command', 671-99.

[49] See the revisionist argument put forward by Webb, *The Governors General*, *passim*.

[50] Webb, *Lord Churchill's Coup*, 14 and Pincus, *op. cit.,* 144-48, Baxter, *William III*, 284.

[51] Pincus, *op. cit.*, 234-35, has recently questioned the real impact of this military *putsch.* The standard account is by Childs, *The Army*; see also the critical account of John Churchill's involvement by Webb, *Lord Churchill's Coup*, 124-68. For the troubled aftermath of these events for the Army see Childs, *The British Army*, 4-33.

[52] *Ibidem*, 43; Dalton, *English Army Lists*, III, 107-23.

[53] The standard published account is by Childs, *The Nine Years' War and the British Army*, but see also the important (unpublished) study by Waddell, who identifies clear benefits to the English by their adoption of Dutch methods of organization, provisioning, musters, management of the baggage train and officer discipline, *op. cit.*, 33-52; also Baxter, *op. cit.*, 281, 284, 298-99. For Marlborough learning the business of a general officer under Waldeck's supervision, see Chandler, *Marlborough as a Military Commander*, 31.

[54] Houlding, *op. cit.,* 174. Had the technique of platoon fire even entered popular understanding? 'Platoons discharge their small Artillery' - Laurence Eusden(?), *The Encomium* (1710), cited in Horn, *op. cit.*, 324. For the reputation of the English troops of William III as being the best armed in Europe, see Walton, *History of the British Standing Army*, 433.

[55] Childs, *British Army of William III*, 29, 53; Baxter, *op. cit.*, 92-93, Childs, ed., 'Lord Cutts' Letters, 1695', 374-79; Guy, *Oeconomy and Discipline*, 32-34.

[56] Scouller, *Armies of Queen Anne*, xii-xiii.

[57] See for example, Marlborough to the Duke of Shrewsbury, 22 March 1707, Murray, *Letters,* III, 337; same to the Earl of Pembroke, 24 Sept 1708, *ibidem*, IV, 235.

[58] Holmes, *British Politics in the Age of Anne*, 27; Scouller, *op. cit.*, 73-74.

[59] Marlborough to Colonel Pennefather, 30 Sept 1709, Murray, *Letters,* IV, 609.

[60] Godolphin to Marlborough 1 July 1709, Snyder, *Marlborough-Godolphin*, III, 1299; Marlborough to Godolphin, 7/18 July 1709, *ibidem*, 1306; Marlborough to Duchess Sarah, 'I think it is a very unreasonable desire', 11/22 July 1709, *ibidem*, 1309; Godolphin to Marlborough, 16 August 1709, *ibidem*, 1346. The regiment was short-lived.

[61] Scouller, *op. cit.*, 52; Walton, *op. cit.*, 405-6.

[62] Scouller, *op. cit.*, 77-78; Marlborough to Albemarle, 26 Feb. 1706, Murray, *Letters*, II, 436-37; same to the Earl of Cardigan, 19 Dec 1707, *ibidem*, III, 653-54.

[63] Scouller, *op. cit.*, 71; for King William's much more rigid attitude, see Waddell, *op. cit.*, 302-03.

[64] Marlborough to St John, 16 July 1711, Murray, *Letters,* V, 412-13.

[65] Marlborough to Robert Walpole, 14 June 1708, *ibidem*, IV, 64; same to same, 18 June 1708, *ibidem*, 67. Sir John Cope, of Prestonpans notoriety (1745) founded his military career on brevets; for this and a detailed explanation of their workings, see Burton and Newman, 'Sir John Cope: Promotion in the Eighteenth Century', 655-68.

[66] Scouller, *op. cit.*, 337.

[67] Childs, *British Army of William III*, 117.

[68] Steppler, 'The Common Soldier in the Reign of George III', especially 85-112, 'Making Ends Meet'.

[69] Guy, 'Colonel Francis Charteris'.

[70] Childs, *British Army of William III*, 118-19, 156-57; Scouller, *op. cit.*, 336-40. For conditions a generation later, see the pioneering article by Kopperman, 'The British High Command and Soldiers' Wives in America, 1755-1783'; also Hendrix, 'In the Army: Women, Camp Followers and Gender Roles in the British Army'. John Lynn has made an important reconnaissance of the entire subject in *Women, Armies and Warfare in Early Modern Europe*, unfortunately without much detail about British Army conditions, but see his third chapter, 118-63: 'Women's Work: Gendered Tasks, Commerce and the Pillage Economy' with its important indicators for future research; for the anonymity of the common soldier as a whole, see Waddell, *op. cit.*, 330-31.

[71] Guy, '"The Stubborn English Spirit": Officer Discipline and Resistance to Authority, 1727-1750'.

[72] Notably during the political fall-out from the

disastrous battle of Almanza on 25 April 1707 where, out of 29,395 English troops voted for Spain and Portugal, it emerged that only 8,660 had been present at the engagement; Scouller, *op. cit.*, 110-17.

[73] *Ibidem.*, 321-26; Waddell, *op. cit.*, 233.

[74] Colonel Henry Hawley, 'Some thoughts, some observations and remarks, quotations, abstracts & opinions, productions of a rainy day after my own way Touchant le Militaire', *c.*1725: manuscript formerly on loan to the National Army Museum, NAM 7411-24-16, now at the Royal Archives, Windsor.

[75] TNA. SP 41/13/172, Return of Officers incapable of performing their Duty, 23 July 1741.

[76] For changes in officers' career trends from 1715, computed from a sample of eleven regiments of horse and 29 of foot, see Houlding, *op. cit.*, 104-16. For expanding horizons in military technique, see in general, Ultee, *Adapting to Conditions*. For Humphrey Bland, see Houlding, 'Bland, Humphrey', and Bland, *A Treatise of Military Discipline*, especially his Preface, 2. Gruber, *Books and the British Army*, 38-39.

[77] *The Spectator*, No 2, 2 Mar 1711. *The Tatler's* earlier version of Captain Sentry was the wonderfully named Major Matchlock, a garrulous veteran of the Civil Wars; Bond, *The Tatler: The Making of a Literary Journal*, 174. For an extended discussion of these literary types, see McNeil, *The Grotesque Depiction of War and the Military*, 144-67.

[78] Reprinted in *The Gentleman's Magazine*, III (1733), 344.

[79] 'From a Military Officer in the Country'; 'On Frank Firelock's Letter'; 'The Subject of Frank Firelock's Letter on the Army further pursued'; *ibidem*, VII (1737), 427-30, 437; VIII (1738), 202-03.

[80] Fluchère, *Laurence Sterne, from Tristram to Yorick*, 306-11; Scouller, *op. cit.*, 336-37; Holmes, *Augustan England*, 262-74. For the relative poverty of junior officer grades see Waddell, *op. cit.*, 318-21.

[81] 'The Land Leviathan; [or] Modern Hydra', London (1712), cited in Horn, *op. cit.*, 374-75; McNeil, *op. cit.*, 113-43, *passim*.

[82] Analysed by Schwoerer, *No Standing Armies*.

[83] See the disconcerting remarks made by Thomas Churchyard, Tudor 'soldier and hack' and others of his kind as exposed by Rapple, *Martial Power and Elizabethan Political Culture*, 73-85 and *passim*.

[84] For the rackety lifestyle of Marlborough's colonels, see Waddell, *op. cit.*, 312-15. For Colonel Parke, see Churchill, *op. cit.*, I, 863, 869-90; Falkner, James, 'Parke, Daniel', and Horn, *op. cit.*, 355-57; for Maccartney, see Dickinson, 'The Mohun-Hamilton Duel: Personal Feud or Whig Plot?'

[85] Davies, 'The Seamy Side of Marlborough's War'.

[86] For a case study of Cadogan 'at home' in his mini-Blenheim country seat at Caversham, Berkshire, see Thompson, *Whigs and Hunters*, 100-02 and *passim*. The rough-and-ready style of the old officer corps is well captured in Dickinson, ed. 'Correspondence of Henry St John and Thomas Erle.' For the nostalgic survival of this style of masculine behaviour into the eighteenth century, see Mackie, *Rakes, Highwaymen and Pirates*, *passim*.

[87] No.16 (23 November 1710), and No.27 (8 February 1711), 'The Letter to Crassus.' For a readable account incorporating long extracts from *The Examiner* see Foot, *The Pen and the Sword*, especially 151-53, where the Duke's 'visible profits' from the War of the Spanish Succession are tallied up by Swift. 'The falsest, as well as the most impudent paper that was ever printed', fumed the Whig *Medley*.

[88] Rogers, *Pope and the Destiny of the Stuarts*, 212-18; McNeil, *op. cit.*, 79-83.

[89] For this episode, see Snyder, 'The Duke of Marlborough's Request of his Captain-Generalcy for Life'.

[90] Holmes, *op. cit.*, 470-71; Guy, *Oeconomy and Discipline*, 28.

[91] Guy, *ibid.*, 28-29; Whitworth, Rex, *William Augustus, Duke of Cumberland*, 145-46, 149-50. For Ligonier as commander-in-chief under Pitt, see Whitworth, *Ligonier*, 201-2, 225-35; Wood, Stephen, 'Ligonier, John', and Middleton, *The Bells of Victory*, 44-46 and *passim*. The Honourable Artillery Company and the Royal Marines, not being regiments, still have a royal captain-general, as General Whitworth points out, but, 'Like the title of Lord High Admiral, it now has a faintly Ruritanian flavour', *ibidem*, 189. For hard-to-handle (royal) commanders-in-chief of a later age, see Stephens, 'Frederick, Prince, duke of York and Albany' and Spiers, 'George, Prince, second duke of Cambridge'.

4 Marlborough and Siege Warfare

[1] Chandler, *Marlborough as Military Commander*, 63, 141-42, 324; Jones, *Marlborough*, 59, 230-31; Scott, 'Marlborough' in Parker and Cowley, *Reader's Companion to Military History*, 287.

[2] Chandler, *The Art of Warfare in the Age of Marlborough*, 234.

[3] Burton, *The Captain-General*, dedicates six pages to Ramillies and a single paragraph to the four sieges (106-07); Tournai earns only a couple of paragraphs (148-49) compared to the battle of Malplaquet (150-58), while the campaigns of 1710 and 1711 receive only a single chapter, most of which deals with the political situation. Chandler spends six pages on the battle of Ramillies and four pages on its aftermath, which included four sieges that consumed 80% of the entire campaign. Jones spends four on the field action and two-and-a-half on its effects. Chandler covers all of the 1710-1711 campaigns (one of siege after siege with no sign of battle) in a single chapter, while Jones gives even less time to them.

[4] Atkinson, 'Marlborough's Sieges', and his 'Marlborough's Sieges: Further Evidence'. These articles were intended only to identify the participation of British regiments in order to secure them battle honours in the 1930s. The recent exception is Falkner, *Marlborough's Sieges*.

[5] For two examples, see Burton, *Captain-General*, 192, and Jones, *Marlborough*, 231.

[6] Churchill, *Marlborough: His Life and Times*, 1, 84-85; also 1, 605.

[7] Chandler, *Robert Parker and the Comte de Mérode-Westerloo*, 236; see also Chandler's *Marlborough as Military Commander*, 77. Other examples in Guerlac, 'Vauban: The Impact of Science on War', 79; Britt, *The Dawn of Modern Warfare*, 89; Jones, *Marlborough*, 56; McLaughlin in Margiotta, *Brassey's Encyclopedia of Military History and Biography*, 465.

[8] Chandler summarized Marlborough's career: 'he forced four major battles and two important actions on evasive foes and unwilling allies alike', in 'John Churchill, First Duke of Marlborough', 215; McJoynt also concluded that 'Marlborough's accomplishments can be summarized by four great battles': see his entry on 'Marlborough,' in *Brassey's Encyclopedia*, 657. See also Ashley, *Marlborough*, 62.

[9] *Marlborough as Military Commander*, 63; also Atkinson, 'Marlborough's Sieges', 195-96.

[10] Dennis Showalter's entry on 'Churchill' in Frey and Frey, *Treaties of the War of the Spanish Succession*, 108; Falkner, *Marlborough's Sieges*, xvi-xviii.

[11] Recent biographies of Vauban include Pujo, *Vauban*; Blanchard, *Vauban*; and Virol, *Vauban*.

[12] It is unlikely that Churchill was a land participant in the 1672 campaign, where, the story goes, the 'handsome Englishman' was singled out for praise by Turenne at the siege of Nijmegen. Atkinson, *Marlborough and the Rise of the British Army*, 40, 49, 65-66.

[13] For Louis XIV's self-centred account of the siege, see Champollion-Figeac, *Oeuvres de Louis XIV*, 3, 317ff. For an English perspective, Watson, *Captain-General and Rebel Chief*, 56-66.

[14] For a full discussion of Vauban's systematic approach to siege craft, see Ostwald, *Vauban under Siege*, 46-90.

[15] The most recent work on Turenne is Bérenger, *Turenne;* see 508-14 for discussion of his strategic style.

[16] For example, Atkinson, *Marlborough and the Rise of the British Army*, 60; Chandler, *Marlborough as Military Commander*, 7.

[17] For Turenne's method of siege warfare in the 1650s, see La Barre Nanteuil, 'La guerre de siège sous Turenne', 143-48.

[18] James occupied himself as a noble volunteer in French military service before he and his elder brother returned to England in 1660. Stuart, James, *The Memoires of James II*, 151-53. He further recounted that the chief French engineer barely escaped a pummelling when his promised mine failed to breach the walls.

[19] For a detailed examination of the widespread military resistance to Vauban's ideas, see Ostwald, *Vauban under Siege*, 173-214.

[20] Vauban, *Les Oisivetés de Monsieur de Vauban*, 43. See more generally Rousset, *Histoire de Louvois*, I, 461-64.

[21] For Cork, see Childs, *The Williamite Wars in Ireland*, 267-73; Simms, 'Marlborough's Siege of Cork', and Stapleton, 'The Blue-Water Dimension of King William's War', 330-34.

[22] On Kinsale, see Childs, *The Williamite Wars in Ireland*, 273-77; and Jordan, 'The Siege of Kinsale, 1690: The Danish Report'.

[23] Childs, *The Williamite Wars in Ireland*, 273-74. The exact state of Charles Fort's fortifications is unclear—some contemporary plans suggest that it had a covered way (one contemporary account indicates a storming of the counterscarp), yet a French engineer's report indicates that the covered way was only traced out, but not actually constructed. See Mulloy, 'French engineers with the Jacobite Army in Ireland, 1688-1691', 230.

[24] A very dismissive view of the Emerald Isle from Continental engineers' perspective can be seen in Mulloy, 'French engineers with the Jacobite Army in Ireland', 222-32.

[25] For Duffy's judgment of the sieges of Cork and Kinsale as un-noteworthy, see Duffy, *The Fortress in the Age of Vauban and Frederick the Great*, 169.

[26] Several seventeenth century contemporaries noted that once engineers starting taking over the details of the siege, the regular army officers quickly lost their facility with the task, though engineers would later question how knowledgeable such officers had actually been in the first place. See, for example, Stuart, *The Memoires of James II*, 152-53.

[27] Churchill, *Marlborough: His Life and Times*, I, 294.

[28] Numerous studies emphasize the backwardness of British fortifications and siege craft vis-à-vis continental Europe (particularly during the British Civil Wars): Duffy, *Siege Warfare*, chapter 6; Loeber and Parker, 'The military revolution in seventeenth century Ireland', 66-88; and Hutton and Reeves, 'Sieges and Fortifications'.

[29] For English engineers, see Dalton, *English Army Lists*; for the years 1702-1707, V, 115-23 and V, Part II: The Blenheim Bounty Roll, March 1705, 9-11. For 1707-1714, consult VI,

43-48. On England's backwardness circa 1700 more generally, see Scouller, *The Armies of Queen Anne*, 173-87; and Chandler, 'Fortifications and Siegecraft,' in *Blenheim Preparations*.
[30] Cambon was William's master-general of fortifications. Another French descendant, Charles Du Puy de l'Espinasse, would succeed him in this post. By 1695 William had informally elevated Menno van Coehoorn to prime advisor in engineering matters. Ostwald, *Vauban under Siege*, 131-32.
[31] Lamont, M. de, *The art of war*, 267-307.
[32] For the details on this table, see the appendices in Ostwald, *Vauban under Siege*.
[33] For example, Falkner, *Marlborough's Sieges*, 7.
[34] For example, see Churchill's account of Menen in *Marlborough*, II, 177.
[35] For example, Chandler, *Marlborough as Military Commander*, 329-30. Falkner's recent survey discusses non-British participants more frequently, although the Dutch engineers running the siege are excluded from the index.
[36] Jones, *Marlborough*, 66, 127-28, is an exception.
[37] Ostwald, *Vauban under Siege*, 106-07, 260-62.
[38] Ostwald, *Vauban under Siege*, 104-11. The Marlborough literature consistently overestimates the strength of these fortifications.
[39] *Le Mercure Galant*, octobre 1702, 430.
[40] Chandler is the only one to mention their names with any regularity (e.g. Hesse-Cassel, Ouwerkerk, the Prince of Orange, Anhalt-Dessau, and a very small number of Englishmen such as Lord Orkney). Notably, he rarely mentioned them by name (or position) after his initial introduction, unless it was to highlight their difficulties.
[41] For Coehoorn's difficulties, see Ostwald, *Vauban under Siege*, 114-16, 235-38.
[42] On Des Rocques, see Veenendaal, Jr.'s entry in Frey and Frey, *The Treaties of the War of the Spanish Succession*, 132-33.
[43] This total figure comes from a count of Ringoir's *Afstammingen en voortzettingen der genie en trein*. F.W.J. Scholten's count of Dutch engineers in the *staten van oorlog* fluctuate between forty and eighty per year over the course of the Spanish Succession. *Militaire topografische kaarten en stadsplattegronden van de Nederlanden, 1579-1795*.
[44] Porter, *History of the Corps of Royal Engineers*; Dickinson, 'The Richards Brothers: Exponents of the Military Arts of Vauban'.
[45] For discussion of specific English engineers, see Dickinson, 'The Richards Brothers: Exponents of the Military Arts of Vauban', and Mason and Barber, '"Captain Thomas, the French engineer", and the teaching of Vauban to the English'; and Hebbert, 'Major-General John Richards (1667-1709)'.
[46] Chandler, *Marlborough as Military Commander*, 295.
[47] Koninklijke Bibliotheek, The Hague, Pamflet #15958, *Journal du siège de Bouchain depuis qu'elle fût investie jusques à sa prise; avec la capitulation*, 13. Confirmed by Porter, 115.
[48] Porter,Whitworth, *History of the Corps of Royal Engineers*, 111. Marlborough's correspondence mentions him only a few times in ten years, while Porter, 115, notes that he disappears completely from the sources for most of his years fighting the Spanish Succession war. Marlborough's few references to Armstrong are in the context of such quartermaster duties. Murray, *Letters and Dispatches*, IV, 45ff and 231.
[49] Only regiments on the English establishment could serve overseas, therefore in the case of the Flanders theatre English and British are synonymous. This also explains why six Scottish regiments were put in Dutch service so that they might serve on the Continent.
[50] In addition to the 60,000 slated for the army, the Dutch paid for an additional 42,000 of their own troops to serve as garrisons. All figures are paper strengths. For discussions of these numerical issues, see Burton, *Marlborough*, 20-21; Hattendorf, *England in the War of the Spanish Succession*, 134ff; and for the Germans, Wilson, *German Armies: War and German Society*, 105-09. For a detailed comparison of Dutch and British units (including those paid by both England and the States), see Wijn, *Het Staatsche Leger*, I, 675-85.
[51] According to Hattendorf, 8,000-12,000 men were stationed in the British Isles for home defence throughout the war, while the Dutch tasked some of their troops with garrison duty as well along their own frontiers.
[52] Bland, *A Treatise of Military Discipline*, 287-92. Table of national contributions on 290-91.
[53] The regimental siege duties are drawn primarily from the siege narratives and Allied casualty lists (by regiment, most of which are reprinted in the appendices) of Wijn, *Het Staatsche Leger*, vols. I-III. These numbers have then been cross-referenced with Atkinson, 'Marlborough's Sieges', and his 'Marlborough's Sieges: Further Evidence'. The total number of English regiments in the Low Countries theatre comes from Hattendorf, *England in the War of the Spanish Succession*, 134-35, confirmed by comparisons with several Orders of Battle. The lack of specificity in Atkinson's two articles, and Falkner's recent book, contrasted with the material available in Dutch accounts, is yet another indication of the need for English historians to consult Dutch sources. I have not included cavalry regiments for three reasons. First, there were usually only a very small number of cavalry units in the besieging army (perhaps a dozen, occasionally two), as they were more useful in the covering army. Second, the size of each cavalry regiment was much smaller than infantry regiments, a theoretical strength of perhaps 150 men versus a one-battalion regiment of perhaps 600-700. Third, the cavalry troopers served a very limited number of functions in sieges after the fortress had been invested, primarily making fascines and carrying them to the trenches, as well as guarding against garrison sorties. The ratio of British to non-British squadrons is comparable in any case.
[54] Johnston, 'Letters of Samuel Noyes, Chaplain of the Royal Scots', 70.
[55] Bland, *A Treatise of Military Discipline*, 257.
[56] Murray, *Letters and Dispatches*, IV, 528; Hoff, B. van 't, *The Correspondence*, 443.
[57] For Marlborough's frequent criticisms of the engineers, see Ostwald, *Vauban under Siege*, 176-80.
[58] Veenendaal, Jr., *Briefwisseling Heinsius*, IX, 35.
[59] Snyder, *Marlborough-Godolphin*, III, 1285.
[60] Veenendaal, Jr., *Briefwisseling Heinsius*, IX, 103 and 115.
[61] *Ibidem*, IX, 103.

[62] Murray, *Letters and Dispatches*, IV, 571.

[63] Veenendaal, Jr., *Briefwisseling Heinsius*, IX, 94 and 103.

[64] Murray, *Letters and Dispatches*, IV, 575.

[65] Veenendaal, Jr., *Briefwisseling Heinsius*, IX, 194.

[66] *Ibidem*, VIII, 668; Service Historique de l'Armée de Terre, Archives de Guerre, série A1 vol. 2159, #408.

[67] On English reliance on Dutch logistics, see Nimwegen, O. van, *De subsistentie van het leger.*

[68] The sieges of Hulst 1702 (which Vauban had never wanted to attack in the first place, and whose lifting was due to the impossible terrain), Liège 1705 (where the French never opened trenches and which was lifted once its objective, drawing Marlborough from the Moselle, succeeded), Brussels 1708 (where the French attackers had expected to surprise the town rather than besiege it, and therefore lacked the manpower to besiege it *dans les formes*, much less hold off a relief force as well), and Landrecies 1712, the only case in Flanders where a relief effort directly led to the abandonment of a serious siege.

5 'By thes difficultys you may see the great disadvantage a confederat army has' Marlborough, the Allies, and the Campaigns in the Low Countries, 1702-1706

[1] I wish to thank Jamel Ostwald, my colleagues at the United States Military Academy Tom Rider, Jackie Whitt and Steve Waddell, and the editors for their helpful suggestions and comments in preparing this essay.

[2] Although Churchill was First Earl of Marlborough through the autumn of 1702 when Queen Anne conferred upon him the title Duke of Marlborough, I refer to him as the Duke of Marlborough throughout this essay.

[3] Chandler lists eight field engagements during the Spanish Succession War, though only Blenheim, Ramillies and Malplaquet were set-piece battles. Oudenaarde was a meeting-engagement of sorts. Chandler lists twenty-six sieges while Marlborough commanded the Confederate Army, while Ostwald's more thorough list cites twenty-seven. For details, see Chandler, *Marlborough as Military Commander*, 334-39; Ostwald, *Vauban Under Siege*, 96-104, 340-47, 367-70.

[4] Churchill, *Marlborough: His Life and Times*, I, 3.

[5] Chandler, *Marlborough as Military Commander*, 313-15. Marlborough's diplomacy is described in detail in Churchill, *Marlborough*, II, 233-56; and Bevin, *Marlborough the Man*, 177-87. For the details of his diplomatic affairs throughout his tenure as Extraordinary Ambassador to the United Provinces, see Schutte, *Repertorium der Buitenlandse Vertegenwoordigers*, 84-87.

[6] Bevin writes 'Where Marlborough deserves high honour and credit was in his tactful handling of his allies. The Dutch generals were as jealous of him as they had been during the Irish campaign and opposed him wherever possible.' Further on, he writes of the Dutch generals' 'lack of co-operation' but that Marlborough 'suppressed his resentment, and tried to mitigate the discontent among his officers who clamoured against the Dutch'. But Marlborough's correspondence to Heinsius, Slingelandt, and others suggest that despite his diplomatic skill, he could not convince the Dutch generals to do what he wished unreservedly. For details, see Bevin, *Marlborough the Man*, 187-89.

[7] Churchill was less direct in his criticism of the Dutch than both his contemporaries and successors in the historical profession. David Chandler's early work reflects a certain xenophobic tone when he called the field deputies 'veritable political commissars' and the Dutch generals 'sulky' when they vetoed his proposed attacks. More vitriolic is Sir John Fortescue who clearly detested the Dutch. In describing the outcome of 1702 campaign, he quipped 'all of [Marlborough's] plans had been wrecked by Dutch jealousy and Dutch stupidity,' a statement characteristic of his xenophobic tone. In the United States, Russell Weigley used similar, disparaging language. For Weigley, Marlborough was the hero while the Dutch were an obstacle to be overcome. He attributed Dutch field deputies to 'the vagaries of Dutch politics,' their territorial concerns unimportant when compared with a decisive battle's war-winning potential. He even went so far as to justify their sacrifices on the battlefield when he wrote of Ramillies 'The Allied losses were a relatively low 5,000, borne disproportionately by the Dutch, who compensated in part for their hesitancies elsewhere by bearing the brunt of this new struggle to stem the advance into their homeland.' For details, see Chandler, *Marlborough as Military Commander*, 99-106; Fortescue, *Marlborough*, 32; Weigley, *Age of Battles*, 77-87, 89-92.

[8] David Chandler is foremost among those historians who believe in the genius behind Marlborough's battle-seeking operations, contrasted with the more cautious Dutch preference for siege operations. He writes: 'In the west…generals were constantly being reminded of the virtues of moderation by economy-minded governments. This trend indubitably encouraged military mediocrity, and only a few commanders of the calibre of Marlborough and Prince Eugene were bold enough to insist on returning a measure of effectiveness and decision to the conduct of warfare by constantly seeking for situations favouring a major engagement, or what Clausewitz in the next century would term 'the bloody solution of the crisis.' The Duke regarded a field success as 'of far greater advantage to the common cause than the taking of twenty towns.' Chandler, *Marlborough as Military Commander*, 62.

[9] Fortescue, *Marlborough*, 160.

[10] Hoff, B. van 't, *Correspondence.*

[11] Jones, J., *Marlborough*, 56.

[12] Marlborough only served in the Low Countries as a general officer during the Nine Years' War during the 1689 and 1691 campaigns. It is

unclear in the literature in what capacity Marlborough served in 1691. Holmes claimed he commanded the English contingent; Chandler maintains that he was on William's staff only. In his history of the Nine Years' War, John Childs makes no mention of Marlborough during the 1691 campaign. For details, see Chandler, *Marlborough as Military Commander,* 30-44, Childs, J., *Nine Years' War,* 156-77; Holmes, *Marlborough: England's Fragile Genius*, 159-62, 172-74.

13 Snyder, *Marlborough-Godolphin,* I, 78-79 (#73).

14 Chandler, *Marlborough as Military Commander*, 10-11.

15 See Veenendaal, Jr.'s essay in this volume, Chapter 6, following.

16 Churchill, *Marlborough*, III, 54; Israel, *The Dutch Republic*, 972; Wijn, *Het Staatsche Leger*, I, 30-34, 109-13.

17 For the importance of experience in officers' education and the role of the army as a 'teaching institution,' see especially Lund, *War For The Every Day*, 68.

18 Chandler, *Marlborough as Military Commander*, 13-21, 34-43; Churchill, *Marlborough*, I, 208-22; II, 26-32; and Stapleton, 'The Blue-Water Dimension of King William's War.'

19 Marlborough's corps should have numbered 10,972 men or 12,907 with its officers. At the time of its arrival in the Low Countries, however, the English corps mustered no more than 6,000 men. For details, see The National Archives, Kew (TNA) SP 8/5, *King William's Chest, 1689*, ff. 25, 46; National Archives, The Hague (NAH), *Raad van State Archief* (RvS) (1.01.19), #626, *Ingekomen Missieven, Jan.-Juni 1689*, 'Memorie waer de Nieuwe Engelsche Regimenten logiren sullen (Zanten, den 16 April 1689)', 'Waldeck to the *Raad van State*, Breda, 25 April 1689'; *Calendar of State Papers Domestic, 1689-90*, 130-31 ('Waldeck to William III, Maastricht, 1 June 1689'); and Childs, *Nine Years' War*, 114.

20 Coxe, *Memoirs of the Duke of Marlborough*, I, 27; Chandler, *Marlborough as Military Commander*, 32-33; Childs, *Nine Years' War*, 114, 121-23; Knoop, *Krijgs- en Geschiedkundige Beschouwingen*, III, 11-19; Raa, F. ten, *Het Staatsche Leger*, VII, 15-16.

21 Nimwegen, O. van, *'Deser landen Crijchsvolck'*, 274-76.

22 According to Churchill, William III said of Marlborough after the Irish operation, 'No officer living who has seen so little service as my Lord Marlborough, is so fit for great commands.' William nevertheless believed that Marlborough still lacked the experience for higher command. Churchill, *Marlborough*, II, 33.

23 *Ibidem.*

24 Baxter, *William III*, 298; Childs, *The British Army of William III*, 73-74.

25 Ringoir, *Afstammingen en voortzettingen der cavalerie*, 65, 67; and Frey and Frey, *Treaties of the War of the Spanish Succession*, 377.

26 Childs, *The British Army of William III*, 28; Hora Siccama, *Aantekeningen en Verbeteringen*, 569; and Knoop, *Krijgs- en Geschiedkundige Beschouwingen*, III, 78-93; Raa, F. ten, *Het Staatsche Leger*, VII, *passim*; Childs, *The Nine Years' War, passim*; d'Auvergne, *The History of the Last Campaign in the Spanish Netherlands*, 1693, 23; NAH, Familie van Wassenaer (3.20.63), #8, 'Ordre de Battaille de l'Armée des Alliés au Camp de Mons St. André 1694' (unfoliated); and NAH, CvdH. (1.10.42), #158, 'Memoires et dispositions touchant le Siège de Namur,' ff.1.

27 For Goslinga's background, see Frey and Frey, *The Treaties of the War of the Spanish Succession*, 189-90.

28 Evertz and Delprat, *Mémoires relatifs à la Guerre de Succession*, 1857, 44. Also cited in Chandler, *Marlborough as Military Commander*, 318; and Holmes, *Marlborough: England's Fragile Genius*, 9-10.

29 Childs, *The British Army of William III*, 73-77.

30 Wijn, *Het Staatsche Leger*, I, 109.

31 *Ibidem*, I, 110-13, 110n.

32 As Jamel Ostwald observes in his essay on the battle of Ramillies, '…a perusal of the large number of English-language works will turn up the surprising fact that none bother to consult the secondary literature written by Dutch historians, much less delve into Dutch primary sources.' In my own research, I have not found a single Anglophone work on Marlborough written in the past twenty-five years that cites a single Dutch work – primary or secondary – apart from Van 't Hoff's, *Correspondence.* For details, Ostwald, 'The 'Decisive' Battle of Ramillies,' 663-64.

33 Fockema-Andreae, *De Nederlandse Staat*, 11-17; Nimwegen, *De subsistentie van het leger*, 20-21; Israel, *The Dutch Republic*, 291-93.

34 Deursen, A. van, 'De Raad van State'; Fockema-Andreae, *De Nederlandse Staat*, 19-22, 116-18; Nimwegen, *De subsistentie van het leger*, 21-24.

35 Although Britain would not exist as a political entity until the Act of Union added Scotland to the English Crown in 1707, for the purposes of this essay, the term 'British Army' refers to the three military establishments together--English, Scottish, and Irish--that comprised the Crown's military forces.

36 Israel, *The Dutch Republic*, 960.

37 Wijn, *Het Staatsche Leger*, I, 30.

38 Israel, *The Dutch Republic*, 960-61, 970-72.

39 Churchill, *Marlborough*, II, 61.

40 Wijn, *Het Staatsche Leger*, I: 111-12, 696-98.

41 *Ibidem*, I, 112-13.

42 Knoop, *Krijgs- en Geschiedkundige Beschouwingen*, III, 20; Nimwegen, *De subsistentie van het leger*, 23.

43 For a good example of this practice during the Nine Years' War, see Stapleton, 'Grand Pensionary at War,' especially 210-14.

44 Wijn, *Het Staatsche Leger*, I, 111-13, 696-98.

45 For Van Vredenburch's account book see NAH, RAZH, 3.20.61.01, *Familiearchief van Vredenburch*, #337, 'Eerste Rekening van Jacob van Vredenburch van Adrichem als Gedeputeerde te Velde Anno 1695.'

46 For Goslinga's and Geldermalsen's participation in the battle of Oudenaarde, see Wijn, *Het Staatsche Leger* II, 294-316, especially 306-09.

47 According to Snyder, in 1707, the Council of State did not send a deputy to the army. Van 't Hoff, on the other hand, notes that Geldermalsen was the Council of State's deputy that year. For details, see Snyder, *Marlborough-Godolphin*, III, 1700-1701; and Hoff, B. van 't, *Correspondence*, 322n.

48 G-4 is the U.S. Army term for General of

Logistics, an army-level post.

49 Olaf van Nimwegen, an authority on the Dutch Army during this period, attributes this document to Slingelandt. For details, see Nimwegen, *De subsistentie van het leger*, 23, 46-47.

50 NAH, CvdH (1.10.40), # 137 (unfoliated), 'Instructie voor den Heer Adr. Van Borssele tot Geldermalsen, Haer Ed. Mo. Gedeputeerde gaande in de expeditie te Velde.'

51 Ivor Burton is exceptional in this, identifying the generals rather than the deputies as the source of friction within the Confederate Army's high command. For details, see Burton, *The Captain-General*, 46-47, 89-90.

52 According to Liddell-Hart, there were eight instances when Dutch generals opposed, and ultimately obstructed Marlborough's attacks on French armies: twice in 1702, three times in 1703, and thrice again in 1705. He found that in none of these instances were the field deputies the source of opposition to Marlborough's plans; rather the opposition came from the generals. For details, see Liddell-Hart, 'Letter to the editor and C.T. Atkinson's response,' *Journal of the Society for Army Historical Research*, 118-19. I thank Jamel Ostwald for this reference. See also Wijn, *Het Staatsche Leger*, I, Bijlage 9, 696-702.

53 In Flanders, Lieutenant-General Baron Menno van Coehoorn commanded 14 battalions and a regiment of dragoons; at Rozendaal (near Arnhem), General of Cavalry Godard van Reede-van Ginkel (= Earl of Athlone) commanded 16 battalions and 39 squadrons, plus the 12 British battalions under Lieutenant-General John, Lord Cutts; at Goch, 16 battalions and 33 squadrons were commanded by Lieutenant-General Claude t'Serclaes, Count Tilly; in Maastricht, Lieutenant-General Daniel Wolf von Dopff had 12 battalions and 14 squadrons available for operations; and finally Prince Walrad von Nassau-Saarbrücken's 14 battalions and 12 squadrons were assembling in the camp at Mühlheim near Cologne in preparation for the siege of Kaiserswerth. For details, see Wijn, *Het Staatsche Leger*, I, 42-43.

54 Ostwald, *Vauban Under Siege*, 97; Nimwegen, *De subsistentie van het leger*, 103-06; Wijn, *Het Staatsche Leger*, I, 47-56; 63-76; 83-94.

55 Chandler, *Blenheim Preparation*, 58; Churchill, *Marlborough*, II, 234-35; Holmes, *Marlborough: England's Fragile Genius*, 219-20.

56 Chandler, *Marlborough as Military Commander*, 70-71; Churchill, *Marlborough*, II, 233-34; Holmes, *Marlborough: England's Fragile Genius*, 210-18.

57 This episode is described with great importance in Churchill, *Marlborough*, III, 128-33; Chandler, *Marlborough as Military Commander*, 100-02; Holmes, *Marlborough: England's Fragile Genius*, 225-27. Wijn, on the other hand, notes that both Marlborough and Athlone were of a like mind. Nassau-Saarbrücken was critical of their decision; he believed they should have attacked Boufflers. For details, see Wijn, *Het Staatsche Leger*, I, 124-26.

58 Holmes, *Marlborough: Britain's Fragile Genius*, 226-27; Wijn, *Het Staatsche Leger*, I, 125.

59 Snyder, *Marlborough-Godolphin*, I, 91-92 (#83).

60 *Ibidem*, I, 92-93 (#84).

61 *Ibidem*, I, 80-81, 84-85, 89-90 (#74, #78, #81); Hoff, B. van 't, *Correspondence*, 16-21 (#33, #34, #35, #40).

62 Van Alphen notes that Marlborough was jealous that William III had appointed Athlone to command allied troops in Ireland after his departure in 1690. For details, see Alphen, G. van, *De Stemming*, 104-10.

63 Geldermalsen to Heinsius, St. Hubert Lille, 1 Aug. 1702, cited in Wijn, *Het Staatsche Leger*, I, 706.

64 Snyder, *Marlborough-Godolphin*, I, 102-103; Wijn, *Het Staatsche Leger*, I, 135-40; Nimwegen, *De subsistentie van het leger*, 112-13.

65 For example Churchill, *Marlborough*, III, 136-40.

66 Snyder, *Marlborough-Godolphin*, I, 103-04 (#91).

67 Churchill states: 'The next day, the 24th, although the battle would have been much more even, Marlborough still wished to engage. But now it was the Deputies who jibbed.' Which deputies Churchill means is not clear since the only deputy with the field army, Geldermalsen, was in Grave preparing the siege of Venlo as his correspondence from that place makes clear. The Anglophone literature has accepted Churchill's interpretation of events almost verbatim, again with no consultation of Dutch sources. It is noteworthy that Holmes makes no mention of this episode since the English sources that support Churchill's conclusions (Milner and Berwick) could not have known why the Allies did not attack on 24 August. For details, see especially Churchill, *Marlborough*, III, 138-39. See also Chandler, *Marlborough as Military Commander*, 102-03; Fortescue, *Marlborough*, 33-34; Jones, *Marlborough*, 65-66. For the Dutch perspective, see Wijn, *Het Staatsche Leger*, I, 135-40.

68 Murray, *Letters and Dispatches*, I, 23-25; Wijn, *Het Staatsche Leger*, I, 138.

69 Joost van Keppel, First Earl of Albemarle, to Heinsius, Maastricht, 30 August 1702, cited in Wijn, *Het Staatsche Leger*, I, 138; see also Veenendaal, Jr., *Briefwisseling Heinsius*, I, 403 (#804).

70 Certainly it was viewed so by Parliament and by Queen Anne who elevated him to the Duke of Marlborough.

71 Burton, *The Captain-General*, 36-38.

72 Veenendaal, Jr., *Briefwisseling Heinsius*, I: 479; Wijn, *Het Staatsche Leger*, I, 183-84.

73 Alphen, G. van, *De stemming*, 102-06.

74 Goslinga, *Mémoires*, 136-37. See also Holmes, *Marlborough: England's Fragile Genius*, 317-18.

75 Waddell, 'The Administration of the English Army in Flanders,' 240-42.

76 Wijn, *Het Staatsche Leger*, I, 232-34.

77 *Ibidem*, I, 325-27; Frey and Frey, *Treaties of the War of the Spanish Succession*, 29.

78 Nimwegen, *De subsistentie van het leger*, 121-22, 175-76; Wijn, *Het Staatsche Leger*, I, 232-34.

79 Churchill maintains that the 'Great Design' was Marlborough's idea, proposed to the Dutch at the end of 1702, while Burton demonstrates that it was likely developed by the States General as a way of forcing Louis XIV to divert forces to the Low Countries away from Germany. In either case, historians agree that Marlborough took ownership of the project. For details, see Burton, *The Captain-General*, 40-41; Churchill, *Marlborough*, III: 220-23; Holmes, *Marlborough: England's Fragile Genius*, 242-42.

[80] Nimwegen, *De subsistentie van het leger,* 121-22; Wijn, *Het Staatsche Leger*, I, 266-69.

[81] The sources are unclear about how many troops the Allies had available to them for this operation. The most detailed description comes from Wijn, who notes that the Anglo-Dutch Confederate Army had 140 battalions and 175 squadrons – between 85,000 and 95,000 infantry and between 21,000 and 26,000 cavalry, depending on the figures used to calculate sizes of the respective battalions and squadrons – at the start of the 1703 campaign. Of these, 50 battalions and 20 squadrons initially were earmarked for garrison duty leaving 90 battalions and 155 squadrons available for field operations. Of those destined for the field, 52 battalions and 110 squadrons were earmarked for the allied army on the Maas at Maastricht while 33 battalions and 45 squadrons commanded by Marlborough and Obdam joined Prussian and Imperial forces at Bonn. When the Bonn operation ended, Marlborough took command of Ouwerkerk's army at Maastricht, augmenting it to 59 battalions and 130 squadrons. Coehoorn's Flanders Army, assembling at Bergen-op-Zoom in early June, had 40 battalions and an unspecified number of squadrons available for operations in Flanders. This figure obviously included garrison troops since the 33 battalions and 45 squadrons from the Bonn operation had not yet arrived from Germany. By the time the allies launched the 'Great Design,' Wijn figures the Confederate Army comprised four separate corps: Sparre's corps (13 battalions, 2 squadrons of cavalry and 4 squadrons of dragoons), Coehoorn's corps (10-14 battalions and 2 squadrons of cavalry), Obdam's 'Army of the Scheldt' (13 battalions and 26 squadrons), and Marlborough's 'Army of the Maas' (59 battalions and 130 squadrons). Based on Wijn's figures, this meant that approximately 99 battalions and 164 squadrons were in the field taking part in the 'Great Design' while approximately 39 battalions and 11 squadrons were left in garrison. For details, see Wijn, *Het Staatsche Leger*, I, 231, 270, 283, 285-86, 293.

[82] Veenendaal, Jr., *Briefwisseling Heinsius*, II, 261-62 (#672); Hoff, B. van 't, *Correspondence*, 71 (#115).

[83] According to Wijn, Coehoorn's 'army' at this time comprised 14 infantry battalions. For details, see Wijn, *Het Staatsche Leger*, I, 270.

[84] For Marlborough's plan and Coehoorn's response, see Murray, *Letters and Dispatches*, I:,105-06; Hoff, B. van 't, *Correspondence,* 70 (#113), 71-72 (#116 and #117), 73 (#119), 74-75 (#122), 75n, 76-77 (#124); Wijn, *Het Staatsche Leger,* I, 268-69.

[85] Wijn, *Het Staatsche Leger*, I, 272.

[86] Veenendaal, Jr., *Briefwisseling Heinsius*, II, 261-62 (#672).

[87] Nimwegen, *De subsistentie van het leger,* 126-28; Wijn, *Het Staatsche Leger*, I, 292-309.

[88] Churchill (and much of the Anglophone historiography) noted that Marlborough pushed for an attack despite the strength of the French positions, while Wijn maintained that all of the allied generals unanimously decided to abandon the project to force the Lines at Antwerp including Marlborough. For details, see Burton, *The Captain-General*, 45-46; Churchill, *Marlborough,* III, 234-36; Snyder, *Marlborough-Godolphin*, 213-14 (#205, #206), 219-20 (#212), 222 (#214); Wijn, *Het Staatsche Leger,* I, 323-24.

[89] *Ibidem.*

[90] *Ibidem*, I, 328-36.

[91] Burton, *The Captain-General*, 46; Churchill, *Marlborough*, III, 241-42.

[92] Burton, *The Captain-General*, 46.

[93] These were Marlborough, British Generals Churchill (Marlborough's brother), Cutts, and Lumley, the Danish Generals Württemberg and Scholten, Hanoverian Generals Sommerfeldt, Bülow, and Brunswick, the Hessian Generals the Prince of Hesse, Von Diesenberg, and Tettau. For details, see Wijn, *Het Staatsche Leger*, I, 336.

[94] To give his argument teeth, Slangenburg recalled the battle of Walcourt, where both he and Marlborough had fought the French fourteen years earlier. During the battle, the Allies, positioned behind a sunken road, held off far larger French forces. See Wijn, *Het Staatsche Leger*, I, 337.

[95] The Dutch submitted two memoranda: one from Slangenburg's '*Kleine Armee*' (formerly the Scheldt Army) and the other from the Dutch generals of the main army's 'Left Wing.' The signatories included, from Slangenburg's army Generals Slangenburg, Hompesch, Van der Nath, Friesheim and Tilly. The signatories from the Left Wing included Generals Ouwerkerk, Dopff, Dompré, Oxenstierna, Rantzau, Noyelles, Albemarle, Heukelom, St. Paul, and Prince of Anhalt-Zerbst. For details, see Wijn, *Het Staatsche Leger*, I, 336-38.

[96] *Ibidem*, 339-43.

[97] Marlborough's letters to Godolphin and Heinsius reflect his frustration with the Dutch generals' decision not to attack the lines, but make no mention of the rationale behind their decision. See Snyder, *Marlborough-Godolphin,* I, 236-39 (#232, 234, 235); Hoff, B. van 't, *Correspondence,* 889-90 (#141, especially #142).

[98] Frey and Frey, *Treaties of the War of the Spanish Succession*, 375-76.

[99] Veenendaal, Jr., *Briefwisseling Heinsius*, II, 402 (#1027).

[100] *Ibidem*, II, 423-24, (#1084); Wijn, *Het Staatsche Leger*, I, 343-44.

[101] Frey and Frey, *Treaties of the War of the Spanish Succession,* 136; Hora Siccama, *Aanteekeningen en Verbeteringen*, 201-02; Nimwegen, *De subsistentie van het leger,* 59.

[102] Veenendaal, Jr., *Briefwisseling Heinsius*, II, 422-23 (#1080).

[103] For Cadogan, see Churchill, *Marlborough,* II, 233-34; and Holmes, *England's Fragile Genius*, 210-19. For Dopff, see Frey and Frey, *Treaties of the War of the Spanish Succession*, 136; Nimwegen, *De subsistentie van het leger,* 59.

[104] Wijn, *Het Staatsche Leger*, I, 601-03.

[105] Veenendaal, Jr., *Briefwisseling Heinsius*, IV, 275 (#722), 281 (#789); Hoff, B. van 't, *Correspondence*, 198 (#316).

[106] For Marlborough's letters and an overview of the operation, see Murray, *Letters and Dispatches*, II, 192; Snyder, *Marlborough-Godolphin*, I, 463-65 (#480 and #481 and Snyder's analysis on 463); Hoff, B. van 't, *Correspondence*, 196-98 (#314 and 316).

[107] In his letter to Heinsius on 30 July 1705, Marlborough clearly obscured the facts when he writes: '...I prevailed with the generals to consent that we should march, as we did last night,

to try if we could to pass that river before the French could know it. I did promis them that if the French army should be there I would not attempt the passage til I had there consent. I am afraid this was known to M. de Villeroy, otherwais I do not think he would have ventured to be there; but God forgive those who that are better pleased when anything goes ill then when wee have success.' Under the circumstances, it is no surprise that Slangenburg and the Dutch generals grew frustrated with Marlborough, and his treatment of them. For the complete letter, see Hoff, B. van 't, *Correspondence*, 198 (#316); also see 198-99 (#318). For Wijn's analysis, see Wijn, *Het Staatsche Leger*, I, 606-10.

[108] Wijn, *Het Staatsche Leger*, I, 620-21. For Churchill's interpretation, see Churchill, *Marlborough*, IV: 229-37.

[109] Although Ouwerkerk supported Marlborough's operation, he was not present at the council-of-war, which may explain why the field deputies asked the opinions of Ouwerkerk's subordinate commanders. For details, see Wijn, *Het Staatsche Leger*, I, 625.

[110] For the details of this council-of-war, see especially Nimwegen, *De subsistentie van het leger,* 175-76; and Wijn, *Het Staatsche Leger*, I, 623-26.

[111] Snyder, *Marlborough-Godolphin*, I, 472-73 (#488).

[112] See also Hoff, B. van 't, *Correspondence*, 203-204 (19 August letter to Slingelandt), 205-07 (#327, #329, #330).

[113] Wijn, *Het Staatsche Leger*, I, 629-31, 775. See *Bijlage* 52 in the same volume, for Slingelandt's 5 September 1705 letter to Sicco van Goslinga.

[114] Wijn, *Het Staatsche Leger*, I, 634-35. Wijn states that Slangenburg was not fired; rather that the States General would not employ him in the same field army as Marlborough.

[115] Nimwegen, *De subsistentie van het leger,* 176.

[116] Wijn, *Het Staatsche Leger*, I, 633-34.

[117] Holmes, *England's Fragile Genius*, 326.

6 Marlborough and Anthonie Heinsius

[1] There is no biography of Heinsius available. Old and definitely out of date is the chapter on Heinsius in De Fouw, *Onbekende raadpensionarissen*. More modern and more informative is the introduction in vol. 1 of Veenendaal, Jr., ed., *Briefwisseling Heinsius*.

[2] Holmes, *Marlborough.*, 104, 110.

[3] His office, now next door to the Meeting Room of the First Chamber (Senate) of the Netherlands Parliament, has little changed, apart from the furniture and modern office equipment.

[4] Stork-Penning, *Het Grote Werk*, 68-69.

[5] Marlborough to Godolphin, 26 July, 1708. Snyder, *Marlborough-Godolphin*, nr.1044.

[6] Veenendaal, Jr., 'Who is in Charge Here?', 18-20.

[7] Marlborough was appointed commander in chief of English forces on the Continent on July 1st, and ambassador to the States General on June 26th, 1702.

[8] For a catalogue of all letters exchanged between Marlborough and Heinsius, see Veenendaal, Jr., *Inventaris Archief Heinsius*, 8-9. Almost all letters between the two men have been printed by Hoff, B. van 't, ed., *The Correspondence*. A few that have been missed by him have been printed by Veenendaal, *Briefwisseling Heinsius.*

[9] A number of Heinsius's letters to Marlborough are lacking for 1702.

[10] Heinsius lived in a large rented house in what is now the Kazernestraat in The Hague, but what was then known as the Denneweg. The house was demolished in the 19th century.

[11] Marlborough to Heinsius, 1 January, 1705. Hoff, B. van 't, *The Correspondence*, nr.251.

[12] Johan van den Bergh to Heinsius, 27 October 1710. Veenendaal, *Briefwisseling Heinsius*, XI, nr.548.

[13] Marlborough to his wife, 17 November 1702. Snyder, *Marlborough-Godolphin*, nr.134.

[14] Marlborough to Godolphin, 27 October 1707. *Ibidem*, nr.933. The intention mentioned was about the role of Eugene of Savoy during the next campaign.

[15] Marlborough to Heinsius, 20 June, 1707. Hoff, B. van 't, *The Correspondence*, nr.527.

[16] 'J'ay trouvé cette affaire d'assez grande importance pour en escrire un mot à V.A. en amy.' Heinsius to Marlborough, 30 June, 1706. *Ibidem*, nr.399.

[17] 'V.A. me pardonnera bien que je luy ouvre mon coeur et je proteste que je n'ay en veue que le bien des alliés, des deux nations et de V.A., et que je n'y ay aucun intérest particulier sinon que d'avoir l'honneur de vous obéir en ce que vous avés désiré mes précis sentimens.' Heinsius to Marlborough, 3 July, 1706. *Ibidem*, nr.402.

[18] Marlborough to Godolphin, 21 August, 1702. Snyder, *Marlborough-Godolphin*, nr.89.

[19] Marlborough to Godolphin, 16 April 1709, and same to same, 24 April 1709. *Ibidem*, nrs.1260, 1265.

[20] Marinus van Vrijbergen to Heinsius, 19 March, 1702: '... pour milord Marlborough on est persuadé qu'il y va d'un bon pié et qu'il fera tout ce qui dépendra de luy que la bonne intelligence entre les deux estats subsiste.' René de Saunière de l'Hermitage to Heinsius, 24 March, 1702. Veenendaal, *Briefwisseling Heinsius*, I, nrs.5, 31.

[21] 'ende ick kan niet anders oordeelen off hij is van seer goede intentie.' Heinsius to Van Vrijbergen, 9 June, 1702. *Ibidem*, I, nr.471.

[22] Marlborough to Heinsius, 27 July, 1705, and same to same, 19 July, 1706. Hoff, B. van 't, *The Correspondence*, nrs.314 and 410.

[23] 'Voicy encore une découverte que j'ay fait déchifrer à la haste. Je vous prie de la bien mesnager, autrement nous perdrions la source.' Heinsius to Marlborough, 16 March, 1708. *Ibidem*, nr.614.

[24] Through his network of informants Heinsius was already advised that Torcy was on his way to

The Hague. Heinsius to Marlborough, 8 May, 1708. *Ibidem*, nr.733.

[25] Marlborough to Heinsius, 19 June, 1709. *Ibidem*, nr.742.

[26] Marlborough to Heinsius, 28 June 1710. Heinsius's reply is of 2 July: 'Je ne croye pas selon mon petit sentiment que la conjuncture présente des affaires est si mauvaise que nous devrions hazarder le tout. V.A. ne s'explique pas sur la dite conjuncture, mais je ne voye pas ausi nullement qu'elle voudroit hazarder le tout par une bataille, si non que la conjuncture le requeroit. La guerre n'estant pas de mon mestier, je ne puis pas entrer en détail de ce qui se peut faire ou non, mais je croye que V.A. et les autres généraux dirigeront et concerteront le tout si bien selon la raison de guerre que nous en aurons une bonne issue.' *Ibidem*, nrs.860, 863.

[27] See for instance Marlborough to Godolphin, 30 May, 1707. Snyder, *Marlborough-Godolphin*, nr.795.

[28] Marlborough to Heinsius, 28 August, 1704; 23 March, 1709; 24 July, 1710. Hoff, B. van 't, *The Correspondence*, nrs.210, 728, 874.

[29] 'qu'il estimoit Mr. le conseiller pensionnaire pour des plus honnêtes hommes qu'il y eust au monde et qui alloit le plus droit . . . il estoit le seul au monde de qui on le peust dire et qu'il estoit le centre.' Saunière de l'Hermitage to Abel Tassin d'Alonne (Heinsius's secretary), 1 March, 1709. Veenendaal, *Briefwisseling Heinsius*, X, nr.622.

[30] Marlborough to Godolphin, 30 October, 1703. Snyder, *Marlborough-Godolphin*, nr.256.

[31] 'Je suis bien aise que vous avez pris la résolution de demeurer à la teste de l'armée.' Heinsius to Marlborough, 9 July and 23 August, 1710. Hoff, B. van 't, *The Correspondence*, nrs.868 and 892.

[32] Heinsius to Marlborough, 8 May, 1709. *Ibidem*, nr.733.

[33] Heinsius to Marlborough, 3 May, 1710; Marlborough to Heinsius, 8 May, 1710. *Ibidem*, nrs.837, 839.

[34] Heinsius to Sicco van Goslinga, 27 August, 1707; Heinsius to Marinus van Vrijbergen, 25 October, 1707. Veenendaal, *Briefwisseling Heinsius*, VI, nrs.998, 1207.

[35] Albemarle to Heinsius, 9 March, 1709; Heinsius to Albemarle, 11 March, 1709. Veenendaal, *Briefwisseling Heinsius*, X, nrs.676, 680.

[36] Marlborough to Heinsius, 28 June, 1706. Hoff, B. van 't, *The Correspondence*, nr.397.

[37] Marlborough to Godolphin, 1 July, 1706. Snyder, *Marlborough-Godolphin*, nr.606.

[38] 'V.A. est si clairvoyante et si zélé pour la cause commune qu'il n'est pas nécessaire que je m'élargisse davantage sur ce sujet, estant persuadé qu'Elle tâchera de prévenir tout ce qui pouroit causer le moindre ombrage et diminuer le fruit de l'avantage que le bon Dieu nous a donné.' Heinsius to Marlborough, 30 June, 1706. Hoff, B. van 't, *The Correspondence*, nr.399.

[39] '. . . je prie V.A. de considérer à quelle jalousie une telle affaire pouroit estre sujette tant en Angleterre que dans ce païs-cy et quelles suites ces jalousies pouroient produire dans l'un et l'autre païs et aussi ailleurs, au préjudice de la cause commune et des avantages que nous venons d'emporter.' Heinsius to Marlborough, 3 July, 1706. *Ibidem*, nr.402.

[40] 'Cette nouvelle instance doit convaincre Leurs Hautes Puissances combien j'ay à coeur leur intérêt et satisfaction particulière, comme celui de la cause commune.' Marlborough to Heinsius, 10 July, 1706. *Ibidem*, nr.406.

[41] '. . . en y adjoutant: voilà cette affaire finie et des expressions fortes et obligeantes des sentimens qu'il avoit pour Mess. les Estats Généraux et pour la liberté et le salut de notre chère patrie.' Veenendaal, [Sr.], *Dagboek Cuper*, 62-63.

[42] Heinsius to Hop, 14 July, 1706. Veenendaal, *Briefwisseling Heinsius*, V, nr.737.

[43] 'Le duc a beau faire le content, je lis le chagrin dans ses yeux.' Goslinga to Heinsius, 17 July, 1706. Veenendaal, *Briefwisseling Heinsius*, V, nr.753.

[44] 'Le duc est d'une dissimulation profonde, d'autant plus dangereuse qu'il la couvre par des manières et des expressions qui paroissent exprimer la franchise meme. Il a une ambition demesurée, est d'une avarice sordide et qui influe dans toute sa conduite,' and: 'Voilà des foiblesses qui ne contrebalancent pas pourtant les rares talents de ce véritablement grand homme.' Evertsz and Delprat, *Mémoires de Sicco van Goslinga*, 43.

[45] Marlborough to Heinsius, 29 April, 1711. Hoff, B. van 't, *The Correspondence*, nr.942.

[46] Marlborough to Heinsius, 29 June, 1705. Heinsius to Marlborough, 1 July 1705: 'Vous avés grande raison d'estre chagrin de tout ce que vous est arrivé sur la Mozelle, mais non pas à un point de vouloir quiter le commandement pour l'année qui vient. J'espère que vous n'y songerés pas et que le bon Dieu vous bénira encore tellement dans cette campagne que vous rentrerés avec plaisir et contentement dans la suivante.' *Ibidem*, nrs.299, 301.

[47] 'J'appris hier par un billet de M. Cardonel que vous [vous] trouviés un peu incommodé. J'espère que cela sera passé et que vous vous serés remis.' Heinsius to Marlborough, 19 September, 1709; Marlborough to Heinsius, 15 September, 1706. *Ibidem*, nrs.795, 445.

[48] Marlborough to Heinsius, 7 May, 1713. *Ibidem*, nr.1009.

[49] Marlborough to Heinsius, 7 May, 1714. *Ibidem*,

7 Marlborough as an Enemy

1 Bérenger, *Turenne*, 401-10.

2 Holmes, *Marlborough: England's Fragile Genius*, 78.

3 '... rendre aux Français leurs propres leçons.' Michelet, *Précis de l'histoire moderne*, 238.

4 Correspondence between the King, the offices of the Secretary of State for War, army officers, and civilians in charge of logistics is preserved at the Service Historique de la Défense (SHD), in sub-series A1 of the War Archives (Archives de la Guerre: AG). The correspondence of the offices of the Secretary of State for Foreign Affairs is preserved in the archives of the Ministry of Foreign Affairs (Ministère des Affaires Étrangères: AE).

5 Jones, *Marlborough*, 44.

6 '... homme inquiet, et qui certainement ne vaut pas mieux pour la guerre que ceux auxquels on le préfère.' Sourches, marquis de, *Mémoires du marquis de Sourches*, vii, 311 (9 July 1702).

7 'qui aime à batailler.' SHD AG, A1 1750, no. 134, memoir by Chamlay on German affairs, Versailles, 17 August 1704.

8 '... respire les occasions d'acquérir de la gloire.' Sourches, *op. cit.*, vii, 326 (22 July 1702).

9 Corvisier, *Louvois*, 364.

10 '... en quelque sorte invincibles.' SHD AG, A1 1750, no. 134, memoir by Chamlay on German affairs, Versailles, 17 August 1704.

11 'Il serait à désirer que milord de Marlebo-rought [sic.] [confirme] les Allemands dans l'habitude dans laquelle ils sont de se laisser battre par les Français [...]. Ce serait une chose nouvelle que de voir une armée ennemie avoir avantage sur la nôtre.' SHD AG, A1 1746, no. 19, Chamillart to Tallard, Versailles, 4 June 1704.

12 Sourches, *op. cit.*, ix, 52 (20 August 1704).

13 'Il courait des bruits confus et peu assurés, comme par exemple qu'il y avait eu onze bataillons taillés en pièces sur le champ de bataille, outre les vingt-six qui étaient prisonniers de guerre tout entiers ; que la cavalerie et la gendarmerie, qui étaient l'élite des troupes du Roi, avaient plié sans résistance [...] Cela paraissait incroyable.' Sourches, *op. cit.*, ix, 53 (22 August 1704).

14 Petitfils, *Louis XIV*, 608.

15 'Mes troupes n'ont point perdu [de batailles] de tout mon règne, à nombre à peu près égal.' SHD AG, A1 1933, 36, Louis XIV to Villeroy, Meudon, 6 May 1706, published in Pelet and de Vault, *Mémoires militaires relatifs à la succession d'Espagne sous Louis XIV*, vi, 17–19.

16 'C'est un aventurier mortifié du peu de succès de sa campagne, et qui ne cherche qu'à tout hasarder.' SHD AG, A1 1838, no. 167, Villeroy to Chamillart, camp at Berlaer, 30 September 1705, published in Pelet and de Vault, *op. cit.*, v, 89–93.

17 'Vous n'aurez pas de peine à obtenir de moi que je n'aie qu'une médiocre opinion de la capacité du duc de Marlborough; ce qu'il a fait pendant cette campagne détruit, à mon sens, la grande opinion qu'on avait eu de lui après la bataille d'Höchstett, dont le gain doit être bien plutôt attribué au seul hasard qu'à la capacité des généraux ennemis; il est vrai qu'ils surent profiter de notre mauvaise disposition.' SHD AG, A1 1829, 2nd part, 1st section, 30, Chamillart to Villeroy, Versailles, 6 September 1705, published in Pelet and de Vault, *op. cit.*, v, 608–09.

18 'Milord Marlborough n'est qu'un fanfaron et il faut espérer que les fanfaronnades finiront bientôt.' Cited in Duc de Noailles, *Mémoires politiques et militaires*, ii–iii, 361.

19 'J'étais à Versailles: jamais on ne vit un tel trouble ni une pareille consternation.' Saint-Simon, *Mémoires*, xiii, 380.

20 '... funeste nouvelle.' Sourches, *op. cit.*, x, 85 (26 May 1706).

21 'On a vraiment besoin maintenant de consolation, car je n'ai jamais vu de temps plus malheureux depuis les trente-cinq ans que je suis en France. Il ne se passe de jour où l'on apprenne quelque mauvaise nouvelle.' Letter from the Princess Palatine to the Duchess of Hanover, Versailles, 30 May 1706, in *Lettres de la princesse Palatine*, Paris, 2004, 368.

22 'Je ferai tout mon possible pour ranimer [les troupes], mais ce ne sera pas une petite affaire. Si j'en puis venir à bout, car tout le monde ici est prêt d'ôter son chapeau quand on nomme le nom de Malbouroug [sic] [...]. Je ne désespère pas cependant de les ranimer par de bons discours et de bons exemples, et je vous puis assurer que je n'oublierai rien pour cela, mais à vous parler franchement la besogne est encore plus difficile que je ne l'avais cru.' SHD AG, A1 1939, no. 36, Vendôme to Chamillart, Valenciennes, 5 August 1706.

23 '... pour y aller voir le fameux général.' Archives Nationales G7 1778, no. 198, Paparel to Desmarets, Le Quesnoy, 9 September 1706.

24 '... ceux qui croient à la sorcellerie penseront que [Marlborough] a fait un pacte avec le diable pour avoir un bonheur aussi inouï.' Letter from the Princesse Palatine to the Duchess of Hanover, Versailles, 30 May 1706, in Lettres de la princesse Palatine, *op. cit.*, 368.

25 'Abattues.' SHD AG, A1 2086, no. 314, Le Blanc to Chamillart, Nieuwpoort, 18 December 1708.

26 SHD AG, A1 2085, no. 171, Bernières to Chamillart, camp at Saussoy, 22 September 1708.

27 SHD AG, A1 2083, no. 49, Vendôme to the King, camp at Pont à Marque, 13 September 1708.

28 SHD AG, A1 2085, no. 59, Bernières to Chamillart, Tournai, 12 July 1708; SHD AG, A1 2085, no. 62, Chamillart to Bernières, Fontainebleau, 14 July 1708.

29 'Villeroy voulait combattre / Car il est brave garçon / Est allé à la rencontre / De Marleborou, se dit-on [...] / Mais quand il fut en présence / Qu'il entendit ses canons / Il eut si grand peur aux fesses / qu'il fit tout sur ses tallons.' Bibliothèque Nationale de France, French manuscript 12693, fol. 403–06.

30 'Quel plaisir pour le Roy d'Espagne / De savoir son frère en campagne, / Accompagné d'un directeur. / Malboroug, ta perte est certaine, / Par le conseil du confesseur, / Et la valeur du capitaine.' Bibliothèque Nationale de France, French manuscript 12626, 160.

31 See O'Reilly, 'A Fall from Grace: Vendôme, Bourgogne, and the Aftermath of Oudenaarde,' and Oury, 'La bataille d'Audenarde du côté français.

32 'Marlborough ce n'est pas à toi / Que tu dois ta double victoire / C'est à Tallard, à Villeroy / Qu'en appartient toute la gloire. / Tu dois un compliment général / A l'un et l'autre général.' Bibliothèque Nationale de France, French manuscript 12693, fol. 457.

33 'Votre Majesté, Sire, aura vu [...] le malheureux succès de l'action dudit jour 11, mais combien ce malheur était accompagné de gloire pour les troupes et les armes de Votre Majesté [...]. Elle le saura par les relations mêmes des ennemis, qui ne peuvent assez exalter, ni vanter l'audace, la valeur, la fermeté et l'opiniâtreté des troupes de Votre Majesté, dont ils ont ressenti bien rudement les effets [...]. Enfin, Sire, la suite des malheurs arrivés depuis quelques années aux armes de Votre Majesté avait tellement humilié la nation française qu'on n'osait quasi plus s'avouer Français: j'ose vous assurer, Sire, que le nom français n'a jamais été tant en estime ni peut-être plus craint qu'il l'est présentement dans toute l'armée des Alliés.' SHD AG, A1 2152, no. 181, Boufflers to the King, camp at Ruesne, 13 September 1709, published in Pelet and de Vault, *op. cit.*, ix, 365–69. See also Corvisier, *La Bataille de Malplaquet, 1709*, 99.

34 '... parlent avec admiration de la beauté de notre retraite, et de la fierté avec laquelle elle a été faite. Ils disent qu'ils ont reconnu en cette action les anciens Français.' SHD AG, A1 2152, no. 181, Boufflers to the King, camp at Ruesne, 13 September 1709, published in Pelet and de Vault, *op. cit.*, ix, 365–69.

35 '... meilleures troupes du monde.'

36 '...élevé aux nues.' Villars, *Mémoires*, ii, 259–60.

37 After the battle Villars explained to the King that he would have won if not for his wound. But Voltaire insists that the Marshal's contemporaries did not at all believe his assertion. Voltaire, *Le Siècle de Louis XIV*, xx, 83.

38 'Ces prodiges d'erreurs, d'aveuglement, de ténèbres, entassées et enchaînées ensemble, si grossiers, si peu croyables, et dont un seul de moins eût tout changé de face, retracent bien, quoique dans un genre moins miraculeux, ces victoires et ces défaites immenses que Dieu accordait ou dont il affligeait son peuple suivant qu'il lui était fidèle, ou que son culte en était abandonné.' Saint-Simon, *op. cit.*, xii, 201.

39 '... pour que l'armée de France pût être battue, il fallait que, dans la situation où elle était, de vingt fautes que l'on pouvait commettre, l'on en fît dix-neuf.' Mérode-Westerloo, *Mémoires*, i, 2.

40 SHD AG, A1 1756, no. 24, Villeroi to Chamillart, Offenburg, 11 August 1704; SHD AG, A1 1756, no. 29, Villeroi to the King, Offenburg, 14 August 1704.

41 '... ni assez d'étendue ni de fermeté dans la tête.' SHD AG, A1 1962, no. 255, Vendôme to Chamillart, camp at Castagnaro, 16 June 1706, published in Pelet and de Vault, *op. cit.*, vi, 639–42.

42 '... très médiocre utilité.' SHD AG, A1 1963, no. 27, Marsin to the King, Strasbourg, 5 July 1706.

43 To this list we may add the Duke de La Feuillade, who owed his dizzying ascent to the title of duke and peer of France, as well as his marriage, to the daughter of the Secretary of State for War. La Feuillade's progress came to a brutal halt against the walls of Turin, a city he proved unable to take after a siege of more than three months. La Feuillade never squared off the Duke of Marlborough directly.

44 Prince Eugene insisted on this point in 1706, when describing Vendôme's character to Marlborough, so as to prepare the English general to meet his future adversary: 'Once he makes a resolution, he follows through, letting nothing deter him [...]. Confound his measures even a little, and he will struggle to recover.' ('Quand il a pris une résolution, [il] la suit, sans que rien l'en puisse détourner [...]. Pour peu qu'on lui rompe ses mesures, il a grand peine à y remédier.') Prince Eugene to the Duke of Marlborough, Castelbaldo, 10 July 1706, published in *Feldzüge des Prinzen Eugen*, viii, Suppl., 186–87.

45 Saint-Simon, *op. cit.*, xvi, 178.

46 '... avoient épuisé leur savoir faire à mettre [l'armée] en bataille sur deux lignes.' Bibliothèque Nationale de France, French manuscript 23323, fol. 229–43, 'relation de la bataille de Ramilly, donnée le 23 may, jour de la Pentecoste, en 1706' (account of the battle of Ramillies, given on 23 May, day of Pentacoste, in 1706'), s.l., s.d.

47 For more on these points, see the chapters by Alan Guy and Jamel Ostwald in this volume.

48 De Mérode-Westerloo, *op. cit.*, i, 301.

49 SHD AG, A1 1933, no. 36, Louis XIV to Villeroy, Meudon, 6 May 1706, published in Pelet and de Vault, *op. cit.*, vi, 17–19.

50 Luxembourg defended himself by citing his own army's lack of supplies, which would have prevented an advance against the retreating enemy. Fonck, 'François-Henri de Montmorency-Bouteville, Marshal Luxembourg (1628–1695)', unpublished thesis, ii, 208.

51 Bibliothèque de l'Arsenal, manuscript 2738, 'Éloge de monsieur le duc de Vendosme,' 72.

52 For more on the subject see Oury, C., 'La prise de décision militaire à la fin du règne de Louis XIV: l'exemple du siège de Turin, 1706,' forthcoming.

53 Annex C of 'Relation über die vorgeweste Unterredung in Haag, Düsseldorf und Hannover,' Vienna, 8 May 1708, published in *Feldzüge des Prinzen Eugen*, x, suppl., 81–84, no. 45.

54 'Je suis persuadé qu'ils joindront; et si c'est en dessein de faire une répétition d'Hocstet, ils pourraient bien se tromper dans le calcul, car je vous réponds que nous les battrons.' SHD AG, A1 2080, no. 291, Vendôme to the King, Braine l'Alleu, 15 June 1708.

55 '... sortes de guerres.' SHD AG, A1 2080, no. 226, La Viérue to Chamillart, Soignies, 29 May 1708.

56 Corvisier, *Louvois*, 364.

57 '... mis en brassières.' Saint-Simon, *op. cit.*, xiii, 342–43.

58 Fonck, 'François-Henri de Montmorency-Bouteville, maréchal de Luxembourg'; Pénicaut, *Michel Chamillart*, 518; Cénat, J.-P., *'Chamlay'*.

59 Rowlands, *The Dynastic State and the Army under Louis XIV*; Oury, 'Les défaites françaises de la guerre de Succession d'Espagne', unpublished thesis, École des Chartes, Paris, 2005.

60 As Prince Eugene would say: 'Nothing will ever get done without a formidable combined army. Past experience, in Bavaria [at the battle of Blenheim], has shown what combined forces are capable of.' ('Sans combiner une armée formidable, on ne fera jamais rien, et l'expérience passée a fait voir en Bavière [à l'occasion de la bataille

de Blenheim] ce que les forces combinées sont capables de faire.'), *Feldzüge des Prinzen Eugen*, x, suppl., 46–50, no. 34.

[61] There were nevertheless a few occasions during the War of the Spanish Succession when a competent general was relieved of his duties for political reasons. One such was at the end of 1703, when Villars, despite the success of his campaign, had to quit the army of Germany, because of bad relations with the Elector. But Villars would serve the following year, in the Cévennes. Certain generals were victims of opposing cabals at court. Very different from the parties in England, these cabals were largely unstructured, even vague, networks of influence. They could include members of the royal family, ministerial leaders, and war chiefs, all seeking mutual advancement through the elimination of adversaries. The Duke of Orléans, close to the 'Ministers' cabal, was dispatched to Spain in 1707 and 1708. He quickly became very popular, thanks to his military successes and high birth. Indeed, he even began talking about possibly inheriting the Iberian crown himself, and thus offering a compromise to settle things between Philip V and Archduke Charles. Philip V, represented by his father, the Grand Dauphin, and by the Duke of Vendôme (both members of the 'Meudon' cabal), as well as by Madame de Maintenon (of the 'Seigneurs' cabal), raised a ruckus before Louis XIV. The King ordered the Duke of Orléans to return to France in 1708 and never again entrusted him with troops. That same year the Duke of Vendôme also fell into disgrace with the King after his disastrous campaign. In this case too royal disfavor had less to do with military failure than with a lack of restraint among the Duke's partisans, for they had slandered the Duke of Burgundy, heir to the throne of France – and eminent representative of the 'Ministers' cabal. Yet in 1710 Vendôme was once again called to service, in Spain, at the side of Philip V, whom he had supported two years earlier. On the cabals, see Le Roy Ladurie, *Saint-Simon ou le système de la Cour*.

[62] Bély, *Espions et ambassadeurs*, 363.

[63] AE Hollande 202, fol. 177–202, 'Mémoire du roi pour le sieur marquis d'Alègre, lieutenant général des armées de Sa Majesté, 6 octobre 1705, à Fontainebleau,' published in *Recueil des instructions données aux ambassadeurs*, xxii, Hollande, 131–51.

[64] '… faire la guerre suivant leur méthode.' *Ibidem*, 146.

[65] '… le seul moyen de gagner.' *Ibidem*, 147.

[66] Legrelle, *La diplomatie française et la Guerre de Succession d'Espagne*, v, 250.

[67] Maximilian-Emmanuel's exact title in the Low Countries changed over time. In December 1691 he had been named governor general by Charles II, who hoped thus to ensure a better defense of those territories. The Elector's own military qualities, and the Bavarian troops that he took with him, were the guarantors. But in May 1702 Louis XIV considered naming the Duke of Burgundy as vicar-general, making him almost equal in rank to his brother Philip V and, in any case, superior to the Elector. France would thus secure a grip on the Low Countries. But this was counting out the implacable opposition of the Elector. Needing to keep him in the party of the Two Crowns, the French were obliged to grant him – through Philip V – the letter patent of vicar general. The term governor-general, improper but more common at the time, has nevertheless been used here. Pirenne, *Histoire de Belgique des origines à nos jours*, iii, 236; Kalken, F. van, *La fin du régime espagnol aux Pays-Bas*, 157–58.

[68] Legrelle, *La diplomatie*, v, 275.

[69] AE Bavière 58, fol. 209–18, Louis XIV to Rouillé, Versailles, 14 August 1706.

[70] Jones, *Marlborough*, 212.

[71] See Chamillart's remark to the negotiator Hennequin: 'Your first letters gave me great hopes of a great success in your negotiations. The last leaves me no room to doubt that Marlborough has ruined it, and that the English, as I had warned, have made themselves the absolute masters of the Dutch government.' ('Vos premières lettres m'avaient donné de grandes espérances d'un heureux succès dans votre négociation. La dernière ne me laisse pas lieu de douter que le mylord Marlborough ne l'ait traversé [i.e. ruiné], et que les Anglais, comme je vous l'avais mandé, ne se soient absolument rendus les maîtres du gouvernement d'Hollande.') SHD AG, A1 1940, no. 10, Chamillart to Hennequin, Versailles, 3 October 1706.

[72] Legrelle, *Une négociation inconnue entre Berwick et Marlborough (1708–1709)*, 15.

[73] *Ibidem*, 17–19.

[74] AE Angleterre 226, fol. 157, Marlborough to Berwick, 30 October 1708, published *ibidem*, 21–22. The French now planned to offer the English general up to three million, without neglecting to extend their generosity, to the tune of three hundred thousand livres, to the Duke's secretary, Cardonnel.

[75] '… l'amitié […] promise il y a deux ans par le marquis d'Alègre.'

[76] *Ibidem*, 58.

[77] Berwick, duke of, *Mémoires du maréchal de Berwick*, ii, 138–39.

[78] 'Le duc de Marlborough ne traversera pas [i.e. ne nuira pas à] la négociation, nonobstant l'intérêt particulier qu'il paraissait avoir à la continuation de la guerre. On ne peut presque douter qu'il ne désire présentement la conclusion de la paix, soit parce qu'il voit augmenter le nombre de ses ennemis en Angleterre et qu'il craint qu'un événement malheureux pour lui ne leur donne les moyens de l'accabler, soit parce qu'il est jaloux de la réputation que le prince Eugène de Savoie s'est acquise aux dépens de la sienne, soit parce qu'il est dégoûté de la défiance que les Hollandais témoignent à son égard et de leur persévérance à s'opposer à l'emploi, que l'archiduc a voulu plusieurs fois lui donner, de gouverneur des Pays-Bas. Enfin, quelque raison nouvelle qu'il y ait à lui faire désirer la paix, on doit croire qu'il la souhaite, et depuis quelques mois il a fait plusieurs démarches empressées pour le persuader.' AE Hollande 221, fol. 61–84, 'Mémoire du roi pour servir d'instruction au sieur président Rouillé sur la conduite et le discours que Sa Majesté veut qu'il tienne aux conférences secrètes pour la paix générale,' Versailles, 3 March 1709, published in *Recueil des instructions*, xxii, Hollande, 185–223.

[79] Legrelle, *La diplomatie*, v, 472.

[80] Torcy, *Mémoires*, i, 166–68 and 184–87.

[81] '… chercher une bataille à quelque prix que ce fût'; '… pénétrer dans le royaume.' Villars, *op.*

cit., ii-iii, 264.

82 AE Hollande supplément 8, fol. 82–99, 'Instruction donnée au sieur marquis d'Huxelles, maréchal de France, chevalier des ordres du roi, etc., et au sieur abbé de Polignac, conseiller ordinaire de Sa Majesté en son conseil d'État, auditeur de la Rote, revêtu de ses pouvoirs pour traiter de la paix générale,' Versailles, 4 March 1710, published in *Recueil des instructions*, xxii, Hollande, 232–67.

83 '... parce qu'elle est conforme à son intérêt.' *Ibidem*, 265.

84 'Il assurera les plénipotentiaires de son zèle pour le service du roi. Ils doivent répondre honnêtement aux protestations qu'il ne manquera pas de leur faire de sa franchise et de sa bonne foi. Mais [...] Sa Majesté est bien persuadée que les sieurs maréchal d'Huxelles et abbé de Polignac n'y seront pas, aussi, trompés.' *Ibidem*.

85 'Ses discours ne trompent personne en Angleterre non plus qu'en Hollande.'

86 'If [England] resolves to make peace, the Duke of Marlborough's objections will come to naught. He dare not disobey. In vain will his confidants point out that he will be giving up huge profits and exposing himself to the hatred and vengeance of his countrymen. He will have to sacrifice his own interests to the laws of his country. If, instead, she wants to continue the war, the Duke of Marlborough will owe her the same obedience. Moreover, the sums that the King wished to offer would fall short of compensating him for what he would believe he stood to lose from relinquishing the fruits of a campaign. Leading the Allied armies is very different from simply being in England and enjoying that rank to which fortune has seen fit to elevate you.' ('Si [l'Angleterre] prend la résolution de faire la paix, les oppositions du duc de Marlborough seront vaines. Il n'osera pas désobéir. Ses confidents auront beau lui faire voir qu'il va perdre des profits immenses et se trouver exposé à la haine et à la vengeance de ses compatriotes, il faudra sacrifier son intérêt particulier aux lois de sa patrie. Si elle veut au contraire continuer la guerre, il faut non seulement la même obéissance de la part du duc de Marlborough, mais il est encore à considérer que les sommes que le roi lui destinait ne le dédommageraient pas de ce qu'il croirait perdre en perdant le fruit d'une campagne, et que la situation est très différente, où de se trouver à la tête des armées de la ligue ou simplement en Angleterre dans le rang où la fortune a pris plaisir à l'élever.') *Ibidem*, 265–66.

87 '... quelques nuages qui s'élevaient en Angleterre sur la faveur de milord Marlborough.' Villars, *op. cit.*, ii-iii, 339–40.

88 '... l'ambition meurtrière [...] sacrifiait les peuples à son intérêt.' de Noailles, *op. cit.*, ii-iii, 232.

89 Nordmann, C., 'Louis XIV and the Jacobites,' in: Hatton, *Louis XIV and Europe*, 90.

90 Duclos, *Mémoires secrets*, 57.

91 Marquis Biron, taken prisoner at Oudenaarde, relates that the Duke of Marlborough had publicly asked him for news of the Pretender, before confiding 'that he could not resist taking a great interest in the young prince' ('qu'il ne pouvait s'empêcher de s'intéresser beaucoup en ce jeune prince'). Saint-Simon, *op. cit.*, xvi, 200.

92 '... de petite noblesse et fort pauvre,' qui devint 'pair d'Angleterre, capitaine général des armées, [....] prince de l'Empire et de Mindelheim'; '... sa vie, ses actions sont si connues qu'on peut s'en taire.' Saint-Simon, *op. cit.*, xl, 272.

93 '... plus heureux capitaine de son siècle.' *Ibidem*.

94 In his *Siècle de Louis XIV*, Voltaire considers that Marlborough was 'more of a king than William had been, just as political, and a greater captain' ('plus roi que n'avait été Guillaume, aussi politique que lui, et beaucoup plus grand capitaine'). He also remarked of Marlborough's embassy to Altranstädt: 'Among all those ambassadors came the famous John, Duke of Marlborough, on behalf of Anne, queen of Great Britain. That man, who has never laid siege to a city that he didn't capture, or fought a battle that he did not win, was at St James a deft courtier, in parliament a party chief, and in foreign countries the ablest negotiator of his century. He did France as much damage by his wit as by his arms. We have heard the secretary of the States General, Mr. Fagel, a man of great merit, say that more than once the States General had resolved to oppose what the Duke of Marlborough intended to propose, and then the Duke would arrive, address them in his very bad French, and persuade them all. This is what Lord Bolingbroke has confirmed to me.' ('Parmi tous ces ambassadeurs vint le fameux Jean, duc de Marlborough, de la part d'Anne, reine de la Grande-Bretagne. Cet homme qui n'a jamais assiégé de ville qu'il n'ait prise, ni donné de bataille qu'il n'ait gagnée, était à Saint-James un adroit courtisan ; dans le parlement un chef de parti; dans les pays étrangers le plus habile négociateur de son siècle. Il avait fait autant de mal à la France par son esprit que par ses armes. On a entendu dire au secrétaire des États Généraux, M. Fagel, homme d'un très grand mérite, que plus d'une fois les États Généraux ayant résolu de s'opposer à ce que le duc de Marlborough devait leur proposer, le duc arrivait, leur parlait en français, langue dans laquelle il s'exprimait très mal, et les persuadait tous : c'est ce que le lord Bolingbroke m'a confirmé.') Voltaire, *Le Siècle*, 19; Voltaire, *Histoire de Charles XII*, 76.

95 Take, for example, the writings of Guibert, who does not include Marlborough in his list of great generals contemporary with the Sun King: 'The armies [of the time of Louis XIV], harder to move and feed, became harder to command. [But] Condé, Luxembourg, Eugene, Catinat, Vendôme, Villars, with their superior genius, could stir such masses.' ('Les armées [de l'époque de Louis XIV], moins faciles à mouvoir et à nourrir, en devinrent plus difficiles à commander. [Mais] Condé, Luxembourg, Eugène, Catinat, Vendôme, Villars, par l'ascendant de leur génie, surent remuer ces masses.') Guibert, *Écrits militaires, 1772–1790*, 73.

96 'Make offensive war, like Alexander, Hannibal, Caesar, Gustave-Adolphe, Turenne, Prince Eugene, and Frederick. Read and reread the history of their eighty-three campaigns. Model yourself after them. It is the only way to become a great captain, and fathom the secrets of the army. Your mind thus quickened will make you reject every maxim contrary to the maxims of these great men.' ('Faites la guerre offensive comme Alexandre, Hannibal, César, Gustave-Adolphe, Turenne, le prince Eugène et Frédéric;

lisez, relisez l'histoire de leurs quatre-vingt-trois campagnes, modelez-vous sur eux; c'est le seul moyen de devenir grand capitaine, et de surprendre les secrets de l'armée; votre génie ainsi éclairé vous fera rejeter des maximes opposées à celles de ces grands hommes.') Cited by Coutau-Bégarie, *Traité de stratégie*, 281.

[97] '… grand général.' Las Cases, *Mémorial de Sainte-Hélène*, 691.

[98] '… capitaine et diplomate.' *Ibidem*, 821.

[99] '… sans esprit, sans générosité, sans foi.' *Ibidem*, 691.

[100] '… un grand homme appartient à tous les peuples et à tous les siècles.' Dutems,, *Histoire de Jean Churchill, duc de Marlborough*, i, i.

[101] '… se glorifiait d'appartenir par son origine à la nation française.' *Ibidem*, i, iv.

[102] 'Quoique les Français n'aient pas besoin de chercher hors de leur pays de grands maîtres dans l'art de vaincre, ils ne seront pas fâchés de pouvoir faire sous Marlborough l'apprentissage de l'art de la guerre (…), ceux qui se destinent à la carrière des négociations trouveront également en lui un guide et un maître; car il fut aussi grand homme d'État que grand capitaine.' *Ibidem*, i, xii.

[103] *Gazette national ou Moniteur universel*, Paris, 12 August 1808, 890–92.

[104] 'Indeed, the campaign seems to have offered Marlborough nothing but easy triumphs. He faced an old king, bereft of ministers and generals whose glory had shone bright throughout Europe. Turenne, Condé, Luxembourg, and Louvois were no more, replaced by Chamillard, Tallard, Villeroi, and Marsin. Villars and Catinat were all but disgraced. The courts of Versailles and Meudon were busy with intrigues proper to women and religious cabals.' ('Cette campagne, en effet, semble n'avoir présenté que des triomphes faciles à Marlborough. Il avait affaire à un Roi vieilli, privé des ministres et des généraux qui avaient rempli l'Europe de l'éclat de leur gloire. Turenne, Condé, Luxembourg, Louvois n'existaient plus; Chamillard, Tallard, Villeroi, Marsin, les remplaçaient ; Villars, Catinat étaient presque disgraciés ; les cours de Versailles et de Meudon s'occupaient d'intrigues de femmes et de cabales religieuses.') *Ibidem*.

[105] '… n'avait pas le génie de la guerre.' Duvivier, *Observations sur la Guerre de la Succession d'Espagne*, i, 356.

[106] 'Issu d'une obscure famille et parti des conditions inférieures, il ne parvint qu'à force d'adresse à occuper les plus hautes positions; ses basses intrigues et ses trahisons contribuèrent autant, sinon plus, à son élévation que ses talents militaires. Marlborough est le type accompli de l'ambitieux, du courtisan qui ne recule pas même devant l'infamie, et pour qui il n'y a pas de déshonneur s'il y a profit.' Larousse, *Grand dictionnaire universel*, x, 1223. Also to the point are the biographical dictionaries of Michaud and Hoefer: 'Eugene, Marlborough, and the Pensionary Heinsius formed a triumvirate who wanted war for personal reasons, and who succeeded in prolonging it, through their credibility.' ('Eugène, Marlborough et le grand pensionnaire Heinsius formaient un triumvirat qui voulait la guerre par des vues personnelles, et qui, par le crédit dont ils jouissaient, réussissait à la prolonger.') Michaud, *Biographie universelle, ancienne et moderne*, xxvii, 4–12. 'Marlborough's ambition had an interest in vigorously pursuing the war. For him it was a source of glory, not to mention power and riches, which he liked even more.' ('L'ambition de Marlborough était intéressée à poursuivre vigoureusement la guerre: c'était pour lui une source de gloire et, ce qu'il appréciait encore plus, de puissance et de richesses.') Hoefer, *Nouvelle biographie générale*, xxxiii, col. 834–50.

[107] '… le teint trouble et faux qui dén once les âmes fangeuses.' Michelet, *Histoire de France*, xvi, 161.

[108] Belloc, *Le Génie militaire du duc de Marlborough*.

[109] '… chef de guerre génial.' Bodinier, 'Marlborough.'

[110] '… un excellent soldat ainsi qu'un redoutable tacticien'; '[ni] l'audace, ni le génie militaire du prince Eugène.' Petitfils, *op. cit.*, 594. The author goes on to denounce 'a shamelessly ambitious man, a high-flying bird of prey, with neither morals nor scruples, hungry for honor and money, willing to do anything to achieve his goal' ('un ambitieux sans vergogne, rapace de haut vol, sans morale ni scrupule, assoiffé d'honneur et d'argent, prêt à tout pour atteindre son but').

[111] 'grand Eugène.' The expression appears in Duvivier, *op. cit.*, 47, 80, 176, 236, 244, and 342.

[112] '… l'un des plus grands capitaines des temps modernes.' Larousse, *Grand Dictionnaire*, vii, 1107.

[113] '… prince plein d'audace et de vivacité, […] philosophe […] mécène.' Petitfils, *op. cit.*, 593.

[114] '… cadet de la maison de Savoie, mais fils du comte de Soissons et d'une nièce de Mazarin, peut être appelé français.' Michelet, *Précis de l'histoire moderne*, 238.

[115] Larousse, *Grand Dictionnaire*, x, 1001–2.

[116] Goncourt, E. and J. de, *Histoire de Marie-Antoinette*, 307.

[117] He nevertheless regrets that 'ridicule […] stigmatizes everything, even victory' ('le ridicule […] stigmatise tout jusqu'à la victoire'). Las Cases, *Mémorial de Saint-Hélène*, 821.

[118] '… homme le plus fatal à la France qu'on n'ait vu depuis plusieurs siècles.' Voltaire, *Le Siècle*, 18.

8 'The only thing that could save the Empire'

[1] Haintz, *Karl XII.*, I, 27.

[2] Duchhardt, *Balance of Power*, 237. For the opposite view see: Bély, *Les relations*, 382-85.

[3] Israel, *The Dutch Republic*, 998; Duchhardt, *Balance*, 178.

[4] Oakley, *War and Peace*, 113.

[5] Zernack, 'Der grosse Nordische Krieg', 167; Mediger, *Mecklenburg*, 6-17.

[6] Roosen, 'The origins', 161; Hattendorf, 'Ursprünge', 138.

[7] Plassmann, *Krieg und Defension*, 37.

[8] Laufs, *Reichstagsabschied*, 88; Kroener, 'Schwungrad', 1-23.

[9] Hüttl, *Max Emanuel*, 336-46.

[10] Hatton, *Georg I.*, 73-79.

[11] Baumgart, 'Ein neuer König', in: Windt, *Preußen 1701*, 173.

[12] Schulz, *Geschichte Hessens*; Taylor, *Indentured to Liberty*; Bernhardi, 'Subsidienverträge', 216-46.

[13] Braubach, 'Kurtrier und die Seemächte'; Dotzauer, *Die deutschen Reichskreise*, 94-100; Aretin, 'Die Kreisassoziationen'; Hantsch, *Reichsvizekanzler*, 69-71.

[15] Fahrmbacher, 'Kurfürst Johann Wilhelms Kriegsstaat'; Hilsenbeck, *Johann Wilhelm*.

[16] Dotzauer, *Die Deutschen Reichskreise*; Aretin, 'Die Kreisassozationen', in: Aretin, *Das Reich*, 167-69.

[17] In general: Tessin, *Die Regimenter*; for Prussia see: Jany, *Geschichte*; for Saxony: Schuster und Franke, *Geschichte*; for Bavaria: Staudinger, *Geschichte*; for the Electoral Palatinate: Bezzel, *Geschichte*; for Hesse-Kassel: Böhme, *Die Wehrverfassung*.

[18] Papke, *Miliz*, 194-200.

[19] Braubach, *Subsidien*; Hartmann, *Die Finanz- und Subsidienpolitik*.

[20] Aretin, 'Das Problem der Kriegführung im Heiligen Römischen Reich', 6.

[21] Plassmann, *Krieg und Defension*, 611-13.

[22] Aretin, 'Die Kreisassoziationen', *Das Reich*; Braubach, 'Reichsbarriere', 231-67.

[23] Hattendorf, *England*.

[24] *Ibidem*, 58-61; Hattendorf, 'Alliance'.

[25] Coombs, *The Conduct*, 280; Black, 'Debating Policy', 38.

[26] Corvisier, *Histoire Militaire*, I, 529-47.

[27] Braubach, *Prinz Eugen*, III, 3; Hohrath und Rehm, *Zwischen Sonne und Halbmond*.

[28] [Einer] von den besten und den gescheidesten in diesem Land'. Cf. Jarnut-Derbolav, *Die österreichische Gesandtschaft*, 71.

[29] Israel, *The Dutch Republic*, 971.

[30] Kroener, 'La planification'; Kroener, 'Militärischer Professionalismus'; Chandler, *Marlborough*, 94-96; Chandler, *The Art of Warfare*, 336-37.

[31] Churchill, *Marlborough*, German edition, II, 421.

[32] On the size of the subsidy troops that were financed by Britain: Wilson, *German Armies*, 108-11; Black, *European Warfare*, 109-10.

[33] Churchill, *Marlborough*, German edition, I, 420.

[34] Hoff, B. van 't, ed., *Correspondence*.

[35] Jarnut-Derbolav, *Die österreichische Gesandtschaft*, 119-20.

[36] Marlborough to Nottingham, 17 July 1702. Murray, *Letters*, I, 21.

[37] Chandler, *Blenheim*, 217; Spencer, *Battle*,123; Holmes, *Marlborough*, 254-56; Jones, *Marlborough*.

[38] Hüttl, *Max Emanuel*.

[39] Heuser, *Die Belagerungen*, 84-92.

[40] Corvisier, *La France*, 331.

[41] Jarnut-Derbolav, *Die österreichische Gesandtschaft*, 123-24; Churchill, *Marlborough*, I, 491.

[42] Holmes, *Marlborough*, 227; Chandler, *Marlborough*, 113-14.

[43] Sturgill, *Villars*, 31-52; Hüttl, *Max Emanuel*, 349-51, 359-62; Plassmann, *Krieg und Defension*, 422-25.

[44] Jones, *Marlborough*, 82.

[45] Hochedlinger, *Austria's Wars*, 184-85.

[46] Ritter, *Politik*, 46-47; Baignol, *La campagne*, 11-15.

[47] Braubach, *Prinz Eugen*, II., 47; Mathis, *Aspekte*,; Chandler, *Marlborough*, 113-14.

[48] Plassmann, *Krieg und Defension*, 431.

[49] *Ibidem*, 422-23.

[50] Stein, 'Festungen', 55-106.

[51] 'To leave the command at the Upper Rhine for the time being to Malb[orough], is an absolutely necessary condition for making progress with this plan' (notes by Wratislav, 18 January 1704). '[Das] Comando dem Malb[orough] an dem ober Rein pro tempore zu überlasen, ist eine conditio qua non ohne welcher in diesem dissegno unmöglich forthzukomen, [...].' Cf. Jarnut-Derbolav, *Die österreichische Gesandtschaft*, 160.

[52] Hattendorf, 'English Grand Strategy', 3-19.

[53] Kauer, *Brandenburg-Preußen*, 32-33.

[54] Spencer, *Battle*, 190; Addison, *The Campaign*.

[55] Snyder, *Marlborough-Godolphin*, I, 289-90. The numbers were used for the encryption of names so that its bearers would not be recognized in case of an unauthorized opening of the letter.

[56] Braubach, *Prinz Eugen*, II, 58-60; Otruba, *Prinz Eugen*, 37-39; Churchill, *Marlborough*, (English edition), II, 773-74.

[57] Sicken, 'Heeresaufbringung', 127-29.

[58] Spencer, *Battle*, 135-47; Chandler, *Blenheim*, 217-30; Junkelmann, 'Feldzug', 64-67.

[59] Plassmann, *Krieg und Defension*, 449.

[60] Naujokat, *England*, 87: quoted from *Defoe's Review*, 102 (7 September 1704), III, 406.

[61] Aretin, 'Kreisassoziationen', *Der Mainzer Kurfürst*, 57-59.

[62] Naujokat, *England*, 89-90; Feckl, *Preußen*, 67.

[63] Hinrichs, *Friedrich Wilhelm I.*, 203.

[64] Kauer, *Brandenburg-Preußen*, 37; Bernay, *König Friedrich I.*, 117.

[65] 'Brandenburg [diente] als Isolator zwischen den diesseitigen und jenseitigen Entladungen, [der] um jeden Preis bei der Stange zu halten [war].' Cf. Noorden, 'Die preußische Politik', 314.

[66] For another view: Braubach, *Subsidien*, 114.

[67] Losch, *Soldatenhandel*.

[68] Holmes, *Marlborough*, 258-59, n. 20.

[69] Kauer, *Brandenburg-Preußen*, 65-66.

[70] Hinrichs, *Friedrich Wilhelm I.*, 245-49.

[71] 'So hat man Unrecht in England zu sagen, daß der Herzog von Marlborough nur von Hof zu Hof gegangen ist, um Geschenke zu bekommen.' Sophia, Princess Electress of Hanover, to Leibnitz, 10 January 1705. Cf. Geerds, R., ed., *Die*

Mutter, 398.

[72] Hassinger, *Brandenburg-Preußen*, 173; Kauer, *Brandenburg-Preußen*, 102.

[73] Braubach, *Subsidien*, 153-55.

[74] Jarnut-Derbolav, E., *Die österreichische Gesandtschaft*, 302-04; Otruba, *Prinz Eugen*, 25-54, Braubach, *Prinz Eugen*, II, 147-48.

[75] Ostwald, 'The 'Decisive' Battle', 649-77.

[76] Haintz, *Karl XII.*, I, 162-63; Oakley, *War*, 120.

[77] Hassinger, *Brandenburg-Preußen*, 201.

[78] Churchill, *Marlborough*, II, 138; Braubach, *Prinz Eugen*, II, 186.

[79] Haintz, *Karl XII.*, I, 272-97; Hassinger, *Brandenburg-Preußen*, 211.

[80] Hinrichs, *Friedrich Wilhelm I.*, 313.

[81] Hatton, *Georg I.*, 109-11; Churchill, *Marlborough*, II, 203-04; Braubach, *Prinz Eugen*, II, 221-23.

[82] Hatton, *Georg I.*, 109; Braubach, *Prinz Eugen*, II, 227; Churchill, *Marlborough*, II, 202-05.

[83] Schmidt, 'Prinz Eugen'.

[84] Hatton, R., *Georg I.*, 109.

[85] Braubach, *Prinz Eugen*, II, 239; Reese, *Das Ringen*, 169; Aretin, 'Die Kreisassoziationen', *Das Reich*, 200.

[86] Braubach, *Prinz Eugen*, II, 232-33; Churchill, *Marlborough*, II, 206-07; Reese, *Das Ringen.*

[87] Mühlhoff, *Die Genesis*, 14-22.

[88] Aretin, 'Die Kreisassoziationen', *Das Reich*, 202; Braubach, 'Holland und die geistlichen Staaten', 185-88.

[89] Reese, *Das Ringen*, 255; Braubach, 'Holland und die geistlichen Staaten', 185-88.

[90] Hahlweg , 'Barriere', 77-78; Geikie and Montgomery, *The Dutch Barrier*, 112-13, 142; Reese, *Das Ringen*, 48.

[91] Braubach, *Prinz Eugen*, II, 280-82; Jarnut-Derbolav, *Die österreichische Gesandtschaft*, 369.

[92] Reese, *Das Ringen*, 171-73; Aretin, *Das Reich*, 294-95.

[93] Reese, *Das Ringen*, 265-68.

[94] 'Man sagt, Hoffart kommt vor dem Fall; also hoffe ich, daß Mylord Marlborough und Prinz Eugens Insolenz auch wird gestraft werden.' Cf. Braubach, *Prinz Eugen*, II, 296.

[95] Corvisier, *La bataille.*

[96] Braubach, *Prinz Eugen*, II, 326, 333.

[97] Hassinger, *Brandenburg-Preußen*, 227; Braubach, *Prinz Eugen*, II, 336; Mediger, *Moskaus Weg*, 28.

[98] [...] für den selbst 'der König und sein Haus eine besondere Devotion' bezeugten. Cf. Hinrichs, *Friedrich Wilhelm I.*, 373-75; Kauer, *Brandenburg-Preußen*, 185.

[99] Hinrichs, *Friedrich Wilhelm I.*; Naujokat, *England*, 253; Fleckl, *Preußen*, 167, 176.

[100] Kauer, *Brandenburg-Preußen*, 272; Braubach, 'Geheime Friedensverhandlungen', 268-88; Press, *Kriege*, 467.

[101] Jarnut-Derbolav, *Die österreichische Gesandtschaft*, 411-12; Reese, *Das Ringen*, 274; Press, *Kriege*, 469.

[102] Braubach, *Prinz Eugen*, II, 371.

[103] *Ibidem*, III, 39.

[104] Jarnut-Derbolav, *Die österreichische Gesandtschaft*, 488.

[105] Churchill, *Marlborough*, II, 572-80; Braubach., *Prinz Eugen*, III, 80-95.

[106] Even in treatises that are imbued with the spirit of National Socialism, Marlborough's achievements are valued positively. Cf. Elze, *Der Prinz Eugen*, 80-81.

9 Friendship and Realpolitik

[1] Churchill, *Marlborough* , II, 774-5.

[2] Braubach, *Eugen*, II, 45.

[3] Bibl, *Prinz Eugen–ein Heldenleben.*

[4] Marlborough to Eugene (4 September 1702): Murray, *Letters*, I, 30. Eugene's answer is in Churchill, *Marlborough* , II, 603.

[5] No less a person than the astronomer Halley had inspected Austria's Adriatic ports in 1703 to find out which one might be suitable to receive an Anglo-Dutch fleet: Alan H. Cook, 'An English Astronomer on the Adriatic'.

[6] Höbelt, 'The Impact of the Rákóczi Rebellion on Habsburg Strategy'. On Britain's role there is Young, Großbritannien und die Rákóczi-Erhebung, but also see Slottman, *Ferenc II Rákóczi and the Great Powers.* The French quotation is from Marlborough to Rákóczy (28 April 1709): Murray, *Letters*, IV, 493-94.

[7] There is an interesting thesis on Churchill's view of the Habsburg Monarchy/Austria. A summary appeared as Neubauer, ‚Österreich und seine Geschichte im Werke Winston S. Churchills'.

[8] Hochedlinger, *Oberösterreich im Spanischen Erbfolgekrieg* (Vienna, 1993).

[9] Mathis, ‚Neue Aspekte zur Planung des süddeutschen Feldzuges von 1704', and his 'Marlborough und Wratislaw. Eine politische Freundschaft als Grundlage des Sieges von Höchstädt 1704'. These are by-products of his massive (unpublished) doctoral dissertation ‚Marlborough und Wratislaw vor der Schlacht von Höchstädt. Neue Aspekte zum Feldzug 1704'.

[10] Churchill, *Marlborough* , II, 773-4.

[11] Marlborough to his wife Sarah (14 August 1704): Coxe, *Memoirs*, I, 315.

[12] Hattendorf, *England*, 218.

[13] Coxe, *Memoirs*, I, 525-542, who also prints a map of Mindelheim; Churchill, *Marlborough* , II, 889-92; III, 47-50. The best treatment is Barber, 'Marlborough as Imperial Prince 1704-1717', based on the relevant literature and the Blenheim Papers. For the general background cf. Klein, ‚Die Erhebungen in den weltlichen Reichsfürstenstand 1550-1806', esp. 161-2, and Schlip, ‚Die neuen Fürsten. Zur Erhebung in den Reichsfürstenstand und zur Aufnahme in den Reichsfürstenrat im 17. und 18. Jahrhundert'. Cox, 'Property law and Imperial and British titles: the Dukes of Marlborough and the Principality of Mindelheim' is unfortunately to be read with caution. I had no access to Wilhelm Eberle, Das Reichsfürstentum Mindelheim unter Marlborough 1705-1715.

[14] Mathis, 'Marlborough und Wratislaw' (thesis 1972), 275-76, 334-36. Stepney was perhaps right in believing that this promotion 'would be

no great addition to his [Marlborough's] present state', but entirely mistaken in declaring that the Duke would prefer a quick settlement between the Emperor and the Hungarians in order to concentrate on the French. That Marlborough had explicitly asked for a substantial reward is clear from Wratislaw's report to Leopold I (Frankfurt, 1 June 1704): Österreichisches Staatsarchiv (ÖStA), Kriegsarchiv *Alte Feldakten Römisches Reich/Diplomatische Korrespondenz* 1704-VI-1. The document is printed in Mathis, *Marlborough* (1972), 385-89. Marlborough to his wife (15 June 1704): Coxe, *Memoirs*, I, 252-53.

[15] Drafts for both diplomas are in ÖStA, Allgemeines Verwaltungsarchiv *Reichsadelsakten* Marlborough 1705 November 14 (Reichsfürstenstandserhebung, also granting a new coat of arms which Marlborough used for his seal, the private seal showed the arms of Mindelheim as an escutcheon of pretence), 1705 November 17 (Erhebung Mindelheims als Mannlehen zum unmittelbaren Reichsfürstentum), copies in ÖStA, Haus-, Hof- und Staatsarchiv (HHStA) *Reichskanzlei* Reichsregister Josephs I., vol I and vol. V. The originals disappeared from the Blenheim Papers before 1910. Marlborough to Staffhorst (25 November 1705): Murray, *Letters*, II, 332; Riedenauer, ‚Kaiserliche Standeserhebungen für Angehörige des Militärstandes von Karl V. bis Karl VI.', in Lindgren, et al., eds., *Sine ira at studio. Militärhistorische Studien zur Erinnerung an Hans Schmidt*, esp. 80-83. There is no evidence that Leopold I had elevated Marlborough to the rank of prince as early as 1704. In reality the Emperor only promised to do so, and the affair remained suspended until after Leopold's death. See Leopold's congratulatory letter of 28 August 1704 and related pieces (Coxe, *Memoirs,* I, 325-27). On the refusal of Munderkingen, see Marlborough to Wratislaw (9 January and 23 February 1705): Murray, *Letters*, I, 573-75, 600. The admission (22 November 1706) of Marlborough's envoy, Christoph Schrader, to the college of Princes (*Reichsfürstenrat*) is described in Johann Christian Lünig, *Theatrum ceremoniale historico-politicum*, I, 1052-3. Schrader was the son of the famous Helmstedt professor Christoph Schrader (1601-1680) and the Hanoverian representative at Regensburg. The Emperor ennobled him in 1708. Also see Marlborough to Schrader (21 June 1706, 7 July 1706, 12 December 1706), to Stepney (15 March 1706): Murray, *Letters,* II, 449-50, 610, 672, 251-52. For Stepney's role see Susan Spens, *George Stepney*, 274-78. After Josephs I's death in 1711 Marlborough had to apply for re-enfeoffment: Marlborough to Sinzendorf (10 November 1711): Murray, *Letters*, V, 564.

[16] Mikoletzky, 'Die große Anleihe von 1706. Ein Beitrag zur österreichischen Finanzgeschichte'; Otruba, ‚Die Bedeutung englischer Subsidien und Antizipationen für die Finanzen Österreichs 1701-1748'. A second loan in 1710 was to yield less than £ 100,000.

[17] The quotation is from Jarnut-Derbolav, *Gesandtschaft*, 235. Churchill, *Marlborough*, III, 137-49; IV, 515-17; Geikie and Montgomery, *The Dutch Barrier.* As a compensation, Marlborough received paintings from the ousted Bavarian Elector's art collections in Munich (summer 1706), among them van Dycks's equestrian portrait of Charles I of England (in the National Gallery since 1885). See Lhotsky, *Die Geschichte der Sammlungen, 1*, 385.

[18] Von Arneth, *Das Leben des kaiserlichern Feldmarschalls Grafen Guido Starhemberg*; Landau, *Geschichte Kaiser Karls VI. als König von Spanien.* Curiously, Charles III later offered Marlborough the post of commander-in-chief in Spain (1710): Charles III to Wratislaw (Barcelona, 28 April 1710), published in Von Arneth, ‚Eigenhändige Correspondenz des Königs Karl III. von Spanien (nachmals Kaiser Karl VI.) mit dem Obersten Kanzler des Königreiches Böhmen, Grafen Johann Wenzel Wratislaw', 123.

[19] Hatton, *Charles XII of Sweden*, 221-27.

[20] See Cameron, *This Master Firebrand.*

[21] Coxe, *Memoirs*, III, 494.

[22] Braubach, *Eugen*, III, 142.

[23] Frey and Frey, *Leopold I*, 30.

[24] Otruba, *Bedeutung*, 205-7.

[25] Hattendorf, *England*, 137; Braubach, *Eugen*, II, 334.

[26] Braubach, *Eugen*, III, 183-4; Gregg, 'Marlborough in Exile 1712-1714'.

[27] Jarnut-Derbolav, *Gesandtschaft*, 235 (fn.). Marlborough to Count Sinzendorf (27 December 1706): Murray, *Letters*, III, 267-68. Count Wratislaw to Marlborough (18 October 1709) assuring the Prince of Mindelheim that despite serious obstacles the Emperor would allow him to pass on his principality to his daughters and their male heirs. A formal diploma was to follow after the peace, a clear hint that Vienna expected Marlborough to act as an advocate of Habsburg interests: ÖStA, Kriegsarchiv, *Alte Feldakten* Niederlande 1709-X-38. Charles VI to Count Sinzendorf (1 February 1713): ÖStA, HHStA, *Staatskanzlei* Staats- und Extraordinariprotokoll 1713, fol. 6v-7r. Sinzendorf informed Marlborough accordingly: Barber, *Marlborough*, 69 and fn. 167.

[28] Marlborough to Charles VI (not dated, before 7 September1714): ÖStA, HHStA *Kriegsakten* 196.

[29] Marlborough to Charles VI (London, 14 January 1715): ÖStA, HHStA *Kriegsakten* 196.

[30] That Marlborough was compensated by Nellenburg is first reported in *Zedlers Universallexicon*, vol. 21, Leipzig and Halle, 1739, col. 304.

[31] ÖStA, HHStA *Kurrentakten* Zl. 1485/1940.

[32] Coxe, *Memoirs,* III, 548-552.

[33] ÖStA, HHStA *Kurrentakten* Zl. 7/1825. There had been an earlier investigation into the Mindelheim case in 1769 but with a view to Austria's claims to the former principality: HHStA *Kleinere Reichsstände* 355 (Mindelheim) and ÖStA, Allgemeines Verwaltungsarchiv *Hofkanzlei* 189 (II A 4 Tirol). Mindelheim was to play a (small) political role during the War of the Bavarian Succession (1778-9) after the extinction of the Munich Wittelsbachs. For a short while Austrian troops occupied the region upon which Vienna now reasserted its old feudal rights, but what really mattered in the 'Age of Reason' was the simple fact that Mindelheim would have nicely rounded off Austria's isolated margraviate of Burgau.

[53] *Reasons why the duke of Marlborough* , 3-4, 6.
[54] [Davenant], *Sir Thomas Double*,15, 25-26, 72-3.
[55] [Swift], *Conduct of the allies*, 58 (page references here and subsequently from the corrected second edition).
[56] *Ibidem*, 60.
[57] *Ibidem*, 64.
[58] *Ibidem*, 60.
[59] *Ibidem*, 13.
[60] See for example, *Remarks upon remarks*; *Full answer to the conduct*; *Defence of the allies*.
[61] [Boyer], *Letter from a foreign minister*, 6; *Reasons why a certain great g——-l*, 7-10; *No Queen*; [Fenton], *M. Manlius Capitolinus*; *Fate of M. Manlius Capitolinus*.
[62] See, for example, [Wagstaff], *Representation*; *Examiner* (23 November and 27 February 1710 – second date 1711 if year taken to start on 1 January); *Fable of Midas*.
[63] *Report of the commissioner*. *The Examiner* was particularly keen to unearth financial irregularity.
[64] *Present negotiations*, 26-7; [Defoe], *Farther search*, 30-6.
[65] *Secret history of Arlus*, 24.
[66] For example, *The Queen*, 11-12; [Swift], *Some remarks*, preface, 1-4; *Trip to Germany*.
[67] *Sense of the nation*.
[68] [Hare], *Bouchain*.
[69] Clarke, *Dedication*; [Hare], *Caveat*, 13-17; Hare, *Charge of God*; *Case of the British*.
[70] Maynwaring, *Three articles*, 15. [The spelling is Maynwaring's. The correct spelling of the town is Blaregnies, located on the border with France in the modern province of Hainault, Belgium. ed.]
[71] Listing earlier praise became a Whig trope: see, for example *Remarks upon the present negotiations*, 1-5.
[72] [Hare], *Negotiations*; [Hare], *History of negotiations*.
[73] Churchill, *Case of his grace; Information against the duke*; [Hare], *Speech*; *Letter from a curate*; *Short narrative*, 33-42.
[74] For example, *French king's thanks; Thoughts of a member*.
[75] For example, [Hare], *Allies and the late ministry*; *Ballance of Power*.
[76] For example, [Hare], *Management of the war*, 20-23, *Short narrative*, 27; *Lives of two*; which stress Marlborough's close collaboration with Prince Eugene and the Dutch.
[77] For example, *Anniversary*.
[78] [Burnet], *True character*, 10.
[79] A particularly tiresome example is [Manley], *Learned comment* – though its target (Hare) was as guilty in his series of published letters to a Tory member.
[80] Examples from across the genres include Henley, *Apotheosis*; Gay, *Epistle to her grace*; *Funeral poem, sacred to the memory; General's pattern*; *Churchill's annals*.
[81] For a recent survey of the origins in England of this style of presentation, see Sharpe, *Selling the Tudor monarchy*.
[82] See Holmes, *Trial of Dr Sacheverell*; Speck ed., *Critical bibliography*.
[63] Here I am partly indebted to a discussion with Mark Knights of these prints.
[84] [Hare], *Conduct of the duke*, 232.
[85] Marlborough's defence of his budgets in *Case of his grace* was a masterpiece of tendentious pleading.
[86] For the imagery of the exclusion crisis, see Harris, *Restoration*, chs. 3-4.
[87] To take typical examples, [Boyer], *Letter*, 8-9; [Hornby], *Fourth and last part*, 86; *Oliver's pocket*.
[88] For instance – *Fable of the widow*; *Perquisite-monger*; *Grand enquiry*.
[89] *Story of St Alb-ns*, 3-5.
[90] See especially, Claydon, *Europe*; Jardine, *Going Dutch;* Pincus, *1688*; Scott, *England's troubles*.

12 'The British Caesar'

[1] For a broader overview of the contrasting academic traditions outlined here see Andrew Lambert, 'Military History', *Making History*, online resource of the Institute of Historical Research, n.d. [www.history.ac.uk/makinghistory/resources/articles/military_history.html – accessed March 2011]; and Bonehill and Quilley, introduction to *Conflicting Visions: War and Visual Culture in Britain and France c. 1700-1830*, 1–14. Although neither text deals directly with Marlborough, many of the issues they raise are pertinent to the concerns of this essay.
[2] For a detailed account of Closterman's career and English patrons, see Rogers, 'John and John Baptist Closterman: a catalogue of their works', in *Walpole Society*, 49 (1983), 224–79.
[3] Closterman's painting and the later portraits it inspired are discussed in Bapasola, *Faces of Fame and Fortune*, esp. 12–19.
[4] Smith produced prints of more than 100 of Kneller's portraits between the late 1680s and the painter's death in 1723. For a detailed history of early mezzotints, including a comprehensive catalogue of Smith's output, see online: National Portrait Gallery, 'Early history of mezzotint', online text and catalogue, n.d. [www.npg.org.uk/research/programmes/early-history-of-mezzotint.php – accessed December 2010].
[5] *An essay towards an English school of painters*, appended to Roger de Piles, *The art of painting, with the lives and characters of above 300 of the most eminent painters* [trans. John Savage], third edition, London, 1750, 393–98. The opinion of Kneller's biographer echoed the printmaker and writer on art George Vertue, who had previously noted: 'In the Talent of an exact likeness Sr. Godfrey has excelld most if not all that have gone before him in this Art.' Vertue, 'Notebooks', 123.
[6] The identification of the sitter as Marlborough was first questioned by Stewart, *Sir Godfrey Kneller and the English Baroque Portrait*, 47. See also British Museum, collection database, n.d. [www.britishmuseum.org/research/search_the_collection_database/search_object_details.aspx?objectId=752079&partId=1 – accessed December 2010].

[7] Royal Collection (RCIN 405322). Establishing a further connection between the two subjects, George Vertue makes reference to a watercolour mentioned in Sarah Churchill's will: a copy in miniature of another equestrian portrait of Charles I by Van Dyck (now in the National Gallery), made by Bernard Lens, in which the face of the King had been replaced by a likeness of Marlborough. (Vertue, 'Notebooks', 35).

[8] For a detailed account of the unusual publishing history of Lombart's 'Headless Horseman' see Griffiths, *The Print in Stuart Britain 1603-1689*, 180–81.

[9] Kneller's equestrian portrait of Schomberg, now at Brocklesby Park, Lincolnshire, was singled out for praise by the gentleman writer on art Marshall Smith, in *The Art of Painting according to the theory and practise of the best French, Italian and Germane Masters*, 24.

[10] The inscription on the reverse of the medal reads: SINE CLADE VICTOR ('A conqueror without slaughter'). The only other medal to feature the Queen and Marlborough together was the unofficial (and now rare) example struck in Berlin by Jan Boskam following the Battle of Blenheim. See Hawkins, *Medallic Illustrations of the History of Great Britain and Ireland to the Death of George II*, esp. vol. 2, 246, 255.

[11] Richard Gwinnett, 'On a Medal with the Queen on One Side, and the General on a prancing Horse on the Other.' Gwinnett's short poem was published posthumously in *Pylades and Corinna: or, memoirs of the lives, amours, and writings of Richard Gwinnett Esq.*, I, 52.

[12] See, for example, the medal struck by John Croker in 1709 to commemorate the Battle of Malplaquet, a silver example of which is in the collection of the Victoria and Albert Museum, London (Museum number: 1894-1902).

[13] Buckeridge, *On Her Majesty's grant of Woodstock Park, etc. To His Grace the Duke of Marlborough, 1704. In a letter to Signior Antonio Verrio at Hampton-Court*, [London, 1705].

[14] Blackmore, *Instructions to Vander Bank: a sequel to the Advice to the poets.*

[15] The most comprehensive study of the building and decoration of Blenheim remains Green's *Blenheim Palace*. Green, however, did not extend his study to the tapestries and other portable decorations commissioned for the palace.

[16] The *Art of War* series has a complicated history, outlined in Wace, *The Marlborough Tapestries at Blenheim Palace*; and Hefford, 'Some problems concerning the Art of War tapestries', and more recently by Bapasola in *Threads of History: the Tapestries at Blenheim Palace*, esp. 33–40.

[17] Marlborough's *Art of War* comprised eight scenes on nine tapestries (*Pillage* reaches across two smaller panels). The other four panels in the series were *The March*, *Ambush*, *Cutting Fascines* and *Foraging*. These have not survived as part of the Blenheim set but are known as part of the first set produced for the Elector of Bavaria, now dispersed in various collections. See Wace, 29–39.

[18] The *Art of War* series proved highly lucrative in other ways. The cartoons were later adapted to form the basis of a second, expanded edition with six additional scenes based on the Blenheim *Victories*. The production of Marlborough's *Art of* War tapestries was contracted to the Antwerp workshops of Jerome Le Clerc and Jasper (or Gaspar) van der Borght in 1705. See Wace, 44–39; and Delmarcel, *Flemish tapestry from the 15th to the 18th century*, 342–51.

[19] Bapasola, *Threads of History*, esp. 91–133.

[20] See Campbell, *Tapestry in the Renaissance: Art and Magnificence*, exh. cat., Metropolitan Museum of Art, New York, 2002; and, by the same author, *Tapestry in the Baroque: Threads of Splendour*, exh. cat., Metropolitan Museum of Art, New York, 2008. See also Wace, esp. 13–28.

[21] The *Histoire du Roi* tapestries comprised fourteen military and diplomatic scenes designed by Van der Meulen and Charles Le Brun and woven at the Gobelins factory in Paris between 1667 and 1672.

[22] From the Blenheim Papers at the British Library, Add. MS. 61216, f. 46; also cited in Bapasola, *Threads of History*, 72.

[23] For a summary of Laguerre's career in England, see Croft-Murray, *Decorative painting in England 1537-1837, vol. 1*, esp. 61–68.

[24] *A short narrative of the life and action of his Grace John, D. of Marlborough* [...] *by an old officer in the army*, London, 1717.

[25] The subscription for the Marlborough House engravings was announced in the *Evening Post*, 6-9 April 1717, cited in Clayton, *The English Print 1688-1802*, 55–56.

[26] British Library Add. MS. 61355, ff. 5–6.

[27] Kneller's account of the commission and description of the painting are transcribed in Green (1951), 298–99. The artist's memoir also reveals how Marlborough insisted that the only recognisable likeness in the painting be that of the Queen.

[28] British Library Add. MS. 61354, ff. 38–39.

[29] Thornhill was eventually paid £978 for his work in the hall. The disagreement arose because, in keeping with his initial bargain with Vanbrugh (though much to Sarah Churchill's disgust), the artist charged the same price per yard for the architectural painting on the walls as for the more elaborate and colourful figurative details on the ceiling. See Green (1951), esp. 306–08.

[30] The lead figure on the column has been variously attributed to the workshop of Henry Cheere and to an otherwise unknown sculptor Robert Pit. See Green, 277–78.

[31] Kent and Rysbrack had recently also collaborated on the monuments to Isaac Newton and James Stanhope, 1st Earl Stanhope, at Westminster Abbey. For a detailed study of monumental sculpture of the period, see Craske, *The Silent Rhetoric of the Body: A History of Monumental Sculpture and Commemorative Art in England, 1720-1770*.

Index

Page references to the subjects of illustrations and other information in the captions to illustrations are indicated by page numbers in italics.

Gunpowder Plot (1605) 28
Haersolte, Johan van, Heer van Cranenburg, Dutch diplomat 83
Hague, The, Holland 8, 10-11, 14, 24, 36, 45-46, 172, 175-*183*, 185, 188, 223, 225-226, 229, 252, 255, 257, 260, 382
Halifax, Lord, *see Montagu, Charles*
Halley, Edmund, English astronomer, 390
Hamilton, George, Earl of Orkney, Scottish officer in English service 71
Hampton Court Palace, London 333-334
Hanover 85
Hanover, Elector of, *see Georg Ludwig*
Hare, Frances, chaplain of Marlborough 99, 302, 308, 313
Harley, Robert, Earl of Oxford, English politician 59, 60, 80, 84, 92, 96-99, 120, 185, 188, 191, 268, 310, 312, 359-367
Hawksmoor, Nicholas, English surveyor 75, 101, 352
Hawley, Henry, English officer 116, 373
Heidelberg 43, 257
Heinrich Friedrich, Duke of Württemberg, general in Dutch service 381
Heinsius, Adriaan, alderman of Delft 173
Heinsius, Anthonie, Grand Pensionary of Holland 5, 10, 33, 60, 76, 88, 93, 146-147, 152, 160, 166, *172*-191, 206, 226, 241, 265, 276, 291
Helchin, Brabant 83
Helchteren, Brabant 157
Herbert, Arthur, Earl of Torrington, English admiral 53
Herbert, Henry 43
Herbert, Thomas, Earl of Pembroke, English politician 323
Hessen-Kassel, Landgrave of, *see Karl*
Hessen-Kassel, hereditary Prince of, *see Friedrich*
Hertford, Lord, *see Seymour, Charles*
Heukelum, Willem van, Heer van Kronenstein, Dutch general 381
Hill, John, English officer 92
Hill, Richard, English envoy in Savoy 35
Höchstädt, battle of (1703) 228
Höchstädt, battle of (1704), *see Blenheim, battle of*
Hoff, B. van 't, Dutch historian 146
Hoffmann, Johann Philip, Imperial diplomat 16
Holland, States of 45, 173-177, 180, 185
Holmes, Sir John 46
Holmes, Richard, English historian 170
Holmes, Sir Robert, English admiral 42
Holstein-Beck, Prince of, *see Anton Günther*
Holstein-Gottorf, Duchy 218, 287
Holy Roman Empire 8, 165, 257, 306
Holy Roman Empire, Emperor of, *see Leopold I, Joseph I, Karl VI*
Holywell House, St. Albans 48, 97, 323
Homann, J.B., Austrian mapmaker *263*, *269*
Hompesch, Reinhart Vincent, Baron, Dutch general 381
Hondt, Lambert de, Brussels weaver *2*, *6*, *81*, *90-91*, *105*, 335, 336, *338-339*, 341
Hondt, Philippe de, Brussels weaver *2*, *6*, *81*, *90*, *91*, *105*, *338-339*
Honywood, Philip, English general 120
Hooghe, Romeyn de, Dutch artist and pamphleteer *36*
Hooke, Nathaniel, English author 101
Hooke, Robert, English artist 352
Hop, Jacob, Treasurer-General of the United Provinces 157, 186-188
Hostun, Camille d', Comte de Tallard, Duc d'Hostun, Marshal of France 67-71, 101, 154, 194, 196, 198-200, 203-204, 211, *336-337*, 355, 388
Houbraken, Jacobus, Dutch painter and etcher *155*
Hove, Michiel ten, Grand Pensionary of Holland 174
Hounslow 49
Huchtenburg, Jan van, Dutch artist *336*
Hudson, Thomas, English painter 323
Hudson's Bay 49, 299
Hudson's Bay Company 49
Huguenots, 16, 28
Hulett, James, English engraver *84*
Hulst, States Flanders, proposed siege of (1702) 378
Hungary, insurrection in 228, 251, 253, 255
Husson, Pierre, French engraver *293*
Huxelles, d', *see Du Blé*
Huy, siege of (1702) 64, 132, 137, 331
Huygens, Constantijn, Junior, secretary of Stadholder-King William III 16
Hyde, Edward, Lord Cornbury, 1709 Earl of Clarendon, English officer 51
Hyde, Henry, Earl of Clarendon, English politician 31, 48, 52
Hyde, Laurence, Earl of Rochester, English politician 23, 60

Iberian Peninsula 226, 228, 276, 279, 287
Ibiza *295*
Ieper (Ypres) 139
Imhof, Joseph, Baron von, caretaker of Mindelheim principality 270
Ingoldsby, Richard, English general 110
Ingolstadt, siege of (1704) 205, 235, 257
Innes, Lewis, Jacobite agent 98
Innsbruck, Austria 356
Ireland 8, 17, 112-113, 128-130, 149, 151, 194, 277-278, 289, 305, 330
Isle of Wight 42, 46
Italy 7-10, 200, 218, 222, 225-226, 228, 252-253, 260

Jacobites 11, 29, 37, 56, 85, 97, 178, 194
James I, King of England 39
James II, King of England 8, 11, 18, 39, *41*, 51, 59, 104, 113, 174, 200, 276, 278-279, 301, 323, 376, 393
James III, Pretender to the throne of Great Britain 8, 30, 32, 35, 59-60, 97, 208, 211, 295
Jeffreys, George, Baron, Lord Chief Justice 49
Jeker, River 64
Jenyns, Sarah, Duchess of Marlborough 9, 44-48, , 51-57, 59-60, 64, 71, 75, 81, 83-89, 91, *93*, 95-98, 101, 155, 174, 213, 231, 266, 323, 337, 343, 347, 352-353, 355, 395
Johann Moritz, Prince of Nassau-Siegen, Dutch general 148
Johann Wilhelm, Count of Pfalz-Neuburg, Elector Palatine 77, *236*, 239, 260
Jones, J.R., English historian 146
Joseph I, King of the Romans, German Emperor 75, 77, 94, 186-188, 211, 239, 246, 253, *259*-260,

266
Joseph Clemens, Archbishop-Elector of Cologne, bishop of Liège 218, 226, 253
Joynes, Henry, comptroller of the building of Blenheim Palace, 75
Jurieu, Pierre, Huguenot minister in Rotterdam 25
Kaiserswerth, siege of (1702) 154, 380
Karl, Landgrave of Hessen-Kassel 218, 229, 237
Karl VI, German Emperor, King of Spain as Carlos III, 64, 79-80, 89, 94, 98, 186-188, 226, 253, 258, 260, 264, 266, 268, 292, 295, 297, 386, 391
–, wife of, *see Elisabeth Christina*
Karl XII, King of Sweden 36, 82-83, 101, 109, *238*-239, 265, 287, 291
Karlowitz, Peace of (1699) 251
Kehl, on the Rhine 228, 253
Kent, William, English architect, 45, 101, *354*
Keppel, Arnold Joost van, Earl of Albemarle, Dutch general 142, 158, 163, 166, 186, 190, 381
King, Richard, English officer 135
King, William, Irish Anglican minister 304-*305*
Kingston, Richard, English spy 56
Kinsale, Ireland 54, *122-123*, 128-130, 136
Kirke, English officer 52
Kit-Cat Club *257*
Kneller, Godfrey, English painter *39*, 60, 94, *151*, *160*, *245*, *257*, *266*, 270, *308*, 323, *327-334*, *346*, 352, 394-395
Knights, Sir John, M.P. 16
Knights, Mark, English historian 394
Koblenz, on the Rhine River 63, 257
Konz, Consarbrück, on the Saar River near Trier 75
Krafft, David, Swedish painter *238*

La Feuillade, Duc de, *see Aubusson*
Laguerre, Louis, French painter *157*, 341, *342-344*, 346, *348*, 351, 395
La Hogue, naval battle of (1692) 19-*20*, 56, *274*-276, 279-*280*, 286
Lake Constance (Bodensee) 98, 270
Landau 132, 200, 226, 228-230, 253, 257
La Tour d'Auvergne, Henri de, Vicomte de Turenne, French general 17, 43-44, 104, 110, 127, 148, *193*, 199, 202, 212-213, 387-388
Leake, Sir John, English admiral 297
Lebrun, Charles, French painter and weaver *193*, 342, 395
Leclerc, Jerome, Antwerp weaver 395
Lediard, Thomas, secretary of Marlborough 101
Leibniz, Gottfried Wilhelm, philosopher and councillor of the Elector of Hanover 239, 389
Leicester, Earl of, *see Dudley*
Leipzig 358, 391
Leke, Nicholas, Earl of Scarsdale, English politician 51
Lely, Peter, English painter 323
Lens, Bernard, French-English painter 395
Leopold I, German Emperor 7-8, *36*, 71, 75, 225-226, 251-252, *255*, *259*, 260, 291, 391
Le Quesnoy, siege of (1712) 268
Lerma, Francisco Gomez de Sandoval y Rojaz, Duke of, Spanish politician 31
Le Tellier, François-Michel, Marquis de Louvois, French minister of war 43-44, 388
Leuchtenberg, Maximilian Philipp von 261
Leuven 79
Levant 276, 281, 283, 287-288
Ley, James, (first) Earl of Marlborough 53
Liddell-Hart, B.H., English military historian, 379
Liège (Luik), siege of (1702) 62
Liège (Luik), bishop of, *see Joseph Clemens*
Ligonier, Sir John, English officer, *108-109*, 110, 121
Lille (Rijssel), siege of (1708) *81*, 86, 87, 124, 132, *136*, 196
Lilly, Edmund, English painter *23*
Lilly, Peter, English painter *41*
Limbourg, siege of (1703) 132, 164, 166, 331
Limerick, siege of (1691) 128-129
Limerick, Treaty of (1691) 29
Lisbon 253, 287, 291, 294
Lombardy 200, 252
Lombart, Pierre, English painter 330, 395
London 8-9, 14, 16, 27, 40, 42, 44-47, 60, 86, 96, 109, 119, 122, 139, 157, 174, 180, 182, 217, 222, 225-226, 229, 233-234, 245, 249, 252-253, 255, 257, 260, 266, 274, 276, 278-280, 284, 288-289, 291, 294, 301, 304-305, 308, 315, 320, 323, 327-329, 331-334, 336, 342-344, 348, 352
Loo, het, palace of Stadholder-King William III 160, 178
Lorraine (Lothringen) 221, 226
Louis XIV, King of France 7-9, 14, 18-19, *36*, 43, *87*, 127, 173-174, 176, 193-195, 198, 200, 218, 226, 251-252, 255, 265, 276, 281, 283, 286, 330, 333
Louis, Duc de Bourgogne (Burgundy), grandson of Louis XIV 85-86, 127, 196, 199, 202-203, 208, 386
Louvois, Marquis de, *see Le Tellier*
Ludwig Wilhelm, Margrave of Baden, Imperial field marshal 67-68, 70-71, 77, 194, 205, *224*-226, 228-229, 231, 235, 240, 257
Lumley, Richard, Earl of Scarborough, English general 381
Lund, Erik, Swedish historian, 107
Luxembourg, Duke of, *see Montmorency*
Luzzara, Lombardy, battle of (1702) 253

Maas, River 62-64
Maastricht 62-63, 134, 158, 381
-, siege of (1673) 17, 43, 62-64, 127-128
Maccartney, George, English general 120, 375
Machado, Antonio Alvarez, Allied contractor 96
Madrid 252, 286
Mahan, Alfred Thayer, American naval historian 277, 362
Maintenon, Madame de 386
Mainwaring, Arthur, English politician 91, 99
Mainz 221, 228, 257, 266
Mainz, Archbishop-Elector of, *see Schönborn, Lothar Franz von*
Majorca *295*
Málaga, naval battle of (1704) 293-*294*, 298
Malplaquet, battle of (1709) 24, 87-88, *90-91*, *102-103*, 109, 119, 131, 171, 198-199, 202, 210, 213, 243, 265, *340-344*, 395
Mantegna, Andrea, Italian painter 334
Mantua 269

Mar, Earl of, *see Erskine*
Marbach, on the Neckar 257
Marchin, Ferdinand, Count of, Marshal of France 69-71, 194, 199-200, 385, 388
Maritime Powers 8, 217-218, 221-222, 228-229, 246, 252-253, 255, 277-278, 280, 284, 286-287
Marlborough, (first) Earl of, *see Ley*
Marlborough, (first, second creation) Earl and (first) Duke of, *see Churchill, John*
Marlborough, (third) Duke of, *see Spencer, Charles*
Marlborough, Duchess of, *see Jenyns, Sarah*
Marlborough House, Westminster 86, 343-345
Marsin, *see Marchin*
Mary, Queen of England, wife of Stadholder-King William III 56, 276
Mary of Modena, Queen of England, wife of King James II 44, 54, 97
Masham, Abigail, confidante of Queen Anne 91-92
Massue, Henri, Marquis de Ruvigny, Earl of Galway, Huguenot general in Dutch and English service 16, 48, 151
Mauritshuis, The Hague *188*
Maximilian II Emanuel, Elector of Bavaria 65, 67-69, 78, 97, 203, 207-208, 211, 218, *220-221*, 226, 240, 253, 255-256, 258, 260-261, 386
Maystetter, Stephan, Austrian painter *230*
Mazarin, Jules, French cardinal and politician 31, 213
Medina, Sir Solomon, Allied contractor 96
Mediterranean 7, 10, 19, 41, 214, 226, 276, 279, 281, 283-284, 288
Meenen (Menin), Flanders 143
Meer, Albert van der, Dutch envoy in Savoy 35
Méhaigne River 77-78, 164
Meldert, Brabant 83
Meredyth, Thomas, English general 120
Mérode, Eugène-Jean-Philippe, Comte de, Marquis de Westerloo, Southern Netherlands nobleman in Spanish service 199
Mesmes, Jean-Antoine de, Comte d'Avaux, French diplomat 59
Methuen, John, English envoy in Portugal 35, 360
Meulen, Adam Frans van der, French weaver *111*, 342, 395
Meuse (Maas) River 154-155, 158, 163, 226, 229, 231, 253
Michelet, Jules, French historian 213
Milan 9
Millner, James, English officer 107, 358
Mindelheim, Bavaria, Principality of 77-79, 97, 211, 239, 260-264, 268-269, 270, 308, 311, 356, 391
Minorca 19, *109*-110, 283, 295
Minterne, Dorset 45
Mol, Herman, cartographer/publisher, *14*
Moniteur, French official publication 357
Monmouth, Duke of, *see Scott, James*
Mons 85
Mons, siege of (1709) 90, 91, 132, 344
Montagu, Charles, Baron Halifax, English politician 52
Montagu, John, Viscount Monthermer, Duke of Montagu, son-in-law of Marlborough 75, 99
Montagu, Ralph, Duke of Montagu, English politician 56
Montalegre, Joseph, engraver *218*
Monte Argentaro, Italy 371
Montmorency-Bouteville, François-Henry de, Duke of Luxembourg, French general 55, 199, 388
Mordaunt, Charles, Earl of Peterborough, English general 41, 266
Morier, David, English painter, *119*
Mortier, David, Dutch engraver, *233*
Moselle (Moesel) River 65, 71, 226, 228-229, 240, 257
Mothe-Houdancourt, Charles, Comte de la, French general, 86
Mündelheim, near Stuttgart, 67, 257
Munderkingen, Bavaria, 391
Musbury, Devon 39

Nantes, Edict of 28
Naples-Sicily 252, 264
Napoleon, Emperor of the French 9, 104-105, 212
Nassau, Cornelis van, Heer van Woudenberg, Dutch officer 86, 160
Nassau, Hendrik van, Heer van Ouwerkerk (Overkirk, Auerquerque), Dutch field marshal 14, 82, 132, 146, 149, 153, *159-160*, 163, 167-170, 208, 381
Nassau, Willem Hendrik van, Heer van Zuylesteyn, Earl of Rochford, Dutch/English officer 16
Nassau-Saarbrücken, Prince of, *see Walrad*
Nassau-Siegen, Prince of, *see Johann Moritz*
Nath, Gerhard von der, Holstein officer in Dutch service 381
Nebel, Bavaria, river 68-69, 71, 202
Nellenburg, County of 98-99, 270, 391
Netherlands, Northern, *see United Provinces*
Netherlands, Southern, (Spanish, Austrian) 19, 24, 181, 199, 218, 223, 252, 283, 306
Netscher, Theodoor, Dutch painter, *145*
Neuchâtel, Principality 245
Neufville, François de, Duc de Villeroi, Marshal of France 67, 78, 163-164, 166-168, 195, 199-200, 202-204, 388
Newcastle, English man-of-war 52
Newfoundland 286-287, 299
Newtown, Isle of Wight 46
Nijmegen 45, 62, 147
Nine Years' War (War of the League of Augsburg) 178, 194, 286
Noailles, Adrien-Maurice de, Comte d'Ayen, Duc de Noailles, French officer and minister 211, 384, 387
Nördlingen, Association of 68, 229, 235, 245-246
Normandy 279
North America 49, 286, 292, 298-299
North Sea 10, 19, 179, 182, 277, 282, 284, 286
Northumberland, Duke of, *see Fitzroy, George*
Nottingham, Earl of, *see Finch*
Nova Scotia 299
Noyelle et Falais, Jacques Louis, Comte de, Dutch general 132, 160, 381
Nürnberger, Georg Friedrich, German medallist, *234*
Nutt, John, English printer *323*

Oates, Titus, 393

Obdam, Heer van, see Wassenaer, Jacob van
Oberglau, Bavaria 70-71
Occasional Conformity Bill 28, 63-64
Olivarez, Gaspar de Guzmán, Duke de, Spanish politician 31
Orchies 139, 142
Orkney, Earl of, *see Hamilton, George*
Orléans, Duc d', *see Philippe II*
Ormonde, Duke of, *see Butler*
Orsbeck, Johann Hugo von, Archbishop-Elector of Trier 221, 228
Osnabrück 323, 361, 364
Ostend (Oostende) 86, 163
Ostend (Oostende), siege of (1706) 63, 79, 132, 137
Ottoman Empire (Turkey) 218, 373
Otway, Thomas, English poet 46
Oudenaarde, battle of (1708) *2*, 82, *84*-86, 109, 124, 131, 171, 196, 199-200, 241, *250*, *340*
Ouwerkerk, Heer van, *see Nassau, Hendrik van*
Overijssche, Brabant 166
Overton, Henry, English publisher *344*, *348*
Oxenstierna, Bengt, Count, Swedish officer in Dutch service 381
Oxford, Earl of, *see Harley, Robert*

Palatinate, Elector of, *see Johann Wilhelm*
Palatinate, Princess of, *see Elisabeth Charlotte*
Pall Mall, London 343
Paparel, French banker 196, 384
Paris 8, 19, 44, 46, 111, 174, 193, 196, 204-205, 207, 209, 214, 286, 323
Parke, Daniel, American officer in English service 71, 120, 372
Parker, Robert, English officer 109, 373
Parliament, of England 9, 16, 31, 46, 52, 55, 58-59, 63, 74-75, 77, 81, 85, 88, 91-92, 94, 97, 99, 115-116, 136, 170, 177, 185, 211, 246, 249, 286, 312-313, 352
Passau 68, 228
Pedro II, King of Portugal 226
Peer, Brabant 154
Pellerin, French printer, *214*
Pembroke, Earl of, *see Herbert, Thomas*
Penal Act 51
Peter I, the Great, Czar of Russia 109, 245
Peterborough, Earl of, *see Mordaunt*
Petitfils, Jean-Christian, French historian, 213
Petitot, Jean, English miniaturist *42*
Philippe II, Duc d'Orléans, Regent of France 202, 204, 386
Philippe d'Anjou, grandson of Louis XIV, King of Spain as Felipe V 28, 35, 58, 79, 89, 195, 200, 207, 252, 371, 386
Philips, John, English poet 310
Pierrepont, Evelyn, Earl/Duke of Kingston-upon-Hull, Marquess of Dorchester, English politician 14
Piombino, Italy 371
Pit, Robert, English sculptor *98*, 101, 372, 395
Pitt, William, the Elder, English politician 121
Pittis, William, English poet 310, 358
Plessen, Christian Sigfred von, Danish diplomat 47
Plymouth 279
Pocock, John G.A., English historian 28
Pointis, Baron de, *see Desjean*
Poland, King of, *see Augustus II*
Polignac, Melchior, Abbott of, French diplomat 210, 387
Poltawa, battle of (1709) 109, 240, 243
Popish Plot (1683) 28
Port Mahon, Minorca 283, 295-296, 299
Portland, Earl/Duke of, *see Bentinck*
Porto Ercole, Italy 371
Porto Longone, Italy 371
Porto Santo Stefano, Italy 371
Portsmouth 52, 54, 278-279
Portugal 8, 10, 19, 25, 35, 37, 64, 226, 235, 245-246, 253, 268, 292
Portugal, King of, *see Pedro II*
Post Man, English newspaper 303
Pretender, *see James III*
Price, Robert, M.P. 16
Prior, Matthew, English poet and diplomat 308
Protestant Succession, in England 29-30, 32, 58, 77, 96, 178, 191, 241, 276, 327

Rákóczy, Ferenc II, Prince of Transylvania, leader of the Hungarian insurrection 255
Ralph, James, English author 101,
Ramillies, battle of (1706) *24*, 78-79, 81, 109-110, 119, 124, 131, 146, 170-171, 195-196, 198, 200, 202, 204, 207, 239, 264, 335, 342-344, *348-349*
Rantzau, Jørgen von, Danish officer in Dutch service, 381
Rastatt, Peace of (1714) 97, 211, 269
Rechteren, Adolf Hendrik van, Heer van Almelo, Dutch politician 67, *165*-166, 190
Regensburg 391
Reede, Godard van, Heer van Ginkel, Earl of Athlone, Dutch general 54, 129, 146, 148-149, *150*-155, 157-158, 160, 380
Resolution, English man-of-war 42, 49, 62, 151, 170, 371
Reynolds, Joshua, English painter *109*, 323, 392
Rhine (Rhein) River 36, 44, 60, 63-65, 67-68, 71, 77, 82-83, 85, 131, 154, 158, 162-163, 193, 200, 202, 225-226, 228-231, 235, 237, 239-241, 243, 245-247, 253, 255, 257, 265-266, 269
Richards, Michael, English officer 135
Richelieu, Armand-Jean du Plessis, Duc de, French cardinal and politician 31
Riga 217
Rigaud, Hyacinthe, French painter, *196*, *200*, *226*
Rijswijk, Peace of (1697), 18, 21, 58, 59, 218, 286
Riley, John, English painter *51*
Rio de Janeiro, Brazil 298
Rivers, Earl, *see Savage, Richard*
Robert, J., English author 101
Robijn, Jacobus, Dutch artist *278*
Robinson, John, English envoy to Sweden 83
Rochester, Earl of, *see Hyde, Laurence*
Rocroi, battle of (1643) 194
Rodger, N.A.M., naval historian, 281
Roermond, siege of (1702) 62, 67, 132-133
Rooke, George, English admiral *284-285*, 287, 291-292
Rouillé de Marbeuf, Pierre, French diplomat 210, 386
Rouvray, Louis de, Duc de Saint-Simon, French courtier 195, 200, 203, 211
Royal Prince, English man-of-war 42
Royal Sovereign, English man-of-war *290-291*
Russell, Edward, Earl of Orford, English admiral 57, 281, 283-284
Russell, John, English officer 41

Russia 8-9, 36, 77, 239
Russia, Czar of, *see Peter I*
Ruvigny, *see Massue*
Rysbrack, Michael, Flemish-English sculptor *99, 101, 354-355*, 395

Sacheverell, Henry, English Anglican minister *27*-28, 92, 315, 393
Sackville, Edward, English officer 57
Sailmaker, Isaac, English marine painter, *294*
Saint-Germain, court of 208
Saint-Simon, Duc de, *see Rouvray*
Salisbury 48, 51-52
Salisch, Ernst Willem van, Dutch general 132, 160, 169
Sandridge 45, 48, 51, 174
Sardinia 35, 269, 295
Saunière de l'Hermitage, René, Dutch diplomatic agent in London 184
Savage, Richard, Earl Rivers, English general 92, 157
Savoy, Duke of, *see Victor Amadeus*
Saxony, Elector of, *see Friedrich August I*
Saxony-Gotha, Duke of, *see Friedrich II*
Scarsdale, Earl of, *see Leke*
Schalcken, Godfried, Dutch painter *15*
Scheldt (Schelde) River 63, 160, 162-164, 200, 283, 336
Schellenberg, storming of (1704) 67, 109, 112, 257, 260
Schenck, Pieter, Dutch mapmaker and engraver *222, 288, 295*
Schmidt, Georg Friedrich, German engraver, *226*
Scholten, Jobst von, general in Dutch/Danish service 381
Schomberg, Friedrich Hermann, Duke of, officer in the service of William III 52, 330, *332*, 395
Schönborn, Lothar Franz von, Archbishop Elector of Mainz 221, 235, 243
Schonenberg, Franciscus van, Dutch envoy in Portugal 35
Schrader, Christoph, representative of Marlborough in Regensburg 391
Schulenburg, Matthias Johann, Count von der -, Saxon general in allied service 132, 142
Schuppen, Jacob van, Dutch painter *249*
Scotland 8, 28-29, 46-47, 51-52, 112, 178, 291, 298
Scott, James, Duke of Monmouth 43, 46, 48-49, 51, 127
Sedgemoor, battle of (1685) 49, 148
Sedley, Sir Charles, English playwright 44
Sedley, Katherine, daughter of the former 44
Seeman, Enoch, Flemish-English painter *35*, 337, *340*
Seine, river 195
Septennial Act (1716) 116
Sersanders, Antonie, agent of Maximilian Emanuel, 208
Sevilla 287
Seymour, Charles, Earl of Hertford, Duke of Somerset 92
Seymour, Sir Edward, English politician 24
Sherlock, William, English Anglican minister 304
Shetland Islands 298
Shovel, Sir Clowdisley, English admiral 84, 297, 406
Shrewsbury, Earl of, *see Talbot, Charles*
Sicily 35, 252, 297
Sidney, Henry, Earl of Romney, Master-General of the Ordnance 54
Silesia (Schlesien) 264-265
Sinzendorf, Philipp Ludwig Wenzel, Count, Imperial diplomat 270-271, 340-341
Sinzheim, battle of (1674) 43, 193
Slangenburg, Heer van, *see Baer*
Slingelandt, Simon van, secretary of the Dutch Council of State 158, 180
Smith, John, English publisher and printmaker *266, 327*, 330-332, 394
Snyder, Henry, American historian 33
Soignies (Brabant), Forest of 83, 167
Sole Bay, naval battle of (1672) 42, 148
Solms-Braunfels, Heinrich Trajectinus, Count of, German officer in the service of King William III 55
Somers, John, Baron Somers of Evesham, English politician 92
Sommerfeldt, Hanoverian general, 381
Sophia, Electress of Hannover 74, 77, 239, 389
Sound 45, 104, 117, 166, 170, 287-288
Sourches, Marquis de, *see Du Bouchet*
Spain 7-10, 24-25, 31-32, 35-36, 58, 64, 80, 83, 94, 96, 106, 110, 117, 194-195, 200, 204, 208, 222, 243, 252-253, 255, 258, 264-266, 269, 281, 283, 289, 291-292, 294, 297-299, 304, 308, 311
Spain, King of, *see Carlos II; Karl VI (Carlos III); Philippe d'Anjou*
Spencer, Charles, Earl of Sunderland, (second) Duke of Marlborough, English politician and son-in-law of Marlborough 14, 24, 58, 77, 80, 93, 98-99, 184, 266
Spencer, Charles, (third) Duke of Marlborough, 99, 355
Spierbach, battle of (1703) 200
Spithead, 291
St. Albans, Hertfordshire 45, 48, 52, 56-57, 63, 98
St. Antoine, M. de, equerry of King Charles I 330
St. James Palace, London 44-45, 47-48, 54, 57, 83-84, *86*, 94, 99, 225, 311, 343
St. John, Henry, Viscount Bolingbroke, English politician 85, 98, 101, 268, 354, 387
St. Kitts, Caribbean island 299
St. Malo, France 286, 298
St. Michael, English man-of-war 42
St. Paul des Estanges, Louis, Hanoverian general in Dutch service 381
St. Venant, siege of (1710) 93, 132, 313
Stair, Earl of, *see Dalrymple*
Stanislaw Leszczyński, King of Poland as Augustus II 82-83; *see also Augustus II*
Starhemberg, Guidobald, Count of, Imperial general 265, 359
Steele, Richard, English author 99
Stepney, George, English diplomat 78, 80, 255, *256-257*, 260-261, 264, 390
Sterne, Laurence, English author 119, 375
Stevensweert, on the Meuse River, siege of (1702) 62, 63, 132-133
Stollhofen, defensive line of 229
Stuart, House of 30
Stuttgart 67, 230, 239
Sunderland, Earl of, *see Spencer*
Superville Jean de, Huguenot minister in Rotterdam 25
Swabian Circle 77, 229
Sweden 8, 36, 77, 82-83, 101, 109, 207, 218, 221, 238, 240, 245, 287, 291
Swift, Jonathan, English pamphleteer *14*, 16, 37, 96-97, 120, 268, 311-312, 319
Switzerland, Confederation of 98, 241

Tagus, river 195, 292, 294
Talbot, Charles, Earl of Shrewsbury, English politician 56-57, 60, 94
Talbot, Richard, Earl of Tyrconnel, Irish Jacobite nobleman 113
Tallard, Comte de, *see Hostun*
Talmash, Thomas, English officer 57
Tangier 17, 41-42, 51, 110, 112, 126, 148, 288, 299
Taniers, Tanières, *see Malplaquet*
Tanjé, Pieter, Dutch engraver *352*
Taxation, in England 21
Telamonte, Italy 371
Test Act 51
Tettau, Albrecht, Freiherr von, Hessian general, 381
Tettau, Julius Ernst von, Prussian military engineer in Danish service 130
Thames River 195
Thornhill, James, English painter *351*-352, 395
Tienen, Brabant *76*
Tilly, Comte de, *see T'Serclaes*
Tirol 356, 391
Torcy, *see Colbert*
Tories 14, 19, 21-24, 28, 30, 59, 80, 87, 211, 266, 269, 291, 301, 306, 310, 313-315, 318-319
Torrington, Earl of, *see Herbert, Arthur*
Toulon 82, 84, 265, 276, 278-279, 283-284, 291-296, 298
Tournai (Doornik), siege of (1709) *87*, 89, 132, 134, *138*-139, *140-141*, 351
Tourville, *see Cotentin*
Townshend, Charles, Viscount, English politician and diplomat 14, 88-89, 183, 356
Trarbach, on the Moselle, siege of (1704) 71, 132, 241
Travendal, Peace of 231
Trier (Trèves), siege of (1704) 71, 75, 228
Trier (Trèves), Archbishop-Elector of, *see Orsbeck*
Trognée, Jean-Gérard Baron de, Liégeois officer in Dutch service 132, 134
Trouvaine, Antoine, French engraver *225*
Troy, François de, French painter 323
T'Serclaes, Claude-Frédéric, Comte de Tilly, Dutch general 169, 380, 381
Turckheim, battle of 44, 127
Turenne, *see La Tour*
Turin (Torino), relief of (1706) 35, 200, 202, 204, 239, 264, 385
Turkey, *see Ottoman Empire*
Turnhout, Brabant 170
Tutchin, John, English pamphleteer 16
Tyrconnel, Earl of, *see Talbot*

Ulm, Bavaria 67-68, 71, 132, 226, 257
Union, Act of (1707) 23, 379
United Provinces (Dutch Republic) 17, 35, 59, 143, 147, 152, 190, 193, 252, 268
United Provinces, Council of State of 152-153, 155, 180, 257, 330
United Provinces, States General of 5, *36*, 59-60, 62, 67, 136, 147, 151-154, 158, 160, 162, 165-166, 170-171, 178, 182, 184, 187, 194, 204, 206, 210, 217, 222-223, 225-226, 228-231, 235, 237, 240-241, 243, 245-246, 255, 264, 297
Utrecht, Peace of (1713) 14, 21-22, 28, 36, 191
Uxelles, *see Du Blé*

Vanbrugh, John, English architect 74-75, 84, 334, 395
Vanderbank, John, English weaver 334
Vasseur, Guillaume le, *see Des Rocques*
Vauban, Sébastien le Prestre de, French military engineer 86, 117, 125-131, 134, 143, 145, 253, 265
Velde, Willem van de, the Younger, Dutch marine painter *274, 291*
Vendôme, Louis-Joseph, Duc de, French general 83, 85-86, 195-196, 199-204, 212, 386, 387
Venlo, siege of (1702) 62, 132
Verrio, Antonio, Italian-English painter 333, 342, 346, 395
Versailles 193-195, 200, 202, 207, 252, 306, 342
Vertue, George, English author 394-395
Victor Amadeus, Duke of Savoy 8-9, 14, 25, 35, 37, 44, 64, 67, 74, 97, 99, 132, 175, 186, 200, 210, 213, 225-226, 230-231, 241, 245-246, 249-253, 260, 266, 268, 306-307
Vienna (Wien) 14, 67, 77, 88, 94, 186, 226, 228-229, 231, 235, 239, 241, 246, 249-253, 255, 257-261, 263-266, 268-270, 314
Vigo, Bay of, naval battle of (1702) *288*-289, 291-292
Villa Hermosa, Duke of, Spanish general 45
Villars, Louis-Hector, Duc de, French general 64, 90-91, 94, 139, *196*-200, 202-204, 210-212, *226*-228, 239, 364, 386-388
Villaviciosa, Spain, battle of (1710) 200
Villeroi, Duc de, *see Neufville*
Villiers, Barbara, Countess of Castlemaine, Duchess of Cleveland, mistress of King Charles II 41, *42*
Villiers, Elizabeth, favourite of King William III 53
Villiers, George, Duke of Buckingham 31, 39
Vivien, Joseph, French painter *221*
Vollevens, Johannes, Dutch painter *296*
Voltaire, François-Marie Arouet, known as -, French philosopher and author 211, 215
Vos, Judocus de, Brussels weaver *2, 6, 20, 81, 90-91, 105*, 335, *338*, 341
Vosges Mountains 44, 193
Vrijbergen, Marinus van, Dutch envoy in London 182, 382-383

Walcourt, battle of (1689) 53, 148, 381
Waldeck, Prince of, *see Georg Friedrich*
Waldensians, 28
Wales 28, 51, 60, 112, 369, 407
Walpole, Sir Robert, English politician, 119
Walrad, Prince of Nassau-Saarbrücken, Dutch field marshal 60, 62, 149, 151, 154, 160, 380
Wassenaer, Arent, Baron van, Heer van Duvenvoorde, Dutch politician 190
Wassenaer, Jacob van, Heer van Obdam, Dutch general 64, 149, 157, 160, 162, 163, 164
Wassenaer, Jan Gerrit, Baron van, Dutch Vice-Admiral 149, 160, 190, 297
Webb, John Richmond, English officer 86-87
Weede, Everard van, Heer van Dijkveld, Dutch politician 15, 49
Weigley, Russell, American historian, 378
Welstead, Leonard, English poet 307, 393
Werff, Adriaen van der, Dutch painter and engraver *217, 223, 236, 352*, 354
West Indies 222, 292, 298
Westminster Abbey 99, 101, 344, 395
Weston Zoyland 49
Westphalia, Peace of 25, 43, *234*, 243
Wharton, Thomas, Baron (Earl) of, English politician 114
Whigs 14, 19, 22-25, 28-30, 37, 56-57, 75, 80, 87-88, 91-92, 268, 291, 301, 310-311, 313-315, 319
White Sea 287

Wight, Isle of 42, 46
Wijnendael, Flanders, battle of (1708), 86
Wildt, Job de, Dutch naval secretary 292
Wilkinson, Robert, English engraver *72, 102*
William, Duke of Gloucester, son of Queen Anne and George of Denmark 32, 58, 304, 359
William III, King of England, Stadholder of Holland 7-9, 11, 15-16, 18-19, 22-23, 29, 31-33, 35, 37, 45, 54-55, 57-60, 62, 112-114, 128, 147-149, 151-152, 155, 158, 160, 166, 170, 173-174, 191, 194, 222, 225, 231, 255, 276, 279, 281, 284, 291, 298, 308, 311, 314, 330, 332-333, 335, 351, 379
William Augustus, Duke of Cumberland, English general *118-119*, 121
Wilson, John, English officer 107
Wilton House 323
Winchester 51
Wise, Henry, English royal gardener *75*
Witt, Johan de, former Grand Pensionary of Holland 173
Wolseley, Sir Garnet, English general 104
Woodstock, Oxfordshire, manor of 74-75, 90, 101, 308, 311, 333-335, 346, 351-352, 354, 359, 395
Wratislaw, Johann Wenzel, Count, Imperial diplomat 60, 65, 67, 231, 253, *254-255*, 257, 260, 265-266, 271-273, 389
Wren, Sir Christopher, English architect 74, 84, *86*, 343
Wren, Christopher Jr 84
Wright, J.M., English painter *39*
Württemberg, Duke of, *see Eberhard Ludwig*; Heinrich Friedrich
Württemberg-Neustadt, Duke of, *see Ferdinand Wilhelm*
Young, Robert, English spy 56
Yssche, River 76, 167, 168

Zincke, Christian Friedrich, German miniaturist *93, 320*
Zinzendorf, see Sinzendorf
Zoutleeuw (Leau), Brabant 132, 164
Zuylesteyn, Heer van, *see Nassau, Willem Hendrik van*

Editors & Contributors

Jaap R. Bruijn (1938) in 2003 became emeritus professor of maritime history at the University of Leiden. He has published numerous books and articles on a variety of topics including the early modern Dutch Navy, shipping and commanders of the Dutch East India Company, privateering, 20th century Dutch whaling, trade unions in the Navy, and a few shorter biographies of 18th and 19th century Dutch naval officers, fishermen, and merchants. With several of these studies, he has enjoyed the cooperation with colleagues and former students. He also served as editor-in-chief of the four volume *Maritieme Geschiedenis der Nederlanden* (1976-78) and, in the same series as this volume, *De Ruyter: Dutch Admiral* (2011).

Tony Claydon (1965) is professor of early modern history, and Head of the College of Arts and Humanities at Bangor University, Wales. He is author of various works on the political and religious culture of late Stuart England, in particular *William III and the Godly Revolution* (CUP, 1996); *William III: Profiles in Power* (Longman, 2002); and *Europe and the Making of England: 1660-1760* (CUP, 2007). He has also been an editor of 'Studies in Church History' (2008-11), and is a convenor of the Bangor Conference on the Restoration.

Alan J. Guy (1950) served at The National Army Museum, London, for many years and was Director from 2004 to 2010. During that time he published a number of books and articles on British Army history from the 17th to the 19th centuries, including: *Oeconomy and Discipline - Officership and administration in the British army, 1714-63* (1985); *Colonel Samuel Bagshawe and the Army of George II, 1731-1762* (1990) and, most recently, with Alastair Massie, *Expedition to the Crimea* (2010), an edition of the manuscript Crimean War journal of Captain Louis Edward Nolan of Charge of the Light Brigade notoriety. He is currently Visiting Fellow at Wolfson College, Cambridge, working on the military system of the English East India Company, 1750-90.

John B. Hattendorf (1941), the editor-in-chief of this volume, has been the Ernest J. King professor of maritime history at the U.S. Naval War College since 1984. In addition to his many contributions to maritime history, he has published a number of articles on early 18th century history. Among other works, his University of Oxford doctoral thesis was published as *England in the War of the Spanish Succession: A Study of the English View and Conduct of Grand Strategy, 1702-1712* (1987) and he contributed some twenty-two biographies of military, naval and diplomatic figures of the period to the *Oxford Dictionary of National Biography* (2004), including the entry for Marlborough.

Michael Hochedlinger (1967) took his PhD from Vienna University. He started his career as head of the early-modern section of the research department at the National Army Museum in Vienna (1995-1999). He has been a senior archivist at the Austrian State Archives since 1999. He has published widely on early-modern diplomatic and military history. His books include *Krise und Wiederherstellung. Österreichische Großmachtpolitik zwischen Türkenkrieg und "Zweiter Diplomatischer Revolution" 1787-1791* (2000) and *Austria's Wars of Emergence 1683-1797. War, State and Society in the Habsburg Monarchy* (Modern Wars in Perspective, 2003).

Rolof van Hövell tot Westerflier (1940) earned an LLM degree and a MA degree from the University of Leiden. He also received a degree in comparative law (MCL) from Columbia University. He has spent the last forty years practicing law in The Netherlands Antilles, Rotterdam and Jakarta. Driven by his life-long passion for history, he founded Karwansaray Publishers in 2007, a company dedicated to promoting and sharing a multi-faceted view of history that crosses cultural and political boundaries. Some of his other productions include the successful *Ancient Warfare* and *Medieval Warfare* magazines. This book is the second in the Protagonists of History in International Perspective series. The first, *De Ruyter: Dutch Admiral*, examines the life of the renowned sea hero and is also available from Karwansaray Publishers. Future releases include an upcoming work on the Duke of Alba (due out in December 2012).

Richard Johns (1973) is an art historian. He has published on several aspects of British art of the late seventeenth and early eighteenth centuries, and is completing a book on the work of the English decorative history painter James Thornhill. More recent, and ongoing, research extends into the nineteenth century and focuses on the art of the sea. He studied at the Courtauld Institute of Art and the University of York, where he earned a PhD in 2004. Since 2008, he has been Curator of Prints and Drawings at the National Maritime Museum, London.

Bernhard R. Kroener (1948) is professor for military history and the cultural history of violence at Potsdam University. He has published numerous books and articles on early modern and modern French and German military history; topics include the logistics of the French Army in the 17th century, the social origins, life and death of soldiers during the Thirty Years' War, and the relationship between state, army and society during the reign of Frederick the Great. His most recent publications are *Der starke Mann im Heimatkriegsgebiet – Generaloberst Friedrich Fromm. Eine Biographie*, (Paderborn u.a. 2005); *Militär, Staat und Gesellschaft im 20. Jahrhundert (1890-1990)* (München 2011) and *Kriegswesen, Herrschaft und Gesellschaft im Spätmittelalter und in der Frühen Neuzeit (1300-1800)* (München 2012). B.R. Kroener has served as co-editor of the 'Krieg in der Geschichte' and 'Herrschaft und soziale Systeme' series and was president of the Arbeitskreis 'Militär und Gesellschaft in der Frühen Neuzeit' between 1995 and 2004.

David Onnekink (1970) is assistant professor of the early modern history of international relations at the University of Utrecht. He is mainly interested in the history of English and Dutch foreign policy and religious conflict in the 17th and 18th century. He is the author of *The Anglo-Dutch Favourite. The career of Hans Willem Bentinck, 1st Earl of Portland* (Aldershot 2007) and edited several volumes of essays on William III, Huguenot soldiering, religious conflict and foreign policy. He is currently finishing a monograph on the Dutch role in the wars against Louis XIV (1672-1713) and the Peace of Utrecht.

Clément Oury (1981), a graduate of the Ecole Nationale des Chartes (2005) and the Ecole Nationale Supérieure des Sciences de l'Information et des Bibliothèques (2006), is a library curator. He holds the position of Head of Digital Legal Deposit at the National Library of France. In 2011, he earned his PhD from the University of Paris-Sorbonne, on the subject: 'The French Defeats of the War of the Spanish Succession, 1704-1708'. He is the author of several papers related to French early modern warfare, and has edited Vauban's *Traité des sièges et de l'attaque des places* as part of the general edition of Vauban's major works (ed. M. Virol, 2007).

Jamel Ostwald (1970) earned his PhD in early modern European history at Ohio State University (2002). He is currently associate professor of history at Eastern Connecticut State University. He has published on warfare in the age of Louis XIV, including 'The «Decisive» Battle of Ramillies,1706: Prerequisites for Decisiveness in Early Modern Warfare' in *The Journal of Military History* (2000), as well as *Vauban under Siege: Engineering Efficiency and Martial Vigor in the War of the Spanish Succession* (2007), winner of the Society for Military History's 2009 Distinguished Book Award in Non-American History.

John M. Stapleton, Jr. (1964) earned his PhD in early modern European history at the Ohio State University (2003). He is currently an Associate Professor of History at the United States Military Academy at West Point, New York. He has published several articles on various aspects of early modern military history, focusing particularly on the Anglo-Dutch military relationship during William III's reign. He is currently completing work on a book exploring coalition warfare and the Anglo-Dutch alliance during Louis XIV's wars.

Augustus J. Veenendaal, Jr. (1940), the associate editor of this volume, earned his PhD at Radboud University Nijmegen in 1976. He retired in 2005 as senior research historian from the Institute of Netherlands History at The Hague, where he edited the correspondence of Grand Pensionary Anthonie Heinsius 1702-1720: *De Briefwisseling van Anthonie Heinsius 1702-1720* (19 vols., The Hague, 1976-2001). He published a catalogue of the Heinsius archives (2001), wrote many articles pertaining to several aspects of the War of the Spanish Succession, and was editor of a volume of articles and contributor to dictionaries on Heinsius and his contemporaries. Besides this work in the early 18th century he also wrote numerous books and articles on Dutch and American railway history and on international railway finance. From 2001 to 2004 he was seconded to Netherlands Railways to write the history of railways in the Netherlands: *Spoorwegen in Nederland van 1834 tot nu* (Amsterdam, 2004).

NB. Les rouges sont les Trouppes des Armées des Alliez, et Les bleues marquent les Trouppes Ennemies, ou francoises.
Berchem
Castel de he
authever

De l'Attaque
la Dyle à Ne
tentée par l
liées, Laquelle
sée, Mais S. A. Le
trouva bon
tourner les A
Ce que c'est passe
Netisch
Nettene